Fodor's

CITYGUIDE
SAN FRANCISCO

2ND EDITION

FODOR'S TRAVEL PUBLICATIONS
NEW YORK • TORONTO • LONDON • SYDNEY • AUCKLAND
WWW.FODORS.COM

STREETFINDER

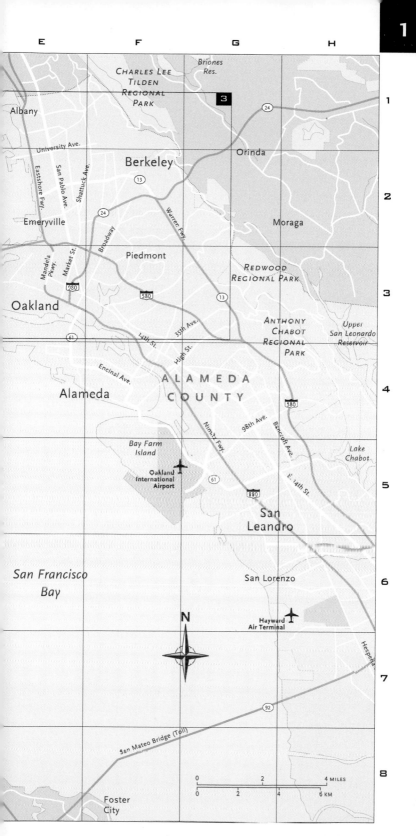

THE BAY AREA

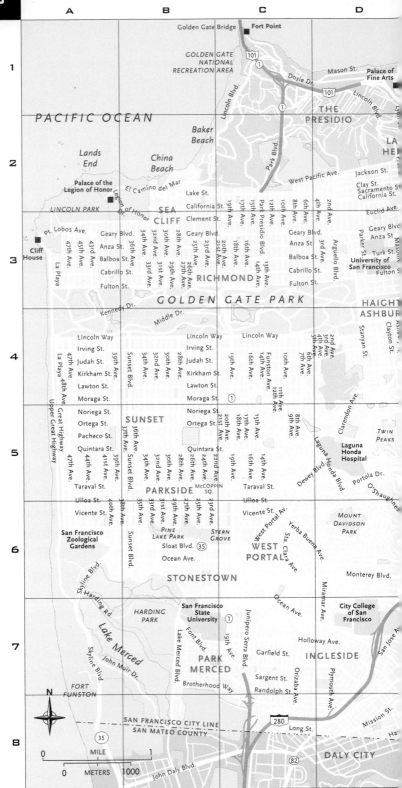

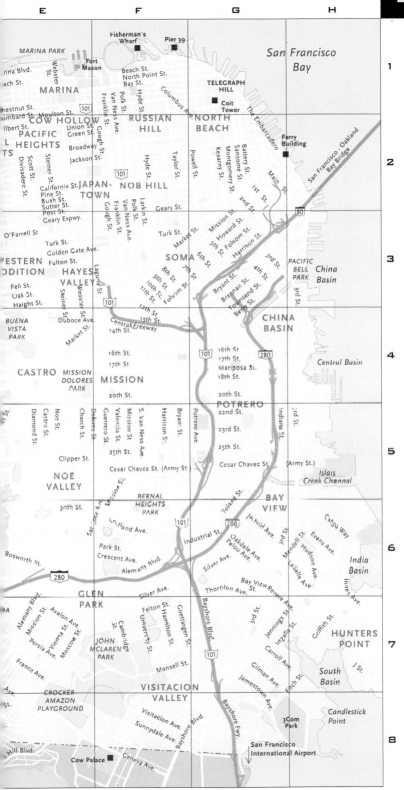

E F G H

San Francisco Bay

1

MARINA PARK

Fisherman's Wharf
Pier 39

Fort Mason

arina Blvd.
ach St.

MARINA

Beach St.
North Point St.
Bay St.

TELEGRAPH HILL
Coit Tower

Webster St.

hestnut St.
ombard St.
ilbert St.

COW HOLLOW

Moulton St.
101

Franklin St.

Van Ness Ave.

Polk St.

Hyde St.

Columbus Ave.

NORTH BEACH

The Embarcadero

Ferry Building

San Francisco-Oakland Bay Bridge

2

PACIFIC HEIGHTS
TS

Union St.
Green St.

Gough St.

RUSSIAN HILL

Broadway

Jackson St.

Taylor St.

Powell St.

Battery St.
Sansome St.
Montgomery St.
Kearny St.

1st St.

Main St.

Scott St.
Steiner St.
Divisadero St.

California St.
Pine St.
Bush St.
Sutter St.
Post St.
Geary Expwy.

JAPAN-TOWN

101

NOB HILL

Hyde St.

Larkin St.

Polk St.

Van Ness Ave.

Franklin St.

Gough St.

Geary St.

Turk St.

Market St.

Mission St.
Howard St.
5th St. Folsom St.
Harrison St.

2nd St.

3rd St.

80

3

O'Farrell St

WESTERN
ADDITION

Turk St.
Golden Gate Ave.
Fulton St.

SOMA

6th St.

8th St.
7th St.

9th St.
10th St.
11th St. Folsom St.

Bryant St.
Brannan St.
Townsend St.
Berry St.

4th St.

3rd St.

PACIFIC BELL PARK

China Basin

Fell St.
Oak St.
Haight St.

HAYES VALLEY

Steiner St.

Webster St.

Laguna St.

101

12th St.
13th St.

CHINA BASIN

BUENA VISTA PARK

Duboce Ave.

Central Freeway

14th St.

Market St.

16th St
17th St.
Mariposa St.
18th St.

101

280

Central Basin

4

CASTRO

MISSION DOLORES PARK

16th St.
17th St.

MISSION

20th St.

20th St.

Noe St.
Castro St.
Diamond St.

Church St.

Dolores St.

Guerrero St.

Valencia St.
Mission St.

S. Van Ness Ave.

Harrison St.

Bryant St.

Potrero Ave.

22nd St.

POTRERO

23rd St.

25th St.

Indiana St.

3rd St.

5

Clipper St.

NOE VALLEY

25th St.

Cesar Chavez St. (Army St.)

Cesar Chavez St. (Army St.)

Islais Creek Channel

30th St.

San Jose Ave.

BERNAL HEIGHTS PARK

101

Toland St.

BAY VIEW

Galvez Way

Bosworth St.

280

Sn. land Ave.

Park St.

Crescent Ave.

Alemany Blvd.

Industrial St.

200

Jerrold Ave.

Oakdale Ave.
Palou Ave.

Silver Ave.

Evans Ave.

Mendell St.

Hudson Ave.

LaSalle Ave.

India Basin

Innes Ave.

6

GLEN PARK

Silver Ave.

Thornton Ave.

Bay View
Bay St.
Revere Ave.

3rd St.

7

A

Alemany Blvd.
Mission St.
Avalon Ave.
Persia Ave.
Vienna St.
Moscow St.

France Ave.

JOHN McLAREN PARK

Cambridge St.

Felton St.
Hamilton St.
University St.

Goettingen St.

Mansell St.

Bayshore Blvd.

101

VISITACION VALLEY

Jennings St.

Ingalls St.

Carroll Ave.

Gilman Ave.

Jamestown Ave.

Fitch St.

Griffith St.

HUNTERS POINT

J St.

South Basin

Ave.

CROCKER AMAZON PLAYGROUND

St.

Visitacion Ave.

Sunnydale Ave.

Bayshore Blvd.

Bayshore Fwy.

3Com Park

Candlestick Point

8

Hill Blvd.

Cow Palace

Geneva Ave.

San Francisco International Airport

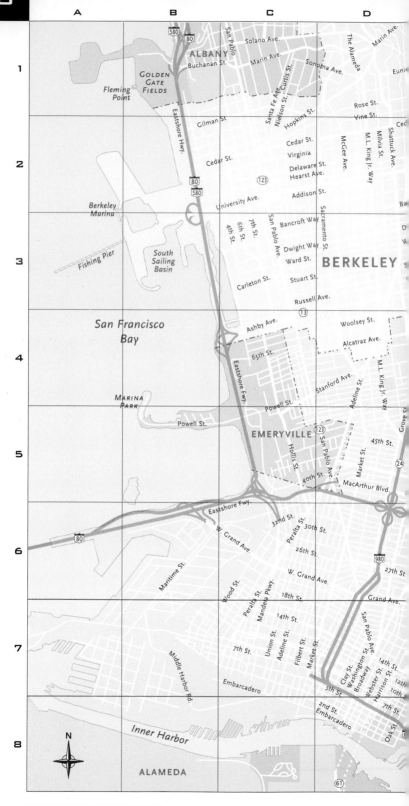

A B C D

1

2

3

4

5

6

7

8

580
80
ALBANY
San Pablo
Solano Ave.
The Alameda
Marin Ave.
GOLDEN
GATE
FIELDS
Buchanan St.
Marin Ave.
Sonoma Ave.
Euni
Fleming
Point
Santa Fe Ave.
Nielson St.
Curtis St.
Rose St.
Eastshore Hwy.
Gilman St.
Hopkins St.
Vine St.
Cec
Cedar St.
McGee Ave.
Shattuck Ave.
Milvia St.
M.L. King Jr. Way
Virginia
Cedar St.
Delaware St.
Hearst Ave.
Ba
80
580
123
Addison St.
University Ave.
San Pablo Ave.
Sacramento St.
Bancroft Way
D
7th St.
6th St.
4th St.
W.
Berkeley
Marina
Dwight Way
BERKELEY
S
Fishing Pier
South
Sailing
Basin
Ward St.
Carleton St.
Stuart St.
Russell Ave.
13
San Francisco
Bay
Ashby Ave.
Woolsey St.
Alcatraz Ave.
65th St.
Eastshore Fwy.
Stanford Ave.
Adeline St.
M.L. King Jr. Way
MARINA
PARK
Powell St.
Powell St.
EMERYVILLE
123
Hollis St.
San Pablo Ave.
Market St.
45th St.
Grove
24
40th St.
MacArthur Blvd.
80
Eastshore Fwy.
32nd St.
Peralta St.
30th St.
W. Grand Ave.
26th St.
980
27th St
Maritime St.
W. Grand Ave.
Wood St.
Peralta St.
Mandela Pkwy.
18th St.
Grand Ave.
14th St.
San Pablo Ave.
7th St.
Union St.
Adeline St.
Filbert St.
Market St.
Clay St.
Washington St.
14th St.
Broadway
12th
Middle Harbor Rd.
Embarcadero
Webster St.
Harrison St.
10th
5th St
2nd St.
Embarcadero
7th St.
St. O
N
Inner Harbor
ALAMEDA
61

STREETFINDER

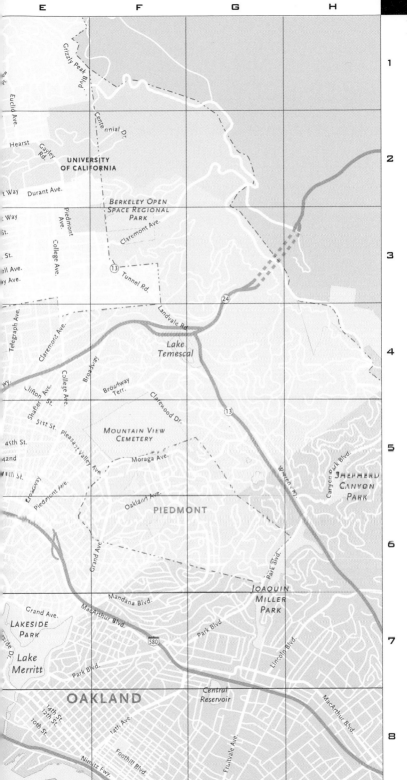

E   F   G   H

1

2

3

4

5

6

7

8

Grizzly Peak Blvd.

Euclid Ave.

Centennial Dr.

Hearst

Gayley Rd.

UNIVERSITY
OF CALIFORNIA

t Way   Durant Ave.

Piedmont Ave.

BERKELEY OPEN
SPACE REGIONAL
PARK

. Way

St.   Claremont Ave.

St.

College Ave.

ll Ave.

13

ay Ave.   Tunnel Rd.

24

Telegraph Ave.   Claremont Ave.   Landvale Rd.

Lake
Temescal

College Ave.

Broadway

Clifton Ave.

Broadway Terr.

51st St.   Clarewood Dr.

45th St.   Pleasant Valley Ave.   13

42nd   MOUNTAIN VIEW
CEMETERY

th St.   Broadway   Moraga Ave.

Piedmont Ave.   Warren Wy.

Canyon Oak Blvd.

SHEPHERD
CANYON
PARK

Oakland Ave.

PIEDMONT

Grand Ave.

Park Blvd.

JOAQUIN
MILLER
PARK

Grand Ave.   Mandana Blvd.

LAKESIDE
PARK   MacArthur Blvd.

Park Blvd.

de Dr.   580

Lake
Merritt   Park Blvd.

Lincoln Blvd.

MacArthur Blvd.

OAKLAND

14th St.   Central
Reservoir

12th St.

10th St.   14th Ave.

Foothill Blvd.

Fruitvale Ave.

Nimitz Fwy.

BERKELEY AND OAKLAND

4

A B C D

1

Municipal Pier

GOLDEN GATE
RECREATION AREA

Pier 45

Pier 43½ Pier 43 Pier 41

Pier 47
Fisherman's
Wharf

East
Harbor

AQUATIC PARK

Gashouse
Cove

FORT
MASON

Mexican
Museum

Maritime
Museum

Jefferson St.

Jones St.
Taylor St.
Mason St.
Powell St.

Marina
Blvd.

GHIRARDELLI
SQUARE

Beach St.

FISHERMAN'S
WHARF

2

North Point St.

Hyde St.

North Point St.

Bay St.

Bergen
Al.

Vandewater
St.

Bret Harte

Bay St.

RUSSIAN
HILL PARK

San Francisco
Art Institute

Francisco St.

Houston
St.
Water St.

North View
Ter.

Francisco St.

Chestnut St.

GEORGE R.
MOSCONE
RECREATION
CENTER

Francisco St.

Culebra Ter.

Lombard St.

Newell

Scotland

Magnolia St.

Chestnut St.

Montclair
Ter.

Larmont
Ter.

Jones St.

Greenwich St.

Mason St.

Via Bufano

3

101

Lombard St.

Gough St.

Lombard St.

Larkin St.

Hyde St.

Leavenworth St.

Filbert St.

Aladdin
Ter.

Kent
Webb
Pl.

Union

Moulton
St.

Greenwich St.

Blackstone

Southard

Bedford

Green

Pixley St.
Buchanan St.

Laguna St.

Harris Pl.

Franklin St.

Van Ness Ave.

Polk St.

Filbert St.

Havens
Amster

Black

Marion
Pl.

Redfield

Macondray La.

Webster St.

Filbert St.

Imperial

Union St.

Allen
Eastman
Pl.
Hastings
Ter.
Warner
Pl.

Russell

Sharp

Delgado

RUSSIAN
HILL

Alta
Vista
Montgomery

August

UNION
STREET

Union St.

Green St.

Green St.

Bonita St.

Vallejo St.

White
St.

Rockland

Waldo Al.

Glover
St.

Florence
St.

COOLBRITH
PARK

Fallon
Pl.

Valle

4

101

Octavia St.

Broadway

Cyrus Pl.

Broadway Tunnel

Bernard St.

Himmelman

Salmon

Auburn

Broa

John

Pacific Ave.

Pacific Ave.

MacArthur

Lynch Al.

Pacific Ave.

Mason

Fallon

Phoenix
Ter.

Marcy

Dixie Al.

Pacific Ave.

Jackson St.

McCormick

Wall Pl.

Burgoyne

Jackson St.

Cable Car
Barn

Bromley Pl.

Jackson St.

Washington St.

Sha
Truett St.

Shepha

5

WEBSTER ST.
HISTORIC
DISTRICT

Washington St.

Washington St.

Torrens
Ct.

Clay St.

Pleasant St.

Malvina D.
Ewer Pl.
Sproule

Sutter

Pacific
Med. Ctr.

LAFAYETTE
PARK

Clay St.

Troy Al.

Sacramento St.

Hyde St.

Kimball Pl.

Golden Ct.
Leroy Pl.

Jones St.

HUNTINGTON
PARK

NO

Webster St.

Buchanan St.

Laguna St.

Gough St.

Franklin St.

Van Ness Ave.

California St.

Acorn Al.

Leavenworth St.

Helen

Taylor St.

Frank
St.
Vine
Ter.

California St.

Pine St.

Touchard

Mulford St.

Orben Pl.

Austin St.

Frank Norris St.

Bush St.

6

Octavia St.

Fern St.

Sutter St.

Meacham

Cosmo Pl.

Hobart Al.

Wilmot St.

101

Hemlock St.

Post St.

Colin Pl.
Shannon St.

I. Duncan
La.

Derby

Cottage
Row

Cedar St.

Geary St.

Larkin St.

Amity Al.

Harlem
Al.

Leavenworth St.

Jones St.

O'Farrell St.

Japanese Cultural
&Trade Center

Myrtle St.

Polk St.

Hyde St.

Antonio

Cohen

Stevelos

Ellis St.

Geary St.

ST. FRANCIS
SQUARE

Cleary Ct.

Olive St.

Ellis St.

Wagner

Eddy St.

Hollis

St. Mary's
Cathedral

Willow St.

7

Webster St.

Hollis

Ellis St.

Eddy St.

Turk St.

Op

Fillmore St.

Willow St.

Larch St.

Dodge

Market St.

Eddy St.

WESTERN
ADDITION

JEFFERSON
SQUARE

Turk St.

Elm St.

Golden Gate Ave.

Breen

BART/MUNI

Main Post
Office

Turk St.

Gough St.

Franklin St.

Redwood St.

McAllister St.

Van Ness Ave.

Fulton St.

CIVIC
CENTER

7th St.

Golden Gate Ave.

McAllister St.

CIVIC
CENTER

8

Western
Addition
Cultural Ctr.

Laguna St.

Birch St.

Octavia St.

Grove St.

Lech Walesa
St.

8th St.

Mission St.
Julia

Fulton St.

Grove St.

Ivy St.

Ivy St.

Hayes St.

9th St.

Jessie St.

Minna St.

Natoma St.

Grove St.

Hayes St.

Fell St.

10th St.

Washburn St.

Howard St.

Tehama St.

Hayes St.

HAYES
VALLEY

Linden St.

Hickory St.

Grace St.

Clementina St.

Steiner St.

Fillmore St.

Fell St.

101

Oak St.

Hickory St.

Oak St.

Lily St.

Page St.

11th St.

Stevenson St.

Minna St.

Natoma St.

Dore St.

Folsom St.

Ringold

Lily St.

Rose St.

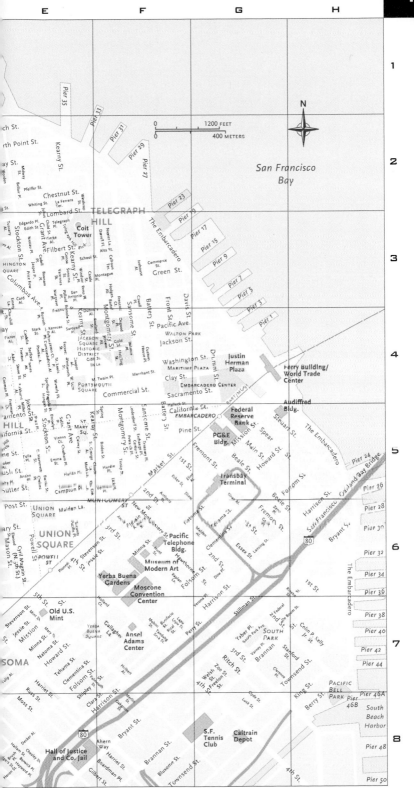

DOWNTOWN SAN FRANCISCO

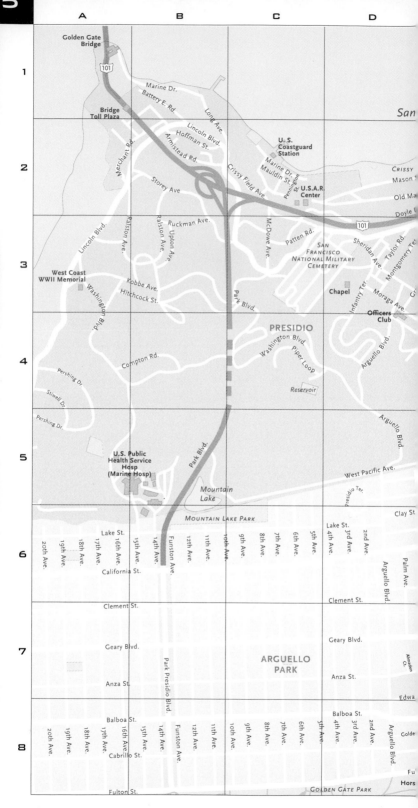

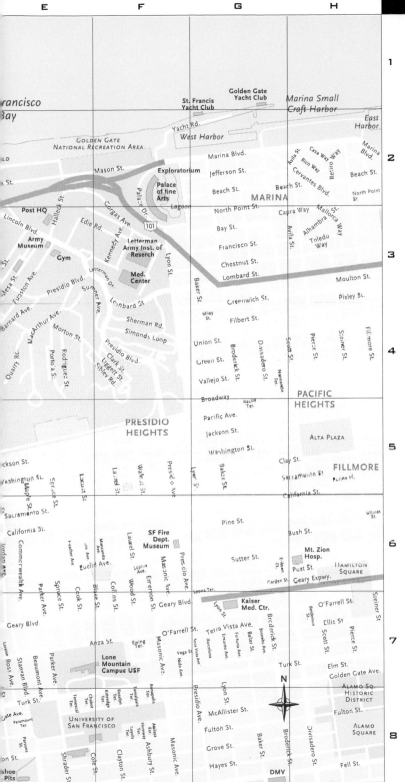

THE PRESIDIO AND RICHMOND DISTRICT

6

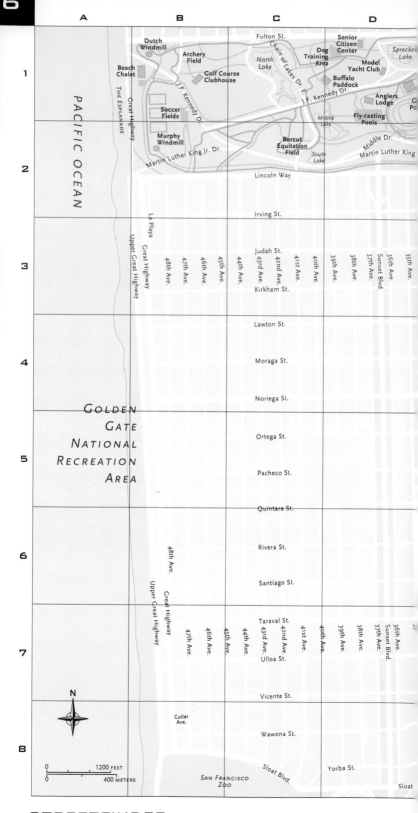

A **B** **C** **D**

1

2

3

4

5

6

7

8

PACIFIC OCEAN

THE ESPLANADE

Great Highway

Upper Great Highway

La Playa

48th Ave.
47th Ave.
46th Ave.
45th Ave.
44th Ave.
43rd Ave.
42nd Ave.
41st Ave.
40th Ave.
39th Ave.
38th Ave.
37th Ave.
Sunset Blvd.
36th Ave.
35th Ave.

Dutch Windmill
Beach Chalet
Archery Field
Golf Course Clubhouse
North Lake
Chain of Lakes Dr. E.
Fulton St.
Dog Training Area
Senior Citizen Center
Sprecke Lake
Model Yacht Club
Buffalo Paddock
J. F. Kennedy Dr.
Anglers Lodge
Fly-casting Pools
J.F. Kennedy Dr.
Soccer Fields
Murphy Windmill
Martin Luther King Jr. Dr.
Bercut Equitation Field
Middle Lake
South Lake
Middle Dr.
Martin Luther King

Lincoln Way

Irving St.

Judah St.

Kirkham St.

Lawton St.

Moraga St.

Noriega St.

Ortega St.

Pacheco St.

Quintara St.

Rivera St.

Santiago St.

Taraval St.

Ulloa St.

Vicente St.

Cutler Ave.

Wawona St.

Sloat Blvd.

Yorba St.

Sloat

GOLDEN GATE NATIONAL RECREATION AREA

48th Ave.
Great Highway
Upper Great Highway

47th Ave.
46th Ave.
45th Ave.
44th Ave.
43rd Ave.
42nd Ave.
41st Ave.
40th Ave.
39th Ave.
38th Ave.
37th Ave.
Sunset Blvd.
36th Ave.

N

0 1200 FEET
0 400 METERS

SAN FRANCISCO ZOO

STREETFINDER

E   F   G   H

Spreckels Lake Dr.

Cross Over Dr.

Marx
Meadow

Transverse Dr.

Boat
House

Redwood
Memorial
Grove

Lindley
Meadow

J.F. Kennedy Dr.

Barbecue
Pits

Lloyd
Lake

Pioneer
Log Cabin

den Gate
k Stables

Speedway
Meadow

Cross Over Dr.

Stow Lake Dr.

en Gate Park
ields/Stables

GOLDEN GATE PARK

Strawberry
Hill

Stow Lake

1

Metson
Lake

Elk Glen
Lake

Metson Rd.

Mallard
Lake

Middle Dr.

Martin Luther King Jr. Dr.

Lincoln Way

Lincoln Way

2

Irving St.

Irving St.

Judah St.

33rd Ave.   32nd Ave.   31st Ave.   30th Ave.   29th Ave.   28th Ave.   27th Ave.   26th Ave.   25th Ave.   24th Ave.   23rd Ave.   22nd Ave.   21st Ave.   20th Ave.   19th Ave.   18th Ave.   17th Ave.   16th Ave.   15th Ave.   14th Ave.

Kirkham St.

Kirkham St.

Lawton St.

3

Lawton St.

Lawton St.

SUNSET
REC.
CENTER

Loraha Ave.

Aloha
Ave.

Aloha Ave.

Moraga St.

Moraga St.

GRAND
VIEW
PARK

4

SUNSET

Noriega St.

Noriega St.

DISTRICT

Ortega St

Ortega St.

19th Ave.

Pacheco St.

Sunset
Reservoir

Pacheco St.

18th Ave.   17th Ave.   16th Ave.   15th Ave.   14th Ave.

5

Quintara St.

Quintara St.

Rivera St.

Rivera St.

Cecilia Ave.

6

Santiago St.

Santiago St.

McCoppin
Square

Taraval St.

34th Ave.   33rd Ave.   32nd Ave.   31st Ave.   30th Ave.   29th Ave.   28th Ave.   27th Ave.   26th Ave.   25th Ave.   24th Ave.   23rd Ave.   22nd Ave.   21st Ave.   20th Ave.   19th Ave.   18th Ave.   17th Ave.   16th Ave.   15th Ave.   14th Ave.

Ulloa St.

7

Vicente St.

Vicente St.

LARSEN PARK

Escolta Way

PARKSIDE
SQUARE

Wawona St.

Wawona St.

Wawona Ave.

Crestlake Dr.

Laguna
Puerca

PINE LAKE PARK

STERN GROVE

19th Ave.

West Portal Ave.

Portola Dr.

orba St.

Crestlake Dr.

Crestlake Dr.

Ardenwood
Way

San Rafael
Way

San Leandro Way

Constanso
Way

Sloat Blvd.

8

A   B   C   D

M.H. de Young Memorial Museum
Multi-Purpose Paved Area
Conservatory of Flowers
McLaren Lodge (Park HQ)
PANHANDLE

Asian Art Museum
John F. Kennedy Dr.
Tea Garden Dr.
California Academy of Sciences
Morrison Planetarium
Lily Pond
Tennis Courts
Page St.
Cole St.

1

Music Concourse
Middle Drive East
Bowling Green Dr.
Stanyan St.
Haight St.

Shakespeare Garden
Steinhart Aquarium
Sharon Meadow

Strybing Arboretum and Botanical Gardens
Lawn Bowling
Children's Playground
Mothers' Meadow
Waller St.
Cole St.
Claytory St.
Belvedere St.

Big Rec. Ball Field
Kezar Dr.
Kezar Stadium
Kezar Pavilion
Beulah St.

Hall of Flowers
Martin Luther King Jr. Dr.
Frederick St.
Frederick St.
SUNSET TUNNEL Pk.

Lincoln Way
Lincoln Way
Carl St.
Carl St.

2

Hugo St.
2nd Ave.
Arguello Blvd.
Frederick St.
Parnassus Ave.
Belvedere St.

Irving St.
Hillway Ave.
Carl St.
Shrader St.
Grattan St.

12th Ave.
11th Ave.
10th Ave.
9th Ave.
8th Ave.
7th Ave.
6th Ave.
5th Ave.
4th Ave.
3rd Ave.
Hill Point
Stanyan St.
Parnassus Ave.
Alma St.

Judah St.
Parnassus Ave.
Woodland Ave.
Willard St.
Belmont Ave.
Rivoli St.

University of California San Francisco (Medical Center)
Edgewood Ave.
17th St.

Kirkham St.
5th Ave.
BUENA VISTA
Carmel St.

3

Lawton St.
Locksley Ave.
Mt. Sutro Dr.
Upper Service Rd.
Belgrave Ave.
Twin Peaks Blvd.

MT. SUTRO
Johnstone Dr.
Mountain Spring
Reco

12th Ave.
Moraga St.
7th Ave.
Oakhurst Ln.
Behr Ave.
Adolf Sutro
St. Germain Ave.
Glenbrook Ave.
Palo Alto Ave.
Twin Peaks Blvd.

4

Warren Dr.
Christopher Dr.
Woodhaven Ct.
La Avanzada
Fairview Ct.
TWIN PEAKS

Noriega St.
Decoshire Way
Forest Knolls Dr.
Dellbrook Ave.
Clairview Ct.

11th Ave.
10th Ave.
9th Ave.
8th Ave.
Oak Park Dr.
Panorama Dr.

Pacifico St.
Ortega St.
Laguna Honda Reservoir
Clarendon Ave.
Dellbrook Ave.
Aquavista Way
Skyline Way
Gladeview Way
Knollview Way
TWIN PEAK

Funston Ave.
GOLDEN HEIGHTS PARK
Linares Ave.
Ventura Ave.
Laguna Honda

5

Cragmont Ave.
Alton Ave.
Laguna Honda
Laguna Honda Hospital
Cityview Way
Longview
Twin Peaks Blvd.
Midcrest Way
Blvd.
Dawn

Quintara St.
Solejo Ave.
Pacifico St.
Castenada Ave.
Magellan Ave.
Pandorama Dr.
Mountain View Ct.
Longview
Glenview
Sue

Funston Ave.
Mendosa Ave.
Mesa Ave.
Santa Rita Ave.
Lopez Ave.
Marcela Ave.
Marcela Sola Ave.
Glenview

9th Ave.
Woodside Ave.
Portola Dr.

San Marcos Ave.
Magellan Ave.
Balceta Ave.
O'Shaughnessy

6

Castenada Ave.
Dewey Blvd.
Merced Ave.
Hernandez Ave.
Idora St.
Teresita Blvd.

Dorantes Ave.
Vasquez Ave.
Garcia Ave.
Ulloa St.
Portola Dr.
Fowler Ave.

Taraval St.
Rockaway Ave.
Rockwood Ct.
Portola Dr.
Juanita Way
Evelyn Way

Kensington Way
Edgehill Way
Rockwood
Del Sur Ave.
Chaves Ave.
Agua Way
Encline Ct.

7

Forest Side Ave.
Madrone Ave.
Wawona Ave.
Lenox Way
Allston Way
Claremont Blvd.
Dorchester Way
Ulloa St.
Rockdale Dr.
Myra Way
Reposa Way
Marietta Dr.

Vicente St.
Wawona Ave.
Portola Dr.
San Lorenzo
Santa Paula Ave.
Marne Ave.
Juanita Al.
Teresita Blvd.
Victoria Way
Arroyo Way

West Portal Ave.
MT. DAVIDSON PARK
Molimo Dr.

Portola Dr.
Terrace Dr.
Miraloma Dr.
San Pablo Ave.
Casitas Ave.
Dalewood Way
Myra Way
Bella Vista Way
Molimo Dr.

San Anselmo
Santa Clara Ave.
Yerba Buena Ave.
Lansdale Ave.
Robin Hood Dr.
Dorcas Way
Verna St.

8

San Benito Way
San Buena Ventura
Casitas Ave.
Cresta Vista Dr.
Los Palmos
Foerster St.

Santa Ana Ave.
San Jacinto Way
Hazelwood Ave.
Los Palmos Dr.
Los Palmos Dr.

San Fernando Way
Brentwood Ave.

STREETFINDER

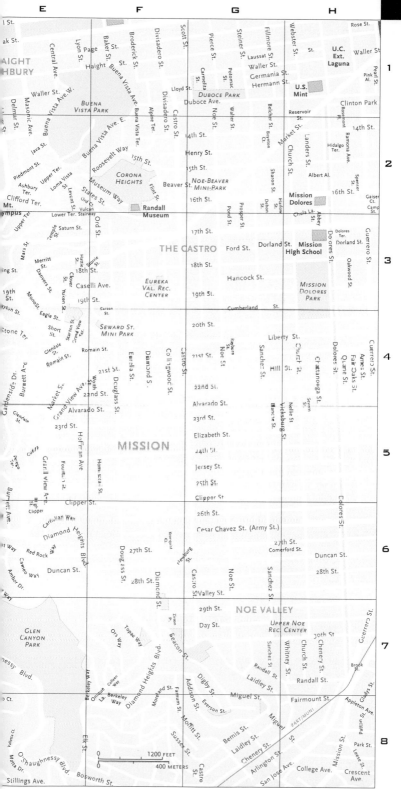

THE CASTRO, NOE VALLEY, AND THE MISSION (WEST)

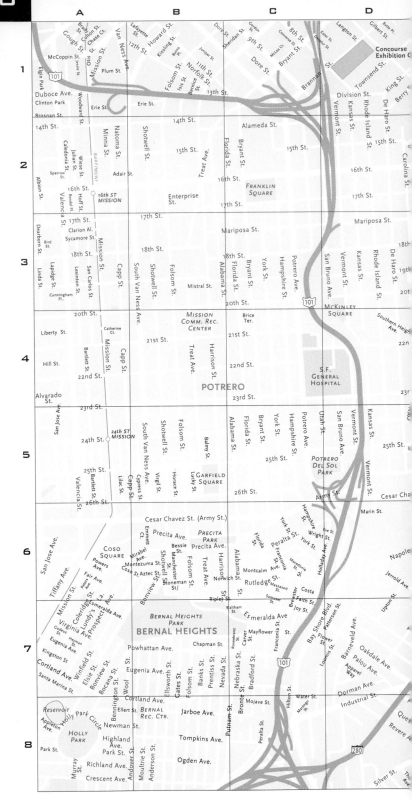

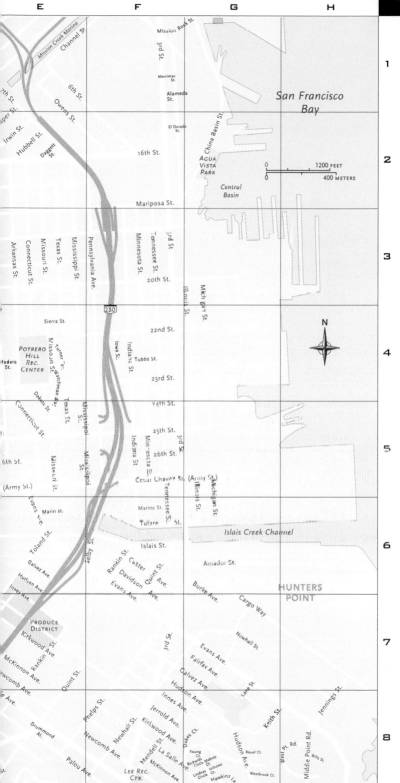

BERNAL HEIGHTS, POTRERO, AND THE MISSION (EAST)

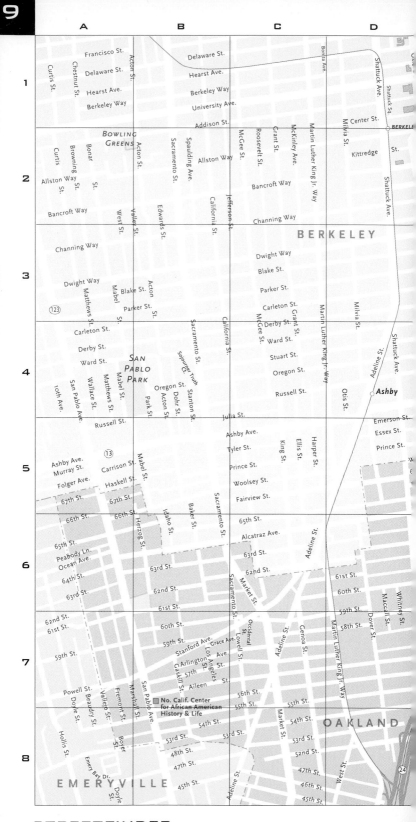

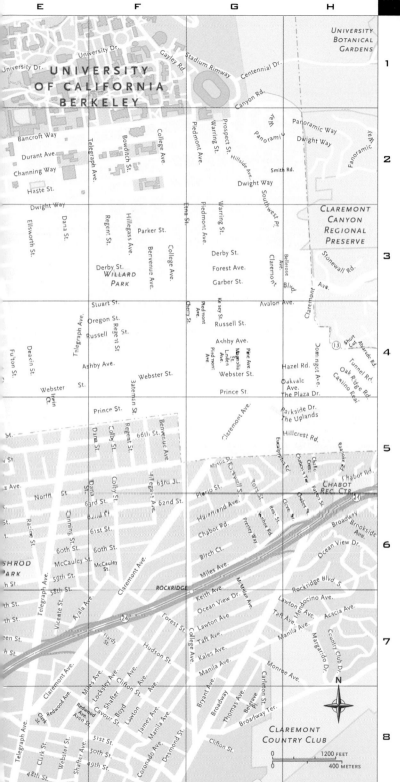

E   F   G   H

1

UNIVERSITY
BOTANICAL
GARDENS

University Dr.
Gayley Rd.
Stadium Rimway
Centennial Dr.

UNIVERSITY
OF CALIFORNIA
BERKELEY

Canyon Rd.

2

Bancroft Way
Telegraph Ave.
Bowditch St.
College Ave.
Piedmont Ave.
Prospect St.
Warring St.
Hillside St.
Panoramic Way
Panoramic Way
Dwight Way
Panoramic Way

Durant Ave.
Channing Way
Haste St.

Smith Rd.
Dwight Way

Dwight Way
Dana St.
Regent St.
Hillegass Ave.
Parker St.
Elms Rd.
Piedmont Ave.
Warring St.
Southwest Pl.

CLAREMONT
CANYON
REGIONAL
PRESERVE

3

Ellsworth St.
Derby St.
WILLARD
PARK
College Ave.
Bervenue Ave.
Derby St.
Forest Ave.
Garber St.
Claremont
Bellrose Ave.
Blvd.
Stonewall Rd.
Ave.
Claremont

Stuart St.
Telegraph Ave.
Oregon St.
Regent St.
Russell
Redmont Ave.
Cherry St.
Kelsey St.
Avalon Ave.
Russell St.

4

Fulton St.
Deakin St.
Ashby Ave.
Webster St.
Ashby Ave.
Magnolia
Piedmont Ave.
Linden
Pine Ave.
Webster St.
Hazel Rd.
Oakvale Ave.
The Plaza Dr.
Domingo Ave.
Oak Ridge Rd.
Camino Real
Tunnel Rd.
Alvarado Rd.
Short Cut
13

Webster St.
Irwin St.
Prince St.
Prince St.
Colby St.
66th St.
Regent St.
Dana St.
Bervenue Ave.
Claremont Ave.
Prince St
Parkside Dr.
The Uplands
Hillcrest Rd.
Eucalyptus Rd.
Baywood

5

North St.
Dana St.
Colby St.
Hillegass Ave.
63rd St.
Mystic St.
Cross St.
Russell St.
Ross St.
Chabot Cres.
Chabot Ct.
Chabot Rd.

Racine St.
62nd St.
62nd St.
61st St.
60th St.
Piedra St.
Harwood Ave.
Chabot Rd.
Presley Way
Yerba St.
Clive St.
Chabot St.
CHABOT
REC. CTR
24

6

SHROD PARK
Telegraph Ave.
McCauley St.
59th St.
58th St.
Claremont Ave.
60th St.
McCauley St.
Birch Ct.
Miles Ave.
ROCKRIDGE
Keith Ave.
McMillan Ave.
Ocean View Dr.
Broadway
Brookside Ave.
Ocean View Dr.
Rockridge Blvd. S

Vicente St.
Ayala Ave.
Claremont Ave.
Forest St.
College Ave.
Ocean View Dr.
Lawton Ave.
Taft Ave.
Manila Ave.
Lawton Ave.
Mendocino Ave.
Taft Ave.
Acacia Ave.
Manila Ave.
Margarido Dr.
Country Club Dr.

7

Hudson St.
Kales Ave.
Manila Ave.
Monroe Ave.
Carleton St.

Telegraph Ave.
Claremont Ave.
Redwood St.
Clark St.
Miles Ave.
Locksley Ave.
Cavour St.
Shafter
Boyd
Clifton St. Ave.
Redwood Aven.
Lawton
James Ave.
Manila Ave.
Bryant Ave.
Broadway
Thomas Ave.
Belgrave St.
Broadway Ter.

8

48th St.
Clark St.
Webster St.
Shafter Ave.
51st St.
50th St.
49th St.
Coronado Ave.
Desmond St.
Clifton St.

CLAREMONT
COUNTRY CLUB

N

0   1200 FEET
0   400 METERS

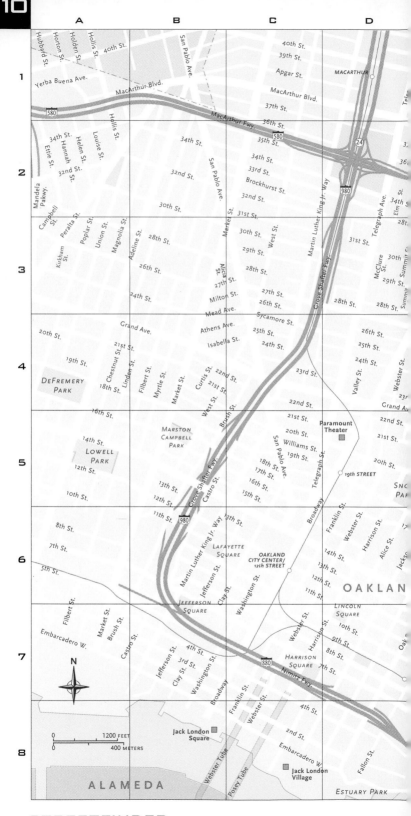

E   F   G   H

MOUNTAIN VIEW CEMETERY

42nd St.
Rich St.
41st St.
40th St.
Ruby St.
38th St.
Shafter Ave.
Opal St.
Webster
Manila Ave.
Emerald St.
Garnet St.
Broadway
Terrace St.
Gilbert St.
Ridgeway Ave.
Montgomery St.
John St.
Pleasant Valley St.
Brandon St.
Clenedon Ave.
Pleasant Valley Ct.
Ramona Ave.
Moraga Ave.
Ramona Ave.
Rosada Ave.
Montecello Ave.
Glen Ave.
Grand Ave.
Arroyo Ave.
York Dr.
Ricardo Dr.
Park Way
Manor Dr.

Howe St.
Piedmont Ave.
Echo Ave.
Rose Ave.
Linda Ave.

MacArthur Blvd.
Manila Ave.
40th Way
Cerrito Ave.
40th St.
Glen Ave.
Monte Vista Ave.
Monte Cresta Ave.
Kingston Ave.
Greenbank Ave.
Cambridge Way
DRACENA PARK

MOSSWOOD PARK
Montell St.
Rio Vista Ave.
Yosemite Ave.
Fairmount Ave.
Rivo Vista St.
Lake Ave.
Nace St.
Howard Ave.
PIEDMONT

thur Fwy.
580
Harrison
Harrison Ave.
Lake Sunnyside Ave.
Olive Ave.
Oakland Ave.
Fairview Ave.
Nova Dr.

Broadway
Brook St.
Richmond Blvd.
Kempton Ave.
Frisbie St.
Frisbie Way
Santa Rosa Ave.
Santa Mariposa St.
ROSE GARDEN PARK
Jean St.
Wildwood Ave.
Sylvan Way

Valdez St.
Richmond Ave.
Fairmount Ave.
Garland St.
Harrison St.
Oakland Ave.
Moss Ave.
Vernon St.
Chetwood St.
Santa Clara Ave.
Jean St.
Crofton Ave.
Fairbanks Ave.
Warfield Ave.

Hamilton Pl.
Orange St.
MacArthur Blvd.
Mira Vista Ave.
Grand Ave.
Walker Ave.
Vermont St.
Prince St.
Rose Ave.
Weldon Ave.

27th St.
Vernon St.
Adams St.
Jayne Ave.
Euclid Ave.
Elwood Ave.
Valle Vista Ave.
Walker Ave.
Warfield Ave.
York St.
Mandana Blvd.
Erie St.
Lakeshore Ave.
Balfour Ave.

Waverly St.
Bay Pl.
Morecito Ave.
Warwick Ave.
Pain Ave.
Bellevue
Santa Clara Ave.
Crescent St.
Rand Ave.

Lakeside Dr.
Farkview Ter.
Lenox Ave.
Lee St.
Perkins St.
Van Buren Ave.
Belmont St.
Staten Ave.
Lagunitas Ave.
Lakeshore Ave.
Longridge Rd.
Trestle Glen Ave.

Children's Fairyland
Grand Ave.
Ellita Ave.
LAKE SHORE PARK
Lake Park Ave.
MacArthur Blvd.
Hillgirt Cir.

LAKESIDE PARK
Bellevue
Natural Science Center
Waterfowl Refuge
Merritt Ave.
Lakeshore Ave.
Merritt Ave.
Wesley Ave.
Radnor St.
Haddon Rd.
Kenwyn
Athol Ave.
Prospect Ave.
McKinley Ave.
Cleveland St.
Spruce St.

side Dr.
Lake Merritt
Wayne Ave.
Hanover Ave.
Lester Ave.
Newton Ave.
Athol Ave.
Brooklyn Ave.
Park Blvd.

Lakeside Dr.
Boat House
Camron-Stanford House
Athol Ave.
Park Blvd.
ATHOL PLAZA
Park Blvd.
Ivy Dr.

kland seum
PERALTA PARK
1st Ave.
2nd Ave.
3rd Ave.
4th Ave.
Foothill Blvd.
5th Ave.
6th Ave.
E. 22nd St.
E. 21st St.
E. 20th St.
E. 19th St.
E. 24th St.
E. 23rd St.

MERRITT
E. 15th St.
E. 14th St.
7th Ave.
8th Ave.
E. 18th St.
E. 17th St.
9th Ave.
10th Ave.
11th Ave.

7th St.
E. 13th St.
CLINTON SQUARE
E. 12th St.
E. 11th St.
E. 10th St.
E. 8th St.
FRANKLIN CENTER
12th Ave.
13th Ave.
14th Ave.
15th Ave.
16th Ave.
17th Ave.
E. 21st St.

880

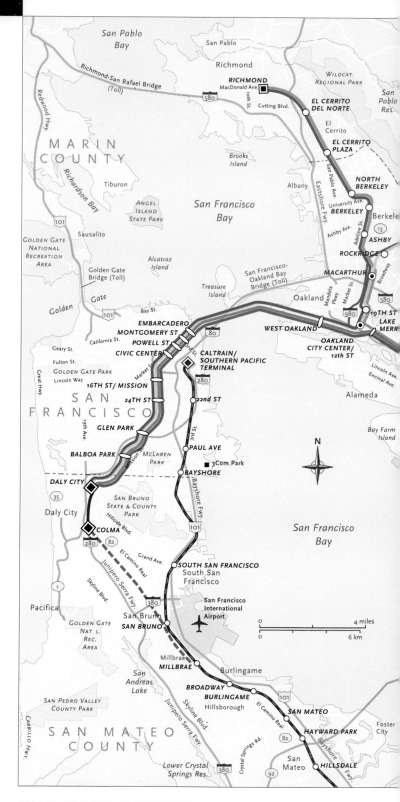

THE BART SYSTEM

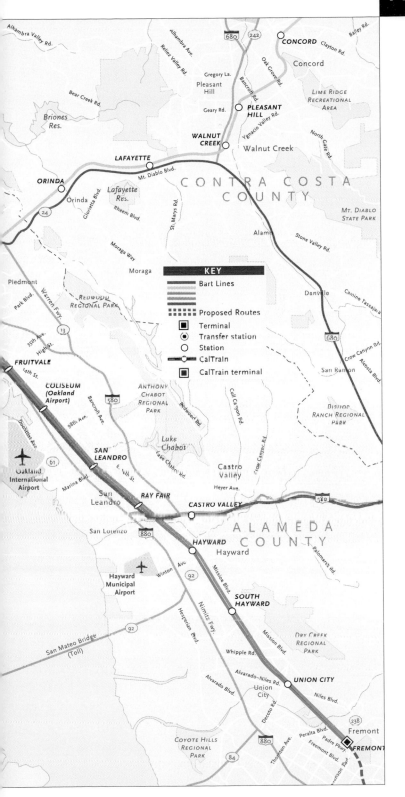

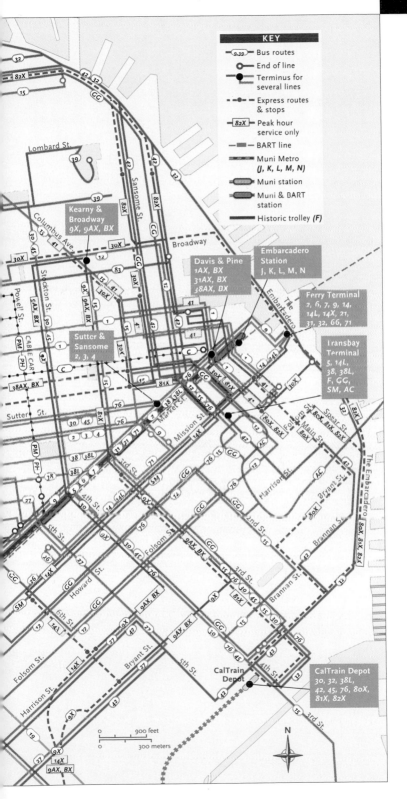

KEY

- **Bus routes** — 9,39
- **End of line** — ○
- **Terminus for several lines** — ●
- **Express routes & stops** — - - ●
- **Peak hour service only** — 82X
- **BART line**
- **Muni Metro** (J, K, L, M, N)
- **Muni station**
- **Muni & BART station**
- **Historic trolley** (F)

Kearny & Broadway
9X, 9AX, BX

Davis & Pine
1AX, BX
31AX, BX
38AX, DX

Embarcadero Station
J, K, L, M, N

Ferry Terminal
2, 6, 7, 9, 14,
14L, 14X, 21,
31, 32, 66, 71

Sutter & Sansome
2, 3, 4

Transbay Terminal
5, 14L,
38, 38L,
F, GG,
SM, AC

CalTrain Depot
30, 32, 38L,
42, 45, 76, 80X,
81X, 82X

Lombard St.
Columbus Ave.
Stockton St.
Powell St.
Sutter St.
Market St.
Mission St.
3rd St.
4th St.
5th St.
6th St.
Folsom St.
Howard St.
Bryant St.
Folsom St.
Harrison St.
2nd St.
Brannan St.
The Embarcadero
Sansome St.
Broadway
The Embarcadero
Spear St.
Main St.
Harrison St.
Bryant St.
Brannan St.

CABLE CAR

CalTrain Depot

0 900 feet
0 300 meters

N

DOWNTOWN SAN FRANCISCO

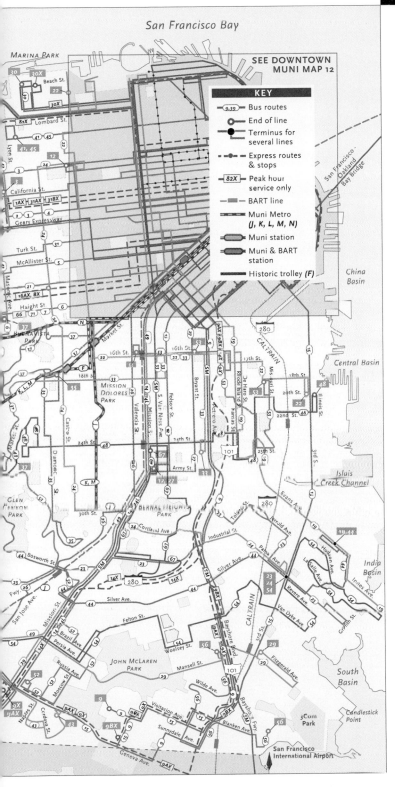

San Francisco Bay

MARINA PARK

SEE DOWNTOWN
MUNI MAP 12

KEY	
○–9,39	Bus routes
○	End of line
●	Terminus for several lines
●–●–	Express routes & stops
82X	Peak hour service only
	BART line
	Muni Metro (J, K, L, M, N)
	Muni station
	Muni & BART station
	Historic trolley (F)

Beach St.

Lombard St.

Lyon St.

California St.

Geary Expressway

Turk St.

McAllister St.

Masonic Ave.

Haight St

BUENA VISTA PARK

Market St.

16th St.

18th St.

MISSION DOLORES PARK

Castro St.

Valencia St.

Mission St.

S. Van Ness Ave.

Folsom St.

Bryant St.

24th St.

Army St.

30th St.

BERNAL HEIGHTS PARK

Cortland Ave.

GLEN CANYON PARK

Bosworth St.

Industrial St.

Silver Ave.

Felton St.

Mission St.

San Jose Ave.

Brazil Ave.

Persia Ave.

Russia Ave.

JOHN McLAREN PARK

Moscow St.

Woolsey St.

Mansell St.

Wilde Ave.

Visitacion Ave.

Sunnydale Ave.

Geneva Ave.

San Francisco Oakland Bay Bridge

China Basin

Central Basin

CALTRAIN

Rhode Island St.

Mississippi St.

Kansas St.

Potrero Ave.

Illinois St.

3rd St.

Islais Creek Channel

Evans Ave.

Toland St.

Arnold Ave.

India Basin

Hudson Ave.

LaSalle Ave.

Innes Ave.

Revere Ave.

Van Dyke Ave.

Griffith St.

Barneveld Ave.

Bayshore Blvd.

CALTRAIN

Fitzgerald Ave.

South Basin

Candlestick Point

3Com Park

Blanken Ave.

Bayshore Fwy.

San Francisco International Airport

SAN FRANCISCO

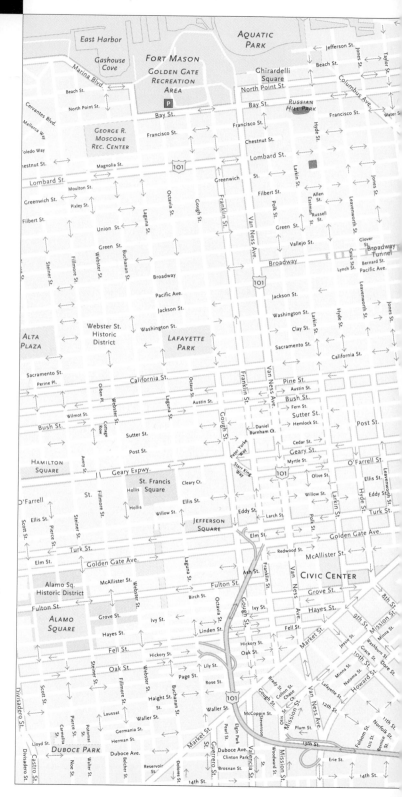

DRIVING AND PARKING

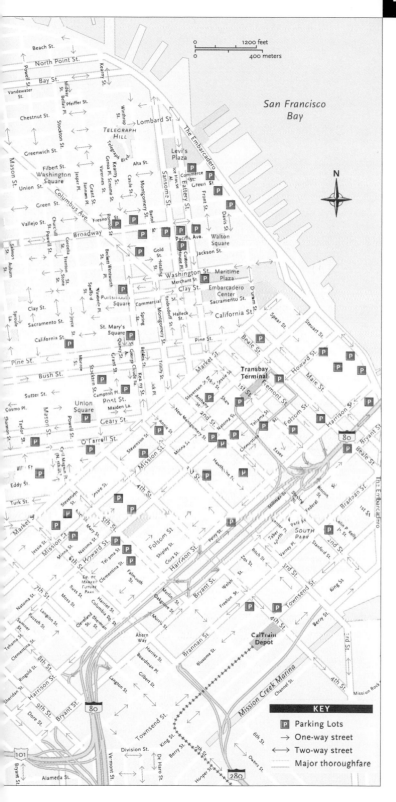

San Francisco Bay

TELEGRAPH HILL

Washington Square

Union Square

Transbay Terminal

South Park

CalTrain Depot

Mission Creek Marina

N

1200 feet
400 meters

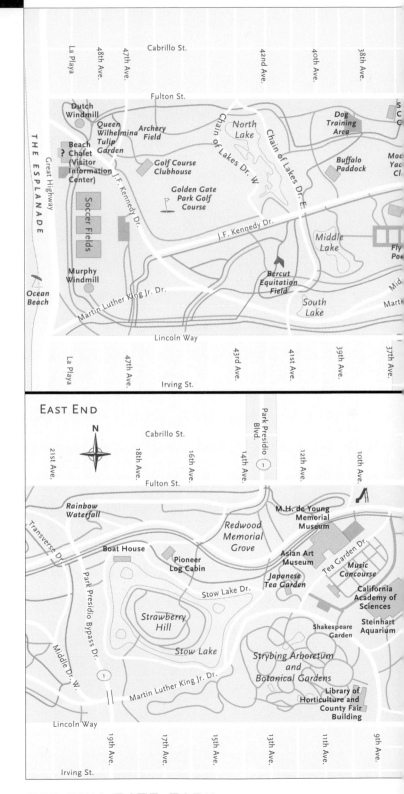

La Playa
48th Ave.
47th Ave.
Cabrillo St.
42nd Ave.
40th Ave.
38th Ave.

Fulton St.

Dutch Windmill
Queen Wilhelmina Tulip Garden
Archery Field
Chain of Lakes Dr. W.
North Lake
Chain of Lakes Dr. E.
Dog Training Area
S C

Beach Chalet (Visitor Information Center) ?
Golf Course Clubhouse
Buffalo Paddock
Mod Yac Cl

J. F. Kennedy Dr.
Golden Gate Park Golf Course

Soccer Fields
J.F. Kennedy Dr.
Middle Lake
Fly Po

Murphy Windmill
Bercut Equitation Field
South Lake
Mid

Ocean Beach
Martin Luther King Jr. Dr.
Marti

Lincoln Way

La Playa
47th Ave.
43rd Ave.
41st Ave.
39th Ave.
37th Ave.

Irving St.

THE ESPLANADE
Great Highway

EAST END

N

21st Ave.
18th Ave.
Cabrillo St.
16th Ave.
14th Ave.
Park Presidio Blvd.
12th Ave.
10th Ave.

Fulton St.

Rainbow Waterfall
Redwood Memorial Grove
M.H. de Young Memorial Museum

Transverse Dr.
Boat House
Pioneer Log Cabin
Asian Art Museum
Tea Garden Dr.
Music Concourse

Park Presidio Bypass Dr.
Japanese Tea Garden
California Academy of Sciences

Stow Lake Dr.
Strawberry Hill
Shakespeare Garden
Steinhart Aquarium

Stow Lake
Strybing Arboretum and Botanical Gardens

Middle Dr. W.
Martin Luther King Jr. Dr.
Library of Horticulture and County Fair Building

Lincoln Way

19th Ave.
17th Ave.
15th Ave.
13th Ave.
11th Ave.
9th Ave.

Irving St.

GOLDEN GATE PARK

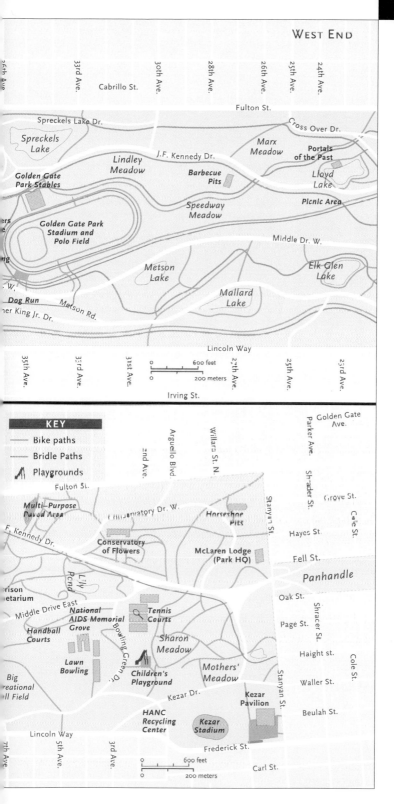

The Sourcebook
For Your City

MANY MAPS • WHERE & HOW

FIND IT ALL • NIGHT & DAY

ANTIQUES TO ZIPPERS

BARGAINS • BAUBLES • KITES

ELEGANT EDIBLES • ETHNIC EATS

STEAK HOUSES • FISH HOUSES

BISTROS • TRATTORIAS

CLASSICAL • JAZZ • CABARET

COMEDY • THEATER • DANCE

BARS • CLUBS • BLUES

COOL TOURS

HOUSECLEANING • CATERING

LOST & FOUND • THE CABLE GUY

GET A LAWYER • GET A DENTIST

GET A NEW PET • GET A VET

MUSEUMS • GALLERIES

PARKS • GARDENS • RINKS

AQUARIUMS TO ZOOS

BASEBALL TO ROCK CLIMBING

FESTIVALS • EVENTS

DAY SPAS • DAY TRIPS

HOTELS • HOT LINES

PASSPORT PIX • TRAVEL INFO

HELICOPTER TOURS

DINERS • DELIS • PIZZERIAS

BRASSERIES • CAFÉS

BOOTS • BOOKS • BUTTONS

BICYCLES • SKATES

SUITS • SHOES • HATS

RENT A TUX • RENT A COSTUME

BAKERIES • SPICE SHOPS

SOUP TO NUTS

Fodor's

CITYGUIDE
SAN FRANCISCO

FODOR'S TRAVEL PUBLICATIONS • NEW YORK, TORONTO, LONDON, SYDNEY, AUCKLAND

WWW.FODORS.COM

FODOR'S CITYGUIDE SAN FRANCISCO

EDITOR
Caragh Rockwood

EDITORIAL CONTRIBUTORS
Jennifer Brewer, Lisa Alcalay Klug, Cathleen Miller, Andy Moore, Sharon Silva,
AnneLise Sorensen, Sharron Wood

EDITORIAL PRODUCTION
Nicole Revere

MAPS
David Lindroth Inc., *cartographer*; Bob Blake, *map editor*

DESIGN
Fabrizio La Rocca, *creative director*; Allison Saltzman, *text design*;
Tigist Getachew, *cover design*; Jolie Novak, *photo editor*

PRODUCTION/MANUFACTURING
Mike Costa

COVER PHOTOGRAPH
Robert Holmes

Series created by Marilyn Appleberg

COPYRIGHT

Second Edition

ISBN 0–679–00419–X

ISSN 1099–8535

SPECIAL SALES

CONTENTS

METROPOLITAN LIFE

On a bad day in a big city, the little things that go with living shoulder-to-shoulder with a few million people wear us all down. But the special pleasures of urban life have a way of keeping us out of the suburbs—and thankful, even, for every second of stress. The field of daffodils in the park on a fine spring day. The perfect little black dress that you find for half price. The markets—so fabulously well stocked that you can cook any recipe without resorting to mail-order catalogs. The way you can sometimes turn a corner and discover a whole new world, so foreign you can hardly believe you're less than a mile from home. The never-ending wealth of possibilities and opportunities.

If you know where to find it all, the city cannot defeat you. With knowledge comes power. That's why Fodor's has prepared this book. It will put phone numbers at your fingertips. It'll take you to new places and remind you of those you've forgotten. It's the ultimate urban companion—and, we hope, your **new best friend in the city.**

It's the **citywise shopaholic,** who always knows where to find something, no matter how obscure. We've made a concerted effort to bring hundreds of great shops to your attention, so that you'll never be at a loss, whether you need a special birthday present for a great friend or some obscure craft items to make Halloween costumes for your kids.

It's the **restaurant know-it-all,** who's full of ideas for every occasion—you know, the one who would never send you to Café de la Snub, because he knows it's always overbooked, the food is boring, and the staff is rude. In this book we'll steer you around the corner, to a perfect little place with five tables, a fireplace, and a chef on her way up.

It's a **hip barfly buddy,** who can give you advice when you need a charming nook, not too noisy, to take a friend after work. Among the dozens of bars and nightspots in this book, you're bound to find something that fits your mood.

It's the **sagest arts maven you know,** the one who always has the scoop on what's on that's worthwhile on any given night. In these pages, you'll find dozens of concert venues and arts organizations.

It's also the **city whiz,** who knows how to get you where you're going, wherever you are.

It's the **best map guide** on the shelves, and it puts **all the city in your briefcase** or on your bookshelf.

Stick with us. We lay out all the options for your leisure time—and gently nudge you away from the duds—so that you can truly enjoy metropolitan living.

YOUR GUIDES

No one person can know it all. To help get you on track around the city, we've hand-picked a stellar group of local experts to share their wisdom.

Globe-trotting freelance writer **Lisa Alcalay Klug**, a former staff writer for the *Los Angeles Times* and the Associated Press, earned her masters at UC Berkeley's Graduate School of Journalism. Her love of the Bay Area's natural beauty—not to mention day spas—is contagious in the chapter she updated, Parks, Gardens & Sports. Her favorite outdoor haunts include the Berkeley Rose Garden, Tilden Park's Lake Anza, and China Beach. Her travel articles appear in *Shape, Men's Fitness*, and other national publications.

Cathleen Miller, our fearless Places to Explore updater, has published essays in the *Washington Post, Denver Post, Times-Picayune, San Francisco Examiner*, and the anthology *Travelers' Tales San Francisco*. After living many years in Baghdad by the Bay, she currently makes her home in Napa—a region with less art, but considerably more wine.

Hotels updater **Andy Moore** holed up in so many hotels in his own hometown that he fears he wore out his white gloves in the line of duty. He is a frequent Fodor's contributor, and also an independent filmmaker.

Local eating-out guru **Sharon Silva**, who broke bread for the Restaurants chapter, contributes regularly to *San Francisco Magazine* and other local publications.

AnneLise Sorensen works as a freelance writer in San Francisco and has written for numerous travel guidebooks. She is also an avid traveler, and at press time was making her way through India, Spain, and France. She scoured her hometown streets, however, for the compilation of City Sources.

Freelancer writer, editor, and web publishing consultant **Sharron Wood** has contributed to more than a dozen travel guides to her favorite city and home of 10 years. For this book she fought overindulgence of various sorts as she revised the Shopping and the Arts, Entertainment & Nightlife chapters.

Marilyn Appleberg, who conceived this series, is a city-lover through and through. She plots her urban forays from an archetypal Greenwich Village brownstone with two fireplaces.

It goes without saying that our contributors have chosen all establishments strictly on their own merits—no establishment has paid to be included in this book.

HOW TO USE THIS BOOK

The first thing you need to know is that everything in this book is **arranged by category and by alphabetical order** within category.

Now, before you go any farther, check out the **city maps** at the front of the book. Each map has a number, in a black box at the top of the page, and grid coordinates along the top and side margins. Listings in the book are keyed to one of these maps. Look for the map number in a small black box preceding each establishment name. The grid code follows in italics. For establishments with more than one location, additional map numbers and grid codes appear at the end of the listing. To locate a museum that's identified in the text as as **7** *e-6*, turn to Map 7 and locate the address within the e-66 grid square. To locate restaurants that are nearby, simply skim the text in the restaurant chapter for listings identified as being on Map 7.

Throughout the guide, as applicable, we name the neighborhood in which each sight, restaurant, shop, or other destination is located. We also give you complete opening hours and admission fees for sights; closing information for shops; and credit-card, price, reservation, closing information, and takeout and delivery for restaurants.

At the end of the book, in addition to an **alphabetical index,** you'll find **directories of shops and restaurants by neighborhood.**

Chapter 7, City Sources, lists essential information, such as entertainment hot lines (for those times you can't lay your hands on a newspaper), and resources for residents—everything from vet and lawyer-referral services to caterers worth calling.

We've worked hard to make sure that all of the information we give you is accurate at press time. Still, time brings changes, so always confirm information when it matters—especially if you're making a detour.

Were the restaurants we recommended as described? Did you find a wonderful shop you'd like to share? If you have complaints, we'll look into them and revise our entries in the next edition when the facts warrant. So send us your feedback. Either e-mail us at editors@fodors.com (specifying *Fodor's CITYGUIDE San Francisco* on the subject line), or write to the *Fodor's CITYGUIDE San Francisco* editor at Fodor's, 280 Park Avenue, New York, New York 10017. We look forward to hearing from you.

Karen Cure

Karen Cure
Editorial Director

chapter 1

RESTAURANTS

San Franciscans are regularly accused of acting smug about their burgeoning restaurant community. But they have reason to be. In a city with less than three-quarters of a million people, there are roughly 4,000 licensed eating establishments. About 1,000 of these shut their doors every year, only to be replaced by an equal number of newcomers. In other words, food matters here and the competition for dining-out dollars is serious business.

Trends are serious business, too. For example, until a few years ago, French food had virtually gone the way of hoop skirts, but now fashionable bistros have opened all over the city. At the same time, a craze for grazing continues: look for tapas, antipasti, and bar snacks at restaurants all over town. Spots devoted to noodles, some pan-Asian and some global, and to fusion food are also blossoming, and restaurant boomlets have hit the blocks of the North Mission and the Inner Sunset districts, turning them into serious spawning grounds for new eateries. High-quality neighborhood restaurants and smart dining rooms catering to the new martini crowd have proliferated, and more than ever folks are piling into their cars and driving to the wine country for a meal among the vineyards.

San Francisco diners remain curious, which means that our legendary ethnic-restaurant mosaic has continued to expand, forming an ever-more-complex culinary landscape. And the city has kept its reputation for imagination and for being a place where chefs are restless if they are not innovating a new dish or discovering new ingredients.

general information

NO SMOKING

Smoking is banned in Bay Area workplaces, including restaurants, although many lounges for cigar smokers have opened. Smoking is banned in all bars as well.

RESERVATIONS

Reservations are hard to come by at many of the hot-ticket restaurants, unless they are booked literally weeks in advance. In some of these same restaurants, there has been a trend toward leaving up to one-third of the seats unreserved for walk-ins. In any case, it is a good idea to call and check a restaurant's policy.

TIPPING

Tipping is about 15% for most restaurants and 20% for classier operations. A good way to figure the gratuity quickly is roughly to double the tax.

PRICE CATEGORIES

CATEGORY	COST*
Very Expensive ($$$$)	over $50
Expensive ($$$)	$30–$50
Moderate ($$)	$20–$30
Inexpensive ($)	under $20

*Prices are per person for a three-course meal, excluding drinks, service, and 8.5% sales tax.

restaurants by cuisine

AFGHAN

 4 e-4

HELMAND
White table linens, Afghan carpets, and colorful photographs set an elegant scene in this modestly priced North Beach restaurant. For first courses, try

the sweetened baked pumpkin with yogurt, or *aushak* (leek-filled ravioli served with yogurt and ground beef). Lamb dishes—kebabs, sliced leg served with sautéed eggplant—are first-rate. There's free nighttime validated parking at Helmand Parking (468 Broadway). *430 Broadway, between Montgomery and Kearny Sts., North Beach, 415/362–0641. AE, MC, V. No lunch weekends. $*

AMERICAN/ CASUAL

3 *e-7*

AUTUMN MOON CAFÉ

Although this friendly Oakland spot advertises its fare as "home-style American café cooking," most home cooks can't hope to turn out roast chicken hash with poached eggs as savory, buttermilk pancakes as airy, or blintzes with sour cream as light as these cooked up in the Autumn Moon kitchen. At midday, the bright, casual dining room outfitted with wooden tables and toys for kids is a good place for sandwiches and such simple plates as sausage with polenta and spinach. In the evening, dishes such as roasted salmon are offered, which you can enjoy on a heater-warmed outdoor patio. *3903 Grand Ave., near Santa Clara Ave., Oakland, 510/595–3200. MC, V. Closed Mon. Takeout. $–$$*

4 *c-7*

BACKFLIP

This bastion of hipness in the Phoenix Hotel has a blue retro bar area with a tropical theme and a green dining room that looks out onto a real motel swimming pool. Foodwise, it's tough to pigeonhole. The chef has dubbed the fare "cocktail cuisine," which is delivered on rolling carts and travels the food chain from tamales to house-smoked salmon to sushi. For the unadventurous, the burger and fries remains the best bet. Ear-splitting music and a drink menu of contemporary martinis adds to the happening mood. *Phoenix Hotel, 601 Eddy St., at Larkin St., Tenderloin, 415/ 771–3547. AE, MC, V. $$*

5 *h-3*

BALBOA CAFÉ

In the mid-'90s, the owners of the popular Plumpjack Café (*see* Mediterranean, *below*) pulled this legendary spot into

their orbit, spiffed up the surroundings, and redid the menu. The food is satisfyingly straightforward, with steaks, grilled fish, and simple salads. Burgers are the number one draw; pair them with the fine house fries and one of the boutique beers regularly stocked at the bar and you'll understand why. The crowd is casual, corporate, and mostly single. *3199 Fillmore St., at Greenwich St., Cow Hollow, 415/921–3944. AE, D, DC, MC, V. $$*

3 *b-2*

BETTE'S OCEANVIEW DINER

In Berkeley's fashionable 4th Street shopping area, this high-profile '50s-style diner serves what many consider the best buttermilk pancakes on the planet. There are also *huevos rancheros* (scrambled eggs with corn tortillas, salsa, guacamole, and other Mexican fixings) for those who like a bit of morning

---

BREAKFASTS AND BRUNCHES

San Franciscans love to eat the first meal of the day out. Here are some dandy choices.

Campton Place (French)
A good place for an elegant power breakfast when money is no object.

Chava's (Mexican)
A barrio favorite when a craving for huevos rancheros and tortillas strikes

Garden Court (American/Contemporary)
Eat brunch in one of San Francisco's most historic—and beautiful—hotel dining rooms.

Home Plate (American/Casual)
House-baked scones and fresh-fruit-topped granola are draws.

Kate's Kitchen (American/Casual)
Join the slackers for cornmeal buttermilk pancakes and New England flannel hash.

Ritz-Carlton Terrace (French)
Bountiful Sunday brunch with live jazz in an upmarket setting.

Suppenkuche (German)
Weekend brunch chased with good German beer.

Ton Kiang (Chinese)
Who needs bacon and eggs? Start the day with dim sum.

spice, and poached eggs and scrapple for homesick Philadelphians. At noontime, sandwiches, bread pudding, and fruit pie move front and center. The jukebox is loaded with old favorites. Expect long lines or opt for the take-out branch next door. *1807 4th St., between Hearst and Virginia Aves., Berkeley, 510/644–3230. Reservations not accepted. No credit cards. No dinner. $*

7 g-3
BLUE
A cool, stark industrial look defines this Castro spot: gray booths and walls, shiny black tabletops, blue ceiling, refrigerator-white plates, high-tech light fixtures. The menu of a first-rate burger topped with blue cheese and caramelized onions, perfectly crisp french fries, macaroni and three kinds of cheese (mozzarella, Cheddar, and Parmesan), chicken potpie, and meat loaf fit the all-American comfort food profile with a detour to a culinary institute. The kitchen sometimes misses the mark, but the reasonable prices make diners forgiving. *2337 Market St., between Noe and Castro Sts., Castro, 415/863–2583. MC, V. Takeout. $*

8 a-3
BURGER JOINT
At first glance, you might wonder if you can eat in this eye-searing sea of turquoise tables and red seats, black-and-turquoise-tiled floor, and bright-orange ceiling decorations. But once you bite into one of the kitchen's hormone-free beef burgers or beef hot dogs, the wild color scheme will be forgotten. Fries cut thick enough for a trencherman show up alongside the burgers, and a nice, thick vanilla milk shake rounds out the all-American meal. Since this is San Francisco, garden burgers are served if you shy away from eating the animal world. *807 Valencia St., between 19th and 20th Sts., Mission, 415/824–3494. Reservations not accepted. No credit cards. Takeout. $*

7 h-2
CHOW
Photographs of film stars decorate this down-to-earth green-and-cream dining room, and an open kitchen with a wood-burning pizza oven stands at the back. There's a little bit of everything on the menu—salads, pastas, pizzas, grills, sandwiches—and the seasonings run the gamut from oregano to ginger. Some of the dishes, such as fire-roasted mussels, Shanghai noodles with peanut sauce, and tomato-topped bruschetta, are decidedly upmarket. Others—Rose's spaghetti and meatballs; meat loaf—are not. A second branch, called Park Chow, calls the Inner Sunset home. *215 Church St., between Market and 15th Sts., Castro, 415/552–2469. MC, V. Takeout. $–$$*

7 a-2
1240 9th St., between Irving St. and Lincoln Way, 415/665–9912.

5 f-6
ELLA'S
On weekends, a line of patient breakfast eaters has already formed before the 9 AM opening of this favorite San Francisco brunch spot with a cozy, flower-filled dining room. In addition to addictive house-made sticky buns, there are buttermilk pancakes, California-inspired omelets, and fresh-squeezed blood-orange juice. On weekdays, lunch and dinner are also served, with grilled fish, chicken potpie, pot roast in gravy, and big burgers showing up on the regularly changing menu of updated grandmother food. *500 Presidio Ave., at California St., Pacific Heights, 415/441–5669. Reservations not accepted. MC, V. No dinner weekends. Takeout and delivery. $$*

4 f-3
FOG CITY DINER
This sleek chrome eatery, with its Edward Hopper counter, had a lot to do with the renaissance of the American diner. It carries the expected fare—burgers and milk shakes—but there are also such local favorites as *chiles rellenos* (stuffed chile peppers). The service falters on occasion, but a crisp french fry dipped into the house-made ketchup should help you forget the staff's lapses. The shareable "small plates"—quesadillas, pork satay—are a good way to explore the menu. *1300 Battery St., at Greenwich St., Embarcadero, 415/982–2000. D, DC, MC, V. $$*

4 h-5
GORDON BIERSCH BREWERY RESTAURANT
German-style beers made on the premises accompany such classy brew-pub fare as pan-roasted chicken with Tuscan bread salad, garlic lamb with

cucumber salad, and tender baby back ribs with garlic fries. There are great views of the bay from the granite- and wrought-iron-filled restaurant, which occupies the historic Hills Brothers Coffee building. Expect to find a gregarious after-work crowd of mostly twentysomethings. *2 Harrison St., at Steuart St., South Beach, 415/243-8246. AE, D, DC, MC, V. Takeout. $$*

5 *h-3*
HOME PLATE
Loyalists of this postage-stamp-size neighborhood spot point to the house-baked scones as reason enough to come here for breakfast. The apple-wood-smoked meats, fresh fruit–topped granola, and egg dishes featuring everything from chicken livers to spinach to smoked salmon are additional enticements. Weekends find the line of hungry brunch goers curling around the corner (you can call ahead and the staff will pen in your name on the waiting list); weekday breakfasts are a calmer affair. *2274 Lombard St., between Steiner and Pierce Sts., Marina, 415/922-4663. MC, V. Closed Mon. No dinner. Takeout. $*

2 *f-3*
IT'S TOPS COFFEE SHOP
A few blocks east of Church Street, this retro diner with knotty pine walls and tabletop jukeboxes dates from the mid-'30s, although some of the furnishings go back only to the '50s. You can take a seat at the counter or slide into a booth on the opposite wall. The burgers—hefty and succulent on a grilled bun—and thick milk shakes are deliciously all-American. The breakfast menu includes pancakes, waffles, and eggs as you like them; dinners revolve around chops and chicken. In true diner style, It's Tops serves food until 3 AM. *1801 Market St., at Octavia St., Castro, 415/431-6395. MC, V. No dinner Sun.–Tues. Takeout. $*

7 *g-1*
KATE'S KITCHEN
It's hard to resist the thick slabs of French toast topped with berries and the New England flannel hash at this funky, comfy American-food outpost. Biscuits and gravy, big cornmeal pancakes, and other breakfast items are equally tempting. For lunch, folks munch on meat loaf sandwiches and slurp big bowls of healthy soup. Save room for a slice of homemade pie. *471 Haight St., between Fillmore and Webster Sts., Lower Haight, 415/626-3984. Reservations not accepted. No credit cards. No dinner. Takeout. $*

2 *h-3*
KELLY'S MISSION ROCK
Here is the perfect place to kick back and enjoy the bay. You can relax at a table and watch a slew of weekend pleasure boats bob in the adjoining marina and follow the water fowl as they skim along the shore. If you want only a quick bite, this wonderful, newly built wood, glass, and sheet metal structure has a café downstairs for grabbing some fish-and-chips or a burger. A more formal upstairs eating space, called Topside, serves weekend brunch, lunch with such rib-sticking fare as hearty corned beef sandwiches and crab BLTs, and dinners of seared duck breast or lamb with whipped potatoes. *817 China Basin St., off 3rd St., South of Market, 415/626-5355. AE, MC, V. No dinner Sun.–Wed. Takeout. $-$$*

4 *e-3*
MO'S
Thick, prime chuck patties sit on a fancy grill that rotates above a glowing fire in this regular haunt for burger fans. The choice of toppings goes beyond the traditional—you can opt for blue cheese or Gruyère in addition to good old American cheese. Sandwiches such as grilled lamb burger or grilled chicken breast with Thai curry paste are also on offer. The black-and-white tile and chrome decor gives Mo's a modern attitude. *1322 Grant Ave., between Vallejo and Green Sts., North Beach, 415/788-3779. MC, V. Takeout. $*

MUSTARDS GRILL
It seems that just about everybody who lives in the valley loves the smoky baby back ribs with slaw served here, making it hard for out-of-towners to find a seat in this lively tavernlike operation. The Mongolian pork chop with mashed potatoes is another signature dish, as are the thread-thin onion rings. You can get Peking duck, California style, or just a burger. Either would be great with a glass of valley wine for sipping. Cap off your repast with a slice of vanilla-bean angel food cake or fresh fruit pie. *7399 St. Helena Hwy., Napa, 707/944-2424. D, DC, MC, V. Takeout. $$*

2 *e-2*

PERRY'S

When Perry Butler arrived in San Francisco from New York in the late '60s, he decided what the city needed was good East Coast saloon food—steak, veal chops, Caesar salad, and the best hamburgers in town. That's precisely what you'll find at his namesake restaurants. The bar at the original Union Street location is a good place to watch whatever major sports event is being broadcast. The second location, Perry's Downtown, serves the same type food in a more upmarket, mahogany-lined space that attracts Financial District suits midday and after five. *1944 Union St., between Laguna and Buchanan Sts., Cow Hollow, 415/922–9022. AE, MC, V. Takeout. $$–$$$*

4 *f-5*

185 Sutter St., between Montgomery and Kearny Sts., Union Square, 415/989–6895.

7 *g-1*

ROSAMUNDE SAUSAGE GRILL

Tiny, with just a couple of stools and a narrow little counter, this first-class sausage joint, which grills your choice to order, stands next door to the Lower Haight's popular Tornado bar. The sausage menu mixes good classics—bratwurst, knockwurst, kielbasa—with the equally good gourmet—smoked lamb, Thai chicken. House-made pepper relish, a tasty curry ketchup, and a choice of mustards—whole grain and smooth, hot and mild—are on hand for slathering on your selection. Grab a bag of chips and your meal is complete. *545 Haight St., between Fillmore and Steiner Sts., Haight, 415/437–6851. No credit cards. Takeout. $*

8 *c-5*

ST. FRANCIS FOUNTAIN

Welcome to Main Street America—in the heart of the barrio. Since 1918 (its opening year), this place has hardly changed, despite the multiethnic history of the neighborhood around it. On one side of the restaurant is the stool-lined counter, where folks make their way through sodas whipped up with ice cream made on the premises, and other nostalgic fare—grilled cheese, tuna salad, and BLT sandwiches. Across from the counter is a display of the homemade candies. *2801 24th St., at York St.,*

Mission, 415/826–4200. Reservations not accepted. MC, V. Takeout. $

1 *b-1*

SAM'S ANCHOR CAFÉ

College students and everybody else have been coming to this Tiburon spot since the 1920s. They sit on the deck; drink cold beer; eat decent burgers, sandwiches, soups, and salads; and try to keep the low-flying gulls from carrying off their lunches. The menu ain't much, but no one comes here for the eats. The homey, familiar atmosphere, however, draws them like lawyers to Washington. *27 Main St., near the ferry terminal, Tiburon, 415/435–4527. AE, D, DC, MC, V. Takeout. $*

7 *g-1*

SPAGHETTI WESTERN

The neighborhood slackers have nicknamed this daytime dive Spag Wag. The exterior has a big cactus painted on it, cattle skulls decorate the walls, and the staffers, in jeans and T-shirts, are all attitude. The food is hearty—pesto-scrambled eggs; fried eggs, home fries, and biscuits in gravy; tuna melts; and BLTs—and it arrives with all the haste of a Republican at a Democratic fundraiser. Nonetheless, the line is out the door on weekend mornings, when carbs are the only answer to the night before. *576 Haight St., between Fillmore and Steiner Sts., Lower Haight, 415/864–8461. Reservations not accepted. No credit cards. No dinner. Takeout. $*

7 *g-1*

SQUAT AND GOBBLE

The name certainly lacks finesse, and the portion sizes do, too. But on sunny days, tables from this mildly grungy Lower Haight mainstay spill out onto the sidewalk, and hungry eaters fuel up on crepes stuffed with savory or sweet fillings, billowy omelets paired with pan-fried potatoes, grilled sandwiches, and outsize salads. Take a number at the counter and wait to hear your order yelled out over the often-cacophonous dining area. The Upper Haight has its own Squat and Gobble. *237 Fillmore St., between Haight and Waller Sts., Lower Haight, 415/487–0551. No credit cards. Takeout. $*

7 *e-1*

1424 Haight St., between Masonic and Ashbury St., Upper Haight, 415/864–8484.

1 *b-1*

SWEDEN HOUSE BAKERY & CAFÉ

Swedish pancakes with lingonberries is a great way to start the day, especially if the day is sunny and you take your breakfast on the patio of this dollhouse-like wood-frame café across the bay. A sign warns you to keep your eyes on your food, however, because the local birds are sneaky. At midday, customers switch to sandwiches filled with shrimp or chicken salad or Swedish meat loaf. *35 Main St., near the ferry terminal, Tiburon, 415/435–4527. Reservations not accepted. MC, V. No dinner. Takeout. $*

AMERICAN/ CONTEMPORARY

AUBERGE DU SOLEIL

The view here is legendary even in the wine country, which has more than its share of gorgeous views. The food is up-to-date American, so no one will be surprised to find a heavy Californian hand and some Asian influences on his or her plate. Seared seafood with luxuriant sauces, variations on sushi, sashimi, and tempura, flavorful local lamb loin, and desserts built on seasonal fruits are regular features. The wine list matches the view. *Rutherford Hill Rd., Rutherford, 707/967–3111. Reservations essential. AE, D, DC, MC, V. $$$$*

7 *a-2*

AVENUE 9

With the Inner Sunset's new burst of trendy commerce has come a handful of new restaurants, including this cheerful American bistro done in bright yellows and wood. A far-from-classic Caesar salad includes blue cheese, walnuts, and pears; nicely cooked local duck is paired with a chile-laced custard; and a flatiron steak joins forces with a mound of mashed potatoes. The warm ginger-bread with vanilla ice cream is a pleasing finale. *1243 9th Ave., between Lincoln Way and Irving St., Sunset District, 415/664–6999. MC, V. $$*

3 *e-5*

BAY WOLF

This Oakland restaurant began fashioning its California-Mediterranean table at a time when many of today's biggest California-cuisine boosters were still in diapers. Now, about a quarter of a cen-

tury later, it still has its many fans who turn up for such dishes as duck rillettes, lamb shanks with polenta, and the house specialty, duck with a fruit sauce. The converted Victorian house, chock-full of art, is a convivial setting, particularly if you can snare a table on the wide front porch. *3853 Piedmont Ave., near Rio Vista Ave., Oakland, 510/655–6004. MC, V. No lunch weekends. $$$*

6 *b-1*

BEACH CHALET

The Beach Chalet is a great place to watch the sun sink below the horizon while sipping a home-brewed pint, or to relax over Sunday brunch after a walk on the beach. It's housed in an historic colonnaded building overlooking the Pacific; inside, handsomely restored Works Project Administration–produced murals portray the city in the mid-1930s. The menu is a mixed bag, with everything from ceviche to buffalo wings to hearty seafood gumbo. Don't miss the chocolate sand castle for dessert. The North Judah streetcar will carry you here from downtown in about 40 minutes. *1000 Great Hwy., at John F. Kennedy Dr., Golden Gate Park, 415/386–8439. MC, V. Takeout. $$*

3 *c-2*

BISTRO VIOLA

The menu served in this small, friendly Berkeley eatery is Californian with a strong French accent. The Gallic influence is evident in such preparations as dandelion salad with a poached egg and chunks of bacon, fried frog legs, and chocolate mousse. But the very American burger on a boutique-bakery bun and the seared rare tuna served with corn and fava beans let the diner know the chef's feet are firmly planted on both continents. You can watch your meal come together in the open kitchen, and in pleasant weather can eat it on the simple enclosed patio that fronts the restaurant. *1428 San Pablo Ave., at Page St., Berkeley, 510/528–5030. AE, D, DC, MC, V. No lunch Sat. $$$*

4 *f-4*

BIX

Occupying a historic building on a charming back alley, this swanky supper club has a bustling bar and dining tables downstairs, and a banquette-filled balcony. Opt for the lower level; the acoustics upstairs are deafening. The menu, which changes with the seasons, lists contemporary renditions of classic American standards such as Waldorf salad and grilled pork chops. A pianist adds to the jazzy mood. 56 Gold St., between Jackson and Pacific Sts. and Montgomery and Sansome Sts., North Beach, 415/433–6300. AE, D, DC, MC, V. No lunch weekends. $$$

4 e-4
BLACK CAT

San Francisco's original Black Cat was a legendary North Beach club that drew a bohemian crowd from the 1930s to the 1960s. Chef-owner Reed Hearon hopes to recapture some of that old glow with this combination restaurant and jazz club. The dining room is outfitted in red booths, red-and-white-checkered table-cloths, and big windows so that you can take in the street action. The menu reflects the cultural mix of the city, with everything from chowder from the wharf to roast duck and noodles from China-

town. There's pasta from North Beach, too, and for dessert, the kind of jelly doughnuts that keep beat cops happy. 501 Broadway, at Kearny St., North Beach, 415/981–2233. AE, DC, MC, V. Takeout. $$

4 g-4
BOULEVARD

Nationally acclaimed chef Nancy Oakes and design partner Pat Kuleto have turned the first floor of the 1889 Aud-iffred Building, a Parisian look-alike and one of the few structures in the area to survive the 1906 earthquake and fire, into an oasis of American seasonal food. Oakes's menu changes regularly, but fresh Sonoma foie gras, wood oven–roasted duck, and wild mushroom risotto are among the irresistible possi-bilities. Simpler fare, such as pizza with braised leeks and pancetta, and crispy calamari with a Thai vinaigrette, prevails at midday. 1 Mission St., at the Embar-cadero, Embarcadero, 415/543–6084. Reservations essential. AE, D, DC, MC, V. No lunch weekends. $$$

3 d-1
CHEZ PANISSE

Alice Waters defined California cuisine at this more than a quarter-century-old culinary temple, where organically grown local ingredients reign supreme. Downstairs, fixed-course meals are served in an elegantly rustic space. Upstairs in the more casual café, an à la carte menu is in force, with pizzas, pastas, salads, and simple meat and fish on the list. The ice cream, which comes in such dreamy guises as crème fraîche and lavender, and fruit desserts (tarts and cobblers) are legendary. 1517 Shattuck Ave., between Cedar and Vine Sts., Berkeley, 510/548–5525 (dining room), 510/548–5049 (café). Reserva-tions essential. AE, D, DC, MC, V. Closed Sun. No lunch in downstairs dining room. $$–$$$$

3 e-4
CITRON

Although the owner-chef who opened this charming, white-tablecloth neigh-borhood spot in the early '90s has since left, the food remains a draw, with such inviting plates as grilled leg of lamb with a savory bread pudding, a gloriously rich duck confit, and a fragrant blood-orange sorbet. A fixed-price three-course menu is offered for those watching their bud-

---

FIREPLACES

When the city's famous fog rolls in, a crackling fireplace chases away the chills.

Auberge du Soleil (American/Contemporary)
A warm spot on a cold wine-country weekend.

Betelnut (Pan-Asian)
A lively stop for tea-smoked duck and Shanghai dumplings.

Greystone Restaurant (American/Contemporary)
This cooking school restaurant boasts a big stone fireplace for chilly wine-country nights.

Guaymas (Mexican)
When San Francisco is fogged in, this Tiburon fireplace looks mighty good.

House of Prime Rib (Steak)
An old-fashioned dining room with silver cart service.

Red Herring (Seafood)
This Embarcadero restaurant spit-roasts chickens in its huge fireplace.

Zuni Café & Grill (Mediterranean)
Front and center, a large brick wood-burning oven is used for cooking and for keeping you warm.

gets. *5484 College Ave., near Lawton, Oakland, 510/653–5484. MC, V. Closed Sun. No lunch. $$–$$$*

4 *f-4*
CYPRESS CLUB

Bulbous light fixtures, curvy banquettes with plush velvet upholstery, and imposing pillars give the celebrated Cypress Club a futuristic look; stone mosaic floors, hammered copper arches, and murals depicting northern California add even more pizzazz. The food is only slightly more down to earth: sweetbread tartlet with caramelized cauliflower, rounds of foie gras terrine wrapped in slices of smoked duck breast, lamb pot-au-feu, and a sophisticated cheese selection are among the high-class selections. *500 Jackson St., between Montgomery and Kearny Sts., Financial District, 415/296–8555. Reservations essential. AE, DC, MC, V. No lunch. $$$–$$$$*

4 *f-6*
EDDIE RICKENBACKER'S

World War II memorabilia, a vintage air plane, and a trio of motorcycles outfit this gathering place for Financial District suits and young SoMa media moguls. A menu of hearty, all-American fare—steaks, burgers, pork chops, chicken, and sandwiches—complements the patriotic decor. When the clock strikes five, it's hard to find a free bar stool at Eddie's, as the regulars crowd in for after-work camaraderie and the bar food. *133 2nd St., between Mission and Howard Sts., South of Market, 415/543 3498. AE, MC, V. Closed Sun. No lunch Sat. $$*

4 *g-6*
ELROYS

When Elroys, a big bar-restaurant, first opened in the mid-'90s, it served contemporary American food with strong fusion and Southwest elements. But a sea change has taken place in the kitchen of this warehouse-turned-restaurant, and the food is on a far more even keel. It is still American food, but the influences are tempered by a wiser staff. The aromatic paella comes punctuated with a bouquet of seafood, chunks of chorizo, and small pieces of green bean; the lamb loin wears a scrumptious coat of minty mustard; and the succulent deep-fried quail are nicely peppery. The bar has not changed, however. It is as lively as ever, with billiards tables that

never rest. *301 Folsom St., between Beale and Fremont Sts., South of Market, 415/882–7989. AE, MC, V. No lunch weekends. $$$*

4 *e-6*
FIRST CRUSH

The name gives it away: this classy place is all about wine, but California wine only. The very street-level wine bar, complete with photographs of some of the state's best-known vintners, stocks close to 300 wines and plenty of suits and sheaths sipping zins and chardonnays before heading home, out on the town, or downstairs to the stylish wine-colored dining room for dinner. The menu skims along from oysters on the half shell to cheese ravioli to thick, full-flavored steaks to fresh fish grilled over a mesquite fire. *101 Cyril Magnin St., at Ellis St., Union Square, 415/982–7874. AE, D, MC, V. Closed Sun. No lunch. $$$*

8 *a-4*
FOREIGN CINEMA

For anyone who wants dinner and a movie, this is the ideal destination. You can order your Cal-French bistro-style meal in the indoor dining room or grab a table at the adjoining enclosed patio and eat while you watch a movie projected on the white concrete wall that forms one side of the patio. The schedule of flicks, made by such cinematic legends as Godard, Fellini, and Bergman, are guaranteed to make any true film lover camp out at a table or on a bar stool until show time (you are not required to order a meal to watch the movies). *2534 Mission St., near 21st St., Mission, 415/648–7600. AE, MC, V. $$*

2 *h-4*
42 DEGREES

A sophisticated menu, an outdoor patio with a view of the bay, a crowded bar, and a sleek overall design pull in a mostly thirtysomething crowd with a few bucks to spend. Dishes on the Mediterranean-influenced menu range from the classic—marrowbones with toasts—to the contemporary—duck breast with fiddlehead ferns. A selection of little plates is ideal for small appetites or folks looking for something to munch on with their drinks. Live music draws a crowd into the wee hours. *235 16th St., near Illinois St., Potrero Hill, 415/777–5559. MC, V. Closed Sat. No dinner Mon.–Tues. No lunch Sat. $$—$$$*

4 *f-6*

GARDEN COURT

This is a stop for Sunday brunch. It is an elaborate affair in one of the most beautiful rooms in a San Francisco hotel, the Garden Court of the Palace. This historic room, with its stunning lead-glass ceiling, crystal chandeliers, and towering Ionic columns, serves an elaborate brunch that stretches from smoked salmon to roast beef, from scones to Danishes, from eggs Benedict to omelets folded before your eyes. Lunch and dinner are served here as well, but only the brunch, an old San Francisco tradition, deserves a visit. *Palace Hotel, 2 New Montgomery St., at Market St., South of Market, 415/546–5011. Reservations essential. AE, DC, MC, V. No dinner Sun. $$$*

GENERAL'S DAUGHTER

Housed in a Victorian home originally built for the daughter of General Vallejo, a Mexican general who was already growing grapes in the valley in the mid-1800s, the General's Daughter is a picture-postcard place with roses climbing over the porches and tables set up in the garden in good weather. The menu is a pastiche, offering everything from seared ahi tuna to lamb chops with a cumin glaze to rib-eye steaks to crisp superthin onion rings. Not surprisingly, Sonoma vintages shine on the wine list. *400 W. Spain St., at 4th St., Sonoma, 707/938–4004. MC, V. Takeout. $$$*

4 *f-4*

GLOBE

Although housed in a building dating from 1911, Globe is an up-to-the-minute eatery with an intriguing contemporary menu. In the small, terra-cotta-floored dining room you may find it hard to choose between a starter of grilled sardines and the utterly French *frisée aux lardons* (curly greens with bacon) and a poached egg. Main courses may include T-bone steak with potato gratin or lamb chops for two with rosemary-scented white beans. Service is excellent if sometimes a bit snooty. *290 Pacific Ave., near Battery St., Financial District, 415/391–4132. Reservations essential. MC, V. No lunch weekends. $$$*

8 *c-3*

GORDON'S HOUSE OF FINE EATS

Located in a warehouse that dates from the 1930s, Gordon's is dressed up in concrete floors, halogen lighting, and yards of expensive wood, and local workers—video artists, public television producers—seem to flock here like kids to an ice-cream truck. The menu has its own mind, listing dishes under columns headlined healthful, luxury, comfort, Continental, and local showcase. The categories don't always make sense—what makes Dungeness crab with scallion buns Continental?—but dishes don't suffer because of it. Music starts up after 9 PM, so conversationalists may want to move on. *500 Florida St., near Mariposa St., Portrero Hill, 415/861–8900. DC, MC, V. No lunch weekends. $$$*

4 *d-6*

GRAND CAFÉ

Eight large, dramatic murals, whimsical sculptures of stylized human figures, striking chandeliers, and big booths outfit this former ballroom inside the trendy Hotel Monaco. The menu is clas-

---

BEST BURGERS

Not in the mood for a Mexican taco or Middle Eastern shawarma? That's when only a burger will do.

Balboa Café (American/Casual)
A Cow Hollow old-timer famous for its burgers.

Burger Joint (American/Casual)
Burgers and their kin in a retro setting.

Chow and Park Chow (American/Casual)
This two-branch minichain makes a big burger.

Fog City Diner (American/Casual)
A sleek chrome diner that serves house-made ketchup with its burgers.

It's Tops Coffee Shop (American/Casual)
America's favorite sandwich in a knotty-pine coffee shop with table-top jukeboxes.

Mo's (American/Casual)
You can watch your burger—lamb or beef—cook on a circular grill that rotates over a glowing fire.

Zuni Café & Grill (Mediterranean)
A thick burger—Gorgonzola optional—slid between focaccia slabs and served with shoestring spuds.

sic California, relying heavily on seasonal local ingredients, but freely draws upon French and Italian culinary traditions. Sandwiches, salads, and pizzas from a wood-burning oven are served in the more casual bar. *Hotel Monaco, 501 Geary St., at Taylor St., Union Square, 415/292–0101. AE, D, DC, MC, V. $$*

GREYSTONE RESTAURANT

In the mid-'90s, the West Coast campus of the Culinary Institute of America installed itself in the former Christian Brothers' winery, redoing the old stone buildings completely and opening this restaurant to the public. The walls of the dining room are thick volcanic stone, dramatic metal sculptures decorate the space, a fireplace warms the space in the cooler months, and the center of the room is dominated by a large, glassed-in kitchen. Much of the food, which is Californian with a strong Mediterranean influence, is served in tapa-size portions, making dedicated grazers happy. *2555 Main St., St. Helena, 707/967–1010. AE, D, DC, MC, V. $$$*

4 *f-6*
HAWTHORNE LANE

This celebrated establishment has helped sustain the boom that first hit SoMa in the early '90s. It is the creation of David and Anne Gingrass, onetime chefs at the famed Postrio, and the setting is grand, from the light-flooded dining room to the spacious, table-filled bar. In the latter, you can order a selection of irresistible small plates—Thai-style squid, tempura-battered green beans, and trendy pizzas—as well as anything on the dinner menu. Dining-room patrons indulge in only the more serious fare, such as grilled quail, foie gras with arugula salad and Napa Valley *verjus* (verjuice), or seared Maine scallops—all prepared with Mediterranean and Asian touches. *22 Hawthorne St., between 2nd and 3rd Sts., South of Market, 415/777–9779. Reservations essential. D, DC, MC, V. No lunch weekends. $$$*

4 *g-7*
INFUSION BAR & RESTAURANT

What's being "infused" here is vodka: glass decanters, lined up behind the bar like chess pieces, contain spirits of mango, pepper, coconut, and more. The idea is to taste a few different flavors, all through the course of several small plates of food, such as roasted mussels.

Main dishes, some of them infused with the flavored vodkas, consist mostly of meats and pastas. Things pick up after 9 PM, when live music precludes conversation. *555 2nd St., between Bryant and Brannan Sts., South of Market, 415/543–2282. AE, DC, MC, V. No lunch weekends. Delivery. $$*

4 *b-8*
JARDINIÈRE

Pricey and elegant, Jardinière is the brainchild of celebrated chef Traci Des Jardins, who built her reputation as chef at Rubicon, and famed restaurant designer Pat Kuleto, creator of such talked-about spaces as Boulevard and Farallon. Jardinière's stunning two-story, black-and-silver interior, complete with gold ceiling, is a suitably flashy setting for Des Jardins's exquisite plates of foie gras with pear salad, ahi tuna carpaccio, juicy roasted quail, and bittersweet chocolate–hazelnut torte. Opera- and symphony goers crowd the showplace before and after performances. *300 Grove St., at Franklin St., Hayes Valley, 415/861–5555. Reservations essential. AE, D, DC, MC, V. No lunch weekends. $$$*

4 *e-8*
JULIE'S SUPPER CLUB

A crowd of twentysomethings sips martinis and snacks on fried calamari in this throwback-to-the-'50s supper club. The sultry cocktail lounge atmosphere fits the menu of New York steak, grilled chicken with corn soufflé, and house-made pastries. The pink, vinyl-covered bar, with lamps that look as if they were whisked away from a midrange hotel of yesteryear, contribute to the charm. *1123 Folsom St., between 7th and Rausch Sts., South of Market, 415/861–0707. AE, DC, MC, V. Closed Sun. No lunch. $$*

8 *a-7*
LIBERTY CAFÉ

Bernal Heights gained its first classy eatery in the mid-'90's with the opening of this sunny yellow café in the heart of the neighborhood. Regulars know to order the chicken potpie, which arrives packed with pearl onions and chunks of chicken, potatoes, and carrots, topped with a puff-pastry crust. A memorable Caesar salad, a choice cut of steak, thin-crust pizzas with contemporary toppings, and a banana cream pie that will put your grandmother's to shame round out the menu. Fans have long grumbled about Liberty's no-reservations policy, but the addition of a wine cottage (and a small bakery) at the rear of the restaurant, where you can sip a cabernet and nosh on a couple of appetizers, has made the wait more comfortable. Locals come for weekend brunch. *410 Cortland Ave., between Bennington and Andover Sts., Bernal Heights, 415/695–8777. Reservations not accepted. AE, MC, V. Closed Mon. $$*

`4` *f-4*

MACARTHUR PARK

San Franciscans have long flocked to this renovated pre-earthquake warehouse for baby back ribs, but the oakwood smoker and mesquite grill turn out other American dishes as well, from steaks, chicken, and sausages to thick burgers and catfish. The crisp onion rings are worth splurging on. *607 Front St., between Jackson St. and Pacific Ave., Financial District, 415/398–5700. AE, DC, MC, V. No lunch weekends. Takeout. $$*

`7` *h-2*

MECCA

This giant, highly popular space combines late-20th-century industrial—aluminum air ducts, shiny metal bar, sharp corners—with mid-20th-century nightclub—velvet drapes, cut-glass chandeliers, good jazz and blues. With the arrival of chef Mike Fennelly, Mecca's onetime Mediterranean menu took a sharp turn and headed back to the United States, pausing long enough in New Orleans to put a bit of Southern flair into the dishes. There are Asian influences too, and the pizzas are still here as well. The cleverly named cocktails—Mecca-Rita, Stellatini, Ima Gimlet—may tempt you to order a drink. *2029 Market St., between Duboce and 14th Sts., Castro, 415/621–7000. AE, DC, MC, V. $$*

`2` *f-2*

THE MEETINGHOUSE

Modernized American dishes and an inviting dining room of warm yellow walls and Shaker furniture make the Meetinghouse a great place to meet—and eat. The menu is always changing, but rock shrimp–filled johnnycakes with a pepper relish and oyster stew are among the most popular first courses, and hominy-crusted catfish and pan-roasted chicken are satisfying entrées. The old-fashioned hot biscuits and sum-

mertime berry shortcakes are addictive. *1701 Octavia St., at Bush St., Pacific Heights, 415/922–6733. AE, MC, V. Closed Sun. No lunch. $$*

`4` *h-7*

MOMO'S

PacBell Park, the new home of the San Francisco Giants, is within almost home-run distance of this trendy American grill. The menu isn't exactly old-fashioned ballpark fare, but the sports fans who fill the bar and dining room and spill onto the heated patio don't seem to mind. Indeed, they seem happy to tuck into the roasted chicken, crispy onion rings, bourbon-flavored baby back ribs, and triflavored ice-cream sandwich that the kitchen turns out. The bar is always crowded, usually with fans tracking scores on the TV set overhead. *760 2nd St., at King St., South of Market, 415/227–8660. AE, MC, V. Takeout. $$*

`4` *f-6*

MONTAGE

Metreon, the glitzy cyber-charged Sony center in Yerba Buena Gardens, boasts a food court on the first floor with everything from sushi to Chinese noodles to American ribs. But for fine dining after a movie or a few video games, head upstairs to the second floor for Montage, with its high-style curved walls, deep blue tiles, and long, narrow tables. The menu lists such contemporary plates as flat bread with Mission figs, Gorgonzola, and walnuts, and sand dabs on a bed of potatoes and fennel. And if you passed on popcorn at the movie, you can order a chocolate popcorn bag, which combines chocolate ice cream, chocolate mousse, and caramel popcorn in a chocolate sack. *101 4th St., at Mission St., South of Market, 415/369–6111. AE, D, DC, MC, V. $$$*

`4` *g-4*

ONE MARKET

Opened in 1993, this large, lively brasserie across from the Ferry Building is the province of well-known chef Bradley Ogden. The spacious dining room, with its large windows looking out on Market Street, is smart and comfortable, and a sizable café-bar serves snacks beginning at noon. Although the kitchen suffered from unevenness in its early years, it has since settled down, and the stylish American fare—soft-shell crabs, salmon tartar, beef tenderloin, grilled fish—has its loyal partisans. *Embarcadero, at the foot of Market St., Embarcadero, 415/777–5577. Reservations essential. AE, DC, MC, V. Closed Sun. No lunch Sat. $$$*

4 *d-6*
POSTRIO

Über-chef Wolfgang Puck periodically commutes from his Los Angeles head-quarters to check the kitchen in this appealing multilevel bar and dining space, complete with a dramatic stair-case for showy entrances. The food has Mediterranean and Asian overtones; roasted Chinese duck and smoked salmon on a giant blini are favorites with many regulars. Good breakfast and bar menus (with great pizza) keep cus-tomers happy from dawn until late at night. *545 Post St., between Mason and Taylor Sts., Union Square, 415/776–7825. Reservations essential. AE, D, DC, MC, V. $$$–$$$$*

3 *c-1*
RIVOLI

Chef Wendy Brucker assembles a mem-orable Californian–Mediterranean menu at this small East Bay restaurant, while her husband, Roscoe Skipper, oversees the dining room. You might start with a beautiful salad of frisée and arugula with spiced hazelnuts and pears, an order of piping-hot vegetable fritters with lemony aioli, or a Caesar salad. Entrées are equally notable: look for duck cooked two ways or pepper-coated sirloin steak. *1539 Solano Ave., at Peralta Ave., Berkeley, 510/526–2542. Reservations essential. MC, V. No lunch. $$*

4 *f-4*
RUBICON

With Robin Williams, Robert De Niro, and Francis Ford Coppola among its investors, this sleek, cherry wood–lined restaurant was fated to be a destination. (Both Williams and Coppola live in the city, a fact that dramatically increases the chance for a celebrity sighting.) Set in a handsome, nearly century-old stone building, Rubicon has the dignified air of a men's club. The superb cuisine, pri-marily sophisticated renditions of seafood and poultry (crab cakes, seared scallops, crisp roast chicken), is served on two floors to Hollywood big shots, Financial District power brokers, and the rest of us. *558 Sacramento St., between Sansome and Montgomery Sts.,*

Financial District, 415/434–4100. Reserva-tions essential. AE, MC, V. Closed Sun. No lunch Sat. $$$

4 *e-5*
RUMPUS

On an old-time alley in the heart of downtown, this appealing bistro is lively from midday through dinnertime. The Caesar salad has been voted the best in town by devoted Rumpus regulars; a handful of pasta and risotto selections, garlic-laced roast chicken, and apple tart made with puff pastry are among the other stars. A bar menu kicks in mid-afternoon. *1 Tillman Pl., off Grant Ave. between Sutter and Post Sts., Union Square, 415/421–2300. AE, MC, V. $$*

8 *c-3*
SLOW CLUB

Plunked down in the middle of a bee-hive of multimedia activity, and marked by a blue neon sign, this trendy spot of cement floors and exposed pipes is named for the bar in David Lynch's eerie *Blue Velvet*. The menu, which changes daily, is as slim as a cigarillo, with just a couple of appetizers, a handful of mains, and a couple of desserts. There might be roasted chicken with grilled vegetables or pasta with chanterelles. A thick hamburger made from hormone-free beef is always available, however, served with a passel of crisp fries. *2501 Mariposa St., at Hampshire St., Lower Potrero, 415/241–9390. MC, V. Closed Sun.–Mon. No lunch Sat. Takeout. $$*

4 *c-7*
STARS

Jeremiah Tower, the superchef who did much to put California cuisine on the culinary map, sold this San Francisco institution in mid-1999 to concentrate on other operations. Stars has long been where many local power brokers break bread, and where operagoers dine late at night in a setting reminiscent of a popular brasserie. Although the place underwent a makeover just before Tower left, the new owner, Andrew Yap, closed it immediately, promising a new look and, of course, a new chef within a few months. Rumor has it that the chef is a favorite of some of the society set, so Stars is likely to remain a magnet when it reopens. *150 Redwood St., between Van Ness Ave. and Polk St., Civic Center, 415/ 861–7827.*

7 g-2

2223

For years this scorchingly popular place was known as No-Name Restaurant, until its fame was so great that its address proved to be all the name it needed. Swarms of people, many of them Castro neighborhood residents, fill the tables and bar stools, creating a noise level that threatens permanent hearing loss. Despite the roar, they seem happy supping on thin-crust pizzas, glazed pork chops with sautéed red cabbage and apples, and lamb kabobs with mint couscous and roasted eggplant. A nice Sunday brunch keeps the crowds coming. *2223 Market St., between 16th and Sanchez Sts., Castro, 415/431–0692. AE, DC, MC, V. No lunch Sat. $$*

8 c-3

UNIVERSAL CAFÉ

Tucked into an industrial-residential neighborhood that is also home to the local PBS station and the well-known artists' live-work space Project Artaud, the high-style, light-filled Universal serves wonderful midday sandwiches of focaccia filled with roast chicken and aioli or meat loaf and provolone. At night the menu changes regularly, but you might start with sesame-coated grilled tuna or grilled flat bread topped with sautéed peppers, tomatoes, and goat cheese; then move on to pan-seared filet mignon with Gorgonzola mashed potatoes or roasted chicken with lemon risotto. Neighborhood residents grab a quick breakfast here, too. *2814 19th St., between Bryant and Florida Sts., South of Market, 415/821–4608. AE, DC, MC, V. Closed Mon. $$*

4 f-6

XYZ

In 1999, stylish visitors to the city's popular San Francisco Museum of Modern Art gained a stylish spot to eat at right next door to the museum. Tucked into the utterly sleek W hotel, XYZ sports curved, suede banquettes, high ceilings, polished wood floors, and a wall of windows, all adding to the big city feel of the spot. The food—roast chicken with fennel-laced risotto; beefsteak resting on a hillock of new potatoes and oyster mushrooms; roasted beets with goat cheese on a bed of arugula—is suave yet hearty enough to satisfy anyone who missed lunch. *W San Francisco, 181 3rd St., at Howard St., South of Market, 415/817–7836. AE, DC, MC, V. $$$*

4 d-2

ZAX

The menu is brief but the delivery is first-rate in this small, flower-decked, chef-owned restaurant, where one partner handles the savory end of the menu and the other handles the sweet end. A towering goat cheese soufflé is a delectable way to begin a meal here, although a salad of heirloom tomatoes, feta, and olives in summer or mixed greens with a sherry vinaigrette the rest of the year is also recommended. Roasted rabbit and swordfish with peppers and roasted garlic are wonderful mains. Be sure to save room for the apple galettes with house-made ice cream. *2330 Taylor St., near Columbus Ave., North Beach, 415/563–6266. MC, V. No lunch. $$*

BARBECUE

2 f-4

BIG NATE'S BAR-B-QUE

The Big Nate here is the famed basketballer Nate Thurman. His barbecue place is pretty stripped down—few seats, lots of linoleum—so most folks come in for takeout. Nate's got smoky ribs, brisket, hot links, and chicken, along with a trio of sauces—hot, midrange, and mild—and all the standard side dishes. Be ready to do some serious washing up when your meal is done. *1665 Folsom St., between 12th and 13th Sts., South of Market, 415/861–4242. MC, V. Takeout. $*

5 h-8

BROTHER-IN-LAW'S BARBECUE

Nobody who loves barbecue can pass up this Western Addition institution. The telltale smell of old-fashioned barbecue pulls folks down the street and in the door for beef brisket, pork ribs, chicken, and beef links, properly slow-cooked and wonderfully smoky all the way through. Don't forget the hot sauce—they'll even mix the hot and not-so-hot blends for timid palates—or the corn muffins. This is a takeout place, but you may find yourself ripping open the bag as you drive home. *705 Divisadero St., at Grove St., Western Addition, 415/931–7427. MC, V. Closed Mon. Takeout. $*

BRAZILIAN

4 c-8

CANTO DO BRASIL

A few years ago, this Brazilian favorite moved from its original Mission District home to the Civic Center, where it now caters to workers at noontime and culture vultures at night. The pale blue interior, with plenty of potted ferns, has a soft tropical feel, and the menu includes dips into a variety of Brazilian favorites, from feijoada (the national dish of Brazil that combines black beans and meats), made weekends only, to roast leg of pork to chicken cooked in coconut milk and served with rice and beans. Order a little dish of the farofa; it is nothing more than ground dried yucca, but it adds a nice texture and flavor to nearly every dish that comes out of the kitchen. 44 Franklin St., at Page St., Civic Center, 415/626 8727. MC, V. No lunch Sun. Takeout. $

2 f-3

TERRA BRAZILIS

Walls done in deep peach and bricks and a line of windows that overlooks the street form the setting for this attractive restaurant, which features Brazilian food turned out with a California hand. You can start with salt-cod croquette or clams and Portuguese sausage, and follow with caldo verde, the classic Portuguese potato soup with greens and sausage. On Thursday through Saturday, the kitchen serves feijoada, but every night a superb pork chop stuffed with apricots and prunes and accompanied with slender ribbons of collard greens is served. For dessert, try the guava paste-stuffed empanadas and crème fraîche ice cream. Weekend brunch is served. 602 Hayes St., at Laguna St., Civic Center, 415/241-1900. MC, V. Closed Mon. No lunch Tues.–Fri. $$

BURMESE

4 d-6

BURMA HOUSE

In Myanmar (formerly Burma), many of the restaurateurs are Chinese, so it comes as no surprise that this downtown restaurant serves a combination of Chinese and Burmese specialties. The ginger salad (a tossed mixture of young ginger, fried garlic, yellow peas, chiles, and other ingredients) and the chicken and coconut curry are among the high-lights. If you want to stick with Burmese dishes, ask the helpful wait staff to direct you to the national dishes. 720 Post St., between Jones and Leavenworth Sts., Union Square, 415/775–1156. MC, V. Takeout. $

5 c-6

MANDALAY

At this venerable Richmond District restaurant, the first Burmese eatery in San Francisco, repeat customers especially enjoy the tea salad of dried shrimp, fried garlic, lentils, coconut, sesame seeds, and other ingredients, all tossed together in a savory blend. Follow it with a peppery thick fish soup with noodles, curried prawns, or beef; or chin mong kyaw, a sour leafy vegetable prepared with shrimp. Colorful fabric and simple Asian artifacts contribute to the pleasant atmosphere. 4348 California St., between 5th and 6th Aves., Richmond District, 415/386–3895. MC, V. Takeout. $–$$

3 e-4

NANYANG ROCKRIDGE

Chef-owner Philip Chu opened his first Burmese restaurant in Oakland Chinatown and later launched this more upscale site on busy College Avenue. Long lines of customers clamor for his plates of garlic noodles served with curried spinach or fresh mango and his hearty curries. His tea and ginger salads, which are actually considered snacks rather than salads by the Burmese and are made up of such ingredients as peanuts, dried shrimp, coconut, and fried yellow split peas, are among the popular dishes served here. 6048 College Ave., at Claremont St., Oakland, 510/655–3298. MC, V. Closed Mon. Takeout. $$

CAJUN/CREOLE

4 c-2

BELLE ROUX
LOUISIANA KITCHEN

Homesick Louisianans can satisfy their culinary cravings at this casual Cannery-site vendor of gumbo and jambalaya. The chef turns out two respectable gumbos, a vegetarian gumbo z'herbes with a bushel of greens, and an old-fashioned crab and crawfish combo. The tasty jambalaya, loaded with shrimp and house-made Creole sausage, carries a wonderful layer of chile heat that's nicely doused with a bottle of Louisiana-brewed Dixie Voodoo beer. Skip the crab cakes, but order the bayou barkers with rémoulade sauce, hush puppy look-alikes that conceal crawfish and *tasso* (smoked pork shoulder). *2801 Leaven-worth St., in the Cannery, at Beach St., Fisherman's Wharf, 415/771–5225. MC, V. Takeout. $$*

CATAHOULA RESTAURANT AND SALOON

The saloon half of this dual operation, located in the Mount View Hotel and Spa, has Cajun music, painted cement floors, plain wooden tables, and pho-tographs of the Catahoula, the official hunting dog of the state of Louisiana, on the walls. The menu, created by cele-brated American chef Jan Birnbaum, can be eaten here or in the classier dining room across the lobby. It offers such down-home, yet sophisticated, plates as cornmeal-fried catfish and pork steak

---

THE KIDS'LL LOVE IT

Despite its reputation as an adult town, San Francisco has its share of kid-friendly restaurants.

Brother-in-Law's Barbecue (Barbecue)
Get the napkins ready. This is a messy proposition.

Ella's (American/Casual)
Sticky buns and pancakes: what more could you ask for?

La Taqueria (Mexican)
A sure way to break the habit of crisp taco shells.

Mifune (Japanese)
You're allowed to slurp your noodles here.

Mo's (American/Casual)
Burgers for young but sophisticated palates.

St. Francis Fountain (American/Casual)
A soda fountain just like the ones mom and dad used to know.

Tommaso's (Pizza)
Every kid loves pizza, so get 'em a good one.

Ton Kiang (Chinese)
The wait staff is used to lots of kids and commotion.

---

with red-eye gravy and grits. There are also pizzas, including one with andouille and fontina cheese, and some delectable desserts, from beignets to buttermilk berry ice cream. *Mount View Hotel and Spa, 1457 Lincoln Ave., near Washington St., Calistoga, 707/942–2275. D, MC, V. No lunch Mon.–Thurs. Take-out. $$$*

7 e-1
CRESCENT CITY CAFÉ

There are no frills here, just red beans and rice, jambalaya, spicy sausages, blackened redfish, and gumbo—plus warm corn bread that's by no means low-fat. The walls are festooned with New Orleans memorabilia, and from the small counter (with less than a dozen seats), you can keep an eye on the culi-nary action. There are also half a dozen tables. A blackboard lists the daily spe-cial. *1418 Haight St., between Masonic and Ashbury Sts., Haight, 415/863–1374. MC, V. Takeout. $*

2 e-2
ELITE CAFÉ

Since the early '80s, the Elite has been serving platters of raw oysters and batches of peel-and-eat shrimp to homesick New Orleaners. The kitchen has had its ups and downs (the gumbo, sadly, is forgettable), but the regulars have stood by it, coming back year after year for the jambalaya, corn-meal-sheathed catfish, and baby back ribs. A strict no-reservations policy means that you will have to wait for one of the big, roomy old-fashioned booths to empty, but a sizzling Cajun martini will help pass the time. *2049 Fillmore St., near California St., Lower Pacific Heights, 415/346–8668. Reserva-tions not accepted. AE, MC, V. No lunch Mon.–Sat. $$$*

9 d-4
LA BAYOU

Po' boys are a specialty here. Also known as heroes, these hearty sand-wiches call for slipping hot or mild Louisiana sausages or boudin into a soft roll spread with mayo and mustard and packed with lettuce, tomato, and onion. For a buck more, you can have this scrumptious sandwich stuffed with fried catfish or oysters. This latter duo can also be ordered on a dinner plate, or you can opt for gumbo, jambalaya, or red beans and rice with sides of collards and hush puppies. The brightly painted dining room has only half a dozen tables, but your food is happily packed for takeout. Come early, as the cooks go home at eight. *3278 Adeline St., near Ashby BART, Berkeley, 510/594–9302. Reservations not accepted. No credit cards. Closed Sun.–Mon. Takeout. $*

CAMBODIAN

R *a-7*
ANGKOR BOREI
For years, the kitchen at this homey neighborhood spot has been educating diners in the intricacies of the Cambodian table. Diners happily munch on the legendary spring rolls, crisp cylinders stuffed with pork, mushrooms, and cellophane noodles; skewers of charbroiled chicken; and a folded crepe hiding vegetables, shrimp, tofu, and pork, served with a garlicky lemon sauce punctuated with ground peanuts for dousing each bite. Curries in a rainbow of colors are popular, as is the dessert of coconut-scented sticky black rice with mangoes. *3471 Mission St., at Cortland Ave., Mission, 415/550–8417. AE, D, MC, V. No lunch Sun. Takeout. $*

5 *c-7*
ANGKOR WAT
Owners Joanna and Keith Dan, who opened this flower-filled restaurant in the early 1980s, still draw diners to their Cambodian table. Among the kitchen's best efforts are lovely catfish fillets in a tart, intriguing lime sauce, a rich and satisfying duck curry, and an aromatic grilled chicken infused with a pantry-full of exotic ingredients. The dining room is outfitted with Cambodian folk art that adds to the overall experience. Don't pass up the creamy, refreshing, and unusual house-made jackfruit custard for dessert. *4217 Geary Blvd., between 7th and 8th Aves., Richmond District, 415/221–7887, AE, D, DC, MC, V. No lunch Sun. Takeout. $$*

CARIBBEAN

7 *d-1*
CHA CHA CHA
Be prepared to jockey for a table at this quirky Haight Street institution. The food is updated Caribbean, and the space is a showplace of bright colors and Hispanic shrines and folk art. Many regulars opt for the dozen or so tapas, such as pork quesadillas, steamed mussels, and garlicky shrimp. The menu changes regularly; among the many possibilities are aromatic Cuban roast pork with black beans, or grilled fish with olives and peppers. A Cha3 has opened in the Mission as well, in a retro space that housed an Irish bar, McCarthy's, for nearly a century. *1805 Haight St., between Shrader and Stanyan Sts., Upper Haight, 415/386–5758. Reservations not accepted. MC, V. Takeout and delivery. $–$$*

2 *f-4*
2327 Mission St., between 19th and 20th Sts., Mission, 415/386–7670.

8 *a-3*
CHARANGA
This lively, casual, exposed-brick spot is named for a well-known style of Cuban salsa music, but the tapas, portioned large enough for the hearty eater, are a mix of tastes from Cuba and other Caribbean ports of call, plus some Latin American, Spanish, and even Asian accents. Among the choices are mushrooms sautéed with shallots and sherry, a Cuban-style beef with *sofrito* (sauce of annatto seeds and rendered pork fat), chicken *chalupas* (fried "boat"-shape tortilla stuffed with meat, vegetables, and/or cheese) on a bed of black beans, a ceviche of snapper chunks and plenty of cilantro, and slices of seared red tuna partnered with a pineapple-mango salsa. *2351 Mission St., between 19th and 20th Sts., Mission, 415/282–1813. MC, V. Closed Mon. No lunch. $*

8 *b-5*
EL NUEVO FRUTILANDIA
The flavors of Puerto Rico and Cuba are here for the picking. At lunchtime, Cuban sandwiches stuffed with roast pork are filling and tasty, as are the Puerto Rican "dumplings" of shredded pork and olives inside a "skin" made from plantains and yucca. For dinner, you might have chicken in salsa verde or green chiles stuffed with cheese. Plantains, yucca, rice, and beans turn up at every meal. As the name would imply, a tropical fruit shake is the drink of choice. *3077 24th St., between Treat Ave. and Folsom St., Mission, 415/648–2958. MC, V. Takeout. $*

CHINESE

4 *e-4*

BOW HON

Here is an oasis for the aficionado of clay pot cooking. The menu of this Formica-and-linoleum-lined gem is a mile long, with everything from rice plates to half a dozen crab preparations, but the dishes prepared in unglazed earthenware vessels are the specialty here. They come in two styles, with rice and without. For the former, a variety of ingredient combinations is strewn over a bed of rice and then cooked, with dried black mushrooms, chicken, and sausage or pork ribs with black beans among the toppings. The house soup and a plate of mustard greens are included with the price of the pot. A long list of regular clay pots is also offered, including a delicious bean cake with chicken and salted fish. *850 Grant Ave., between Clay and Washington Sts., Chinatown, 415/362–0601. Reservations not accepted. No credit cards. Takeout. $*

6 *e-4*

CHEUNG HING

This is a bare-bones combination Chinese take-out "roast house" and casual eatery. Nearly every day, the line trails out the door, everyone patiently waiting their turn at the counter to order a roast duck or marinated duck, soy sauce chicken or white poached chicken, crispy skin pork or barbecued pork to take home to the family dinner table. You can also take a seat at one of eight tables and enjoy what may be the largest rice plates in the city, each order topped with a pile of greens and your choice of one of the above proteins. There are also noodles, in and out of soup, and wontons. *2339 Noriega St., between 30th and 31st St., Sunset District, 415/665–3271. Reservations not accepted. MC, V. Takeout. $*

8 *e-3*

ELIZA'S

Although the cooking here is far from authentic Chinese, Ping and Jan Sung have a large, loyal following for their sunflower beef with scallions and enoki mushrooms, slightly sweet shrimp tossed with pine nuts, portly pot stickers, and other California-influenced dishes. The food arrives on colorful Italian plates, and the room is full of lovely Chinese carved-wood antiques and blue-and-white porcelains. A pot of orchids tops each of the tables. A second location stands within a high C of the Opera House. *1457 18th St., between Missouri and Connecticut Sts., Potrero Hill, 415/648–9999. MC, V. Takeout. $–$$*

4 *b-8*

205 Oak St., at Gough St., Civic Center, 415/621–4819.

4 *e-4*

GREAT EASTERN

The busy dining room of this bi-level Cantonese restaurant is home to large tanks of swimming Dungeness crabs, black bass, abalone, catfish, shrimp, rock cod, and other creatures of the sea; a wall menu in both Chinese and English lists the prices of the various choices. Conch stir-fried with yellow chives, crab with vermicelli in a clay pot, and shrimp steamed with garlic are among the chef's many specialties. Late-night appetites favor the tasty noodle dishes. *649 Jackson St., between Kearny St. and Grant Ave., Chinatown, 415/986–2550. AE, MC, V. Takeout. $–$$*

2 *d-3*

HAPPY FAMILY

Sample the cuisine of China's Shandong province: boiled dumplings filled with pork or shrimp, and such classic cold dishes as garlic-scented cold seaweed, pig's ear salad, and wine-cooked chicken. Of particular note are the hand-pulled noodles, made without the aid of a knife (a mound of dough is pulled, stretched, and twisted until it forms long, uniform strands); these are served in soup or with various sauces. Kimchi arrives automatically with every order, an acknowledgment of Shandong's border with North Korea. *3809 Geary Blvd., between 2nd and 3rd Aves., Richmond District, 415/221–5095. MC, V. Closed Tues. Takeout. $*

4 *f-3*

HAPPY VALLEY SEAFOOD RESTAURANT

The specialty here is the hot pot, a bubbling cauldron of broth into which diners dip meats, seafood, and vegetables. There are four different hot pots, but shrimp, scallops, white fish, mushrooms, pea shoots, and more than half a dozen other items are usually part of the mix. The cost heads upward as the individual ingredients become more pricey, so if you want lobster, bamboo pith (a pricey fungus that grows near bamboo plants), and the like, expect to pay more. *1255 Battery St., between Filbert and Greenwich Sts., Embarcadero, 415/399–9393. MC, V. Takeout. $$*

4 g-4

HARBOR VILLAGE

Dim sum lunches, fresh seafood from the restaurant's own tanks, and Chinese classics from Peking duck to roast suckling pig are the hallmarks of this deluxe branch of a top-flight Hong Kong–based operation. The dining areas are outfitted with Chinese antiques and teak furnishings, and the main dining room usually hosts a slew of business moguls and various large family groups. A gallery of private rooms is used for weddings, anniversaries, and other special occasions. *4 Embarcadero Center, at Sacramento and Drumm Sts., Embarcadero, 415/781–8833. AE, DC, MC, V. Takeout. $$*

4 e-4

HING LUNG

A good place for night owls (it's open until 1 AM), Hing Lung is a well-known destination for Chinese comfort food such as *jook* (thick rice porridge laced with various ingredients, from roast duck to preserved egg), stir-fried rice or wheat noodles, bowls of wontons, and plates of crispy roast pork. More substantial meals are available, too: try steamed catfish in black bean sauce, stir-fried crab with ginger and scallions, or salt-and-pepper squid. The dining room is a sea of bamboo chairs and bare-topped tables, with a small, glass-enclosed kitchen up front. *674 Broadway, between Stockton St. and Columbus Ave., Chinatown, 415/398–8838. MC, V. Takeout. $*

5 a-7

H. K. SHANGHAI LO JING HING RESTAURANT

Names carry a certain cachet in the Chinese world, restaurant names included. One of the best Shanghainese restaurants in Hong Kong is called Lo Jing Hing, and this modest Richmond District outpost has acquired the right to call itself this as well, thus elevating its status among name-conscious local Chinese diners. Order some steamed dumplings or panfried pork buns to start. The smoked fish, crystal jade shrimp, sautéed eel with garlic and

chives, soy-braised pork shank, and bean curd with shrimp roe are all as commonly eaten on the Bund as hot dogs are on Coney Island. *5423 Geary Blvd., between 18th and 19th Sts., Richmond District, 415/876–2828. MC, V. Takeout. $*

2 b-6

JUST WON TON

This modest, white-walled Sunset storefront specializes in delicate wontons. You can order them in plain broth or partnered with noodles, fish balls, chicken, duck, pork, beef, or assorted innards. If you're still hungry, order up a plate of *chow fun* (rice noodles) or *chow mein* (wheat noodles), stir-fried with meat and vegetables. If you've no time to sit, take out a batch of wontons and cook them at home. *1241 Vicente St., between 23rd and 24th Aves., Sunset District, 415/681–2999. No credit cards. Takeout. $*

4 e-4

NEW ASIA

Hundreds of people can sit down at once in this lively, warehouse-like dim sum parlor. Once you take a seat, start flagging down the carts rolling past you: they're stacked with small plates and bamboo baskets holding translucent shrimp dumplings, pork spareribs with black bean sauce, lotus leaves stuffed with glutinous rice, turnip cake, and more. The waiting line for a table is usually lengthy, but the size of the place means your number comes up pretty quickly. At night, a dinner menu takes over and wedding parties are often part of the scene—but dim sum remains their strong suit. *772 Pacific Ave., between Grant Ave. and Stockton St., Chinatown, 415/391–6666. MC, V. Takeout. $*

1 b-2

NORTH SEA VILLAGE

The draw here, in addition to the great view, is Cantonese seafood: steamed fish, crab with scallions and ginger, salt-baked prawns, stir-fried lobster, clams in black bean sauce, scallops with pine nuts. At lunchtime, a full selection of dim sum is served, from pearly skinned dumplings to pint-size spareribs to shrimp-stuffed rice-noodle rolls to tiny, sunny yellow custard tarts. *300 Turney St., at Brideway St., Sausalito, 415/331–3300. AE, MC, V. Takeout. $*

2 c-3
PARC HONG KONG RESTAURANT

Whatever is making news in Hong Kong restaurants turns up here in no time, cooked by chefs who are considered masters. The kitchen is known for its seafood—crabs, shrimp, catfish, lobsters, scallops—prepared in classic as well as contemporary variations. (Always check the price before ordering.) Dim sum is available at midday. The signature green roof tiles outside should prevent you from passing this place by. *5322 Geary Blvd., between 17th and 18th Aves., Richmond District, 415/668–8998. AE, D, DC, MC, V. Takeout. $$*

4 e-4
R&G LOUNGE

Despite the name, this is not a smoky dive with a bluesy piano player, but a first-rate Cantonese restaurant on two floors. Downstairs (entrance on Kearny Street) is a no-tablecloth dining room that is always packed at lunch and dinner. The more upscale second-floor space (entrance on Commercial Street), complete with shoji-lined private rooms, is a favorite stop for folks on expense accounts. A menu with photographs helps you decide among the many intriguing dishes, including panfried salted fish with minced pork, drunken scallop soup, and steamed bean curd with shrimp meat. *631 Kearny St., at Commercial St., Chinatown, 415/982–7877 or 415/982–3811. AE, DC, MC, V. Takeout. $–$$*

2 b-4
SAN TUNG

This is one of the few Shandong restaurants in the city. It boasts a second, larger location, San Tung No. 2, also in the Sunset. Dumplings, which are assembled in the small kitchen to your left as you enter, come one dozen to an order, filled with shrimp and garlic chives or pork. They are delicious dipped in a blend of soy and hot sauce. Various noodle preparations, in soup or panfried, are good here as well. Round out your meal with a plate of stir-fried greens or a salad of jellyfish and cucumbers and a small plate of cold Shaoxing wine-marinated chicken. *2240 Irving St., between 23rd and 24th Aves., Sunset District, 415/661–4233. MC, V. Closed Mon. Takeout. $*

2 b-3
1031 Irving St., between 11th and 12th Aves., Sunset District, 415/2442–0828.

2 c-4
SHANGHAI RESTAURANT

Admittedly, some of the best dishes in this plain-Jane neighborhood restaurant appear only on the Chinese-language chef's specialties menu, but there are plenty of eastern Chinese classics on the regular English menu to satisfy anyone in search of the Shanghainese classics.

WINE COUNTRY DINING

California's internationally recognized wine region is home to some extraordinary restaurants.

Auberge du Soleil (American/Contemporary)
> *One of the valley's most beautiful restaurant settings.*

Bistro Don Giovanni (Italian)
> *A taste just south of Napa.*

Bistro Jeanty (French)
> *A bistro that looks like it was plucked from the French countryside.*

Bouchon (French)
> *The newest enterprise of brothers Thomas and Joseph Keller.*

Catahoula Restaurant and Saloon (Cajun/Creole)
> *Chef Jan Birnbaum gives Calistoga a taste of the South.*

French Laundry (French)
> *Thomas Keller's kitchen, the most coveted reservation in the valley.*

General's Daughter (American/Contemporary)
> *Old Victorian house with a sunny, rose-covered porch.*

Greystone Restaurant (American/Contemporary)
> *West Coast home of the Culinary Institute of America.*

La Toque (French)
> *Traditional French food in an elegant setting.*

Tomatina (Pizza)
> *A kid-friendly pizza place in the adult world of wine.*

Tra Vigne (Italian)
> *Eat in the dining room or take out from the Cantinetta.*

Pass up the standard Cantonese fare and hone in on the bite-size steamed dumplings served with vinegar and ginger for dipping; cold appetizers of drunken chicken, smoked fish, and vegetarian goose; pearly pink sautéed shrimp, braised eels, and braised pork shank with greens. At midday, enjoy dim sum, Shanghai style. *420 Judah St., Sunset District, 415/661–7755. MC, V. Takeout. $*

4 *f-4*
TOMMY TOY'S
With its elaborate decor, Tommy Toy's would have made the Empress Dowager feel right at home. The preparations, which meld Eastern and Western influences, sometimes falter, but the roast duck, minced squab, lobster tossed with pine nuts, and seafood bisque in a coconut shell topped with puff pastry are popular with the regulars. The place is usually crowded with businesspeople out to impress their clients; don't expect to show up in a T-shirt and be served. *655 Montgomery St., between Clay and Washington Sts., Financial District, 415/397–4888. Reservations essential for lunch. Jacket required. AE, D, DC, MC, V. $$–$$$*

2 *b-3*
TON KIANG
Here you will find the rustic Hakka cuisine of southern China, rarely found in this country. Among the regional specialties are salt-baked chicken, braised stuffed bean curd, wine-flavored dishes, and delicate fish and beef balls. Do not overlook the seafood dishes, including salt-and-pepper squid or shrimp, and silky bean curd stuffed with shrimp meat, or the exotic vegetables such as *ong choy* (water spinach). A full menu of excellent dim sum is served at midday, and some dim sum selections are served at dinnertime as well. *5821 Geary Blvd., between 22nd and 23rd Aves., Richmond District, 415/386–8530. MC, V. Takeout and delivery. $–$$*

4 *f-4*
YANK SING
The oldest teahouse in the city (its original location was in Chinatown), this is still considered by some locals to be the best dim sum kitchen in town; five dozen or so versions of the classic midday Cantonese meal are served on a rotating basis. The handsome Battery

Street location seats 300; the older Stevenson Street site is far smaller, a cozy refuge for nearby office workers who crave dumplings at noontime. *427 Battery St., between Clay and Washington Sts., Financial District, 415/362–1640. AE, DC, MC, V. No dinner. Takeout. $*

4 *f-5*
49 Stevenson St., between 1st and 2nd Sts., Financial District 415/541–4949. Closed weekends.

DELICATESSENS

4 *d-6*
DAVID'S DELICATESSEN
San Francisco's best-known deli, in the Theater District, has been serving New York deli food for what seems like forever. Some of the food is not as good as it should be; still, the sinfully rich blintzes are rightfully famous, and the sandwiches are serious skyscrapers filled with all the traditional fixings: pastrami, corned beef, tongue, chopped liver. Pastry lovers will swoon at the countless caloric choices. Grab a seat at the counter, or settle into a table or booth. *474 Geary St., between Mason and Taylor Sts., Union Square, 771–1600. AE, DC, MC, V. Takeout. $–$$*

8 *e-3*
KLEIN'S
At midday, Klein's fills up with Potrero Hill workers and residents who come for hearty, whimsically named sandwiches. The tongue and cheese tucked between slices of pungent dark rye is called the Abzug, while the Minnie Mouse is a trio of cheeses stacked in a kaiser roll. In addition, pastrami, corned beef, chicken, and turkey sandwiches are all freshly made and filling. Klein's closes in the early evening, so be sure to pick up your deli ration early. *501 Connecticut St., at 20th St., Potrero Hill, 415/821–9149. MC, V. Takeout. $*

4 *c-7*
MAX'S OPERA CAFE
No one will ever accuse Max's of skimpy servings. One corned beef and Swiss on rye will nearly feed a family of four. Dinner plates—brisket, chicken, and the like—are equally generous. The waiters and waitresses take turns at the microphone, singing everything from opera to Broadway show tunes. Max's is packed before and after opera and symphony

performances, but there's also a take-out counter for those nights when you don't want to wait. *601 Van Ness Ave., at Golden Gate Ave., Civic Center, 415/771–7301. Reservations not accepted. AE, DC, MC, V. Takeout. $–$$*

EASTERN EUROPEAN

4 *d-2*

ALBONA RESTAURANT

At this comfortable, well-staffed restaurant you can sample the food of Istria, the peninsula near Trieste that once was Italian but became part of the former Yugoslavia after World War II. *Crafi*, dumplings stuffed with cheese, raisins, and nuts, are served with a meat sauce laced with mildly sweet spices. Puffy fried gnocchi arrive with a similar sauce. Stuffed pork loin, lamb in pomegranate sauce, and shredded cabbage braised with prosciutto are among the other distinctly Istrian specialties. *545 Francisco St., between Mason and Taylor Sts., North Beach, 415/441–1040. MC, V. Closed Sun.–Mon. $$*

8 *a-7*

HUNGARIAN SAUSAGE FACTORY

Despite the name, this modest, homey spot is more than a sausage factory, although the pork sausages and pork-liver-and-rice sausages made on the premises are unquestionably first rate. You can easily make a meal of the stuffed cabbage leaves, or opt for chicken fricassee or pork cutlets. Don't miss the Hungarian sweets, especially the traditional poppy seed roll. For wine, choose the Hungarian Bull's Blood. *419 Cortland Ave., between Bennington and Andover Sts., Bernal Heights, 415/648–2847. MC, V. Closed Mon. No lunch weekdays. Takeout. $*

ECLECTIC

2 *f-3*

CARTA

The Carta kitchen travels the globe: each month there's a different menu from a different country or region. The versatile chefs, who have cooked at some of San Francisco best-known restaurants, transport diners to such varied destinations as the American Southwest, Oaxaca, Turkey, Sicily, Morocco, and New

England, to name just a few. There are usually about 10 small plates, four main courses, and four desserts. The space doubled in size in 1999, and the bar menu is served until midnight every day. A mailing list keeps regulars abreast of the kitchen's itinerary. *1772 Market St., between Gough and Ocatavia Sts., Civic Center, 415/863–3516. AE, MC, V. Closed Mon. No lunch Sat. $$*

7 *f-3*

FUZIO

The crafty marketing folks at Fuzio are cashing in on the surefire wisdom that everybody loves noodles. This slowly growing chain offers an East-West chile prawn noodle salad, a respectable pad Thai (with or without meat), tofu-loaded Japanese *udon* (wheat noodles), linguine with calamari, and pasta al pomodoro, all from under the same stove hood. It's fast food with a little flair at bargain-basement prices, which makes the steady clamor for a table understandable. Moviegoers from the just-steps-away Castro Theatre love to stop in before or after the show. The Embarcadero Center has its own Fuzio, again perfectly placed for moviegoers, plus a third Fuzio is fueling the Marina's young professionals. *469 Castro St., between 17th and 18th Sts., Castro, 415/863–1400. Reservations not accepted. AE, D, MC, V. Takeout. $*

5 *h-3*

2175 Chestnut St., near Pierce St., Marina, 415/673–8804.

4 *f-4*

1 Embarcadero Center, between Battery and Front Sts., Embarcadero, 415/392–7995.

2 *d-4*

POMELO

You may have to wait until the nurses and interns finish chowing down at this global noodle and grain eatery. Just down the road from the ever-expanding UCSF medical center, Pomelo's counts only about 20 seats and they are usually taken by neighborhood regulars. There are noodles from Lanzhou, Saigon, Phnom Penh, and Bologna; fried rice from Bangkok; and quinoa from Peru, all put together in attractive fashion in the small, but efficient, open kitchen. Grab one of the stools at the sleek black counter so that you can watch the cooks in action. *92 Judah St., near 5th Ave., Sunset District, 415/731–6175. No credit cards. Takeout. $*

5 g-3
WORLD WRAPPS
What's being wrapped here is a bevy of global burritos: everything from Peking duck to teriyaki tofu is stuffed inside a plain, spinach, or tomato tortilla. High energy, good-for-you fruit smoothies—papaya, blackberry, banana-date—are paired with the hearty wraps, which can be eaten on the spot or easily toted away. Not surprisingly, the crowd is mostly young, athletic, and enthusiastic about the food. That enthusiasm has translated into new locations springing up all over the Bay Area. *2257 Chestnut St., between Pierce and Scott Sts., Marina, 415/563–9727. No credit cards. $*

4 c-4
2227 Polk St., between Vallejo and Green Sts., Russian Hill, 415/931–9727.

2 e-4
2012 Market St., Castro, 415/487–4300.

ENGLISH

7 g-1
MAD DOG IN THE FOG
British expats regularly turn up at this soccer-crazy pub as early as 6 AM to catch major matches on cable TV. Later on, they come back for pub grub and pints. Shepherd's pie, bangers and mash, ploughman's lunch, and a few sandwiches are as fancy as it gets, but the crowd is loyal—thanks especially to the well-used dartboard. For those who care, there's a major bar-towel collection. *530 Haight St., between Fillmore and Steiner Sts., Lower Haight, 415/626–7279. No credit cards. Takeout. $*

ETHIOPIAN

7 g-1
AXUM
This tiny, unpretentious Lower Haight combination café and restaurant draws both young, hip neighborhood residents and the Eritrean exiles who occupy the same blocks. As with all Eritrean and Ethiopian restaurants, the food at Axum is served on large, round, spongy slabs of bread known as *injera*. *Tshebie derho*, chicken in a peppery tomato sauce; lamb *tibsie*, grilled lamb in a smoky marriage with onions and peppers; and *alicha*, a highly seasoned vegetable ragout, are among the best dishes here.

Sip a glass of *tej*, an East African honey wine, along with the food. *698 Haight St., at Pierce St., Haight. 415/252–7912. No credit cards. No lunch Tues. Takeout. $*

7 d-1
MASSAWA
Named for the Eritrean city of Massawa, this Haight Street favorite serves all the traditional Ethiopian fare, from stews to vegetarian dishes to vegetable fritters laced with chile pepper. The dishes—*doro wat* (spicy chicken stew), red and yellow lentils with braised greens, fish and vegetables, and others—are piled on injera: just tear off a corner, scoop up some lentils, and you've got a mouthful. There's a sidebar of Italian food as well. The dining room is dressed up with basketry and African fabrics. *1538 Haight St., between Ashbury and Clayton Sts., Haight, 415/621–4129. MC, V. Closed Mon. Takeout. $*

7 a-2
NEW ERITREA RESTAURANT
The best way to enjoy this place is to go with a group and order two combinations, one with meat and one without. The meat selection will include lamb, beef, and chicken, and the nonmeat dishes usually feature squash, okra, and mixed vegetables. Don't pass up the *berberé*, the dynamite chile sauce of East Africa. The simply decorated dining room stands beyond a friendly front-room bar. *907 Irving St., near 10th Ave., Sunset District, 415/681–1288. MC, V. No lunch Mon. Takeout. $*

5 g-6
RASSELAS
Along with some of the best Ethiopian food in the city, you get first-rate jazz at Rasselas. The dining room adjoins a large bar where musicians start playing after 8 PM Sunday through Thursday and after 9 PM on Friday and Saturday, so if you want to carry on a dinner conversation easily, eat early. The traditional meat and vegetable stews are served on a round of injera. Try several different dishes to sample the culinary talents of the chef, who was a well-known cook in Ethiopia. At press time, a second location was slated to open in the new Fillmore Jazz District in 2000. *2801 California St., at Divisadero St., Pacific Heights, 415/567–5010. AE, MC, V. No lunch. $$*

FRENCH

`4` b-8

ABSINTHE

From the day it opened, in 1998, the sophisticated space of burgundy walls, dark wood, and luxurious banquettes drew the city's social set. The name is taken from the long-banned, cloudy green liqueur that turn-of-the-century Europeans sipped with abandon. But the menu, which includes such fare as cassis-braised short ribs, squab with risotto, and ricotta dumplings with truffles, is up-to-date French with Mediterranean and Californian touches. A cold seafood bar, a bar menu, and a first-rate selection of imported French cheeses add to the appeal. A late-night menu feeds post-performance goers. *398 Hayes St., at Gough St., Civic Center, 415/551–1590. AE, DC, MC, V. Closed Mon. $$–$$$*

`4` e-5

ANJOU

French expats swoon for the sautéed calves' brain seasoned with sage, and the asparagus spears in puff pastry with a morel sauce. Just steps away from the hubbub of Union Square, this comfortable French bistro on two levels is ideal for folks looking for a place to dine before heading to the theater. Duck confit fans should not pass up the kitchen's excellent rendition. *44 Campton Pl., between Post and Sutter Sts. and Grant and Stockton Sts., Union Square, 415/392–5373. AE, D, MC, V. Closed Sun.–Mon. $$*

`5` g-3

BAKER STREET BISTRO

Not much bigger than a postage stamp, the Baker Street Bistro has a four-course menu that's one of the best bargains in town. If you decide to order à la carte, you can choose from such Gallic standards as snails cooked with butter and garlic, rabbit in mustard sauce, and lamb stew with vegetables. At lunch, salads, omelets, and the sandwiches built on baguettes are satisfying and bargain priced. *2953 Baker St., between Greenwich and Lombard Sts., Cow Hollow, 415/931–1475. MC, V. Closed Mon. $–$$*

`5` h-3

BISTRO AIX

Named for the southern French town of Aix-en-Provence, Bistro Aix is a classic, with banquettes, paper-topped tablecloths, and friendly service. On weekdays there's a bargain two-course prix fixe dinner of soup or salad, plus roast chicken, sirloin steak, or seafood pasta. Thin, crisp-crust pizzas, salads of young, tender greens, house-baked breads, and fruit tarts are all worth ordering à la carte. *3340 Steiner St., between Lombard and Chestnut Sts., Marina, 415/202–0100. MC, V. No lunch. $–$$*

`2` f-3

BISTRO CLOVIS

With its discreet lace curtains, small flower vases on white-cloth-covered tables, wooden bar backed by an antique mirror, and light wood floors, Bistro Clovis looks like what it is: a cozy French bistro. Savvy opera- and symphony goers know they can savor rabbit cooked with Dijon mustard, a tasty lamb salad, a formidable house-made pâté, a robust onion soup, duck with green peppercorns, and nearly addictive profiteroles at this Civic Center spot. At lunchtime, the *croque monsieur* (grilled, egg-dipped ham-and-cheese sandwich) will have you believing you are sitting alongside the Seine. *1596 Market St., at Franklin St., Civic Center, 415/864–0231. MC, V. No lunch weekends. $$*

BISTRO JEANTY

Window boxes, green wooden shutters, and a striped awning in red and white greet you at this Yountville outpost of French food good enough to compete with what's served in the old country. Many of the dishes are familiar souls: cassoulet, coq au vin, mussels steamed in wine, foie gras with pears, escargots, and lamb's tongue salad with potatoes and frisée. Others are a tiny bit fancier, like a tomato soup in puff pastry and truffle oil–doused rabbit ragout with sweetbreads and white beans. Chef Philippe Jeanty is often on hand in the dining room to make sure his diners are happy. *6510 Washington St., Yountville, 707/944–0103. Reservations essential. MC, V. $$*

`4` g-8

BIZOU

Award-winning chef Loretta Keller prepares homey bistro fare in this small, sunny dining room. Regulars point to the thin, crisp pizza topped with caramelized onions, featherlight batter-fried green beans, and grilled sardines as evidence of Keller's ability—although first courses tend to outshine the mains. Imaginative yet familiar desserts such as berry pudding (in warmer months only) and crème brûlée are a good way to cap off any meal. *598 4th St., at Brannan St., South of Market, 415/543–2222. AE, MC, V. Closed Sun. No lunch Sat. $$*

BOUCHON

Two Frenchmen are behind this wine-country restaurant, Thomas Keller, of the famed French Laundry (*see below*), and his brother, Joseph. Bouchon boasts a raw bar, the first in the valley according to the brothers. They also serve such classic French bistro appetizers as leeks in vinaigrette, terrine of duck foie gras, and onion soup au gratin; and eight main dishes, from steak frites to leg of lamb with flageolet beans to mussels *marinières* (with garlic and parsley). The zinc bar was hand-crafted in France, and the plush wine-color banquettes invite lingering. *6534 Washington St., Yountville, 707/944–8037. AE, MC, V.*

4 *f-5*
CAFÉ BASTILLE

The Bastille has a double life: it's a mid-day destination for suits who hunger for onion soup or a few slices of pâté; and it's also a nighttime haunt for folks in search of jazz along with their poulet rôti. When weather permits, the outdoor tables are hard-won. Every year on Bastille Day, this simple bistro, along with its French neighbors, celebrates as if this were Paris instead of San Francisco. *22 Belden St., between Bush and Pine Sts. and Kearny and Montgomery Sts., Financial District, 415/986–5673. AE, MC, V. Closed Sun. Takeout. $–$$*

4 *e-5*
CAFÉ CLAUDE

A favorite spot of Francophiles, Café Claude is hidden in an alley in the heart of San Francisco's French quarter. A zinc bar, comfy banquettes, and posters that once outfitted a Paris bar create a suitably Gallic scene, and on mild days the tables spill into the alley in true French form. Order a croque monsieur, some pâté, a *salade niçoise* (salad with green beans, tuna, eggs, and herbs), or a simple daube, and dream of the City of Light. *7 Claude La., off Bush St., Financial District, 415/392–3505. AE, DC, MC, V. Closed Sun. Takeout. $*

4 *e-3*
CAFÉ JACQUELINE

This cozy storefront operation is a serious soufflé outpost. The egg-leavened concoctions arrive at the white-cloth-topped tables in fine form: tall and puffy, with a crusty crown and a savory or sweet interior. There are a couple of salads and plenty of French bread to accompany the towering soufflés, which are made with wild mushrooms, broccoli and cheese, or spinach, among other ingredients. Consider dropping by after dinner for one of chef Jacqueline's billowy chocolate creations. *1454 Grant Ave., between Green and Union Sts., North Beach, 415/981–5565. MC, V. Closed Mon.–Tues. No lunch. $$–$$$*

4 *e-5*
CAMPTON PLACE

In 1984, chef Bradley Ogden put new American food on the culinary map with the opening of this elegant dining room,

---

LATE-NIGHT BITES

It's late and you're hungry. Here are some spots where you can fuel up.

Absinthe (French)
A smart place to linger after the opera.

Bouchon (French)
A place for frites on the late side.

El Zocalo (Salvadoran)
For some of the best pupusas in the city.

Globe (American/Contemporary)
A first-class kitchen that hums until 1 AM.

Great Eastern (Chinese)
Steamed fish and chow mein until 2 AM.

It's Tops Coffee Shop (American/Casual)
For burgers until the wee hours.

Kabuto Sushi (Japanese)
For lovers of late-night sushi.

Koryo Wooden Charcoal Barbecue (Korean)
When some smoky barbecue's the only thing that'll do.

LuLu (Mediterranean)
A great food and bar scene until midnight.

housed in one of America's premier small hotels. Although other chefs have followed, they all kept the American influence until now. Laurent Manrique, the current top toque, has shifted the focus to southern France, with such dishes as goat cheese salad and ravioli stuffed with foie gras and chanterelles. Power breakfasts and weekend brunches are an institution here, with fluffy omelets and beautiful breads always part of the table. *Campton Place hotel, 340 Stockton St., between Post and Sutter Sts., Union Square, 415/955–5555. Reservations essential. AE, D, DC, MC, V. $$$–$$$$*

5 *h-3*
CASSIS BISTRO
Sit down in this small, sunny yellow bistro and you'll feel as if you've been transported to a town in the south of France. The servers have charming Gallic accents, and the food—warm sausage slices resting in rounds cut from a slice of bread, onion tart, spinach ravioli, veal ragout—has the appeal of good home cooking. If the chef has made tarte Tatin, be sure to sample a wedge. *2120 Greenwich St., between Webster and Fillmore Sts., Cow Hollow, 415/292–0770. No credit cards. Closed Sun.–Mon. No lunch. $–$$*

5 *b-7*
CHAPEAU!
About a dozen hats hang on the walls of this small, light-filled dining room—thus the name. The food has a contemporary French bistro flair: snails in garlic butter, wilted bitter greens with crisp bits of bacon and a poached egg, sweetbreads on parslied mashed potatoes, and a near-perfect crème brûlée. The lovely wine list is a pleasant surprise in such a small restaurant. Unfortunately, the tightly spaced tables and the noise can dampen your enthusiasm for the good food. *1408 Clement St., near 15th Ave., Richmond District, 415/750–9787. AE, DC, MC, V. Closed Mon. No lunch. $$*

4 *d-5*
CHARLES NOB HILL
Elegant and pricey, this small, formal restaurant is housed in what was once a private club. It still has a slightly exclusive mood; most of the men in the dining room wouldn't be caught dead without a tie except on the golf course. The food is contemporary French; sautéed foie gras

with a fruit compote, parchment-cooked fish with red pepper rouille, and pan-roasted poussin are among the favorites. Tasting menus let you sample the full range. *1250 Jones St., between Sacramento and Clay Sts., Nob Hill, 415/771–5400. Reservations essential. AE, DC, MC, V. Closed Mon. No lunch. $$$$*

1 *b-2*
CHRISTOPHE
The chalkboard menu, the bilingual staff, the tiny white lights, the fresh flowers, the lace curtains: this could be a neighborhood bistro in a provincial French town. And once you bite into the duck liver mousse, the slow-cooked cassoulet, or the decadent chocolate mousse, you'll be humming "La Marseillaise." Dinners are all four course and prix fixe, at prices that are throwbacks to an earlier decade. Come early, before six o'clock, and the price drops even further. *1919 Brideway St., at Spring St., Sausalito, 415/332–9244. MC, V. No lunch. $–$$*

5 *d-6*
CLÉMENTINE
This very French restaurant—the *plats du jour* (daily specials) are handwritten on a handsome mirror, suave Gallic men sip pastis at the bar, flower boxes grace the entrance—is a Western culinary outpost in the mostly Asian Inner Richmond. The menu changes every few weeks, but the properly garlicky escargots always seem to be available, and mustard-cloaked rack of lamb and roasted salmon with mashed potatoes are commonly offered. For dessert, the *pain perdu* served with sautéed apple wedges and caramel sauce will make you forget every other French toast you've ever eaten. *126 Clement St., between 2nd and 3rd Aves., Richmond District, 415/387–0408. AE, DC, MC, V. Closed Mon. $$*

4 *e-4*
DES ALPES
This old-fashioned restaurant harkens back to a time when North Beach was home to a handful of boardinghouses catering to Basque residents. Huge, modestly priced prix fixe dinners are the custom: soup, salad, *two* entrées—pan-fried sand dabs and roast leg of lamb are a typical pair—ice cream, and coffee. With wood-paneled walls and bright cloths on the tables, it's an unpreten-

tious spot with family-style service and a crowd of all ages. *732 Broadway, between Stockton and Powell Sts., North Beach, 415/788–9900. D, DC, MC, V. Closed Mon. No lunch. $*

`4` *d-5*

FLEUR DE LYS

With its elegantly canopied dining room, this romantic, pricey Union Square showplace has long been one of the premier French restaurants in town. Chefpartner Hubert Keller's creative cuisine can be sampled in preset menus, including a vegetarian one, or from an à la carte list. The dishes change constantly, but you can count on finding lobster bisque, salmon with wild mushrooms, and seared venison medallions most of the time. Desserts are heavenly, and the wine list is impressive. *777 Sutter St., between Taylor and Jones Sts., Union Square, 415/673–7779. Reservations essential. AE, DC, MC, V. Closed Sun. $$$$*

`2` *e-2*

FLORIO

A ceiling the color of a good Burgundy, gold-tan walls, snow-white linen tablecloths, and bentwood chairs give this small brasserie the feeling of Paris. The crisp roasted chicken and fashion model–slim french fries are both traditional and wonderful. The small menu also includes steak frites, a fine lobster bisque, and a seafood stew that is a kissing cousin of bouillabaisse. Plenty of suits of both sexes show up here after work, usually perching on bar stools to wait their turn for a table. *1915 Fillmore St., between Pine and Bush Sts., Lower Pacific Heights, 415/775–4300. MC, V. $$$*

FRENCH LAUNDRY

Recognized as one of the finest restaurants in the country, French Laundry is nearly always fully booked. But plan ahead or pray for a cancellation and you will sit down to a regular five-course menu or a six-course tasting menu (plus you always get some unannounced bites, too) that you won't soon forget, such as melt-in-your-mouth beef cheeks partnered with veal tongue and baby leeks, seared skate wing with *cippollini* onions and savoy cabbage, and cinnamon-sugared doughnuts with cappuccino *semifreddo* (frozen enriched ice cream). The prices are not for the fainthearted, of course, but many folks believe the exquisite French food prepared by chef Thomas Keller and served

in the comfortable dining room and adjoining garden is worth a trip to the pawn shop. *6640 Washington St., at Creek St., Yountville, 707/944–2380. Reservations essential. AE, DC, MC, V. No lunch Mon.–Thurs. $$$$*

`4` *g-8*

FRINGALE

Chef Gerald Hirigoyen has put his dazzling bistro on the regular route of a well-turned-out crowd from the Financial District and beyond, although his reasonable prices draw everyday pocketbooks, too. They come for his French Basque–inspired dishes such as frisée aux lardons, steamed mussels, bouillabaisse, and duck confit. Hirigoyen trained as a pastry chef in Paris, so leave room for one of the fine desserts for which this kitchen is known—crème brûlée is a must. The small dining room is furnished with classic bistro wood furniture and paper-topped white cloths. *570 4th St., between Bryant and Brannan Sts., South of Market, 415/543–0573. Reservations essential. AE, MC, V. Closed Sun. No lunch Sat. $$*

`4` *c-2*

GARY DANKO

Gary Danko, who won the James Beard Best Chef in California award in the mid-'90s and spent several years winning over fussy palates at San Francisco's Ritz-Carlton Dining Room, opened his own place in 1999, and, in true French style, gave it his name. This very sophisticated spot offers three-, four-, five-, and six-course dinners at prices to match the elegant surroundings. The food is first class, too, from sautéed duck breast with figs to lobster with chanterelles to an addictive chocolate soufflé. *800 North Point St., at Hyde St., Fisherman's Wharf, 415/749–2060. Reservations essential. AE, D, DC, MC, V. No lunch. $$$$*

`4` *c-4*

LA FOLIE

You can explore the elegant food at this pretty storefront restaurant by ordering the five-course set meal or by selecting from the à la carte menu. Chef Roland Passot creates seasonally changing, artful presentations in the form of tasty terrines, tender *galettes* (flat, round cakes), and savory napoleons. The roasted birds—quail, squab—are always excellent; but so is everything else Passot dreams up. *2316 Polk St., between Green and Union Sts., Russian Hill, 415/776–5577. Reservations essential. AE, D, DC, MC, V. Closed Sun. No lunch. $$$$*

LA TOQUE

At La Toque, a white-linen restaurant with brocade-upholstered chairs, a glassed-in exhibition kitchen, and outdoor seating, only a five-course prix-fixe meal is offered, with a handful of choices for each course. The menu changes daily, and the dishes are prepared in a traditional French style, with such appealing combinations as foie gras ravioli with pork confit and balsamic sauce, grilled lamb with Provençal bean ragout, and lemon-ginger crème brûlée. The fare, alas, can be as rich as a Louis XIV credenza, so pace yourself. *1140 Rutherford Cross Rd., off Hwy 29, Rutherford, 707/963–9770. AE, MC, V. Closed Mon.–Tues. No lunch Wed.–Sat. $$$$*

4 *e-5*

LE CENTRAL

Power lunchers have occupied the tables and stood alongside the zinc bar in this quintessential bistro for years. All the classics are served here—leeks vinaigrette, steak with Roquefort sauce, cassoulet, grilled blood sausage with crisp french fries—although not always with the finesse they deserve. The service generally shines, however, especially if you are in the company of regulars. *453 Bush St., between Kearny St. and Grant Ave., Financial District, 415/391–2233. AE, DC, MC, V. Closed Sun. $$*

4 *f-7*

LE CHARM

In the early '90s, Alain Delangle and Linda Yew, a formidable culinary husband-and-wife team, opened this cozy bistro, complete with outdoor patio, in an anonymous strip of SoMa. It was wildly popular almost immediately. Recently, they have redone the exterior, adding bigger windows and a pretty doorway, making it more inviting than ever. The prix fixe dinner is an unqualified bargain, with a choice of sautéed chicken livers on a tangle of greens or rich onion soup, followed by roast chicken with puréed potatoes or salmon on a bed of greens. Yew's tarte Tatin is outstanding. *315 5th St., between Folsom and Harrison Sts., South of Market, 415/546–6128. MC, V. Closed Sun. No dinner Mon. No lunch Sat. $$*

4 *e-5*

MASA'S

This legendary flower-filled dining spot, with its burgundy walls and small marble bar, is housed in the Vintage Court Hotel. Chef Chad Callahan carries on the tradition of the late Masa Kobayashi, who put Masa's on the national map, and chef Julian Serrano, who kept it on the map. Pricey items such as foie gras and truffles figure largely on the menu in such intriguing preparations as ragout of lobster and baby vegetables with truffle shavings and foie gras sautéed with Madeira truffle sauce. Dinners are all prix fixe; book a table at least two weeks in advance. *Vintage Court Hotel, 648 Bush St., between Stockton and Monroe Sts., Union Square, 415/989–7154. Reservations essential. AE, D, DC, MC, V. Closed Sun.–Mon. and 1st 2 wks of Jan. No lunch. $$$$*

4 *f-3*

PASTIS

A cement bar, exposed brick walls, and handsome wooden banquettes give Pastis a casual yet upmarket ambience. At lunchtime, well-heeled workers from the surrounding blocks come in for prawns marinated in pastis (anise-flavored French liqueur) and seared scallops with leeks. The evening menu may include foie gras with a verjus sauce or duck confit. If you're not a fan of oxtails, you may well become one when you try the braised oxtails with *sauce gribiche* (an oil-based sauce of hard-boiled egg yolks, capers, gherkins, and herbs). *1015 Battery St., near Green St., Embarcadero, 415/391–2555. AE, MC, V. Closed Sun. No lunch Sat. $$*

4 *f-5*

PLOUF

The catchy name means "splash," a good moniker for this sleek spot with its mussel-heavy menu. There are seven hefty-portioned mussel preparations from which to choose, including marinière, apple cider, leeks and cream, and crayfish and tomato. Big appetites might want to start with a mixed seafood salad or crab cakes. French vintages are well represented on the carefully selected wine list. *40 Belden St., between Bush and Pine Sts. and Kearny and Montgomery Sts., Financial District, 415/986–6491. MC, V. Closed Sun. No lunch Sat. $$*

`4` *e-5*

RITZ-CARLTON DINING ROOM AND TERRACE

This Nob Hill showplace holds both the Dining Room, a pricey, formal space with urbane French cuisine served in three- to five-course dinners, and The Terrace, which has a garden patio for outdoor dining and hosts a popular Sunday brunch with live jazz. The Dining Room executive chef is Sylvain Portay, previously chef de cuisine at New York's celebrated Le Cirque. *600 Stockton St., at Pine St., Nob Hill, 415/296–7465. AE, D, DC, MC, V. Dining Room: closed Sun., no lunch. $$$–$$$$*

`4` *g-7*

SOUTH PARK CAFÉ

Tucked into a pleat of the city's hip Multimedia Gulch, South Park Café is an utterly Gallic stop. An order of frisée with baked goat cheese, steak with *pommes frites* (french fries), *boudin noir* (blood sausage) with sautéed apples, or perfectly cooked duck breast is solid evidence of the kitchen's commitment to the Paris culinary tradition. Weekdays, you can grab a simple breakfast of café au lait and a croissant while practicing your French with the wait staff. *108 South Park Ave., between 2nd and 3rd Sts. and Bryant and Brannan Sts., South of Market, 415/495–7275. MC, V. Closed Sun. No lunch Sat. $$*

`0` *a-2*

TI COUZ

When crepes came back into fashion in the mid-'90s, this Breton-style crêperie was leading the pack. Working in an assembly-line setup, cooks wrap the large, thin pancakes around your choice of fillings—ratatouille, salmon, mushrooms, or spinach. In 1999, Ti Couz grew, taking over part of the building next door. Two bars have been installed, one for seafood, both raw and cooked, and one offering mixed drinks. *3108 16th St., between Guerrero and Valencia Sts., Mission, 415/252–7373. MC, V. $*

`8` *a-4*

WATERGATE

Nixon never ate here. Nor is this a high-rise apartment building. It is, however, an interesting kitchen ruled by classic French technique that borrows freely from the Chinese pantry. Chef Walter Liang stuffs wontons with butternut squash, braises lamb shanks in Shaoxing wine, and tops a sea bass with sweet Chinese red dates, rosemary, and white wine before sealing it in parchment. The buttery yellow walls, white tablecloths, and Chinese paintings are a nice balance of East and West. Order a tea from the superb selection; it comes in a beautiful purple earthenware pot. *1152 Valencia St., between 22nd and 23d Sts., Mission, 415/648–6000. AE, DC, MC, V. No lunch. $$–$$$*

`7` *d-2*

ZAZIE

When San Francisco's bone-chilling winds blow, those seeking comfort head to Zazie for a warming beef daube or some garlicky roast chicken. The staff of this small, brick-walled dining room serves waffles and omelets in the early morning, filling sandwiches at lunch, and full-scale dinners at night. The Provençal-style fish stew is a good bet, and the desserts, including wonderful fruit crisps, are homey and delicious. *941 Cole St., between Carl and Parnassus Sts., Upper Haight, 415/564–5332. MC, V. Takeout. $–$$*

FUSION

`4` *d-8*

ASIASF

The tasty food at this combination restaurant and nightclub is meant for grazing. It is out of the ordinary fare lemongrass-seasoned hamburger with wasabi cream, quesadillas stuffed with tea-smoked duck and jack cheese, shiitake-filled pot stickers. But the food is not nearly as unusual as the all-male Asian wait staff of "gender illusionists." In other words, these are men dressed as women, from their feather boas to their stiletto heels. When they are not delivering your food, they are delivering your entertainment from atop a 40-ft-long red-vinyl bar. Expect lip-synched show tunes and sundry other melodies at ear-splitting volume and a nice show of dance steps. *201 9th St., at Howard St., South of Market, 415/255–2742. AE, D, DC, MC, V. No dinner Mon.–Tues. No lunch. $$*

`4` *a-6*

CAFÉ KATI

The location is decidedly low profile: next door to the Japan Center. But chef Kirk Webber's dishes are decidedly high profile: *pappadam* (crispy lentil flour bread) and *raita* (cucumber yogurt sauce) instead of bread and butter, bass glazed with miso and served with avocado sushi, sweet-onion-and-salmon tacos, Caesar salad of bundled romaine standing straight up, ready for deconstruction. A surprisingly small kitchen is set between two long, narrow dining rooms; the one at the rear is especially pleasant because of its Asian accents. *1963 Sutter St., between Webster and Fillmore Sts., Lower Pacific Heights, 415/775–7313. MC, V. Closed Mon. No lunch. $$$*

7 *d-2*

EOS RESTAURANT & WINE BAR

Chef Arnold Wong churns out intriguing East-West dishes such as tea-smoked salmon and mango spring rolls, grilled New York steak with Thai spiced butter, and lemongrass-skewered bass with wasabi mashed potatoes. Sometimes diners may find the competing flavors more confusing than comforting, but Wong's loyal following keeps the place busy. The attached wine bar, with some 400 vintages, is a good place for friends to meet, and any of the wines on hand can make the trip to your table next door. *901 Cole St., at Carl St., Haight, 415/566–3063. Reservations essential. AE, MC, V. No lunch. $$$*

7 *a-2*

HOUSE ON NINTH

A sharply angled window and doorway—almost like at an amusement park fun house—might make you feel slightly off balance when you approach this stylish Inner Sunset eatery. And chef-owner Larry Tse's fusion fare is equally quirky. He fries up green beans in light tempura batter, serves East Coast soft-shell crabs with a spicy cilantro mignonette, tosses golden-fried scallops into his Caesar salad, and serves slim taro-pork spring rolls. Tse's original House, a smaller and less showy space, straddles the border between Chinatown and North Beach, in a perfect East-West echo of the menu. *1269 9th Ave., between Lincoln St. and Irving Way, Sunset District, 415/682–3898. AE, MC, V. Closed Mon. No lunch weekends. Takeout. $$*

4 *e-3*

11230 Grant Ave., near Columbus Ave., North Beach, 415/986–8612. AE, MC, V. Closed Sun.–Mon. Takeout. $$

1 *b-2*

ONDINE

Ondine has been around, off and on, in this same Sausalito location for more than 40 years, and nowadays folks are flocking to this pricey East-West outpost for the drop-dead gorgeous, 180-degree bay view and the equally memorable menu. The choices seem designed for the pocketbook of an Internet executive: foie gras and langoustine in a port sauce, pan-roasted salmon with truffle-chervil butter, and a whole lobster reclining on fresh noodles dressed with a truffle-rich lobster sauce. Even the desserts are for the Armani-clad, if the Grand Marnier soufflé with bittersweet chocolate sauce is any indication. *558 Bridgeway Blvd, Sausalito, 415/331–1133. AE, D, DC, MC, V. No lunch Mon.–Sat. $$$$*

4 *e-5*

ORITALIA

The name tips you off as to what you'll find at this stylish eatery: the foods of the Orient— Japan, China, Thailand, Vietnam—and, of course, Italy. Highlights include *sale* (salt) steamed sea bass, poached shrimp wontons in roasted garlic-sesame broth, crab cakes with rice paddy herb sauce, and satsuma potato gnocchi with nuggets of lobster. The restaurant recently moved from its small original home in Pacific Heights to a large downtown space filled with handsome Asian artifacts. *586 Bush St., at Stockton St., Union Square, 415/782–8122. AE, DC, MC, V. No lunch. $$*

GERMAN

4 *d-6*

GERMAN COOK

This tiny, no-frills downtown restaurant has a small counter with just a few stools and a wall of cozy wooden booths. The hearty fare is home-style, with such old-fashioned items as stuffed cabbage, meat loaf, bratwurst, sauerbraten, and stuffed pork chops. The small staff does a fine job, and always with a smile. *612 O'Farrell St., between Leavenworth and Hyde Sts., Tenderloin, 415/776–9022. No credit cards. No lunch Sat.–Tues. Takeout. $*

7 *h-6*

SPECKMANN'S

In the heart of San Francisco's original German neighborhood, Speckmann's houses both a delicatessen and a restaurant. The dining room, with its photographs of snowy mountain tops and atmospheric Dortmunder beer lanterns, brings to mind a *gasthaus* somewhere in the Black Forest. Among the generous entrées are veal kidneys in mushroom gravy and smoked pork chops with mashed potatoes, all best accompanied by a stein of any of the excellent German beers. *1550 Church St., at Duncan St., Noe Valley, 415/282–0565. MC, V. Takeout. $$*

4 *b-8*
SUPPENKUCHE
At this hip outpost of German cuisine and brews, bratwurst and red cabbage are standards, along with smoked pork chops, schnitzel with spaetzle, and delicious house-made soups. The place is often crowded and strangers regularly end up seated together at the long, unfinished pine tables—a good way to meet new friends. There's also a bountiful weekend brunch. *601 Hayes St., at Laguna St., Hayes Valley, 415/252–9284. AE, MC, V. No lunch Mon.–Sat. Takeout. $–$$*

GREEK

4 *f-4*
KOKKARI
This is not a simple little taverna, but some of the food will make you daydream longingly for sparkling, whitewashed villages plunked down alongside the deep blue Aegean. Admittedly, the fireplace at Kokkari is larger than your first studio apartment, and the dining room runs half a block, but once the food arrives—superb grilled octopus salad, a trio of classic dips with warm pita bread, superb moussaka—you'll be back on that Greek island and ready for another glass of retsina. *220 Jackson St., at Davis St., Embarcadero, 415/98–0983. AE, DC, MC, V. $$–$$$*

HAWAIIAN

7 *g-3*
TITA'S HALE AINA
Homesick Hawaiians flock to this small, sunny, plant-filled space decorated with black-and-white photographs of hula dancers and walls the soothing color of deep-sea coral. Breakfast is served all day, with eggs and Spam (a Hawaiian standard) or *pao douce* (Portuguese-style French toast) among the offerings. At lunch and dinner, big eaters opt for the King Kamehameha plate, which delivers a taste of just about everything in the kitchen: teriyaki beef, chicken adobo, *kalua* pork (baked until tender enough to cut with a fork), *lomi-lomi* salmon (a salted fillet mixed with onion and tomato), plenty of rice, a big scoop of macaroni salad, and more. *3870 17th St., at Noe St., Castro, 415/626–2477. Reservations not accepted. No credit cards. Closed Mon. Takeout. $*

INDIAN

8 *a-2*
BOMBAY ICE CREAM AND CHAAT
Attached to the large Indian food emporium known as Bombay Bazaar is this small, three-table space that serves bargain-priced Indian *chaat* (snacks) and ice cream in dreamy flavors. On the snack part of the menu you will find samosas, curries, and *aloo puri* (puffy

---

DESPERATELY SEEKING CAFFEINE

San Franciscans are fussy about their coffee, which means there's stiff competition among espresso purveyors.

Antica Trattoria (Italian)
The espresso is short and serious.

Café Claude (French)
Where Francophiles take their café express.

Mario's Bohemian Cigar Store Café (Italian)
Cappuccino is the neighborhood benchmark.

Pacific Restaurant (Vietnamese)
Ultraslow-drip Vietnamese filtered coffee sweetened with condensed milk.

South Park Café (French)
Order a café au lait and pick up yesterday's Le Monde.

Vineria (Italian)
A stellar espresso.

Zuni Café & Grill (Mediterranean)
Icy espresso granita laced with a ribbon of cream.

wheat bread filled with potatoes, coriander, and yogurt), all in portions sized to quell your hunger until the next meal. The exotic tastes of the ice cream are as yummy as the names are intriguing: cardamom, rose petal, fig, and saffron and pistachio. *552 Valencia St., near 16th St., Mission, 415/431–1103. MC, V. Closed Mon. Takeout. $*

9 b-3
BREADS OF INDIA

No reservations, only seven tables, and low prices mean that just about everyone who shows up at this storefront restaurant ends up milling around outside for a bit before a seat opens up. Don't come here if you don't want to share a table. But you will be missing a tasty chicken *biryani* (rice cooked with chicken and spices) or chicken tandoori, a home-style curry of peas, cauliflower, and potatoes, and especially the wonderful breads, from *kulcha* stuffed with spiced potatoes or cauliflower to blistered nan sprinkled with exotic seeds. *2448 Sacramento St., at Dwight Way, Berkeley, 510/846–7684. Reservations not accepted. No credit cards. $*

7 c-2
THE GANGES

Strictly vegetarian food—no eggs, no gelatin—is served at this small storefront restaurant. Waitresses in saris deliver delicious curries of potato and cauliflower with black mustard seeds or "meatballs" made with black-eyed peas. The *pakoras* (vegetable fritters) are featherlight and served with two chutneys. On some nights, live Indian music helps set the mood. *775 Frederick St., between Arguello Blvd. and Willard St., Haight, 415/661–7290. MC, V. Closed Sun.–Mon. No lunch. Takeout. $–$$*

4 b-2
GAYLORD'S

A tandoor oven is used to prepare the mildly spiced foods of northern India: delicate salmon, succulent lamb, and other tempting choices. The kitchen falters on occasion, but beautiful bay views help keep diners happy. The elegant dining rooms are full of handsome Indian antiques and fine fabrics in rich browns, greens, and golds. The daily lunch is replaced with brunch on Sunday. *Ghirardelli Square, 900 North Point St., at Polk St., Fisherman's Wharf, 415/771–8822. AE, D, DC, MC, V. No lunch Sun. $$–$$$*

7 g-1
INDIAN OVEN

Tandoori chicken is arguably the best thing to order at this Victorian storefront restaurant. The bird arrives succulent and flavorful, complemented by breads and vegetarian curries. A complete meal, called a *thali* for the metal plate on which it arrives, includes a choice of entrée, plus soup, a curried vegetable, basmati rice, nan, and chutney. *223 Fillmore St., between Haight and Waller Sts., Lower Haight, 415/626–1628. MC, V. No lunch. Takeout. $$*

2 e-1
NORTH INDIA

An old-timer among the city's Indian restaurants, the burgundy-outfitted North India has long seduced a regular clientele with its fine tandoori preparations. The kitchen is visible behind glass walls, so you can easily watch as chickens, shrimp, and lamb speared on long skewers are slipped into the clay oven. The curries are tasty as well, and the breads are addictive. The service is uneven, but the spicy fare is worth the inconvenience. *3131 Webster St., between Moulton and Lombard Sts., Cow Hollow, 415/931–1556. AE, DC, MC, V. No lunch weekends. $$*

3 c-3
VIK'S CHAAT CORNER

There is no pretense here: you walk up to the counter, place your order, grab a seat, and enjoy some great traditional Indian food in the heart of Berkeley. On the walls around you are travel posters depicting exotic Indian locales, and in front of you are chaat—snacks—that run the gamut from pakoras and samosas to *chole batura* (chickpeas in spicy sauce served on a puffy wheat bread). Two curries, one vegetarian and one meat, are offered on the specials board each day. Don't plan on dinner here unless you eat very early; Vik's serves only until six o'clock. *726 Allston Way, between 4th and 5th Sts., Berkeley, 510/644–4412. MC, V. Closed Mon. No dinner. Takeout. $*

INDONESIAN

5 c-8
JAKARTA

Batik, shadow puppets, and masks from Indonesia decorate this handsome representative of Southeast Asian cuisine. Seating is in two dining rooms, both with white walls and dark carpeting. Shrimp cakes with fruit chutney for dipping or spicy ground fish cooked in a banana leaf are good ways to start. Follow up with satay dipped in creamy peanut sauce; the long-cooked *gudeg* (curry) of beef and jackfruit; or chile-dusted fried chicken. *615 Balboa St., between 7th and 8th Aves., Richmond District, 415/387–5225. AE, D, MC, V. Closed Mon. No lunch weekends. Takeout. $$*

IRISH

4 *e-3*

O'REILLY IRISH PUB AND RESTAURANT

If you're looking for corned beef and cabbage, head for this lively pub-cum-restaurant. The dish, which also includes potatoes and turnips, is considerably more sophisticated than what is served in most pubs in Ireland, but the Gaelic spirit is intact. You can also order steak-and-kidney pie, finnan haddie (smoked haddock), Irish stew (lamb and potatoes), and roast chicken and *champ* (mashed potatoes with green onions), all in hearty portions. Chase your meal with one of the many brews on tap. *622 Green St., between Powell and Stockton Sts., North Beach, 415/989–6222. AE, MC, V. Takeout. $$*

ITALIAN

4 *c-5*

ACQUERELLO

This quiet restaurant, one of the most romantic spots in town, serves contemporary Italian food in an elegant setting of watercolors and fine table service. Ingredients of the highest quality are assembled into memorable plates that, understandably, don't come cheaply. The gnocchi and tortellini are always flavorful and refined, and the fish dishes and stuffed roasted quail are superb. *1722 Sacramento St., between Polk St. and Van Ness Ave., Nob Hill, 415/567–5432. Reservations essential. AE, D, DC, MC, V. Closed Sun.–Mon. No lunch. $$$$*

4 *c-3*

ANTICA TRATTORIA

Classy yet straightforward in both food and atmosphere, this charming neigh-borhood restaurant has a small but intriguing menu and a first-rate kitchen. For a great opener, order the antipasto of *coppa*, cured pork-sausage slices topped with a few fresh fava beans and a thread of extra-virgin olive oil; or chicken liver–topped crostini. Rare venison medallions, roasted whole bass, and beef fillet riding atop polenta are among the main courses. For dessert, the custard topped with berries and cream is delectable. *2400 Polk St., at Union St., Russian Hill, 415/928–5797. AE, DC, MC, V. Closed Mon. No lunch. $$–$$$*

8 *e-3*

APERTO

Portrero Hill's restaurant community is centered on the corner of 18th and Connecticut streets, and Aperto is one its most important members. The food is generous and rustic, from polenta topped with Gorgonzola to penne tossed with eggplant. Braised lamb shanks and roast chicken with olives are among the main courses. A pair of big picture windows brings light and openness to the always bustling dining room. *1434 18th St., at Connecticut St., Portrero Hill, 415/252–1625. Reservations not accepted. MC, V. Takeout. $$*

BISTRO DON GIOVANNI

Pastas and pizzas are the focus here, such as the linguine with mushrooms, artichokes, and truffle oil or pizza topped with mozzarella, tomato, and basil. Among the antipasti, the fried zucchini sticks with a shower of Parmesan are popular. At lunchtime, the thick focaccia sandwiches are a good choice, especially if they are eaten on the outdoor patio while you look across the vineyards. *4110 St. Helena Hwy., between Salvador and Oak Knoll, Napa, 707/224–3300. AE, D, DC, MC, V. Takeout. $$*

4 *e-4*

CAFÉ NIEBAUM-COPPOLA

The Coppola in this café name is none other than that of film director Francis Ford Coppola, and the combination café and wine bar is named after the Napa Valley winery he co-owns. Located on the first floor of the historic Sentinel building, which upstairs houses Coppola's Zoetrope film company, the space is done up in marble-topped tables, stone floors, and a copper-topped bar. On the down side, just about everything seems to be for sale, from film posters to pasta bowls to T-shirts. Cracker-thin pizzas, some antipasti and sandwiches, and a few pastas make up the slim snack/small-meal menu. Outdoor seating lets you sip a heady Italian espresso while you watch the world go by. *916 Kearny St., at Columbus Ave., North Beach, 415/291–1700. Reservations not accepted. AE, MC, V. No dinner Sun. Takeout.* $

4 b-8

CAFFE DELLE STELLE

The food at this cheerful trattoria is homey and hearty and the portions are bountiful—the kitchen's faithful fans love to eat the big bowls of pasta tossed with sausage, eggplant, tomatoes, and greens. The brightly dressed dining room has a familial Italian feel, and large windows on two sides keep diners up to date on who's heading to the nearby opera house. Those in the know cap off their meals with an order of tiramisu. *395 Hayes St., near Gough St., Hayes Valley, 415/252–1110. MC, V. Closed Sun. Takeout.* $$

DINING ROOMS WITH A VIEW

. *A number of restaurant views make it easy to understand why San Francisco is one of the most-photographed cities in the United States.*

Auberge du Soleil (American/Contemporary)
   Vineyards, vineyards, vineyards.

Greens (Vegetarian)
   Sailboats bob in nearby slips, with a backdrop of the Golden Gate Bridge.

Julius' Castle (Italian)
   Treasure Island, Alcatraz, the East Bay hills, and both bridges.

McCormick & Kuleto's (Seafood)
   Look for hardy swimmers in the San Francisco Bay.

Mad Dog in the Fog (English)
   A gritty urban sidewalk scene.

Moose's (Mediterranean)
   A bird's-eye view of Washington Square.

Ondine (Fusion)
   A panoramic view of San Francisco from Sausalito.

---

4 d-3

CAPPS'S CORNER

This North Beach favorite is a throwback to the days when family-style Italian dinners were the neighborhood norm. Hearty meals of minestrone, a green salad, pasta (usually with tomato sauce or pesto), a main course (the roast lamb or beef is a good choice), and dessert (spumoni) are served at old-fashioned prices. The tables are covered with red-and-white-checkered cloths, and the bar is a friendly slice of yesteryear. *1600 Powell St., at Green St., North Beach, 415/989–2589. MC, V. No lunch weekends.* $

4 d-3

DA FLORA

Located in a North Beach corner storefront, this unpretentious *osteria* bills itself as a Venetian kitchen. Proof of its commitment is a satisfying antipasto of fresh sardines prepared *in saor* (marinated in olive oil and white wine vinegar), and *bottarga* (tuna roe), another pantry staple of the region, is mixed with olive oil and spread on *bruschetta* (grilled bread hunks) with delicious results. If you're an anchovy lover, pasta tossed with a sauce of the pleasantly salty fish and sweet onions is pure comfort food. *701 Columbus Ave., at Filbert St., North Beach, 415/981–4664. MC, V. Closed Sun.–Mon.* $$

7 h-3

DELFINA

When Delfina first opened, the 35 seats were among the most coveted dining-out spots in town. The owners quickly decided to take over the space next door and add a heat-lamp-warmed patio to accommodate the crowd. The commotion is for chef Craig Stoll's daily changing menu of Italian dishes with plenty of French plates tossed into the mix. That means you might put together a dinner of *brandade* (puree of salt cod) or fried squash blossoms, ravioli stuffed with ricotta and nettles or rabbit with olives, and chocolate profiteroles or *panna cotta* (caramel custard), all washed down with a fine French or Italian wine. *3621 18th St., between Guerrero and Dolores Sts., Mission, 415/552–4055. MC, V. No lunch.* $$

4 d-3

GIRA POLLI

A large Palermo-built rotisserie capable of holding scores of rotating birds stands near the center of the handsome dining room. The big, succulent, garlic-and-herb-rubbed roast chickens are served with potatoes and crusty bread rolls. There's a good selection of salads to start, and tasty cheesecake to finish. A steady stream of nearby residents stops by for takeout. *659 Union St., between Columbus Ave. and Powell St., North Beach, 415/434–4472. MC, V. No lunch. Takeout. $*

1 f-3
IL FORNAIO

This upscale trattoria, with its hand-painted ceiling and marble counters, has a lovely outdoor seating area as well as a heated patio. The kitchen is known for its pizzas from a wood-burning oven, including one with Gorgonzola, onions, and pine nuts. The various pastas are popular too, as are the spit-roasted meats, including rabbit. Special Italian regional menus are available on occasion. *Levi's Plaza, 1265 Battery St., between Filbert and Greenwich Sts., Embarcadero, 415/986 0100. AE, DC, MC, V. Takeout. $$*

5 h-5
JACKSON FILLMORE TRATTORIA

The atmosphere in this simply decorated Upper Fillmore trattoria is infectiously festive, and the southern Italian food is a hit. Grilled Portobello mushrooms served on a tangle of arugula, mammoth-size artichokes stuffed with herbed crumbs, or tomato-topped bruschetta are good ways to start a meal. The pastas are paired with full-flavored sauces, and the main courses of baked fish and chicken with sausage and mushrooms are satisfying. There's a long counter as well as tables. Reservations are taken only for parties of three or more; otherwise, expect a wait. *2506 Fillmore St., near Jackson St., Pacific Heights, 415/346–5288, MC, V. No lunch. Takeout. $$*

4 e-3
JULIUS' CASTLE

Arguably, this restaurant claims the best view in the city: both bridges, Treasure Island, Alcatraz, sailboats on the San Francisco Bay, and the curve of the East Bay hills. In the past, the food was no match for the stunning panorama, but in recent years it has improved, with some decent—albeit pricey—pastas and

antipasti available, among them gnocchi with sautéed scallops and pasta with wild mushrooms. *1541 Montgomery St., between Greenwich and Lombard Sts., Telegraph Hill, 415/392–2222. Reservations essential. AE, DC, MC, V. No lunch. $$$*

4 e-6
KULETO'S

The contemporary cooking of northern Italy, the atmosphere of old San Francisco—imparted in part by the large, beautiful carved bar—and a terrific bar menu showcasing contemporary and traditional antipasti have long made Kuleto's a hit. Comfortable booths and an open kitchen fill one side of the restaurant; a skylighted room lies beyond. The chefs are not always in top form, but the lively ambience keeps the crowds coming. The adjoining Caffè Kuleto dispenses coffees, morning pastries, and sandwiches. *221 Powell St., at O'Farrell St., Union Square, 415/397–7720. AE, D, DC, MC, V. $$*

4 e-3
L'OSTERIA DEL FORNO

A truly low-tech kitchen—everything is done in a little oven or on simple burners—turns out some of the neighborhood's best Italian food: tiny white onions dressed in balsamic vinegar, tuna-and-white-bean salad, polenta with Gorgonzola, thin-crust pizzas, pork cooked in milk, sandwiches of house-made focaccia. A handful of tables fills the two front windows, and the staff is always friendly and helpful. *519 Columbus Ave., between Union and Green Sts., North Beach, 415/982–1124. Reservations not accepted. No credit cards. Closed Tues. Takeout. $–$$*

4 e-3
MARIO'S BOHEMIAN CIGAR STORE CAFÉ

There is a wonderful conviviality in this narrow space overlooking Washington Square. Neighborhood denizens ease their way through the crowd to a table or a counter-side stool to down a powerful espresso made with beans from nearby Graffeo's coffee store or to munch on a thick meatball sandwich on focaccia from a nearby bakery. There are sandwiches of chicken or turkey and mozzarella and a wonderful, old-fashioned tuna melt; the cannelloni is another good choice. A slice of ricotta cheesecake is the sentimental finish. The branch on Polk Street between Green and Vallejo lacks the same charm. *566 Columbus Ave., at Union St., North Beach, 415/362–0536. No credit cards. $*

4 *c-4*

2209 Polk St., between Vallejo and Green Sts., Russian Hill, 415/776–8226.

9 *e-4*

MAZZINI

The home cooking of Tuscany and Umbria is featured in this handsome yet casual Berkeley restaurant. Marble-topped tables are set in a room lined with solid mahogany wainscoting, and two trompe l'oeil murals depicting the Italian countryside decorate one of the two dining rooms. Among the intriguing menu offerings are marinated roasted peppers; *orecchiette* ("little ears" pasta) with broccoli rabe, garlic, and chile pepper flakes; and rabbit with fennel sausage stuffing. A wedge of fresh fruit tart or marsala-infused chocolate and almond cake makes a good finish. *2826 Telegraph Ave., Berkeley, 510/848–5599. Reservations not accepted. MC, V. $$*

3 *e-4*

OLIVETO

Celebrated throughout the Bay Area, this superb Italian restaurant on the corner of a bustling gourmet marketplace shows off the considerable culinary skills of famed chef and co-owner Paul Bertolli. He prepares such classics as chicken cooked under a brick, ravioli stuffed with pumpkin, a salad of grilled quail and greens, house-made sausages, and simply grilled fresh fish. The upstairs dining room has an elegant yet comfortable ambience, and the service is attentive without being intrusive. Downstairs, a more casual menu prevails. *5655 College Ave., at Shafter St., Oakland, 510/547–5356. Reservations essential. AE, DC, MC, V. No lunch weekends. $$$*

4 *f-5*

PALIO D'ASTI

Businesspeople from surrounding offices swarm here at lunchtime for Piedmontese dishes such as fresh ravioli in sage-butter sauce and thin-crust pizzas topped with prosciutto and arugula. In the evening, the small wine bar at the front fills with people interested in a few antipasti or a pizza and a glass or two of great wine. A second branch, called Paninoteca Palio d'Asti, is a hit for its stylish takeout or eat-in lunchtime *panini* (Italian sandwiches) on house-made bread. *640 Sacramento, near Kearny St., Financial District, 415/395–9800. AE, MC, V. Closed Sun. No lunch Sat. $$$*

4 *f-5*

505 Montgomery St., at Sacramento St., Financial District, 415/362–6900. Takeout. $

5 *h-4*

PANE E VINO

The Italian-born owner-chef favors the dishes of Tuscany and northern Italy, with roasted whole fish, sausages with peppers and polenta, *vitello tonnato* (cold veal with a tuna sauce), and comforting risotto among the popular choices. The small, rustic dining rooms have wooden furniture and bright white walls punctuated with colorful pottery. Expect a long wait for a table if you haven't made reservations. *3011 Steiner St., between Union and Filbert Sts., Cow Hollow, 415/346–2111. MC, V. No lunch Sun. $$–$$$*

5 *h-3*

PASTA POMODORO

This is the first location of a homegrown multibranch Italian pasta operation where good-quality pasta, salads, and sandwiches cost less than a first-run-movie ticket. The tiny storefront has counter seating only, and folks queue up to eat noodles tossed with Gorgonzola and cream; penne with *puttanesca* sauce (spicy tomato sauce with olives and anchovies); and spaghetti tossed with scallops, squid, and mussels. The salads range from simple tossed greens to more elaborate concoctions with vegetables, cheeses, and olives. *2027 Chestnut St., near Fillmore St., Marina, 415/474–3400. Reservations not accepted. MC, V. Takeout. $*

4 *d-3*

655 Union St., near Columbus Ave., North Beach, 415/399–0300.

7 *g-2*

2304 Market St., between 16th and Noe Sts., Castro, 415/558–8123.

7 *g-1*

598 Haight St., at Steiner St., Lower Haight, 415/436–9800. No lunch.

`4` a-6

1865 Post St., between Webster and Fillmore Sts., Lower Pacific Heights, 415/674–1826.

`4` a-4

1875 Union St., between Octavia and Laguna Sts., Cow Hollow, 415/771–7900.

`4` e-3

RISTORANTE IDEALE

This fun-loving spot, with its tile floors, high ceilings, and yards of wine racks, has the spirit of a Roman restaurant: the waiters, oozing with Italian charm, are friendly and relaxed; the antipasti, including the mixed grilled vegetables and the carpaccio, are satisfying; and the pasta is perfectly al dente, whether it is *pappardelle* (wide ribbons) with a lamb sauce or fettuccine with chunks of lobster. An espresso granita delivers a sublime Italian finish. 1309–15 Grant Ave., between Vallejo and Green Sts., North Beach, 415/391–4129. D, MC, V. Closed Mon. No lunch. $$

`4` e-3

ROSE PISTOLA

Named for one of North Beach's best-known barkeeps, Rose Pistola is a wildly successful outpost of Italian food with a contemporary flair. The menu favors the dishes of Liguria, plus some local favorites such as cioppino, a tomato-laced seafood stew. The assortment of antipasti—roasted peppers, house-cured fish, fava beans and pecorino cheese, baby artichokes—is every bit as interesting as the mains, such as whole roasted fish, and rabbit with polenta. A crowd of regulars fills the dining room and the large and inviting bar area and, often, the sidewalk tables outside. 532 Columbus Ave., between Union and Green Sts., North Beach, 415/399–0499. AE, DC, MC, V. Takeout. $$

`5` h-4

ROSE'S CAFÉ

This is an offshoot of North Beach's wildly popular Rose Pistola, with similar food at lower prices. A wood-fired pizza oven lets you know that thin, crisp pies are offered. Rose's opens early in the morning for folks on their way to work, satisfies lunchtime drop-ins with thick sandwiches loaded with wonderful cheeses, meats, and grilled vegetables, and seduces the dinner crowd with mussels roasted in the pizza oven,

creamy polenta blended with mascarpone cheese, and a no-nonsense grilled chicken. Top off the meal with an order of hazelnut crepes and an espresso and you are on your way. 2298 Union St., at Steiner St., Cow Hollow, 415/775–2200. AE, DC, MC, V. Takeout. $$

`4` e-5

SCALA'S BISTRO

A modish bi-level dining room and a large, intriguing menu have given this hotel restaurant a sterling reputation. Carpaccio topped with slivers of raw artichoke and Parmesan cheese, grilled Portobello mushrooms, and a tower of fried calamari are among the best antipasti, and the pastas, grilled meats, and poultry, including a bronzed roast chicken, satisfy most main-course appetites. The kitchen's Bostoni cream pie, a rich custard-and-orange chiffon cake topped with chocolate sauce, is too rich for good health—and very popular. Sir Francis Drake Hotel, 432 Powell St., between Post and Sutter Sts., Union Square, 415/395–8555. Reservations essential. AE, D, DC, MC, V. $$

TRA VIGNE

To reach this high-ceilinged, spacious restaurant with its stone walls and exhibition kitchen, you pass under a picturesque trellised arch and through a tree-rimmed courtyard complete with fountain, leaving behind the hustle and bustle that accompanies nearly every wine country visit. The kitchen can be uneven, but when the cooks are on, the pizzas, fresh pastas, and grilled meats are superb. You can also buy a glass of wine and various prepared foods—polenta-stuffed peppers, slices of cheese-laden pizza—at Cantinetta, the adjoining deli, and enjoy it at a table in the courtyard. 1050 Charter Oak Ave., at Washington St., St. Helena, 707/963–4444. D, DC, MC, V. Takeout. $–$$$

`3` f-4

VINERIA

A long, slim space with a brushed-metal bar, track lights, and sleek, colorful chairs, Vineria is a welcome addition to the hip, lively North Mission. Run by the same people who operate L'Osteria del Forno in North Beach (see above), Vineria serves many of the same dishes, including flavorful little balsamic-dressed onions and fine "white pizzas" of mozzarella cheese and porcini.

Pumpkin-stuffed ravioli with sage and butter, orecchiette tossed with broccoli rabe, and thin slices of rare roast beef with oven-roasted potatoes are simple and satisfying. *3228 16th St., between Guerrero and Dolores Sts., Mission, 415/ 552–3889. MC, V. Closed Mon.–Tues. No lunch. $–$$*

2 *e-2*

VIVANDE PORTA VIA

This pricey combination Italian delicatessen-restaurant draws a crowd at lunch and dinner for both its sit-down and take-out fare (a cold case that runs along one wall holds all kinds of Italian gourmet delicacies). The regularly changing menu lists half a dozen pastas and risottos, including a classic Sicilian pasta *alla Norma* (with eggplant), and northern specialties such as risotto with radicchio, pancetta, and pine nuts. *2125 Fillmore St., between California and Sacramento Sts., Pacific Heights, 415/ 346–4430. AE, DC, MC, V. Takeout. $$$*

4 *c-7*

VIVANDE RISTORANTE

Owner-chef Carlo Middione, who also operates the popular Vivande in Pacific

---

A ROMANTIC MEAL

Places to take your honey for a romantic evening.

Aqua (Seafood)
An elegant, flower-filled room for when you want to dress up.

Café Jacqueline (French)
Soufflés are always romantic, and that's all Jacqueline serves.

French Laundry (French)
Win her (or his) heart with the best French food in the wine country.

Murasaki (Japanese)
A homey, little place when you want to seduce a sushi lover.

Ondine (Fusion)
180-degree panoramic view of San Francisco—when you're not staring at each other of course.

Waterfront Restaurant (Seafood)
Another seductive view, this time of the Bay Bridge and beyond.

Zodiac Club (Mediterranean)
Romance for astrology believers.

Heights (*see above*), oversees this sublime restaurant near the Opera House, a favorite after-hours supper stop. The menu is full of irresistible choices: grilled radicchio, pasta tossed with assorted mushrooms, bass dressed with lemony oil, and risotto laced with shrimp. *670 Golden Gate Ave., between Van Ness Ave. and Franklin St., Civic Center, 415/673–9245. AE, DC, MC, V. $$$*

4 *d-3*

WASHINGTON SQUARE BAR AND GRILL

National journalists, political power brokers, and other celebrities have long flocked to "the Washbag," drawn by its nightly piano music and the no-nonsense ambience of the darkly wainscoted dining room. The food is Italian with some Californian accents. Simply cooked fish, a mound of fried calamari, and a nicely seared veal chop are the best dishes here; the pastas are average at best. *1707 Powell St., at Union St., North Beach, 415/982–8123. AE, DC, MC, V. $$*

5 *g-3*

ZINZINO

The thin, asymmetrical pizza topped with prosciutto and arugula is a favorite at this popular Chestnut Street destination, as is its cousin that comes crowned with chunks of fennel sausage and caramelized onions. The food is Italian, although American-born chef Andrea Rappaport adds plenty of her own national touches. The crisp-skinned roast chicken arrives with creamy polenta, and the desserts are generally delectable, including house-made ice creams and a warm chocolate truffle cake. The slim dining room, which was dressed up with new chairs and tables and other appointments just before the millennium, ends in a patio for outdoor dining. *2355 Chestnut St., between Scott and Divisadero Sts., Marina, 415/346–6623. AE, DC, MC, V. No lunch. Takeout. $$*

JAPANESE

2 *c-3*

CLEMENT OKAZU YA

The *teishoku* (complete) dinners at this reasonably priced Japanese eatery are a remarkable buy. In fact, the generous *hamaichi* (yellowfin tuna) sashimi dinner, which comes with a bowl of miso soup, rice, pickles, and ice cream, is a downright steal. A large sushi selection is also modestly priced. There are a dozen interesting appetizer-size dishes and a number of noodle and *donburi* (meat- or chicken-topped rice bowls) selections. *914 Clement St., between 10th and 11th Aves., Richmond District, 415/668–1638. MC, V. Closed Tues. Takeout. $*

7 *g-5*

HAMANO SUSHI

Noe Valley residents pack into this small, serene sushi bar and restaurant in search of fresh fish and a masterful sushi hand. The sushi chef is particularly adept at assembling *makizushi*—rolls of vinegared rice and vegetables or fish in a seaweed wrapper. Dinner, served in the rear of the narrow restaurant, ranges from tempura to grilled fish; entrées are served with miso soup, rice, and a saucer of pickled vegetables. *1332 Castro St., between 24th and Jersey Sts., Noe Valley, 415/826–0825. MC, V. No lunch. Takeout. $*

2 *c-4*

HOTEI

Outside, Hotei has a whitewashed facade and rough-hewn logs holding up a canopy of tiles—in other words, the building would look right at home in the Honshu countryside. Inside, in a pale pumpkin room lined with dark wood wainscoting, diners dig into bowls of soup noodles, plates of panfried noodles, and a score of appetizers and snacks. The dining room is always crowded, and the efficient waiters are quick to deliver your *zarusoba* (cold buckwheat noodles), panfried *gyoza* (pot stickers), or *nabeyaki udon* (udon noodles topped with seafood, chicken, and vegetables) and keep your mug filled with hot green tea. *1290 9th Ave., between Irving St. and Lincoln Way, Sunset District, 415/753–6045. Reservations not accepted. MC, V. Takeout. $*

2 *e-3*

JUBAN

Yakiniku, or grilled beef, is the specialty at this large, contemporary restaurant. Down-draft grills installed in each table clear the smoke away from diners and keep the beef grilling over perfect heat. In addition to rib-eye, short ribs, and tongue, there are squid, scallops, and other items for cooking over the flames. The house-made pickles are addictive,

and a fine selection of sake complements the meal. *Kinokuniya Bldg., 1581 Webster St., between Geary Blvd. and Post St., Japantown, 415/776–5822. AE, DC, MC, V. $$*

2 *c-3*

KABUTO SUSHI

Master sushi chef Sachio Kojima flashes his knives with the grace of a samurai warrior. Take a seat at the sushi bar and put yourself in his hands: a succession of exquisite sushi is sure to be your reward. In addition to first-rate sushi and sashimi, a number of small plates—seaweed salad, sake-marinated black cod—and traditional Japanese dinners are served, and tatami seating is available in the adjoining dining room. A sophisticated sake list is available. *5116 Geary Blvd., between 15th and 16th Aves., Richmond District, 415/752–5652. MC, V. Closed Mon. and the last Sun. of the month. No lunch. Takeout. $$*

9 *d-4*

KIRALA

Before the doors open for the dinner crowd at Kirala, a knot of people is always standing outside, ready to bolt over the threshold. The no-reservations policy has made a wait at the usual dinner hour almost inevitable, especially for the seats at the combination sushi and *robata* bar. The sushi is as fresh as a good looking guy in his first year in college, and the robata selections, small skewers of grilled meats, seafood, vegetables, are deliciously charred and smoky. Don't miss the steamed monkfish liver, a kind of Japanese foie gras. *2100 Ward St., at Shattuck Ave., Berkeley, 510/549–3486. Reservations not accepted. AE, MC, V. No lunch weekends. Takeout. $$*

2 *e-3*

KUSHI TSURU

The specialties of this simple Japanese restaurant are deep-fried, skewered vegetables and meats served with a quartet of dips. Other sure-bet orders are the Osaka-style *battera sushi* (preserved fish molded with rice), and the eel and salmon dishes. Start with a small plate of sesame-tossed spinach or boiled soybeans. The long, narrow dining room opens onto one of the busiest passageways in the Japan Center. *Kintetsu Mall, Japan Center, between Webster and Laguna Sts., Japantown,*

415/922–9902. AE, DC, MC, V. Closed Tues. Takeout. $–$$

4 f-6

KYO-YA

This extraordinarily authentic restaurant, housed in the historic Palace Hotel, serves tempuras, one-pot dishes, deep-fried and grilled meats, and more. The grilled bass is simple and exquisite, and eel on rice in a lacquer box is superb. The sleek, cypress sushi bar is manned by chefs from Japan, and the raw fish prices match their mastery. The lunch menu is more limited and more reasonably priced than the dinner list. *Palace Hotel, 2 New Montgomery St., at Stevenson St., South of Market, 415/546–5000. AE, D, DC, MC, V. Closed Sun. No lunch Mon. and Sat. $$–$$$*

2 e-3

MAKI

The owner, clad in a lovely kimono, watches over her tiny, attractive dining room, where many of the diners order the house special of *wappa meshi*, fish and/or vegetables steamed atop rice in individual bamboo steamers. The kitchen also delivers a fine sukiyaki and *shabu shabu* (raw beef cooked at the table in broth); other Japanese standards—tempura, teriyaki—are given a respectable turn. Various sakes are available; ask the waitress to describe the selection. *Kinokuniya Bldg., Japan Center, between Fillmore and Webster Sts., Japantown, 415/921–5215. AE, MC, V. Closed Tues. No lunch. Takeout. $$*

2 e-3

MIFUNE

You're often faced with a queue at this Japan Center institution—a testament to the quality of Mifune's signature thin, brown *soba* (buckwheat) and thick, white udon (wheat) noodles, all made on the premises. Served both hot and cold and with more than a score of toppings, they are well worth the wait. Pass the time by studying the fine plastic food models lined up in the front windows; they are a visual record of the menu. Seating is at rustic wooden tables. There is even a children's noodle dish that arrives aboard a bullet-train look-alike. *Kintetsu Bldg., Japan Center, between Webster and Laguna Sts., Japantown, 415/922–0337. Reservations not accepted. AE, D, DC, MC, V. $*

2 d-3

MURASAKI

A small sushi bar and four tables are all the seating this homey and comfortable little storefront holds. Sushi buffs come here for the perfectly fresh fish and the camaraderie of the crowd made up mostly of locals and discriminating Japanese. The rest of the menu is given over to tempura, a couple of noodle dishes, and a few appetizers. *211 Clement St., between 2nd and 3rd Aves., Richmond District, 415/668–7317. AE, MC, V. Closed Sun. No lunch. Takeout. $$*

7 h-2

NIPPON SUSHI

This offbeat wedge of a sushi bar has been around for years, and it still lacks an outdoor sign to identify it. The sushi is inexpensive and very good for the price, and the sushi makers are wonderfully eccentric. There's almost always a line, rain or shine, for one of the only two dozen or so seats. The rustic interior has the patina of a well-worn restaurant, which only adds to its charm. *314 Church St., at 15th St., Castro, no phone. Reservations not accepted. No credit cards. Closed Sun. $*

2 e-2

SANPPO

This longtime restaurant serves an enormous selection of Japanese food—*nabemono* dishes (one-pot meals), grills, donburi, udon and soba, tempura, and sushi—and does it well. Wood screens and a wood ceiling impart a rustic air, and a good-size list of small dishes provides plenty of grazing possibilities. *Buchanan Mall, 1702 Post St., at Buchanan St., Japantown, 415/346–3486. Reservations not accepted. MC, V. No lunch Sun. Takeout. $*

4 d-5

SANRAKU

Here you'll find a two-fer: on one side is a boisterous, inexpensive restaurant with everything from sushi to teriyaki to tempura to nabeyaki udon; on the other side is a serene, 20-seat dining room serving *kaiseki* dinners (traditional seasonal menus that commonly number seven or more courses). The foods are exquisitely prepared and presented, each one made with ingredients at their peak of taste and texture. If you wish to go the formal route, reserve one day in advance. A second Sanraku is located in the food court of the new Metreon center at 4th and Mission streets. *704 Sutter St., at Taylor St., Union Square, 415/771–0803. AE, D, MC, V. Kaiseki meals dinner only. Takeout. $–$$*

2 *e-2*
SUSHI-A
A television set, usually tuned to a ball game, keeps diners entertained. Those who are more interested in food watch the chef, who does magic with raw fish. A menu board lets eaters know which fish are featured that day. In addition to sushi, good choices are the light and crisp tempura; and the seafood *nabemono*, a one-pot dish packed with shellfish, noodles, and vegetables. Several tatami rooms at the rear of the dining room may be reserved for kaiseki (seasonal) feasts. *Buchanan Mall, 1737 Buchanan St., between Post and Sutter Sts., Japantown, 415/931–4685. AE, DC, MC, V. Closed Tues.–Wed. Takeout. $$*

1 *h-2*
SUSHI RAN
Raw fish lovers can't resist this place: perfectly fresh ingredients, nearly a score of different types of sake, and friendly sushi chefs keep the place packed every night of the week. All the customary *nigiri* and *maki* sushi are made here; buttery hamaichi and *maguro* (tuna) are among the popular options from the nigiri side of the menu, and salmon skin rolls and spider rolls (soft-shell crab) are two of the favorites from the maki side. You can get your fish cooked, too, plus order the usual Japanese plates. *107 Caledonia St., between Turney and Pine Sts., Sausalito, 415/332–3620. AE, D, MC, V. No lunch weekends. Takeout. $$*

2 *f-4*
TOKYO GO GO
Retro '60s is where it's at for this oh-so-hip combination sushi bar and restaurant. The chairs are popsicle green, and the ceiling is dressed up in the same green plus baby-girl pink and lunch-box orange, with a series of large hanging globes lighting the length of the room. Twentysomethings sip sake while waiting for a table or a seat at the sushi bar to empty, so that they can slide back nigiri and maki sushi or such cooked plates as satay (tiger shrimp, fried tofu, or scallops), mussels steamed in sake,

or miso-rubbed steamed bass. *3174 16th St., between Guerrero and Valencia Sts., Mission, 415/864–2288. MC, V. Closed Mon. No lunch. Takeout (1st hr only). $$*

3 *e-4*
UZEN
The raw fish here is first-rate. It turns up in memorable nigiri sushi—sweet shrimp, pale yellow hamaichi, silky snapper—of course, and in various rolls. But it is served in a couple of very California salads, too, such as spring mix with raw scallops. The cooked side of the menu has the classics, including chicken teriyaki made with hormone-free birds. The decor is ultramodern: halogen lamps, black tables, and walls without art. *5415 College Ave., at Manila St., Oakland, 510/654–7753. MC, V. Closed Sun. No lunch Sat. $$*

KOREAN

2 *d-3*
BROTHERS RESTAURANT
The local Korean community fills up this smoky spot until the wee hours. They come mainly to sit down at a tabletop grill and cook beef, although other items such as beef heart and tongue, pork, and chicken are also available. Small bowls filled with everything from kimchi to sesame-doused spinach to tiny dried fish tossed with chiles arrive with your grilling order, along with rice and a clear soup. Be prepared to toss your smoky clothes in the washer when you get home. *4128 Geary Blvd., between 5th and 6th Aves., Richmond District, 415/387–7991. MC, V. Takeout. $–$$*

3 *d-3*
4014 Geary Blvd., between 4th and 5th Aves., Richmond District, 415/668–2028.

3 *e-5*
KORYO WOODEN CHARCOAL BARBECUE
Tucked in an all-Asian mini-mall, complete with beauty salon, sushi parlor, karaoke bar, and social center, this large Korean restaurant is generally packed past midnight. Once you've ordered, nearly a score of kimchi arrive, small dishes holding such tasty bites as tiny salted dried fish, chile-laced cabbage and daikon, crisp seaweed rectangles, and batter-fried potatoes. The tabletop hibachis are regularly loaded up with short ribs, chicken, squid, pork, tripe, or

tongue. Don't want to cook? Order a big bowl of wheat noodles, raw skate and hot sauce, or one of the many other dishes offered. *4390 Telegraph Ave., at 44th St., Oakland, 510/652–6707. MC, V. Takeout. $*

2 *e-3*
NEW KOREA HOUSE
If you are interested in tracking down an authentic Korean breakfast, this Japantown institution is where you'll find it. (The morning menu is hidden from anyone who doesn't read Korean, but you can usually charm the wait staff into doing a quick translation.) The authentic dishes include Korean sashimi, which combines raw tuna with cooked octopus, clams, julienned vegetables, strips of omelet, and pine nuts—just toss and eat. Standard grilling items are available, along with some tasty soups, noodles, and simmered casseroles. *1620 Post St., between Buchanan Mall and*

TAPAS

Everybody is crazy for small plates with a Latin beat.

César (Spanish)
Berkeley's top tapas destination.

Cha Cha Cha (Caribbean)
The Upper Haight's longtime small-plates outpost.

Cha Cha Cha at McCarthy's (Caribbean)
The Mission branch of the original Cha3.

Charanga (Caribbean)
A heady mix of Caribbean, South American, Spanish, and even Asian flavors.

Esperpento (Spanish)
A favorite with Mission District singles and families alike.

Pinxtos (Spanish)
The name says it all: pinxtos means "small savory bites" in Basque.

Thirstybear (Spanish)
A combination brewpub and tapas bar.

Timo's (Spanish)
A hip, colorful spot with small plates galore.

Zarzuela (Spanish)
A lively tapas refuge for Russian Hill dwellers.

Laguna St., Japantown, 415/931–7834. MC, V. Takeout. $$

2 *e-3*
SEOUL GARDEN
Despite this restaurant's location in the East Wing of the Japan Center, it is strictly Korean. Beyond the handsome doorway, topped by a blue-tiled roof, are a bar and a pair of dining rooms. All the classics are here: cellophane noodles tossed with beef and green onions, large *mandoo* (beef dumplings) in broth, fish and tofu casserole, grilled octopus, Korean-style steak tartare, grilled short ribs, and more. Check the board for the daily Korean specialties. *Japan Center, between Webster and Laguna Sts., Japantown, 415/563–7664. AE, DC, MC, V. Takeout. $$*

MEDITERRANEAN

8 *a-3*
BRUNO'S
In the late 1930s, Bruno's was a favorite of local power brokers and fans of Italian-American food. After closing briefly in 1994, it made a comeback within several months, this time as one of the hottest dining and music spots in town. The opening chef left, so the glow has gone off the kitchen, but the retro-'50s, giant red-leather booths—the only seating in the dining room—are still filled with diners. The Mediterranean menu with Californian elements changes regularly. *2389 Mission St., between 19th and 20th Sts., Mission, 415/550–7455. Reservations essential. MC, V. Closed Sun.–Mon. No lunch. $$*

4 *f-6*
CAFFÈ MUSEO
When San Francisco's classy Museum of Modern Art opened in the mid-'90s, this equally classy eating spot, with its granite floors and leather directors' chairs, started feeding throngs of art lovers. It serves hearty soups, grilled-vegetable or chicken focaccia sandwiches, saffron rice laced with rock shrimp, and couscous with vegetables. In the mornings, stop by for an espresso and one of the irresistible pastries. Next door to the museum's main entrance, it's primarily a lunch spot, but on Thursdays, when the museum stays open until 9 PM, the café follows suit. *151 3rd St., between Mission and Howard Sts., South of Market,*

415/357–4500. MC, V. Closed Wed. No dinner Fri.–Tues. Takeout. $

4 f-5
FAZ
Sample food from around the Mediterranean in this second-story ocher dining room. A wonderful meal might include creamy *baba ghanoush* (eggplant spread) or dolmas; greens tossed with pomegranate seeds and walnuts; a pasta or pizza dish prepared with Italian flair; and a house-smoked fish platter, with salmon, trout, and sturgeon. Midday, suits from the surrounding towers enjoy hearty sandwiches made with rosemary-flecked focaccia. *161 Sutter St., between Montgomery and Kearny Sts., Union Square, 415/362–0404. AE, DC, MC, V. Closed Sun. No lunch Sat. Takeout. $$*

7 f-3
FIREWOOD CAFÉ
The formula here works well: a nice-looking space, good prices, and generally tasty Mediterranean food promptly served. The thin-crust pizza topped with mozzarella, prosciutto, and arugula is wonderful, as is citrus-marinated roasted chicken served with herbed potatoes. You can order a Caesar salad large enough to satisfy two hungry souls, or a variety of different pastas. Order at the counter and grab a table, and your meal is delivered. A second Firewood is located in SoMa's Metreon. *4248 18th St., at Diamond St., Castro, 415/252–0999. Reservations not accepted. MC, V. Takeout. $*

3 c-1
LALIME'S
Berkeley denizens dote on this top-flight kitchen, which has a regular fixed-priced menu in addition to an enticing à la carte list. Both types of menu span the globe: you might find Moroccan couscous, French duck foie gras, Spanish paella, or Italian pasta tossed with springtime vegetables on any given night. The comfortable two-story space is bright and peaceful, and always crowded, so call ahead for reservations. Put your name on the mailing list to keep up on the restaurant's many special dinners. *1329 Gilman St., near Neilson St., Berkeley, 510/527–9838. MC, V. No lunch. $$*

4 g-4
LAVASH
Done in lovely earth tones and marble floors, and owned by Faz Poursohi, who also operates Faz (*see above*), the spacious Lavash offers a menu that successfully marries the tables of the eastern and western Mediterranean. House-made aged pickled garlic and pickled vegetables (cauliflower, peppers, cucumbers, carrots) are among the appetizers, and Turkish chicken kabobs, rigatoni with Gorgonzola, and pizza *margherita* (with mozzarella, tomato, and basil) round out the larger plates. Delicious sandwich fillings (beef, chicken, eggplant) are wrapped with the house-made organic *lavash* (paper-thin flat bread). *4 Embarcadero Center, at Market St, 415/982–2233. AE, MC, V. Closed Sun. Takeout. $–$$*

4 f-7
LULU
Chef Jody Denton presents a regularly changing menu at this continuing SoMa hotspot. The *fritto misto* of deep-fried artichoke hearts, fennel, and thin lemon slices is dynamite, as are the mussels roasted on an iron platter. Main courses, from spit-roasted rabbit to herb-laced pork roast, are generous and generally first-rate. The atmosphere in the bar is SRO and rather boisterous; a table in the smaller, quieter room off to one side makes dinner conversation easier. The café on the opposite side serves food from morning until late at night. *816 Folsom St., near 4th St., South of Market, 415/495–5775. AE, DC, MC, V. Takeout. $$*

4 e-3
MOOSE'S
A top celebrity destination from the moment it opened in 1992, Moose's remains the fueling station of choice for politicians, media types, actors, and those who enjoy supping within throwing distance of fabled Washington Square. Executive chef Brian Whitmer cooks up such prize-winning fare as king salmon with ratatouille, guinea fowl on whipped parsnips, and beef fillet with Gorgonzola-stuffed ravioli. Try to reserve one of the hard-won window seats with a view of the square. Live music keeps you entertained until your first course appears. *1652 Stockton St., between Union and Filbert Sts., North Beach, 415/989–7800. Reservations essential. AE, DC, MC, V. $$–$$$*

5 h-3
PLUMPJACK CAFÉ
The name is the title of an opera composed by famed oil tycoon and music

lover Gordon Getty, whose sons are two of the partners here. They also run the Balboa Café (*see* American/Casual, *above*), just down the street; a nearby respected wine store, PlumpJack Wines (making for excellent wine prices here); and a restaurant in Lake Tahoe. But this dinner house is their most stylish operation. Chef Maria Helm oversees a regularly changing menu that spans the Mediterranean, with gravlax and blini and herbed chicken flanked by polenta among the possibilities. The crowd is generally well-heeled and carefully attired. *3201 Fillmore St., at Greenwich St., Cow Hollow, 415/463–4755. AE, MC, V. Closed Sun. $$$*

2 c-3
SOCCA

Socca is a crisp, flat, savory chickpea cake native to the south of France. It is just one of the specialties at this Mediterranean dinner house, where neighborhood residents go for a salad of quickly cooked rock shrimp, a main of lamb shanks and white beans, and crème brûlée in three flavors: pumpkin, lime, and maple. The bright blue, green, and yellow walls and cool tile floors evoke the sun and the sea, and the attentive service makes you feel right at home. *5800 Geary Blvd., at 22nd Ave., Richmond District, 415/379–6720. MC, V. Closed Mon. No lunch. Takeout. $$*

4 g-4
SPLENDIDO

A crisp, brick oven–cooked pizza will set you to thinking about Italy, and a warm goat-cheese salad will transport you to France. But the stunning view of San Francisco Bay from the wall of windows will bring you back home. The chefs have come and gone, but now the talented Giovanni Perticone is at the helm and the food is superb. The handsome dining room has always been a wonderful place to sit and enjoy the sunsplashed cuisine of the Mediterranean. *Embarcadero 4, at Sacramento and Drumm Sts., Embarcadero, 415/986–3222. AE, DC, MC, V. $$–$$$*

7 h-2
ZODIAC CLUB

Remember when people used to ask each other what their sign is? Well, that's in fashion again at the Zodiac Club, the look of which is a conscious knockoff of the bar where Stewart and Novak hung out in the late-'50s' film *Bell, Book and Candle*. Stars and planets hang overhead, Zodiac signs adorn the light fixtures (including the candles), and yards of fabric decorate the walls. Even drinks are keyed to the signs, such as the double (twin) martini for Geminis. Grilled octopus salad, salmon in grape leaves served with *romesco* sauce (with tomatoes, bell peppers, and almonds), and steak frites keep the mostly thirtysomethings fueled into the wee hours. *718 14th St., between Church and Market Sts., Castro, 415/626–7827. MC, V. No lunch. $$$*

4 c-8
ZUNI CAFÉ & GRILL

Zuni's Mediterranean menu carries a heavy dose of Italian culinary influence. A spacious, window-filled balcony dining area overlooks the large bar, where shellfish, one of the best oyster selections in town, and drinks are dispensed. Perhaps the most popular main course here is a whole roast chicken and Tuscan bread salad for two, but the house-cured anchovies, Caesar salad, shoestring potatoes, and heavenly burgers on focaccia are also the stuff of food myths. The eclectic crowd regularly orders the icy espresso granita with cream to cap off the evening. *1658 Market St., between Franklin and Gough Sts., Hayes Valley, 415/552–2522. Reservations essential. AE, MC, V. Closed Mon. $$–$$$*

MEXICAN

8 a-6
BRISAS DE ACAPULCO

There is nothing like a big bowl of homemade soup on a cold night. But for folks too busy to stand at the stove, Brisas de Acapulco is an ideal option. A big bowl of fish or chicken soup, loaded with protein and carbs, will keep you fueled through any rainstorm, plus it's ladled up at price that makes you feel like a burglar. The ceviche arrives with a crown of avocado, the grilled shrimp show up still in their shells, and a menu sidebar of Salvadoran dishes will satisfy those who crave *pupusas* (cheese or meat stuffed cornmeal rounds) and fried plantains. *3137 Mission St., between Cesar Chavez St. and Coso Ave., Mission, 415/826–1496. MC, V. Takeout. $*

5 g-3

CAFÉ MARIMBA

In the midst of a hip, youthful neighborhood, this colorful Mexican café full of playful folk art serves contemporary yet authentic versions of Mexico's regional fare: tamales with mole *negro* (sauce of chiles and chocolate) from Oaxaca; shrimp with roasted tomatoes in the style of Zihuatanejo; and grilled chicken from Yucatán, packed into a tortilla. Two kinds of house-made salsa, usually one red and one green, come with a mountain of freshly fried chips that always seem to get eaten. The list of tequilas is a connoisseur's dream. *2317 Chestnut St., near Scott St., Marina, 415/776–1506. MC, V. No lunch Mon. Takeout. $$*

8 b-3

CHAVA'S

On Saturdays, *menudo* aficionados head for this barrio favorite, where they sit down to huge portions of the famed Mexican tripe-and-hominy stew cherished as a surefire antidote to a hangover. Regulars also know that weekends are the time to sample the kitchen's fine *birria*, braised goat with onions and cilantro. You can scoop up anything you order with house-made corn tortillas, including excellent huevos rancheros and huevos *con nopales* (with cactus). The brightly painted dining room attracts families, couples, and singles. *3748 18th St., at Shotwell St., Mission, 415/552–9387. No credit cards. Takeout. $*

1 b-1

GUAYMAS

A margarita and a warm afternoon are all you need at Guaymas. From a seat on the deck, you can sip your ice-cold drink and stare at the beautiful San Francisco skyline. But if that's all you did, you would be missing the Mexican classics prepared by a kitchen devoted to delivering classy south-of-the-border food. All the favorites are here—tacos, guacamole, ceviche, tamales, chiles rellenos, plus duck with a pumpkin-seed sauce, a mixed seafood platter, and mesquite-grilled fish. On sunny Sunday mornings, the deck fills with brunchers, so book ahead. *5 Main St., at the ferry terminal, Tiburon, 415/435–6300. AE, MC, V. Takeout. $$*

8 a-5

LA TAQUERIA

The operation's logo claims "The Best Tacos & Burritos in the Whole World"—and in fact, it's not far from the truth. Choose from *carne asada* (grilled beef), *carnitas* (braised pork), or hefty chunks of chicken, and watch the staff stuff your request into piping-hot tortillas. The burritos are packed with tasty beans and rice, and the salsas come in varying levels of hotness. Cool down with a glass of *agua fresca* (fresh juice). It's mostly takeout, although there is limited seating. *2889 Mission St., between 24th and 25th Sts., Mission, 415/285–7177. No credit cards. Takeout. $*

8 b-4

LOS JARRITOS

Jarritos, tiny earthenware cups used for drinking tequila, hang from the ceiling and walls of this brightly colored restaurant located on a sunny Mission District corner. Beneath them, diners young and old, families, and singles feast on wonderful tacos de carne asada, quesadillas stuffed with nopales, chiles, and cheese-, cilantro-, and onion-topped carnitas. *901 South Van Ness, between 20th and 21st Sts., Mission, 415/648–8383. Reservations not accepted. No credit cards. Takeout. $*

4 g-7

MAYA

The Sandoval family opened their first upscale Mexican restaurant in New York and followed it a couple of years later, in 1999, with this West Coast twin. The names of the tasty dishes are familiar, but the preparations are far classier—and pricier—than their barrio counterparts. The tuna taco uses seared rare fish, the buttery guacamole comes in a silver bowl, and the chile relleno conceals scallops, shrimp, and squid. Mexican artwork covers the walls, showy sunbursts serve as chairbacks, and an outdoor terrace is a nice place to perch on a warm day. *303 2nd St., at Harrison St., South of Market, 415/543–2989. AE, DC, MC, V. No lunch weekends. $$$*

8 a-2

PANCHO VILLA

The line here usually snakes out the door, and the women making tacos and burritos behind the counter never have a moment's rest. Carne asada is usually sizzling away on the griddle, alongside green onions. Full-dinner plates include everything from chiles rellenos to grilled tequila-marinated prawns, but most people settle on the tortilla-wrapped specialties. *3071 16th St., between Valencia and Mission Sts., Mission, 415/864–8840. No credit cards. Takeout. $*

8 *a-5*
PAPALOTE MEXICAN GRILL
In the heart of the barrio, this colorful outpost, done up in bright, cheery blues and reds, is primarily a place to get a good taco or burrito. The freshly grilled carne asada is superb tucked into a big flour tortilla along with some beans, rice, and a spoonful of the house-made salsa. First-rate quesadillas are offered here as well, as are full dinner plates that include a tasty jícama salad and specials that change monthly. Sip a glass of sangria or a fragrant agua fresca

---

A COUNTER PERSPECTIVE

Watching cooks at work from across the counter is a favorite San Francisco pastime.

Il Fornaio (Italian)
In this handsomely decorated ristorante, you can watch your pizza slip right into the wood-burning oven.

Kabuto Sushi (Japanese)
Take a seat at the sushi bar to watch the fastest sushi master in the West.

Los Jarritos (Mexican)
Watch your tortillas being made by hand in this Mexican family favorite.

Pancho Villa (Mexican)
Order your burrito at the counter, oversee its filling and wrapping, and then snag a table.

St. Francis Fountain (American/Casual)
Ice-cream sundaes and banana splits made right before your eyes.

Swan Oyster Depot (Seafood)
Pick up tips on shucking oysters from a ringside seat.

Ti Couz (French)
Watch your authentic Breton-style crepes go together.

---

made from hibiscus along with your meal. On weekends, stop in for a breakfast of huevos rancheros. *3409 24th St., at Valencia St., 415/970–8815. AE, MC, V. Takeout. $*

8 *a-6*
TAQUERIA CANCUN
Despite the name, don't expect beach umbrellas and swaying palms. But do expect a large TV set turned to Mexican programming and some good tacos and burritos. You can opt for carnitas, carne asada, *cabeza* (beef head), and *lengua* (tongue) for either package. A big non-meat burrito is available, too, packed with beans, rice, onions, cheese, sour cream, and avocado. No matter what you order, load up your choice with the house-made red and green salsas. *3211 Mission St., at Valencia St., Mission, 415/550–1414. No credit cards. Takeout. $*

8 *a-3*
2288 Mission St., between 18th and 19th Sts., Mission, 415/252–9560.

8 *a-5*
TAQUERIA SAN JOSÉ
This is the real thing. The tacos, served in paper-lined plastic baskets, are classics: soft tortillas wrapped around a choice of meat—carne asada, *al pastor* (barbecued pork), chorizo, lengua, cabeza, *sesos* (brains)—along with fiery or mild salsa, onions, and cilantro. Everything is perfectly fresh, right down to the bowls of tomatillo salsa on the tables. Bigger appetites can try the burritos filled with the same meats, plus rice and beans. *2830 Mission St., near 24th St., Mission, 415/282–0203. No credit cards. Takeout. $*

MIDDLE EASTERN

8 *a-3*
AMIRA
Belly dancers take to the stage, and itinerant mariachis sometimes stop by, but the pan-Arabic Amira is known for more than its music and dance. Big plates of couscous surrounded with chicken, lamb, or sausages, and kebabs on mounds of rice are two popular choices, as are the appetizers, including the chef's signature walnut dip. The fabric-draped ceiling, low benches, and large, round brass trays evoke the feeling of a Casbah transplanted to the trendy North

Mission. *590 Valencia St., between 16th and 17th Sts., Mission, 415/621–6213. MC, V. Closed Mon. No lunch. $–$$*

7 *g-2*

JUST LIKE HOME

At the front of this neighborhood deli–restaurant stands a large glass case holding many of the kitchen's tasty Middle Eastern creations: pizzalike flat breads topped with seasoned ground lamb, tabbouleh, hummus, baba ghanoush, *kibbeh* (balls of ground lamb), and stout dolmas filled with rice, pine nuts, and spices. You can order piping-hot falafel stuffed into pocket bread, a plate of *musakhan* (oven-roasted chicken smothered in onions), or, if you're feeling adventurous, spleen stuffed with onions and spinach. The house-made phyllo sweets are packed with nuts and honey. *1024 Irving St., between 11th and 12th Aves., Sunset District, 415/681–3337. MC, V. Takeout. $*

4 *e-3*

MAYKADEH

Teheran-born San Francisco opera director Lotfi Mansouri eats in this handsome Persian restaurant whenever he wants a taste of his homeland. Grilled lamb brains with saffron butter, rice-filled dolmas, and tangy feta cheese and fresh herbs are all delicious ways to launch your meal. Kebabs of marinated chicken, lamb, and beef served with fluffy white rice are favorite main courses. Or try the classic Persian *ghorme sabzee*, lamb shanks with red beans, onions, tomatoes, and a mix of Middle Eastern spices. *470 Green St., between Grant Ave. and Kearny St., North Beach, 415/362–8286. MC, V. $$*

9 *d-1*

PAPA'S RESTAURANT

Although the operation has the look of an all-American coffee shop, the Papa in this case is Iranian. One taste of the combination meze platter—dolmas stuffed with beef, thinly sliced eggplant, sliced tomatoes, pita, and *kookoo sabzi*, a Middle Eastern omelet of sorts thick with herbs and vegetables—and you'll be glad he is. There are wonderful main dishes with lamb shanks, chicken breasts, and kabobs, and mounds of fluffy Persian rice. For dessert, try the ice cream flavored with rose water or almond-laced baklava. *2026 University Ave., near Shattuck Ave., Berkeley, 510/ 841–0884. D, MC, V. Closed Mon. Takeout. $*

2 *f-4*

TRULY MEDITERRANEAN

Tucked next door to the popular Roxie Cinema, an outpost of intelligent film programming, this tiny storefront serves *shawarma*, sandwiches made from spit-roasted lamb or chicken. The meats are wrapped in the paper-thin Middle Eastern flat bread known as lavash, along with tahini sauce, seasoned onions, cucumbers. Falafel is folded up in a sheet of lavash as well, plus there are pita sandwiches stuffed with feta, baba ghanoush, and hummus. There are less than half a dozen seats, so plan on walking away with your meal. *3109 16th St., between Valencia and Guerrero St., Mission, 415/252–7482. Reservations not accepted. No credit cards. Takeout. $*

7 *f-4*

YAYA CUISINE

In a dining room brightened by green and blue tiles and a mural depicting ancient Mesopotamia, Yahya Salih serves dinners of everything from lamb shanks to chicken kebabs, all with a California touch. In an adjoining space he calls Ur, named for the ancient birthplace of the patriarch Abraham, he serves a great midday buffet at bargain-basement prices. tabbouleh, hummus, baba ghanoush, pomegranate chicken, lamb with yogurt, *leffa* (a Middle Eastern flat bread wrapped around meats or vegetables, hummus, marinated onions, and other condiments), and *laham bea'ajeen*, a close relative of pizza. *663 Clay St., between Kearny and Montgomery Sts., Financial District, 415/434–3567. MC, V. Closed Sun. No lunch Sat. Takeout. $–$$*

PAN-ASIAN

4 *a-4*

BETELNUT

Although the service is too often dismally bad, this fashionable pan-Asian outpost remains popular. The adventurous drinks list—with everything from house-brewed rice beer to martinis—draws a mostly young crowd to the bar area, where lacquered walls, bamboo ceiling fans, and hand-painted posters create a comfortably exotic mood. A plate of tasty stir-fried dried anchovies, chiles, peanuts, garlic, and green onions is arguably the best dish from the kitchen, although many diners also rave about the Vietnamese five-spice grilled chicken, fiery green papaya salad, and sweet, garlicky spareribs. *2030 Union St., between Buchanan and Webster Sts., Cow Hollow, 415/929–8855. D, DC, MC, V. $$*

2 *d-4*

CITRUS CLUB

You won't get the same authentic noodles you would sit down to in Ho Chi Minh City or Shanghai, Tokyo or Bangkok, but if you are looking for a big serving of noodles at a bargain price in a place nicely done up in a kind of faux Asian exoticism, take a seat at the long counter or at one of the tables here. In no time at all, you will be digging into an order of chicken and rice noodle soup fragrant with cilantro or hot-sour shrimp noodle soup laced with vegetables. If you are in the mood for some wok-tossed noodles, there are various chicken, meat, seafood, and vegetable permutations from which to choose. End your meal with a sake martini (sake shaken with citrus juice) and a passion-fruit sorbet. *1790 Haight St., at Shrader St., Upper Haight, 415/387–6366. Reservations not accepted. MC, V. Takeout. $*

4 *e-5*

E & O TRADING COMPANY

The look is turn-of-the-century Asian trading house, complete with bamboo, dragons, flowing fabric, and high ceilings. The menu jumps from Vietnamese salad rolls to chicken satay, Thai green curry, Indian nan with raita and tomato chutney, and Indonesian fried rice. Draft beer, brewed on the third floor, is yet another draw: try India pale ale, unfiltered wheat beer, or malty brown ale. *314 Sutter St., near Grant Ave., Union Square, 415/693–0303. AE, MC, V. No lunch Sun. $$*

4 *g-5*

LONGLIFE NOODLE COMPANY AND JOOK JOINT

This slick, black-gray-and-red pseudo-cafeteria space is the first in what the owners hope will be a string of Asian noodle houses. The noodles are principally adaptations from Thailand, China, Japan, Singapore, Malaysia, and Vietnam. They turn up in broths, stir-fried,

and cold, usually with too-cutesy names such as *laksa luck* (rice noodles in a spicy coconut milk broth), and dragon's breath (garlic noodles tossed with vegetables). Various buns, spring rolls, wontons, and pot stickers round out the menu. The food and service have both been uneven, but still the crowds throng here, especially around midday. The Metreon food court, at 4th and Mission streets (*see map 4, grid f-6*), has a branch. *139 Steuart St., between Mission and Howard Sts., Embarcadero, 415/281–3818. Reservations not accepted. MC, V. No lunch weekends. Takeout. $*

8 *b-8*

MOKI'S SUSHI AND PACIFIC GRILL

When this cheerful spot, decorated with Southeast Asian artifacts and rattan furniture, opened in Bernal Heights in the late '90s, it seemed like a strange interloper in this mostly working class family neighborhood. But its menu of sushi and Pacific-islands fare has caught on, and a legion of fans can now be found at the dozen-seat sushi bar or one of the half dozen or so tables. The cooked plates are mostly fish grilled and served with tropical sauces. Weekend brunch has been on hiatus for a while, but it promises to return with its fabulous banana French toast. *830 Cortland Ave., at Gates St., Bernal Heights, 415/970–9336. Reservations for parties of 5 or more. AE, MC, V. No lunch. Takeout. $$*

2 *d-3*

STRAITS CAFÉ

Although not a true pan-Asian restaurant, this highly popular eatery serves the cuisine of Singapore, a combination of the culinary traditions of China, India, and the Malay archipelago. Chef-owner Chris Yeo serves an exotic list of complex curries, sticks of fragrant satay, and seafood noodle soups. He also adds a contemporary twist to many classic Asian dishes: raw tuna with pickled ginger, shallots, and greens tossed with a ginger-plum dressing; and sea bass fillet baked in parchment with ginger, mushrooms, rice wine, and *longans* (small, perfumy Asian fruit). One wall in the handsome dining room is decorated with partial re-creations of the old pastel-painted shop-house fronts of Singapore. *3300 Geary Blvd., at Parker St., Richmond District, 415/668–1783. AE, MC, V. Takeout. $$*

5 h-5
ZAO NOODLE BAR
No sooner did the doors open at the trendy Zao than lovers of Asian noodles swooped down on the place, ready to slurp up everything from Thai chicken in lemongrass-coconut broth to Vietnamese rice noodles with seared pork to Shanghai noodles tossed with chile pepper—flecked chicken and prawns. The space recalls a trendy spot in Hong Kong or Singapore, and generously sized portions are priced to feed folks who are saving their pennies for that next trip to Asia. *2046 California St., between Fillmore and Steiner Sts., Pacific Heights, 415/345–8088. Reservations not accepted. MC. V. Takeout. $*

PERUVIAN

8 a-3
FINA ESTAMPA
Even though the hipsters have been slowly taking over the Mission, some fine old spots have remained. This storefront Peruvian favorite serves the classics, so order like the Andean expats: *anticuchos,* grilled marinated beef heart accompanied with a sizzling green chile sauce; *chicharrón de pollo,* crispy chunks of chicken with a lime sauce and a side of marinated onions and tomatoes; *lomo saltado,* a vinegary sauté of beef strips, potatoes, onions, and tomatoes; and *parihuela,* a spicy seafood stew. *2374 Mission St., between 19th and 20th Sts., Mission, 415/824–4437. MC, V. Closed Mon. Takeout. $*

PIZZA

4 e-3
NORTH BEACH PIZZA
The Italian-Brazilian owners have figured out just what their customers want: American pizza. Their thick-crust pies are blanketed with cheese and loaded with toppings—pepperoni, mushrooms, clams, olives, and more. The pastas and other Italian standards on the menu are less worthwhile. If you want to eat your pizza at home, this is the place to call for fast delivery that puts the other chains to shame. *1310 Grant Ave., near Vallejo St., North Beach, 415/433–2444. AE, D, DC, MC, V. Takeout and delivery. $*

4 e-3
1499 Grant Ave., at Union St., North Beach, 415/433–2444.

7 c-1
800 Stanyan St., near Haight St., Haight, 415/75186–2300.

2 e-7
4787 Mission St., near Ocean Ave., Outer Mission, 415/586–1400.

2 a-5
3054 Taraval St., between 40th and 41st Aves., Sunset District, 415/242–9100.

8 a-1
PAULINE'S PIZZA
Pauline's made its name with its pesto pizza, whose prebaked crust prevents the basil from turning bitter from too much heat. Their crisp crusts also hold a slew of other classic and contemporary toppings: tomatoes and mozzarella; leeks and Kalamata olives; and Cajun tasso with parsley and lemon zest are a few of the best. Salads are hearty and suitable for sharing. The neighborhood is a little gritty, but Pauline's is a sure beacon. *260 Valencia St., at Brosnan St. off Duboce Ave., Mission, 415/552–2050, MC, V. Takeout. $–$$*

4 f-7
PAZZIA
Folks who work at the Italian consulate turn up here for thin, crisp pizzas that remind them of home. The margherita, made with mozzarella, tomato, and basil, is classic. Other toppings show the same Italian restraint, including one of arugula and prosciutto, and another with Gorgonzola. The calzones are substantial enough for two people to share. Order a salad of radicchio and arugula and a glass of Chianti and you'll think you're in Rome. *337 3rd St., between Folsom and Harrison Sts., South of Market, 415/512–1693. MC, V. Takeout. $–$$*

TOMATINA
An offshoot of Tra Vigne, Tomatina is the place to stop when you want just a pizza, a salad, and a glass of wine. It's big, casual, efficient, and penny-wise, thus giving fast food a good name. You order at the counter when you enter, take a seat at one of the tables, all of which are already set with silverware, and your pizza shows up in no time. *1016 Main St., St. Helena, 707/967–9999. D, DC, MC, V. Takeout. $*

4 *e-4*

TOMMASO'S

For more than 60 years, both locals and visitors have been lining up to step down into this dark North Beach institution for one reason: pizza. It comes in more than a dozen-and-a-half guises, with memorable tomato sauce and whole-milk mozzarella playing major roles. The crusts are thin, crisp, and classic, cooked in San Francisco's original wood-burning pizza oven. Accompany the Italian pies with a room-temperature vegetable such as broccoli, green beans, or asparagus, tossed simply with olive oil and lemon juice. No reservations are taken, but your meal will be worth the wait. *1042 Kearny St., between Broadway and Pacific Ave., North Beach, 415/398–9696. Reservations not accepted. MC, V. Closed Mon. No lunch. Takeout. $–$$*

4 *b-8*

VICOLO

This is the home of gourmet pizza: crisp cornmeal crusts topped with andouille and smoked mozzarella, blue cheese and roasted eggplant, house-made sausage, garden-fresh tomatoes, wild mushrooms, and imported cheeses. The pies come in paper-lined cast-iron pans; a tossed green salad or one of the marinated vegetable salads is a perfect accompaniment. The opera house and symphony hall are just a stone's throw away, making this busy, cathedral-ceilinged spot a nice stop before you head off for a concert. *150 Ivy St., at Franklin St., Hayes Valley, 415/863–2382. MC, V. Takeout. $*

RUSSIAN

2 *c-3*

CINDERELLA RESTAURANT AND BAKERY

In the evenings, the bakers roll their cooling racks of freshly baked breads to the doorway of this local institution, to enjoy a curbside smoke. During the day, a stream of regulars comes through the doors to buy the sturdy Russian loaves and the more delicate rolls and sweets, or to sit down in the modest dining room for bowls of *pelmeni* (small meat-filled dumplings in broth) and plates of cabbage rolls, lamb and kasha, or cheese-filled dumplings. *436 Balboa St., between 5th and 6th Aves., Richmond District, 415/751–9690. MC, V. Closed Mon. Takeout. $*

2 *d-3*

KATIA'S

There are floor-to-ceiling windows and flowers on every table at this charming corner-storefront restaurant. The delicious borscht arrives with a dollop of sour cream, a perfect opener to your meal. Or you might start with small plates of smoked salmon and blini, marinated mushrooms, and meat- or vegetable-filled piroshki. The pelmeni are delicate and satisfying, as is the chicken Pozharski, seasoned minced chicken formed into a cutlet and sautéed. Save room for a meringue drizzled with berry sauce or a flaky, caloric napoleon. *600 5th Ave., at Balboa St., Richmond District, 415/668–9292. AE, DC, MC, V. Closed Mon. $$*

SALVADORAN

8 *a-6*

EL ZOCALO

Ever yearn for a late-night pupusa, the stuffed cornmeal round that is more or less the hamburger of El Salvador? This always-busy Formica-and-linoleum restaurant keeps the stove stoked until the wee hours—indeed, until the paper boys are almost ready to pedal out on their routes. That means that those who love not only pupusas, but also a whole fried snapper with rice and salad, fried plantains and *crema* (a kind of Central American sour cream), or a mountain of *chicharrónes* and yucca can stop in for a bite just about whenever hunger strikes. *3230 Mission St., between Valencia and 29th Sts., Mission, MC, V. Takeout. $*

8 *c-4*

LA PAZ RESTAURANT

The cooks here are experts at making El Salvador's national snack, the pupusa. With a few swift pats of their hands, they seal a filling of cheese, pork, or a combination of the two inside a chewy cornmeal disk and cook it on a griddle. The tasty morsels are served hot and accompanied by a pile of vinegary shredded cabbage. An order of fried *platanos* (plantains) and cream is a good accompaniment, or you might try the pork tamales or rice and beans. *1028 Potrero Ave., between 22nd and 23rd Sts., Mission, 415/550–8313. MC, V. Takeout. $*

2 e-6

LA SANTANECA

Even though the ambience is as plain as a shoe box, the food from this Salvadoran kitchen shines. Everything from pupusas to chubby tamales crammed with pork and potatoes are served here. Regulars like to sit down to one of the bathtub-size soups, from shrimp with vegetables to chicken with corn. Try a *licuado*, a kind of Central American smoothie made with cherimoya, banana, or strawberry, or a mixture. *3781 Mission St., between Park and Richland Sts., Mission, 415/648–1034. No credit cards. Takeout. $*

SEAFOOD

4 f-5

AQUA

This quietly glamorous spot, with its monumental floral arrangements and stylish lighting, is arguably the city's most important seafood restaurant. It serves contemporary versions of Mediterranean and American classics: mussel or lobster soufflé; chunks of lobster alongside lobster-stuffed ravioli; and ultrarare ahi tuna paired with foie gras are especially good. Save room for the regularly changing list of desserts, nearly all of them miniature museum pieces. Don't stint on wine, since this food deserves the best. *252 California St., between Front and Battery Sts., Financial District, 415/956–9662. Reservations essential. AE, DC, MC, V. Closed Sun. No lunch Sat. $$$*

4 e-6

FARALLON

There was plenty of talk about this $4 million, Pat Kuleto–designed restaurant before it opened in mid-1997. One reason was Kuleto and all that money. The other reason was chef Mark Franz, who spent 10 years guiding the kitchen at the fabled Stars. That seafood is the specialty here comes as no surprise once you see the scallop-shell entryway, jellyfish-shape chandeliers, and kelp-covered columns. Soft-shell crab resting on a bed of vine-ripened tomatoes, lobster and prawns paired with nugget-size gnocchi, and braised pike with Yukon Gold mashed potatoes are just a few of Franz's elaborate creations. Desserts are by Emily Luchetti, another Stars alum; don't miss the warm chocolate cake. *450*

Post St., between Powell and Mason Sts., Union Square, 415/956–6969. Reservations essential. AE, DC, MC, V. No lunch Sun. $$$–$$$$

4 b-8

HAYES STREET GRILL

Consult the blackboard for the seafood selections du jour at this Hayes Valley mainstay, with its classic decor of white walls, wood wainscoting, bentwood chairs, and white-cloth-topped tables. The fish is simply grilled, with a choice of sauces ranging from tomato salsa to a spicy Szechuan peanut concoction to beurre blanc or fruity olive oil. Also recommended are the crab cakes and the various salads, including one of grilled quail and another that combines calamari and fennel. The crème brûlée is famous. *320 Hayes St., between Franklin and Gough Sts., Hayes Valley, 415/863–5545. Reservations essential. AE, D, DC, MC, V. No lunch weekends. $$–$$$*

4 c-2

MCCORMICK & KULETO'S

Here is a visitor's dream come true: a fabulous view of the Bay from every seat in the house and dozens of varieties of fish and shellfish prepared in scores of globe-circling ways, from tacos and pot stickers to grills and pastas. The kitchen often stumbles, so the best advice is not to challenge it: stick to the simplest preparations—and enjoy that priceless view. *Ghirardelli Square at Beach and Larkin Sts., Fisherman's Wharf, 415/929–1730. AE, D, DC, MC, V. Takeout. $$–$$$*

4 h-5

RED HERRING

The long-popular Bistro Roti morphed into the inventive Red Herring in mid-1999, throwing over its old chef and menu for a new cast in the kitchen and a nearly all-seafood list—but keeping its million-dollar bay view. The food introduces flavors from around the world, reaching into pantries in the Middle East, the Caribbean, the Indian subcontinent, Asia, and even Cajun-Creole country. The result is dishes such as Maine crab cakes served with a mango-habanero salsa, squid stuffed with tasso and rice, scallop carpaccio with ahi tuna stuffed in a cannoli-like seaweed wrapper, and tandoori-style snapper paired with a banana raita. *155 Steuart St., between Mission and Howard Sts.,*

Embarcadero, 415/495–6500. AE, D, DC, MC, V. No lunch weekends. $$$

4 *f-5*
SAM'S GRILL
Fresh seafood draws crowds of local bankers and brokers to this longtime, no-nonsense grill at lunchtime, where regulars are pampered by the veteran wait staff. The retro, wood-lined space, with its seemingly countless coat hooks, has curtained booths at the rear that recall the dining room of a stuffy men's club. Charbroiled seafood and sautéed sole are the standard mains, although steaks and chops keep the red-meat eaters happy. The seafood is sometimes too long on the stove; request it rare if you so desire. *374 Bush St., between Montgomery and Kearny Sts., Financial District, 415/421–0594. AE, DC, MC, V. Closed weekends. $$–$$$*

4 *c-5*
SWAN OYSTER DEPOT
This renowned fish purveyor and seafood bar has remained unchanged for decades, and that's just fine with the legions of San Franciscans who flock here. It's a delightfully atmospheric operation, with sawdust-covered floors, a marble counter and spinning stools, and a steamy kitchen. The convivial counter-men serve old-fashioned clam chowder and fresh oysters on the half shelf. The doors close early, so plan on dinner before 5 PM. *1517 Polk St., between California and Sacramento Sts., Nob Hill, 415/673–1101. No credit cards. Closed Sun. $$*

4 *f-5*
TADICH GRILL
Owners and locations have changed many times since this old-timer opened during the Gold Rush era, but it has kept its 19th-century San Francisco atmosphere. The kitchen is best at simple sautés—petrale and rex sole are favorites—although an order of cioppino during crab season is mandatory. The old-fashioned house-made tartar sauce that accompanies deep-fried items and the smooth, rich rice pudding have kept locals smiling for more decades than anyone cares to count. There is seating at the counter as well as in private booths, but expect long lines for a table at lunchtime. *240 California St., between Front and Battery Sts., Financial District, 415/391–1849. Reservations not accepted. MC, V. Closed Sun. $$–$$$*

4 *g-3*
WATERFRONT CAFÉ
You are sold on this place the moment you see the spacious, airy dining room and outdoor patio that looks out on the bay and the bridge. Although called a café, this is really a full-fledged seafood restaurant, the name coined in deference to the very upmarket Waterfront Restaurant on the second floor, which boasts a completely different menu and a higher profile—and price list. The house-smoked salmon or crab cakes are good starters here, and the wood-fired pizza oven delivers not only individually sized pies, but also roasted mussels and Dungeness crab. Halibut, tuna, salmon, and their water-borne neighbors regularly appear on the menu. *Pier 7, on the Embarcadero at Broadway, Embarcadero, 415/391–2696. AE, DC, MC, V. Takeout. $$–$$$.*

4 *g-3*
WATERFRONT RESTAURANT
First-class seafood and an East-West flair are the hallmarks of this upmarket dining room. The signature dish is a heavenly garlic flan paired with fresh crabmeat and diced daikon. Smoked sturgeon with Osetra caviar, monkfish braised with lotus, and lobster with Jap-

---

WATERFRONT DINING

Everyone loves to eat near the water, and San Francisco offers plenty of opportunity to do just that.

**Beach Chalet
(American/Contemporary)**
   The ocean turns an inky black when the sun goes down.

McCormick & Kuleto's (Seafood)
   A great view of the East Bay can be seen from this Ghirardelli Square restaurant.

Red Herring (Seafood)
   Glass doors open out onto the Embarcadero and a view of the waterfront.

Waterfront Café (Seafood)
   Great view of the Bay Bridge from this ground-level dining room.

Waterfront Restaurant (Seafood)
   Upstairs from the café (see above), the view widens.

anese *shiso* (an aromatic green) leaves turn up on the regularly shifting menu. The dining room, elegant and outfitted with orchids, has a wall of windows that shows off the Bay Bridge at its most handsome. *Pier 7, on the Embarcadero at Broadway, Embarcadero, 415/391–2696. AE, DC, MC, V. $$$*

4 *c-4*

YABBIES

For those unable to score a table, there are two seafood bars—one a sturdy concrete number fronting a couple of oyster shuckers hard at work, and the other a see-through glass beauty; both are perfect perches for a meal. Crab cocktail with mango and lemongrass; raw tuna with sesame oil, ginger, and avocado; big, scrumptious crab cakes; and porcini-dusted sea bass are among the outstanding choices. *2237 Polk St., between Vallejo and Green Sts., Russian Hill, 415/474–4088. Reservations essential (except for seafood bars). MC, V. No lunch. $$–$$$*

SPANISH

3 *d-1*

CÉSAR

Tucked right next door to Chez Panisse, and opened by folks who have worked there, this spacious, contemporary tapas bar offers a wonderful selection of small plates that are up to the standards of its legendary neighbor. You will almost believe you are in Spain when you dip into a dish of thin slices of serrano ham laid alongside grilled green onions, or a wedge of the classic Spanish tortilla, a cake of thin slices of potato and onion bound together with egg. Catalan romesco sauce arrives with roasted potatoes, and a cluster of shiny black olives are paired with house-marinated anchovies. A good selection of sherries and other wines complement the Iberian table. *1515 Shattuck Ave., between Cedar and Vine Sts., Berkeley, 510/883–0222. Reservations not accepted. MC, V. No lunch. $*

8 *a-4*

ESPERPENTO

With its Dali-derivative art and hand-painted tabletops, the restaurant has a quirky look, but the food is surprisingly straightforward. Three dozen tapas cater to all different tastes: shrimp arrive flecked with garlic and chiles; squid comes nicely deep-fried; and the blood sausage is outstanding. There are simpler plates, too, of olives, cheeses, and hams. Lines of mostly neighborhood residents sometimes form on the weekends, and local mariachi bands occasionally drop in to jam. *3295 22nd St., near Mission St., Mission, 415/282–8867. No credit cards. Takeout. $$*

8 *a-2*

PINXTOS

The super-hot North Mission got even hotter with the arrival of this sophisticated Spanish-Basque outpost, all dressed up in distressed tabletops, halogen lights, striking collages, and lots of robust plates. *Pinxtos* is Basque for small savory bites, and the little plates here are the kitchen's best efforts: mussels and artichoke hearts, sweet peppers stuffed with squid and shrimp, sautéed quail, and roasted peppers and eggplant with anchovies and black olives. Cap off your Iberian evening with a wedge of almond and pear tart and a glass of amber sherry. *557 Valencia St., between 16th and 17th Sts., Mission, 415/565-0207. MC, V. Closed Mon. No lunch. Takeout. $$*

4 *f-6*

THIRSTYBEAR

This combination brewpub-and-tapas outpost stands right around the corner from the Museum of Modern Art. Its small plates and brews are a welcome treat after serious gallery cruising. The cavernous interior of concrete floors, brick walls, and shiny tanks holding homemade brews is cool and utilitarian, but the small plates of sherry-infused fish cheeks, steamed mussels, *tortilla española* (egg-and-potato omelet), and white beans with house-made sausage will take away the chill. If you prefer ordering in bulk rather than grazing, request the paella. *661 Howard St., between Hawthorne La. and 3rd St., 415/ 974–0905. MC, V. No lunch Sun. $$*

8 *a-3*

TIMO'S

When the ultrahip Timo's first opened in the North Mission a few years back, you couldn't snag a table. Lovers of the small plates kept the tiny kitchen busy creating cakes of salt cod and potato; shrimp with garlic; and skewers of chicken or pork. Now, however, tapas bars are blooming, so the crowds have thankfully eased up. At the same time, Timo's is serving more kinds of tapas than ever to meet the competition. The paint job in bright yellows, greens, and purple creates a cheerful mood. *842 Valencia St., between 19th and 20th Sts., Mission, 415/647–0558. MC, V. No lunch. Takeout. $$*

4 c-3
ZARZUELA

The small, crowded storefront with stucco and brick walls serves nearly 40 different hot and cold tapas, plus a dozen or so main courses. There is a tapa to suit every palate, from poached octopus on new potatoes to seared scallops with barely wilted greens; slabs of Manchego cheese with paper-thin slices of serrano ham is one of the best. If you haven't filled up on tapas, order the paella—saffron-scented rice laced with prawns, mussels, and clams. The amiable staff will answer any questions. *2000 Hyde St., at Union St., Russian Hill, 415/346–0800. Reservations not accepted. MC, V. Closed Sun. $$*

OLD-TIMERS

San Francisco may be a youthful city, but some of its restaurants show their years with respectable dignity.

Beach Chalet (American/Contemporary)
Known for its restored WPA murals.

Boulevard (American/Contemporary)
The gorgeous brick building predates the '06 earthquake.

Chez Panisse (American/Contemporary)
The birthplace of Californian cuisine.

It's Tops Coffee Shop (American/Casual)
A burger joint since the '30s.

Sam's Grill (Seafood)
A favorite of bankers and brokers for more than 50 years.

Swan Oyster Depot (Seafood)
Serving oysters since 1912.

Tadich Grill (Seafood)
In 1849, folks were already saying, "meet me at Tadich."

Tommaso's (Pizza)
Site of the city's first brick pizza oven, installed in the '30s.

STEAK

4 b-4
HARRIS'

Regularly dubbed the best steak house in San Francisco, Harris' is the creation of Ann Harris, who grew up on a Texas cattle ranch and was married to the late Jack Harris of Harris Ranch fame. In her New York–style restaurant at the bottom of Russian Hill, she serves top-quality dry-aged steaks cooked exactly as you request. Start with a trendy martini and an order of sweetbread pâté, and accompany your slab of meat with a baked potato dressed with sour cream and bits of bacon. Save room for a wedge of pecan pie. *2100 Van Ness Ave., at Pacific Ave., Russian Hill, 415/673–1888. AE, DC, MC, V. No lunch. $$$*

4 b-5
HOUSE OF PRIME RIB

This isn't a place for steak, but it's only a whisper away. For decades, San Franciscans have been faithful to the tableside service at this venerable institution. A shiny silver cart rolls up, the cover slips back, and before you sits an absolutely gorgeous prime rib. In no time at all, a thick slab of meat is on your plate, along with horseradish sauce, a baked potato topped by sour cream and bacon bits, creamed spinach, and Yorkshire pudding. Salad is included, too, in this fixed-price meal. Order a martini (it comes in an individual shaker) and forget your cholesterol worries for one evening. *1906 Van Ness Ave., between Washington and Jackson Sts., Russian Hill, 415/885–4605. AE, DC, MC, V. No lunch. $$*

5 h-3
IZZY'S STEAK & CHOP HOUSE

Izzy's, named for a legendary San Francisco barkeep, has a wonderful, saloon-like ambience that steak house frequenters love. The menu is naturally heavy on steaks, most of which seem large enough to serve two average appetites. There are chops and seafood, too, plus all the trimmings: scalloped potatoes, roasted carrots, and some of the best creamed spinach in town. A blizzard of Izzy memorabilia and antique advertising art covers almost every inch of wall space, and a long shelf shows off an impressive collection of steak sauces and related condiments.

3345 Steiner St., between Lombard and Chestnut Sts., Marina, 415/563–4487. AE, DC, MC, V. No lunch. $$

THAI

2 b-3
BAI SOM
Thai restaurants are popular in San Francisco, and the menus of many of them vary little from one to the other. But the comfortable, no-frills Bai Som offers a handful of interesting dishes not easily found elsewhere, such as grilled liver with onions and lemongrass with a spicy dressing, northern Thai Issahn sausage, and a refreshing bamboo salad tossed with chiles, lemon, toasted rice powder, and mint. The curries are tasty as well, especially a coconut-milk rich green curry with chicken, eggplant, and basil. 2121 Clement St., between 22nd and 23rd Sts., Richmond District, 415/751–5332. MC, V. Takeout. $

4 d-8
BASIL
Wood floors, a glass-brick wall, and deep blue and rich yellow accents create a stylish setting for Thai food prepared with modern flair. Intriguing dishes include warm duck salad on watercress, paper-thin pork with garlic and pepper, and beef short ribs in mild curry. The kitchen turns out a sublime version of the classic Thai sweet dessert, sliced mango and sticky rice drizzled with coconut milk. 1175 Folsom St., between 7th and 8th Sts., South of Market, 415/552–8999. MC, V. No lunch weekends. Takeout. $$

5 d-6
KING OF THAI KITCHEN
Although the surroundings are sparse, the food at this modest operation has the authentic taste of Thailand. Curries and other simmered dishes are served with rice for sit-down or walkaway diners. Particularly tasty is the suki hang, a heady mix of shrimp, squid, chicken, vegetables, and cellophane noodles in a spicy bean curd sauce; another standout is the thinly sliced beef mixed with chiles, onion, ground roasted rice, and mint. 346 Clement St., between 4th and 5th Aves., Richmond District, 415/831–9953. MC, V. Takeout. $

8 b-1
MANORA
Not far from the Performing Arts Center, this popular restaurant, with its fresh flowers, good table linens, and an efficient staff, is a natural stop before an evening of Mozart or Verdi. Standout dishes are fried soft-shell crabs with a tamarind dipping sauce; rice paper–wrapped seafood, black fungus, and sausage; and whitefish steamed in banana leaves. Traditional Thai curries featuring meats, poultry, or seafood are also worth a try. SoMa clubbers often fuel up here before heading out on the town. 1600 Folsom St., at 12th St., South of Market, 415/861–6224. MC, V. No lunch weekends. Takeout. $

2 d-3
THAI CAFÉ
This little café is a bright, light space with a discreet altar niche at the back. The food is generously portioned and modestly priced, which keeps the tables full for most of the evening. The seafood soup with straw mushrooms in a rich coconut milk broth is a treat, as are the tod mun (fried fish cake), squid with garlic and pepper, and deep-fried chicken wings with sweet-hot sauce. 3407 Geary Blvd., near Jordan Ave., Richmond District, 415/386–4200. MC, V. Takeout. $

7 g-1
THEP PHANOM
Food critics and restaurant goers have been singing the praises of Thep Phanom ever since it opened in 1985. Duck is deliciously prepared in a variety of ways—in a fragrant curry, minced for salad, or resting atop a bed of spinach—and the squid salad nicely balances the coolness of lime with the sizzling heat of chiles. Daily specials supplement the regular menu, many of them based on seafood. A wonderful mango sorbet is sometimes available for dessert. 400 Waller St., at Fillmore St., Lower Haight, 415/431–2526. AE, D, DC, MC, V. No lunch. Takeout. $

TIBETAN

5 g-3
LHASA MOON
Outside of Tibet, this type of restaurant is few and far between—which is one of the reasons Lhasa Moon is such a treat

for San Franciscans. The other reasons are friendly service and the many unusual and delicious dishes served here: *momos*, traditional plump, juicy dumplings filled with meat or vegetables; light beef soup flavored with blue cheese; mild curries; interesting breads; sturdy noodles; and exotic braises. Beautiful photographs of Tibet decorate the walls of the comfortable dining room. *2420 Lombard St., between Scott and Divisadero Sts., Marina, 415/674–9898. MC, V. No lunch weekends. Closed Mon. Takeout. $*

VEGETARIAN

4 *a-2*

GREENS

The Bay Area's Zen Buddhist Center has operated this famed vegetarian restaurant for more than two decades. It is also the site of the Tassajara Bakery outlet, which is known for its outstanding breads and desserts. Even nonvegetarians rave about the meatless cooking at Greens: the black bean soup, crisp-crust pizzas, enchiladas verdes, and eggplant fritters are all divine. Dinners are à la carte on weeknights, but only a five-course prix fixe dinner is served on Saturday. A sweet after the theater? A late-evening dessert service will satisfying any craving. *Bldg. A, Fort Mason, Marina Blvd. at Laguna St., Marina, 415/771–6222. MC, V. No lunch Mon., no dinner Sun. Takeout. $$*

4 *c-7*

MILLENNIUM

Tucked into the former carriage house of the venerable Abigail Hotel, Millennium, with its black-and-white checkered floors and sponged walls, is a gold mine for anyone who eschews meat and appreciates imagination. The literature describes the food as "organic cuisine"; almost everything on the menu is not only vegetarian, but also low-fat, low-salt, and dairy-free. The Mediterranean is the inspiration for most dishes, with pastas, polenta, risotto, and grilled fresh vegetables among the most popular choices. Dishes made with *seitan*, a whole-wheat meat substitute, convince believers that veal piccata tastes better without the veal. A list of organic wines rounds out the health-conscious theme. *246 McAllister St., between Hyde and Larkin Sts., Civic Center, 415/487–9800. MC, V. No lunch. $$*

VIETNAMESE

4 *d-6*

BA LE

In the Vietnamese community, Ba Le is probably best known for its house-made charcuterie items, including pâté, head cheese, and ham. They form the bulk of the sandwiches, which are built on large French rolls and stuffed to the brim with shredded carrot, onion, tomatoes, fresh coriander, and a "secret sauce." The kitchen also assembles excellent rice and noodle dishes, among them grilled marinated pork chop and pork sausage atop rice, and shredded pork skin dusted with roasted rice powder over vermicelli. A combination plate lets you eat around the menu. *511 Jones St., between O'Farrell and Geary Sts.,*

BEST HOTEL
DINING ROOMS

Some of the best eating in these parts is done in hotel restaurants.

Campton Place (French)
> *A sophisticated room in one of the city's classiest small hotels.*

Catahoula Restaurant and Saloon (Cajun/Creole)
> *Calistoga's Mount View Hotel and Spa houses chef Jan Birnbaum's lively eatery.*

Grand Café (American/Contemporary)
> *A commodious restaurant in a former ballroom in the Hotel Monaco.*

Kyo-ya (Japanese)
> *Fine sushi and sashimi in the historic Palace Hotel.*

Masa's (French)
> *This legendary destination is tucked into downtown's Vintage Court Hotel.*

Postrio (American/Contemporary)
> *Wolfgang Puck's Northern California outpost is in the Prescott Hotel.*

Ritz-Carlton Dining Room (French)
> *Elegance and fine food in one of the city's most serene dining rooms.*

Scala's Bistro (Italian)
> *A glitzy but fun dining room in the historic Sir Francis Drake Hotel.*

Tenderloin, 415/474–7270. No credit cards. Takeout. $

7 h-2
ELEPHANT BLEU

In the oh-so-hot North Mission, this small, handsomely but simply designed, budget-friendly spot is a welcome sight. A nice list of rice vermicelli dishes, matched up with charbroiled prawns, pork, and crisp imperial rolls in various combinations, and rice noodle soups, with chicken, beef, or shrimp, squid, and fish balls, are priced for the penurious. So, too, are the rice plates, which arrive topped with your choice of five-spice chicken, barbecued pork, curry chicken, spicy bean curd, or half a dozen other options, each one costing far less than the price of a movie. 3232 16th St., between Dolores and Guerrero Sts., Mission, 415/553–6062. MC, V. No lunch Mon. Takeout. $

2 b-3
LA VIE

The informative, congenial staff here is always willing to lead you to such traditional fare as nep chien (deep-fried balls of sticky rice stuffed with a mixture of finely cut pork, shrimp, and mushrooms) or "shaking beef," cubes of tender beef with a lime-and-pepper dipping sauce. For a starter, order the small shrimp cakes dotted with yellow mung beans; you wrap up the cakes in crisp lettuce leaves and dip them in a spicy fish sauce. Seafood dishes often dominate the list of specials. 5830 Geary Blvd., between 22nd and 23rd Aves., Richmond District, 415/668–8080. AE, MC, V. Takeout. $

10 c-6
LE CHEVAL

Oakland Chinatown is home to a variety of Asian cuisines, including the Vietnamese food served at this highly popular destination. A glance at the surrounding tables reveals that big, steaming bowls of pho (beef noodle soup), hubcap-size noodle dishes, and crisp, packed spring rolls are affordable favorites here. If you are feeling wealthier, go for the salt and pepper squid or grilled pork on a bed of rice vermicelli. Sip an iced Vietnamese coffee to finish. 1007 Clay St., near 10th St., Oakland, 510/763–8957. MC, V. No lunch Sun. Takeout. $

4 d-6
LE COLONIAL

Old French colonials would sigh knowingly to see this romantic throwback to imperialism: rattan furniture in the bar, a stamped iron ceiling, black-and-white photos of old Saigon, a gaggle of society types sipping cocktails, polished service, and white tablecloths. The food is Vietnamese with a strong shot of French style. Among the most popular dishes are sea bass scented with lemongrass, doused with butter, and cooked in a banana leaf; seared beef tenderloin; sautéed morning glory; and fried bananas with a tapioca sauce. 20 Cosmo Pl., between Jones and Taylor Sts., Union Square, 415/931–3600. AE, DC, MC, V. No lunch. $$$

5 d-6
LE SOLEIL

As its name implies, Le Soleil is full of sunlight and pastel colors. An eye-catching painting of Saigon hangs on one wall, and a large aquarium of tropical fish stands near the door. The kitchen prepares traditional dishes from every part of Vietnam: try the excellent raw-beef salad; crisp, flavorful spring rolls; a southern-style pancakelike omelet encasing a filling of shrimp, pork, and bean sprouts; or large prawns simmered in a clay pot. 133 Clement St., between 2nd and 3rd Aves., Richmond District, 415/668–4848. MC, V. Takeout. $

3 d-6
PACIFIC RESTAURANT

Although only a simple noodle house, this restaurant is head and shoulders above much of the competition. Their pho, the beef and rice noodle soup that is the daily meal of Hanoi, is a big, full-flavored bowl fragrant with spices. You can order the bovine soup in any number of ways—with meatballs, rare thin slices, or tendon. A plate of lime wedges, bean sprouts, and fresh herbs arrives with the soup, along with chile pepper sauce. There are also cold noodles and other refreshing dishes. 337 Jones St., between Eddy and Ellis Sts., Tenderloin, 415/928–4022. No credit cards. Closed Tues. No dinner. Takeout. $

1 c-7
607 Larkin St., near Eddy St., Tenderloin, 415/441–6722.

8 a-2
SLANTED DOOR

Since opening in early 1996, owner-chef Charles Phan has developed a steady following for his self-described "real Vietnamese home cooking." There are fresh spring rolls packed with rice noodles, pork, shrimp, and pungent mint leaves, and fried imperial rolls concealing shrimp, pork, black fungus, and vegetables. You usually can't go wrong with the deep-fried pompano with ginger dipping sauce; lightly battered soft-shell crab; or lamb chops with lemongrass. The menu changes every two weeks, but popular dishes are never abandoned. This place is no secret, so plan on waiting for a table. *584 Valencia St., between 16th and 17th Sts., Mission, 415/861–8032. Reservations for groups of 5 or more. MC, V. Closed Mon. Takeout. $$*

10 c-6
VI'S VIETNAMESE CUISINE

On days when you want a salad, but a chef or a Cobb just isn't exotic enough, you can head to the modest Vi's for a wonderful, highly seasoned Southeast Asian creation built from rice noodles, grilled chicken or pork, chunks of imperial roll, and slivered vegetables, all dressed with a chile pepper–laced concoction based on fish sauce and lime juice. In the mood for a big bowl of soup? You might order the duck noodle soup, a favorite here, or the Saigon-style seafood noodle soup. Another good choice is the fresh steamed rice noodle rolls stuffed with mushrooms, pork, and onion and served with bean sprouts and sausage on the side. *724 Webster St., between 7th and 8th Sts., Oakland, 510/835–8375. No credit cards. Takeout. $*

chapter 2

SHOPPING

San Francisco is one of the great shopping cities of the world. Downtown, around Union Square, you'll find both small boutiques selling designer fashions and vast department stores, and in funky neighborhoods such as the Mission and Hayes Valley you can pick through rare jazz LPs or vintage watches.

What you won't find are the shopping malls so common throughout much of America. Rather, in San Francisco your shopping experience will take you hither and yon, to neighborhoods known for a particular good or service: antiques shops in Jackson Square, fine jewelers in Union Square, men's fashion in the Castro, rare- and secondhand-book shops in the Mission District, and bargains of all kinds in SoMa (South of Market), where many of the city's discount outlets are clustered. To add to the allure, most of the city's shops—particularly clothing shops—have seasonal sales from January through February and July through August.

shopping areas

DEPARTMENT STORES

4 e-6
GUMP'S
In business since 1861, Gump's is famous for its large selection of high-quality collectibles and its amusing Christmastime window displays. It carries exclusive lines of dinnerware, flatware, and glassware, as well as contemporary decorative items, Asian artifacts, antiques, and furniture. The jewelry department has extensive displays of jade and freshwater pearls. Gump's is one of the city's most premier stores for bridal registries. *135 Post St., between Grant Ave. and Kearny St., Union Square, 415/982–1616. Closed Sun.*

4 e-6
MACY'S
Fantastic for one-stop shopping, Macy's has designer fashions and an extensive selection of shoes, cosmetics, fragrances, jewelry, housewares, furniture, electronics, and food. The Cellar is devoted to cooking gadgets and gourmet goodies. The men's department (one of the world's largest) occupies its own building across Stockton Street. *170 O'Farrell St., at Stockton St., Union Square, 415/397–3333.*

4 e-6
NEIMAN MARCUS
With its Philip Johnson–designed checkerboard facade, gilded atrium, and stained-glass skylight (see Architecture & Historic Sites *in* Chapter 4), Neiman Marcus showcases its high-end goods in luxury surroundings. Eclectic and high-fashion women's and men's clothing, top-brand cosmetics, gem-studded jewelry, and fancy household wares are the draws at this outpost of the Texas-based company. Its biannual "Last Call" sales—in January and July—draw quite a crowd. *150 Stockton St., at Geary St., Union Square, 415/362–3900.*

4 e-6
NORDSTROM
The Seattle-based Nordstrom company is known worldwide for its exceptional customer service, and its downtown San Francisco store is no exception. It's housed on the top five levels of the nine-story San Francisco Shopping Centre building (see below) and has spiral escalators circling a four-story atrium. Designer shoes, accessories, and cosmetics are among its specialties. *865 Market St., between 4th and 5th Sts., Union Square, 415/243–8500.*

4 e-6
SAKS FIFTH AVENUE
The West Coast outpost of this New York City institution has opulent jewelry, cosmetics, and accessories departments that are not to be missed. Designer fashions for women range from the conservative to trend setting. The bulk of the men's items are housed at a separate store a few blocks away (see Clothing for Men/General, *below*). The restaurant, Saks Fifth Avenue Café, on the top floor overlooking Union Square, serves California-accented Continental food, such as salads, pastas, filet mignon, and rack of lamb. *384 Post St., at Powell St., Union Square, 415/986–4300.*

MALLS & SHOPPING CENTERS

4 *c-2*

THE ANCHORAGE

Multicolored nautical flags snap in the wind at this open-air complex in Fisherman's Wharf, a block from the Hyde Street cable car turnaround. Dozens of shops—from touristy T-shirt shops to chain stores like Benetton—sell everything from casual apparel to jewelry, luggage, and shoes. There are also several specialty shops selling great gift items such as music boxes and redwood furniture. A dozen restaurants serve snacks and sit-down meals. *2800 Leavenworth St., at Beach St., Fisherman's Wharf, 415/775–6000.*

4 *c-2*

THE CANNERY

The former Del Monte peach cannery (built in 1906) now houses dozens of shops, restaurants, art galleries, and cafés with views of San Francisco Bay. A glass elevator travels up and down the three levels of the redbrick building; in a courtyard filled with 100-year-old olive trees, mimes, magicians, and jugglers perform for free. This is where you'll find Cobb's Comedy Club (*see* Comedy *in* Chapter 5) and the Museum of the City of San Francisco (*see* History Museums *in* Chapter 4). *2801 Leavenworth St., at Beach St., Fisherman's Wharf, 415/771–3112.*

4 *f-5*

CROCKER GALLERIA

With its spectacular glass dome, this beautiful Financial District shopping complex is modeled after the Galleria Vittorio Emanuele in Milan, Italy. Some 40 boutiques and restaurants on three levels cater to discerning downtown business types, with accessories, shoes, home furnishings, jewelry, stationery, flowers, gifts, gourmet foods, and more. The two rooftop gardens are perfect for picnicking. *50 Post St., between Montgomery and Kearny Sts., Financial District, 415/393–1505.*

4 *f-4, g-4*

EMBARCADERO CENTER

Four modern towers of shops, restaurants, and offices make up the Embarcadero Center, on the waterfront near Market Street. The eight-block, 10-acre complex contains more than 120 chichi shops catering to harried Financial District workers on their lunch breaks. Here you'll also find nationally known clothing, housewares, and gift stores, as well as the Skydeck (*see* Viewpoints *in* Chapter 4), a five-screen movie theater specializing in art films, and the Hyatt Regency (*see* Very Expensive Lodgings *in* Chapter 6). There is free validated parking at the center's four underground garages on evenings and weekends. *Clay and Sacramento Sts. between Battery and Drumm Sts., Embarcadero, 415/772–0700.*

4 *b-2, c-2*

GHIRARDELLI SQUARE

Although its oldest redbrick building dates from 1864, this beloved manufacturing complex is best known as the site of Domingo Ghirardelli's chocolate factory from 1893 until the early 1960s. Today it's a charming open-air complex with 70 boutiques and restaurants. You can still watch Ghirardelli chocolate being made in some of the original vats and ovens at the old-fashioned soda fountain on the plaza level, or watch street performers gambol on the West Plaza stage. *900 North Point St., at Polk St., Fisherman's Wharf, 415/775–5500.*

4 *a-6*

JAPAN CENTER

Since 1968, this graceful 5-acre complex has been a center for San Francisco's Japanese community. Boutiques on Japan Center's three-block-long shopping arcade sell gifts and artifacts from Japan; there are also art galleries, antiques shops, bookstores, restaurants, a Japanese-style spa, and the eight-screen Kabuki movie theater. The center's Japanese architecture includes a magnificent Peace Pagoda. Special events and free entertainment take place on weekends. *Geary Blvd., between Fillmore and Laguna Sts., Japantown, 415/922–6776.*

4 *e-6*

METREON

Sony has redefined the modern shopping experience with this four-story entertainment and shopping complex in SoMa. Behind the four-story glass wall, which overlooks Yerba Buena Gardens, 15 theaters, a Sony IMAX theater, a *Where The Wild Things Are* playspace, Sony Style, PlayStation, and the Metreon

Marketplace are just some of the amazing features in store. *101 Fourth St., SoMa, 415/369–6000.*

4 *d-1, e-1*

PIER 39

This 1,043-ft former cargo pier, once abandoned and decaying, now has a carnival atmosphere that makes it a first stop for many tourists to San Francisco. You'll find more than 100 shops, many selling San Francisco–themed items, 10 restaurants with bay views, numerous fast-food stands, a 350-berth marina, a double-decked carousel, an entertainment complex, and the UnderWater World aquarium (*see* Zoos & Aquariums *in* Chapter 3). Street performers show off their antics daily, and the Blue & Gold Fleet departs nearby. Just offshore is a colony of barking California sea lions. *The Embarcadero and Beach St., Fisherman's Wharf, 415/981–7437.*

4 *g-5*

RINCON CENTER

Rincon Center's glass-roofed atrium has a central, free-falling fountain surrounded by cafés, shops, restaurants, business offices, and landscaped terraces with public seating. The net result is a relaxed, inviting oasis where you can eat and shop just steps away from the frenzied pace of the Financial District. *101 Spear St., at Mission St., South of Market, 415/243–0473.*

4 *e-6*

SAN FRANCISCO SHOPPING CENTRE

The newest of the city's shopping complexes houses a Nordstrom department store (*see above*) and 90 other trend-setting shops, art galleries, restaurants, and cafés, all surrounding a dizzying nine-story atrium encircled by spiral escalators. It's across from the Powell Street cable car turnaround, three blocks from Union Square. Valet parking is available on 5th Street. *865 Market St., between 4th and 5th Sts., Union Square, 415/495–5656.*

2 *c-6*

STONESTOWN GALLERIA

This indoor mall with vaulted glass skylights and Italian marble floors and walls has a rare, invaluable bonus: ample free parking. The fine collection of fashionable shops and boutiques caters to people of all ages. There are also banks, beauty salons, a pharmacy, and a movie theater. Stores here include Macy's, Nordstrom, Eddie Bauer, Imaginarium, and Williams-Sonoma. *19th Ave. and Winston Dr., Stonestown, 415/759–2626.*

SHOPPING NEIGHBORHOODS

the castro

Often called the gay capital of the world, the Castro is a premier shopping and entertainment district for nongays as well. The neighborhood bustles day and night, with much of the activity revolving around the intersection of Castro and 18th streets, near where the famous Castro Theatre stands (*see* Architecture & Historic Sites, *in* Chapter 4). Here are cutting-edge clothing boutiques, quirky antiques stores, and various specialty shops such as A Different Light (*see* Books, *below*), one of the country's premier gay and lesbian bookstores. *Best shopping: Castro St. between Market and 19th Sts.*

chinatown

The intersection of Grant Avenue and Bush Street marks the gateway to Chinatown, a 24-block neighborhood of shops, restaurants, markets, and nonstop human activity. Almost anything made or grown in any Asian country can be found here: crates of bok choy, tanks of live crabs, and hanging whole chickens fill the food shops and stalls, and Chinese silks, toy trinkets, inexpensive electronic goods, colorful pottery, baskets, and figurines of ivory and soapstone are displayed in boutique windows. Jewelry shops specializing in jade and pearls are on every block, as are herb pharmacies selling ginseng and roots. *Best shopping: Grant Ave. between Bush and Washington Sts.*

civic center/hayes valley

The only real attraction for shoppers around Civic Center is the small Opera Plaza, where A Clean Well-Lighted Place for Books (*see* Books, *below*) draws a steady stream of browsers. Just southwest of Opera Plaza, Hayes Valley is a small, up-and-coming shopping neighborhood packed with art galleries, furniture stores, and unusual gift boutiques. *Best shopping: Hayes St.*

financial district

The shops in this area complement those of nearby Union Square, catering mostly to the needs of rushed office workers running errands on their lunch break. The Embarcadero Center and Crocker Galleria (see Malls & Shopping Centers, above) are full of stylish stores and restaurants. Much of this area shuts down on Sunday, but the shopping centers remain open. Embarcadero Center: Clay and Sacramento Sts. between Battery and Drumm Sts.; Crocker Galleria: 50 Post St., between Montgomery and Kearny Sts.

fisherman's wharf

Tourists throng to Fisherman's Wharf, with good reason: Pier 39, the Anchorage, Ghirardelli Square, and the Cannery are all here (see Malls & Shopping Centers, above), providing the shopper in you a vast selection of restaurants, souvenir shops, and clothing and gift boutiques. In the outdoor spaces, musicians, mimes, and magicians create a circus atmosphere. Best of all are the wharf's view of the bay and proximity to the cable car lines, which can take you directly to Union Square. Down at the piers, fishermen still haul in their catch of the day. Best shopping: Jefferson St. between the Cannery and Pier 39.

the haight

Haight Street is always of interest, if only to see the sign at Haight and Ashbury streets, the geographic center of the hippie movement during the 1960s. These days, shops here abound with vintage clothing (and the rock stars and movie costumers who frequent them), used books and records, and high-quality handmade jewelry and folk art. There are also plenty of bicycle, skateboard, and in-line-skating shops, reflecting the neighborhood's proximity to Golden Gate Park. The less-traveled Lower Haight—around Webster, Pierce, and Fillmore streets, has one of the best video stores in town, Le Video (see Videos, below), and a mix of odd and inexpensive boutiques catering to the twentysomething set that lives here. Best shopping: Haight St. between Stanyan St. and Masonic Ave.

jackson square

Just north of the Financial District, tiny Jackson Square was once the center of the raffish Barbary Coast. Now fully gentrified, the area is home to two dozen of San Francisco's finest antiques dealers, most of them occupying two-story, 19th-century brick town houses on narrow lanes. Every store has a specialty, and all are appointed like small museums.

japantown

Unlike Chinatown, North Beach, or the Mission District, where ethnic shops and restaurants fill block after block, the social and commercial focal point of San Francisco's Japanese community, southwest of Nob Hill, is the 5-acre Japan Center (see Malls & Shopping Centers, above). The three-block complex includes an 800-car public garage, a cinema, and three shop-filled buildings. In the Kintetsu and Kinokuniya buildings, shops and showrooms sell cameras, CDs and tapes, futons, food items, art, new and old porcelain, and all manner of antiquities. Japan Center: Geary Blvd., between Fillmore and Laguna Sts.

the marina/cow hollow

The Marina District's main shopping street is Chestnut Street, one block north of Lombard Street and stretching from Fillmore Street to Divisadero Street. The street caters to the well-to-do Marina District residents with stylish restaurants, cafés, and bars. Just four blocks south of and parallel to Chestnut Street, Union Street is the heart of Cow Hollow. The restored Victorian buildings that line the street between Steiner and Octavia streets house contemporary fashion, home furnishing, and custom jewelry shops, along with a few antiques shops and florists. Like the Marina, Cow Hollow attracts a crowd of young professionals who swarm the area's many bars after sundown. Best shopping: Chestnut St. between Fillmore and Divisadero Sts.; Union St. between Steiner and Octavia Sts.

the mission

The Mission is a large neighborhood sprawling both east and west of its main thoroughfares, the parallel Mission and Valencia streets. The Mission is one of the city's most ethnically diverse neighborhoods, with a large Latino population as well as a thriving contingent of young artists, musicians, and new bohemians. Bargain shoppers frequent the area's overflowing thrift shops for secondhand clothing and furniture. Look for one-of-a-kind music and bookstores, avant-garde art galleries, and botanicas and other "magic" shops where you can flirt with the occult. *Best shopping: 16th St. between Mission and Guerrero Sts.; Valencia St. between 16th and 24th Sts.*

noe valley

Many flower children settled in Noe Valley, south of the Castro and the Mission, when they grew up and had children of their own, so it figures that kids' clothing, book, and educational toy stores fill the streets. The neighborhood is also full of natural-fiber clothing boutiques, record and art supply stores, ethnic crafts shops, restaurants, health food stores, and gourmet shops. *Best shopping: 24th St. between Castro and Church Sts.*

north beach

Most of the businesses in this Italian neighborhood are small, chic clothing and gift stores. A few art galleries and antiques and vintage shops have taken up residence as well. Once the center of the beat movement, North Beach is also home to the city's most famous bookstore, City Lights (*see Books, below*), where the bohemian spirit lives on. Stop to enjoy an espresso at one of many European-style cafés, or look for gourmet goodies at the plentiful Italian delicatessens, bakeries, and restaurants. *Best shopping: Grant and Columbus Aves.*

pacific heights/ laurel heights

Pacific Heights residents seeking practical services head straight to busy Fillmore Street, whose many boutiques, bars, and upscale restaurants are concentrated mostly between Post Street and Pacific Avenue. West of Pacific Heights, Laurel Heights is a small, mostly residential neighborhood that has some attractive stores along Sacramento Street, where private residences alternate with good bookstores, fine clothing and gift shops, thrift stores, and art galleries. *Best shopping: Fillmore St. between Post St. and Pacific Ave.; Sacramento St. between Divisadero and Maple Sts.*

polk gulch

In the "gulch" between the hilly Pacific Heights, Nob Hill, and Russian Hill

neighborhoods is the lively strip of Polk Gulch. Inexpensive trendy and vintage clothing stores, record shops and bookstores, movie theaters, and gift boutiques make this a favorite meeting spot for young San Franciscans. *Best shopping: Polk St. between Geary St. and Greenwich St.*

richmond district

In the past several decades this old Russian neighborhood has gone international. Chinese bakeries, Russian tearooms, Irish pubs, Japanese and Korean markets, and Palestinian delis do business side by side on its main shopping thoroughfare, Clement Street. *Best shopping: Clement St. between 14th Ave. and Arguello Blvd.*

south of market

Dozens of discount and factory outlets can be found on SoMa's streets and alleyways. The former warehouse district has recently blossomed with restaurants, nightclubs, art galleries, and designer boutiques as well. For unique gifts, don't skip the district's excellent museums, such as the San Francisco Museum of Modern Art and the Center for the Arts at Yerba Buena Gardens (*see Art Museums in Chapter 4*); their gift shops sell handmade jewelry and various other artsy gift items. *SFMOMA: 151 3rd St., between Mission and Howard Sts.*

union square

Determined shoppers head straight to Union Square, one of the nation's most prestigious downtown shopping districts, on par with those of New York and Chicago. Indeed, Union Square could lay claim to being one of the world's biggest outdoor shopping malls. Within a half-mile radius of the square are most of the city's department stores, as well as the pricey international boutiques of Hermès of Paris, Gucci, Celine of Paris, Alfred Dunhill, Louis Vuitton, and Cartier. Appealing to other tastes are entertaining megastores such as F. A. O. Schwarz, Virgin Megastore, the Disney Store, and Nike-Town. On Post Street alone, between Powell Street and Grant Avenue, you'll find Giorgio Armani, Ralph Lauren, Bulgari, Brooks Brothers, Coach, Williams-Sonoma, Versace, and Eddie Bauer. A dedicated shopper could walk from one of the major hotels or city parking garages and spend an entire day browsing. *Best shopping: Union Square; Post St. between Powell St. and Grant Ave.; Maiden La.*

specialist shops

ANTIQUES

american & european

5. *c-6*

THE ANTIQUE TRADERS

This shop specializes in stained- and beveled-glass windows and lamps, with famous names such as Tiffany, Handel, and Pairpoint. Count on finding interesting examples of American and European artisanship. *4300 California St., at 5th Ave., Richmond District, 415/668–4444.*

4 *f-8*

ANTONIO'S ANTIQUES

Antonio specializes in 17th-, 18th-, and early 19th-century English, French, and Continental furniture. He has an especially good collection of French chinoiserie and of Louis XIV, XV, and XVI pieces. His restoration work is world-renowned. *701 Bryant St., at 5th St., South of Market, 415/781–1737. Closed weekends.*

4 *f-4*

DILLINGHAM & COMPANY

In this Jackson Square shop, 17th- and 18th-century English and Dutch furniture and accessories abound. There are some French and Italian pieces as well, and unusual small items such as snuff boxes. *700 Sansome St., at Jackson St., Jackson Square, 415/989–8777. Closed Sun.*

4 *f-4*

FOSTER-GWIN ANTIQUES

English and Continental country and formal furniture from the 17th to the early 19th centuries are top quality at this Jackson Square shop. There are also some fine accessories. In summer it is open by appointment only on Saturday. *38 Hotaling Pl., between Montgomery and Sansome Sts., at Jackson St., Jackson Square, 415/397–4986. Closed Sun.*

4 *c-8*

GRAND CENTRAL STATION ANTIQUES

The staff will tell you that "small, pretty, and practical" items are what sell to San Franciscans living in tiny apartments. Which means that they have lots of useful storage pieces such as armoires, highboys, and commodes, as well as beautiful wooden beds for reasonable prices. Most pieces are 19th- and early 20th-century European and American furniture. *1632-A Market St., between Franklin and Gough Sts., Hayes Valley, 415/252–8155.*

7 *f-3*

595 Castro St., between 18th and 19th Sts., Castro, 415/863–3604.

4 *f-4*

HUNT ANTIQUES

Hunt Antiques feels like an English town house, with fine 17th- to 19th-century English and Continental furniture, longcase clocks, porcelains, paintings, and some silver. It's in the heart of antiques country, Jackson Square. *478 Jackson St., at Montgomery St., Jackson Square, 415/989–9531. Closed Sun.*

4 *c-4*

INTERIOR VISIONS

A good deal friendlier than your average antiques dealer, the proprietor of this store welcomes each customer into her store and is happy to answer questions. And it's hard not to like someone with taste like hers: witness the charming, turn-of-the-century American oak highboys, early 20th-century French armoires, and glass-paned barrister bookcases. *2206 Polk St., between Vallejo and Green Sts., Russian Hill, 415/771–0656.*

4 *f-4*

JOHN DOUGHTY ANTIQUES

This Jackson Square dealer carries fine 18th- and 19th-century English furniture and accessories, including an incredible collection of desks from the late 18th century through the Edwardian period. *619 Sansome St., between Washington and Jackson Sts., Jackson Square, 415/398–6849. Closed weekends.*

4 *c-8*

ONE-EYED JACKS

Come here for Western artifacts such as antique cowboy boots and saddles, as well as 19th-century American furniture. The shop also rents out props. *1645 Market St., between Gough and Franklin Sts., Hayes Valley, 415/621–4390. Closed Fri.*

`4` *f-4*

ROBERT DOMERGUE & CO.

Well stocked with 17th- and 18th-century French and Continental furniture and art objects, Domergue & Co. carries rare and expensive furniture, tapestries, screens, mantels, architectural drawings, and prints. *560 Jackson St., at Columbus Ave., Jackson Square, 415/781–4034. Closed Sun.*

`4` *c-4*

RUSSIAN HILL ANTIQUES

This shop has a fine collection of Eastern European furniture, plus antique glassware, pottery, and costume jewelry. Antique cocktail paraphernalia is a specialty. *2200 Polk St., at Vallejo St., Russian Hill, 415/441–5561.*

`8` *d-2*

THERIEN & COMPANY

Therien & Company sells fine 17th- and 18th-century Continental furniture and decorations, including Sheffield silver and porcelain as well as museum-quality Chinese, Vietnamese, and Greco-Roman antiquities. Its showroom at the Design Center carries custom-designed and custom-made period reproductions. *411 Vermont St., at 17th St., Potrero Hill, 415/956–8850. Closed weekends.*

art deco

`4` *c-8*

ANOTHER TIME

This shop is a Deco lover's delight, with a good selection of furniture and accessories by Heywood Wakefield and others. It's conveniently close to a whole host of other stores that also stock vintage collectibles. *1586 Market St., at Franklin St., Hayes Valley, 415/553–8900. Closed Mon.*

`4` *b-8*

JET AGE

Although it looks a little tatty from the outside, inside are some fine Art Deco and '30s and '40s furniture, plus later pieces designed by Eames, Noguchi, and others. *250 Oak St., at Gough St., Hayes Valley, 415/864–1950. Closed Sun. and Mon.*

asian

`4` *a-6*

ASAKICHI JAPANESE ANTIQUES

This shop in Japantown's Kinokuniya Building carries antique blue-and-white Imari porcelains and handsome tansu chests. *1730 Geary Blvd., between Fillmore and Webster Sts., Japantown, 415/921–2147.*

`4` *e-5*

DRAGON HOUSE

Unlike many other Chinatown stores that peddle cheap reproductions of Chinese art, Dragon House sells genuine antiques and Oriental fine arts. The ivory carvings, ceramics, and jewelry for sale date back 2,000 years and beyond. *455 Grant Ave., between Pine and Bush Sts., Chinatown, 415/781–2351.*

`4` *a-4*

FUMIKI FINE ARTS

Two specialties here are tansu chests and Japanese bamboo baskets. Also for sale are fine Asian art and antiques including Imari porcelains, Chinese silk paintings, and Japanese and Korean furniture. Small items include ceramics, Yixing teapots, and uncommonly beautiful chopsticks. *2001 Union St., at Buchanan St., Cow Hollow, 415/922–0573.*

THE JACKSON SQUARE ANTIQUES DISTRICT

Jackson Square is chock-full of art and antique dealers selling fine English and Continental furniture and accessories. A few shops you won't want to miss:

Dillingham & Company
English and Dutch furniture and accessories.

Foster-Gwin Antiques
English country and formal furniture.

Hunt Antiques
Like an English town house, with paintings and long-case clocks.

John Doughty Antiques
Fine desks from the late 18th century through the Edwardian period.

Robert Domergue & Co.
French and Continental furniture and objets d'art.

4 *a-6*

GENJI ANTIQUES INC.
In addition to beautiful antique Japanese tansu chests, Genji Antiques carries Japanese furniture, folk arts, and some 17th-century kimonos. *22 Peace Plaza, at Buchanan and Post Sts., Japantown, 415/931–1616.*

4 *a-6*

NARUMI JAPANESE ANTIQUES AND DOLLS
Hand-painted Imari porcelain and beautiful tansu chests share the shop with dozens of antique Japanese dolls, many from the 19th century. You'll find an especially large selection of antique geisha dolls. *1902-B Fillmore St., between Pine and Bush Sts., Japantown, 415/346–8629. Closed Sun.*

8 *d-1*

ORIGINS ART AND ANTIQUES
In SoMa's Baker Hamilton Square complex, this shop imports unusual collector's items, Chinese furniture, porcelain, silk, and jade. Antiques here are up to 400 years old. *680 8th St., at Townsend St., South of Market, 415/252–7089. Closed Sun.*

4 *a-6*

SHIGE ANTIQUE KIMONOS
On the Webster Street Bridge that spans Geary Boulevard, this small shop has antique hand-painted, silk-embroidered kimonos and a fine selection of obis. *1730 Geary Blvd., Japantown, 415/346–5567.*

4 *a-4*

A TOUCH OF ASIA
Most of the high-end 19th- and 20th-century Asian antiques here are from Japan and Korea. Exquisite elm and cherry wood furniture, curio cabinets, and chests are the main attractions, although the store also carries Asian sculptures, prints, paintings, and antique vases. *1784 Union St., at Octavia St., Cow Hollow, 415/474–3115.*

auction houses

8 *d-2*

BUTTERFIELD & BUTTERFIELD
The city's premier auction house, founded in San Francisco in 1865, is the oldest and largest in the western United States. Each month brings estate sales and special auctions of fine furniture, rugs, jewelry, art, wine, stamps, and entertainment memorabilia. Free appraisal clinics take place on the first and third Monday of every month. *220 San Bruno Ave., at 15th St., Potrero Hill, 415/861–7500.*

8 *c-2*

BUTTERFIELD WEST
The low-key annex of San Francisco's premier auction house holds monthly auctions of "intermediate property"— furniture, objects, and art that are not quite top-of-the-line. Call for an auction schedule. *164 Utah St., at 15th St., Potrero Hill, 415/861–7500, ext. 308.*

show

4 *a-2*

SAN FRANCISCO FALL ANTIQUES SHOW
Some 100 dealers of quality furniture and decorative antiques showcase their wares at this benefit show held in late October. *Festival Pavilion, Fort Mason, Laguna St. at Marina Blvd., Marina, 415/546–6661.*

victorian & vintage

4 *c-8*

BEAVER BROS.
The sign over this eclectic shop reads "This is not a museum. This is junk for sale." The owners sell whatever strikes their fancy: Louis XVI furniture, Art Deco clocks and telephones, 19th- and 20th-century armoires, silver, cut glass, and rugs. Movie companies have rented many an item here; *Star Trek IV* used the entire store in one scene. *1637 Market St., at Franklin St., Hayes Valley, 415/863–4344.*

8 *d-3*

CARNEGIE ANTIQUES
This Potrero Hill shop sells whatever it pleases, including porcelains, jewelry, signed paperweights, and some furniture. It has the largest collection of bronzes in the Bay Area. *601 Kansas St., at 18th St., Potrero Hill, 415/641–4704. Closed Mon. and Tues.*

`4` *c-2*

FRANK'S FISHERMAN'S SUPPLY

Everything here has a seafaring theme: antique marine lamps, clocks, sextants, and ships in bottles are the specialties. *366 Jefferson St., between Jones and Leavenworth Sts., Fisherman's Wharf, 415/775–1165.*

`4` *a-3*

GREAT AMERICAN COLLECTIVE

At this antiques mini-mall you'll find 38 dealers selling all kinds of goodies, from an antique purse to a Federal-era chest of drawers. The overall feel is upscale garage sale, with prices that range from reasonable to ridiculous. *1736 Lombard St., at Octavia St., Cow Hollow, 415/922–2650.*

`2` *b-3*

OLD STUFF

The gems are mixed in with the merely dated at this shop that resembles a grandmother's attic. The furniture and collectibles date from the Victorian period through the 1920s, with plenty of jewelry, silver, and porcelain. *2325 Clement St., between 24th and 25th Aves., Richmond District, 415/668–2220.*

`7` *d-1*

REVIVAL OF THE FITTEST

This is the place to find funky vintage telephones, dishes, clocks, jewelry, lamps, and vases—as well as excellent reproductions of the same stuff. *1701 Haight St., at Cole St., Haight, 415/751–8857.*

`7` *f-3*

THE SCHLEP SISTERS

This intriguing shop has a fine selection of secondhand American dinnerware, art pottery, and glass, as well as home accessories from the 1920s through the '60s, such as cookie jars and salt-and-pepper shakers. The largest selection is from the 1950s. *4327 18th St., between Diamond and Eureka Sts., Castro, 415/626–0581. Closed Mon. and Tues.*

`4` *e-3*

TELEGRAPH HILL ANTIQUES

The diverse objets d'art at this tiny North Beach store include crystal, art glass, china, porcelain, silver, cloisonné, and bronzes. There's also a nice selection of Wedgwood pieces, Victoriana, and paintings. *580 Union St., at Stockton St., North Beach, 415/982–7055. Closed Sun.*

`5` *e-6*

WOODCHUCK ANTIQUES

Original American Victorian furniture can be found here, along with other treasures of the Victorian era, such as advertising memorabilia, toys, and a large selection of bronze lamps. *3597 Sacramento St., at Locust St., Laurel Heights, 415/922–6416. Closed Sun.*

`4` *b-8*

ZONAL

The sign on the window here reads ALWAYS REPAIR, NEVER RESTORE—a perfect prelude to the Depression-era American country furniture within. Inside is an assortment of forgotten treasures, such as antique gardening equipment, vintage porch gliders, old croquet sets, and vintage-1930s iron bed frames. *568 Hayes St., at Laguna St., Hayes Valley, 415/255–9307.*

`4` *c-4*

2139 Polk St., between Broadway and Vallejo St., Russian Hill, 415/563–2220.

ART SUPPLIES

`5` *a-7*

AMSTERDAM ART

The largest art supply store in town and a favorite of local artists for years, Amsterdam Art stocks supplies for painting, printmaking, ceramics, and more. There's also a full selection of do-it-yourself frames and a helpful staff. *5424 Geary Blvd., at 19th Ave., Richmond District, 415/387–5354.*

`3` *c-2*

1013 University Ave., near San Pablo Ave., Berkeley, 510/649–4800.

`7` *g-5*

COLORCRANE ARTS AND COPY CENTER

This Noe Valley shop carries a complete line of art, graphics, and office supplies. Fax, binding, and color copying services are also available. *3957 24th St., at Sanchez St., Noe Valley, 415/285–1387.*

`4` *f-8*

DOUGLAS & STURGESS

Tools and supplies for the sculptor are the specialties at Douglas & Sturgess—

including all kinds of clays and glazes. General art supplies are also available here. *730 Bryant St., between 5th and 6th Sts., South Beach, 415/896–6283. Closed weekends.*

8 *a-1*

FLAX ART & DESIGN

Some 32,000 items are sold at competitive prices at this upscale warehouse for art supplies. There are bargains on decorative papers, stationery, frames, portfolio cases, easels, paints, drafting tables and lamps, and sketch books. *1699 Market St., at Valencia St., Mission, 415/552–2355. Closed Sun.*

7 *d-1*

MENDEL'S ART AND STATIONERY SUPPLIES/ FAR-OUT FABRICS

A longtime Haight-Ashbury favorite, Mendel's carries art, graphics, and office supplies. *1556 Haight St., between Ashbury and Clayton Sts., Haight, 415/621–1287.*

4 *e-7*

PEARL ART AND CRAFT SUPPLIES

What it lacks in charm or fancy displays, it makes up for with a good selection and good prices. Come here for your basic inventory of art supplies—paints, brushes, and canvas. The bottom floor is full of craft items. *969 Market St., between 5th and 6th Sts., Union Square, 415/357–1400.*

1 *d-1*

SAN FRANCISCO ART INSTITUTE STORE

The art supply store at the renowned San Francisco Art Institute has bargain prices on all kinds of art, printmaking, photo, and filmmaking supplies. The store is the cheapest in the city for paper, whether it's watercolor board or decorative handmade sheets. *800 Chestnut St., between Jones and Leavenworth Sts., Russian Hill, 415/749–4555. Closed Sun.*

BASKETS

4 *f-8*

FANTASTICO

Baskets of all shapes and sizes are here, in more than 50 different styles. Most are made of willow, but there are also unique woven baskets from Africa and Asia. (*Also see* Craft & Hobby Supplies, *below.*) *559 6th St., between Brannan and Bryant Sts., South of Market, 415/982–0680. Closed Sun.*

3 *d-1*

NINEPATCH

Tucked away in a residential neighborhood, this grandmotherly Berkeley store sells all sorts of quilts—both new and antique—as well as baskets. Items include picnic baskets, whitewashed hampers, and African woven baskets with sturdy leather handles. *2001 Hopkins St., at El Dorado Ave., Berkeley, 510/527–1700.*

5 *e-7*

PIER 1 IMPORTS

Part of a national chain, this popular import store is known as one of the best places in the city to shop for baskets. Its enormous basketry department has all types, from giant wicker hampers to woven picnic baskets to miniature baskets made of delicate reeds. *3535 Geary Blvd., at Stanyan St., Richmond District, 415/387–6642.*

BEADS

7 *f-3*

THE BEAD STORE

Here you'll find a daunting collection of more than a thousand kinds of strung and unstrung beads, including stones such as lapis and carnelian, Czechoslovakian and Venetian glass, African trade beads, Buddhist and Muslim prayer beads, and Catholic rosaries. Premade silver jewelry is another specialty, along with religious masks, figurines, and statues from India and Nepal. *417 Castro St., at Market St., Castro, 415/861–7332.*

7 *e-1*

GARGOYLE BEADS

Why buy jewelry when you can make your own from Gargoyle's exotic beads, seeds, and polished stones? Hanks of seed beads, Czech and German glass, African cowrie shells, glow-in-the-dark beads, and a small selection of semiprecious stones are just some of the treasures here. *1324 Haight St., between Masonic and Central Aves., Haight, 415/552–4274.*

5 *a-7*

THE HOBBY COMPANY OF SAN FRANCISCO

In addition to all kinds of miscellanea (*see* Craft & Hobby Supplies, *below*), this store has a whole room full of exotic beads. *5150 Geary Blvd., at 16th Ave., Richmond District, 415/386–2802.*

4 *e-3*

YONE

This shop opened in 1965 and now carries so many types of beads that the owner has lost track—somewhere between 5,000 and 10,000, he thinks. The beads—made of glass, wood, plastic, bone, sterling silver, and semiprecious stones—come from Africa, Indonesia, Thailand, China, Sri Lanka, India, and many other far-off lands. *478 Union St., at Grant Ave., North Beach, 415/986–1424. Closed Sun.*

BEAUTY

fragrances & skin products

4 *a-5*

THE BEAUTY STORE

This San Francisco minichain, founded on Fillmore Street in 1980, carries a full line of traditional and organic beauty supplies, including cosmetics previously available only to professionals. The staff is very friendly and will explain how to use each product. *2124 Fillmore St., at California St., Pacific Heights, 415/346–2511.*

7 *e-1*

1560 Haight St., at Ashbury St., Haight, 415/552–9696.

7 *g-2*

3600 16th St., at Noe St., Noe Valley, 415/861–2019.

5 *h-3*

2085 Chestnut St., at Steiner St., Marina, 415/922–2526.

4 *g-4*

4 Embarcadero Center, Clay and Sacramento Sts. between Battery and Drumm Sts., Embarcadero, 415/982–5599.

2 *c-6*

Stonestown Galleria, Upper Level, 19th Ave. and Winston Dr., Stonestown, 415/681–0779.

4 *a-5*

BENEFIT

Here the staff imbues the makeup with a spirit of fun, selling products like a black kohl eye pencil called "Bad Gal" and self-tanning cream called "Aruba in a Tuba." Friendly salespeople let you experiment with the products in a low-pressure setting. *2117 Fillmore St., between California and Sacramento Sts., Pacific Heights, 415/567–0242.*

5 *g-2*

2219 Chestnut St., between Scott and Pierce Sts., Marina, 415/567–1173.

4 *a-4*

BODY TIME

This Berkeley-based minichain sells some of the best concoctions around for the face and body: its own line of glycerine soaps, lotions, creams, perfumes, and body oils. It also carries domestic and imported hair ornaments, bathrobes and kimonos, hair brushes, and other toiletries. Call for the four Berkeley and Oakland locations. *2072 Union St., at Webster St., Cow Hollow, 415/922–4076.*

7 *e-1*

1465 Haight St., at Ashbury St., Haight, 415/551–1070.

4 *a-6*

1932 Fillmore St., at Bush St., Pacific Heights, 415/771–2431.

7 *g-5*

COMMON SCENTS

Most of the bath and skin-care products at this shop are made in the Bay Area. You'll find all kinds of bath oils, gels, and salts, as well as rubber duckies and other bath toys. Massage oils and lotions, perfumes and incense, and exotic skin-care products round out the selection. Many products can be custom-scented. *3920 24th St., near Sanchez St., Noe Valley, 415/826–1019.*

4 *a-6*

FUJIYA COSMETICS

Fujiya has all of your favorite Shiseido-brand cosmetics, plus Shiseido sun and hair-care products and fragrances for men and women. Makeovers are available by appointment. *1662 Post St., at Buchanan St., Japantown, 415/931–3302.*

4 *e-6*

JACQUELINE PERFUMERY

Since 1969, Jacqueline has carried one of the city's largest and finest selections of perfumes and men's toiletries. Once you've picked out a scent, choose a beautiful crystal perfume bottle to put it in. There's also a choice selection of European skin-care products. *103 Geary St., between Stockton St. and Grant Ave., Union Square, 415/981–0858. Closed Sun.*

4 *a-4*

MAC

Many women (and a few men) swear by MAC, which stocks the latest colors of lipstick and eye shadow, as well as all the makeup basics, in a fun, trendy atmosphere. The latest is glittery powder, sold in five glitzy colors. *1833 Union St., between Laguna and Octavia Sts., Cow Hollow, 415/771–6113.*

4 *e-6*

SEPHORA

The cosmetics superstore that first opened in Paris is like a multilevel, red-carpeted makeup playground for women. Products are arranged by type rather than brand, which means that in the lipstick section hundreds of tubes vie for your attention. The staff are helpful but not intrusive, leaving you to squirt, rub, and dab in peace. Sephora.com is yet another alluring emporium. *1 Stockton St., at Market St., Union Square, 415/392–1545.*

7 *f-3*

SKIN ZONE

At this environmentally aware shop, many of the men's and women's bath-and skin-care products are sold in refillable bottles—including 103 varieties of scented oils. The Skin Zone carries popular brands such as Caswell-Massey and Aubrey Organics. *575 Castro St., at 18th St., Castro, 415/626–7933.*

hair care

7 *g-1*

AQUARIUS BARBER SHOP

What's old is new again, and this old-fashioned barbershop with rusting antique barber's chairs is back in fashion. Although the clientele is largely Gen-X men, a few women and older men use the shop as well. *505 Haight St., at Fillmore St., Lower Haight, 415/621–9295. Closed Mon.*

7 *f-1*

MAIRE RUA

This funky Lower Haight shop gives fun and fashionable cuts to an appreciative crowd of twentysomethings. The stylists specialize in "corrective color," so if you've had a mishap with a bottle of peroxide, you might want to give this place a call. *798 Haight, at Scott St., Lower Haight, 415/626–6674.*

7 *f-3*

NOTORIOUS FOR HAIR

Gay men and young fashion-forward professionals are the primary clients at this airy spot on a busy stretch of Castro Street. Prices are extremely reasonable, especially for your first haircut at the salon. *561 Castro St., between 18th and 19th Sts., Castro, 415/558–0401. Closed Mon.*

5 *h-4*

NOVELLA SALON AND SPA

At this salon dedicated to relaxation and rejuvenation, haircuts are a treat, preceded by a scalp and neck message and with attentive service throughout. The fragrant and cozy salon also offers a full array of spa services. *2238 Union St., between Fillmore and Steiner Sts., Cow Hollow, 415/673–1929.*

4 *b-8*

OXENROSE

Don't be alarmed when you see that everyone that works here has a palette of tattoos or improbably colored hair—they won't dye your hair electric blue unless you ask them to. Instead, they'll give you an up-to-the-minute cut, style, or color in this slick salon, complete with coffee bar. Co-owner Carl is a Houdini with the scissors. *500 Hayes St., at Octavia St., Hayes Valley, 415/252–9723.*

4 *e-5*

VIDAL SASSOON

This was voted "Best Place to Get Your Hair Cut" in a recent San Francisco Bay Guardian poll. Call and ask about student training sessions, during which you can enjoy a deep discount off the usual rates. *359 Sutter St., between Stockton St. and Grant Ave., Union Square, 415/397–5105. Closed Sun.*

4 *e-6*

YOSH FOR HAIR

This is the downtown salon of the moment, where clients pay to be pampered by Yosh Toya while getting a fabulous cut. If the prices are beyond your budget but you still want to be able to say you go to Yosh's, call two weeks in advance for a deeply discounted cut by an apprentice. *173 Maiden La., between Stockton St. and Grant Ave., Union Square, 415/989–7704.*

4 *e-5*

ZENDO URBAN RETREAT

At this Aveda concept salon you'll get more than a haircut; you'll come away relaxed after a shampoo like no other and a scalp massage with scented oils. Antique and other hardwood furniture makes the salon feel more like a home than a place of business. *256 Sutter St., between Grant Ave. and Kearny St., Union Square, 415/788–3404.*

BICYCLES

3 *e-4*

THE BENT SPOKE

This friendly shop specializes in second-hand bikes that the owners have purchased from California police auctions and then reconditioned (although they do not fix cosmetic troubles such as dents or chipped paint). You'll find a wide range of bargains (40 to 60 bikes at any given time), including many kid's bikes. *6124 Telegraph Ave., at 62nd St., Oakland, 510/652–3089.*

3 *d-2*

MISSING LINK BICYCLE COOPERATIVE/ MISSING LINK ANNEX

The East Bay's best bike shop carries Trek, Kona, Ibis, and Bianchi bikes, plus clothing and accessories. The Missing Link Annex, across the street from the main store, houses rental bikes, used bikes, and a repair shop. Used bikes are fully reconditioned and range in price from $50 to $1,000; many come with a 90-day warranty. *Missing Link: 1988 Shattuck Ave., at University Ave., Berkeley, 510/843–4763.*

3 *d-2*

Missing Link Annex: 1961 Shattuck Ave., at Durant Ave., Berkeley, 510/843–4763.

7 *c-1*

START TO FINISH BICYCLES

One of the Bay Area's largest bike shop chains, Start to Finish has three San Francisco shops with rentals, high-end demos, free lifetime service on sales, and free maintenance classes. Among the other brands for sale are Gary Fisher, Trek, and Marin. For information on any of their nine stores around the Bay Area, call 800/600–2453. *672 Stanyan St., between Haight and Page Sts., Haight, 415/750–4760.*

4 *g-7*

599 2nd St., at Brannan St., South of Market, 415/243–8812.

5 *g-3*

2530 Lombard St., at Divisadero St., Marina, 415/202–9830.

8 *a-4*

VALENCIA CYCLERY

This low-key shop has the largest selection of new bikes, parts, and accessories in San Francisco, all priced competitively. There are mountain bikes, hybrids, kid's bikes, and even low-rider bicycles. The repair shop a few doors down at 1065 Valencia Street handles all makes and models, many done while you wait. *1077 Valencia St., between 21st and 22nd Sts., Mission, 415/550–6600 for sales, 415/550–6601 for repair shop.*

1 *c-7*

WINDSURF BICYCLE WAREHOUSE

At this 7,200-square-ft warehouse in South San Francisco, you'll find exceptional customer service and great deals on mountain, road, hybrid, and BMX bikes. The low-price guarantee: if within 30 days you find the identical item with a lower price somewhere else, it will refund you the difference plus 10%. There's also a fine selection of snowboarding, windsurfing, and in-line skating gear. *428 S. Airport Blvd., Airport Blvd. exit from U.S. 101, South San Francisco, 650/588–1714.*

BOOKS

8 *a-2*

THE ABANDONED PLANET BOOKSTORE

This is a snug little shop, with an old piano in one corner and a pair of pet cats. Music, theater, and art history are particularly well represented, and it occasionally has publishers' overstock books at bargain prices. *518 Valencia St., near 16th St., Mission, 415/861–4695. Closed Sun.*

4 *f-5*

ALEXANDER BOOK CO.

With three floors of titles, this "old-fashioned, full-service, independent bookstore" is particularly well stocked with literature, art books, and poetry. It also has an excellent children's books section. *50 2nd St., between Market and Mission Sts., South of Market, 415/495–2992. Closed weekends.*

4 *d-2*

BARNES & NOBLE BOOKSELLERS

Everything you've come to expect from this national book lover's chain is here, including the bountiful magazine racks and tolerant attitude towards browsing. *2550 Taylor St., at Bay St., Fisherman's Wharf, 415/292–6762.*

9 *d-1*

BLACK OAK BOOKS

This Berkeley shop is well known for its sophisticated literature, classics, and poetry sections; it also carries quite a few imports. This is usually the first store to get used copies of literary fiction. Best selling and critically acclaimed authors hold weekly readings. *1491 Shattuck Ave., at Vine St., Berkeley, 510/486–0698.*

7 *d-1*

BOOKSMITH

Founded in 1976, this fine neighborhood bookshop is chock-full of current releases, children's titles, and literary treasures. Reflecting the interests of its Haight clientele, it also carries plenty in the areas of science fiction, counterculture, and alternative medicine. *1644 Haight St., between Clayton and Cole Sts., Haight, 415/863–8688.*

4 *e-6*

BORDERS BOOKS AND MUSIC

The Union Square outpost of the national chain is always at the top of the list of San Franciscans' favorite bookstores. It has three floors of books on every subject, plus a friendly staff to help navigate the aisles. Other draws are a large music section with dozens of listening stations and an in-store café. *400 Post St., at Powell St., Union Square, 415/399–1633.*

4 *e-4*

CITY LIGHTS

This North Beach establishment—the city's most famous bookstore—has been a literary landmark since 1955, when it was a meeting place for Beat poets like Jack Kerouac, Gregory Corso, and Allen Ginsberg. Lawrence Ferlinghetti still owns the place, and his old friends still stop by—as do subsequent generations of San Francisco literati. City Lights is particularly well stocked with poetry, contemporary literature, small-press publications, literary reviews, and translations of Third World literature. Many titles are published in-house. *261 Columbus Ave., at Broadway, North Beach, 415/362–8193.*

4 *c-7*

A CLEAN WELL-LIGHTED PLACE FOR BOOKS

This locally owned bookstore, whose main branch is in the Opera Plaza, bills itself as carrying "a large selection of paperbacks and hardbacks in all fields for all ages." Paperback literature and books on opera and San Francisco history are particularly well stocked in the San Francisco branch. It's known for its well-organized, easy-to-browse shelves. *601 Van Ness Ave., at Turk St., Civic Center, 415/441–6670.*

9 *e-2*

CODY'S BOOKS

This Berkeley institution stocks every imaginable genre, from poetry and philosophy to self-defense and women's studies. It also has an impressive newsstand, a cheery children's room, an extensive selection of foreign-language books, and an information desk with a well-read staff. Readings by local and nationally known authors are always crowded; arrive early. *2454 Telegraph Ave., at Haste St., Berkeley, 510/845–7852.*

3 *b-2*

1730 4th St., between Hearst and Virginia Sts., Berkeley, 510/559–9500.

5 *c-6*

GREEN APPLE BOOKS

This has been a local favorite since 1967 and is voted the Bay Area's best bookstore by *Bay Guardian* readers year after year, despite the fact that you can find lower prices elsewhere. It has one of the largest used-book departments in the city, as well as new books in every field. The atmosphere is like Grandma's attic, with strange and wonderful books tucked into every dusty corner. Specialties are comic books and a rare-books collection. Sale-priced books spill out into bins on the sidewalk. A new- and used-fiction annex is two doors down, at 520 Clement Street. *506 Clement St., at 6th Ave., Richmond District, 415/387–2272.*

8 *a-3*

MODERN TIMES BOOKSTORE

Named after Charlie Chaplin's politically subversive film, Modern Times is a large shop that stocks quality literary fiction and nonfiction, much of it with a political bent. Strong subjects include Spanish language, art, current affairs, gay and lesbian issues, cultural theory, multicultural children's books, and underground newspapers and 'zines. Author readings and public forums are held on a regular basis. *888 Valencia St., between 19th and 20th Sts., Mission, 415/282–9246.*

3 *e-2*

MOE'S BOOKS

See Secondhand & Antiquarian, *below.*

2 *e-2*

SOLAR LIGHTS BOOKS

In the heart of the Union Street shopping district, Solar Lights is a fine independent bookstore carrying contemporary literature, travel, mysteries, New Age psychology, and more. Although it's easy to miss—below street level, down a short flight of stairs— inside it's surprisingly large. *2068 Union St., at Webster St., 415/567–6082.*

4 *e-5*

TILLMAN PLACE BOOKSHOP

You can find this shop tucked away in a tiny alley off Grant Avenue near Union Square. It has a good selection of children's books and a strong literature department. *8 Tillman Pl., off Grant Ave. between Post and Sutter Sts., Union Square, 415/392–4668. Closed Sun.*

4 *e-6*

VIRGIN MEGASTORE

Best known for its extensive musical offerings, the Virgin Megastore also has great selections of popular culture and travel books. *See* Music, *below.*

secondhand & antiquarian

7 *h-1*

AARDVARK BOOKS

Pick up high-quality used books at reasonable prices, or browse among a small selection of new titles. Pluses include book buyers who won't make you feel like a cretin when you try to sell the dregs of your collection, and one of the most aloof bookstore cats in San Francisco. *227 Church St., at Market St., Castro, 415/552–6733.*

4 *c-5*

ACORN BOOKS

Customers in search of an antiquarian, out-of-print, or used book know that the dedicated staff at this Polk Gulch shop would scour the earth's four corners to find it. Chances are, however, that the well-stocked store probably already has it somewhere on the shelves. *1436 Polk St., between Pine and California Sts., Polk Gulch, 415/563–1736.*

8 *a-2*

ADOBE BOOK SHOP

Adobe specializes in used and rare books, particularly those about art and modern philosophy. The staff is erudite but affable, and the prices are some of the lowest in the city. *3166 16th St., between Valencia and Guerrero Sts., Mission, 415/864–3936.*

4 *d-5*

ARGONAUT BOOK SHOP

First editions and other rare books fill the shelves here. There is an excellent selection of history books on San Francisco and the American West, in addition to many art books and collector's maps. *786 Sutter St., between Taylor and Jones Sts., Union Square, 415/474–9067. Closed Sun.*

3 *d-1*

BLACK OAK BOOKS

See above.

4 *e-6*

BRICK ROW BOOK SHOP

Since 1915, Brick Row has specialized in first editions and rare books of 18th- and 19th-century English and American literature. *49 Geary St., between Kearny St.*

and Grant Ave., Union Square, 415/398–0414. Closed weekends.

5 c-6

GREEN APPLE BOOKS

See above.

4 e-6

JEFFREY THOMAS

This shop in the 49 Geary Street building that houses many of the city's finest art galleries sells rare books, prints, and manuscripts in all fields of interest. 49 Geary St., between Kearny St. and Grant Ave., Union Square, 415/956–3272. Closed weekends.

4 d-6

MCDONALD'S BOOK SHOP

McDonald's is a throwback to the good old days of used-book selling, with haphazardly stacked shelves that encourage browsing. It has the best, if most disorderly, selection of old magazines in the city. 48 Turk St., near Market St., Tenderloin, 415/673–2235. Closed Sun.

3 e-2

MOE'S BOOKS

This beloved Berkeley institution has five floors of secondhand and antiquarian books, as well as a good selection of new books, periodicals, and reviews. The foreign language and art book sections are particularly impressive. 2476 Telegraph Ave., near Haste St., Berkeley, 510/849–2087.

3 e-3

SHAKESPEARE & CO. BOOKS

This used-book store has not changed a bit over the years; it's dusty and disorganized, but filled with treasures in the art, literature, classics, and philosophy genres. If you wish to spend the afternoon book browsing, Moe's Books (see above) is across the street. 2499 Telegraph Ave., at Dwight Way, Berkeley, 510/841–8916.

6 g-2

SUNSET BOOKS

This is a solid general-interest used bookshop with many titles on art, psychology, music, history, literature, and philosophy. 2161 Irving St., at 23rd Ave., Sunset District, 415/664–3644.

8 a-2

TALL STORIES

Tucked away on the second floor of an inconspicuous building, Tall Stories is difficult to find but worth the search if you're interested in rare, collectible, or first-edition books. Nineteenth- and 20th-century fiction are particularly well represented. 2141 Mission St., between 16th and 17th Sts., Mission, 415/255–1915. Closed Sun.

special interest

4 f-8

AUTOMOBILIA

The bookstore at the FAA Automotive Center is packed tighter than a Volkswagen at a circus, and all of the books it stocks are about cars. Look for fiction, nonfiction, technical manuals, glossy coffee-table books, and a fine selection of miniature car models and automotive art. 601 Brannan St., at 5th St., South of Market, 415/292–2710.

1 a-1

BOOK PASSAGE

This excellent Marin County shop has all kinds of books, including used and remaindered, but travel books are the specialty. There's an entire room devoted to travel literature, and another room full of travel guides to every nook and cranny on the planet. 51 Tamal Vista Blvd., Corte Madera, 415/927–0960.

7 e-1

BOUND TOGETHER ANARCHIST BOOK COLLECTIVE

This is an old-school anarchist entity founded in the 1970s and staffed entirely by volunteers, with profits contributed to anarchist projects. In addition to an ample supply of books on anarchist themes, there are also books on women's studies, African-American studies, and literature, and a small Spanish-language section. 1369 Haight St., at Masonic Ave., Haight, 415/431–8355.

4 b-2

BUILDERS BOOKSOURCE

Books about architecture, interior design, gardening, crafts, and construction abound in this beautifully laid out bookstore, along with a some cookbooks and children's books. A mecca for contractors and construction workers, it's a great source of information on building codes and other technical matters. *Ghirardelli Square, 900 North Point St., at Polk St., Fisherman's Wharf, 415/440–5773.*

3 *b-2*

1817 4th St., at Hearst St., Berkeley, 510/845–6874.

3 *d-2*

2138 University Ave., at Shattuck Ave., Berkeley, 510/843–5002.

7 *f-1*

COMIX EXPERIENCE

This shop sells all kinds of comics, from the popular to the obscure. It occasionally holds in-store signings. *305 Divisadero St., between Oak and Page Sts., Haight, 415/863–9258.*

3 *f-3*

DARK CARNIVAL OF CRIME, MYSTERY, SUSPENSE, AND TRUE CRIME BOOK STORE

Make a trip to Berkeley to browse the Bay Area's largest selection of sci-fi and fantasy. Mysteries and crime fiction are plentiful as well. *3086 Claremont Ave., between Alcatraz and Ashby Aves., Berkeley, 510/595–7637.*

7 *f-3*

A DIFFERENT LIGHT

Part of a national chain, this is the place for lesbian, gay, and transgender literature and history, as well as everything from sci-fi and fantasy to religion and film criticism. Added attractions: a large magazine section, stacks of free weekly newspapers, and dozens of flyers about community events. Book signings and readings take place weekly. *489 Castro St., near 18th St., Castro, 415/431–0891.*

4 *e-3*

EASTWIND BOOKS AND ARTS

This shop deals exclusively in new books on all aspects of Asia, particularly China, as well as Asian America. There are both Chinese- and English-language sections. *1435 Stockton St., 2nd floor, at Columbus Ave., Chinatown, 415/772–5899.*

4 *c-6*

EUROPEAN BOOK COMPANY

Travelers bound for Europe will want to stop here first to stock up on French-, German-, Italian-, and Spanish-language books, magazines, and newspapers, as well as foreign-language dictionaries, learning cassettes, maps, and travel guides. *925 Larkin St., between Post and Geary Sts., Tenderloin, 415/474–0626. Closed Sun.*

4 *c-6*

FANTASY, ETC.

Fantasy, Etc., is a great source for all kinds of new and used pulp fiction, science fiction, detective stories, and adventure books. Even though it's tiny, you can't miss this shop, right next to a huge adult cinema. *808 Larkin St., at O'Farrell St., Tenderloin, 415/441–7617.*

3 *d-1*

GAIA BOOKSTORE

This is a longtime Bay Area favorite for New Age books. It also sells New Age music and instruments, tarot cards, and meditation supplies. *1400 Shattuck Ave., at Rose St., Berkeley, 510/548–4172.*

7 *h-1*

GET LOST TRAVEL BOOKS, MAPS, & GEAR

Sure, you can find a travel guide to Paris or New York at almost any bookshop. But when you're looking for a book about Malta or Polish-language instruction tapes, come visit Get Lost, where the selection of guides is first rate. It also stocks travel accessories and luggage by outfitters such as Eagle Creek. *1825 Market St., at Guerrero St., Mission, 415/437–0529.*

4 *a-6*

KINOKUNIYA BOOKSTORE

This shop has one of the finest selections of English-language books on Japanese subjects in the United States. A major attraction is the collection of beautifully produced graphics and art books; there are also periodicals in Japanese and English. *Japan Center, Kinokuniya Bldg., 2nd floor, 1581 Webster St., at Post St., Japantown, 415/567–7625.*

7 *h-1*

LIMELIGHT FILM AND THEATRE BOOKSTORE

This establishment carries new and used film and theater titles, plus special-interest periodicals. *1803 Market St., at Octavia St., Civic Center, 415/864–2265.*

`3` *e-4*

MAMA BEARS

Mama Bears is more than a bookstore: it's a women's community center, with a coffee house, crafts, music, bulletin boards, and networking opportunities galore. Books are primarily by women and deal mostly with women's issues; there are some books for children as well. *6536 Telegraph Ave., at 66th St., Oakland, 510/428–9684.*

`4` *a-6*

MARCUS BOOKS

Books, periodicals, cards, and gifts here celebrate and reflect on African and African-American reality. *1712 Fillmore St., at Post St., Japantown, 415/346–4222.*

`3` *d-5*

3900 Martin Luther King Way, at 39th St., Oakland, 510/652–2344.

`4` *c-2*

THE MARITIME BOOKSTORE

Sailors will want to set a course for this Hyde Street Pier shop, where literature of the sea, boat-building books, and maritime histories abound. *Hyde St. Pier, 2905 Hyde St., at Jefferson St., Fisherman's Wharf, 415/775–2665.*

`4` *b-8*

PSYCHIC EYE

Books on astrology, metaphysics, the occult, and self-help are this shop's specialty. The staff will not only sell you books, but also do a psychic reading or an astrology chart. *301 Fell St., at Gough St., Hayes Valley, 415/863–9997.*

`4` *f-5*

RAND MCNALLY MAP & TRAVEL STORE

See Maps, *below.*

`7` *f-5*

SAN FRANCISCO MYSTERY BOOKSTORE

Shelves of quality new and used detective fiction make this the shop of choice for the armchair Sherlock Holmes. The shop even carries some first editions. *4175 24th St., between Castro and Diamond Sts., Noe Valley, 415/282–7444. Closed Mon.*

`3` *e-3*

SHAMBHALA BOOKSELLERS

Shambhala sells books on Eastern and Western religious traditions, Jungian

psychology, acupuncture, astrology, Wicca, and magic. *2482 Telegraph Ave., near Dwight Way, Berkeley, 510/848–8443.*

`4` *f-5*

STACEY'S BOOKSTORE

Once a solely professional bookstore, with computer, technical, medical, business, travel, and reference titles forming the bulk of its inventory, Stacey's is now one of San Francisco's best bookstores—with literary fiction, nonfiction, travel guides, the whole nine yards. More than 100,000 titles are displayed on three floors. *581 Market St., between 1st and 2nd Sts., Financial District, 415/421–4687.*

`4` *f-4*

THOMAS BROS. MAPS AND BOOKS

See Maps, *below.*

`3` *e-2*

UNIVERSITY PRESS BOOKS

This shop appeals to academics and deep thinkers with books published by more than 100 university presses, plus academic lines including Penguin, Routledge, Sage, and Beacon. *2430 Bancroft Way, between Dana St. and Telegraph Ave., Berkeley, 510/548–0585.*

`5` *h-4*

VEDANTA SOCIETY BOOKSHOP

At the entrance to the Vedanta Society Old Temple (*see* Churches, Synagogues & Temples *in* Chapter 4), this shop carries books on Hindu philosophy, in Sanskrit and in English, as well as those about other Eastern and Western religions. *2323 Vallejo St., at Fillmore St., Cow Hollow, 415/922–2323. Closed Tues.*

`4` *f-4*

WILLIAM STOUT ARCHITECTURAL BOOKS

Architecture and design books and periodicals are the specialty at this Jackson Square bookshop. The majority of the books are new, although there's an impressive out-of-print collection as well. *804 Montgomery St., between Jackson and Pacific Sts., Financial District, 415/391–6757. Closed Sun.*

CANDLES

4 *e-5*

CANDELIER

Recently relocated into a more spacious shop, Candelier sells candles of every size, shape, color, and fragrance, with a large selection of aromatherapy candles. It also stocks a small collection of home decor books. *33 Maiden La., between Grant Ave. and Kearny St., Union Square, 415/989–8600. Closed Sun.*

BOOK SHOPPING IN BERKELEY

Berkeley brims with excellent bookstores, not surprisingly, considering that it's home to a world-class university. Whether you're seeking classical philosophy or a Tom Clancy thriller, these Berkeley shops merit a trip across the Bay:

Black Oak Books
> *A discriminating collection of new and used literature, classics, and poetry.*

Cody's Books
> *Berkeley's best, with every imaginable genre.*

Dark Carnival of Crime, Mystery, Suspense, and True Crime Book Store (Special Interest)
> *The Bay Area's largest selection of sci-fi and fantasy.*

Gaia Bookstore (Special Interest)
> *A longtime favorite for New Age books.*

Moe's Books (Secondhand & Antiquarian)
> *Five floors of secondhand and antiquarian books.*

Shakespeare & Co. Books (Secondhand & Antiquarian)
> *A small, dusty shop with all kinds of treasures.*

Shambhala Booksellers (Special Interest)
> *Eastern and Western religious traditions, psychology, acupuncture, astrology, Wicca, and magic.*

University Press Books (Special Interest)
> *Books by more than 100 university presses.*

---

2 *c-6*

THE CANDLEMAN STORE

Wafting from this shop are the scents of gardenia, cinnamon, and mulberry. In addition to scented and potpourri candles, there are clever candles shaped like dogs, dragons, and fish, and more than 100 styles of oil candles. *Stonestown Galleria, 19th Ave. at Winston Dr., Stonestown, 415/566–6773.*

8 *a-2*

LADY LUCK CANDLE SHOP

The friendly proprietor of this tiny shop can convince even the most bitter cynic to buy a hope candle. There's a wide selection of incense, devotional candles, and love potions. *311 Valencia St., between 14th and 15th Sts., Mission, 415/621–0358. Closed Sun.*

CELLULAR PHONES

4 *c-5*

MYRON GROUP WIRELESS COMMUNICATION

This is a one-stop shop for cellular communications and home office needs, selling cellular phones and pagers, as well as offering fax services. It carries phones by Mitsubishi, Ericsson, Nokia, and others, including the tiny Motorola Startac. *1472 California St., between Larkin and Hyde Sts., Tenderloin, 415/928–8338. Closed Sun.*

4 *e-6*

SAN FRANCISCO CELLULAR AND PAGING, INC.

On sale are phones by Ericsson, Motorola, and Nokia, as well as a wide selection of pagers. You can rent cell phones for periods as short as one day. *325 Mason St., between Geary St. and O'Farrell St., Union Square, 415/922–8319.*

4 *g-5*

TOTALLY WIRELESS

A wide selection of phones is sold with a similarly wide selection of carriers: you can choose from CellularOne, Nextel, and Sprint. Another bonus is the free loaner phone it'll provide if your purchase should ever need repairs. *245 Market St., between Beale and Main Sts., Financial District, 415/543–5555. Closed weekends.*

CHARITABLE CAUSES

7 g-5

GLOBAL EXCHANGE FAIR TRADE CRAFT CENTER

The nonprofit Global Exchange organization aims to help world artisans and farmers achieve self-sufficiency through trade. To that end, the shop sells hundreds of handcrafted gift items, plus handmade clothing, jewelry, musical instruments, and food items from 40 countries. *4018 24th St., between Noe and Castro Sts., Noe Valley, 415/648–8068.*

7 d-1

PLANETWEAVERS TREASURE STORE

San Francisco's official UNICEF store stocks crafts, clothing, masks, drums, music, books, and toys from around the world. *1573 Haight St., at Clayton St., Haight, 415/864 4415.*

7 f-3

UNDER ONE ROOF

Affiliated with the NAMES Project (*see* Statues, Murals & Monuments *in* Chapter 4), this shop sells high-quality gift items gathered from 50 AIDS organizations: aromatherapy candles, stationery, Christmas ornaments, queer pride T-shirts, picture frames, and more. All profits go directly to AIDS service providers and researchers. *519 Castro St., between 18th and 19th Sts., Castro, 415/252–9430.*

CLOTHING FOR CHILDREN & INFANTS

5 d-6

CITY KIDS BABY NEWS STORE

This is a veritable kiddie department store, selling clothing, nursery furniture, and diapers—plus books, games, and toys. *152 Clement St., at 3rd Ave., Richmond District, 415/752–3837. Closed Sun.*

5 e-6

DOTTIE DOOLITTLE

Dottie Doolittle is where Pacific Heights mothers buy Florence Eiseman dresses for their little girls. The shop has a good selection of domestic and imported clothing for boys and girls from infants to age 14. It also carries baby furniture

and accessories. *3680 Sacramento St., at Spruce St., Laurel Heights, 415/563–3244.*

7 d-1

KIDS ONLY

There's a little bit of everything here, from sturdy clothing to amusing games and toys. Clothes range from tiny rompers for infants to party dresses in size 5. *1608 Haight St., at Clayton St., Haight, 415/552–5445.*

4 a-4

MINIS

See Clothing for Women/Specialty, *below.*

4 a-4

MUDPIE

This charming shop overflows with unique children's wear such as velvet dresses and handmade booties. Quilts, toys, books, and overstuffed child-size furniture make this a fun store for browsing. *1694 Union St., at Gough St., Cow Hollow, 415/771–9262.*

7 g-5

SMALL FRYS

In the heart of family-friendly Noe Valley, Small Frys carries a complete range of colorful cottons, mainly for infants but also for older children—including OshKosh B'gosh and Levi's for Kids. It also stocks kiddie accessories. *4066 24th St., between Castro and Noe Sts., Noe Valley, 415/648 3954.*

5 h-5

YOUNTVILLE

This upscale shop carries clothing for children up to age eight, with some European fashions and many California designs. *2416 Fillmore St., at Washington St., Pacific Heights, 415/922–5050.*

CLOTHING FOR WOMEN/GENERAL

classic & casual

4 e-5

ANN TAYLOR

This national chain is famous for high-quality yet affordable fashions suitable for work, play, and formal occasions. You can accessorize from head to toe with AT hats, scarves, jewelry, perfume, bags, belts, stockings, and shoes. 240

Post St., between Stockton St. and Grant Ave., Union Square, 415/788–0716.

`4` g-4
Embarcadero Center, Clay and Sacramento Sts. between Battery and Drumm Sts., Embarcadero, 415/989–5355.

`4` b-2
Ghirardelli Square, 900 North Point St., at Polk St., Fisherman's Wharf, 415/775–2872.

`2` c-6
Stonestown Galleria, 19th Ave. and Winston Dr., Stonestown, 415/564–0229.

`4` e-6
San Francisco Shopping Centre, 865 Market St., between 4th and 5th Sts., Union Square, 415/543–2487.

`4` e-5
BANANA REPUBLIC
Basic items (T-shirts, sweater sets, jerseys) in basic colors (black, gray, sky blue, oatmeal), but in comfortable (say stretch), not-so-basic fabrics (cashmere, merino wool) are the rub at this national chain. The stores are filled with those pieces we all need—but with modern styling and often luxurious fabrics that make them a cut above. It also carries a small selection of linens in similarly muted colors. 256 Grant Ave., at Sutter St., Union Square, 415/788–3087.

`2` c-6
Stonestown Galleria, 19th Ave. and Winston Dr., Stonestown, 415/753–3330.

`4` f-4
2 Embarcadero Center, Embarcadero, 415/986–5076.

`4` e-5
BROOKS BROTHERS
See Clothing for Men/General, below.

`4` e-5
BURBERRY
Burberry has been selling its famed plaid-lined trench coats since World War I. The shop also carries stylish yet distinctive English-country weekend wear: shirts, blouses, jackets, blazers, sweaters, hats, and umbrellas. 225 Post St., at Stockton St., Union Square, 415/392–2200.

`4` a-4
CP SHADES
CP Shades produces an extremely appealing line of California-casual separates and dresses. Everything is made of 100% natural fibers and is machine washable. 1861 Union St., at Laguna St., Marina, 415/292–3588.

`7` d-1
DALJEETS
Get mod in all kinds of trendy merchandise, from T-shirts and jeans to jackets and halter tops. 1744 Haight St., at Cole St., Haight, 415/752–5610.

`4` e-3
DONNA
Donna's unconstructed linens, cottons, and knits are easy to wear. 1424 Grant Ave., at Union St., North Beach, 415/397–4447.

`4` e-6
GAP
Of the many Gap stores in San Francisco, this branch on Market Street is one of the biggest and best-stocked. You'll find all your favorite weekend basics, like T-shirts and jeans, plus shoes, belts, scarves, sleepwear, and hats. 890 Market St., at Powell St., Union Square, 415/788–5909.

`4` g-4
3 Embarcadero Center, Embarcadero, 415/391–8826.

`7` e-1
1485 Haight St., at Ashbury St., Haight, 415/431–6336.

`4` b-4
GEORGIOU
Georgiou excels at dressing the contemporary woman. Career and special-occasion fashions are sold under the shop's own label. 1725 Union St., at Gough St., Cow Hollow, 415/776–8144.

`4` f-4
Embarcadero Center, Clay and Sacramento Sts. between Battery and Drumm Sts., Embarcadero, 415/981–4845.

`4` e-6
152 Geary St., between Grant Ave. and Stockton St., Union Square, 415/989–8614.

`7` g-5
GLADRAGS
Natural-fiber apparel is the specialty here, from lingerie to special-occasion dresses. The staff is especially friendly. 3985 24th St., at Noe St., Noe Valley, 415/647–7144.

4 *e-6*
J. CREW
The popular mail-order company sells its nouveau-preppy couture here. *San Francisco Shopping Centre, 865 Market St., between 4th and 5th Sts., Union Square, 415/546–6262 or 415/434–2739.*

7 *g-5*
JOSHUA SIMON
This Noe Valley shop stocks unusual women's garments: flowing pants, romantic dresses, woven vests, and hand-painted shirts. Many items are by local designers. *3915 24th St., between Noe and Sanchez Sts., Noe Valley, 415/821–1068.*

4 *e-3*
MAC (MODERN APPEALING CLOTHING)
MAC merchandise ranges from dressy to casual. Trendy fashions are by designers such as Todd Oldham, Marc Jacobs, and San Franciscan Hank Ford. *1543 Grant Ave., between Filbert and Union Sts., North Beach, 415/837–1604.*

1 *o 5*
5 Claude La., between Bush and Sutter Sts., at Kearny St., Financial District, 415/837–0615.

7 *c-2*
NANA
The San Francisco branch of this national chain sells clothes and shoes to ultrahip Gen Xers. Funky, chunky shoes are a specialty. *2276 Market St., at Noe St., Noe Valley, 415/861–6262.*

8 *c-2*
OLD NAVY
This spin-off of the Gap sells everyday basics—jeans, T-shirts, cargo pants, jackets, belts, and sweaters—to a mostly high school–age crowd. The selection is wide and prices reasonable—you can snag most items for less than $25. *Potrero Center, 2300 16th St., at Potrero Ave., Potrero Hill, 415/255–6814.*

7 *e-1*
POSITIVELY HAIGHT STREET
Here you'll find all the 1960s apparel and accessories that the Haight is so firmly associated with. Little flowery halter tops, peasant skirts, and an endless procession of tie-dye are big sellers, as are iron-on "peace" and "love" patches.

1400 Haight St., at Masonic St., Haight, 415/252–8747.

5 *h-4*
THREE BAGS FULL
Most of the beautiful—and expensive—sweaters here are hand-knitted out of luxurious yarns. *2181 Union St., at Fillmore St., Cow Hollow, 415/567–5753.*

4 *e-5*
500 Sutter St., at Powell St., Union Square, 415/398–7987.

4 *b-8*
WORLDWARE
San Francisco's most ecologically correct store features men's, women's, and children's clothing made from organic hemp, wool, or cotton. It also carries great furniture and gift items (*see Gifts & Souvenirs, below*). *336 Hayes St., between Franklin and Gough Sts., Hayes Valley, 415/487–9030.*

conservative

4 *e-5*
LAURA ASHLEY
If your image of Laura Ashley clothes is of flowery dresses with Peter Pan collars, you apparently haven't been into one of its stores lately. Loosely fitted cotton dresses come in subtle colors, and flax-colored linen pants are suitable for a casual office environment. The store also sells bedding, upholstery fabrics, and other housewares. *253 Post St., between Stockton St. and Grant Ave., Union Square, 415/788–0190.*

4 *f-6*
THE RAFAEL'S
Conservative and classy suits for women are the mainstay of this service-oriented shop. Owner Mona Rafael and her staff will help you put together the outfit to wear on your interview for that corporate job. *643 Market St., at New Montgomery St., Financial District, 415/974–6772. Closed Sun.*

4 *e-6*
285 Geary St., between Powell and Stockton Sts., Union Square, 415/956–3489. Closed Sun.

4 *e-5*
TALBOTS
Classic cashmere sweaters, wool jackets, linen pants, and ballet flats are Tal-

bots stock in trade. Its faux pearl jewelry goes with just about anything sold in the store. The large, commodious Post Street store has plenty of comfy seating. *128 Post St., between Kearny St. and Grant Ave., Union Square, 415/398–8881.*

4 *f-4*

2 Embarcadero Center, Clay and Sacramento Sts. between Battery and Drumm Sts., Embarcadero, 415/781–2128.

2 *c-6*

Stonestown Galleria, 19th Ave. and Winston Dr., Stonestown, 415/566–7311.

contemporary

7 *e-1*

AMBIANCE

At this inviting Haight-Ashbury shop, the mix of sportswear and separates (some under the shop's own label) is eclectic but attractively priced. During the holiday season it has a dandy selection of party dresses. *1458 Haight St., at Masonic Ave., Haight, 415/552–5095.*

4 *a-5*

BEBE

Sassy casual pieces, vampy suits, and provocative evening wear—many with plunging necklines—are the draws at this national chain. The styling is unmistakably European. *2133 Fillmore St., at California St., Pacific Heights, 415/771–2323.*

4 *e-6*

San Francisco Shopping Centre, 865 Market St., between 4th and 5th Sts., Union Square, 415/543–2323.

4 *a-4*

2095 Union St., at Webster St., Cow Hollow, 415/563–2323.

7 *e-1*

BEHIND THE POST OFFICE

Here's all the latest and greatest hip-hop gear: T-shirts, roller-girl dresses, and capri and cargo pants. Look for original shirts with bold graphic designs by local designer Sil Cappuccio. *1510 Haight St., at Ashbury St., Haight, 415/861–2507.*

4 *e-6*

DIESEL

A veritable shrine to youth culture, this store seems to be more about image than clothing. A DJ booth upstairs is the scene for occasional performances by

local and touring DJs, and fliers around the store advertise upcoming concerts and club events. But in case you were coming for the clothes, they sell colorful T-shirts, ski jackets, bike messenger bags, accessories, and reams of jeans: the house label jeans fill a wall full of shelves that stretch two stories high. *101 Post St., at Kearny St., Union Square, 415/982–7077.*

4 *e-3*

KNITZ AND LEATHER

Mother-daughter team Anna Martin and Anna Katherina operate this small shop, selling original-design coats, sweaters, scarves, and handbags. *1429 Grant Ave., at Green St., North Beach, 415/391–3480.*

4 *d-8*

ROLO

This SF minichain keeps the club set up to date. Men's and women's designer-brand denim, sportswear, shoes, and accessories reveal a distinct European influence. *See also* Clothing for Men/General, *below. 1301 Howard St., at 9th St., South of Market, 415/861–1999.*

7 *d-1*

SOLO MIA

Although you can pick up a simple pair of pants or a sweater here, the real reason to come is for the special occasion dresses and accessories like vaporous organza wraps. A collection of slinky ivory-colored dresses, like a sleeveless Nicole Miller number, are suitable for brides. *1599 Haight St., at Clayton St., Haight, 415/621–0342.*

4 *e-6*

URBAN OUTFITTERS

A hodgepodge of trendy, youthful clothing, inexpensive housewares, and gift items is the formula at this successful chain of stores for the twentysomething shopper. The clothes have a neo-hippie attitude—witness flowing floral-print dresses that wouldn't have been out of place when the chain began in 1970. Cosmetics by Urban Decay are another draw. *80 Powell St., at Ellis St., Union Square, 415/989–1515.*

7 *d-1*

VILLAINS

A mega fashion store for club kids and those who can still get away with dressing like one, Villains stocks a wide variety of clothes and accessories like sunglasses and watches. You'll find a large collection of wide-leg pants, including bootleg-cut Levi's and matching denim jackets. An attached shoe store sells many shoes by Diesel and Vans. *1672 Haight St., between Clayton and Cole Sts., Haight, 415/626–5939.*

5 *h-5*

ZOE LTD.

These beautifully styled clothes have a decidedly noncorporate look. Natural-fiber separates and gorgeous sweaters range from casual to dressy. *2400 Fillmore St., at Washington St., Pacific Heights, 415/929–0441.*

designer

4 *a-4*

ARMANI EXCHANGE

The exchange sells Armani's casual lines—jeans, sweaters, jackets, handbags, T-shirts, and socks. *2090 Union St., at Webster St., Cow Hollow, 415/749–0891.*

4 *b-8*

BELLA DONNA

The discriminating selection of dresses and accessories by talented New York and Los Angeles designers sets this store apart. Owner Justine Kaltenbach designs all the hats on display. *539 Hayes St., between Octavia and Laguna Sts., Hayes Valley, 415/861–7182.*

4 *a-5*

BETSEY JOHNSON

Postmodern designer Betsey Johnson brings you outrageous women's fashions in a campy, neon-lit shop. The styling is youthful and fun, and you come away with her trademark, undeniably pink bag. *2033 Fillmore St., between Pine and California Sts., Pacific Heights, 415/567–2726.*

4 *e-6*

160 Geary St., between Stockton St. and Grant Ave., Union Square, 415/398–2516.

4 *e-6*

CELINE OF PARIS

In addition to elegant women's clothing by the famous Parisian couture house, the shop carries lovely Celine shoes, handbags, and scarves. There are also Celine ties, wallets, and belts for men. *216 Stockton St., at Geary St., Union Square, 415/397–1140. Closed Sun.*

4 *e-6*

CHANEL

Chanel's world-famous couture clothing, accessories, perfumes, cosmetics, and jewelry fill this stylish shop. *155 Maiden La., at Stockton St., Union Square, 415/981–1550.*

7 *g-5*

DESIGNERS TOO

The local and national designers represented here use natural fibers and sumptuous fabrics. In addition to clothing, a wide selection of hats, handbags, and locally made jewelry is sold. *3899 24th St., at Sanchez St., Noe Valley, 415/648–1057.*

4 *e-6*

EMPORIO ARMANI

The designer's hip San Francisco flagship store has fashionable jackets, pants, and shirts. Accessories, of

---

ONE-OF-A-KIND SHOPS IN HAYES VALLEY

If, like a lot of San Franciscans, you'd rather scour small, original boutiques then get lost in big chain stores, you'll love Hayes Valley. So you might want to browse these only-in-San Francisco shops before Gap and Starbucks invade this up and coming neighborhood.

Bella Donna (Clothing for Women/General)
Trendy looks by New York and Los Angeles designers.

Nomads (Clothing for Men/General)
Upscale grunge threads.

Oxenrose (Beauty)
A trendy salon with first-rate stylists.

Polanco (Folk Art & Handicrafts)
Mexican arts and crafts.

Worldware (Clothing for Women/General)
Clothing made from organic hemp and cotton plus recycled decorative items.

Zeitgeist Timepieces & Jewelry (Watches & Clocks)
Meticulously restored vintage watches.

Zonal (Antiques)
Forgotten treasures from Depression-era America.

course, are no mere sideline. Down-stairs is the more casual apparel. *1 Grant Ave., at Market St., Union Square, 415/677–9400.*

4 *f-5*

GIANNI VERSACE

Versace turns out very sophisticated and dramatic high fashions. The service is exceptional. *Crocker Galleria, 50 Post St., between Montgomery and Kearny Sts., Financial District, 415/616–0604. Closed Sun.*

4 *e-6*

GUCCI

Gucci's three levels are filled with the famous designer's men's and women's apparel, jewelry, and leather goods, including those with the classic "G"s. Gorgeous architecture and artwork make shopping here an experience. *200 Stockton St., at Geary St., Union Square, 415/392–2808.*

4 *e-5*

JAEGER INTERNATIONAL SHOP

British workmanship and beautiful fabrics are the hallmarks of Jaeger's classic jackets, sweaters, pants, blouses, skirts, and accessories. *272 Post St., at Stockton St., Union Square, 415/421–3714. Closed Sun.*

4 *e-6*

JIL SANDER

Women with a definite sense of self come here for the complete line of Jil Sander's beautifully tailored fashions. *135 Maiden La., at Stockton St., Union Square, 415/273–7070.*

4 *a-5*

JIM-ELLE

"Clothes for the fashion confident" is the motto here. The interchangeable separates are by designers such as Romeo Gigli, Harriet Selwyn, Peter Cohen, and Matsuda. *2237 Fillmore St., at Sacramento St., Pacific Heights, 415/567–9500.*

4 *e-5*

JOANIE CHAR

Silk fashions are what first made Joanie Char famous, although now there's a wider variety of fashions in linen, cotton, and wool as well. *404 Sutter St., at Stockton St., Union Square, 415/399–9867.*

4 *e-5*

MIX

If you're tired of arriving at the party dressed like everyone else, you can pick up one of the unusual and beautiful outfits here, crafted by designers like Illoni Pelli and by in-house designers. Innovative treatments of fabrics—take starched linen molded into almost architectural forms—set the clothes apart. Outfits can run way beyond several hundred dollars. *309 Sutter St., at Grant Ave., Union Square, 415/392–1742. Closed Sun.*

4 *f-5*

NICOLE MILLER

Flirty, strappy dresses and clingy cashmere cardigans are Nicole Miller's specialty. If your figure doesn't accommodate one of the little silk dresses, you can indulge in her fun tiny evening purses, sexy sandals, or other accessories. *Crocker Galleria, 50 Post St., between Montgomery and Kearny Sts., Financial District, 415/398–3111. Closed Sun.*

4 *f-5*

POLO STORE– RALPH LAUREN

Ralph Lauren's classic American clothing collections for men, women, and children are beautifully displayed. *90 Post St., at Kearny St., Union Square, 415/788–7656.*

discount & outlet

8 *c-1*

CHRISTINE FOLEY

Beautiful hand-loomed cotton sweaters for men, women, and children are sold at discounts of about 50% at this factory outlet. In the small front room you'll find pillows and other knickknacks at retail prices. *430 9th St., between Harrison and Bryant Sts., South of Market, 415/621–8126. Closed Sun.*

8 *f-2*

ESPRIT FACTORY OUTLET

San Francisco–based Esprit manufactures hip sportswear, shoes, and accessories, primarily for young women and children. In-season clothing from Esprit's women's and children's lines, as well as shoes and accessories, are sold at 30% to 70% discounts. *499 Illinois St., at 16th St., China Basin, 415/957–2550.*

4 b-8
560 HAYES VINTAGE BOUTIQUE

The '70s are in style at 560 Hayes, where the stock of vintage and used clothing includes pants, coats, and dresses. Most of the fashions here are women's. *560 Hayes St., between Laguna and Octavia Sts., Hayes Valley, 415/861–7993.*

4 g-7
JEREMY'S

Big-name seconds and samples of a practical yet stylish nature are sold here for 40% to 60% off. You may find such brands as Prada and Jil Sander. *2 South Park Rd., at 2nd St., South of Market, 415/882–4929.*

4 e-5
LOEHMANN'S

Savvy shoppers will find astounding bargains at Loehmann's, which stocks labels like Karl Lagerfeld, Calvin Klein, and Eileen Fisher at drastically reduced prices. It helps to know designers' merchandise, however, as the labels are often removed. *222 Sutter St., between Kearny St. and Grant Ave., Union Square, 415/982–3215.*

4 e-7
YERBA BUENA SQUARE

The square is a collection of 10 shops selling discount apparel, shoes, and toys. Spend a few hours weeding through the racks and you'll find gems by Armani, Calvin Klein, and Dior. *899 Howard St., at 5th St., South of Market 415/543–1275.*

unusual sizes

4 a-6
THE COMPANY STORE

Stylish sports and career wear, jewelry, scarves, and other accessories are made for women sizes 14 and up. *1913 Fillmore St., at Bush St., Pacific Heights, 415/921–0365.*

4 g-8
HARPER GREER

Stylish and stylish career attire comes in sizes 14 and up, with a full line of scarves, belts, and jewelry to complete the look. Most of the clothing is in natural, easy-care fabrics. *580 4th St., at Brannan St., South of Market, 415/543–4066.*

4 e-6
LIZ CLAIBORNE PETITES

Women 5'5" and shorter can finally find shorts and skirts that don't need to be hemmed. Liz Claiborne's classic clothes are heavy on the dressy sweaters, linen and wool slacks and skirts, and office-appropriate dresses. *San Francisco Shopping Centre, 865 Market St., between 4th and 5th Sts., Union Square, 415/495–8982.*

vintage & resale

4 c-6
AMERICAN RAG

The huge selection features new and used men's and women's clothes from the United States and Europe that are all in excellent shape. You'll find racks of stylish suits, classy jackets, and black vintage dresses, plus shoes and accessories such as sunglasses, hats, belts, and scarves. *1305 Van Ness Ave., between Sutter and Bush Sts., Pacific Heights, 415/441–0537.*

7 e-1
BUFFALO EXCHANGE

Part of a national chain, Buffalo Exchange sells both new and recycled clothing and will also trade or buy items. It has a wide selection of Levi's, leather jackets, vintage dresses, and flannel shirts, as well as sunglasses and other accessories. *1555 Haight St., between Masonic Ave. and Ashbury St., Haight, 415/431–7733.*

4 c-4
1800 Polk St., between Washington and Jackson Sts., Polk Gulch, 415/346–5726.

4 a-6
CROSSROADS TRADING CO.

At this upscale resale clothing emporium, San Francisco hipsters can conjure up the complete retro look. The prices are a little higher than at other local shops, but so is the quality. *1901 Fillmore St., at Bush St., Pacific Heights, 415/775–8885.*

7 g-2
2231 Market St., between Sanchez and Noe Sts., Castro, 415/626–8989.

4 a-5
DEPARTURES FROM THE PAST

Along with vintage clothing, shoes, and hats, you'll find some costumes, formal attire, and casual wear. *2028 Fillmore St., between California and Pine Sts., Pacific Heights, 415/885–3377.*

7 *d-1*

THE WASTELAND

Wasteland brings you trendy and outrageous treasures, as well as vintage gowns, suits, and costume jewelry. It's one of the city's most popular—but priciest—secondhand stores. Expect it to be packed on weekends. *1660 Haight St., between Belvedere and Clayton Sts., Haight, 415/863–3150.*

7 *f-3*

WORN OUT WEST

Budget-conscious cowboys and western wanna-bes come here for secondhand western wear and leather goods. *582 Castro St., near 19th St., Castro, 415/431–6020. Closed Mon.*

CLOTHING FOR WOMEN/SPECIALTY

furs

4 *e-5*

ROBERTS FURS

In addition to fine furs by top designers, this Union Square salon carries leather and shearling coats for men and women. The staff travels the world to buy furs, so it is very knowledgeable about the inventory. Services include storage, cleaning, repairs, and restyling. *272 Post St., at Stockton St., Union Square, 415/362–6608. Closed Sun.*

handbags

4 *e-5*

COACH

Women treasure their Coach handbags for their versatility, classic styling, and high quality. This shop carries only the Coach handbags and women's belts; a second location up the street carries men's leather goods and luggage (*see* Leather Goods & Luggage, *below*). *190 Post St., at Grant Ave., Union Square, 415/392–1772.*

4 *e-6*

HERMÈS

The entire range of elegant, high-status Hermès leather bags, wallets, and accessories is here. So are the famous silk scarves and ties, equestrian items, and sundry other treasures. This Union Square shop, designed by architect Madam Rena Dumas, is a beauty. *212 Stockton St., at Geary St., Union Square, 415/391–7200.*

hats

4 *e-6*

HATS ON POST

This Union Square boutique is San Francisco's best-known ladies' millinery. You'll find elegant hats with all the trimmings, rain hats, summer hats made of straw, and extravagant winter fur hats. Custom designs for brides are available. It also stocks a small collection of men's hats. *210 Post St., 2nd floor, at Grant Ave., Union Square, 415/392–3737. Closed Sun.*

lingerie & nightwear

4 *f-5*

ARICIE LINGERIE DE MARQUE

The beautiful lingerie, loungewear, and sleepwear sold here is by top designers such as Valentino, Wacoal, and Jezebel. The shop also has silk pajamas, boxers, and briefs for men. *50 Post St., between Montgomery and Kearny Sts., Financial District, 415/989–0261. Closed Sun.*

4 *a-4*

CAROL DODA'S CHAMPAGNE AND LACE LINGERIE BOUTIQUE

Let the legendary and alluring Carol Doda—who led the vanguard to legalize topless dancing in the 1960s—help you find just the right bra, teddy, bustier, corset, garter belt, slinky dress, or bikini. She also carries lingerie in larger sizes. *1850 Union St., between Laguna and Octavia Sts., Cow Hollow, 415/776–6900.*

5 *h-3*

CHADWICK'S OF LONDON

Bras, panties, and negligees are romantic rather than naughty at this old-fashioned store. Beautiful Eileen Fisher nightgowns take you back to the 19th century. *2068 Chestnut St., between Fillmore and Steiner Sts., Marina, 415/775–3423.*

7 *g-5*

GLADRAGS

See *Clothing for Women/General,* above.

4 e-1

MIDSUMMER NIGHTS LINGERIE

The intimate apparel here ranges from slinky to snuggly. Everything is reasonably priced, and there are even choices for petites and larger sizes. *Pier 39, The Embarcadero and Beach St., Fisherman's Wharf, 415/788–0992.*

4 a-5

TOUJOURS

This perfumed Presidio Heights boutique specializes in elegant and expensive lingerie of cotton, silk, and other natural fibers. It's a great place to go gift shopping. *2484 Sacramento St., at Fillmore St., Pacific Heights, 415/346–3988.*

4 e-6

VICTORIA'S SECRET

The famed lingerie chain has an especially large and well-stocked shop on Union Square, staffed with friendly and helpful personnel. There's plenty here for her, as well as a small selection of silk boxer shorts, robes, pajamas, and briefs for him. *335 Powell St., at Post St., Union Square, 415/433–9671.*

5 h-3

2061 Chestnut St., between Fillmore and Steiner Sts., Marina, 415/923–9750.

4 e-6

San Francisco Shopping Centre, 865 Market St., between 4th and 5th Sts., Union Square, 415/882–0864.

maternity

4 a-6

MATERNITÉ

Perfect for the working mother-to-be, this shop carries sophisticated maternity clothing for the office, as well as stylish evening wear and comfortable casual ensembles. *San Francisco Shopping Centre, 865 Market St., between 4th and 5th Sts., Union Square, 415/227–0825.*

4 a-4

MINIS

This small shop stocks everything from basic maternity clothes to children's outfits up to size 10. The maternity clothes include the usual jumpers and the "classic men's shirt." Popular baby clothes include San Francisco–themed T-shirts and rompers. *2042 Union St.,*

between Webster and Buchanan Sts., Cow Hollow, 415/567–9537.

shoes & boots

7 g-5

ASTRID'S RABAT

Astrid's concentrates on inexpensive, comfortable shoes, clogs, and boots for men and women. *3909 24th St., at Sanchez St., Noe Valley, 415/282–7400.*

4 e-5

BALLY OF SWITZERLAND

The Bally store sells high-quality men's and women's dress shoes. *238 Stockton St., at Sutter St., Union Square, 415/398–7463.*

4 e-6

BIRKENSTOCK NATURAL FOOTWEAR

Birkenstock has come a long way since it produced only its classic "Arizona" style. You'll be surprised at the variety of comfortable—and almost fashionable—shoes for sale here, including clogs and slip-ons with an embossed bubble pattern. *42 Stockton St., between Market and O'Farrell Sts., Union Square, 415/989–2475.*

4 b-8

GIMME SHOES

Hip European-designed shoes are styled for those willing to make an investment in quality footwear. Especially popular are shoes by such French designers as Robert Clergerie. *416 Hayes St., at Gough St., Hayes Valley, 415/864–0691.*

5 h-5

2358 Fillmore St., at Washington St., Pacific Heights, 415/441–3040.

4 e-6

JOAN & DAVID SHOES

The handsome, Italian-made shoes, handbags, and belts are all by the famous Joan & David designers. *172 Geary St., at Stockton St., Union Square, 415/397–1958.*

7 d-1

JOHN FLUEVOG SHOES

This branch of the Canada-based chain with stores in New York, Seattle, and Toronto is perhaps the largest and best stocked in the Haight. Here you'll find all the shoes you need to go clubbing, or simply look like you do. Improbably tall platform shoes are all the rage. *1697 Haight St., at Cole St., Haight, 415/436–9784.*

4 *e-6*

KENNETH COLE

High-quality, high-fashion footwear for work and for play is Kenneth Cole's bread and butter. Purses, briefcases, jackets, and belts complete the look. The Union Street location even stocks a Kenneth Cole diaper bag. *San Francisco Shopping Centre, 865 Market St., between 4th and 5th Sts., Union Square, 415/227–4536.*

4 *a-4*

2078 Union St., at Webster St., Cow Hollow, 415/346–2161.

7 *g-2*

NANA

See Clothing for Women/General, *above.*

7 *e-1*

SHOE BIZ

Come to this Haight-Ashbury shop for 7-inch platform sneakers, spiky heels, or whatever else might be the latest rage in Europe. The emphasis is on fun and style. *1446 Haight St., at Masonic Ave., Haight, 415/864–0990.*

swimsuits

4 *a-4*

CANYON BEACHWEAR

The only store in the city dedicated solely to women's swimwear, and one of the few places you can find a swimsuit out of season, the shop was named by *Vogue* as one of the best in the country. The staff will work with you to find you the suit that fits you perfectly. It also stocks some athletic suits, including a few Speedos. *1728 Union St., at Octavia St., Cow Hollow, 415/885–5070.*

CLOTHING FOR MEN/GENERAL

classic & casual

4 *e-6*

ALFRED DUNHILL OF LONDON

The American outpost of posh London-based Alfred Dunhill carries everything

for the man who enjoys spending lots of money on himself. Besides clothing with a decidedly British feel, you'll find luggage, toiletries, and fine cigars *(see* Tobacconists, *below)*. *250 Post St., at Stockton St., Union Square, 415/781–3368.*

4 *e-5*

BANANA REPUBLIC

See Clothing for Women/General, *above.*

4 *e-6*

BILLY BLUE

Financial District types who know what they like in clothing come to this 600-square-ft shop for its tiny but impeccably chosen collection of classic Italian clothes. Cashmere sweaters, camel hair coats, and shirts and suits custom made for the shop are examples of what you'll find here. *54 Geary St., between Grant Ave. and Kearny St., Union Square, 415/781–2111. Closed Sun.*

4 *e-5*

BROOKS BROTHERS

This classic men's store was established in 1818 and still sells the private-label button-down oxford shirts that first made it famous. The store has women's shirts, sweaters, blazers, slacks, and coats as well. *201 Post St., at Grant Ave., Union Square, 415/397–4500.*

4 *e-6*

BULLOCK & JONES

Bullock & Jones has been a favorite among successful businessmen since it was established in San Francisco in 1853. Best-sellers include its pima cotton dress shirts, linen and wool slacks, and private-label silk ties. *340 Post St., at Stockton St., Union Square, 415/392–4243.*

4 *e-5*

BURBERRY

See Clothing for Women/General, *above.*

4 *e-5*

CABLE CAR CLOTHIERS

A San Francisco tradition since 1939, this shop carries British and American classics in 100% cotton and pure wool. Its old-fashioned, high-quality pajamas and robes have long been favorites, as have their undergarments, gloves, tweed hats, caps, and scarves. *441 Sutter St., between Stockton and Powell Sts., Union Square, 415/397–4740. Closed Sun.*

`4` *e-6*

GAP

See Clothing for Women/General, *above.*

`4` *f-5*

THE HOUND GENTLEMEN'S CLOTHIERS

This shop carries clothing and accessories for the ambitious young Financial District professional. It has a good selection of robes and pajamas, too. *140 Sutter St., between Kearny and Montgomery Sts., Financial District, 415/989-0429. Closed Sun.*

`4` *f-5*

275 Battery St., between Sacramento and California Sts., Financial District, 415/982-1578. Closed weekends.

`4` *e-6*

J. CREW

See Clothing for Women/General, *above.*

`4` *e-5*

MAC (MODERN APPEALING CLOTHING)

See Clothing for Women/General, *above.*

`8` *c-2*

OLD NAVY

See Clothing for Women/General, *above.*

`4` *e-5*

SAKS FIFTH AVENUE, THE MEN'S STORE

Like most department stores, this one opens onto a fragrance counter and accessories like gloves, umbrellas, and wallets. But the difference is that this entire store is dedicated to men. The clothing is mostly a selection of classics. *220 Post St., between Stockton St. and Grant Ave., Union Square, 415/986-4300.*

`4` *e-5*

WILKES BASHFORD

A legendary San Francisco haberdashery, Wilkes Bashford carries menswear and accessories, both classic and trendy. Mayor Willie Brown has been known to shop here, among other prominent San Franciscans. The shop is famous for its customer service; its tailors will even make house and office calls. *375 Sutter St., between Grant Ave. and Stockton St., Union Square, 415/986-4380. Closed Sun.*

contemporary

`7` *f-3*

ALL AMERICAN BOY

If this shop stocks it, it must be the fashion of the moment among the gay men in the Castro. Eclectic barely begins to describe the selection here: choose from variously colored bandanas, itty-bitty Speedo bathing suits, and fashionably loud shirts. Top it all off with the sort of hat your father wears when mowing the lawn—to be worn with irony, surely. *463 Castro St., between Market and 18th Sts., Castro, 415/861-0444.*

`7` *e-1*

BEHIND THE POST OFFICE

See Clothing for Women/General, *above.*

`4` *d-6*

COURTOUÉ

The fine Italian suits here range in style from classic to avant-garde. Evening wear, sportswear, shoes, and accessories are also by Italian designers. If you want custom-made suits, there's an excellent fabric selection right on the premises. The shop's tie selection is one of the best in town. *459 Geary St., between Taylor and Mason Sts., Union Square, 415/775-2900. Closed Sun.*

`7` *a-6*

DAVID STEPHENS CLOTHIERS

David Stephens provides fine Italian menswear for the fashion conscious. Designer lines include Ermenigildo Zegna, Canali, Byblos, and the Redaelli line by Freer. *50 Maiden La., between Kearny St. and Grant Ave., Union Square, 415/982-1612. Closed Sun.*

`4` *e-6*

DIESEL

See Clothing for Women/General, *above.*

`4` *f-4*

KENNETH CHARLES

San Francisco's on-the-rise menswear designer, Kenneth Charles, showcases his fashions in an art gallery–like setting. The suits, jackets, shoes, sportswear, and accessories are stylish but affordable. *582 Washington St., between Sansome and Montgomery Sts., Financial District, 415/399-1059. Closed Sun.*

4 *b-8*

NOMADS

A must for artists and rock stars, this shop has cornered the market on upscale grunge fashions. It sells shepherd's vests, cowhide pants, and other clever necessities and accessories. *556 Hayes St., at Laguna St., Hayes Valley, 415/864–5692.*

7 *g-5*

OCEAN FRONT WALKERS

Printed T-shirts, boxer shorts, and pajamas with designs ranging from animal wildlife to 1950s iconography are all available at this friendly neighborhood store. *4069 24th St., at Noe St., Noe Valley, 415/550–1980.*

7 *f-3*

ROLO

This Rolo and the Market Street location sell groovy club gear for men. (*See also* Clothing for Women/General, *above.*) *450 Castro St., at 18th St., Castro, 415/ 626–7171.*

7 *f-3*

2351 Market St., at Castro St., Castro, 415/ 431–4545.

4 *e-5*

THE TAILORED MAN

The helpful, multilingual staff will help you choose stylish menswear by top American and European designers. This shop has one of the largest tie selections in the Bay Area. *360 Sutter St., between Stockton St. and Grant Ave., Union Square, 415/397–6906. Closed Sun.*

custom

4 *d-6*

COURTOUÉ

See above.

discount & outlet

4 *f-5*

THE MEN'S WEARHOUSE

Fine men's suits, sport coats, accessories, and shoes by top designers are sold 20% to 30% below retail at this shop, part of a national chain. The sales staff is pleasant and dedicated to customer service. *601 Market St., at 2nd St., Financial District, 415/896–0871.*

4 *e-6*

17 Stockton St., between Ellis and O'Farrell Sts., Union Square, 415/544–0627.

unusual sizes

4 *f-6*

CALIFORNIA BIG AND TALL CLOTHING MART

This off-price and clearance center is a great place for great values for hard-to-fit men. Shoes by Bally, Capezio, and Zodiac sell for as much as 60% below retail. *625 Howard St., between 2nd and 3rd Sts., South of Market, 415/495–4484. Closed Sun. and Mon.*

4 *f-6*

ROCHESTER BIG AND TALL

Rochester has a good selection of suits, sport coats, trousers, sportswear, and formalwear in sizes ranging from 46 regular to 60 extra-long. Their shoe department also deals in hard-to-find sizes. *700 Mission St., at 3rd St., South of Market, 415/982–6455.*

4 *f-6*

THE SHORT SHOP

Men from 4'10" to 5'7" can finally find clothes that fit at this downtown store, where even the socks and ties come proportioned differently for the short-statured man. The fashions run the gamut from bright Hawaiian shirts to tuxedos. Shoes come in sizes 5 to 8. *49 Kearny St., between Geary St. and Post St., Financial District, 415/296–9744. Closed Sun.*

vintage & resale

See *Clothing for Women/General*, above.

CLOTHING FOR MEN/SPECIALTY

formalwear

2 *c-6*

GINGISS FORMALWEAR

The advantage of doing business with this chain, which has more than 200 stores nationwide, is the ability to coordinate services between cities for major events. Designer tuxedos are available for sale or rent, in addition to shoes, ties, and cummerbunds. *Stonestown Galleria, 19th Ave. and Winston Dr., Stonestown, 415/665–1144.*

4 f-5

SELIX

Selix has branches all over the Bay Area, all linked by computer to coordinate wedding information. Designer tuxedos are available for sale or rent, and all accessories are sold. *123 Kearny St., between Post and Sutter Sts., Financial District, 415/362–1133.*

2 b-6

2622 Ocean Ave., at 19th Ave., Stonestown, 415/333–2412.

shoes & boots

4 e-6

BIRKENSTOCK NATURAL FOOTWEAR

See Clothing for Women/Specialty, *above.*

4 f-5

CASSERD SHOES

This Financial District shoe store has a good selection of dress and casual men's shoes at reasonable prices. It covers narrow and extra-wide sizes, as well as elevator shoes. *310 Kearny St., at Bush St., Financial District, 415/421–5690. Closed Sun.*

4 f-5

CHURCH'S ENGLISH SHOES LTD.

This shop carries the famed high-quality Church's English-made shoes as well as expensive Italian and American footwear for men. Rounding out the selection: ties, slippers, and small leather goods. *Crocker Galleria, 50 Post St., between Montgomery and Kearny Sts., Financial District, 415/433–5100. Closed Sun.*

4 e-6

KENNETH COLE

See Clothing for Women/Specialty, *above.*

ties

4 e-5

THE TAILORED MAN

See Clothing for Men/General, *above.*

underwear

4 f-5

ARICIE LINGERIE DE MARQUE

See Clothing for Women/Specialty, *above.*

4 e-6

VICTORIA'S SECRET

See Clothing for Women/Specialty, *above.*

COINS

2 c-6

DON'S VILLAGE COINS

Don's buys and sells American coins, particularly those from the 18th century. The shop also deals in gold coins from all countries. *2536 Ocean Ave., at 19th Ave., Stonestown, 415/584–2515. Closed Sun.*

4 f-5

WITTER COINS

Established in 1959, this shop in the Hobart Building of the Financial District buys, sells, and appraises American and foreign coins. *582 Market St., Suite 1409, at Montgomery St., Financial District, 415/781–5690. Closed weekends.*

COMPUTERS & SOFTWARE

4 e-7

CENTRAL COMPUTER SYSTEMS INC.

This Silicon Valley–based company has everything for the PC: modems, monitors, printers, scanners, CDs, and software. *837 Howard St., between 4th and 5th Sts., 415/495–5888.*

4 f-6

COMP USA

This mammoth newcomer sells computers and all its accoutrements—software, cables, joysticks, carrying cases, you name it. Although service is spotty, the selection is huge and prices are among the lowest in the city. *750 Market St., at 3rd St., Financial District, 415/391–9778.*

4 e-8

MACADAM COMPUTERS

Mac users drop by this Mac-only store on a regular basis to check out the latest software and gadgets. There's a full range of hardware, especially monitors, and of software, especially graphics programs. If you pay by cash or check instead of credit card, you receive a 3%

discount. *1062 Folsom St., between 6th and 7th Sts., South of Market, 415/863–6222.*

4 *e-6*

MICROSOFT SF

Opened in 1999 as the only Microsoft retail store in the world, this glitzy shop in the Metreon sells the usual Microsoft software—including Encarta encyclopedias and Web publishing tools—as well as desk accessories and souvenirs. Mugs, notepads, and CD holders come in funky, fashionable colors. *Metreon, 4th and Mission Sts., South of Market, 415/369–6030.*

4 *a-7*

PERSONAL COMPUTERS FOR LESS

This shop stocks some new computers, and many used computers (mostly PCs). Let owner Don Marshall help you choose the hardware and software that suits you best. It's open on Saturday by appointment. *1309 Fillmore St., at Eddy St., Western Addition, 415/346–1692. Closed weekends.*

CRAFT & HOBBY SUPPLIES

7 *h-5*

CRADLE OF THE SUN

In addition to a fine collection of hand-blown art glass, Tiffany-style lamps, and stained-glass panels, you'll find stained-glass window tools, supplies, and training at this unusual crafts store. Sign up far in advance; there's a six-month waiting list for beginners classes. *3848 24th St., between Church and Sanchez Sts., Noe Valley, 415/821–7667. Closed Mon.*

4 *f-8*

FANTASTICO

This SoMa discount warehouse stocks supplies for any and all kinds of crafts. It has an enormous assortment of dried and silk flowers, ribbons, and wire for bouquet making, as well as hundreds of baskets. *559 6th St., between Brannan and Bryant Sts., South of Market, 415/982–0680. Closed Sun.*

5 *a-7*

THE HOBBY COMPANY OF SAN FRANCISCO

For hobbyists, this is the best shop in San Francisco. It's stocked with all sorts of goodies, including model cars, airplanes, and boats; dollhouses and miniatures; paints, thread, and yarn; stenciling and stamp making supplies. *5150 Geary Blvd., at 16th Ave., Richmond District, 415/386–2802.*

4 *a-2*

ORION TELESCOPES AND BINOCULARS

Everything a stargazer could want is here, at the Bay Area's largest shop devoted to astronomical telescopes. The small refractor telescopes cost around $100, and top models sell for well over $1,000. *3609 Buchanan St., at Bay St., Marina, 415/931–9966. Closed Mon.*

ELECTRONICS & AUDIO

7 *f-3*

EBER ELECTRONICS

Although Eber specializes in large-screen home-theater equipment, it's also well stocked with electronic essentials like TVs, VCRs, camcorders, speakers, telephones, and fax machines. The staff is extremely knowledgeable. *2355 Market St., at Castro St., Castro, 415/621–4332.*

4 *f-5*

THE GOOD GUYS

At this full-service audio/video showroom, part of a national chain, try for good deals on TVs, VCRs, and stereo components. You can almost always get 10% off the list price on big-ticket items simply by looking like you mean it when you ask. *1400 Van Ness Ave., at Bush St., Financial District, 415/775–9323.*

4 *c-8*

LASER CITY HOME ENTERTAINMENT

Specializing in home theater items, this store sells large-screen TVs, DVD and laser disc players, and even karaoke systems. *1390 Market St., at Polk St., Civic Center, 415/241–9664.*

5 *g-6*

PERFORMANCE AUDIO

Audiophiles and those who demand the best in home theater shop here for high-definition TVs, Zenith Pro components, and other high-performance items. The staff will arrange custom installment of components at your home. *2847 Califor-*

nia St., at Divisadero St., Pacific Heights, 415/441–6427.

4 *e-6*

SONY STYLE

All of Sony's highest-tech items are here, displayed artfully on shelves as if it were a gallery. Some of the mini stereo systems here look so sleek you expect them to fly. As well as a huge selection of every type of Sony Walkman and Discman, you'll also find videophiles clustered around high-definition TVs. Pick up a large-screen version for a mere $12,000. *Metreon, 4th and Mission Sts., South of Market, 415/369–6050.*

EROTICA

8 *a-5*

GOOD VIBRATIONS

This friendly, woman-owned-and-operated shop describes itself as a "clean, well-lighted place to shop for sex toys, books, and videos." *1210 Valencia St., at 23rd St., Mission, 415/974–8980.*

3 *c-3*

2504 San Pablo Ave., at Dwight Way, Berkeley, 510/841–8987.

7 *g-2*

ROMANTASY

At this "sensual, erotic shop for loving couples and romantic singles," you can purchase such essentials *d'amour* as liquid latex, lacy underthings, tantra love swings, and chinchilla-lined G-strings. It specializes in custom-made corsets. *2191 Market St., at Sanchez St., Castro, 415/487–9909. Closed Mon.*

EYEWEAR

7 *h-2*

EYEDARE

In this small shop, fashionable frames, mostly by European and Japanese designers, are displayed like the artwork they are. *3199 16th St., at Guerrero St., Mission, 415/241–0240. Closed Sun.*

5 *h-5*

INVISION OPTOMETRY

In addition to frames by companies like Saki and Oliver Peoples, you'll see eyewear by designers not carried in most other stores. Check out the unbelievably tiny, rimless spectacles by Kazuo

Kawasaki. *1907 Fillmore St., between Bush and Pine Sts., 415/563–9003.*

4 *e-5*

OPTICAL UNDERGROUND DESIGNER OUTLET

Designer frames are sold at a discount of at least 30% at this well-stocked shop, where Alain Mikli, Donna Karan, and Modo are just some of the designers on display. It also specializes in high-end lenses, which will make your old Coke-bottle lenses seem like a distant nightmare. *280 Sutter St., at Grant Ave., Union Square, 415/982–5106. Closed Sun.*

1 *o-5*

RIMS AND GOGGLES

Fashionable French and Italian frames are the specialty here. Most glasses can be ready the same day. *445 Sutter St., between Stockton and Powell Sts., Union Square, 415/397–3110. Closed Sun.*

5 *f-6*

3568 Sacramento St., between Laurel and Locust Sts., Laurel Heights, 415/346–0304. Closed Sun.

4 *e-6*

SITE FOR SORE EYES

Almost everyone can find something to suit them at this friendly, well-respected chain store that often shows up in the *Bay Guardian* "Best of the Bay" issue. Many glasses can be made in one hour. *901 Market St., at 5th St., Union Square, 415/495–2020.*

4 *f-5*

140 Battery St., between California and Pine Sts., Financial District, 415/421–2020. Closed Sun.

4 *e-6*

SPECTACLE SHOPPE

Classic and not-too-cutting-edge frames by Cartier, Mont Blanc, and Alain Mikli line the walls here. There's an unusually good selection of Escada sunglasses. *177 Maiden La., at Stockton St., Union Square, 415/781–8556. Closed Sun.*

7 *g-2*

URBAN EYES

Hip but not haughty, the staff here is happy to answer questions about the wide array of specs by Oliver Peoples and LA Eyeworks, as well as the many Ralph Lauren sunglasses. *2253 Market*

St., between Noe and Sanchez Sts., Castro, 415/863–1818. Closed Sun. and Tues.

FABRICS & ZIPPERS

4 *e-6*

BRITEX FABRICS

A San Francisco institution since 1952, Britex has the West Coast's largest selection of fabrics and notions on four spacious, well-organized floors. Alongside the latest in bridal, couture, menswear, and home decorating fabrics, you'll find trims, tassels, and more than 30,000 buttons. *146 Geary St., between Stockton St. and Grant Ave., Union Square, 415/392–2910. Closed Sun.*

7 *e-1*

DISCOUNT FABRICS

The satin, wool, and cotton fabrics are cheap here, and there is a limited selection of patterns for sale: Simplicity patterns are only 99 cents. Buttons are 10 for $1 in the discount button bin, and you can buy zippers by the yard. *1432 Haight St., at Masonic Ave., Haight, 415/621–5584.*

4 *e-4*

FAR EAST FASHIONS

There are a few fabric stores in Chinatown to browse through, but this shop has one of the neighborhood's better selections of Chinese embossed silks. *953 Grant Ave., between Jackson and Washington Sts., Chinatown, 415/362–8171 or 415/362–0986.*

7 *d-1*

FAR-OUT FABRICS

In the back of Mendel's Art and Stationery Supplies (*see Art Supplies, above*) is a collection of "far-out" fabrics, particularly of the wild '60s genre. Day-Glo and fuzzy fabrics are well represented. *1556 Haight St., between Ashbury and Clayton Sts., Haight, 415/621–1287.*

3 *d-2*

KASURI DYEWORKS

Come here for traditional Japanese fabrics including handwoven and hand-dyed silk, cotton, and wool. Services include custom-made futon covers, clothing, and bedspreads. *1959 Shattuck Ave., at University Ave., Berkeley, 510/841–4509. Closed Sun. and Mon.*

8 *c-1*

SAL BERESSI FABRICS

This warehouse is an excellent resource for fine upholstery, drapery, and bedspread fabrics, usually priced 40% below wholesale. The best bargains can be found at its two annual sales, which run from mid-April through May and mid-October through November. *1504 Bryant St., 2nd floor, near 11th St., South of Market, 415/861–5004. Closed Sun.*

9 *d-3*

STONEMOUNTAIN AND DAUGHTER

Beautiful fabrics for dressmaking and quilting are the specialty at this East Bay store, spread out over two floors and three rooms. You'll find a good selection of cotton prints and bridal fabrics. *516 Shattuck Ave., at Dwight Way, Berkeley, 510/845–6106.*

FLEA MARKETS

2 *f-6*

FLEA MARKET

This flea market has lots of cast-off knickknacks, plus small selections of clothing, household appliances, furniture, and some antiques and collectibles. Prices tend to be lower than at other city flea markets. *100 Alemany Blvd., at Crescent Ave., Bernal Heights, 415/647–2043. Sun. only.*

4 *f-2*

PIER 29 ANTIQUE AND COLLECTIBLES MARKET

This is the largest weekly indoor antiques and collectibles market in California. The city's upscale flea market, it has around 100 indoor booths selling antique furniture, rare books, vintage clothing, kitchenware, jewelry, and collectibles. Unlike other San Francisco flea markets, it charges admission: $2, or $10 before 9:30 AM. *Pier 29, between Sansome and Battery Sts., Embarcadero, no phone. Sun. only.*

8 *a-1*

SAN FRANCISCO FLEA MARKET

Most of the items for sale here are junk: plastic toys, Chinese-made batteries, and used clothes that were never in fashion. However, it's worth a look if you're searching for new or used kitchen appliances, clock radios, and other small electronics. *1651 Mission St., between S. Van Ness Ave. and 12th St., South of Market, 415/646–0544. Weekends only.*

1 *d-3*

TREASURE ISLAND FLEA MARKET

San Francisco's newest flea market, scenically situated off the Bay Bridge between San Francisco and Oakland, is a winner: the usual odds and ends are mixed in with an interesting selection of antiques and crafts. It opens Sunday at 6 AM, and, as always, early birds will be rewarded. *Avenue of the Palms at 4th St., Treasure Island, 415/255–1923. Sun. only.*

FLOWERS & PLANTS

4 *c-2*

BEACH BONSAI

Cypress and pomegranate are only a few of the miniature bonsai trees lining the walls. You can also pick up bonsai accessories such as trays and pebbles. The staff will pack and ship trees to almost anywhere. *500 Beach St., Suite 120, between Leavenworth and Jones Sts., Fisherman's Wharf, 415/771–7998.*

5 *h-4*

A BED OF ROSES

This neighborhood florist has a wonderful selection of cut flowers, interesting vases and baskets, and old-fashioned wrought-iron plant stands. *2274 Union St., between Fillmore and Steiner Sts., Cow Hollow, 415/922–5150. Closed Sun.*

7 *h-2*

CHURCH STREET FLOWERS

This fragrant little shop stocks a beautiful selection of perfectly fresh flowers. The charming and friendly florists will wrap up your selections, tying a little cluster of lisianthus or other flowers to them for good measure. *212 Church St., at Market St., Castro, 415/553–7762.*

5 *g-3*

FIORI

This is where society ladies call when they need armloads of flowers for their luncheons or Christmas parties: Fiori is well respected for its event-planning team that can arrange spectacular flowers for any event. The rest of us can just go into their shop and inhale deeply, maybe picking up a phalaenopsis orchid to take home. *2314 Chestnut St., between Scott and Divisadero Sts., Marina, 415/346–1100.*

4 *a-6*

FLEURTATIONS

Even on Sundays you can buy unusual fresh flowers at this Upper Fillmore shop. It also has one of the city's best selections of silk and dried flowers. *1880 Fillmore St., between Sutter and Bush Sts., Japantown, 415/923–1070. Closed Mon.*

4 *a-3*

HOOGASIAN FLOWERS

This full-service FTD florist will whip up a beautiful floral or balloon bouquet for you in minutes flat. It also has a handy outdoor flower stand downtown, at 250 Post Street. *1674 Lombard St., at Octavia St., Marina, 415/885–4321.*

7 *g-3*

HORTICA

Inside what looks like just a small plant shop, with orchids and other potted plants in the window, is a full-fledged little nursery selling everything from seed to fertilizer to small garden tools. Behind the store, in the backyard, you'll find everything from tomato plants to Icelandic poppies. *566 Castro St., between 18th and 19th Sts., Castro, 415/863–4697.*

4 *b-5*

THE PLANT WAREHOUSE

All kinds of plants are available at this 5,000-square-ft shop, from the common to the exotic. The emphasis is on tropical indoor plants; there's also a large selection of orchids. *1355 Bush St., between Polk and Larkin Sts., Polk Gulch, 415/885–1515.*

4 *f-8*

PODESTA BALDOCCHI

This friendly, old-fashioned florist has been in business since 1871 and is one of the largest in the city. In addition to cut flowers and indoor plants, you can pick up balloon bouquets, fruit baskets, and other creative bouquets. *508 4th St., at Bryant St., South of Market, 415/346–1300. Closed Sun.*

4 c-8

RED DESERT

Red Desert is worth a visit even if you're not planning to buy: hundreds of species of cacti are for sale here, tall and small, rare and common, for indoors or out. *1632 Market St., at Franklin St., Hayes Valley, 415/552–2800.*

4 c-7

ROSE BOWL FLORIST

Conveniently located in the Opera Plaza, this florist does stunningly beautiful work with exotic flowers and plants. The staff will also assemble impressive gift baskets that include California wines, French champagnes, and gourmet food items. The shop is open some weekends; call ahead to find out. *601 Van Ness Ave., between Turk St. and Golden Gate Ave., Civic Center, 415/474–1114. Closed weekends.*

5 h-4

VALENTINE & RIEDINGER

As you walk through a narrow passageway to this store, a sign warns "Danger: Walking Beyond This Point You Could be Subject to Stress Reduction." The sign is right. The passageway leads to a peaceful, shady, and aromatic garden and ramshackle shop selling whimsical flowerpots, plants, garden accessories, and cut flowers. *2164 Union St., between Webster and Fillmore Sts., Cow Hollow, 415/346–1001.*

FOLK ART & HANDICRAFTS

See also *Charitable Causes,* above.

4 b-8

AFRICAN OUTLET

This shop carries beautiful handmade goods from all over Africa—masks from Kenya, Berber and Tuareg jewelry, brilliant Senegalese textiles, and authentic Zulu spears, among other things. *524 Octavia St., at Hayes St., Hayes Valley, 415/864–3576.*

4 a-4

ANOKHI

Clothing, home furnishings, and accessories from India are the stock-in-trade here. The small shop is crowded with unusual treasures such as Indian tea caddies, bolts of hand-printed fabrics, hand-thrown pottery, and wooden chil-

dren's toys. *1864 Union St., at Laguna St., Cow Hollow, 415/922–4441.*

4 a-6

ASAKICHI

Drop by this cozy little shop for beautifully crafted Japanese items such as wind chimes, teapots, and handmade chopsticks. The store also carries small pieces of furniture, such as tansu chests. *Japan Center, on the bridge between Kinokuniya and Kintetsu Bldgs., Japantown, 415/921–3821.*

5 h-3

ASIAN POINT OF VIEW

Asian knickknacks come in both beautiful and whimsical varieties: lovely bonsai dogwood trees sit next to small candles so realistically shaped like sushi you're tempted to eat them. There's also a good selection of origami instruction books and paper. *2260 Chestnut St., at Avila St., Marina, 415/351–2742. Closed Mon.*

8 e-3

COLLAGE GALLERY

The work of more than 50 Bay Area artists is featured at this studio gallery. The selection of handmade crafts varies but usually includes some mosaic mirrors, handblown glass objects, handmade jewelry, and delicate glazed vases. *1345 18th St., near Arkansas St., Potrero Hill, 415/282–4401. Closed Mon.*

4 e-6

FOLK ART INTERNATIONAL/ XANADU TRIBAL ARTS/ BORETTI AMBER & DESIGN

Three stores have teamed up to create an enchanting shop in the landmark Frank Lloyd Wright building on Maiden Lane, where the central spiral staircase is reminiscent of the Guggenheim Museum in New York City. Beautiful items like Chinese lacquer bride's boxes and painted pottery come with a hefty price tag. *140 Maiden La., between Stockton St. and Grant Ave., Union Square, 415/392–9999. Closed Sun.*

4 f-4

JAPONESQUE

Japonesque's owner travels to Japan once or twice each year to collect items for the shop, and all are of very high quality. Unlike the mass-produced goods for sale in most stores in Japantown, the antique and contemporary stone, wood, glass, ceramic, and lacquer objects here are fine art pieces. There are also sculptures, paintings, and handcrafted wooden boxes. *824 Montgomery St., between Jackson St. and Pacific Ave., Jackson Square, 415/391–8860. Closed Sun. and Mon.*

4 *a-6*

MA-SHI'-KO FOLKCRAFT

In Japan Center, Ma-Shi'-Ko carries handcrafted pottery from Japan. A specialty is *mashiko*, the style that has been in production longer than any other. There are also masks and other antique and handcrafted goods, all from Japan. *Kinokuniya Bldg., 2nd floor, 1581 Webster St., at Post St., Japantown, 415/346–0748. Closed Tues.*

4 *a-6*

NILE TRADING CO. AFRICAN ART GALLERY

African masks, sculpture, beaded jewelry, and baskets fill this jumbled little shop. Owner Rose Okello is happy to explain the significance of the ethnographic art in the shop. *1856 Fillmore St., between Sutter and Bush Sts., Pacific Heights, 415/776–2233.*

4 *b-8*

POLANCO

More like a gallery than a shop, Polanco showcases the arts and crafts of Mexico—everything from antiques and folk crafts to fine contemporary paintings. Its collection of Day of the Dead figures and religious statues is impressive. *393 Hayes St., between Franklin and Gough Sts., Hayes Valley, 415/252–5753. Closed Sun. and Mon.*

8 *c-5*

STUDIO 24

Part of the acclaimed Galería de la Raza (*see* Art Galleries *in* Chapter 4), Studio 24 is a fabulous spot to shop for Latin American folk art, works by contemporary artists, or kitschy Mexican products like strings of jalapeño Christmas lights. Proceeds support the gallery. *2857 24th St., at Bryant St., Mission, 415/826–8009.*

5 *g-5*

V. BREIER

Every piece in this colorful gallery is one-of-a-kind, from jewelry and ceramics to light fixtures and furniture. The bulk of

what's sold is contemporary and traditional North American crafts, mostly by emerging artists, with a sprinkling of items from Asian countries such as Japan and India. *3091 Sacramento St., between Baker and Broderick Sts., Pacific Heights, 415/929–7173.*

7 *g-5*

XELA

This wonderful Noe Valley shop (the name is pronounced "shay-la") sells ancient and contemporary art and crafts from Africa, central Asia, Indonesia, Latin America, and elsewhere. The collection of ethnic jewelry is superb. *3925 24th St., between Sanchez and Noe Sts., Noe Valley, 415/695–1323.*

FOOD & DRINK

baked goods

8 *a 3*

ANNA'S DANISH COOKIE CO.

Anna's has been baking Danish cookies—as well as cakes, brownies, and pastries—since 1936. It also has a large assortment of cookie jars and tins for sale. *3560 18th St., between Valencia and Guerrero Sts., Mission, 415/863–3882. Closed Sun. and Mon.*

4 *c-4*

THE BAGELRY

Transplanted New Yorkers recommended this down-to-earth shop for fresh bagels, bialys, lox, whitefish, and cream-cheese spreads. *2139-A Polk St., at Broadway, Russian Hill, 415/441–3003.*

4 *a-4*

BEPPLES PIES

This San Francisco legend is most famous for mouthwatering fruit pies, but also makes tasty meat- and vegetable-filled pies. Most people get their pies to go, but the shop also has a small café area for salads, soups, and (of course) pies. *1934 Union St., between Laguna and Buchanan Sts., Cow Hollow, 415/931–6225.*

4 *d-8*

THE CAKE GALLERY

Some of the cakes on display here would make a sailor blush. The shop specializes in funny and novel custom cakes, and will bake one to look like *anything*, in any size, and can even copy a photo in full living color on the cake of your choice. Naturally this is the bakery of choice for bachelor parties. *290 9th St., between Folsom and Howard Sts., South of Market, 415/861–2253. Closed Sun.*

8 *c-5*
CASA SANCHEZ
Heavenly soft, fresh tortillas are the draw at this small taquería. Several varieties and sizes are available daily. *2778 24th St., between York and Hampshire Sts., Mission, 415/282–2400. Closed Sun.*

5 *c-8*
CINDERELLA BAKERY, DELICATESSEN & RESTAURANT
The best piroshki and piroghi in the city are made here fresh daily. The deli also sells such delicacies as borscht, blini, and cabbage rolls. The tearoom is a gathering place for the neighborhood's Russian immigrants. *436 Balboa St., between 5th and 6th Aves., Richmond District, 415/751–9690. Closed Mon.*

4 *e-3*
DANILO
Baked fresh daily in this North Beach shop are Italian country-style bread loaves, grissini bread sticks, anise-flavored cookies, Genovese-style panettone, and to-die-for chocolate tortes. *516 Green St., between Stockton St. and Grant Ave., North Beach, 415/989–1806.*

8 *a-5*
DIANDA ITALIAN-AMERICAN PASTRY
Elio Dianda worked as a pastry chef in Lucca, Italy, for four decades before setting up this pair of San Francisco stores. Today his sons carry on the same fine tradition, making fresh biscotti, *torte de mandorle* (almond tortes), *zuppa inglese* (liquor-soaked sponge cake layered with custard and/or whipped cream), *panforte* (dense fruit, nut, and cocoa cake), St. Honoré cakes, panettone, and other treats. *2883 Mission St., between 24th and 25th Sts., Mission, 415/647–5469.*

8 *c-5*
DOMINGUEZ MEXICAN BAKERY
Hot and crispy *churros* (Mexican doughnuts dusted with cinnamon) are the specialty here. The bakery also makes

Latin American treats such as eggbread, crescent rolls, and *panes dulces* (pastries) and sells imported groceries and colorful piñatas. *2951 24th St., at Alabama St., Mission, 415/821–1717.*

7 *h-2*
JUST DESSERTS
This Bay Area favorite carries delectable chocolate velvet mousse cake, almond-flavored chocolate-chip blondies, and other sinful splurges. *248 Church St., at Market St., Castro, 415/626–5774.*

4 *g-4*
3 Embarcadero Center, Embarcadero, 415/ 421–1609.

4 *a-2*
3735 Buchanan St., between Marina Blvd. and North Point St., Marina, 415/922– 8675.

7 *h-3*
LADY BALTIMORE CAKE CO.
At this new bakery, opened in 1999, eclairs, glistening fruit tarts, and decadent little chocolate cakes tempt you. It also bakes custom cakes for special occasions. *600 Guerrero St., at 18th St., Mission, 415/437–5151.*

8 *c-5*
LA VICTORIA MEXICAN BAKERY AND GROCERY
The venerable La Victoria is the Mexican cookie capital of the Mission. You'll also find Mexican breads, cakes, and other goodies at this old favorite. *2937 24th St., at Alabama St., Mission, 415/ 550–9292.*

4 *e-3*
LIGURIA BAKERY
Delicious focaccia bread is the only product of this North Beach bakery— and it's baked the Italian way, in an old-fashioned brick oven. *1700 Stockton St., at Filbert St., North Beach, 415/421–3786.*

7 *g-5*
MANHATTAN BAGEL
To find this San Francisco bagelry, just follow the aroma of fresh bagels, bialys, challah, hamentaschen, *rugelach* (fruit-, nut-, or jam-filled cookies), and *mandelbrot* (sweet almond bread). New York–style deli items include pickles, lox, whitefish, and cream-cheese spreads. *3872 24th St., at Sanchez St., Noe Valley, 415/647–3334.*

7 *e-1*

1206 Masonic Ave., at Haight St., Haight, 415/626–9111.

5 *h-3*

NOAH'S NEW YORK BAGELS

What started as a single shop in Berkeley has grown to become a California bagel empire. The dozen or so San Francisco Noah's are known for fresh, delicious, New York–style Kosher bagels and spreads, and friendly service. On Sunday mornings the line at any given neighborhood Noah's often snakes outside the door. *2075 Chestnut St., at Steiner St., Marina, 415/775–2910.*

7 *f-3*

400 Castro St., at Market St., Castro, 415/552–2256.

4 *a-4*

1887 Union St., between Laguna and Octavia Sts., Cow Hollow, 415/346–4095.

2 *g-2*

221 Montgomery St., at Bush St., Financial District, 415/398–3378.

4 *b-8*

PENDRAGON BAKERY

San Francisco city and county employees flock to this tiny, inconspicuous bakery near the Civic Center. In the mornings they come for blueberry scones, streusel, and strong coffee, and in the afternoons for quiche, pastries, and cakes. *400 Hayes St., at Gough St., Hayes Valley, 415/552–7017.*

7 *g-2*

SWEET INSPIRATION

Muffins, scones, tarts, tortes, cheesecakes, and breads are all part of this popular bakery's repertoire, although it also makes beautiful wedding cakes. The indoor table seating provides a tranquil retreat. *2239 Market St., at Sanchez St., Noe Valley, 415/621–8664.*

4 *a-5*

2123 Fillmore St., at California St., Pacific Heights, 415/931–2815.

7 *b-2*

TART TO TART

At this bustling Sunset hangout, many of the tarts, scones, muffins, and other desserts look like works of art. The emphasis is on natural, wholesome ingredients. *641 Irving St., between*

7th and 8th Aves., Sunset District, 415/753–0643.

4 *e-4*

VICTORIA PASTRY CO.

This North Beach bakery has been around since the beginning of the century. Its specialties are Italian pastries (try the horseshoes) and St. Honoré cakes. *1362 Stockton St., at Vallejo St., North Beach, 415/781–2015.*

chocolate & other candy

4 *e-1*

CHOCOLATE HEAVEN

This is the place to get silly treats like milk-chocolate tool kits, golf clubs, champagne bottles, dog bones, playing cards, and bingo games. There are more than 1,000 different chocolate items to choose from. *Pier 39, The Embarcadero and Beach St., Fisherman's Wharf, 415/421–1789.*

4 *e-6*

CHOCOLATES BY BERNARD CALLEBAUT

Although not as well known as other city chocolatiers, this shop is quickly earning kudos for its decadent, and expensive, chocolates. After you have one of its walnut-shape dark-chocolate candies filled with a white chocolate ganache, you may never be able to go back to

---

THE BAY AREA'S BEST CHOCOLATE

It seems no one can quite agree which of San Francisco's chocolate shops sells the most decadent treats. Try a piece from each of the following contenders and decide for yourself:

Chocolates by Bernard Callebaut
Dark chocolate candies define the genre.

Faerie Queene Rococoa Chocolates
Fanciful chocolates made from the best ingredients.

Joseph Schmidt Confections
Sold at boutiques around town and at their own store.

Teuscher Chocolates of Switzerland
Famous for its champagne-filled truffles.

Hershey's. *75 O'Farrell St., between Stockton and Grant Sts., Union Square, 415/781–2601.*

4 *g-4*

CONFETTI LE CHOCOLATIER
Come here for candy from all over the world: chocolate imported from France and Belgium, licorice and Gummi Bears from Germany, and hard candies from Spain, among many other choices. *4 Embarcadero Center, Clay and Sacramento Sts. between Battery and Drumm Sts., Embarcadero, 415/362–1706.*

4 *c-2*

The Cannery, 2801 Leavenworth St., at Beach St., Fisherman's Wharf, 415/474–7377.

7 *f-3*

FAERIE QUEENE ROCOCOA CHOCOLATES
Some of the city's most extravagant chocolates and fudge are made and sold in this tiny shop. The amusing decor extends to the exceedingly long names of the chocolates: Try the "Slap in the Face" or the "Roll Me Over in the Clover." *415 Castro St., between Market and 18th Sts., Castro, 415/252–5814.*

4 *b-2*

GHIRARDELLI CHOCOLATE MANUFACTORY AND SODA FOUNTAIN
The Ghirardelli company is San Francisco's most famous chocolate maker. At the shop in Ghirardelli Square you can buy bars of Ghirardelli chocolate to take home, or sit down to a triple hot-fudge sundae. *Ghirardelli Square, 900 North Point St., at Polk St., Fisherman's Wharf, 415/771–4903.*

7 *g-2*

JOSEPH SCHMIDT CONFECTIONS
This is the best place to buy gourmet chocolate in San Francisco. Joseph Schmidt, a Swiss-trained candy maker, sculpts chocolates into fanciful shapes, ranging from chocolate windmills to life-size chocolate turkeys. Egg-shape truffles, which come in more than 30 flavors, are another best-seller; they're also sold in specialty boutiques around the city. *3489 16th St., at Sanchez St., Noe Valley, 415/861–8682. Closed Sun.*

8 *c-5*

ST. FRANCIS FOUNTAIN
This family-owned soda fountain has sold homemade candy and other old-fashioned treats since 1918 (*see* American/Casual *in* Chapter 1). *2801 24th St., at York St., Mission, 415/826–4200.*

4 *e-5*

TEUSCHER CHOCOLATES OF SWITZERLAND
Teuscher is best known for its dreamy champagne-filled chocolate truffles, sold singly or by the box. These ultimate Swiss treats are flown in from Geneva once a week. *255 Grant Ave., at Sutter St., Union Square, 415/398–2700.*

cheese

5 *h-5*

CALIFORNIA STREET CREAMERY
As well as a large number of cheeses, the shop stocks a good selection of dairy products. You'll also find pâtés, including vegetable and goose liver. *2413 California St., between Fillmore and Steiner Sts., 415/929–8610.*

7 *f-3*

CASTRO CHEESERY
In addition to a good selection of domestic and imported cheeses, this Castro shop has the best cheap coffee in town. It sells some fine stuff for as little as half the price at other gourmet java shops. *427 Castro St., at Market St., Castro, 415/552–6676.*

4 *h-8*

COUNTRY CHEESE INC.
This shop sells a wide range of imported and domestic cheeses in bulk at good prices, including delicious locally made mozzarella. Dried fruit, beans, grains, nuts, and spices are also sold in bulk. *415 Divisadero St., between Oak and Fell Sts., Western Addition, 415/621–8130. Closed Sun.*

7 *d-6*

CREIGHTON'S CHEESE & FINE FOODS
Creighton's carries wines and baked goods in addition to 300-plus varieties of imported and domestic cheeses. Noncheese goodies include coffee beans, fresh pâtés, salads, sandwiches, and

desserts. There's a coffee bar on the premises. *673 Portola Dr., near O'Shaughnessey Blvd., Twin Peaks, 415/753–0750.*

7 *d-2*

SAY CHEESE

This Haight-Ashbury shop routinely wins votes in polls of San Franciscans' favorite food shops. It carries more than 400 kinds of fine cheese from around the world, plus gourmet goodies like fresh pâtés and wonderful house-made spreads. The staff is helpful and quick. *856 Cole St., at Carl St., Haight, 415/665–5020.*

7 *g-5*

24TH STREET CHEESE COMPANY

This is Noe Valley's cheese center. It's stocked with exotic cheeses and salamis, gourmet crackers, oils, vinegars, mustards, and other delectables. *3893 24th St., at Sanchez St., Noe Valley, 415/821–6658.*

coffee & tea

8 *b-1*

CAPRICORN COFFEES

This very established SoMa business is a favorite of San Franciscans for fresh-roasted beans that can be custom ground and blended. Teas, spices, and coffee-making equipment are also available. Capricorn beans are sold to many fine restaurants around town. *353 10th St., at Folsom St., South of Market, 415/621–8500. Closed Sun.*

7 *f-3*

CASTRO CHEESERY

See Cheese, *above.*

7 *d-1*

COFFEE, TEA & SPICE

This place has a good selection of coffee beans, but it's really known for its diverse assortment of teas. Spices are sold by the ounce, so you can buy just as much fenugreek or garam masala as you need. Coffee beans are roasted on the premises. *1630 Haight St., between Cole and Clayton Sts., Haight, 415/861–3953.*

4 *c-5*

FREED TELLER & FREED

This coffee roaster and tea blender has been doing business in San Francisco since 1899. More than 20 fine blends of coffee beans are available, plus 30 varieties of teas. The shop also carries herbs, spices, jams, preserves, and chocolates. *1326 Polk St., at Bush St., Polk Gulch, 415/673–0922. Closed weekends.*

4 *d-3*

GRAFFEO COFFEE ROASTING COMPANY

Since 1938, this North Beach emporium has been supplying San Franciscans with fine Italian-roast coffee beans. The air is thick with the aroma of beans roasting for the special Graffeo blends. *735 Columbus Ave., at Filbert St., North Beach, 415/986–2420. Closed Sun.*

6 *g-4*

HOUSE OF COFFEE

This family-run Sunset District coffee business is now in its third generation. The specialties are finely ground Turkish-style coffee, plus teas, spices, and Middle Eastern deli items. Beans are roasted fresh daily. *1618 Noriega St., at 23rd Ave., Sunset District, 415/681–9363. Closed Sun*

5 *f-6*

PEET'S COFFEE & TEA

Although Dutch coffee buyer Alfred Peet began with a single Berkeley store in 1966, today Peet's shops are all over the Bay Area, and their beans are even used in the national Au Bon Pain chain. Long-running favorites among the traditional and creative blends include Major Dickason's blends, Garuda, and Sulawesi-Kalossie beans. Peet's also has excellent selections of green and black teas, and all kinds of coffee- and tea-making equipment. *3419 California St., at Laurel St., Laurel Heights, 415/221–8506.*

5 *h-3*

2156 Chestnut St., between Steiner and Pierce Sts., Marina, 415/931–8302.

7 *g-2*

2257 Market St., between Sanchez and 16th Sts., Castro, 415/626–6416.

4 *c-4*

2139 Polk St., at Broadway, Russian Hill, 415/474–1871.

4 *a-5*

2197 Fillmore St., at Sacramento St., Pacific Heights, 415/563–9930.

5

TEA & COMPANY

Full leaf teas sold in bulk are the specialty here, as well as a small assortment of tea-brewing accessories. Teas are divided into no-, low-, and full-caffeine varieties. Try the caffeine-free African Nectar, with tropical fruits and herbs, or the low-caffeine Kyoto Rice, a green tea with toasted rice. *2207 Fillmore St., between Sacramento and Jackson Sts., Pacific Heights, 888/832–4884.*

4 *e-4*

TEN REN TEA COMPANY OF SAN FRANCISCO

This Chinatown business has one of the largest selections of teas in the Bay Area. The staff is well versed in the healing and/or energizing properties of each blend. *949 Grant Ave., at Jackson St., Chinatown, 415/362–0656.*

5 *h-5*

TULLY'S COFFEE

The many San Francisco outlets of this coffee beanery are popular for espresso and coffee bars. Coffee beans are sold whole or custom ground. *2455 Fillmore St., at Jackson St., Pacific Heights, 415/929–8808.*

7 *g-5*

3966 24th St., at Noe St., Noe Valley, 415/550–7416.

7 *d-2*

919 Cole St., between Carl and Parnassus Sts., Haight, 415/753–2287.

7 *f-3*

504 Castro St., at 18th St., Castro, 415/241–9447.

4 *f-4*

2 Embarcadero Center, Embarcadero, 415/391–6166.

ethnic foods

8 *a-3*

BOMBAY BAZAAR

Here's where you'll find everything you need to prepare an Indian meal: Indian flours, spices, chutneys, chiles, pickles, even paper-thin sheets of gold and silver for making special desserts. *548 Valencia St., at 16th St., Mission, 415/621–1717.*

8 *c-5*

CASA LUCAS MARKET

Spanish, Caribbean, and Latin American fresh produce are sold here, along with wines and cheeses. Regularly in stock are hard-to-find products like dried hominy, palm oil, Andean potatoes, salt cod, tamarind, and cherimoyas. *2934 24th St., at Alabama St., Mission, 415/826–4334.*

4 *e-4*

GOLDEN GATE FORTUNE COOKIES

If you have always been curious about how the fortune gets into the cookie, stop by for a glimpse of the process at this store. You can pick up a bag on your way out. *56 Ross Alley, between Washington and Jackson Sts., Chinatown, 415/781–3956. Closed Sun. and Mon.*

5 *c-6*

HAIG'S DELICACIES

Middle Eastern, Indian, Indonesian, Greek, and Armenian groceries are all carried here: feta cheese, phyllo dough, Kalamata olives, *soujouk* sausage (spicy sausage), and Armenian dried beef. *642 Clement St., at 8th Ave., Richmond District, 415/752–6283. Closed Sun.*

5 *c-6*

HAPPY SUPERMARKET

This is your one-stop shop for Chinese groceries: dried fish, dried mushrooms, pot stickers, every grade of soy sauce, tofu, abalone, Chinese vegetables and pickles, Chinese herbs and medicines, and many varieties of rice. There are supplies for Philippine, Thai, and other Asian cuisines as well. *400 Clement St., at 5th Ave., Richmond District, 415/221–3195.*

4 *a-6*

K. SAKAI UOKI CO.

This beautiful, clean supermarket in the heart of Japantown has great Asian produce and fresh sushi-quality fish. Come here for Japanese fish cakes, barbecued pork, pickled vegetables, and anything else needed for preparing a Japanese meal. *1656 Post St., between Laguna and Buchanan Sts., Japantown, 415/921–0514.*

8 *c-5*

LA PALMA MEXICATESSEN

The handmade tortillas from this "Mexican deli" are excellent. It also stocks all kinds of wonderful dried chiles, beans, hot sauces, and corn husks for making tamales, plus prepared Mexican food. *2884 24th St., at Florida St., Mission, 415/647–1500.*

5 h-3
LUCCA DELICATESSEN
Lucca has been serving the Marina community since 1932. It's famous for its handmade ravioli and huge selection of Italian gourmet goods: imported olive oils, Parmesan cheese, fresh pastas, Italian sausages, Chianti and other Italian wines, polenta, pancetta, roast chickens, and prepared salads. *2120 Chestnut St., at Steiner St., Marina, 415/921–7873.*

4 e-3
MOLINARI DELICATESSEN
Billing itself as the oldest delicatessen west of the Rockies, Molinari has been making its own salami, sausages, and cold cuts since 1896. Other homemade specialties include meat and cheese ravioli, tortellini with prosciutto filling, homemade tomato sauces, and fresh pastas. Cured meats, cheeses, and Italian wines fill the room with tantalizing sights and smells. *373 Columbus Ave., at Vallejo St., North Beach, 415/421–2337. Closed Sun.*

8 a-5
SAMIRAMIS IMPORTS
This import shop is crowded with all sorts of edible goodies from the Middle East. *2990 Mission St., at 26th St., Mission, 415/824–6355. Closed Sun.*

7 h-6
SPECKMANN'S
Adjacent to the restaurant of the same name, Speckmann's is filled to the rafters with German foods. Bratwurst, Swiss *bundenfleisch* (salt-cured, air-dried beef), liverwurst, Westphalian ham, and the house-made pork and veal loaf known as *leberkase* are just a few of the meats it carries. About 20 varieties of German beer round out the stock quite nicely. *1550 Church St., at Duncan St., Noe Valley, 415/282–6850.*

fish & seafood

4 d-1
CRESCI BROS.
If you're visiting Fisherman's Wharf, stop by Cresci Bros. for live and cooked crabs in season, as well as shrimp,

prawns, clams, oysters, and lobsters. Your seafood can even be packed for long trips. *Stall No. 2, Fisherman's Wharf, 415/474–8796.*

4 a-2
MARINA SAFEWAY
The fish counter at this supermarket outlet has one of the city's largest and best-priced selections of seafood. There are usually more than 25 varieties of shellfish, including live lobster and crab, and more than 30 kinds of fish from around the world, weather and season permitting. Cleaning and scaling are complimentary. Fish arrives fresh Monday through Saturday. *15 Marina Blvd., at Buchanan St., Marina, 415/563–4946.*

4 g-4
SAN FRANCISCO FARMERS' MARKET
See Produce, below.

3 c-2
SPENGER'S FISH GROTTO
The famed Berkeley seafood restaurant, founded in 1890, also has an outstanding fish market. There are always plenty of local catches, plus fish and seafood from around the world. *1919 4th St., near University Ave., Berkeley, 510/845–7771.*

4 c-5
SWAN OYSTER DEPOT
The best place in the city to purchase fresh local shellfish, Swan Oyster Depot also has counter seating and a delicious chowder to warm the cockles of your heart (*see* Seafood *in* Chapter 1). The oysters, fish, and other seafood vary according to availability. *1517 Polk St., between California and Sacramento Sts., Nob Hill, 415/673–1101. Closed Sun.*

8 a-3
WANG FAT FISH MARKET
It's not fancy—more like a hole-in-the-wall—but the fish, manila clams, and live crabs are fresh and very reasonably priced. Most fish are sold whole, but there's a small selection of fillets, whether you're looking for catfish or sea bass steaks. *2199 Mission St., at 18th St., Mission, 415/61–7203.*

6 g-2
YUM YUM FISH
This Chinese market has fish and seafood, including tanks with live fish.

Buy the fish whole or ask them to clean, scale, and fillet it. *2181 Irving St., between 22nd and 23rd Aves., Sunset District, 415/566–6433.*

gourmet goodies

6 *h-2*

ANDRONICO'S MARKET

The Sunset District's best full-service grocery is loaded with gourmet specialties: jams, crackers, pickles, olives, vinegar, and prepared foods. *1200 Irving St., at 14th Ave., Sunset District, 415/661–3220.*

4 *e-6*

THE CELLAR AT MACY'S

The Cellar at Macy's department store is a wonderland of cooking gadgets and gourmet goodies. It's got everything: coffee, tea, meats, candy, smoked fish, cheese, packaged foods, and wine. The selection of international food items is impressive. *170 O'Farrell St., at Stockton St., Union Square, 415/397–3333.*

5 *f-8*

FALLETTI'S FOODS

Falletti's is famed for its produce, but its separate deli, meat, fish, poultry, dessert, bread, and liquor boutiques are also full of mouthwatering gourmet delights. *1750 Fulton St., at Masonic Ave., Western Addition, 415/567–0976.*

4 *e-6*

HARVEST MARKET

The prepared foods here—sesame noodles, barley soup, and orzo salad are just a few possibilities—are so delicious that few make it home with them; many sit on one of the benches outside and eat right then and there. It also stocks decadent baked goods, produce, and an interesting cheese selection. *2285 Market St., between Sanchez and Noe Sts., Castro, 415/626–0805.*

4 *c-7*

OPERA PLAZA GROCERY & DELICATESSEN

Though it's small, this place has an amazing selection of quality gourmet foods and spices. Saffron threads and other hard-to-find ingredients are in abundance. *601 Van Ness Ave., at McAllister St., Civic Center, 415/441–2727.*

4 *a-5*

VIVANDE PORTA VIA

This just might be the best gourmet shop in the city, if also the priciest. Choose from such delights as pâtés, terrines, meats, cheeses, sausages, salads, and pastries. Especially delicious are the torta Milanese, the rotisserie, and the breads. Or sit down at a table to enjoy a fine Italian feast (*see* Italian *in* Chapter 1). *2125 Fillmore St., between Sacramento and California Sts., Pacific Heights, 415/346–4430.*

health food

7 *f-3*

BUFFALO WHOLE FOOD & GRAIN CO.

Everything at this lovely shop is well organized and displayed, prices are good, and the quality is high. In addition to organic produce, there's a large selection of bulk grains, flours, pastas, nuts, spices, and dried fruits. *598 Castro St., at 19th St., Castro, 415/626–7038.*

4 *a-5*

ORGANIC CITY NATURAL FOODS

As well as organic packaged foods, nutritional supplements, and herbal beauty products, this store sells organic vegetable and fruit juices, fresh vegan sandwiches, and hot entrées. *2047 Fillmore St., between California and Pine Sts., Pacific Heights, 415/922–3811.*

8 *b-1*

RAINBOW GROCERY

This vast cooperatively owned-and-run grocery has every food item a vegetarian, vegan, or natural-foods fan could dream of, including organic produce, baked goods, deli items, cheeses, oils, grains, pastas, herbs, and spices—and prices are reasonable. It's a great place to shop for vitamins, health books, juicers and cookware, and natural body-care products. *1745 Folsom St., at 13th St., South of Market, 415/863–0620.*

4 *c-3*

REAL FOOD COMPANY

One of the city's most successful health food stores, Real Food has some of the best fresh produce you'll find outside the farmers' markets, as well as a full line of fresh fish, meat, and grains. The Stanyan Street branch has a small delicatessen. Vitamins and other herbal products are carried at all the stores. The prices may not be the best in town, but the variety is certainly the widest. *2140 Polk St., between Broadway and Vallejo St., Russian Hill, 415/673–7420.*

7 *c-1*

1023 Stanyan St., at Carl St., Haight, 415/564–2800.

7 *g-5*

3939 24th St., between Noe and Sanchez Sts., Noe Valley, 415/282–9500.

2 *b-3*

THOM'S NATURAL FOODS
This roomy organic produce and grocery store has bulk herb and grain bins and a deli counter. *5843 Geary Blvd., at 23rd Ave., Richmond District, 415/387–6367.*

herbs & spices

4 *e-4*

GREAT CHINA HERB CO.
One of the largest herb shops in Chinatown has familiar items like ginseng and teas and hundreds of things you may have never seen before. And it's perhaps the only store in the United States that will still add up your bill on an abacus. *857 Washington St., between Grant and Stockton Sts., Chinatown, 415/982–2195.*

3 *e-3*

LHASA KARNAK HERB CO.
Berkeley's best herb shop has two branches. *2513 Telegraph Ave., at Dwight Way, Berkeley, 510/548–0380.*

3 *d-2*

1938 Shattuck Ave., at Berkeley Way, Berkeley, 510/548–0372.

8 *a-2*

SAN FRANCISCO HERB CO.
In business since 1973, this outlet store is well stocked with herbs, spices, teas, essential and fragrance oils, flavoring extracts, and all kinds of potpourri ingredients and recipes. *250 14th St., at Mission St., Mission, 415/861–3018. Closed Sun.*

8 *a-4*

SCARLET SAGE HERB CO.
Choose from more than 250 herbs and spices, many of them organic, and all sold in bulk. There are also vitamins, extracts, oils, teas, and herbal body-care products. *1173 Valencia St., between*

22nd and 23rd Sts., Mission, 415/821–0997.

meat & poultry

5 *h-6*

HONEYBAKED HAM COMPANY
Delicious hams, back ribs, smoked turkey, sauces, hearty soup mixes, cheeses, and salads are sold at this small, tidy store. *2190 Geary Blvd., at Divisadero St., Western Addition, 415/931–7383. Closed Sun.*

4 *f-8*

KWONG JOW SAUSAGE FACTORY
This SoMa business sells dried sausages, barbecued pork, and bacon rind. *753 Bryant St., at 6th St., South of Market, 415/398–4348.*

4 *e-3*

LITTLE CITY MARKET
Range-fed veal, cut any way you like, is this North Beach butcher's specialty. *1400 Stockton St., at Vallejo St., North Beach, 415/986–2601. Closed Sun.*

nuts & seeds

4 *e-6*

MORROW'S NUT HOUSE
Fresh roasted nuts fill the glass-fronted bins that line the walls here, and still more nuts fill the fancy gift tins stacked on the shelves. Dried fruits are also for sale. *111 Geary St., between Grant Ave. and Stockton St., Union Square, 415/362–7969. Closed Sun.*

8 *d-8*

SAN FRANCISCO POPCORN WORKS
Pesto, cheddar Cajun, sour cream, caramel, and golden macadamia crunch are among the 40-odd wacky flavors of popcorn sold here. Buy the stuff from gift shops around the city, or direct from the factory store. *1028 Revere Ave., near Silver St., Bayview, 415/822–4744 or 800/777–2676. Closed weekends.*

pasta & noodles

4 *e-4*

NEW HONG KONG NOODLE CO.
This Chinatown shop has Hong Kong and Shanghai style noodles, plus won-

ton and pot sticker skins. Prices are very reasonable. *874 Pacific Ave., at Powell St., Chinatown, 415/982–2715.*

produce

3 *d-3*

BERKELEY BOWL MARKETPLACE

Recently relocated into more spacious digs, this vast market is worth the trip across the Bay Bridge. The vegetable and fruit selection (including organic produce) is seemingly endless, the bulk grains well priced, and the adjoining seafood and cheese departments are both superb. Most local bakeries stock their loaves here. *2020 Oregon St., at Shattuck St., Berkeley, 510/843–6929.*

4 *f-3, g-4*

SAN FRANCISCO FARMERS' MARKET/FERRY PLAZA

The Saturday-only outdoor farmers' market on the Embarcadero at Green Street is more upscale than the one at United Nations Plaza (*see below*). It has the same fresh, locally grown produce, plus homemade yogurts, cheeses, preserves, salsas, breads, and desserts. In season, it's also one of the best places in the city for shellfish straight out of Tomales Bay. In summer an additional market is held Tuesday at Justin Herman Plaza. *415/981–3004.*

4 *c-7*

SAN FRANCISCO FARMERS' MARKET/UNITED NATIONS PLAZA

Many of the farmers who sell their produce on Wednesday and Sunday at this sprawling outdoor market are from Southeast Asia, so the selection ranges from the expected to the exotic—you can even find live chickens. Produce varies by season, but is always cheap. *United Nations Plaza, 415/558–9455.*

FRAMING

6 *h-5*

AL BERNZWEIG FRAMING

Al has been doing custom framing at his well-stocked shop since 1967. For those in a hurry, there's one-hour service. *1100 Ortega St., at 18th Ave., Sunset District, 415/664–8052. Closed Sun.*

5 *a-7*

AMSTERDAM ART

See Art Supplies, above.

5 *c-7*

CHEAP PETE'S

At this factory outlet, choose from hundreds of ready-made picture frames in all sizes and styles. Prices run 30%–70% below retail. *4249 Geary Blvd., at 7th Ave., Richmond District, 415/221–4720.*

4 *f-6*

MUSEUM WEST

Across the street from the San Francisco Museum of Modern Art, Museum West does museum-quality framing of fine art. There's an excellent selection of elegant gold-leaf and period frames, and the staff knows how to handle oversized works. *170 Minna St., at 3rd St., South of Market, 415/546–1113. Closed Sun.*

GIFTS & SOUVENIRS

4 *d-5*

AUSTRALIAN FAIR

Everything in this Union Square shop comes from the land down under. This includes lambskin rugs and coats, toy koala bears and duckbill platypuses, rabbit-pelt Acubra hats, Aussie chocolates, and tins of Vegemite. Best-sellers include RM Williams boots and stockman's coats. *700 Sutter St., at Taylor St., Union Square, 415/441–5319. Closed Sun.*

4 *e-1*

THE CABLE CAR STORE

After you've fallen in love with San Francisco's charming cable cars, take home a miniature. This Pier 39 shop carries cable-car music boxes, memorabilia, and other clever souvenirs. *Pier 39, The Embarcadero and Beach St., Fisherman's Wharf, 415/989–2040.*

4 *d-1*

CELL BLOCK 41

You'll find Cell Block 41 next to the dock where ferries depart for Alcatraz. It's filled with souvenirs of the famous former prison—everything from T-shirts to handcuffs. *Pier 41, Fisherman's Wharf, 415/249–4666.*

4 f-6

CENTER FOR THE ARTS GIFT SHOP

The Yerba Buena Gardens gift shop carries beautiful handmade jewelry, tableware, and crafts from both regional and national artists. It also has unusual children's books, T-shirts, and greeting cards. *701 Mission St., at 3rd St., South of Market, 415/978–2710.*

4 a-4

THE ENCHANTED CRYSTAL

Dozens of crystal candleholders, vases, and art deco sculptures fill this friendly shop. Many of the pieces—including a large selection of handcrafted glass jewelry—are made by Bay Area artists. *1895 Union St., at Laguna St., Cow Hollow, 415/885–1335.*

4 e-4

FAR EAST FLEA MARKET

All sorts of inexpensive objects and souvenirs—San Francisco memorabilia, ceramic rice bowls, Buddha figurines—make this the place to come when you need to stock up on little mementos and things that make a house a home. *729 Grant Ave., between Sacramento and Clay Sts., Chinatown, 415/989–8588.*

5 a-1

GOLDEN GATE BRIDGE GIFT CENTER

Trinkets featuring the world-famous bridge are for sale at the Round House Building, on the south (San Francisco) side of the Golden Gate Bridge. *Golden Gate Bridge, 415/923 2331.*

4 c-4

GREEN WORLD MERCANTILE

Whether you're searching for a gift or just want to treat yourself, stop by for a wide array or natural home products, urban gardening items, aromatherapy candles, decorative papers, and luxury bath items. Look for inexpensive jewelry made by local artisans. *2340 Polk St., between Green and Union Sts., 415/ 771–5717.*

4 e-1

HOLLYWOOD USA

For movie and radio buffs, this place is a delight: it sells unusual (and sometimes silly) Hollywood-themed souvenirs. You'll find plates painted with scenes from *Star Trek* and replica Oscars for

"Best Shopper." *Pier 39, The Embarcadero and Beach St., Fisherman's Wharf, 415/982–3538.*

4 e-1

MAGNETRON

Only at San Francisco's Pier 39 can you find a shop devoted exclusively to refrigerator magnets. Of the hundreds stuck to this shop's walls and ceiling, many have San Francisco motifs. *Pier 39, The Embarcadero and Beach St., Fisherman's Wharf, 415/989–2361.*

7 e-1

PIPE DREAMS

Perfect for your favorite Deadhead, this place sells Day-Glo posters, tie-dye T-shirts, incense, candles, and all kinds of exotic pipes. *1376 Haight St., at Masonic Ave., Haight, 415/431–3553.*

4 f-6

SFMOMA STORE

The San Francisco Museum of Modern Art's gift shop is famous for its exclusive line of watches and jewelry, as well as its artists' monographs, Picasso dishes and other dinnerware, children's art-making sets and books, and extensive collection of art books for adults. *151 3rd St., South of Market, 415/357–4035.*

4 f-5

THE SHARPER IMAGE

This purveyor of high-end gadgetry, now a national chain, was founded in San Francisco. It carries everything from five-language translators and noiseless rowing machines to vibrating massage chairs and Walkman-size computers. *532 Market St., at Sansome St., Financial District, 415/398–6472.*

4 c-2

Ghirardelli Square, 900 North Point St., Fisherman's Wharf, 415/776–1443.

4 f-3

680 Davis St., at Broadway, Embarcadero, 415/445–6100. Closed Sun.

4 b-8

WORLDWARE

At this shop, recycling is art. The picture frames and candlesticks are made from aluminum cans, and purses and wallets are cut from discarded tires. The owner, Shari Sant, designs her own line of clothing made from organic hemp, wool, and cotton (*see* Clothing for

Women/General, *above*). *336 Hayes St., between Franklin and Gough Sts., Hayes Valley, 415/487–9030.*

HATS

4 *b-2*

THE HAT GENERATION

Panama hats, sun hats, and garden party hats are just a few of the choices here. Kids have their own selection of fanciful items, including striped Cat in the Hat–style hats and pointy fairy princess caps. *Ghirardelli Square, 900 North Point St., at Polk St., Fisherman's Wharf, 415/749–1734.*

4 *e-6*

HATS ON POST

See Clothing for Women/Specialty, *above.*

2 *b-3*

PAUL'S HAT WORKS

Since 1918 Paul's has specialized in fine Panama straw hats. The owner takes pride in finding and selling the finest hats available—including some types that take more than a year to make. *6128 Geary Blvd., at 25th Ave., Sunset District, 415/221–5332. Closed Sun. and Mon.*

HOME FURNISHINGS

8 *c-1*

BED, BATH, & BEYOND

This vast store, part of a national chain, has seemingly endless household wares, from chic to cheap. There are two floors of bed, bath, and kitchen necessities, plus picture frames, sculptures, and other decorative items. *555 9th St., at Bryant St., South of Market, 415/252–0490.*

4 *e-5*

CRATE & BARREL

The Union Square store was the chain's first in the western United States, and it is still the largest. It sells affordable but stylish bed linens, kitchen accessories, dishware, glassware, furniture, and other home furnishings. The outlet store in Berkeley has irregular or discontinued products priced 30%–50% below retail. *125 Grant Ave., at Post St., Union Square, 415/986–4000.*

3 *b-2*

Outlet: 1785 4th St., at Hearst Ave., Berkeley, 510/528–5500.

bedroom & bath

4 *e-7*

DREAMS DOWN BEDDING

Although mattresses and box springs are available for reasonable prices upstairs, the real reason to come to this shop is for its selection of luscious down pillows and comforters. Bring in your feather or down items and have them expertly cleaned here, or even have down added or removed according to your specifications. *921 Howard St., at 5th St., South of Market, 415/543–1800.*

4 *e-6*

SCHEUER LINENS

Designers and everyday shoppers flock to Scheuer for its luxurious linens for the bed, bath, and dinner table—by the very best makers from the United States and Europe. Many of the down comforters, duvet covers, and pillows are imported from Europe. There is also a wide variety of gifts, such as candles, hand-embroidered handkerchiefs, and soaps. *340 Sutter St., at Stockton St., Union Square, 415/392–2813. Closed Sun.*

4 *e-6*

STROUDS

A huge selection of bed linens, pillows, and bath accessories are sold at a discount from department store prices. *731 Market St., between 3rd and 4th Sts., Union Square, 415/979–0460.*

5 *g-5*

SUE FISHER KING

Fine bedroom linens and an aromatic mix of soaps, perfumes, and candles are among the many choice items here (*see* Furniture & Accessories, *below*). *3067 Sacramento St., between Baker and Broderick Sts., Pacific Heights, 415/922–7276. Closed Sun.*

4 *a-6*

TOWNHOUSE LIVING

This Japan Center store sells futons and pillows as well as household accessories (*see* Furniture & Accessories, *below*). *1825 Post St., at Fillmore St., Japantown, 415/563–1417.*

carpets & rugs

8 c-8

CARPET CONNECTION

This store has San Francisco's largest inventory of new name-brand carpeting. Area rugs and remnants, draperies, miniblinds, and vinyl flooring are all sold at warehouse prices. *390 Bay Shore Blvd., at Industrial St., Bayview, 415/550–7125. Closed Sun.*

4 f-4

CARPETS OF THE INNER CIRCLE

Owner Roger Cavanna was an architect and city planner before going into the antique carpet business. His shop carries a marvelous range of beautiful kilims and carpets. It is open weekends by appointment. *444 Jackson St., at Montgomery St., Jackson Square, 415/398–2988. Closed weekends.*

8 d-1

JALILI INTERNATIONAL, INC.

Jalili carries an extensive collection of dhurries, kilims, and other fine antique Oriental carpets, as well as contemporary handmade rugs. *101 Henry Adams St., Suite 355, at Division St., South of Market, 415/788–3377. Closed weekends.*

8 f-1

OMID ORIENTAL RUGS

This large showroom is piled with Persian, Turkish, Pakistani, Indian, Chinese, Nepalese, and other new, used, and antique rugs. The staff is knowledgeable and helpful. *590 9th St., at Brannan St., South of Market, 415/626–3466.*

5 h-4

SILKROUTE INTERNATIONAL

Of the many antique and new kilims and carpets here, many are from Afghanistan. The shop also has Afghani imports such as brass and copper works, jewelry, and needlework. *3119 Fillmore St., between Union and Filbert Sts., Cow Hollow, 415/563–4936.*

ceramic tiles

8 d-1

ANN SACKS TILE & STONE

The ceramic, marble, slate, limestone, and terra-cotta tiles here come from around the world. There are handcrafted tiles, antique tiles, and tile mosaics. *2*

Henry Adams St., at Division St., South of Market, 415/252–5889. Closed weekends.

8 d-2

TILE VISIONS

Roger Chetrit of Tile Visions designs delightful trompe l'oeil tiles, as well as tile murals. Much of his work is custom, but he also has ready-made

---

SETTING UP HOUSE IN SAN FRANCISCO

You've just spent a fortune on security deposits and rent to move into that fabulous new San Francisco apartment, and now you need all sorts of new things. The following are spots where you can pick up items for your new apartment without putting yourself in the poorhouse.

Alemany Flea Market (Flea Markets)
  Household appliances and furniture can be unearthed here.

Bed, Bath & Beyond (Home Furnishings)
  Endless bed linens and bath and kitchen necessities, all reasonably priced.

Busvan for Bargains (Home Furnishings)
  Inexpensive, functional furniture for those just starting out.

Butterfield West (Antiques)
  Items from liquidated estates are auctioned here, sometimes for a song.

Cookin': Recycled Gourmet Appurtenances (Housewares & Hardware)
  Although not everything is cheap here, there are bargains among the used cookware.

Crate & Barrel (Home Furnishings)
  The Berkeley outlet store has housewares priced 30%–50% below retail.

The Good Guys (Electronics & Audio)
  Reasonable prices on TVs, stereos, telephones, answering machines, and much more.

The Plant Warehouse (Flowers & Plants)
  Tropical indoor plants are a specialty here.

Sal Beressi Fabrics (Fabrics & Zippers)
  Upholstery, drapery, and bedspread fabrics are sold at deep discounts.

designs, some by European designers. *299-A Kansas St., between 16th and 17th Sts., Potrero Hill, 415/621–4546. Closed Sun.*

china, glassware, porcelain, pottery, silver

4 *e-3*

BIORDI ART IMPORTS

This established family business imports gorgeous hand-painted Italian Renaissance–style majolica. You could invest thousands in a complete set of dinnerware, or less than a hundred on small decorative items like vases, soap dishes, or masks. *412 Columbus Ave., at Vallejo St., North Beach, 415/392–8096. Closed Sun.*

4 *e-6*

GUMP'S

San Francisco's fabled department store (*see* Department Stores, *above*) stocks a dizzying assortment of fine china, crystal, and silver—including exclusive lines of dinnerware, flatware, and glassware. *135 Post St., between Kearny St. and Grant Ave., Union Square, 415/982–1616. Closed Sun.*

8 *d-7*

HERITAGE HOUSE TABLEWARE SHOWROOM

Shop here first: there more than 500 patterns by more than 100 manufacturers on display, including all the fine brands like Ginori and Lenox. There's crystal and silverware, too. Prices on many items run 15%–40% below retail. The staff members recommend calling ahead to let them know you're coming. Patterns are not priced, so they prefer to make someone available to show you around. *2190 Palou Ave., at Industrial St., Bayview, 415/285–1331.*

4 *f-5*

PESARESI CERAMICS

Brightly painted plates, vases, and other decorative items come straight from Pesaro, Italy, a center for ceramics production since the Renaissance. Prices reflect the fact that the pieces are both molded and painted by hand. *Crocker Galleria, 50 Post St., between Montgomery and Kearny Sts., Financial District, 415/362–4570. Closed Sun.*

7 *g-5*

TERRA MIA CERAMIC STUDIOS

This place lets you create ceramic pieces using your own designs and the store's art supplies and kiln. Teapots, mugs, goblets, and tiles are among the items that can be fired and ready to display within a week. Relive your childhood and make mom a gift for Mother's Day. *4037 24th St., between Noe and Castro Sts., Noe Valley, 415/642–9911.*

5 *h-4*

2122 Union St., between Webster and Fillmore Sts., Cow Hollow, 415/351–2529.

4 *e-6*

TIFFANY & CO.

Very fine china, crystal, and silver are sold in this renowned treasure house. The jewels are famed worldwide (*see* Jewelry, *below*). *350 Post St., between Powell and Stockton Sts., Union Square, 415/781–7000. Closed Sun.*

furniture & accessories

4 *d-3*

ABITARE

This popular North Beach shop stocks a quirky and eclectic mix of home furnishings: soaps and bath supplies, candleholders, picture frames, lamps, and one-of-a-kind furniture, artwork, and decorations. *522 Columbus Ave., at Union St., North Beach, 415/392–5800.*

8 *d-2*

AMBIENTE

Dining room sets, dressers, sofas, and chairs are among the mildly trendy and reasonably priced contemporary home furnishings here. *390 Kansas St., at 17th St., Potrero Hill, 415/863–9700.*

4 *a-3*

THE BOMBAY COMPANY

This national chain specializes in affordable reproductions of 18th- and 19th-century American and British furniture and accessories. *2135 Union St., at Webster St., Cow Hollow, 415/441–1591.*

2 *c-6*

Stonestown Galleria, 19th Ave. and Winston Dr., Stonestown, 415/753–2955.

`4` *f-3*

BUSVAN FOR BARGAINS

A favorite of San Franciscans looking for cheap furniture, Busvan specializes in those pieces that everyone needs when they're setting up house: dressers, bookshelves, desks, and the like. Most pieces are more functional than fashionable but it does sell custom-upholstered chairs and couches as well. *900 Battery St., at Vallejo St., Embarcadero, 415/981–1405.*

`5` *d-6*

244 Clement St., between 3rd and 4th Aves., Richmond District, 415/752–5353.

`4` *d-8*

EVOLUTION

Evolution carries an unusual selection of imported furniture, home accessories, crafts, and housewares, with many pieces from Indonesia. It also has Amish, Shaker, and Arts and Crafts reproduction furnishings such as armoires, love seats, and hope chests. *271 9th St., between Folsom and Howard Sts., South of Market, 415/861–6665*

`5` *h-5*

FILLAMENTO

This Pacific Heights favorite has three floors of home furnishings. You'll find everything from dinnerware and bedding to rugs and furniture to bath and baby accessories, in styles ranging from traditional to contemporary. *2185 Fillmore St., at Sacramento St., Pacific Heights, 415/931–2224.*

`4` *b-2*

GORDON BENNETT

See Housewares & Hardware, *below.*

`4` *e-6*

HOLD EVERYTHING

If you dream of getting control of clutter in your house, you could go mad in this shop, which carries baskets, bookshelves, hampers, wine racks, and other storage items. Clothes hangers come in dozens of shapes and sizes. *San Francisco Shopping Centre, 865 Market St., between 4th and 5th Sts., Union Square, 415/546–0986.*

`4` *g-8*

LIMN COMPANY

This is San Francisco's best outlet for designer furniture, as well as fine lamps and home accessories. You'll find classic and modern designs by international and local talents. *290 Townsend St., at 4th St., South Beach, 415/543–5466.*

`4` *g-7*

MAISON D'ETRE

Eclectic luxury items for the home include gorgeous wrought-iron light fixtures, luxurious pillows, and ornate mirrors. *92 S. Park Ave., between 2nd and 3rd Sts., South Beach, 415/357–1747. Closed Sun.*

`4` *a-5*

MIKE FURNITURE

The stylish furniture here tends to be conservative and expensive. The shop does custom work as well. *2142 Fillmore St., at Sacramento St., Pacific Heights, 415/567–2700.*

`4` *d-8*

NEXT EXPRESS

If the home furnishing stores in Pacific Heights strike you as a tad stuffy (and expensive), take a look at Next's trendy offerings. Couches are available in curvy, asymmetric forms, and chairs come clad in purple velvet. Traditionalists have plenty of choices, too, since most of the pieces come upholstered in the fabric of your choice. *1315 Howard St., at 9th St., 415/255–1311.*

`4` *c-6*

NIGEL IMPORTS

Nigel has a stunning selection of solid rosewood furniture. All pieces are handcrafted in Asia in either traditional or contemporary styling. Accessories such as Chinese standing screens, Japanese wall screens, and lamps round out the selection. *1244 Sutter St., at Van Ness Ave., Polk Gulch, 415/776–5490.*

`4` *a-5*

PASCUAL'S FURNITURE

Choose from a range of fabrics—from conservative to bright and lively—to cover any of the custom sofas, chairs, headboards, and other furniture available here. *2116 Fillmore St., at Sacramento St., Pacific Heights, 415/346–1098.*

`4` *f-5*

POLO STORE– RALPH LAUREN

The genteel look that designer Ralph Lauren has popularized does not come cheap. This shop displays his version of gracious living, with home furnishings, linens, and elegant accessories. *90 Post St., at Kearny St., Union Square, 415/ 788–7656.*

5 *g-5*

SUE FISHER KING

A favorite among designers and neighborhood residents, Sue Fisher King has decorative pillows and luxurious throws, Italian dinnerware, fine linens for the bedroom and kitchen, and books on gardening and home decoration, among other things. A small garden area gives the store a homey mood. *3067 Sacramento St., between Baker and Broderick Sts., Pacific Heights, 415/ 922–7276. Closed Sun.*

8 *a-2*

THERAPY

Re-live the '60s and '70s with a plastic chair molded into the shape of a hand, mohair throw pillows, or a crystal ball lamp. A mix of new and vintage items are perfect for furnishing and accessorizing a space-age bachelor pad. *545 Valencia St., between 16th and 17th Sts., Mission, 415/861–6213.*

8 *a-4*

1051 Valencia St., between 21st and 22nd Sts., Mission, 415/648–7565. Closed Mon. and Tues.

4 *f-5*

568 Mission St., between 1st and 2nd Sts., South of Market, 415/371–0821. Closed weekends.

4 *a-6*

TOWNHOUSE LIVING

Lamps, frames, Japanese fabrics, tatami mats, vases, and other graceful household accessories are available at this Japan Center outpost. *1825 Post St., at Fillmore St., Japantown, 415/563–1417.*

4 *a-4*

Z GALLERIE

The home furnishings and accessories here—including dinnerware, desks, chairs, and lamps—are sleek, high-tech, and sometimes playful. Pair a black butterfly chair with one of their many posters. This was recently voted "Best Urban Chic Furniture Store" by *Bay Guardian* readers. *2071 Union St., at Webster St., Cow Hollow, 415/346–9000.*

5 *h-4*

2154 Union St., between Webster and Fillmore Sts., Cow Hollow, 415/567–4891.

lamps & lighting

8 *b-1*

CITY LIGHTS LIGHTING SHOWROOM

The art deco– and art moderne–style lamps are made of oxidized brass, limed woods, and other unique materials. City Lights also has a good selection of garden-lighting fixtures. *1585 Folsom St., at 12th St., South of Market, 415/863–2020. Closed Sun.*

5 *b-7*

LAMPS PLUS

Lamps by leading manufacturers are available here. *4700 Geary Blvd., at 11th Ave., Richmond District, 415/386–0933.*

4 *c-2*

SHADES OF TIFFANY

Tiffany-style lamps with shades of colored glass are the only items you'll find here. Styles range from simple floriform shades in a single muted color to bright scenes in rainbow hues. *The Cannery, 2801 Leavenworth St., at Beach St., Fisherman's Wharf, 415/345–8529.*

paint & wallpaper

5 *a-7*

CREATIVE PAINT

A wide selection of paints, computer color matching, and expert service set this shop apart. It also carries wallpaper. *5435 Geary Blvd., between 18th and 19th Aves., Richmond District, 415/666–3380.*

5 *a-7*

PAINT EFFECTS

All the tools and paints you need for decorative painting, whether stenciling, marbling, glazing, or even gilding, are here. If you don't know how to paint, you can take one of the many classes here, or buy a video explaining various techniques. *2426 Fillmore St., between Washington and Jackson Sts., Pacific Heights, 415/292–7780.*

HOUSEWARES & HARDWARE

7 *g-3*

BAUERWARE CABINET HARDWARE

Never in your life have you seen so many drawer knobs and pulls. Floor-to-ceiling cases house fixtures made of ceramic, brass, wood, glass, and iron, including pulls shaped like mixing spoons, letters of the alphabet, or dominoes. Prices range from modest to exorbitant. *3886 17th St., at Noe St., Castro, 415/864–3886. Closed Sun.*

2 *c-6*

BROOKSTONE CO.

Every gadget and tool imaginable is found at this shop, whether it's for home repairs, cooking, cleaning fish, barbecuing, figuring your income taxes, or gardening. *Stonestown Galleria, 19th Ave. and Winston Dr., Stonestown, 415/731–8046.*

4 *e-6*

San Francisco Shopping Centre, 865 Market St., between 4th and 5th Sts., Union Square, 415/546–6667.

4 *c-2*

THE CAPTAIN'S WHARF

Brassware is the specialty here: Look for doorknobs, door knockers, hooks, towel bars, lamps, candleholders, and clocks. Many items have a nautical theme. *Ghirardelli Square, 900 North Point St., Fisherman's Wharf, 415/921–0889.*

7 *f-1*

COOKIN': RECYCLED GOURMET APPURTENANCES

Cookin' carries quality used fondue makers, espresso machines, food processors, cookie cutters, Jell-O molds, pots, pans, and other kitchen gadgets, all at excellent values. *339 Divisadero St., between Oak and Page Sts., Haight, 415/861–1854. Closed Mon.*

5 *f-5*

FORREST JONES INC.

This shop has a full range of French and Italian household goods, including dishes, glassware, kitchen tools, cutlery, and complete table settings. *3274 Sacramento St., at Presidio Ave., Laurel Heights, 415/567–2483.*

4 *b-2*

GORDON BENNETT

Housewares and ceramics made by local artists are some of the delights you'll find here. There's a good selection of garden sculptures, garden tools, and wrought-iron outdoor furniture, too. *Ghirardelli Square, 900 North Point St., Fisherman's Wharf, 415/929–1172.*

5 *e-6*

JUDITH ETS-HOKIN HOMECHEF KITCHEN STORE

Associated with a cooking school of the same name, the Homechef Kitchen Store has just about every low- or high-tech cooking utensil you might need, from egg whisks to KitchenAids. Sign up for weekday and weekend cooking classes while you're here. *3525 California St., at Locust St., Laurel Heights, 415/668–3191.*

4 *a-6*

SOKO HARDWARE

Run by the Ashizawa merchant family in Japantown since 1925, Soko Hardware specializes in beautifully crafted Japanese dishware, gardening tools, carpentry instruments, kitchenware, and housewares such as vases and lamps. *1698 Post St., at Buchanan St., Japantown, 415/931–5510. Closed Sun.*

4 *e-6*

SUR LA TABLE

This two-story shop sells serious cookware, as well as wonderfully obscure kitchen gadgets. Look no further for a larding needle or paper bonbon cups. Racks of deeply discounted items are at the back of the basement. *77 Maiden La., between Grant Ave. and Kearney St., Union Square, 415/732–7900.*

4 *e-1*

WE BE KNIVES

This tiny shop is filled with wicked-looking sharp things: kitchen cutlery, all kinds of pocket and hunting knives, and even a few swords. *Pier 39, The Embarcadero and Beach St., Fisherman's Wharf, 415/982–9323.*

4 *e-5*

WILLIAMS-SONOMA

The retail outlet of the famous mail-order catalog house (which began life as a hardware store in Sonoma County) has stylish cooking equipment, tabletop items, and knickknacks, plus dozens of cookbooks and gourmet food items. *150 Post St., at Grant Ave., Union Square, 415/362–6904.*

4 *e-6*

San Francisco Shopping Centre, 865 Market St., between 4th and 5th Sts., Union Square, 415/546–0171.

2 c-6

Stonestown Galleria, 19th Ave. and Winston Dr., Stonestown, 415/681–5525.

4 f-4

2 Embarcadero Center, Clay and Sacramento Sts. between Battery and Drumm Sts., Embarcadero, 415/421–2033.

4 e-5

THE WOK SHOP

Although the shop specializes in Chinese woks, it stocks other Chinese cookware as well—plus Chinese baskets, cookbooks, and aprons. *718 Grant Ave., at Sacramento St., Chinatown, 415/989–3797.*

JEWELRY

antique & collectible items

7 f-3

BRAND X ANTIQUES

Estate jewelry and other gems from the early 20th century are available here. You'll also find cut and blown glass, and European, American, and Asian objets d'art. *570 Castro St., at 18th St., Castro, 415/626–8908.*

4 e-5

LANG ANTIQUES AND ESTATE JEWELRY

Lang has one of the widest selections of vintage jewelry in San Francisco. In addition to a large assortment of engagement rings, this store sells objets d'art, silver hollowware and flatware, and vintage timepieces. *323 Sutter St., at Grant Ave., Union Square, 415/982–2213.*

5 h-4

OLD AND NEW ESTATES

This shop has antique and estate jewelry, timepieces, crystal, objets d'art, antiques, and silver. It specializes in Art Deco jewelry, including wedding and engagement rings. *2181 Union St., at Fillmore St., Cow Hollow, 415/346–7525. Closed Wed.*

4 a-4

VERSAILLE

Beautiful vintage watches by makers like Grüen, Hamilton, and Mido are a favorite of owner Alex Koretsky, who might give you a little break on the price if he senses he's met a fellow watch collector. Estate jewelry is also for sale. *1954 Union St., between Buchanan and Laguna Sts., Cow Hollow, 415/440–0932. Closed Mon.*

contemporary pieces

4 e-6

AMIR H. MOZAFFARIAN

One of the city's most elite jewelers sells diamond-encrusted bracelets, dazzling Harry Winston watches, Fabergé decorative items, and other pricey luxuries. It also sells a small selection of estate jewelry. *155 Post St., at Grant Ave., Union Square, 415/391–9995. Closed Sun.*

4 e-5

CARTIER

Treasures of gold, silver, and platinum, often crusted with precious gems, are the trademarks of this world-renowned jeweler. *231 Post St., at Stockton St., Union Square, 415/397–3180. Closed Sun.*

4 a-3

EARTHEART HEALING JEWELRY

Signs around the store describe the healing properties attributed to the semiprecious stones set into beautiful necklaces, bracelets, and earrings, almost all handmade by local artists. The helpful staff will also repair your jewelry. *1980 Union St., between Laguna and Buchanan Sts., Cow Hollow, 415/921–8358.*

4 e-6

GUMP'S

This Union Square institution (see *Department Stores*, above) *has one of the world's finest collections of jade and freshwater pearls. Much of the opulent jewelry is crafted exclusively for Gump's; prices are appropriately high.* 135 Post St., between Kearny St. and Grant Ave., Union Square, 415/982–1616. Closed Sun.

4 e-4

JADE EMPIRE

One of the many fine jewelry stores in Chinatown, Jade Empire has good selections of jade, diamonds, and other gems, as well as freshwater pearls, beads, porcelain dolls, and lanterns. *832 Grant Ave., at Clay St., Chinatown, 415/982–4498.*

4 *e-6*

PEARL EMPIRE

Pearl and jade pieces are the specialties here. There's also a selection of coral jewelry imported from Hong Kong and Japan. *127 Geary St., at Stockton St., Union Square, 415/362–0606. Closed Sun.*

4 *e-5*

SHREVE & CO.

Founded in 1852, this is one of the city's most elegant jewelers and the oldest retail store in San Francisco. An exquisite selection of fine diamonds, precious stone jewelry, gold, and Mikimoto pearls, plus gift items such as Lalique crystal and Limoges porcelain, adorn the cases. *200 Post St., at Grant Ave., Union Square, 415/421–2600.*

4 *e-5*

SIDNEY MOBELL FINE JEWELRY

This award-winning jeweler is often lauded as San Francisco's most creative and witty. His custom work has included gold toilet seats, diamond mousetraps, and a million-dollar Monopoly set. *200 Post St., at Grant Ave., Union Square, 415/986–4747. Closed Sun.*

4 *a-4*

STUART MOORE GALLERY OF DESIGNER JEWELRY

Here you'll find Moore's own elegant, sleek rings, most crafted from 18k gold or platinum, as well as the handmade pieces created by 25 different European designers. *1898 Union St., at Laguna St., Cow Hollow, 415/292–1430.*

4 *e-6*

TIFFANY & CO.

The San Francisco outpost of the famous New York City jewelry store is just as stunning as you'd expect. Exclusive jewelry designs by Paloma Picasso and others are a large part of why Tiffany's remains America's favorite fine jeweler. The store also carries sterling silver, china, and crystal. *350 Post St., between Powell and Stockton Sts., Union Square, 415/781–7000. Closed Sun.*

4 *a-3*

UNION STREET GOLDSMITH

A local favorite since 1976, Union Street Goldsmith specializes in custom work. Among the wide selection of rare gemstones are golden sapphires, black Tahitian South Seas pearls, and violet tanzanite. *1909 Union St., at Laguna St., Cow Hollow, 415/776–8048.*

4 *e-6*

WHOLESALE JEWELERS EXCHANGE

This is the place to find gems and finished jewelry at less-than-retail prices. More than 20 independent jewelers display their own merchandise. *121 O'Farrell St., between Powell and Stockton Sts., Union Square, 415/788–2365. Closed Sun.*

4 *e-5*

YOKOO PEARLS

Yokoo deals exclusively in pearls of all colors and lusters. It sells custom-designed jewelry as well, and will open on weekends by appointment. *210 Post St., at Grant Ave., 415/982–5441. Closed weekends.*

costume jewelry

7 *f-1*

COSTUMES ON HAIGHT

See Theatrical Items, *below.*

7 *g-5*

GALLERY OF JEWELS

Most of the costume jewelry here—in rhinestone, glass, and silver—is crafted by local artisans. The styles are eclectic, and the prices reasonable. *4089 24th St., at Castro St., Noe Valley, 415/285–0626.*

4 *a-4*

JEST JEWELS

You'll find wonderfully witty *bijoux* at this Marina District shop, as well as a good selection of contemporary watches. *1869 Union St., between Laguna and Octavia Sts., Cow Hollow, 415/563–8839.*

4 *g-4*

3 Embarcadero Center, Clay and Sacramento Sts. between Battery and Drumm Sts., Embarcadero, 415/986–4494.

KITES

6 *b-8*

AIRTIME SAN FRANCISCO

This shop specializes in stunt kites, and has a large selection of kites and accessories. It also handles hang-gliding and paragliding instruction and equipment. *3620 Wawona St., at 47th Ave., Sunset District, 415/759–1177.*

4 e-5
CHINATOWN KITE SHOP

Many of the kites for sale here seem too pretty to subject to a day at the park. Colorful dragon kites, complex stunt kites, and those plain old diamond-shape ones you flew as a kid fill the shelves at this store. *717 Grant Ave., between Clay and Sacramento Sts., Chinatown, 415/989–5182.*

4 e-1
KITE FLITE

Kites of all colors, shapes, and sizes festoon this Pier 39 shop. Their basic single-line parafoil kites start at $25, but there are also plenty of two-line stunt kites, and even some 17-, 25-, and 35-ft dragon kites. *Pier 39, The Embarcadero and Beach St., Fisherman's Wharf, 415/956–3181.*

LEATHER GOODS & LUGGAGE

4 e-6
BOTTEGA VENETA

When your own initials aren't enough, you can always go with the BV monogram. The Italian-made leather goods—luggage, attachés, handbags, wallets, belts, and purses—are designed to last a lifetime. *108 Geary St., between Stockton St. and Grant Ave., Union Square, 415/981–1700. Closed Sun.*

4 e-5
COACH

This shop carries classically styled Coach luggage, as well as beautiful, distinctive briefcases, wallets, and men's belts. A second, nearby Coach store carries the famous Coach handbags, women's belts, and other accessories (*see* Clothing for Women/Specialty, *above*). *170 Post St., at Grant Ave., Union Square, 415/391–7770.*

4 e-3
EAST/WEST LEATHER

This North Beach shop has been selling fine leather boots, jackets, belts, purses, and backpacks for women and men since the late 1960s. *1400 Grant Ave., at Green St., North Beach, 415/397–2886.*

4 g-4
EDWARDS LUGGAGE

The luggage, briefcases, and portfolios at Edwards appeal to its Financial District clientele. Top brands such as Hartmann, Travelpro, Samsonite, Eagle Creek, Coach, and Ghurka are all represented. *3 Embarcadero Center, Clay and Sacramento Sts. between Battery and Drumm Sts., Embarcadero, 415/981–7047.*

4 e-6
EL PORTAL LUGGAGE

This is a one-stop travel shop, with luggage, briefcases, shaving kits, and other necessities by Polo/Ralph Lauren, Hartmann, Samsonite, and others. The staff is multilingual and helpful. *San Francisco Shopping Centre, 865 Market St., between 4th and 5th Sts., Union Square, 415/896–5637.*

4 e-5
GHURKA

Beautiful purses, briefcases, and backpacks come in the softest, most supple leather. Slightly less expensive accessories include leather eyeglass cases and daily planners. *170 Post St., at Kearny St., Union Square, 415/392–7267. Closed Sun.*

7 e-1
LA RIGA

This leather shop sells an odd mix of fairly conservative leather jackets and leather fetish wear—studded collars, bustiers, and barely-there dresses. The only unifying theme seems to be that everything must be black. *1391 Haight St., at Masonic Ave., Haight, 415/552–1525.*

4 e-5
LOUIS VUITTON

A quality French leather goods and luggage maker since 1854, Louis Vuitton produces the ultimate status symbol: LV-embossed bags, briefcases, luggage, and steamer trunks. The classic Monogram line is available, along with the blue, green, red, and yellow pieces of the colorful Epi line. *230 Post St., at Grant Ave., Union Square, 415/391–6200.*

4 e-6
THE LUGGAGE CENTER

Convenient to Moscone Convention Center, the Luggage Center sells top-quality luggage, attachés, backpacks, and travel accessories at up to 50% off regular retail prices. Bring your damaged suitcase here for expert repairs. *828 Mission St., between 4th and 5th Sts., South of Market, 415/543–3771.*

`4` e-5

MALM LUGGAGE

This upscale shop has been supplying San Francisco with fine luggage and leather goods since 1868. The emphasis is on luggage, travel accessories, and gifts for business executives. *222 Grant Ave., between Post and Sutter Sts., Union Square, 415/392–0417.*

`4` f-5

Crocker Galleria, 50 Post St., between Montgomery and Kearny Sts., Financial District, 415/391 5222. Closed Sun.

`7` g-2

MICHAEL BRUNO

This incredibly crowded little shop is packed floor to ceiling with a wide variety of suitcases, backpacks, duffel bags, and totes. In return for threading your way through the shop and stepping over the resident black lab, you get helpful service and a discount of about 20%–30% off other stores' prices. *2267 Market St., between Sanchez and Noe Sts., 415/552 3970. Closed Wed. and Sun.*

`4` e-5

NORTH BEACH LEATHER

This is the city's best source for high-quality leather garments—skirts, jackets, trousers, dresses, and accessories. *224 Grant Ave., between Post and Sutter Sts., Union Square, 415/362–8300.*

MAPS

`4` e-6

JOHN SCOPAZZI GALLERY

The gallery sells a marvelous selection of antique maps from the 16th through the 19th centuries, both framed and unframed. *130 Maiden La., between Stockton St. and Grant Ave., Union Square, 415/362–5708. Closed Sun.*

`4` f 5

RAND MCNALLY MAP & TRAVEL STORE

The famous Rand McNally road maps and atlases are available here, together with maps, language tapes, globes, and domestic and international travel guides from all publishers. The shop carries topographical maps for the Bay Area and Sierras, and can order topo maps for any other area in the United States. *595 Market St., at 2nd St., South of Market, 415/777–3131.*

`4` f-4

THOMAS BROS. MAPS AND BOOKS

This place has a selection, similar to Rand McNally's, of domestic and international maps, travel books and CD-ROMs, atlases, and globes. *550 Jackson St., at Columbus Ave., Financial District, 415/981–7520. Closed weekends.*

MEMORABILIA

`4` d-6

CINEMA SHOP

This tiny storefront, opened in 1967, is jammed with more than 250,000 original posters, stills, lobby cards, and rare videotapes of Hollywood classics and schlock films. *606 Geary St., at Jones St., Union Square, 415/885 6785. Closed Sun.*

`6` e-3

LET IT BE RECORDS

See Music, below.

`4` d-3

SAN FRANCISCO ROCK POSTERS AND COLLECTIBLES

The huge selection of rock-and-roll memorabilia here includes posters, handbills, and original art, most of it from the 1960s. Also available are posters from more recent shows at the legendary Fillmore, with musicians like George Clinton, Porno for Pyros, and Johnny Cash. *1851 Powell St., between Filbert and Greenwich Sts., North Beach, 415/956–6749 or 800/949–1965. Closed Sun. and Mon.*

`4` e-4

SHOW BIZ

Stock up here on movie, rock-and-roll, jazz, and theater memorabilia from several decades—posters, playbills, photos, figurines, and the like. Posters advertising concerts at the Fillmore date from 1966 to the present. Some of it is sensibly priced, some not. *1318 Grant Ave., at Vallejo St., North Beach, 415/989–6744.*

MINIATURES

`5` a-7

THE HOBBY COMPANY OF SAN FRANCISCO

See Crafts & Hobbies, above.

MUSIC

cds, tapes & vinyl

3 *e-3*

AMOEBA

Amoeba stocks more than 100,000 new and used CDs, LPs, and tapes and is always at the top of local "best of" lists. If you're looking for a rare or hard-to-find release, this is where you'll find it. The San Francisco store stages frequent live music by both local and national bands. *2455 Telegraph Ave., at Haste St., Berkeley, 510/549–1125.*

7 *d-1*

1855 Haight St., between Stanyan and Shrader Sts., Haight, 415/831–1200.

8 *a-4*

AQUARIUS RECORDS

Aquarius began as *the* punk rock store in the 1970s, but has since diversified to include indie rock, dance music, experimental electronica, and a great selection of imports. The swank space carries mostly vinyl, but there are tapes and CDs—both new and used—as well. *1055 Valencia St., between 21st and 22nd Sts., Mission, 415/647–2272.*

4 *b-8*

BPM MUSIC FACTORY

Bay Area club DJs shop here for imports and domestic products. The store's 12-inch collection includes house, techno, acid jazz, and progressive. *573 Hayes St., at Laguna St., Hayes Valley, 415/487–8680.*

8 *b-5*

DISCOLANDIA

This Mission District shop is far and away the city's best bet for current and vintage Latin music. *2964 24th St., between Harrison and Alabama Sts., Mission, 415/826–9446.*

7 *g-1*

GROOVE MERCHANT

Groove Merchant's owners run the highly recommended Luv 'n Haight and Ubiquity labels, both of which put the spotlight on the local acid jazz scene. *687 Haight St., between Pierce and Steiner Sts., Haight, 415/252–5766. Closed Mon.*

3 *b-2*

HEAR MUSIC

The collection here is a mix of roots, folk, jazz, hip-hop, international music, and rock. But what really makes this place worth the trip to Berkeley are its 60 listening stations where you can hear *any* CD in the store before you buy. *1809-B 4th St., at Hearst St., Berkeley, 510/204–9595.*

4 *e-6*

Metreon, 4th and Mission Sts., South of Market, 415/369–6070.

6 *g-2*

JAZZ QUARTER

This snug Sunset District shop is tops for jazz lovers. It specializes in new and rare jazz LPs, but also carries new and used CDs. *1267 20th Ave., between Irving St. and Lincoln Way, Sunset District, 415/661–2331. Closed Sun.*

6 *e-3*

LET IT BE RECORDS

With a name like this, could this Sunset District store specialize in anything but the Beatles? It carries many rare and out-of-print rock-and-roll records from the 1950s through 1980s, as well as rock memorabilia. *2434 Judah St., between 29th and 30th Aves., Sunset District, 415/681–2113. Closed Sun. and Mon.*

7 *e-1*

RECKLESS RECORDS

One of several shops that make Haight Street a must stop for music lovers, Reckless buys and sells rock, hip-hop, and indie recordings, with a large section devoted to vinyl. Collectible LPs and picture discs, all for sale, line the walls. *1401 Haight St., at Masonic Ave., Haight, 415/431–3434.*

7 *g-2*

THE RECORD FINDER

Visit this Upper Market shop for new and used vinyl, cassettes, and CDs—if you can't find it yourself, the staff will help you search for it. Its strengths are rock, soul, R&B, and classical music. *258 Noe St., near Market St., Castro, 415/431–4443.*

7 *e-1*

RECYCLED RECORDS

A Haight Street favorite, Recycled doesn't have anything new. Instead, it buys, sells, and trades a vast collection of rock, jazz, soul, pop, blues, reggae, folk, and hard-to-find imports, mostly on LPs. The collection of CDs in the back seems an afterthought. *1377 Haight St., at Masonic Ave., Haight, 415/626–4075.*

5 *h-8*

REGGAE RUNNINS VILLAGE STORE

This reggae wonderland carries records, tapes, videos, T-shirts, jewelry, and other paraphernalia in the Rasta colors of red, gold, black, and green. *505 Divisadero St., between Fell and Hayes Sts., Western Addition, 415/922–2442.*

8 *a-4*

RITMO LATINO

In the heart of the Mission, this colorful Latin-music store sells ranchero, mariachi, salsa, merengue, *conjunto*, *norteño*, and more. You can sample CDs at the listening stations before buying. *2401 Mission St., at 20th St., Mission, 415/824–8556.*

8 *a-5*

SAMIRAMIS IMPORTS

There's a fine selection of Middle Eastern CDs here, in addition to imported gourmet delicacies (*see* Food, *above*).

4 *b-8*

STAR CLASSICS

Star stocks only classical, opera, symphonic, ballet, New Age, and jazz tapes and CDs. The adjoining Star Classics Recital Hall hosts weekly vocal and musical performances. *425 Hayes St., at Gough St., Hayes Valley, 415/552–1110.*

7 *g-5*

STREET LIGHT RECORDS

A San Francisco institution since the 1960s, Street Light buys and sells thousands of used tapes and CDs, with a vast selection of rock, jazz, soul, and R&B, as well as plenty of vinyl. The selection is usually offbeat and always fresh. The Noe Valley store is smaller, but has a better selection of vinyl. *3979 24th St., between Noe and Sanchez Sts., Noe Valley, 415/282–3550.*

7 *f-3*

2350 Market St., at Castro St., Castro, 415/282–8000.

4 *c-2*

TOWER RECORDS

This international megachain is excellent for CDs in every category. Its three huge San Francisco branches—open daily until midnight—carry full selections of all types of music. The North Beach store is the largest, with a great classical music annex across the street. The outlet store has a more limited selection, but its remaindered items are great for bargain-hunters. *2525 Jones St., at Columbus Ave. and Bay St., North Beach, 415/885–0500.*

7 *g-2*

2280 Market St., at Noe St., Castro, 415/621–0588.

2 *c-6*

Stonestown Galleria, 19th Ave. and Winston Dr., Stonestown, 415/681–2001.

4 *g-7*

Outlet: 660 3rd St., between Townsend and Brannan Sts., South Beach, 415/957–9660.

4 *e-6*

VIRGIN MEGASTORE

This towering monolith near Union Square has hundreds of listening stations, a separate classical music room, and an extensive laser disc department, as well as a bookstore and a café. It's the best place in the city to buy import CDs, according to annual *Bay Guardian* surveys, although you can find lower prices elsewhere. *2 Stockton St., at Market St., Union Square, 415/397–4525.*

music boxes

4 *c-2*

CABLE CAR MUSIC BOX CO.

This shop has about 3,000 different music boxes from around the world. Its

---

HAIGHT-ASHBURY HIGH NOTES

The Upper Haight is heaven for music-lovers. Browse for obscure imports, classic punk—whatever you fancy, it's here.

Groove Merchant
Plenty for the collector, DJ, or serious amateur.

Haight Ashbury Music Center
One of the largest sellers of musical instruments on the West Coast.

Reckless Records
Everything from new imports to vintage rock posters.

Recycled Records
A Haight Street favorite for used vinyl, cassettes, and CDs.

cable car music boxes range from a basic model for less than $10 to a model that spins and lights up for about $150. *Anchorage Shopping Center, 395 Jefferson St., at Leavenworth St., Fisherman's Wharf, 415/771–7402.*

4 *e-6*

THE SAN FRANCISCO MUSIC BOX COMPANY

Choose from 2,000 different music boxes, costing anywhere from a song to an arm and a leg, plus a wide variety of San Francisco–themed snow globes. The company started here in 1978, and there are now 175 stores across the United States. *San Francisco Shopping Centre, 865 Market St., between 4th and 5th Sts., Union Square, 415/546–6343.*

4 *e-1*

Pier 39, The Embarcadero and Beach St., Fisherman's Wharf, 415/433–3696.

musical instruments

4 *e-5*

CLARION MUSIC CENTER

This is routinely praised as the best place in the city to "see, hear, and buy" musical instruments of the world: *didgeridoos* (a type of Australian wind instrument), sitars, Tibetan singing bowls, African drums, Native American flutes, Chinese stringed instruments, and more. Don't forget the books and CDs, and live performances on Friday nights. *816 Sacramento St., at Grant Ave., Chinatown, 415/391–1317. Closed Sun.*

WORLD MUSIC

For those who crave something other than good ole American rock and roll, here are a few alternatives:

Discolandia
  Good selections of current and vintage Latin music.

Hear Music
  World music is a specialty here.

Reggae Runnins Village Store
  Reggae records, tapes, and videos.

Ritmo Latino
  Ranchero, mariachi, salsa, and other Latin sounds.

Samiramis Imports
  Middle Eastern music.

---

2 *e-6*

DRUM WORLD

This is easily one of the best-stocked drum stores in the Bay Area, if not the entire country. The shop buys and sells vintage and used drums, and also has a good selection of books and videos. *5016 Mission St., between Geneva and Ocean Aves., Excelsior, 415/334–7559. Closed Sun.*

5 *b-7*

GUITAR SOLO

While all the rock star wannabes are across town at the Guitar Center, serious classical and acoustic guitarists are at Guitar Solo fondling their selection of high-end instruments by Ramirez, Contreras, Hirade, and others. It's also a good place to pick up obscure music and information about guitar-related happenings around town. *1411 Clement St., at 15th Ave., Richmond District, 415/386–0395.*

7 *d-1*

HAIGHT ASHBURY MUSIC CENTER

This is one of the largest sellers of musical instruments on the West Coast, with mixers, mikes, amps, sheet music, magazines, cables, musical instruments, and hundreds of acoustic and electric guitars, all brought to you by pleasant, knowledgeable salespeople. If it doesn't have what you're looking for, the staff will refer you to someone who does. *1540 Haight St., between Clayton and Ashbury Sts., Haight, 415/863–7327.*

4 *c-2*

LARK IN THE MORNING

Portuguese mandolas, concertinas, and steel drums are just a few of the hundreds of instruments sold at this world music emporium. Instructional books and videos will help you figure out what to do with your new tenor banjo. Serious shoppers should ask to use one of the practice rooms in back to escape the crowds thumping on and strumming everything in sight. *The Cannery, 2801 Leavenworth St., at Beach St., Fisherman's Wharf, 415/922–4277.*

7 *g-5*

NOE VALLEY MUSIC

The *Bay Guardian* calls this the "Best place to buy musical equipment without being treated like a cretin." It specializes in stringed instruments, many of them

Finally, a travel companion that doesn't snore on the plane or eat all your peanuts.

MCI WORLDCOM   WorldPhone®

123 456 7891 2345
J.D. SMITH

When traveling, your MCI WorldCom℠ Card is the best way to keep in touch. Our operators speak your language, so they'll be able to connect you back home—no matter where your travels take you. Plus, your MCI WorldCom Card is easy to use, and even earns you frequent flyer miles' every time you use it. When you add in our great rates, you get something even more valuable: peace-of-mind. So go ahead. Travel the world. MCI WorldCom just brought it a whole lot closer.

You can even sign up today at www.mci.com/worldphone or ask your operator to make a collect call to 1-410-314-2938.

EASY TO CALL WORLDWIDE

1 Dial 1-800-888-8000.
2 Dial or give the operator your MCI WorldCom Card number.
3 Dial or give the number you're calling.

EARN FREQUENT FLYER MILES

AmericanAirlines®
A'Advantage®

Continental Airlines
OnePass

▲ Delta Air Lines
SkyMiles®

HAWAIIANMILES
HAWAIIAN AIRLINES

MIDWEST EXPRESS AIRLINES   FREQUENT FLYER
PROGRAM PARTNER

SOUTHWEST AIRLINES®
RAPIDREWARDS
A SYMBOL OF FREEDOM™

MILEAGE PLUS.
United Airlines

U·S AIRWAYS
DIVIDEND MILES

*You will earn flight credits in the Southwest Airlines Rapid Rewards Program. All airline names and logos are proprietary marks of the respective airlines. All airline program rules and conditions apply.

MCI WORLDCOM.

Fodor's

Distinctive guides packed with up-to-date expert
advice and smart choices for every type of traveler.

Fodor's. For the world of ways you travel.

vintage. *3914-A 24th St., between Noe and Sanchez Sts., 415/821–6644.*

sheet music

B *b-2*

BYRON HOYT SHEET MUSIC

Whether you're a professional musician or a just a shower warbler, you'll find what you're looking for in this warehouse space filled with pop, with classical and jazz sheet music. *2525 16th St., between Bryant and Harrison Sts., Mission, 415/431–8055. Closed Sun. and Mon.*

4 *e-6*

MUSIC CENTER OF SAN FRANCISCO

Under one roof you'll find jazz, pop, and classical sheet music, the largest such selection on the West Coast. The shop also sells accessories such as metronomes, tuners, and books. *207 Powell St., between Geary and O'Farrell Sts., Union Square, 415/781–6023.*

6 *g-5*

MUSIC RACK

The San Francisco Conservatory of Music runs this shop stocking new and used sheet music and books. It is closed Saturday in summer. *1201 Ortega St., at 19th Ave., Sunset District, 415/759–3440. Closed Sun.*

NEEDLEWORK & KNITTING

4 *f-5*

ARTFIBERS GALLERY

Artfibers specializes in high-fashion and exotic fiber yarns for knitting and weaving, including imported yarns custom-made for European fashion designers. *124 Sutter St., 2nd floor, between Montgomery and Kearny Sts., Financial District, 415/956–6319.*

5 *g-5*

ATELIER YARNS

Among this shop's extensive selection of yarns for knitting, weaving, spinning, and crocheting is a wide selection of natural fibers, including silky domestic cashmere. In addition, Atelier has day, evening, and weekend classes for all levels. *1945 Divisadero St., at California St., Pacific Heights, 415/771–1550. Closed Sun. and Mon.*

5 *f-5*

ELAINE MAGNIN

This appealing shop stocks well over 1,500 designs of hand-painted needlepoint canvases, and some 145 different kinds of fibers. It also has expert finishing and custom canvas designs, just in case you can't find what you want in the vast collection. *3310 Sacramento St., at Presidio Ave., Laurel Heights, 415/931–3063.*

4 *e-1*

FUN STITCH

Needlepoint, cross-stitch, and crewel are the specialties here, and there are also plenty of supplies, how-to books, and wonderful patterns. Best-selling patterns include those of San Francisco's cable cars and of the Golden Gate Bridge. *Pier 39, The Embarcadero and Beach St., Fisherman's Wharf, 415/956–3037.*

4 *e-6*

NEEDLEPOINT, INC.

A staff of seven artists designs and produces unique hand-painted needlepoint canvases exclusively for this shop. The house brand of 100% Chinese silk thread comes in 427 different colors. It has every kind of fiber and tool needed for needlepoint. *275 Post St., 2nd floor, between Stockton St. and Grant Ave., Union Square, 415/392–1622 or 800/345–1622. Closed Sun.*

NEWSPAPERS & MAGAZINES

3 *d-7*

DE LAUER SUPER NEWSSTAND

News junkies appreciate that this East Bay stand is open 24 hours. In addition to foreign and domestic newspapers, the newsstand also has a huge magazine inventory, as well as maps and paperbacks. *1310 Broadway Ave., between 13th and 14th Sts., Oakland, 510/451–6157.*

4 *f-5*

EASTERN NEWSSTAND CORP.

This is the biggest newsstand corporation in San Francisco, with several downtown stands stocking many newspaper and magazine titles—including about 20 titles from England, France, Germany, and Italy. *101 California St., at*

Front St., Financial District, 415/989–8986. Closed Sun.

4 f-5

444 Market St., at Battery St., Financial District, 415/397–1721. Closed Sun.

4 g-4

3 Embarcadero Center, Clay and Sacramento Sts. between Battery and Drumm Sts., Embarcadero, 415/982–4425.

7 g-5

GOOD NEWS

Noe Valley's favorite newsstand carries out-of-town papers and periodicals. It's open late every Sunday. 3920 24th St., between Noe and Sanchez Sts., Noe Valley, 415/821–3694.

4 d-6

HAROLDS INTERNATIONAL NEWSSTAND

Just two blocks from Union Square, Harolds carries many out-of-town papers, most major periodicals, and plenty of postcards. 524 Geary St., at Taylor St., Union Square, 415/441–2665.

5 h-5

JUICY NEWS

Get your morning news and a healthy start to the day at this combination newsstand/juice bar. It stocks a good selection of foreign (mostly European) newspapers, as well as a wide selection of magazines, heavy on home decor titles. 2453 Fillmore St., between Washington and Jackson Sts., Pacific Heights, 415/441–3051.

7 g-1

NAKED EYE NEWS AND VIDEO

This quirky shop in the Haight can be counted on for an eclectic stock of periodicals and newspapers, and a full array of 'zines. Their video collection is tops (see Videos, below). 533 Haight St., between Fillmore and Steiner Sts., Haight, 415/864–2985.

NOTIONS

7 f-3

CLIFF'S VARIETY

The annex next door to the main hardware store stocks mostly sewing notions and craft items: buttons, ribbon and trim, and the like. A small selection of wares for the bed and bath (mattress pads, shower curtains, soap dishes) rounds out the selection. 479 Castro St., between Market and 18th Sts., Castro, 415/431–5365. Closed Sun.

8 c-2

RIBBONERIE

If you can't find the ribbon you want here, you're just not looking—more than a thousand types line the shelves. Trims, buttons, braid, and silk flowers round out the offerings. 191 Potrero St., at 15th St., Potrero Hill, 415/626–6184. Closed Sun. and Mon.

OFFICE SUPPLIES

5 a-7

GABLES OFFICE SUPPLIES AND STATIONERY

Gables has an old-time feel, with serious business supplies in the back and gifts, stationery, writing instruments, and cards as you enter. 5636 Geary Blvd., between 20th and 21st Aves., Richmond District, 415/751–8152.

5 f-7

OFFICE DEPOT

The San Francisco outlets of the national chain provide a full range of office supplies, plus furniture and computers. Each has an in-house copy and print shop. 2675 Geary Blvd., at Masonic Ave., Western Addition, 415/441–3044.

4 f-7

855 Harrison St., at 5th St., South of Market, 415/243–9959.

8 c-2

Potrero Center, 2300 16th St., at Potrero Ave., 415/252–8280.

7 a-2

SUNSET STATIONERS

Stock up here on office products, computer supplies, and rubber stamps, as well as pens and gifts, unusual greeting cards, wedding invitations, fine stationery, legal forms, and artists' materials. Prices are extremely competitive, and service is friendly. 653 Irving St., at 8th Ave., Sunset District, 415/664–0937. Closed Sun.

4 f-4

WALDECK'S OFFICE SUPPLIES

For decades Waldeck's has been supplying the downtown area with fine pens, stationery and invitations, San Francisco postcards, and all kinds of office supplies. *500 Washington St., at Sansome St., Financial District, 415/981–3381. Closed weekends.*

4 *g-4*

3 Embarcadero Center, Clay and Sacramento Sts. between Battery and Drumm Sts., Embarcadero, 415/986–2275.

PENS

4 *e-6*

GOLDEN GATE PEN SHOP

This shop has one of the largest selections of fine writing instruments in San Francisco. It carries 20 lines—including Mont Blanc, Shaeffer, Aurora, Cross, Cartier, and Caran d'Ache—with many limited editions. *260 Stockton St., 5th floor, at Post St., Union Square, 415/781–4809. Closed Sun.*

4 *e-6*

PENULTIMA

If a Bic just won't do, try out one of the fountain, rollerball, or ballpoint pens sold here, many made by Shaeffer, Waterman, and Mont Blanc. It also sells accessories like bottles of ink and handmade stationery. *San Francisco Shopping Centre, 865 Market St., between 4th and 5th St., Union Square, 415/543–7274.*

PETS & PET SUPPLIES

4 *c-4*

CATNIP & BONES

Human companions of pampered pets shop here for toys and treats. As well as the store's namesake catnip plants and wide selection of bone-shape doggie treats, you'll find sunglasses and accessories for the well-dressed pet. Wedding and other fancy-dress collars are a specialty. *1463 Broadway, between Polk and Larkin Sts., Russian Hill, 415/674–8686.*

5 *h-3*

2220 Chestnut St., at Pierce St., Marina, 415/359–9100.

3 *c-2*

EAST BAY VIVARIUM

The United States' largest collection of reptiles is at this Berkeley shop. Snakes, lizards, and turtles, as well as frogs, toads, and tarantulas, are a specialty.

1827 5th St., at Hearst Ave., Berkeley, 510/841–1400.

4 *g-7*

GEORGE

Named after a wire-hair fox terrier, George stocks "products he and his cat and dog friends would enjoy using." Apparently his friends are fond of luxury items like pet beds, catnip toys, decorative dog bowls, and "Good Dog" bath towels. *2411 California St., at Fillmore St., Pacific Heights, 415/441–0564.*

8 *c-2*

SAMMY'S PET WORLD

Voted "Best Pet Store in San Francisco" by the *SF Weekly*, Sammy's is the largest of the city's pet stores. Come here for dog and cat grooming, premium pet foods, fish and aquariums, birds and other small animals, and every type of pet accessory. *16th and Bryant Sts., Mission, 415/863–1840.*

4 *c-5*

1677 Washington St., at Polk St., Russian Hill, 415/865–4400.

tropical fish and accessories

5 *e-7*

NIPPON GOLDFISH COMPANY

Goldfish aren't the only slippery critters at the largest aquarium store in San Francisco; fresh and saltwater fishes of every hue and size fill the tanks that cover the 10,000-ft store. Minimalists can invest in a simple fishbowl and goldfish, but the real enthusiast can invest thousands in high-tech tanks, filters, and temperature control systems to keep their aquatic companions happy. *3109 Geary Blvd., between Cook and Spruce Sts., Laurel Heights, 415/668-2203.*

PHOTO EQUIPMENT

4 *f-6*

ADOLPH GASSER

Gasser has the largest inventory of photography and video equipment in northern California, including good-quality used gear. The shop rents video and still cameras and has an on-site photo lab. *181 2nd St., between Howard and Mission*

Sts., South of Market, 415/495–3852. Closed Sun.

2 b-3

5733 Geary Blvd., between 21st and 22nd Aves., Richmond District, 415/751–0145. Closed Sun.

4 f-6

DISCOUNT CAMERA

Check the prices here before buying elsewhere: part of a chain, Discount Camera sells major brands of cameras, VCRs, camcorders, telephones, binoculars, and tape recorders. It also buys, sells, and trades used cameras and lenses. 33 Kearny St., between Post and Market Sts., Union Square, 415/392–1100.

3 e-3

LOOKING GLASS

This small store is great for tripods, paper, film, books, and other photographic supplies. It also offers classes and rents darkroom space. 2848 Telegraph Ave., at Oregon St., Berkeley, 510/548–6888.

4 g-7

PHOTOGRAPHER'S SUPPLY

This place has the best prices in San Francisco and is a favorite of Bay Area professional photographers. Novices may find shopping here a bewildering experience, but it's worth the effort of sifting through their huge supply of film, paper, chemicals in bulk, and the lowest-priced Kodak film in town. 436 Bryant St., between 2nd and 3rd Sts., South of Market, 415/495–8640.

POSTCARDS

4 e-3

QUANTITY POSTCARDS

This North Beach shop has about 15,000 postcards—its own designs, vintage cards, and more. Celebrity, geographical, art, and camp are just a few categories. 1441 Grant Ave., at Green St., North Beach, 415/986–8866.

4 e-3

TILT

Under the same ownership as Quantity Postcards (see above), Tilt specializes in postcards with an Americana theme. The whimsical selection includes old snapshots of San Francisco, '50s family scenes, long-forgotten Hollywood stars,

and schmaltzy nature scenes, among other things. 507 Columbus Ave., near Stockton St., North Beach, 415/788–5566.

7 e-1

1427 Haight St., near Masonic Ave., Haight, 415/355–1155.

POSTERS

See also Memorabilia, above.

4 a-4

THE ARTISANS OF SAN FRANCISCO

Historical posters and photos of San Francisco are the specialty here. Look at images of the city's heady Gold Rush days, Barbary Coast hedonism, wrath of the 1906 earthquake, and more. 1964 Union St., at Buchanan St., Cow Hollow, 415/921–0456. Closed Mon.

4 d-8

ART ROCK GALLERY

This funky shop sells handmade silk-screened posters, many in a clever faux-vintage style. Like an art gallery, it frequently displays rare and vintage posters on its walls. 1155 Mission St., between 7th and 8th Sts., South of Market, 415/255–7390. Closed Sun. and Mon.

4 e-1

POSTER SOURCE

To pass the time at Pier 39, browse the contemporary art, rock, sports, and celebrity posters. Pier 39, The Embarcadero and Beach St., Fisherman's Wharf, 415/433–1995.

4 e-3

TILT

Although it's best known for postcards (see above), Tilt is also the exclusive distributor of silkscreened, limited-edition rock posters by famed local artist Frank Kozik, whose psychedelic art has advertised Green Day and other bands.

SPORTING GOODS & CLOTHING

7 d-1

CAL SURPLUS

Woolly socks, old-fashioned sleeping bags, Jansport backpacks, and Swiss Army knives are some of the useful items you can pick up here. 1541 Haight

St., between Clayton and Ashbury Sts., Haight, 415/861–0404.

`4` b-6

FTC SKI & SPORTS

An all-around excellent sporting goods store, FTC has golf, swimming, and tennis equipment, as well as selections of skateboards, snowboards, and wakeboards (*see Skating and Skiing & Snowboarding, below*). *1586 Bush St., at Franklin St., Pacific Heights, 415/673–8363.*

`4` b-8

G & M SALES

The "Great Outdoors Store" has been a local institution since 1948. It has one of the city's best selections of camping gear—with dozens of fully erected tents on display—plus a large selection of outerwear, hiking boots and shoes, ski goods, and an extensive fishing department. *1667 Market St., at Gough St., Civic Center, 415/863–2855.*

`4` c-4

LOMBARDI SPORTS

Like G & M, Lombardi has been serving its devoted clientele since 1948. It's a one-stop shop for ski, camping, and golf equipment; it also has the city's best selection of exercise equipment, shoes, apparel, sunglasses, and other accessories. The shop's annual bike and ski sales draw big crowds. *1600 Jackson St., at Polk St., Russian Hill, 415/771–0600.*

`4` e-5

NIKETOWN

One of the most hyped shops on Union Square, the three-story NikeTown is equal parts theme park, sports museum, and store. High-priced Nike-emblazoned shoes and apparel are displayed next to video screens showing endless loops of Michael Jordan and his namesake sneakers. *278 Post St., at Stockton St., Union Square, 415/392–6453.*

`4` e-5

THE NORTH FACE

The Bay Area-based company is famous for its top-of-the-line, expedition-quality tents, sleeping bags, backpacks, and outdoor apparel, including Gore-Tex jackets and pants. The outlet store is the place to find last season's jackets, sleeping bags, and other gear for 20%–70% less. *180 Post St., between Kearny St. and Grant Ave., Union Square, 415/433–3223.*

`4` d-8

Outlet: 1325 Howard St., between 9th and 10th Sts., South of Market, 415/626–6444.

`4` c-2

PATAGONIA

Along with sportswear and casual clothing, Patagonia carries body wear for backpacking, fly-fishing, kayaking, and the like. The equipment and clothing is for serious outdoors enthusiasts and tends to be expensive. *770 North Point St., at Hyde St., Fisherman's Wharf, 415/771–2050.*

`7` a-7

PLAY IT AGAIN SPORTS

Here you can trade in your old golf clubs, exercise equipment, in-line skates, or skis. The shop buys, sells, trades, and consigns good-quality sporting equipment of all sorts, but the largest selections are of new and used in-line skates, golf accessories, and exercise gear. *45 West Portal Ave., between Vicente and Ulloa Sts., Sunset District, 415/753–3049.*

`3` c-1

REI

The popular retail cooperative has a 30,000-square-ft store in Berkeley, complete with a 35-ft-tall climbing wall and gear for most outdoor pursuits. Monthly events include slide shows and equipment demonstrations; the biannual blowout sales are legendary. A rental department outfits weekend campers and skiers. *1338 San Pablo Ave., at Gilman St., Berkeley, 510/527–4140.*

`5` a-7

SULLIVAN'S SPORT SHOP

Sullivan's has equipment and clothing for camping, fishing, hunting, boxing, baseball, backpacking, swimming, snorkeling, tennis, badminton, table tennis, skiing, boccie, croquet, in-line skating, and in-line hockey. The repair shop handles tennis rackets, camping gear, and skis; the rental department takes care of volleyball, softball, badminton, camping, croquet, and skiing equipment. *5323 Geary Blvd., between 17th and 18th Aves., Richmond District, 415/751–7070 or 415/751–2738.*

`4` e-6

TIMBERLAND

Some people buy the Polartec vests and twill pants for wilderness excursions. For others, the flannel shirts, denim jackets, and Timberland logo sweatshirts are their fashion statement. Many who wear their sturdy leather hiking boots swear by them. *100 Grant Ave., at Geary St., Financial District, 415/788–1690.*

3 *c-2*

WILDERNESS EXCHANGE

Most of the mountaineering, rock-climbing, cross-country skiing, backpacking, and camping gear here are closeouts and seconds sold for 30%–50% off. There are smaller selections of used merchandise and new equipment. *1407 San Pablo Ave., near Gilman St., Berkeley, 510/525–1255.*

fishing

2 *b-3*

GUS'S DISCOUNT TACKLE

The devoted clientele of this friendly, familiar shop drop by before a day's fishing to see what's on sale. Gus's stocks everything for salmon, trout, freshwater, saltwater, and surf fishing, at prices 10%–80% below retail. *3710 Balboa St., between 38th and 39th Aves., Richmond District, 415/752–6197. Closed Sun.*

2 *b-3*

HI'S TACKLE BOX

This spacious shop stocks everything you need to catch any kind of fish, including fly-fishing equipment and deep-sea fishing gear. It also has an excellent repair shop that can build you a custom rod and reel. You can arrange 4- to 16-day deep-sea fishing trips departing from San Diego here as well; the very popular trips fill up almost a year in advance. *3141 Clement St., at 33rd Ave., Richmond District, 415/221–3825. Closed Sun.*

4 *e-5*

ORVIS SAN FRANCISCO

Orvis is a mail-order outdoor store chain with around 25 stores nationwide; the shop in San Francisco has an especially large and fine fly-fishing department, as well as durable outdoor clothing and luggage. *300 Grant Ave., between Bush and Sutter Sts., Union Square, 415/392–1600.*

5 *a-7*

SULLIVAN'S SPORT SHOP

Fishing gear is a specialty at this general sports store: Look for fly-tying tools and materials for fly-fishing, plus rods and reels for freshwater and saltwater fishing. *5323 Geary Blvd., between 17th and 18th Aves., Richmond District, 415/751–7070 or 415/751–2738.*

golf

4 *e-5*

DON SHERWOOD GOLF AND TENNIS WORLD

The selection of clubs is first-rate (*see* Tennis, *below*).

1 *c-7*

FRY'S WAREHOUSE GOLF AND TENNIS

The computerized club fitting at Fry's is free (*see* Tennis, *below*).

1 *c-7*

THE GOLF MART

The San Francisco branch of this store is next to the Mission Bay Golf Center (*see* Golf *in* Chapter 3); but the enormous warehouse-style store south of the city is several times as large as the San Francisco branch. Year-round prices on top-of-the-line golf equipment and apparel are discounted 5%–10% at both stores; get on the mailing list for the scoop on seasonal sales. *470-A Noor Ave., at El Camino Real, South San Francisco, 650/583–4653.*

8 *e-1*

Mission Bay Golf Center, 1200 6th St., at Channel St., China Basin, 415/703–6190.

4 *f-5*

MCCAFFERY'S GOLF SHOP

What sets this shop apart is that it has two PGA professionals on staff, who can assist you with choosing clubs and improving your swing. The pro golf equipment and apparel is reasonably priced. *80 Sutter St., at Montgomery St., Financial District, 415/989–4653.*

riding

2 *b-2*

TAL-Y-TARA TEA & POLO SHOPPE

Here's a place that serves a proper British tea, complete with crumpets and scones, to the folks who stop by to buy English riding apparel and equipment. The shop sells polo mallets to members of the city's Polo Club, and can special order whatever equestrian equipment is not in stock. *6439 California St., between 26th and 27th Aves., Richmond District, 415/751–9275. Closed Sun.*

skating

4 h-8

BLADIUM

The pro shop at the Bladium indoor in-line hockey rink (*see* Hockey *in* Chapter 3) is the city's best source of hockey equipment, including sticks, pucks, blades, and jerseys. *1050 3rd St., near Berry St., South Beach, 415/442–5060.*

7 h-1

DLX

The city's coolest skateboard shop draws a regular posse of skaters who kick back and watch skate videos or peruse the boards, accessories, and clothing from designers like Thunder, Spitfire, and Adrenalin. Local skater and artist Kevin Ancell designs one of the long boards for sale here. *1831 Market St., at Guerrero St., Mission, 415/626–5588.*

4 b-6

FTC SKI & SPORTS

The skate shop within FTC has skateboards, Rollerblades, roller skates, safety gear, clothing, and rentals. *1586 Bush St., at Franklin St., Pacific Heights, 415/673–8363.*

5 g-2

MARINA SKATE AND SNOWBOARD

Super friendly service is what distinguishes this shop: Show up Saturday at 8 AM for a free in-line skating lesson, which includes free rental for the duration of the lesson. The shop sells and rents three kinds of in-line skates—recreational, hockey, and aggressive—for skaters who enjoy jumping off stairs and performing tricks. Snowboards are also a specialty. *2271 Chestnut St., near Scott St., Marina, 415/567–8400.*

7 a-7

PLAY IT AGAIN SPORTS

Come here for new and used in-line skates (*see above*).

6 d-2

SKATE PRO SPORTS

The staff at Skate Pro can tell you anything you want to know about the city's skating scene, including information on racing and league play. It also will sell you in-line skating and hockey equipment and accessories; with purchase of skates you get a free two-hour lesson. *3401 Irving St., at 35th Ave., Sunset District, 415/752–8776.*

7 c-1

SKATES ON HAIGHT

At the Stanyan Street entrance to Golden Gate Park, Skates on Haight is a great place for in-line skate sales and rentals, skateboard sales, and snowboarding sales and rentals. Prices are some of the lowest in town. Free in-line skating lessons are given Sunday at 8:30 AM to those who rent (free lessons are also given with purchase of any pair of in-line skates). *1818 Haight St., at Stanyan St., Haight, 415/752–8375.*

skiing & snowboarding

See also Skating, *above.*

4 d-2

ANY MOUNTAIN

This outdoors store, part of a local chain, has an excellent selection of skis for beginners; experts will appreciate its super-slick skis by Rossignol, Fischer, K2, Atomic, and Salomon. It also stocks a variety of outdoor gear: Kelty sleeping bags, Columbia outerwear, and polar fleece jackets, as well as in-line skates. *2598 Taylor St., at Bay St., Fisherman's Wharf, 415/345–8080.*

DEMO-SPORTS

This tiny San Rafael shop has skis and snowboards for 10%–20% less than its Bay Area competitors. Its April demo-ski sale is legendary, with skiers signing up for particular models beginning in February. In summer the shop sells water skis, in-line skates, and wakeboards. *1101 E. Francisco Blvd., at Bellam Blvd., San Rafael, 415/454–3500.*

4 b-6

FTC SKI & SPORTS

Let FTC help you with custom boot fitting, or top-of-the-line ski and snowboard equipment. It also sells and rents kids' skis and ski car racks, too. *1586 Bush St., at Franklin St., Pacific Heights, 415/673–8363.*

5 g-2

**MARINA SKATE
AND SNOWBOARD**

See Skating, above.

3 d-3

MARMOT MOUNTAIN WORKS

Berkeley's superb outdoors store is also the Bay Area's cross-country ski center. By mid-October it's usually fully stocked with cross-country skis of all types—skating and diagonal stride, waxless metal edge and nonmetal edge, and telemark skis. Rentals are available. 3049 Adeline St., at Ashby Ave., Berkeley, 510/849–0735.

7 d-1

SFO SNOWBOARDING

For top-of-the-line snowboarding equipment and clothing, SFO can't be beat. It has more than 100 top brands, including a full line of clothing for women snowboarders. Look for off-season deals on last year's rental equipment. 618 Shrader St., at Haight St., Haight, 415/386–1666. Closed Mon. in summer.

4 g-7

SOMA SKI & SPORTZ

The skiing and snowboarding equipment here—by Blizzard, Nordica, K2, Nitro, and Airwalk—is top-notch, and the prices tend to be 10%–20% lower than at other San Francisco stores. You can also get overnight tune-ups on your skis. 689 3rd St., at Townsend St., South Beach, 415/777–2165. Closed Sun. Jun.–mid-Oct.

soccer

6 e-2

SUNSET SOCCER SUPPLY

The only specialty soccer shop in the city, this place has brand-name shoes, balls, bags, shorts, and jerseys. Drop by for information on local leagues, or to browse the collection of soccer-team souvenir memorabilia that's also for sale. 3214 Irving St., between 33rd and 34th Aves., Sunset District, 415/753–2666. Closed Tues.

tennis

5 f-5

BAYSPORT

Buy a new racquet, or choose from the stock of high-quality trade-ins. Or don't buy at all; with the demo program you can test as many racquets as you care to try in 25 days, for $25. 3375 Sacramento St., between Presidio Ave. and Walnut St., Laurel Heights, 415/771–4830.

4 e-5

**DON SHERWOOD GOLF
AND TENNIS WORLD**

The tennis equipment and clothing is top-of-the-line, and it also has an excellent racquet-demo program: $10 for five days, and you can apply unlimited demo fees to the purchase of a new racquet. 320 Grant Ave., at Sutter St., Union Square, 415/989–5000.

1 c-7

**FRY'S WAREHOUSE
GOLF & TENNIS**

All of the big name brands like Prince, Dunlop, and Wilson are here, and all at deep discounts. Although the 16,500-square-ft store feels like a warehouse, the salespeople go out of their way to make it feel like a small shop. Tennis-racquet stringing is among the services offered. 164 Marco Way, at S. Airport Blvd., South San Francisco, 650/583–5034.

4 f-4

**JOHN VETTRAINO'S TENNIS
AND SQUASH SHOP**

This place has served Financial District tennis and squash enthusiasts since 1976, with a full line of racquets, clothing, and shoes. Demo racquets are $5 apiece, for two days. 424 Clay St., at Battery St., Financial District, 415/956–5666. Closed Sun.

STATIONERY

4 a-6

**KINOKUNIYA STATIONERY
AND GIFTS**

The usual assortment of pens and notebooks is accompanied by beautiful decorative Japanese papers, washi boxes, and Asian zodiac birthday cards. Notepads and other desk items come in whimsical Japanese designs. Japan Center, Kinokuniya Bldg., 2nd floor, 1581 Webster St., at Post St., Japantown, 415/567–8901.

4 a-4

KOZO ARTS

The specialty papers at Kozo are made of materials such as bark and papyrus. The shop imports hand-silk-screened papers directly from Japan and occasionally from Korea and Italy. Also for sale are various objets d'art, such as hand-bound photo albums and journals, and frames artfully wrapped in handmade paper. *1969-A Union St., between Buchanan and Laguna Sts., Cow Hollow, 415/351–2114.*

4 e-6
PAPYRUS

This chain store with locations throughout the city sells cards for every occasion, wrapping paper, Crane's stationery, and small gift items. It also does custom printing for special occasions. *San Francisco Shopping Centre, 865 Market St., between 4th and 5th Sts., Union Square, 415/543–4246.*

4 a-4
UNION STREET PAPERY

The Bay Area's largest selection of custom-printed stationery and invitations is Union Street Papery's claim to fame. Calligraphers on staff will lend a special touch to your invitations and announcement cards. *2162 Union St., at Webster St., Cow Hollow, 415/563–0200.*

THEATRICAL ITEMS

AMERICAN CONSERVATORY THEATER (ACT)

ACT (*see Theaters & Theater Companies in* Chapter 5) rents out the gorgeous costumes it's collected over three decades of critically acclaimed performances. Unique, meticulously detailed, well-crafted period costumes are what you'll find, with plenty to choose from in the Victorian, Renaissance, and 18th-century periods. *415/439–2379, by appointment only.*

4 f-5
CAPEZIO FOOTLIGHT COSTUME SHOP

At San Francisco's best costume and dance wear shop you can buy or rent clown ruffles, ball gowns, and sinister capes. Choose from masks, wigs, hats, makeup, and other accessories to put together the perfect costume. *180 Sutter St., 2nd floor, at Kearny St., Financial District, 415/421–5657.*

7 g-1
COSTUMES ON HAIGHT

This fun Haight-Ashbury shop carries period, character, and seasonal costumes for sale or rent. Also here is a

selection of contemporary clothing, formal wear, and interesting inexpensive jewelry. *735 Haight St., between Scott and Pierce Sts., Haight, 415/621–1356.*

5 h-3
HOUSE OF MAGIC

Not just for Houdini fans, the House of Magic stocks costumes and professional theatrical makeup. Zany accessories include tiaras, beards, feather boas, and scary masks. *2025 Chestnut St., at Fillmore St., Marina, 415/346–2218.*

7 e-1
PIEDMONT BOUTIQUE

Drag queens come here for sparkly, spangly outfits, feather boas, and rhinestone jewelry of every sort. Women are welcome, too, to try on any of the campy outfits and tutus for ballerinas of all sizes. *1452 Haight St., between Masonic and Ashbury Sts., Haight, 415/864–8075.*

COSTUME SHOPS

Whether Halloween is approaching and you need a knockout costume or you simply enjoy playing dress up, you'll find what you're looking for at one of the following shops.

American Conservatory Theater (ACT) (Theatrical Items)
   The renowned theater company rents its quality costumes.

Capezio Footlight Costume Shop (Theatrical Items)
   All sorts of costumes, wigs, makeup, and accessories.

Costumes on Haight (Theatrical Items)
   Period, character, and seasonal costumes for sale or rent.

Departures from the Past (Clothing for Women/General)
   Vintage clothing with a theatrical flair.

House of Magic (Theatrical Items)
   Masks, theatrical makeup, and costumes.

Piedmont Boutique (Theatrical Items)
   Clothes for drag queens or girls who just want to look like one.

Stagecraft Studios (Theatrical Items)
   Worth the trip to Berkeley, especially if you need custom work done.

3 *d-3*
STAGECRAFT STUDIOS
Serious costume-shoppers will want to make the trip to Berkeley to hunt through this shop's collection of 13,000 costumes. In business since 1928, Stagecraft has some new and vintage costumes for sale, and a huge selection for rent. Period costumes from the 17th and 18th centuries, the Renaissance, Middle Ages, and ancient Rome and Egypt are particularly well represented. A talented designer on staff does custom-orders and costume repairs. Look here for wigs, makeup, lighting, and other theatrical supplies as well. *1854 Alcatraz Ave., between Adeline St. and Shattuck Ave., Berkeley, 510/653–4424. Closed Sun. and Mon.*

TOBACCONISTS

4 *e-6*
ALFRED DUNHILL OF LONDON
The American outpost of the posh, London-based Alfred Dunhill carries the very expensive and high-quality Dunhill tobaccos, cigars, humidors, pipes, lighters, and other smokers' requisites. *250 Post St., at Stockton St., Union Square, 415/781–3368.*

7 *e-1*
ASHBURY TOBACCO CENTER
The heady Haight-Ashbury wouldn't be complete without a well-stocked smoke shop, and the Ashbury Tobacco Center is just that: Alongside premium and imported cigars and fine tobaccos you'll find Middle Eastern hookahs and exotic pipes. *1524 Haight St., at Ashbury St., Haight, 415/552–5556.*

4 *f-5*
GRANT'S TOBACCONISTS
Discerning Financial District power brokers go to Grant's for pipes, cigars, tobaccos, humidors, and accessories of very high quality. High rollers have been purchasing premium cigars here since 1849; the shop currently claims a stock of 100,000 cigars in its walk-in humidor. *562 Market St., between Montgomery and Sansome Sts., Financial District, 415/981–1000. Closed Sun.*

5 *h-4*
THE HUMIDOR
Many cigar smokers peg this as their favorite tobacconist in the city. Several large humidors house premium cigars by Dunhill, Padron, Bode, and others. If you're unsure of what to get, try one of the samplers, each featuring five or so different cigars. *2201 Union St., at Fillmore St., 415/563–5181.*

4 *d-6*
JIM MATE'S PIPE AND TOBACCO SHOP
Well known for its international selection of fine pipes, tobacco, and cigars, Jim Mate's is especially sought out for its house tobacco blend—Jim Mate's Famous Blend—priced at $8.50 for half a pound. *575 Geary St., at Jones St., Tenderloin, 415/388–8964. Closed Sun.*

4 *f-5*
SHERLOCK'S HAVEN
The fictional pipe-smoking British detective Sherlock would surely approve of this smart shop, with its premium cigars, humidors, fine tobaccos, and, of course, handsome pipes. Owner Marty Pulvers is renowned for his cigar knowledge. *275 Battery St., between Sacramento and California Sts., Financial District, 415/362–1405. Closed Sun.*

4 *e-5*
VENDETTA
Although this small shop carries men's clothes and accessories, the real reason to come is for the two humidors stocked with rare cigars—mostly pre-embargo Cuban cigars. Fumo Blu, the small smoking lounge upstairs, is open to members only, but owner Bruce Rothenberg is likely to allow you in if you purchase one of his cigars. *12 Tillman Pl., off Grant Ave. between Sutter and Post Sts., 415/397–7755. Closed Sun.*

TOYS & GAMES

collectibles

3 *d-3*
SCOOBY'S TOYS AND COLLECTIBLES
Baby boomers will recognize most of the vintage toys at this Berkeley shop. Lunch boxes and collectible tin toys from the

1940s and '50s are the specialty. *2750 Adeline St., at Stuart St., Berkeley, 510/ 548–5349. By appointment only.*

7 *g-2*

UNCLE MAME

A shrine to American pop culture, this shop deals strictly in collectible cereal boxes, lunch pails, action figures, and the like, mostly from the 1970s and '80s. You'll wish you had hung onto your childhood toys when you see a Farrah Fawcett doll in its original box for $150. *2241 Market St., between Noe and Sanchez Sts., Castro, 415/626–1953.*

new

8 *d-3*

BASIC BROWN BEAR FACTORY

Pick out any teddy bear pattern and you can watch your new friend being put together; you can even use a big machine to stuff the bear yourself. Bears cost $12 to $150, depending on the size and complexity of the pattern. The De Haro Street location is the company factory, and gives free drop-in tours. *444 De Haro St., at Mariposa St., Potrero Hill, 415/626–0781.*

4 *c-2*

The Cannery, 2nd floor, 2801 Leavenworth St., at Beach St., Fisherman's Wharf, 415/ 931–6670.

4 *e-6*

THE DISNEY STORE

Books, toys, games, and clothing await you inside this store, part of a national chain. The building itself is amusing, with colorful walls and gargoyle-shape pillars. Beyond toys, there are collectibles such as framed animation cells, as well as Disney-oriented table- and glassware for sale. *400 Post St., at Powell St., Union Square, 415/391–6866.*

4 *e-1*

Pier 39, The Embarcadero and Beach St., Fisherman's Wharf, 415/391–4210.

5 *f-2*

EXPLORATORIUM STORE

The store in San Franciscan's favorite science museum allows you to take the fun home. Many of the educational and just plain fun playthings here are exclusive to the store, developed by Exploratorium staff. *3601 Lyon St.,*

between Marina Blvd. and Lombard St., Marina, 415/563–7337. Closed Labor Day– Memorial Day.

4 *e-6*

F. A. O. SCHWARZ

Every child's dream is fulfilled at the lavish San Francisco branch of the famed New York–based toy emporium. The beautiful collection of toys from around the world includes dollhouses, dancing bears, carousel rocking horses, life-size stuffed animals, and motorized miniature cars—as well as more mundane toys like Barbie and G. I. Joe. On display (but not for sale) is the giant keyboard used by Tom Hanks in the movie *Big. 48 Stockton St., at O'Farrell St., Union Square, 415/394–8700.*

4 *f-4*

GAME GALLERY

Board games, puzzles, fantasy card games, and chess computers are among the thousands of games for adults and young adults. *1 Embarcadero Center, Clay and Sacramento Sts. between Battery and Drumm Sts., Embarcadero, 415/433–4263.*

7 *f-1*

GAMESCAPE

The shop sells new and used board, computer, and role-playing games, as well as puzzles; it's got everything from Monopoly and chess to crazy Nintendo adventures. *333 Divisadero St., between Page and Oak Sts., Lower Haight, 415/ 621–4263.*

5 *e-6*

HEARTHSONG TOYS

The wooden automobiles, creative puzzles, educational books, and construction toys are examples of the "toys that run on imagination" sold here. *3505 California St., at Locust St., Laurel Heights, 415/379–9900.*

5 *h-3*

HOUSE OF MAGIC

Hundreds of gag gifts (backwards clocks, celebrity face masks) and goofy gadgets (hand buzzers, wind-up toys) make pranksters of all ages merry. The shop also sells magic sets, magic tricks, how-to books and videos, costume supplies such as wigs and wax lips, and even used crystal balls and other used magician's supplies and antique apparatuses. *2025 Chestnut St., at Fillmore St., Marina, 415/346–2218.*

8 *a-3*

HOWLING BULL SYNDICATE

Plastic Godzillas, Devilman stickers, and the ultrapopular Ultraman figurines are some of the Japanese toys you can buy here. Japanese books, videos, magazines, and comic books are also among the pop-cultural treasures this recently opened store stocks. *826 Valencia St., between 19th and 20th Sts., Mission, 415/282–0339. Closed Mon.*

5 *e-6*

IMAGINARIUM

A California-based chain of stores, Imaginarium manufactures its own learning-oriented games and gadgets and imports European brands rarely found in larger stores. You won't find toy guns or any other war toys in these shops, but there are lots of creative toys—fun, colorful, and educational stuff for all ages. *3535 California St., between Laurel and Spruce Sts., Laurel Heights, 415/387–9885.*

4 *f-6*

JEFFREY'S TOYS

A San Francisco institution since 1968, Jeffrey's brims with games, stuffed animals, comic books, crafts, and a fine selection of educational toys. Comic books and trading cards attract children of all ages. *7 3rd St., at Market St., Union Square, 415/546–6551.*

4 *e-1*

PUPPETS ON THE PIER

Marionettes dance in this shop's front window; inside there are reasonably priced finger puppets, storytelling puppets, marionettes, and dolls. The shop also sells a few antique Pelham puppets from the 1930s and '40s. *Pier 39, The Embarcadero and Beach St., Fisherman's Wharf, 415/781–4435.*

4 *e-6*

SANRIO

Castles, rainbows, and stars decorate this two-floor shop devoted to pop icon Hello Kitty and all her friends. You'll find a plethora of items ranging from lunch boxes to huge plush toys. *39 Stockton St., at Market St., Union Square, 415/981–5568.*

8 *c-1*

TOYS R US

The San Francisco outlet of this national chain has toys, games, puzzles, dolls—everything a child could wish for. *555 9th St., at Bryant St., South of Market, 415/252–0607.*

5 *f-7*

2400 O'Farrell St., at Masonic Ave., Laurel Heights, 415/931–8896.

4 *e-1*

WOUND ABOUT

Walk into this shop and you'll be greeted by dozens of windup and battery-operated toys yapping, clapping, swinging, and singing. Some are quite lifelike; others are hilariously cartoony. *Pier 39, The Embarcadero and Beach St., Fisherman's Wharf, 415/986–8697.*

UMBRELLAS

4 *f-5*

ADORNME

The shop's best-sellers are the Sistine Chapel umbrella and the Winnie the Pooh umbrella (in children and adult sizes). There are practical umbrellas, including fine European brands such as Brigg, and fanciful umbrellas; there's even one made of waterproof velvet. *Crocker Galleria, 50 Post St., between Montgomery and Kearny Sts., Financial District, 415/397–4114. Closed Sun.*

VIDEOS

7 *f-3*

CASTRO VIDEO

The city's largest selection of gay-themed videos are available for sale and for rent. *525 Castro St., between 18th and 19th Sts., 415/552–2448.*

7 *a-2*

LE VIDEO

Le Video annually wins the *Bay Guardian* reader poll for best video store, possibly because of its exhaustive collection of more than 40,000 titles in all genres. It has the city's widest selection of foreign and independent film titles for sale or rent, and a sizable stock of Hollywood releases. Le Video Vault, the shop's annex three doors down, contains all of the cult, sci-fi, horror, documentary, and independent titles. *1231 9th Ave., between*

Lincoln Way and Irving St., Sunset District, 415/566–3606.

7 *a-2*

Le Video Vault, *1239 9th Ave., between Lincoln Way and Irving St., 415/242–2120.*

8 *a-3*

LEATHER TONGUE

This Mission District institution sells and rents mainly cult films, film noir, and sci-fi. Its greatest claim to fame is the extensive collection of films by independent filmmakers, conveniently organized by the name of the director. *714 Valencia St., at 18th St., Mission, 415/552–2900.*

7 *g-1*

NAKED EYE NEWS AND VIDEO

This place deals in video rentals only. It's noted for its eclectic assortment of odd foreign and cult titles, plus classic and recent Hollywood films. *533 Haight St., between Fillmore and Steiner Sts., 415/864–2985.*

WATCHES & CLOCKS

antique

5 *h-4*

OLD AND NEW ESTATES

Fully restored vintage watches of all kinds are a specialty here, particularly vintage Grüen, Rolex, and Hamilton watches. Wedding rings, art glass, jewelry, and lamps are also for sale. *2181 Union St., at Fillmore St., Cow Hollow, 415/346–7525. Closed Wed.*

7 *d-1*

URBAN ANTIQUES

Although this shop looks minuscule from the street, it's actually 125 ft deep and filled with clocks and music boxes from America, Great Britain, France, Germany, Austria, and Switzerland. *1767 Waller St., at Stanyan St., Haight, 415/221–0194. Closed Mon.–Wed.*

4 *b-8*

ZEITGEIST TIMEPIECES & JEWELRY

The owners of Zeitgeist—Carsten Marsch, master watchmaker, and Mac Garmen, clock maker—repair and restore clocks, jewelry, and fine watches. They also sell beautiful vintage wrist- and pocket watches such as Grüen and Bulova. If you buy one of their watches, expect to be admonished to treat it well and sent home with care instructions. *437-B Hayes St., at Gough St., Hayes Valley, 415/864–0185. Closed Mon.*

contemporary

6 *e-4*

CALIFORNIA WATCH, CLOCK, AND JEWELRY CO.

This shop has the largest selection of clocks in the city: grandfather clocks, wall clocks, cuckoo clocks, digital clocks, and more. Most are new, although it does have a few antiques. *2436 Noriega St., at 32nd Ave., Sunset District, 415/566–9902. Closed Sun.*

4 *f-5*

CRESALIA JEWELERS

One of the city's top jewelers since 1912, Cresalia carries fine watches such as Movado, Lassale, Concord, Seiko, and Robindino. Prices are about 25% less than those at shops on Union Square. *111 Sutter St., between Montgomery and Kearny Sts., Financial District, 415/781–7371. Closed Sun.*

4 *f-5*

RAVITS WATCHES AND CLOCKS

Among the choices of clocks and watches are Omega, Tag Heuer, Movado, Tissot, Swiss Army, Timex, Casio, Seiko, Lassal, Raymond Weil, and many other notable brands. *Crocker Galleria, 50 Post St., between Montgomery and Kearny Sts., Union Square, 415/392–1947. Closed Sun.*

4 *e-5*

SHREVE & CO.

Fine watches such as Rolex, Omega, and Patek Philippe fill the elegant cases at Shreve & Co. Since 1852, the company has been famous for diamonds, gold, Mikimoto pearls, and luxury watches. *200 Post St., at Grant Ave., Union Square, 415/421–2600.*

1 *e-1*

THE SWATCH STORE

Brightly colored, plastic Swatch watches with whimsical designs and funny faces fill this Pier 39 shop. The basic models start at $35, and go up to $130. *Pier 39, The Embarcadero and Beach St., Fisherman's Wharf, 415/788–4543.*

4 e-6

ZWILLINGER & CO.

Owners Mel and Sheilah Wasserman offer excellent service and competitive prices—20%–35% less than the norm—on fine watches, diamonds, and designer jewelry. *760 Market St., Suite 800, at Grant Ave., Union Square, 415/392–4086. Closed Sun. and Mon.*

WIGS

4 d-3

ROSALIE'S NEW LOOK

This shop has a huge selection of women's wigs and a full-service salon. The staff is friendly and happy to let you try on as many wigs as you please. *782 Columbus Ave., at Greenwich St., North Beach, 415/397–6246.*

WINES & SPIRITS

5 h-3

CALIFORNIA WINE MERCHANT

Its all-American selection is predictably heavy on California vintages, especially hard-to-find wines from small collections. The staff promises that "anything you want, we'll try to get." You'll also find good Washington and Oregon wines here. *3237 Pierce St., at Chestnut St., Marina, 415/567–0646.*

4 e-3

COIT LIQUORS

Owner Tony Giovanzana has a wide selection of grappas as well as good values on champagnes and Italian, French, and California wines. *585 Columbus Ave., at Union St., North Beach, 415/986–4036.*

4 d-2

COST PLUS WORLD MARKET

This outlet of the popular import chain sells wines and microbrews from California and Oregon, plus liqueurs and spirits from around the world. The quality is good, prices low, and selection unique. *2552 Taylor St., at Bay St., Fisherman's Wharf, 415/928–6200.*

5 h-5

D & M WINE AND LIQUOR CO.

D & M stocks wines from small California boutiques, but San Franciscans come here mainly for the 225 brands of single-malt whiskies; 200 different French champagnes; and the world's largest collection of Armagnacs, dating from 1928. *2200 Fillmore St., at Sacramento St., Pacific Heights, 415/346–1325.*

4 f-5

JOHN WALKER & CO.

In business since 1933, John Walker & Co. has a vast selection of California wines, plus French, Italian, South American, and South African wines; cognacs; and champagnes. Come here for rare and older-vintage California and French wines. *175 Sutter St., between Kearny and Montgomery Sts., Financial District, 415/986–2707. Closed Sun.*

4 f-7

K & L WINE MERCHANT

At this spacious, well-stocked, and reasonably priced showroom, the friendly staff members promise not to sell any wines they haven't tasted themselves. *766 Harrison St., between 3rd and 4th Sts., South of Market, 415/896–1734.*

7 a-6

MR. LIQUOR

Despite the silly name, Mr. Liquor is a serious store. Some 1,000 wines are available here, all at warehouse prices. Mr. Liquor takes pride in carrying well-known Bay Area importer Kermit Lynch's line of wines. Free delivery is available with a minimum $100 purchase. *250 Taraval St., at Funston Ave., Sunset District, 415/731–6222.*

4 d-6

NAPA VALLEY WINERY EXCHANGE

Stocking only California wines and sparkling wines, the Napa Valley Winery Exchange has a wide selection, knowledgeable staff, and hard-to-find labels from small vineyards such as Solitude (Sonoma County), Schweiger Vineyards (Napa Valley), and Au Bon Climat (Santa Barbara). *415 Taylor St., between Geary and O'Farrell Sts., Union Square, 415/771–2887 or 800/653–9463.*

5 *h-3*

PLUMPJACK WINES

Connected to the popular café of the same name (*see* Mediterranean *in* Chapter 1), this stylish shop has hard-to-find California wines, along with a small selection of Italian wines. Approximately 100 wines are priced less than $10. You'll also find gift baskets and other gift items here. *3201 Fillmore St., at Greenwich St., Cow Hollow, 415/346–9870.*

5 *a-7*

SAN FRANCISCO BREWCRAFT

This is the shop to come to whether you just want to learn about brewing beer or you actually know what to do with that wort oxygenation system on sale. It carries beer-making kits and books explaining the process for the beginner, as well as equipment and ingredients for the serious brewer. *1555 Clement St., between 16th and 17th Aves., Richmond District, 415/751–9338. Closed Tues.*

5 *h-5*

VINO

Voted one of the best wine shops in the Bay Area two years in a row by *San Francisco Focus*, Vino prides itself on its knowledgeable service. Don't be intimidated by the wide selection of California and imported wines; the staff is happy to educate you about your options. Each month it features a "taster's six-pack special"—six wines at a specially discounted price. *2425A California St., between Fillmore and Steiner Sts., Pacific Heights, 415/674–8466.*

4 *f-8*

THE WINE CLUB

This place makes up for its bare-bones, warehouse feel with a huge selection of high-quality wines at some of the best discount prices in the city. The largest selection is of French wines, particularly burgundies, Bordeaux, and Alsatians. There's also a wide variety of wine paraphernalia, including glasses, books, openers, and decanters, plus cigars, premium beers, and Russian caviar. Frequent shoppers will want to request the Wine Club's monthly newsletter. *953 Harrison St., between 5th and 6th Sts., South of Market, 415/512–9086.*

4 *g-7*

WINE HOUSE LIMITED

The highly informed and friendly sales staff will help you find the perfect wine for any occasion. Occupying a spacious exposed-brick warehouse, the store has an excellent selection of French wines, and small but well-chosen selections of Italian, Austrian, German, and California wines, all at reasonable prices. It also stocks rare vintage California and Italian wines and vintage champagnes and ports. *535 Bryant St., between 3rd and 4th Sts., South Beach, 415/495–8486. Closed Sun.*

5 *f-6*

WINE IMPRESSIONS

For discount prices on thousands of California, French, Italian, Spanish, and Australian wines, try Wine Impressions. This large shop keeps many bottles of wines and champagnes chilled, and also has a good number of rare California and French wines. The liquor department is well known for its rare tequilas, as well as good selections of cognac, sherry, port, and dessert wines. On Friday you can sample 4 to 12 wines for 10% of the price of each bottle ($1 and up). *3461 California St., at Laurel St., Laurel Heights, 415/221–9463.*

chapter 3

PARKS, GARDENS & SPORTS

L iving in San Francisco means enjoying one of the finest urban playgrounds in the country. In the city's 3,500 acres of parks and open spaces, San Franciscans gather for everything from tennis to lawn bowling. Seemingly countless parks and gardens offer venues for strolls, picnics, or indulging in a great read under a shady tree. The city's unique position on the Bay and the Pacific Ocean also primes it for water sports in the shadow of the picturesque Golden Gate Bridge. Sailing, windsurfing, sea kayaking, sculling, and surfing are all possible. For information on races, tournaments, and other sporting events around the city, pick up a copy of the monthly City Sports magazine, available free at sporting-goods stores and many fitness centers.

parks

For the addresses and telephone numbers of city, state, and national parks departments, see Parks Information in Chapter 7. For information on particular sports in each of the parks, see Sports & Outdoor Activities, below.

5 h-5
ALTA PLAZA PARK
This grassy Pacific Heights park has superb views of the city and beyond. Dog lovers will want to pay their respects at the Dog Park Walk of Fame—two long cement gutters on the north side of the park, in which neighborhood dog owners have carved the names of their four-legged friends. Bordered by Jackson, Steiner, Clay, and Scott Sts., Pacific Heights.

4 b-2, c-2
AQUATIC PARK
Although it's known primarily for its beach, Aquatic Park also has large manicured lawns that are great for picnics and lounging in the sun. Jefferson St., west of Hyde St., Fisherman's Wharf, 415/556–2904.

7 e-1
BUENA VISTA PARK
Long ago this steeply sloped hillside park was named Buena Vista (Spanish for "good view") with good reason. From the cypress- and eucalyptus-covered summit, the views north and west are among the finest in the city. The Golden Gate, the Pacific Ocean, the Bay Bridge, and downtown are all visible. Buena Vista used to be a famous spot for gay trysts. These days it's appreciated by all sorts of San Francisco residents. But, like many parts of the Haight, it's best in daylight. Haight and Buena Vista Sts., Haight.

7 c-1
CHILDREN'S PLAYGROUND
The best and biggest playground in the city went up in 1887, but this magical place is continually being refurbished. Kids love the vintage carousel. Kezar and Bowling Green Drs., Golden Gate Park.

4 a-2
FORT MASON
The fort itself, once a military command post, is now the headquarters of the Golden Gate National Recreation Area (see below), in the Marina. The Fort Mason Visitors Center (open weekdays 9:30–4:30) dispenses information on the Golden Gate National Recreation Area as well as all national parks in California, Oregon, and Washington. West of the fort, the gently rolling Great Meadow is a pleasant spot for walks, with lovely views of the northern waterfront. North of the Great Meadow is Fort Mason (see Architecture & Historic Sites in Chapter 4), a series of warehouses built atop three piers, used as a headquarters for various artistic, cultural, recreational, and environmental organizations. The park and center are frequently the sites of fairs and concerts. Pick up the Fort Mason monthly newsletter (available free at any of the museums) for details on classes, lectures, concerts, and special exhibitions, or call the Fort Mason Center hot line (415/979–3010). Marina Blvd., at Laguna St., Marina.

7 e-7
GLEN CANYON PARK
Tucked away in a southwest corner of the city that is rarely visited by tourists, Glen Canyon Park is a complete escape

from city life. Explore stands of eucalyptus, grassy hills, a bubbling stream, and even a few climbing boulders—but stay on the marked paths to avoid poison oak. *Between O'Shaughnessy and Diamond Heights Blvds., Diamond Heights.*

2 *c-3*

GOLDEN GATE PARK

San Francisco's most well-used playground encompasses 1,017 acres, making it one of the world's largest man-made parks. It's 3 mi long and ½ mi wide, stretching from the Pacific Ocean into the geographical heart of the city. In 1870, when William Hall, who later became the first park supervisor, was retained to design Golden Gate Park, the land consisted of scrubby sand dunes. By 1943, it was a shady paradise. An ongoing multimillion dollar renovation has been making the park even better. It contains 6,000 varieties of plants, a paddock field with bison, 11 lakes, vast green lawns for lolling, bridle paths, play areas for every manner of sports activity including golf and tennis, the runner-filled Panhandle, and Sunday band concerts on the Music Concourse. You'll also find the tranquil Japanese Tea Garden, two Dutch windmills (built in 1902 and used for 20 years to irrigate the park), the beautiful Conservatory of Flowers, the Steinhart Aquarium and the Morrison Planetarium (both components of the California Academy of Sciences; *see* Science Museums *in* Chapter 4), the M. H. de Young Memorial Museum and the Asian Art Museum of San Francisco (*see* Art Museums *in* Chapter 4), and Strybing Arboretum. Free guided walking tours focusing on various aspects of the park depart frequently from the visitors centers; call for a current schedule (415/263 0991). Most tours last about two hours. On Sundays, John F. Kennedy Drive, the park's main thoroughfare, is closed to car traffic between Stanyan Street and 19th Avenue, and flocks of bicyclists, in-line skaters, runners, and skateboarders take over. For park information and maps, drop by the **McLaren Lodge** (501 Stanyan St., near John F. Kennedy Dr., 415/831–2700) daily between 8 and 5. A second visitor center is on the western edge of the park in the charming, historic **Beach Chalet** (John F. Kennedy Dr., at Great Hwy.), which also houses a microbrewery and restaurant (*see* American/Contemporary *in* Chapter 1). *Bordered by Fulton St., Stanyan St., Lincoln Way, and the Great Hwy., Golden Gate Park.*

2 *a-7*

HARDING PARK

Within Harding Park are two golf courses, Jack Fleming Golf Course and Harding Park Municipal Golf Course, as well as Lake Merced, the San Francisco Water Department's emergency reser-

---

INSIDE GOLDEN GATE PARK

You could easily spend a day exploring Golden Gate Park's many attractions. The M. H. de Young Memorial Museum and the Asian Art Museum alone deserve several hours (see Art Museums in Chapter 4). In addition, you'll find the following major landmarks as you move through the park, from east to west.

Children's Playground (Parks)
   Kids love the vintage carousel.

Conservatory of Flowers (Gardens)
   Golden Gate Park's oldest structure is currently under renovation with no scheduled reopening date.

Golden Gate Park Polo Fields (Stadiums)
   The San Francisco Marathon starts and ends here.

Golden Gate Park Stables (Stadiums)
   San Francisco's only stable.

Japanese Tea Garden (Gardens)
   Sip green tea while gazing at colorful koi fish.

Music Concourse (Gardens)
   Site of free summer concerts.

National AIDS Memorial Grove (Gardens)
   A moving national monument in the midst of Golden Gate Park.

Queen Wilhelmina Tulip Garden (Gardens)
   Blooms to full splendor by early spring.

Shakespeare Garden (Gardens)
   Bring along your Folio edition of Romeo and Juliet.

Steinhart Aquarium (Zoos & Aquariums)
   Gaze at the sharks, touch the starfish, and watch the penguins being fed.

Strybing Arboretum and Botanical Gardens (Gardens)
   70 acres of formal gardens.

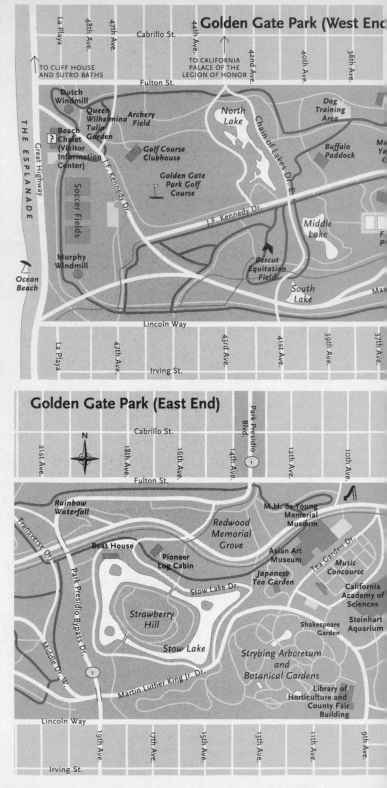

Golden Gate Park (West End)

La Playa
48th Ave.
47th Ave.
Cabrillo St.
44th Ave.

TO CLIFF HOUSE AND SUTRO BATHS

42nd Ave.
40th Ave.
38th Ave.

TO CALIFORNIA PALACE OF THE LEGION OF HONOR

Fulton St.

THE ESPLANADE

Great Highway

Dutch Windmill

Queen Wilhelmina Tulip Garden

Archery Field

? Beach Chalet (Visitor Information Center)

Golf Course Clubhouse

Golden Gate Park Golf Course

J. F. Kennedy Dr.

Soccer Fields

North Lake

Chain of Lakes Dr. E.

Dog Training Area

Buffalo Paddock

Me
Ye
G

J. F. Kennedy Dr.

Middle Lake

Murphy Windmill

Bercut Equitation Field

South Lake

F
P

Ocean Beach

Ma

Lincoln Way

La Playa
47th Ave.
43rd Ave.
41st Ave.
39th Ave.
37th Ave.

Irving St.

Golden Gate Park (East End)

21st Ave.
18th Ave.
16th Ave.
14th Ave.
Cabrillo St.
Park Presidio Blvd.
12th Ave.
10th Ave.

N

1

Fulton St.

Transverse Dr.

Rainbow Waterfall

Boat House

Pioneer Log Cabin

Redwood Memorial Grove

M. H. de Young Memorial Museum

Asian Art Museum

Japanese Tea Garden

Tea Garden Dr.

Music Concourse

Park Presidio Bypass Dr.

Stow Lake Dr.

Strawberry Hill

Stow Lake

California Academy of Sciences

Steinhart Aquarium

Shakespeare Garden

Middle Dr. W.

1

Martin Luther King Jr. Dr.

Strybing Arboretum and Botanical Gardens

Library of Horticulture and County Fair Building

Lincoln Way

19th Ave.
17th Ave.
15th Ave.
13th Ave.
11th Ave.
9th Ave.

Irving St.

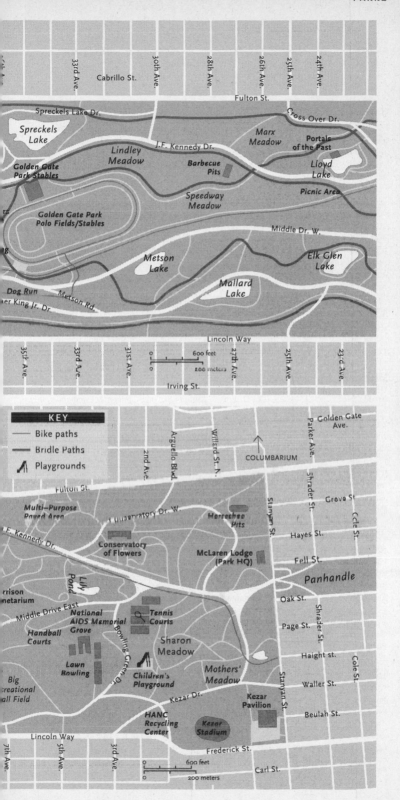

33rd Ave. · Cabrillo St. · 30th Ave. · 28th Ave. · 26th Ave. · 25th Ave. · 24th Ave.

Fulton St.

Spreckels Lake Dr. · Cross Over Dr.

Spreckels Lake

Marx Meadow

Portals of the Past

J. F. Kennedy Dr.

Lindley Meadow

Barbecue Pits

Lloyd Lake

Golden Gate Park Stables

Picnic Area

Speedway Meadow

Golden Gate Park Polo Fields/Stables

Middle Dr. W.

Metson Lake

Mallard Lake

Elk Glen Lake

Dog Run

er King Jr. Dr.

Metson Rd.

Lincoln Way

35th Ave. · 33rd Ave. · 31st Ave. · 27th Ave. · 25th Ave. · 23rd Ave.

0 — 600 feet
0 — 200 meters

Irving St.

KEY

— Bike paths

— Bridle Paths

Playgrounds

Golden Gate Ave.

Arguello Blvd.

2nd Ave.

Willard St. N.

Parker Ave.

COLUMBARIUM

Shrader St.

Fulton St.

Grove St.

Cole St.

Multi–Purpose Paved Area

Conservatory Dr. W.

Horseshoe Pits

Hayes St.

J.F. Kennedy Dr.

Conservatory of Flowers

Stanyan St.

McLaren Lodge (Park HQ)

Fell St.

Panhandle

Oak St.

rrison netarium

Lily Pond

Middle Drive East

Shrader St.

National AIDS Memorial Grove

Tennis Courts

Page St.

Handball Courts

Bowling Green Dr.

Sharon Meadow

Haight st.

Cole St.

Big creational all Field

Lawn Bowling

Children's Playground

Mothers' Meadow

Stanyan St.

Waller St.

Kezar Dr.

Kezar Pavilion

HANC Recycling Center

Kezar Stadium

Beulah St.

Lincoln Way

7th Ave. · 5th Ave. · 3rd Ave.

Frederick St.

0 — 600 feet
0 — 200 meters

Carl St.

voir and a popular spot for fishing and boating. A 5-mi running path encircles the lake, wending through stands of eucalyptus, cypress, and pine, as well as fields of wildflowers, ferns, and ice plants. *Harding Rd., near Skyline Blvd., Park Merced.*

4 *d-4*

INA COOLBRITH PARK

The funky little staircase at Vallejo and Mason streets will transport you to handkerchief-size Ina Coolbrith Park, which has shady trees and views of Oakland and the Bay Bridge. Continue straight through the intersection of Taylor and Vallejo streets to a flower-lined path that ends at a small landing, where you'll find amazing views of Alcatraz and the East Bay. *Vallejo and Taylor Sts., Russian Hill.*

4 *g-4*

JUSTIN HERMAN PLAZA

In the shadow of the Ferry Building, Justin Herman Plaza is a favorite haunt of brown-bagging office workers. The center of the plaza is dominated by Vaillancourt Fountain, a free-form sculpture made of 101 concrete boxes. Jean Dubuffet's mammoth stainless-steel sculpture, *La Chiffonière,* is also here. During the winter holiday season, Justin Herman Plaza converts to an ice-skating rink. At other times of year it hosts free concerts, usually Wednesday or Friday at noon. *Market and Steuart Sts., Embarcadero.*

4 *a-5, b-5*

LAFAYETTE PARK

Visited by dog walkers, picnickers, and sunbathers, this Pacific Heights park has expansive lawns that slope to a wooded crest—just as those of any well-behaved English-style garden should. Although not as dramatic or expansive as other parks in the neighborhood, it's a pleasant stop. *Bordered by Washington, Gough, Sacramento, and Laguna Sts., Pacific Heights.*

2 *b-2*

LINCOLN PARK

This 270-acre stretch runs along the headlands of Point Lobos, in the Richmond District. The 200-ft cliffs add drama to the breathtaking view of the Golden Gate Bridge. At the park's eastern end are the beautiful California Palace of the Legion of Honor and the city's oldest golf course, whose fairways

are lined with large Monterey cypresses. *North of Clement St., west of 33rd Ave., Richmond District.*

2 *e-1*

MARINA GREEN

This wide waterfront lawn is a favored spot of runners (there's a 2½-mi running and exercise course), in-line skaters, bicyclists, kite-fliers, sunbathers, and those in need of a restful place to gaze out across the water to the Golden Gate Bridge. On weekends, people come here for pickup games, especially soccer and volleyball. Offshore, you'll find the sailboat-filled Marina Small Craft Harbor. *Marina Blvd., at Webster St., Marina.*

2 *f-7*

MCLAREN PARK

Although McLaren Park is somewhat inconveniently located in a southern corner of the city, it's a gem for those who live near it. Besides wide green lawns and eucalyptus groves, the park has two small ponds, a playground, boccie courts, tennis courts, and the Gleneagles International Golf Course. *Mansell St., near University St., Visitacion Valley, 415/337–4700.*

7 *h-3*

MISSION DOLORES PARK

The views of downtown San Francisco, the Bay Bridge, and the East Bay are superb from the north end of Mission Dolores Park, in the midst of a well-to-do residential section of the Mission district. Set on a gently sloping hill, it's a favorite among picnickers and sunbathers on pleasant days; it also has tennis courts, a basketball court, a playground, and a popular dog-run area. Look for the gold fire hydrant at the park's southwest corner. When all the other hydrants went dry during the firestorm that followed the 1906 earthquake, this one kept pumping. *Bordered by 18th, Dolores, 20th, and Church Sts., Mission District.*

5 *f-3*

THE PRESIDIO

The Presidio, a 1,480-acre stretch of prime waterfront land stretching from the western end of the Marina all the way to the Golden Gate Bridge, began its life as a Spanish military installation in 1776 (*see* Architecture & Historic Sites *in* Chapter 4). On October 1, 1994, it became part of the National Park system, although the army will remain here for a while longer in a reduced capacity. By 2012 it will be fully converted for use as a park, with an additional 200 acres of open space restored and more than 100 additional acres replanted with native vegetation—but for now you can still count on finding rolling hills crossed by 11 mi of hiking trails and 14 mi of biking routes; 620 historic buildings; and stunning views of the bay, the city, the Pacific Ocean, and the Golden Gate Bridge. A few paths lead through a man-made forest of 400,000 pine, cypress, and eucalyptus trees; these were planted in the 1880s by schoolchildren and soldiers to make the area look more vast than it actually is. Stop by the **William Penn Mott, Jr. Visitor Center** (Bldg. 102 in the Main Post area of the Presidio, 415/561 4323) to pick up maps or trail guides. It's open daily 9–5. Most weekends, rangers and docents lead free hikes ranging from one to three hours, and moderate to difficult skill levels. These typically cover the natural, cultural, and military history of the Presidio. Topics vary depending on the season and the staff.

Stretching along the bay side of the Presidio is Crissy Field, a popular area for pickup sports, picnicking, kite flying, and windsurfing. Recent renovations (scheduled to be completed by the summer of 2000) have restored Crissy Field, its historic wetlands, and a 1921 airfield. Baker Beach (*see* Beaches, *below*) is on the Pacific Ocean side of the Presidio. Along the south side of the Presidio are the Presidio Golf Course and Julius Kahn Playground, which has basketball courts. *W. Pacific Ave., between Spruce and Locust Sts., Presidio, 415/292–2004.*

4 g-7
SOUTH PARK

South Park's proximity to the city's "Multimedia Gulch" sector of SoMa has earned it the moniker "South Spark." The tree-filled, Parisian-style square is a welcome oasis in an area otherwise glutted with warehouses and office buildings; on weekdays its dozens of inviting benches are peopled with graphic artists, writers, architects, attorneys, and computer programmers. Surrounding the park are several cafés and restaurants. For kids, there's a playground. *South Park Ave., between 2nd and 3rd Sts., South of Market.*

6 g-8
STERN GROVE

Most San Franciscans think of this 63-acre park as the spot for free Sunday concerts (*see* Events *in* Chapter 4), which have been held here every summer since 1937. During the rest of the year it's an enchanting place for a walk through groves of eucalyptus, redwood, and fir. Besides the natural amphitheater, the park has a playground (just

---

THE BIGGEST URBAN PARK IN THE WORLD

With 76,500 acres of maritime parks, yacht harbors, ocean beaches, islands, and historic points of interest stretching along 28 mi of coastline in San Francisco and the counties of Marin and San Mateo, the Golden Gate National Recreation Area (GGNRA) maintains more urban parkland than any other city in the world. Congress created the GNNRA in 1972, in part to protect the coastal lands of San Francisco and Marin County from commercial development. In the Marin Headlands, across the Golden Gate Bridge, the GGNRA encompasses wildlife sanctuaries, 100 mi of trails through vast areas of undeveloped lands, and picnic facilities. A few of the highlights:

Baker Beach (Beaches)
Prime views of the Golden Gate Bridge, Marin Headlands, and the Pacific.

China Beach (Beaches)
A swimming beach in the midst of an elegant neighborhood.

Fort Funston (Beaches)
Hang gliders soar from Funston's cliffs.

Fort Mason (Parks)
Once a former military command post, now a thriving cultural center.

Lands End (Beaches)
Secluded enough for nude sunbathing.

Marin Headlands Golden Gate National Recreation Area (Hiking)
Sweeping, windswept views of the Golden Gate.

Ocean Beach (Beaches)
Wild and windy; and at its north end, near the Cliff House, a prime spot for viewing sea lions.

inside the 19th Avenue entrance), picnic and barbecue facilities, croquet lawns, and a small putting green. *Wawona St. and 19th Ave., Sunset District.*

2 *d-4*

SUTRO FOREST

Behind the University of California at San Francisco Medical Center stretches a hilly tract of land thickly forested with eucalyptus and pine trees. Although it isn't neatly groomed like nearby Golden Gate Park, it does have some pleasant hiking trails and far fewer crowds. Overlooking the forest is Mt. Sutro (elevation 908 ft), one of the city's tallest hills. *Parnassus Ave., at 2nd Ave., Twin Peaks.*

4 *f-4*

TRANSAMERICA REDWOOD GROVE

This cool pocket-size park is adjacent to the landmark Transamerica Building. It's one of the few places in San Francisco outside Golden Gate Park where mighty California Redwood trees grow—a welcome sight for businesspeople on their lunch hour. *Between Washington and Clay Sts., west of Montgomery St., Financial District.*

4 *e-6*

UNION SQUARE

All day long shoppers stroll through palm tree–filled Union Square and underneath it. (It covers a subterranean parking lot.) As the park in the heart of the city's most fashionable shopping district, Union Square hosts many enter-

tainment and civic events—including a winter ice-skating rink and Christmas tree and Hanukah menorah lightings. City planners recently held a contest to redesign the park, and a complete face-lift is due in the near future. *Bordered by Post, Stockton, Geary, and Powell Sts., Union Square.*

4 *f-4*

WALTON PARK

Near the Ferry Building, Embarcadero Center, and the Jackson Square Historical District is this attractive downtown park with a soothing fountain as its centerpiece. Plantings of grass, willows, and pine trees offer refuge from the city's urban jungle. *Bordered by Pacific Ave. and Davis, Jackson, and Front Sts., Embarcadero.*

4 *e-3*

WASHINGTON SQUARE

This small park has a European feel. In the midst of the bustling, charmingly Italian North Beach, Washington Square faces the Romanesque church of Sts. Peter and Paul. Afternoons, flocks of old men chew cigars and reminisce in their mother tongue. In the early morning, Chinese and other locals practice graceful, meditative tai chi. *Bordered by Filbert, Stockton, and Union Sts. and Columbus Ave., North Beach.*

other green spaces

BEACHES

4 *b-2, c-2*

AQUATIC PARK

Surrounded on three sides by the bustle of Fort Mason, Fisherman's Wharf, and Ghirardelli Square is a quiet, quarter-mile stretch of sandy beach. Aquatic Park was created as a Works Progress Administration project in 1937. Now, its cove and manicured lawns are part of the San Francisco Maritime National Historic Park. Arrive early and you might spot members of the city's Dolphin Club. They swim in its ice-cold waters almost daily; the largest turnout occurs on New Year's Day. Also here: the gleaming white National Maritime Museum

---

URBAN PARKS WITH HIKING TRAILS

Who said you need to leave San Francisco to hike through the great outdoors?

Glen Canyon Park (Parks)
Follow a bubbling brook through a canyon.

Golden Gate Park (Parks)
Meander past gardens, museums, forests, and even a pair of Dutch windmills and a herd of bison.

Lincoln Park (Parks)
Ends at beautiful Lands End beach.

The Presidio (Parks)
1,480 acres of prime waterfront land.

Sutro Forest (Parks)
Groves full of eucalyptus and pine.

Building (originally a bathhouse), built in the 1930s. Down the hill, you'll find a collection of historic ships docked at the Hyde Street Pier. Cost to board the ships is $5 for adults, $2 seniors and youths ages 13 to 18, kids under 12 are free. *900 Beach St., west of Hyde St., Fisherman's Wharf, 415/556–2904.*

2 b-2
BAKER BEACH

This 1-mi-long sandy beach is a local favorite, especially among anglers, picnickers, and sunbathers (including nudists who gather north of Battery Chamberlin). Treacherous waves make swimming here dangerous (there are no lifeguards); but you can enjoy stunning views of the Golden Gate Bridge and Marin Headlands. The first weekend of every month, rangers provide tours of the 95,000-pound cannon at Battery Chamberlin, which overlooks the beach. Although the 1904 cannon is no longer used to defend the San Francisco harbor from seafaring invaders, it can still spring into firing position. The beach's facilities include grills, drinking water, rest rooms, and picnic tables. *Gibson Rd., off Bowley St., Presidio, 415/561–1323.*

2 b-2
CHINA BEACH

One of the city's safest swimming beaches is also the most convenient, with free changing rooms and showers. China Beach was named for the poor Chinese fishermen who camped here in the 1870s (although it's sometimes marked on maps as Phelan Beach). It comprises a 600-ft sandy strip just south of the Presidio, surrounded by multimillion-dollar homes, including a massive pink structure owned by the actor, Robin Williams. Grills, drinking water, rest rooms, picnic tables, changing rooms, and showers are among the facilities. *Seacliff Ave., off 26th Ave., Richmond District, 415/561–4323.*

2 a-7
FORT FUNSTON

The beach at Fort Funston, south of Ocean Beach, is often buffeted by strong winds. That's what makes it so popular with Bay Area hang gliders. They launch from Funston's high cliffs, then soar overhead. Stay clear from takeoff and landing areas. There's a marked viewing area for spectators. A short, gentle paved loop trail provides

bird's-eye views of the Pacific and a few pleasant picnic spots. *Off Skyline Blvd. (Rte. 35), south of Sloat Blvd., Sunset District, 415/239–2366. Phones, rest rooms, picnic tables.*

2 a-2
LANDS END

The secluded beach at Lands End may be difficult to reach, but it rewards visitors with breathtaking coastal views. To get there, follow the 1-mi-long Lands End trail from the parking lot near the Sutro Baths. This trail through pine and cypress draws hikers, mountain bikers, and picnickers. The beach itself is largely clothing-optional. Dangerous offshore currents make swimming unsafe. *Trailhead at Merrie Way and Point Lobos Ave., Richmond District, 415/556–8642.*

2 a-3
OCEAN BEACH

Stretching along the Great Highway at the Pacific Ocean is this 4-mi-long wide sand beach. The waves are mighty, the wind is gusty, and it's often shrouded by fog. But Ocean Beach remains dear to San Franciscans, and for a long walk or run it's ideal, especially during a fog-free sunset. Lovers gather at dusk and tourists come to peer at Seal Rocks. Sea lions used to sun themselves atop these stony offshore islands; the public mis-

---

PICNIC-PERFECT

When the fog burns off, you'll find San Franciscans rushing, often with wine and cheese in tow. The following are all excellent backdrops for your next meal alfresco.

Baker Beach (Beaches)
   Stunning views of the Golden Gate Bridge.

Golden Gate Park (Parks)
   The crown jewel in the city's park system.

Lafayette Park (Parks)
   A grassy slope surrounded by Pacific Heights mansions.

Mission Dolores Park (Parks)
   Look for ice-cream salesmen on summer days.

Stern Grove (Parks)
   Site of free summer concerts since 1973. Performances begin at 2 PM Sunday, mid-June to mid-August.

took them for seals, giving the place its current moniker. Although most of these marine mammals have relocated to Pier 39, you might still spot a few. Extremely dangerous currents make swimming risky. But daredevil surfers consider it their beach of choice. While here, don't miss a visit to the historic Cliff House restaurant and the Cliff House Visitors Center at Ocean Beach (*see* Architecture & Historic Sites *in* Chapter 4). *Great Hwy., between Balboa St. and Sloat Blvd., Richmond District, 415/556–8642.*

GARDENS

Golden Gate Park is an urban paradise, with a number of smaller collections in addition to the larger gardens described below. Most gardens in and outside of Golden Gate Park are open daily from dawn until dusk.

3 *e-1*

BERKELEY ROSE GARDEN

Built during the Depression, this terraced rose garden is perched in the Berkeley hills, not far above the University of California campus. The garden draws visitors all day long, but at sunset, it's particularly appealing for a picnic and expansive views of the bay. More than 3,000 flowering rosebushes flourish in Berkeley's typically sunny but brisk microclimate. *Euclid Ave. and Bayview Pl., Berkeley.*

7 *b-1*

CONSERVATORY OF FLOWERS

This magnificent classic Victorian structure, shipped from England and reconstructed on this site in 1879, is the oldest building in Golden Gate Park. It is listed in the National Register of Historic Places as a civil-engineering landmark. The Conservatory is currently closed for renovations and will reopen sometime after the year 2000, when it will once again bloom with rare tropical plants. *John F. Kennedy Dr., at Conservatory Dr. West, Golden Gate Park.*

FILOLI

In addition to its gracious mansion, Filoli is justly known for its 16 acres of lovely formal gardens. These were planned and developed over a period of more than 50 years. Among the designs are a sunken garden, walled garden,

woodland garden, and yew alley. The rose garden alone, developed by the last private owner, Mrs. William P. Roth, features more than 50 bushes of all types and colors. There's also a charming Italian Renaissance–style teahouse. Spring is the best time to visit, although blooms come up as early as February, and the mild California climate means the gardens are enjoyable through October. The house and gardens are open from mid-February through the end of October, 10 to 2 Tuesday through Saturday for self-guided tours. (No admittance after 2.) For guided tours, call for more information. *Cañada Rd., near Edgewood Rd., Woodside, 650/364–8300. Admission: $10, $1 children 2–12.*

7 *b-3*

GARDEN FOR THE ENVIRONMENT

The San Francisco League of Urban Gardeners (SLUG) operates a greenhouse and drought-tolerant garden. Through workshops, community programs, and tours, the group also educates visiting gardeners about benefits of water-wise and pesticide-free gardening and composting. Vegetables grown on the premises are distributed to the homeless. Although the park is open daily to the public, it is only staffed Wednesday between 9 and 2, and Saturday from 10 to 4. In spring and fall, there is usually a free garden tour one Sunday afternoon per month; call for a current schedule. *7th Ave. and Lawton St., Sunset District, 415/285–7584.*

7 *a-1*

JAPANESE TEA GARDEN

This beautiful 3½-acre garden in Golden Gate Park was created in 1894 as a Japanese village for the California Mid-Winter Exhibit. It is a tranquil oasis of koi-filled pools, streams, bridges, a pagoda, an 18th-century bronze Buddha, torii gates, and, in spring, a dazzling array of pink and white cherry blossoms and azaleas. The Hagiwara family took care of the garden until World War II when they, along with other Japanese Americans, were detained in internment camps. In 1994, on the garden's 100th-year anniversary, a cherry blossom tree was planted in their memory. A Peace Lantern that hangs in the garden was presented to the city by Japanese schoolchildren. A teahouse near the main gates serves green tea and fortune cookies for an additional charge. The garden is in the eastern half of the park, next to the M. H. de Young Memorial Museum. *Tea Garden Dr., between John F. Kennedy and Martin Luther King Jr. Drs., Golden Gate Park, 415/752–4227. Admission: $3.50, $1.25 children 6–12 and senior citizens, free children under 6.*

7 *a-1*
MUSIC CONCOURSE
This little patch of Golden Gate Park has hosted free summer Sunday concerts (weather permitting) since 1882. *Near John F. Kennedy and Tea Garden Drs., Golden Gate Park.*

7 *b-1*
NATIONAL AIDS MEMORIAL GROVE
In 1991, hundreds of volunteers labored to create the first living memorial to those lost to AIDS. You'll find this 7-acre wooded area (a portion of which was formerly deLaveaga Dell) at the east end of Golden Gate Park. In 1996 Congress and President Clinton signed a bill that granted the Memorial Grove status as a national monument to people with AIDS. *Middle Dr. East, at Bowling Green Dr., Golden Gate Park, 415/750–8340.*

6 *b-1*
QUEEN WILHELMINA TULIP GARDEN
In the northwest corner of Golden Gate Park, adjacent to the historic Dutch Windmill, stands this collection of tulips. Some 10,000 bulbs are planted every October and burst into full bloom in February and March. *John F. Kennedy Dr., at Great Hwy., Golden Gate Park, 415/753–7110.*

7 *a-1*
SHAKESPEARE GARDEN
This is a small garden with more than 200 flowers mentioned in the Bard's works, together with related quotations engraved on bronze plaques. It's in Golden Gate Park, just southwest of the California Academy of Sciences. *Middle Dr. East, near Martin Luther King Jr. Dr., Golden Gate Park.*

7 *a-2*
STRYBING ARBORETUM AND BOTANICAL GARDENS
One of the finest botanical gardens in the country, Strybing's 55 acres are filled with some 7,000 plants displayed in 17 formal gardens. Arrangements are by country of origin, genus, and even—for the visually impaired—fragrance. You'll see plants from Australia, South Africa, Chile, and Asia. Highlights include the California Native Plants Garden, the Succulent Garden, and two separate Old and New World Cloud Forest gardens. Don't miss the Redwood Trail, which winds through a stand of these California giants. Free guided walks take place daily at 1:30 PM with additional tours weekends at 10:30 AM. Call for a current schedule, or pick up maps and brochures for a self-guided tour at the Strybing bookstore. The adjacent Helen Crocker Russell Library of Horticulture is an 18,000-volume library that also has rotating exhibits of botanical art. *9th Ave., at Lincoln Way, Golden Gate Park, 415/661–1316.*

3 *f-2*
UNIVERSITY OF CALIFORNIA BOTANICAL GARDEN
The university's garden is a valuable research and education center with a diverse collection of plants—more than 10,000 neatly labeled species from around the world. Most are arranged by region, everything from the South African desert to Himalayan forest. There are also specialized plots, such as the Chinese Medicinal Herb Garden and the Garden of Economic Plants, as well as three greenhouse exhibits and an excellent rhododendron collection. In the hills of Strawberry Canyon, the garden also offers superb views of the bay and the Golden Gate Bridge. Admission to the garden is $3, $2 for seniors, $1 for kids 3 to 18, and free on Thursday. Parking is available across from the entrance. *200 Centennial Dr., on U.C. Berkeley campus, Berkeley, 510/642–3343. Free tours weekends at 1:30.*

4 *f-6*
YERBA BUENA GARDENS
This $2 billion SoMa arts, performance, garden, and residential complex opened to much fanfare in 1993, after more than 30 years of planning and bureaucratic disputes. The core of the Yerba Buena Gardens complex comprises the Moscone Convention Center and the Center for the Arts (*see Art Museums in* Chapter 4), and two major garden spaces, the Esplanade and the East Garden. The Esplanade is a blend of art and flora, including an outdoor stage, a grass meadow, and two cafés with outdoor terraces. A city garden is filled with

native plants from San Francisco's sister cities: carpet bugle, a ground cover, from Haifa, Israel; orchid rockrose, a shrub, from Assisi, Italy; and white and yellow marguerite chrysanthemums from San Francisco. A reflecting pool cascades down a 22-ft high, 50-ft wide waterfall that leads to an etched-glass Martin Luther King, Jr. Memorial. At the northeastern part of the Esplanade meadow is the Cho-En (Butterfly Garden), planted with wildflowers that attract various species of native San Francisco butterflies. At the 3rd Street entry to the complex, the East Garden mixes eastern and western ideas: European sycamores are planted in a triangle, which is the Japanese symbol for Heaven, Earth, and Man. Also in the East Garden are a quiet lawn and a terrace, a cascading fountain, and a small performance area. Both gardens are scattered with interesting sculptures. Zeum, a children's center, includes a historic, turn-of-the-century carousel, learning garden, play stream and fountain, labyrinth, outdoor amphitheater, and more open lawn areas. *3rd and 4th Sts., between Mission and Howard Sts., South of Market, 415/978–ARTS.*

zoos & aquariums

6 *b-8*

CHILDREN'S ZOO

More than 250 mammals, birds, reptiles, and amphibians are housed at the Children's Zoo. Seven acres adjacent to the San Francisco Zoo features a baby animal nursery, nature trail, exhibit of native American animals, nature theater, barnyard petting zoo, and fascinating insect zoo. During the Petting Zoo "Livestock Stampede" (weekends at 10:45 AM) kids help feed breakfast to the goats and sheep. *Sloat Blvd., at Great Hwy., Sunset District, 415/753–7080. Admission free; $2 for ages 3 and up the first Wed. of the month, "Free Day" at the San Francisco Zoo. Open weekdays 11–4, weekends 10:30–4:30.*

6 *c-8*

SAN FRANCISCO ZOO

Northern California's largest zoological park is home to 220 species of birds and animals, including 18 endangered species such as the snow leopard,

orangutan, and black rhino. The zoo's enclosures have been carefully designed to create as natural a setting as possible for these wild inhabitants. Gorilla World, a $2 million exhibit, is one of the largest and finest gorilla habitats of any zoo, with three generations of gorillas. Several endangered monkey species live in the Primate Discovery Center. The Feline Conservation Center is a 20,000-square-ft sanctuary for rare and endangered cats such as the jaguar, fishing cats, and snow leopard. Other enclosures of note include Koala Crossing, Otter River, the Lion House, and the Australian Walkabout. Don't forget to say hello to the zoo's newest acquisitions, a group of Madagascar aye-ayes, one of the world's rarest primate species. Feeding time is 2 PM Tuesday to Sunday for the big cats in the Lion House. The penguins are fed at 3 PM daily. Additional admission fees apply to the Children's Zoo (*see above*), the circa 1921 carousel ($2 per person), and the Safari Tour Train ($2.50 per person), which winds through the park. *Sloat Blvd. and 45th Ave., Sunset District, 415/753–7080. Admission: $9, $6 senior citizens over 64 and children 12–17, $3 children 3–11, free children 2 and under; free 1st Wed. of month. Discounts for residents with proof of residency: $7, $3.50, and $1.50. Open daily 10–5.*

7 *a-1*

STEINHART AQUARIUM

Steinhart, part of the California Academy of Sciences complex (*see* Science Museums *in* Chapter 4) in Golden Gate Park, houses a splendid collection of marine life. Six hundred species of fresh and saltwater fish live here, as do reptiles and amphibians, and even a flock of adorable black-footed penguins. Piranhas, manatees, jellyfish, sea horses, and other creatures live in 189 displays designed to approximate natural habitats as closely as possible. The Fish Roundabout is a 100,000-gallon circular tank with saltwater fish such as tuna and salmon swimming in schools. The Touch Tidepool is a collection of starfish, anemones, hermit crabs, and sea urchins that visitors can look at and touch. Two of the newest exhibits are the Living Coral Reef display, which features dazzling tropical fish and corals, and the Sharks of the Tropics display, with sleek 3- to 5-ft nurse sharks, black tips, and white tips. The penguins are fed daily at 11:30 AM and 4 PM. The Fish Roundabout feeding time is 1:30 PM daily. Admission to the aquarium gives you access to the Natural History Museum as well. *California Academy of Sciences, between John F. Kennedy and Martin Luther King Jr. Drs., Golden Gate Park, 415/750–7145. Admission: $8.50; $5.50 students and youths 12–17 and senior citizens 65 and older; $2 children 4–11; free for children under 3; free 1st Wed. of month. Open daily 10–5, extended summer hrs, 9–6 (until 8:45 PM 1st Wed. of month).*

4 *e-1, e-2*

UNDERWATER WORLD

This unique aquarium gives visitors a "diver's-eye view." You'll listen to a taped 30-minute tour while traveling through a 300-ft-long transparent tunnel surrounded by swimming creatures of the sea. It's a lot like taking a submarine to the bottom of the ocean. Two main tanks, which hold a total of 707,000 gallons, are stocked exclusively with fish of San Francisco Bay and offshore waters, including monkey face eels, spiny dogfish, sharks, sturgeons, Northern anchovy, and bat rays. *Embarcadero, at Beach St., east of Pier 39, 415/623–5300 or 888/732–3483 for tickets. Admission: $12.95, $6.50 children 3–11, $9.95 senior citizens 65 and older. Open June–Sept., daily 9–9; Oct.–May, daily 10–dusk.*

stadiums

There are seven major sporting venues in the Bay Area, including the new Pacific Bell Park, which opened in 2000. Together, they host everything from professional baseball, basketball, football, and hockey to circuses and gun shows. Purchase tickets by calling the individual box office, or by phoning BASS (510/762–BASS), which requires an extra surcharge. For information on specific teams mentioned here, *see* the individual listings *in* Sports & Outdoor Activities, *below*.

2 *e-8, f-8*

COW PALACE

The Cow Palace hosts sporting events such as tournament tennis and professional wrestling, as well as the Grand National Rodeo (*see* Events *in* Chapter 4). Indoor seating capacity is 10,500 to 14,500. From downtown San Francisco, drive south on U.S. 101 to the Cow

Palace/3rd Street exit; follow signs to Geneva Avenue, then head west seven blocks. Or take BART to the Balboa Park Station and transfer to Muni Bus 15. *2600 Geneva Ave., at Santos St., Daly City, 415/469–6065 for box office.*

6 *d-1, e-1*

GOLDEN GATE PARK POLO FIELDS/STABLES

The Polo Fields, which are used by the public for running and other sporting activities, also host special events. You'll find rock concerts, soccer, and the start and finish of the San Francisco Marathon here. It's a far cry from 1967, when Allen Ginsberg and hordes of flower children meditated and chanted together at their legendary Be-In—a mass effort to alter consciousness. *Between John F. Kennedy and Middle Drs., west of 30th Ave., Golden Gate Park, 415/831–5500.*

7 *2-c*

KEZAR STADIUM

The San Francisco 49ers used to play at Kezar before they moved to Candlestick. Now it's used for the city's Pro Am summer basketball games. It's also available for rental for soccer, football, baseball, and softball games. The stadium's history dates from 1925. It was built, in part, with $1 million left to the city's Park Commission from the estate of Mary A. Kezar, who wanted to memorialize her mother and uncles, all San Francisco pioneer residents. The city and county added another $2 million to erect Kezar Stadium. *Frederick St., at Arguello Blvd., 415/753–7028 or 415/753–7029.*

1 *g-5*

OAKLAND-ALAMEDA COUNTY COLISEUM COMPLEX

The Oakland Coliseum Complex includes an indoor arena with a seating capacity of 15,040 and an outdoor stadium seating 39,875. Both received extensive renovations in 1996 and 1997. The Coliseum's newest addition, the West Side Club, is one of the largest sports bars west of the Mississippi. The stadium is home to the American League baseball team the Oakland Athletics (A's) and the NFL football team the Oakland Raiders. The NBA basketball team the Golden State Warriors play their home games in the indoor arena. The arena also occasionally hosts ice skating and other sporting events; contact the box office for a current schedule. From San Francisco, cross the bridge and follow I–880 south to the Coliseum exit. Or take BART to the Coliseum/Oakland Airport Station; the stadium is connected via an elevated walkway with the BART station. *7000 Coliseum Way, off I–880, north of Hegenberger Rd., Oakland, tel. 510/639–7700 for box office.*

SAN JOSE ARENA

In the South Bay, the San Jose Arena is a relatively new indoor stadium that seats up to 19,500. It's home to the National Hockey League team, the San Jose Sharks. From San Francisco, take I–280 south to the Guadalupe Parkway exit, then turn left on Santa Clara Street. *525 W. Santa Clara St., near Autumn St., San Jose, 408/287–9200 for event information or 408/999–5721 for box office.*

2 *h-3*
PACIFIC BELL PARK

China Basin's new Pacific Bell Park debuted on Opening Day in April 2000 with the Giants playing the Los Angeles Dodgers. This 13-acre site is the first privately funded ballpark built for major league baseball play since Dodger Stadium opened in 1962. For ticket information, call the Giants (415/972–2000). *24 Willie Mays Plaza, at King and 3rd Sts., China Basin, 415/972–BALL.*

2 *h-8*
3COM PARK AT CANDLESTICK POINT

It's windy, but where else can you warm up with a caffè latte while watching a game? 3Com Park (formerly Candlestick Park) is an outdoor stadium in South San Francisco with a seating capacity of 70,497. It's been home to the National League baseball team the San Francisco Giants and the NFL football team the San Francisco 49ers. Each team will eventually move to its own new stadium, headed by the Giants, who moved to Pacific Bell Park in April 2000. Within a few years, the 49ers will move to a stadium to be constructed in the parking facility of 3Com Park. Express city shuttle buses run from numerous bus stops throughout San Francisco on game days; call Muni (415/673–6864) for the stop nearest you. Or take U.S. 101 south to the 3Com Park exit. *Jamestown Ave. and Harney Way, South San Francisco, 415/467–1994.*

sports & outdoor activities

The two best resources for outdoor enthusiasts are **Cal Adventures** (100 Centennial Dr., in Strawberry Canyon Center, Berkeley, 510/642–4000), a nonprofit affiliated with the University of California at Berkeley; and **Outdoors Unlimited Cooperative Adventures** (500 Parnassus Ave., at 3rd Ave., 415/476–2078), on the University of California at San Francisco campus. Both offer courses to the general public on everything from fly-fishing to rock climbing. They also rent equipment and organize backpacking trips and other excursions.

ARCHERY

Archers practice their sport in Golden Gate Park. The best source for equipment is **The Bow Rack,** in San Pablo (1085 Broadway, San Pablo, 510/236–8303), just off the Richmond–San Rafael Bridge about an hour northeast of San Francisco. In addition to their stock of nearly 400 bows, the store also has a 16-lane indoor range, as well as classes and coaching for all levels, and a "Junior Olympics" for kids on Saturday mornings. It's closed on Sunday.

6 *b-1*
GOLDEN GATE PARK ARCHERY FIELD

At the west end of the park, just north of the municipal golf course, this archery field is open daily from dawn until dusk. One block north of the field is the **San Francisco Archery Shop** (4429 Cabrillo St., 415/751–2776) where, during summer, you can rent an archery package ($25 per day) that includes bow, arrow, arm and finger protection, and target. The store is closed on Sunday. *John F. Kennedy Dr. and 47th Ave., Golden Gate Park.*

BASEBALL & SOFTBALL

teams to watch

For credit-card purchases of either A's or Giants tickets, call the BASS Baseball Line (510/762–BALL). There is a per-call processing charge of $2.50, and per-ticket handling fees may also apply.

OAKLAND A'S

The American League's four-time World Champions ('72, '73, '74, and '89) play home games in the Oakland Coliseum. Bleacher seats cost $5, plaza level $10 to $14. Same-day tickets can usually be purchased at the stadium's ticket office. Tickets may also be purchased at any BASS ticket center or through the BASS Baseball Line (510/762–BALL). *510/638–0500 for ticket office, 510/430–8020, ext. 4040, for A's Promotional Hotline; 510/568–5600 for ticket information.*

SAN FRANCISCO GIANTS

The National League's Giants hosted Opening Day against the Los Angeles Dodgers in their brand-spanking-new Pacific Bell Park in China Basin. Tickets cost $10 for bleachers; $15 for view-reserved seats (third level); $18 for arcade seating (beyond right-field wall) and view box seats (lower third level); and $23 for lower box seats (first level). Purchase tickets at the stadium; at any BASS ticket center; through the BASS Baseball Line (510/762–BALL); or from the city's Giants Dugout Stores (4 Embarcadero Center, 415/951–8888; 123 Serramonte Shopping Center, Daly City, 650/755–7571). Game-day tickets are usually available at the stadium's ticket office. *800/734–4268.*

STANFORD UNIVERSITY CARDINAL

Stanford's home games at the sunny Sunken Diamond often sell out. Tickets cost $3 to $5 and may be purchased by telephone or in person at the Stanford Athletic Ticket Office (Gate 2, at the south end of Stanford Stadium, Stanford University campus, Palo Alto). *800/232–8225.*

UNIVERSITY OF CALIFORNIA GOLDEN BEARS

The Bears play ball at Evans Diamond, at Bancroft Way and Oxford Street. Tickets cost $5 for adults, $3 for seniors, kids 6 to 17, and people with disabilities, and are free for children under 5. Tickets may be purchased by phone or in person at the Cal Athletic Ticket Office (2223 Fulton St., at Bancroft Way, Berkeley). *800/462–3277.*

where to play

Reservations for the city's five regulation baseball fields and approximately 65 softball fields are handled through the **San Francisco Recreation and Parks Department's Athletic Fields Reservations office** (415/831–5510). Reservations may be made every Tuesday up to two weeks in advance; the cost is $20–$25 for 1½ hours of play. One of the most popular playing fields is in Golden Gate Park: The **Big Rec Ball Field** (near 7th Ave. and Lincoln Way) is for baseball only. For softball, try **Moscone Park** (between Chestnut and Buchanan Sts., Bay and Laguna Sts.).

Softball and baseball in San Francisco aren't pickup sports; most people who are interested in playing join a league. Contact the office of the **Municipal Softball League** (415/753–7022 or 415/753–7023) for information. There are two seasons: spring (end of March through late June) and summer (end of July through end of October). The cost to join is $405.

BASKETBALL

teams to watch

GOLDEN STATE WARRIORS

The Warriors play NBA basketball at the Arena in Oakland from November through April. Tickets ($15 to $200 for season tickets) go on sale in early October and sell out quickly; call BASS Tickets (510/762–2277). *510/986–2200.*

STANFORD UNIVERSITY CARDINAL

The Cardinal teams are hot. The women's team is a consistent NCAA championship contender, and the men's team typically continues into postseason play. Both leagues play at the Stanford Maples Pavilion. Tickets to men's and women's games cost $15 for reserved tickets. General admission prices are $6 for adults; $4 for kids ages 2 to 17, under 2 free. For men's games, there's a long wait-list for tickets. For women's games, purchase tickets by telephone or in person at the Stanford Athletic Ticket Office (Gate 2, at the south end of Stanford Stadium) or, on the day of the game, at Maples Pavilion (Campus Dr. and Galvez St.). *Stanford University campus, Palo Alto, 800/232–8225.*

UNIVERSITY OF CALIFORNIA GOLDEN BEARS

UC Berkeley's basketball games are played in the new Haas Pavilion on campus, the former site of Harmon Gym on Bancroft Way at Dana Street. Men's tick-

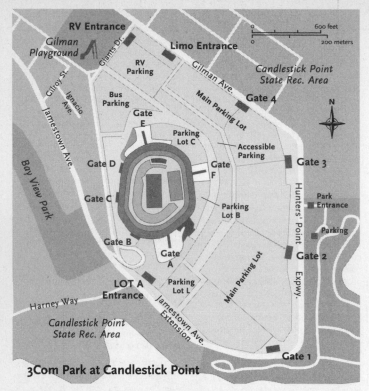

3Com Park at Candlestick Point

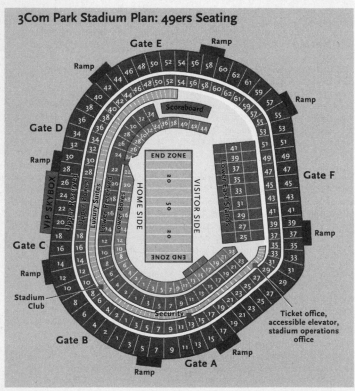

3Com Park Stadium Plan: 49ers Seating

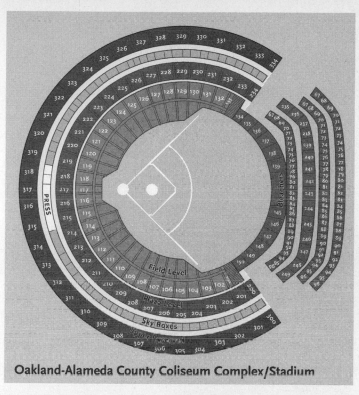

Oakland-Alameda County Coliseum Complex/Stadium

Oakland-Alameda County Coliseum Complex/Arena

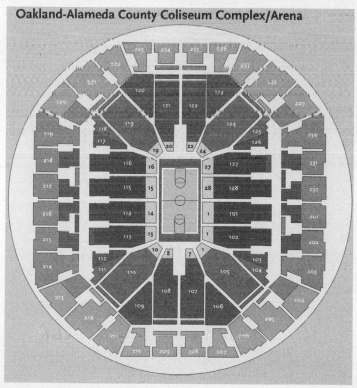

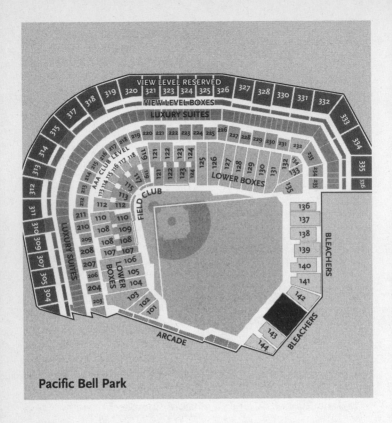

Pacific Bell Park

ets often sell out the day they go on sale. Tickets to men's basketball games cost $22; women's games cost $6 to $8 for reserved seats and $3 to $6 general admission. They may be purchased by phone or in person at the Cal Athletic Ticket Office (2223 Fulton St., at Bancroft Way, Berkeley). *800/462–3277.*

where to play
Pickup basketball games can be found all over the city. The following courts usually get going weekday afternoons and weekend mornings between 8 and 11.

7 *f-3*
EUREKA VALLEY RECREATION CENTER
On Monday nights women play full court. *100 Collingwood St., between 18th and 19th Sts., Castro, 415/554–9528.*

7 *d-2*
GRATTAN PLAYGROUND
The courts at Grattan see casual play weekday afternoons; weekends draw larger crowds and more ferocious com-

petition. *Alma and Stanyan Sts., Haight, 415/753–7039.*

7 *g-5*
JAMES LICK MIDDLE SCHOOL
Relatively low-key four-on-four games begin early on weekends here. The two full-length courts are often taken up with four half-court games by a talented pool of weekend warriors—lawyers, artists, and other professionals in the 20-to-40 age category who still enjoy shooting hoops. *Castro St., between Clipper and 25th Sts., Noe Valley.*

4 *a-3*
MOSCONE RECREATION CENTER
These popular courts (one indoor, one outdoor) have night lighting and unforgiving double rims. *1800 Chestnut St., at Buchanan St., Marina, 415/292–2006.*

7 *d-1*
PANHANDLE PLAYGROUND
The single full outdoor court and two minicourts in the Panhandle have highly

competitive games going nearly all the time. Most players are guys in their twenties and thirties. *Corner of Oak and Ashbury Sts., Haight, 415/554–9530.*

8 *e-4*

**POTRERO HILL
RECREATION CENTER**
Games here are highly competitive, every day of the week. *Arkansas and 22nd Sts., Potrero Hill, 415/695–5009.*

4 *e-7, e-8*

**SOUTH OF MARKET
RECREATION CENTER**
As an alternative to Monday night football, a sole court here hosts pickup games for adults on Monday night, 7 to 9:45. *270 6th St., between Howard and Folsom Sts., South of Market, 415/554–9532.*

7 *g-7, h-7*

**UPPER NOE RECREATION
CENTER**
Although the single full outdoor court is unlighted, it's adjacent to a single lighted outdoor tennis court. Low-key pickup games take place almost every weekend. *Day and Sanchez Sts., Noe Valley, 415/695–5011.*

BICYCLING

Two handy publications for San Francisco cyclists are *The San Francisco Biking/Walking Guide* ($2.50), which indicates street grades and delineates biking routes that avoid major hills and heavy traffic; and *City Sports* magazine, which lists local and regional biking activities in the Calendar section. The *Biking/Walking Guide* is sold in select city bookstores; *City Sports* is free at fitness centers and athletic supply stores. For additional information about bicycling in San Francisco, *see* Public Transportation *in* Chapter 7.

where to ride
San Francisco's legendary hills hold countless challenges for cyclists, but there are plenty of scenic routes that traverse level ground. A number of bike shops provide rentals as well as sales and service. One surefire place to find them is along so-called "Bike Row"—Stanyan Street adjacent to Golden Gate Park. The Great Highway along Ocean Beach (at the end of Golden Gate Park near Lincoln Way) has still more ven-

dors renting mountain bikes, tandem bikes, and bikes with child trailers that hook onto the back. One of the largest local chains is **Start to Finish Bicycles** (672 Stanyan St., between Haight and Page Sts., Haight, 415/750–4760; 599 2nd St., at Brannan St., South of Market, 415/243–8812; 2530 Lombard St., at Divisadero St., Marina, 415/202–9830).

1 *c-2*

ANGEL ISLAND STATE PARK
Angel Island is possibly the best spot in the Bay Area for a scenic, moderately difficult cycling excursion. Start by taking the ferry (*see* Public Transportation, *in* Chapter 7) to the island (bikes are allowed on the ferry). The bike path begins behind the Visitors Center (where you can pick up a map of the island's roads and trails); it's a fairly steep climb uphill to the bike path, but once there you can cruise the 5-mi road that meanders around the perimeter of the island. For the most part the bike path is paved, with only one difficult hill and some scattered inclines. You'll discover secluded picnic spots, attractive beaches, a few historic points of interest, and spectacular views of the city, the Golden Gate Bridge, and the rest of the bay. If you don't want to bring your own bike, you can rent one on the island, at the **Angel Island Tram Tours & Catered Events** (415/897–0715), near the Ayala Cove Visitors Center. Rentals are available from April through October. *Angel Island, 415/435–1915 or 415/435–5390.*

6 *a-1*

BAY TRAIL (GOLDEN GATE PARK—THE PRESIDIO—GOLDEN GATE BRIDGE—MARIN COUNTY)
For a full day's cycling adventure, start at the west end of Golden Gate Park, where John F. Kennedy Drive meets the Great Highway. Follow JFK Drive through the park (the road is at a slight incline), turn left on Conservatory Drive, left again on Arguello Boulevard, exit the park, and head through residential neighborhoods and onto the curvy, downhill roads of the Presidio. Make a right onto Moraga Avenue, then take another right onto Presidio Boulevard for a quick tour of the historic former military base. Make a hard left onto Lincoln Boulevard almost immediately; it leads to the Golden Gate Bridge toll plaza, where posted signs will instruct

you on which lanes to use for crossing (depending on time and day of the week). Expect delays on weekends. From Golden Gate Park to the Golden Gate Bridge Vista Point in Marin County, it's about 8 mi one-way. You can add some additional miles by following signs to the town of Sausalito (a 1½-mi downhill coast one-way), from which you can catch a ferry back to San Francisco (see Ferry in Chapter 7). If you plan to return to San Francisco on bike via Golden Gate Bridge, follow Lincoln Boulevard west; it turns into El Camino del Mar and runs through the beautiful, grand Sea Cliff neighborhood. At the Palace of Legion of Honor, the road veers left and becomes Legion of Honor Drive before dropping you back onto Clement Street. Turn right on Clement, and when it dead-ends, take Point Lobos Avenue past the historic Cliff House. From here it's easy to follow the Great Highway south to your starting point at Golden Gate Park.

2 g-1
THE EMBARCADERO
A completely flat route along the waterfront at the heart of downtown San Francisco, the Embarcadero runs a spectacular 3-mi course between the San Francisco Bay on one side and sleek high-rises on the other. The wide waterfront promenade extends from Townsend Street in SoMa north to Fisherman's Wharf, passing the historic Ferry Building (at the foot of Market Street) and Pier 39.

2 c-3
GOLDEN GATE PARK
For cycling, Golden Gate Park is spectacular. More than 7 mi of paved trails wind past rose gardens, lakes, waterfalls, and forests. All ultimately end at the Pacific Ocean. Additionally, on Sunday, the park's main road, John F. Kennedy Drive, closes to motor vehicles between Stanyan Street and 19th Avenue. Best of all, the roads and paths in the park are on level ground or slope over only moderate hills. Get maps and information at one of two visitors centers in the park: McLaren Lodge, at the park's east end; or the Beach Chalet, near the Pacific Ocean at the park's west end. From end to end, the park is about 3 mi long and just over ½ mi wide. Once you reach the ocean, you can opt to continue your ride along the Sunset Bike

Path (see below), which follows the Great Highway. For bike rentals, try **Surrey Bikes & Blades at Stow Lake** (415/668–6699), in the northwest corner of the park near 19th Avenue; or, for mountain bikes, **Park Cyclery** (1749 Waller St., at Stanyan St., Haight, 415/751–7368), just outside the park.

2 e-1
MARINA GREEN
The Marina Green's ¾-mi flat, paved promenade is a popular place to cycle; most extend their ride by continuing along the Golden Gate Promenade in the Presidio (see below). The Marina Green is also the starting point of a route to the Golden Gate Bridge and beyond: follow Lombard Street west into the Presidio to Lincoln Boulevard. From here, you can cycle onto the Golden Gate Bridge following the Bay Trail directions (see above).

MT. TAMALPAIS
STATE PARK
Mt. Tam, as the locals call it, is known for spectacular mountain biking over rugged but scenic terrain. In fact, in 1974, this is where Bay Area bicycle racer Gary Fisher invented the mountain bike. Pick up one of several topographic maps ($1 to $6) at the park's Pantoll Ranger Station (Panoramic Hwy., at Pantoll Rd., Mt. Tamalpais, 415/388–2070). Take care to distinguish fire trails, where biking is allowed, from walking trails, where biking may net you a fine up to $120.

5 f-3
THE PRESIDIO
Within the Presidio, 14 mi of meandering bicycle routes wind past coastal bluffs, forested hills, and historic military buildings. One popular ride follows Presidio Avenue into the park, where it first becomes Presidio Boulevard and then turns into Lincoln Boulevard. The road dips and loops through the Presidio before it reaches Baker Beach (see Beaches, above). If you want a less hilly ride, follow Lincoln Boulevard to Long Avenue (at the "Y" in the road after Lincoln passes under U.S. 101) and then turn left onto Marine Drive, which ends at historic Fort Point. From Long Avenue you may also turn left onto the Golden Gate Promenade Bike Path, which runs east along the water and eventually links up with the Marina Green. The first ¹⁄₁₀ mi of the promenade

is often wet from the crashing waves, so it's best to walk your bike to the corner where Long and Marine separate. For more information and a map of Presidio routes, stop by the park visitors center (Lincoln Blvd., at Montgomery St., Presidio, 415/561–4323).

6 *a-2, a-8*

SUNSET & LAKE MERCED BIKE PATHS

On a fogless day, the Sunset Bike Path along the Pacific Ocean (one block east of the Great Highway) may take your breath away. This gorgeous but moderate 2-mi raised bike path extends south from Lincoln Way (the southern border of Golden Gate Park) to Sloat Boulevard (the northern border of the San Francisco Zoo). To add another 5 mi to your ride, from Sloat, pick up the Lake Merced Bike Path to loop around the lake and the golf course.

BILLIARDS

4 *e-4*

AMUSEMENT CENTER

This no-frills billiard parlor and arcade has 15 pool tables and three snooker tables for the best prices in town: $4 per hour for one player, $6 per hour for two players. While you're waiting for a table, try out one of 10 pinball machines or 80 of the latest video games. *447 Broadway, between Kearny and Montgomery Sts., Chinatown, 415/398–8858.*

4 *g-5*

CHALKERS BILLIARD CLUB

With 30 custom-made and antique tables on the floor and Brie served at the café, this elegant billiard hall caters to discerning players. Children over eight are welcome with their parents on weekend afternoons. *Rincon Center, 101 Spear St., at Mission St., South of Market, 415/512–0450.*

2 *g-3*

GREAT ENTERTAINER

The Bay Area's largest billiards club has 42 pool and snooker tables, plus shuffleboards, table-tennis, darts, Foosball, a video arcade, and a full bar and restaurant. There is also a "pool school" for beginners and a pro shop for experts. *975 Bryant St., at 8th St., South of Market, 415/861–8833.*

4 *d-7*

HOLLYWOOD BILLIARDS

The late local columnist Herb Caen once described Hollywood Billiards as "a pool player's dream of paradise." The city's oldest pool room has 34 custom-made and antique tables, low cue prices, and reportedly the longest bar in San Francisco. *61 Golden Gate Ave., between Taylor and Jones Sts., Tenderloin, 415/252–9643.*

BIRD-WATCHING

The Bay Area is home to more than 200 species of birds. You'll spot many of them in the region's parks. For guided bird-watching tours, contact the **Golden Gate Audubon Society** (2530 San Pablo Ave., Suite G, Berkeley, 510/843–2222). The group leads half-day birding forays to Bay Area Parks. The **Oceanic Society** (Fort Mason Center E-230, 415/474–3385 or 800/326–7491) offers naturalist-led boat tours off the Farallon Islands National Wildlife Refuge, 27 mi west of the Golden Gate. On peak days, you'll see tufted puffins, pigeon guillemots, rhinoceros auklets, cormorants, and oystercatchers. Trips run June through November and depart from the Marina.

BOATING

Weekend boaters and picnickers frequent Stow Lake in Golden Gate Park, whereas more serious crew teams and fishermen and women head to the much larger Lake Merced. Children, big and small, sail toy boats on Golden Gate Park's Spreckels Lake.

2 *a-7, b-7*

LAKE MERCED

Lake Merced's large expanse is great for fishing and rowing. The city's rowing clubs maintain boathouses at Merced. There are always boats out on the lake, but it's never too crowded. You can rent rowboats and canoes at **Lake Merced Boating & Fishing Company** (1 Harding Rd., off Skyline Blvd., 415/753–1101). Call for seasonal hours. *Between Skyline and Lake Merced Blvds., Sunset District.*

6 *h-1*

STOW LAKE

At Golden Gate Park's largest lake, you can row, paddle, or motor the day away. Picnickers head for Strawberry Hill, an island in the middle of the lake. Rent boats at the **Stow Lake Boathouse** (Lake Dr. and 19th Ave., off John F. Kennedy Dr., 415/752–0347), in the northwest corner of Stow Lake, near 19th Avenue. The lake is open daily year-round, weather permitting; call for seasonal hours.

BOCCIE

4 b-2, c-2

AQUATIC PARK

The boccie court at Aquatic Park is enormously popular with elderly Italian men. *Jefferson St., west of Hyde St., Northern Waterfront.*

2 e-8

CROCKER-AMAZON PLAYGROUND

The Crocker-Amazon boccie court is adjacent to McLaren Park, in the southeast section of San Francisco. *Moscow St., at Geneva Ave., Visitacion Valley.*

4 d-3

NORTH BEACH PLAYGROUND

In the heart of a lively neighborhood, this boccie court has recently been repainted and the playing surface refinished. *Columbus Ave. and Lombard St., North Beach.*

BOWLING

In a break from the recent past, San Francisco now has three bowling lanes in different parts of the city: at the Presidio, downtown, and in Japantown.

4 a-6

JAPANTOWN BOWL

The massive Japantown Bowl has 40 lanes with automatic scorekeepers, plus an on-site coffee shop and three hours of free parking across the street at the Japan Center Garage. On Tuesday, Saturday, and Sunday nights, it hosts Cyber Bowl, a bowling extravaganza with black lights, fog machines, and the latest dance music. Two cameras pan the lanes and post shots of players on two 15-ft DVD screens; they also screen music videos. Reservations are recommended for Cyber Bowl and required for parties; call 415/575–2902. On Friday and Saturday the bowling alley is open all night long. All other nights it closes

at 1 AM. *1790 Post St., at Webster St., Japantown, 415/921–6200.*

5 d-3

PRESIDIO BOWL

Twelve lanes with automatic scorekeepers are open every night at this former U.S. military base. Tuesday and Thursday host league nights, so get here early to get one of the few lanes available on a first-come, first-served basis. Parking is free and there is a snack bar on-site. Presidio Bowl is open 9 PM to midnight Sunday through Friday and 9 PM to 2 AM Saturday. *63 Moraga Ave., at Montgomery St., Presidio, 415/561–2695.*

4 f-6

YERBA BUENA BOWLING CENTER

If you've got to have a cappuccino *and* bowl a strike before noon, you can do it at this new downtown bowling center. There are 12 lanes with automatic scoring, locker rooms, and a vending machine that serves up espresso drinks. If you'd rather have a handmade coffee, head to Mo's, the restaurant upstairs. Lessons and league play are available. The lanes are open Monday 11:30–10; Sunday and Tuesday–Thursday 9 AM–10 PM; and weekends 9 AM–midnight. Evenings and Sunday, limited street parking tends to open up. Otherwise, try the lot at 5th and Mission streets. *750 Folsom St., at 3rd St., South of Market, 415/777–3726.*

BOXING

5 g-6

GORILLA SPORTS

In addition to boxing and kickboxing, you can try out spinning, free weights, tae kwon do, and yoga at these two San Francisco locations. A $15 day pass is good for any class. *2450 Sutter St., at Divisadero St., Pacific Heights, 415/292–2699.*

2 1-e

2324 Chestnut St., at Scott St., Marina, 415/292–8470.

CAMPING

Camping is one of the greatest ways to escape San Francisco's hurried urban pace without depleting your bank account. Although there are many great spots scattered along the bay, here are some of the best.

Unless otherwise noted, place reservations with Reserve America at 800/444–PARK. You can reserve a cabin or campsite up to seven months in advance. You'll usually need that much time to capture one of these prime sites for a holiday weekend. Reserve America can also suggest alternative destinations if you're calling last minute or if sites are already booked on your weekend of choice.

1 1-c, 2-b, 2-c
ANGEL ISLAND STATE PARK
Rising up out of the bay, Angel Island is a camper's dream. You'll have 360-degree views as well as access to relics of the island's military history. You can explore abandoned forts and even a small museum at a former immigration station for this Ellis Island of the west. Trails snake around the mountain, and tiny secluded beaches beckon. Nine environmental sites mean you'll be roughing it: be prepared to use an outhouse and, for washing up, a simple spigot. Showers are not available. Flush toilets are located in the public visitor centers only. Pack lightly because you'll need to hike about an hour to get to most of them. Once you land, you can always rent a tiny wagon to transport your gear up the hill to your site. Campsite fees vary from $7 to $11 depending on the season and day of the week. Most sites accommodate about eight people. A small snack bar and souvenir shop operate at the ferry landing. Ferry service is available every day, except during winter, when ferries operate on weekends only. For ferry service from San Francisco, call 415/773–1188; from Tiburon, call 415/435–2131. *Angel Island State Park, Tiburon, 415/435–1915 or 415/435–5390.*

CHINA CAMP STATE CAMP
This former fishing village now hosts day-trippers and campers along the bay. You can hike to the remains of the shrimp fishery, ride bikes along picturesque mountain trails, or, on the hottest of days, swim in the chilly bay. Thirty campsites, accommodating eight people each, are $12 to $15 per night, depending on the season. Coin-operated showers require a stack of quarters. Most sites allow you to barbecue or

light a campfire, so bring charcoal and firewood along. You'll walk a short distance from the parking lot—50 to 300 yards maximum—so don't worry about heavy loads. China Camp doesn't always fill up far in advance, so it's a good last-minute option. *Rte. 1, San Rafael, 415/456–0766.*

1 a-2
MARIN HEADLANDS GOLDEN GATE NATIONAL RECREATION AREA
This is one of the few spots where you camp for free in the Bay Area, with beautiful views of the city and the Pacific. There are also fee campsites, right off the road, including a military camp built in the early 1900s. Other historic military sites as well as great trails add to the draw. Many microclimates exist within the park alone; the weather changes quickly, so come prepared. To reserve Battery Alexander ($20 per night for 80 people) or Kirby Cove ($20 per night for 10 people), call 415/561–4304 up to 90 days in advance. For reservations at the park's three free sites, call the main number below. A visitor center is located at Bunker and Field roads. Call for maps and more information, daily 9:30 AM to 4:30 PM. *948 Fort Barry, Marin Headlands, 415/331–1540.*

MT. TAMALPAIS STATE PARK
Mt. Tamalpais, home to three campgrounds, is known as the sleeping lady for its majestic profile. Ten rustic cabins and six primitive environmental campsites make up its Steep Ravine Environmental Campground. Situated on a picturesque coastal bluff, they overlook the Pacific Ocean. One is wheelchair accessible, and all are a short walk from the parking lot. The second site, the Alice Eastwood Group Camp, accommodates parties of 10 to 75 people each at two campsites. The third location, the Pantoll Campground, is the only one that accepts campers on a first-come, first-served basis. For the others, contact Reserve America (*see above*). Cabin fees are $30 per night. Campsite fees vary from $7 to $11 depending on the season and day of the week. Other than the group camp, standard sites accommodate five people each. For information about guided hikes during your stay, including moonlight or moonrise hikes, call 415/258–2410. *801 Panoramic Hwy., Mill Valley, 415/893–1580.*

POINT REYES NATIONAL SEASHORE

For backcountry camping, Point Reyes is the place. This national seashore is filled with trails and breathtaking ocean views. You'll also hike past grazing cattle and enjoy good birding, tide pooling, and whale-watching. Four hike-in and 20 boat-in campsites are available. Permits are administered by park rangers, not Reserve America. The cost for one to six people is $10 per night; 7 to 14 people, $20; 15 to 25 people, $30. The maximum stay is four nights. For more information, call 415/663–8054, weekdays 9 AM to 2 PM. Trail maps are available by mail from the Bear Valley Visitor Center (off Bear Valley Rd. and Hwy. 1, in the big red barn at the entrance to Point Reyes National Seashore). Call for more information. *Point Reyes, 415/663–1092.*

SAMUEL P. TAYLOR STATE PARK

If you're planning a family reunion, these 3,000 acres of wooded country-side with steep rolling hills, fern groves, oaks, madrones, and coastal redwoods might be your pick. A stream runs through the bottom of the canyon, with campgrounds on both sides. There are 60 campsites here, two groups sites for up to 75 people each, and three sites accessible to people with disabilities. Another unique feature: a horse camp allows campers to bring along their equine pets. Each standard site accommodates eight campers at a cost of $12 to $15 per night depending on the season. You park close to campsites, so bring wood for campfires and charcoal for grilling. Pay showers require quarters. *8999 Sir Francis Drake Blvd., Lagunitas, 415/488–9897.*

CROQUET

Croquet reservations are handled by the **San Francisco Croquet Club** (415/928–5525). The SFCC gives free introductory courses at 10 AM on the first Saturday of every month. Reservations are required and participants must wear flat-soled shoes. The club also hosts free open play on the first and third Wednesday of each month from 1 PM to 4 PM in the northeast corner of Stern Grove. Reservations are required for groups of four or more.

6 *g-8*
STERN GROVE

Tournament croquet in San Francisco is played on two 10,000-square-ft croquet lawns at Stern Grove. *Wawona St. and 19th Ave., Sunset District.*

DARTS

About 35 bars and pubs in San Francisco are affiliated with dart leagues, offering eight levels of play, from beginners to serious competitors. To join a league you'll need to pay seasonal dues ($8 to $20). During the two seasons, January to May and July to December, game time is typically Wednesday or Thursday at 8 PM. For a comprehensive listing of pubs with teams and competitions, send a self-addressed, stamped envelope to the **San Francisco Dart Association** (Box 192085, San Francisco 94119-2085, 415/781–7332). Or contact the **Golden Gate Darting Organization**, 415/731–8107.

SLEEPING WITH THE STARS

Beautiful surroundings make pitching a tent and starting a campfire much more inviting. Here are some of the Bay Area's most attractive campgrounds.

Angel Island State Park
　Historical sites, secluded beaches, and 360-degree views of the bay.

China Camp State Camp
　Swim in the bay, hike or bike along trails, and learn about the Chinese immigrants who once made this their home.

Marin Headlands Golden Gate National Recreation Area
　Camp in a military battery from the early 1900s.

Mt. Tamalpais State Park
　Wake up to sunrises over the Pacific Ocean from your campsite on a marine terrace.

Point Reyes National Seashore
　Backcountry or boat-in camping with death-drop ocean views and bountiful wildlife.

Samuel P. Taylor State Park
　Camp along a stream in a canyon or with your equine pet at a special horse camp.

8 *a-5*

DOVRE CLUB

It's a young crowd here, and the games are casual. The Club has only one board. *1498 Valencia St., at 26th St., Mission District, 415/285–4169.*

6 *g-4*

EAGLE'S DRIFT-IN LOUNGE

The crowd here is mellow, except when it comes to darts. Expect intense competition on seven boards. *1232 Noriega St., at 19th Ave., Sunset District, 415/661–0166.*

7 *g-1*

MAD DOG IN THE FOG

Guinness-drinking Brits put the two boards here to good use. *530 Haight St., between Fillmore and Steiner Sts., Haight, 415/626–7279.*

8 *c-3*

POTRERO BREWING COMPANY

This friendly pub with two boards also has a huge deck and a cozy atmosphere, thanks to its fireplace. *535 Florida St., at 17th St., Potrero Hill, 415/552–1967*

7 *g-3*

THIRSTY BEAR BREWING CO.

This microbrewery with two boards serves up Spanish cuisine and delicious pints. It's housed in a hip warehouse with exposed beams and high ceilings. *661 Howard St., at 3rd St., South of Market, 415/974–0905.*

8 *b-1*

TWENTY TANK BREWERY

On the weekends, Twenty Tank takes on the air of a fraternity house. There are plenty of microbrews on tap, and two boards for playing darts. *316 11th St., at Folsom St., South of Market, 415/255–9455.*

4 *a-4*

UNION ALE HOUSE

The Ale House is clubby and collegiate, and on weekend nights there's usually a line to use its two boards. *1980 Union St., at Buchanan St., Cow Hollow, 415/921–0300.*

FISHING

Sporting goods stores sell the $27.55 state fishing license that is required for seasonal ocean and freshwater fishing. One-day licenses, good for ocean fishing only, are available for $7 on charter boats.

charters

Charter boats leave from San Francisco and other cities around the bay, including Sausalito, Berkeley, and Emeryville. They search for salmon and halibut outside the bay or striped bass and giant sturgeon within. Unfortunately, heavy environmental pollution may lower the quality of your catch. Most charter boats depart daily from Fisherman's Wharf during the salmon-fishing season, from March through October. Reservations are advised.

CAPTAIN JOHN'S

Captain John leads salmon and rock cod fishing excursions and whale-watching trips in scenic Half Moon Bay. *Pillar Point Harbor, off Hwy. 1, Half Moon Bay, 650/726–2913 or 800/391–8787 for reservations.*

3 *b-5*

EMERYVILLE SPORT FISHING

The friendly staff leads all kinds of fishing excursions daily. "You name the fish, we'll go catch it" is the very unofficial motto. Excursions depart at 5:30 AM and return between 3 and 4:30 PM. Price is $55; license and equipment are extra. *Emeryville Marina, foot of Powell St., off I-80, Emeryville, 510/654–6040.*

4 *c-1*

HOT PURSUIT SPORT FISHING

Captain Ray Crawford specializes in salmon, tuna, and rock cod fishing aboard a super-fast, 25-knot boat. Trips depart from a slip to the east of Castagnola's Restaurant on Fisherman's Wharf. Lessons are free. Whale-watching trips and bay tours are also available. *At the foot of Jefferson and Jones Sts., Fisherman's Wharf, 415/567–7610.*

4 *c-1*

LOVELY MARTHA'S SPORTFISHING

Captain Frank Rescino has been leading salmon-fishing excursions and bay cruises since 1965. *Berth 3, Fisherman's Wharf, 650/871–1691.*

4 *c-1*

WACKY JACKY

Jacky Douglas, a.k.a. Wacky Jacky, is one of the Bay Area's few female skippers. Since 1973 she's been leading salmon fishing excursions in a sleek, fast, and comfortable 50-ft boat. Whale- and bird-watching trips are available, too. *Pier 45, Fisherman's Wharf, 415/586–9800.*

WATER SPORTS

Although San Francisco can't live up to southern California in terms of sunny swimming beaches, there are enough stretches of sandy shoreline—plus lakes, ponds, and swimming holes—to satisfy any landlocked biped. The following spots are great for boating, fishing, swimming, surfing, and more.

Aquatic Park (Beaches)
Serious open-water swimming.

Baker Beach (Beaches)
Angle here, or kick back in repose, just gazing out at the view.

Candlestick Point State Recreation Area (Windsurfing)
Smooth water, strong winds.

China Beach (Beaches)
One of the city's best swimming beaches.

Crissy Field (Windsurfing)
Windsurfing strictly for experts.

Fort Point (Fishing)
Surf's up and the fish are bitin'.

Golden Gate Park Fly-Casting Pools (Fly-Fishing)
Cast your rod just a stone's throw away from the Buffalo Paddock in Golden Gate Park.

Lake Merced (Boating, Fishing)
Rent a rowboat or a canoe and try your luck at trout fishing.

Ocean Beach (Beaches)
Daredevil surfers ride the big waves.

San Francisco Municipal Pier (Fishing)
Rent a rod, buy a bucket of bait, and try your luck.

Stow Lake (Boating)
Pack a picnic and paddle to Strawberry Hill.

---

where to fish

4 *b-2, c-2*

AQUATIC PARK

Bring a net to Aquatic Park and you might land some red rock crabs. Depending on the season, you may also hook perch and king fish from shore. *Jefferson St., west of Hyde St., Fisherman's Wharf.*

2 *b-2*

BAKER BEACH

Anglers come to Baker Beach to catch perch and striped bass, whenever the surf isn't too rough. *Gibson Rd., off Bowley St., Presidio.*

3 *b-3*

BERKELEY MARINA PIER

This is the place to catch tiny sharks and, once in a while, bass. *University Ave. and Marina Blvd., Berkeley.*

5 *a-1*

FORT POINT

You'll find Fort Point's fishing areas (*see* Architecture & Historic Sites *in* Chapter 4) along the seawall and pier. *Marine Dr., off Long Ave., Presidio.*

2 *a-7, b-7*

LAKE MERCED

Rent boats here to fish for trout, catfish, and bass. The North Lake contains trophy-size fish; those in the South Lake are smaller. Bring your own fishing gear or rent it on-site. *Between Skyline and Lake Merced Blvds., Sunset District.*

2 *a-3*

OCEAN BEACH

Anglers catch perch and stripers here. For general information about the beach, *see* Beaches, *above.*

4 *b-1*

SAN FRANCISCO MUNICIPAL PIER

One of the city's best fishing spots, this area is loaded with flounder, sand dabs, cod, bass, and perch, as well as crabs for netting. *North extension of Van Ness Ave., just west of Aquatic Park, Fisherman's Wharf.*

FLY-FISHING

Purchase equipment from **Fly Fishing Outfitters** (463 Bush St., between Grant

Ave. and Kearny St., Financial District, 415/781–3474). For instruction, contact the **Mel Krieger School of Flycasting** (800/669–3474).

6 *d-1*
GOLDEN GATE PARK FLY-CASTING POOLS
These fly-casting ponds in the middle of Golden Gate Park are among the best in the country. The Anglers Lodge beside them was built during the Great Depression as a Works Progress Administration project. Both pools and lodge are managed by the Golden Gate Angling and Casting Club; visitors are welcome to drop by the lodge on Tuesday, Thursday, Saturday, or Sunday. Regular club events include tying seminars and casting clinics; some are free and open to the public. *Across John F. Kennedy Dr. from Buffalo Paddock, west of 36th Ave., Golden Gate Park, 415/386–2630.*

FLYING

Aspiring and experienced pilots flying over San Francisco get a bird's-eye view of some of the most beautiful coastline in California. The following companies all offer flying lessons.

1 *f-5*
CAL-PACIFIC ASSOCIATES
This flight school has been offering lessons since 1978. You can study here for a private pilot's license, commercial license, flight instructor certification, and instrument ratings. Rentals are also available to licensed members of its flying club. *Oakland Airport, 510/489–3585.*

NORTH BAY AVIATION
This company bills itself on its personal approach to flight lessons. It also prides itself on its instructors and a first-time pass rate of more than 90%. It offers instruction for the private pilot certificate, the first step toward becoming a career pilot. Instrument rating is also available. *351 Airport Rd., Gross Field, Novato, 415/899–1677.*

1 *f-5*
SIERRA ACADEMY OF AERONAUTICS
This East Bay flight school offers courses approved for Veterans Administration benefits. Ab initio training is available for aspiring airline, corporate, and helicopter pilots with no previous experience. *Oakland International Airport, Oakland, 510/568–6100 or 800/243–6300.*

STANFORD FLYING CLUB
This nonprofit organization, founded back in 1935, specializes in flight training. Members include students and faculty from Stanford University, but 20% of the available memberships are open to the public. Federal Aviation Administration–certified instructor-pilots are available for private, instrument, or commercial pilot certification, flight instructor license, or advanced pilot ratings. The club claims to have the highest percentage of Bay Area students to complete a pilot's license after joining. *Palo Alto Airport, Palo Alto, 650/858–2200.*

FOOTBALL

When San Franciscans gather to play a game on a weekend afternoon, they prefer soccer to touch football—but when it comes to cheering the pros, they are fanatical about their home team, the 49ers. Tickets to home games sell out in a nanosecond. Football season runs from August into December.

teams to watch

OAKLAND RAIDERS
In 1995 the Raiders returned to the Bay Area after a 15-year sojourn in Los Angeles, and so far local residents have given the "L.A. Traitors" a warm reception. Their AFC West Conference home games are played at the newly renovated Oakland Coliseum (*see* Stadiums, *above*). Tickets are usually available. *800/949–2626.*

SAN FRANCISCO 49ERS
The 49ers play their NFC West Conference home games at 3Com Park (*see* Stadiums, *above*), at least until they are relocated to a new stadium that is in the works but still years off. Tickets are difficult to obtain as most seats are taken by season-ticket holders; when remaining seats go on sale in July, they usually sell out in one day. Take U.S. 101 south to the 3Com exit. *3Com Park, at Candlestick Point, Jamestown Ave. and Harney Way, San Francisco, 415/656–4900.*

STANFORD UNIVERSITY CARDINAL
The Bay Area's two big universities—Stanford University in Palo Alto and the

University of California at Berkeley—have been arch rivals for almost a century. Their Pac-10 football teams duke it out every year during the Big Game (usually late November). The Cardinal plays all its home games on campus at Stanford Stadium, near the town of Palo Alto, 33 mi south of downtown San Francisco. Tickets cost $10 to $30 ($50 for the Big Game) and may be purchased by telephone or in person at the Stanford Athletic Ticket Office (Gate 2, at the south end of Stanford Stadium, Stanford University campus, Palo Alto). *800/232–8225.*

UNIVERSITY OF CALIFORNIA GOLDEN BEARS

All of the Bears' football home games are played in U.C. Berkeley's Memorial Stadium, on Piedmont Avenue near Bancroft Way. Tickets cost $25 to $30 for reserved seats; $50 for all seats in the Big Game: Cal vs. Stanford. Otherwise, day of the game, general admission price is $14 for adults; $10 for kids under 17, seniors, and people with disabilities; and free under 5. Purchase tickets by phone or in person at the Cal Athletic Ticket Office (2223 Fulton St., at Bancroft Way, Berkeley). *800/462–3277.*

where to play

4 *a-3*

MOSCONE RECREATION CENTER

The flag football league of the Golden Gate Sport & Social Club (415/921–1233) holds games at this rec center. *1800 Chestnut St., at Buchanan St., Marina, 415/292–2006.*

6 *d-1, e-1*

POLO FIELD

To reserve the Polo Field, contact the San Francisco Recreation and Parks Department (415/831-–2700). *Between John F. Kennedy and Middle Drs., west of 30th Ave., Golden Gate Park.*

GOLF

courses

All of the courses listed below are open to the public. The city-run golf courses are Golden Gate Park, Harding Park, Jack Fleming, Lincoln Park, and Sharp Park. To make reservations for tee times at any of these (for a $1 per player surcharge), call the **San Francisco automated tee time reservation system and information line** (415/750–4653). The hot line also provides information about greens fees, golf cart and club rentals, and hours of operation for each municipal course.

The **San Francisco Recreation and Parks Department Golf Division** (415/831–2737) maintains practice putting greens at Moscone Recreation Center (1800 Chesnut St., at Buchanan St., Marina) and at two locations in Stern Grove (19th Ave. at Wawona St. and 19th Ave. at Sloat Blvd.).

2 *f-8*

GLENEAGLES INTERNATIONAL GOLF COURSE

In McLaren Park at the south end of the city, Gleneagles is a full-size, challenging nine-hole, par-36 course. *2100 Sunnydale Ave., at Mansell St., Visitacion Valley, 415/587–2425.*

6 *b-1, c-1*

GOLDEN GATE PARK GOLF COURSE

Just above Ocean Beach at the west end of Golden Gate Park is this small but tricky "pitch and putt" nine-hole course. All of the holes are par three, and all are tightly set and well wrapped with small greens. Nearby are a practice putting green and a snack bar. *47th Ave., between John F. Kennedy Dr. and Fulton St., Golden Gate Park, 415/751–8987.*

2 *a-7, b-7*

HARDING PARK GOLF COURSE

This 18-hole, par-72 course adjacent to attractive Lake Merced is heavily forested with Monterey cypress and pine trees. The well-wrapped golf course is older, with postage stamp greens, and is close to the Pacific. It's also walkable. The other facilities include a practice putting green, driving range (with practice balls available for rent), and full-service restaurant. Several professional tournaments have taken place here. *Harding Rd., near Skyline Blvd., Lake Merced, 415/664–4690.*

2 *b-7*

JACK FLEMING GOLF COURSE

Inside the second nine of the Harding Park Golf Course (*see above*) is the par-

32 Fleming course, with all the characteristics of the famed championship course—except that it's shorter, flatter, and less difficult. *Harding Rd., near Skyline Blvd., Lake Merced, 415/664–4690.*

2 *a-2, b-2*

LINCOLN PARK GOLF COURSE

This 18-hole, par-68 course is the oldest in San Francisco. Short and hilly though it may be, Lincoln Park has magical views of the city skyline and the Golden Gate Bridge. The rugged course has small greens and strategically located traps. Facilities include a practice putting green and full-service restaurant. *34th Ave. and Clement St., Richmond District, 415/221–9911.*

5 *c-5*

PRESIDIO GOLF COURSE

This magnificent 18-hole, par-72 course, managed by Arnold Palmer's company, opened to the public in 1995 and has been a hit ever since. On the grounds are a driving range, café, and pro shop. *300 Finley Rd., at Arguello Blvd., Presidio, 415/561–4661 or 415/561–4664.*

1 *b-7*

SHARP GOLF COURSE

A flat, par-72 oceanside course with numerous traps, this 18-holer is south of the city in the community of Pacifica. You'll find a practice putting green and full-service restaurant here. *Hwy. 1, at Fairway Dr. exit, Pacifica, 650/359–3380.*

driving ranges

The driving range listed below rents golf clubs and buckets of balls on the premises. Call for prices and hours of operation. Additionally, you'll find a driving range at Harding Park Golf Course (*see above*).

8 *e-1*

MISSION BAY GOLF CENTER

There are 66 stalls on this 300-yard two-tiered range, plus a putting green, pro shop, and full-service restaurant with an outdoor deck. *1200 6th St., at Channel St., China Basin, 415/431–7888.*

lessons

To brush up on your stroke, you can chose from commercial outfits or lessons at ranges operated by the city.

2 *g-2*

DRIVING OBSESSION/ GOLFIT

The PGA recently named owner David Mutton Teacher of the Year for Northern California. His PGA instructors teach at all levels. Initial swing analysis and training runs about $95 for a one-hour session. After that, classes are $55 for a 30-minute lesson. *23 Stevenson St., between 1st and 2nd Sts., South of Market, 415/357–5970.*

2 *a-7, b-7*

HARDING PARK GOLF COURSE

For $30 you get a half-hour lesson with a PGA pro. If you buy a series of classes, you get a nice discount. It's $145 for six 30-minute sessions. *Harding Rd., near Skyline Blvd., Lake Merced, 415/664–4690.*

2 *a-2, b-2*

LINCOLN PARK GOLF COURSE

Lessons are $40 for a 30-minute session with the head PGA pro or $30 for the assistant pro. For a series, it's six sessions for the price of five. *34th Ave., at Clement St., Richmond District, 415/221–9911.*

2 *g-3*

MISSION BAY GOLF CENTER

Class A and other experienced pros charge $50 per half hour and $90 per hour for lessons here. Five half-hour sessions cost $220; five one-hour sessions are $405. Students can also put their own groups together to save on lessons. For two players, one-hour classes are $100; for three players, $120; for four players, $140. *1200 6th St., at Channel St., China Basin, 415/431–7888.*

5 *d-5*

PRESIDIO GOLF COURSE

Lessons here cost $30 per half hour, or $145 for a series of six, with an assistant instructor. A full instructor charges an additional $10 per half hour or $200 for a series of six. All teachers are PGA pros. *300 Finley Rd., at Arguello Blvd., Presidio, 415/561–4653 or 415/561–4664.*

HANDBALL

7 *a-1, c-1*

GOLDEN GATE PARK

There are two indoor handball courts in the park, across the street from the rear of Steinhart Aquarium. Reservations are not required. *Middle Dr. East, between Martin Luther King Jr. and Bowling Green Drs., Golden Gate Park.*

8 *b-4*

MISSION RECREATION CENTER

Handball players are allowed to use the two squash courts at Mission Rec for free, although they're too small for true handball. Reservations may be made up to 1½ hours in advance (in person only). *2450 Harrison St., between 20th and 21st Sts., Mission District, 415/695–5012.*

HANG GLIDING & PARAGLIDING

For instruction, the **San Francisco Hang Gliding Center** (510/528–2300) is one of the few licensed schools in northern California. (Others abound, but most are not insured or licensed.) This school specializes in tandem hang gliding flights. It also offers paragliding instruction on Mt. Tamalpais. No experience is necessary to fly in its two-person gliders with an experienced pilot.

2 *a-7*

FORT FUNSTON

On sunny weekends you can watch brightly colored hang gliders swooping along the cliffs at Fort Funston, a site for experienced pilots only. Call the Fort Funston Weather Hotline (415/333–0100) for recorded up-to-the minute information on temperature and wind conditions. *Off Skyline Blvd. (Rte. 35), south of John Muir Dr., Sunset District, 415/556–8371.*

HIKING

A hiking day trip makes for a mini-vacation from San Francisco. Parks in the region offer hikes ranging from easy to strenuous.

1 *c-2*

ANGEL ISLAND STATE PARK

Among it's other features, Angel Island makes for great hiking. Start by taking the ferry (*see* Public Transportation *in* Chapter 7) to the island. Then pick up a map of the island's roads and trails. You can hike to a hilltop with 360-degree views and past historic points of interest, including a former immigration sta-

tion, abandoned military installations, small museums, and even a Nike missile station. Don't miss a stop at the island's beautiful beaches, where you can ponder San Francisco from a different perspective. *Angel Island State Park, 415/435–1915 or 415/435–5390.*

1 *f-1*

CHARLES LEE TILDEN REGIONAL PARK

This jewel atop the ridge between Berkeley and Orinda, in the East Bay Regional Park District, is only a 10-minute drive from the UC Berkeley campus. But once you arrive, you'll feel as if you've escaped to the country. Follow signs along the winding road to Inspiration Point. You'll find sweeping views of the hills to your right and, as you continue on the Nimitz Trail, the bay to your left. If you're still up for more when this paved 4-mi trails ends, you can continue amidst the cows and up and down hills, where occasional mountain bikers will keep you company. Look for turkey vultures, banana slugs, and, best of all, deer, who may also cross your path. Or start your hike at Wild Cat Canyon, which leads from the inside of the park up to Inspiration Point. Follow the signs to the pony rides, and turn right at the stop sign until you see the parking lot for Wild Cat Canyon. For tours and guided hikes, call the Interpretation Division at 510/544–2550. For maps and more information on Tilden and other parks, contact the East Bay Regional Parks District, 510/635–0135. *Charles Lee Tilden Regional Park, Berkeley.*

1 *a-2*

MARIN HEADLANDS GOLDEN GATE NATIONAL RECREATION AREA

Hiking within the Marin Headlands brings panoramic views of the Golden Gate Bridge and exotic wildlife, such as bobcats and coyotes. You can also tour a former Nike missile installation and other military sites. A visitor center is located at Bunker and Field roads. Call for maps and information daily 9:30 to 4:30. *948 Fort Barry, Marin Headlands, 415/331–1540.*

MT. DIABLO STATE PARK

This massive park, 20,000 acres in all, features more than 150 mi of trails and fire roads. You can also bike, picnic, or camp here (call 800/444–7275 for camping information). Maps are available at entrance stations and at the Summit Visitors Center, which is open Wednesday through Sunday 11–5. Parking costs are $5 per vehicle and $4 for senior citizens. Guided hikes ranging in difficulty from easy to moderate are led periodically. Call 925/837–0904 for current schedules. The park is open daily from 8 AM to sunset. Take the Diablo Road exit off Highway 680 and follow signs east to the park. *Danville, 925/ 837–2525.*

MT. TAMALPAIS STATE PARK
Mt. Tam's scenic terrain and its extensive web of trails are among the best in the bay area. For information on a wide variety of guided hikes, including moderate Saturday hikes, strenuous Sunday hikes, or moonlight hikes by flashlight, call 415/258–2410. Or pick up a maps ($1–$6) for self-guided tours at the park's Pantoll Ranger Station. *Panoramic Hwy., at Pantoll Rd., Mt. Tamalpais, 415/388–2070.*

POINT REYES NATIONAL SEASHORE
Nothing quite compares to the majesty of Point Reyes. This national seashore is beloved by Bay Area residents for its breathtaking scenery: towering redwoods, bubbling streams, coastal morning glories, and drop-dead views of the violent, crashing sea. You'll also enjoy good birding and spot sea lions here, so bring binoculars, especially from December to March, when you can whale-watch from the Chimney Rock Trail. Point Reyes Bear Valley Visitors Center is open weekdays 9–5 and weekends 8–5. Guided hikes are available. Call for current schedules and a thorough listing of self-guided hikes from one to six hours. Hike-in, back-country camping is also available. For more information call 415/663–8054 weekdays 9–2. *Point Reyes, 415/663–1092.*

SAN PEDRO VALLEY COUNTY PARK
Adjacent to McNee Ranch State Park, these 1,100 acres butt up against other open spaces: Montara Mountain and the San Francisco Watershed. The park is packed with 10 mi of hiking trails, two forks of San Pedro Creek, and Brooks Falls, a 175-ft waterfall in three tiers. Look for up to six to eight weeks after heavy rains. Early mornings and evenings, you might also spot occa-

sional deer in meadow areas. The visitor center is open and staffed on weekends. The park is open daily 8 AM to 5 PM in winter and to 8 PM in summer. *600 Oddsted Blvd., Pacifica, 650/355–8289.*

HOCKEY

teams to watch

SAN JOSE SHARKS
This popular National Hockey League team plays home games at the San Jose Arena (*see* Stadiums, *above*), where they have been swatting pucks and generating a wild buzz since the 1993–94 season. Purchase tickets at the box office or from Ticketmaster (408/999–TIXS or 415/421–TIXS). The season runs from October through April. *408/287–4275.*

where to play

Year-round skating is available at the downtown **Yerba Buena Ice Skating Center** (415/777–3726). A two-tier adult league consisting of 20 teams plays

---

OFF-ROAD ON YOUR FEET

Bay area hikes are a great option for weekend adventure. You'll breathe in fresh air, catch the smell of the sea, or spot wildlife in the back country.

Angel Island State Park
Hike a series of trails and beaches on this historic island

Charles Lee Tilden Regional Park
Watch turkey vultures soar ahead, geckos hide in the woods, and the sun set over the bay.

Marin Headlands Golden Gate National Recreation Area
Explore military installations dating from the early 1900s.

Mt. Diablo State Park
Don't get lost on 150 mi of trails.

Mt. Tamalpais State Park
Hike by moonlight.

Point Reyes National Seashore
Sea lions play in the surf while waves crash against the cliffs below you.

San Pedro Valley County Park
Spot deer in the evenings or a 175-ft waterfall after heavy rains.

here. The individual fee is $350 plus U.S.A. Hockey membership. Call for more information.

Hockey enthusiasts also get their fix by strapping on their in-line skates. Contact **Skate Pro Sports** (415/752–8776) for information on local in-line hockey leagues.

4 h-8
BLADIUM

In-line hockey is the drill at this indoor rink, with adult and youth leagues, clinics, and camps. In addition, you can find pickup games here Monday to Wednesday and Friday 4:30 PM–6 PM and Saturday noon–1:30 PM. The cost for beginner clinics is $15 per Sunday-afternoon sessions, or $125 for the season. Male, female, and coed league play is available on all levels. Fees range from $125 to $135 per person per season.There's also a sports bar with satellite TV on the premises. Equipment is available for rent ($3–$10), and the **Pro Shop at Bladium** sells all types of equipment for both roller and ice hockey. *1050 3rd St., between Berry and 4th Sts., China Basin, 415/442–5060.*

7 b-1, c-1
GOLDEN GATE PARK

Pickup roller-hockey is played near the park's tennis courts. *John F. Kennedy Dr., near Bowling Green Dr., Golden Gate Park.*

7: g-5
JAMES LICK
MIDDLE SCHOOL

The playground at James Lick is a popular spot for pickup in-line hockey games. *Castro St., between Clipper and 25th Sts., Noe Valley.*

ROLLADIUM ROLLER RINK

This San Mateo rink sponsors in-line hockey league games and sells a full line of hockey and in-line skating equipment. The rink is open Tuesday–Thursday and Sunday 1–4 in the summer, and year-round it's open Friday 7:30 PM–11 PM; in the winter, it's also open Sunday 1–4. Saturday schedules vary year-round. Call for more information. *363 N. Amphlett Blvd., Poplar Ave. exit off U.S. 101, San Mateo, 650/342–2711. Admission: $5, $4 on Sat. in winter (parents skate free 10–noon); $8 on Fri. Rollerskate rentals included in admission; in-line skate rentals $3 per person.*

HORSEBACK RIDING

6 d-1
GOLDEN GATE STABLES

San Francisco's only stable offers instruction in English and western riding, as well as dressage and jumping. Group lessons start at $26 per hour, private lessons start at $46 per hour. Daily scenic trail rides along the 12 mi of equestrian trails in Golden Gate Park cost $26 per hour. For kids, there's a summer camp. All trail rides and lessons are by reservation only; call at least two days in advance. *John F. Kennedy Dr., at 36th Ave., Golden Gate Park, 415/668–7360.*

HORSE RACING

BAY MEADOWS RACECOURSE

Thoroughbred racing at Bay Meadows takes place from August through November. Post times vary widely by season, so call for more information. General admission is $3, and it's free for ages 17 and under. *2600 S. Delaware St., San Mateo, off U.S. 101, 20 mi south of San Francisco, 650/574–7223.*

3 b-1
GOLDEN GATE FIELDS

At Golden Gate Fields, the thoroughbred racing season is mid-November to mid-January and April through June. Post time from Wednesday through Sunday is 12:45. Call for information on twilight post times. General admission is $2, free ages 17 and under. *1100 Eastshore Hwy., off Hwy. 80, Albany, 510/559–7300.*

ICE SKATING

With its Olympic contenders, Kristi Yamaguchi, Brian Boitano, and Rudy Galindo, the Bay Area has a winning figure skating tradition. If you're lucky, you might find one of them practicing when you're on the ice.

3 d-3
BERKELEY ICELAND

Berkeley Iceland has provided a cold, well-lighted place to skate since 1944. Daytime admission is $6 ($5 ages 17 and under); evening admission is $6 for all ages. A full range of skating classes

($60 for six lessons) is geared toward all ages, from five-year-olds to adults. Private instruction is also available (510/647–1605). Skate rentals are $2 per person. The rink is closed Monday. *2727 Milvia St., between Ward and Derby Sts., Berkeley, 510/843–8800.*

4 g-4
HOLIDAY ICE SKATING RINK AT EMBARCADERO CENTER
From mid-November until early winter, skaters enjoy this charming, outdoor ice-skating rink adjacent to Embarcadero Center. The lighting is particularly nice at sunset. Skating hours are daily 10 to 10, holidays included. Call for information about group reservations, lessons, and admission prices, which change seasonally. *Market and Steuart Sts., Embarcadero, 415/952–6688.*

4 f-6
YERBA BUENA ICE CENTER
The additions made to Yerba Buena Gardens (*see* Gardens, *above*) include a 32,000-square-ft ice-skating rink with an NHL-regulation-size surface for hockey play and practice, figure skating, and recreational skating. Skating hours are subject to change and vary widely. At night and on Sunday, limited street parking tends to open up. Otherwise, try the lot at 5th and Mission streets. *750 Folsom St., at 3rd St., South of Market, 415/777–3726. Admission: $6 adults, $4.50 seniors or children under 12, rentals $2.50.*

IN-LINE SKATING & ROLLER SKATING

Skaters of all levels are welcome to take part in Friday Night Skate, an evening ramble around town. Depending on the weather, anywhere from several dozen to more than 500 skaters may attend. The group meets on Friday at 8 PM at the Embarcadero at Brannan Street and departs at 8:30 PM. The route varies weekly. Drop by **Skate Pro Sports** (3401 Irving St., at 35th Ave., Sunset District, 415/752–8776) for the scoop on other local skating activities.

4 h-8
BLADIUM
This indoor rink is devoted exclusively to in-line hockey (*see* Hockey, *above*). *1050 3rd St., between Berry and 4th Sts., China Basin, 415/442–5060.*

2 e-4
THE CELL ROLLERDISCO PARTY
This is the closest thing to a roller rink for a night of roller skate dancing on a nice wooden floor. The Cell is a nonprofit grassroots event held in a massive warehouse that has been converted into a loft/theater venue, complete with a nice wooden floor perfect for skating. Bring your own skates or rent free from Skates on Haight (415/752–8375). It's held Tuesday 8 PM–11 PM. *2050 Bryant St, between 18th and 19th Sts., Mission District.*

1 f-1
CHARLES LEE TILDEN REGIONAL PARK
Advanced skaters head to Berkeley's Tilden Park for challenging routes and brilliant views. Follow signs to the parking lot at Inspiration Point and the trailhead for Nimitz Way. A 4-mi, nicely paved path stretches along a ridge overlooking San Francisco Bay and the East Bay hills. *Charles Lee Tilden Regional Park, Berkeley.*

2 c-3, d-3
GOLDEN GATE PARK
There are more than 7 mi of paved trails in and around the park. On Sunday, John F. Kennedy Drive, the park's main thoroughfare, is closed to motor traffic between Stanyan Street and 19th Avenue, making it a paved paradise for in-line skaters of all levels. Beginners practice stopping, and artistic skaters perform their newest moves to music in the large, flat area between the Conservatory and the M. H. de Young Memorial Museum. There's often a slalom course set up near the Conservatory. **Skates on Haight** (1818 Haight St., at Stanyan St., Haight, 415/752–8375), conveniently located at the Stanyan Street entrance to the park, includes a free lesson with in-line skate rentals every Sunday morning at 9 AM. You can also rent skates at **Surrey Bikes & Blades at Stow Lake** (*see* Bicycling, *above*).

2 e-1
THE MARINA
For beginners, the paved path along the Marina is an easy 1½-mi (round-trip) route on a flat, well-paved surface, with glorious views of San Francisco Bay.

ROLLADIUM ROLLER RINK
The closest indoor roller rink is south of San Francisco in San Mateo, where in-

line hockey league games often take place. There's a full line of hockey and in-line skating equipment for sale here, although rentals are mostly of roller skates. Summer and winter hours vary so call for more information. *363 N. Amphlett Blvd., Poplar Ave. exit off U.S. 101, San Mateo, 650/342–2711. Admission: $4–$8 (see Hockey, above).*

LAWN BOWLING

7 *b-1*

GOLDEN GATE PARK

The three lawn-bowling greens at Golden Gate Park are managed by the **San Francisco Lawn Bowling Club** (415/753–9298), which you must contact for reservations. Look for the lawns at the east end of the park between the tennis courts and Children's Playground, on Bowling Green Drive between Middle Drive East and Martin Luther King Jr. Drive.

MARTIAL ARTS

With its embrace of ethnic diversity, San Francisco is a magnet for martial arts from around the world and every discipline.

3 *d-2*

CAPOEIRA ARTS CAFE

At this unique Berkeley establishment, you can sip a cappuccino and watch Capoeira at the same time. Capoeira is an Afro-Brazilian form of self-defense with a system of belts to designate expertise, as in karate. Men and women learn together in this contact sport, which is practiced on mats. The Cafe has two professional *mestres* (masters); one of them, Bira Acordeon Almeida, in his sixties, is revered as a tribal elder. Classes are available Monday to Saturday, at all levels. Poetry readings are held Thursday from 8:30 PM to 10:30 PM. It's closed Sunday. *2026 Addison St., near Shattuck Ave., Berkeley, 510/666–1349.*

2 *f-3*

CARLEY GRACIE JIU-JITSU ACADEMY

One of the earliest martial arts is jiujitsu, dating from the days of Prince Siddharta, the first Buddha in India. As Buddhism spread, so did jiujitsu, which is based on elements of physics, such as balance, torque, and leverage. Carlos Gracie, a Brazilian with an eighth-degree red and black belt, has been teaching a modified form of the traditional Japanese jiujitsu in the United States since 1972. His is a very efficient method of street fighting and self-defense. Group classes are held Monday through Saturday for all levels, with separate classes for women. Courses teach stand-out aggression and defenses, take downs, ground fighting (wrestling), finishing holds, and weapons defense. *30 7th St., at Market St., South of Market, 415/788–0454.*

2 *c-5*

DOC-FAI WONG MARTIAL ARTS CENTERS AND ACUPUNCTURE CLINIC

This kung fu and tai chi chuan school has been operating since 1968. Doc-Fai Wong, the founder of the school and a licensed acupuncturist, was inducted in the Black Belt Hall of Fame in 1991 and voted one of the most influential martial arts personalities by *Inside Kung Fu* magazine in 1988. He serves as Grand Master of the school. His son, Jason Wong, is the *Sifu* (head instructor). They both teach a variety of classes, including traditional Chinese lion dancing and Chi Kung meditation in three forms: standing, sitting, and moving. The younger Wong also teaches kickboxing. Sparring is optional. Men and women learn together. Separate classes are held for kids beginning at age four. Another school operates in Sausalito. Call for hours and class schedules (415/331–8838). It's closed on Sunday. *925 Taraval St., at 19th Ave., Parkside, 415/665–2488.*

2 *e-4*

GOJU-KAI KARATE-DO, USA

Gosei Yamaguchi, in his sixties, has been teaching Goju-Kai karate in the city for 35 years. He is also a teacher and faculty member at San Francisco State University. Men and women study together. There is no direct contact. It's open every day but Sunday. *97 Collingwood St., near Castro and 18th Sts., Upper Market, 415/861–9987.*

2 *f-2*

KARATE ONE

David Shanas, a thirtysomething third-degree black belt, has been teaching for 10 years. He focuses on traditional Japanese karate, mostly Shotokan. Men and women learn together; children's classes are separate. Kickboxing classes are also available. The school operates in a former fitness center with showers on-site. *2001 Van Ness Ave., at Jackson St., Nob Hill, 415/474–3322.*

2 *c-6*

WEST PORTAL KARATE AND FITNESS
Certified Kempo karate black belts teach all levels, from children to adults, at this school. The focus is on the Shaolin style, which is a blend of Japanese and Chinese methods. Men and women study in the same classes. There is only light contact up to brown belt. Personal trainers are also available, as are classes in stretching, tai chi, aerobics, and aikido, another Japanese martial art that is only about 100 years old. A weight room is also available. It's closed Sunday. *66 West Portal Ave., between Ulloa and Vicente Sts., West Portal, 415/752–7283.*

WEST WIND SCHOOLS
West Wind operates five kung fu schools around the Bay Area, in Vallejo, Berkeley, Alameda, Fairfield, and Daly City, using teachers from its own academy. Instruction focuses on the Bok-Fu method,

---

MARTIAL ARTS

San Francisco's wealth of martial arts schools can teach you nearly every discipline, from Asia to Brazil.

Capoeira Arts Cafe
Sip a cappuccino while you watch Capoeira, an Afro-Brazilian form of self-defense.

Carley Gracie Jiu-Jitsu Academy
Experiment with a Brazilian school of this medieval Japanese martial art.

Doc-Fai Wong Martial Arts Centers and Acupuncture Clinic
Offers kung fu, tai chi, chi kung, kickboxing, and lion dancing, as well as acupuncture.

Goju-Kai Karate-Do, USA
Learn with a master of the craft.

Karate One
Study Shotokan karate with a thirtysomething instructor who's been teaching since he was 19.

West Portal Karate and Fitness
Combines karate with weight lifting.

West Wind Schools
Learn the fast, aggressive "white tiger" method of kung fu.

---

which translates to "white tiger," a fast, aggressive form of self-defense. Men and women study together. Contact begins at the purple belt level, ascending from white to orange, purple, blue, green, brown, and black. Teachers instruct with red belts. *7340 Mission St., at San Pedro Ave., Daly City, 415/421–0888.*

RACQUETBALL & SQUASH

4 *g-5*

EMBARCADERO YMCA
A day pass ($12) gives you access to either of the two racquetball courts at the Embarcadero Y. Make reservations on arrival at the club. *169 Steuart St., between Mission and Howard Sts., South of Market, 415/957–9622.*

8 *b-4*

MISSION RECREATION CENTER
At the Mission Rec you'll find two courts available for squash or racquetball play. You may reserve the courts up to 1½ hours in advance (reservations must be made in person). Use of the courts is free. *2450 Harrison St., between 20th and 21st Sts., Mission District, 415/695–5012.*

4 *d-2*

NORTHPOINT HEALTH CLUB
The single racquetball court at Northpoint is open to drop-in guests with the purchase of a day pass ($7). *2310 Powell St., at Bay St., Fisherman's Wharf, 415/989–1449.*

4 *a-7*

SAN FRANCISCO ATHLETIC CLUB
The club has one squash and one racquetball court, and reservations are required (drop-in guests may make reservations up to two days in advance). The drop-in fee is $15. Hours are weekdays 6 AM–10 PM and weekends 8–8 PM. *The Fillmore Center, 1755 O'Farrell St., at Fillmore St., Japantown, 415/776–2260.*

4 *f-3*

SAN FRANCISCO BAY CLUB
One of the city's best private health clubs has seven squash courts and one racquetball court. Drop-in guests pay $15 and must be accompanied by a member. *150 Greenwich St., between*

Sansome and Battery Sts., Telegraph Hill,
415/433–2550.

ROCK CLIMBING

The Bay Area's two outstanding climbing gyms are the place to take classes, find a climbing partner, or get the lowdown on climbing in surrounding parks.

3 *c-3*
BERKELEY IRON WORKS

The East Bay's premiere climbing center—affiliated with Mission Cliffs (*see below*)—has a 42-ft-high wall, 40 top ropes, and 14,000 square ft of climbing terrain. Classes are available daily for beginners, no advance registration required. Experienced climbers must pass a safety test before climbing. There are also private lessons for all skill levels, monthly clinics, and one- or two-day outdoor climbing programs. Nonmembers pay $16 for a day pass ($8 for ages 14 and under), with special discount days for women and students (Monday, Wednesday, and Friday 6:30 AM–3 PM, Tuesday and Thursday 11 AM–3 PM). Shoe and harness rental is $6. On the premises are a complete weight room, locker rooms, wet and dry saunas, and showers. The facility is open Monday, Wednesday, and Friday 6:30 AM to 10 PM, Tuesday and Thursday 11 to 10, and weekends from 10 to 6. *800 Potter St., Suite 400, at Doyle St., off 7th St. near the Ashby Ave. exit of I–80, Emeryville, 510/981–9900.*

4 *f-5*
CLUB ONE AT CITICORP

The outdoor climbing wall here is part of a full-service gym (*see Fitness Centers, Health Clubs & Spa Services, below*), and walk-ins must purchase a $20 day pass. The wall is 24 ft high, with 800 square ft of climbing terrain; it is closed during inclement weather, so call ahead. On Tuesday, Wednesday, and Thursday 5 PM to 7 PM, ropes are set up along 15 of its 35 routes, and the wall is open for supervised climbing. At all other times it is open for bouldering only. Private lessons cost $56 per lesson for club members and nonmembers, with discounts for small groups (up to three persons) and for those who purchase a 3-, 5-, or 10-lesson package. *1 Sansome St., at Sutter St., Financial District, 415/399–1010.*

8 *b-3*
MISSION CLIFFS ROCK CLIMBING CENTER

Mission Cliffs is affiliated with Berkeley Iron Works in the East Bay (*see above*). Its 14,000-square-ft climbing area has a 50-ft-high wall and more than 40 top and lead ropes, plus 2,000 square ft of bouldering terrain. Day passes for nonmembers cost $16 and include use of a weight room, locker rooms and showers, and sauna. Weekdays admission is $8 before 3 PM; special discount days for women and students are also available. Beginners classes are held daily; no advance reservation is required. The center also has a full range of outdoor programs, monthly clinics, private lessons, and kids' activities. You can rent shoes and harness for $6. *2295 Harrison St., at 19th St., Mission District, 415/550–0515.*

ROWING

Early mornings, when the water is still calm, scullers and kayakers take to Aquatic Park and Lake Merced. A few intrepid souls even commute by kayak from San Francisco to the East Bay. Unless otherwise stated, the following private clubs have annual membership dues and require new members to take rowing lessons.

4 *c-2*
DOLPHIN SWIMMING & BOATING CLUB

The Dolphin Club has a semiannual membership fee. A two-day rowing class (included in the membership package) is required of all new members. The main boathouse is at Aquatic Park, and a second boathouse is at Lake Merced. The club keeps singles, doubles, and six-person boats for members' use. *502 Jefferson St., at Hyde St., Aquatic Park, 415/441–9329.*

4 *c-2*
SOUTH END ROWING CLUB

The private South End Rowing club requires new members to take lessons (for no additional fee). The main boathouse, at Aquatic Park, has open-water singles, doubles, and a six-person boat. There is a smaller boathouse at Lake Merced. *500 Jefferson St., at Hyde St., Fisherman's Wharf, 415/776–7372.*

2 *a-6*

UCSF ROWING CLUB

The UCSF Rowing Club, although not affiliated with the university, nevertheless gives discounts for UCSF students and faculty. The club has 11 boats (10 singles and one double) at its Lake Merced boathouse. Sculling lessons are required for new members unless they show proof of prior training. Beginners lessons cost $50 for the first lesson and $25 for each additional one; make reservations at least one day in advance. *1 Harding Rd., off Skyline Blvd., Lake Merced, 415/675–9744.*

RUNNING & WALKING

A handful of running clubs in the city provide a forum for group training and racing. Among the preeminent clubs are **Pamakid Runners** (415/333–4780), which emphasizes competitive track work, and **San Francisco FrontRunners** (415/978–2429), a mostly gay and lesbian club that sponsors weekend runs followed by brunch as well as competitive weekday runs. In addition, the **South End Running Club** (500 Jefferson St., at Hyde St., Fisherman's Wharf, 415/776–7372) and the **Dolphin Swimming & Boating Club** (502 Jefferson St., at Hyde St., Aquatic Park, 415/441–9329) both sponsor running clubs.

The city hosts two major races: the colorful, rollicking Bay to Breakers 12K (May) and the San Francisco Marathon (July). For more information, *see* Events *in* Chapter 4.

In Golden Gate Park you'll find a Parcourse at the Polo Field and a senior citizens' course behind the Senior Citizens Center (36th Ave. and Fulton St.). Here are a few favorite routes for runners and walkers:

2 *b-2*

BAKER BEACH

For a short but spectacular oceanside run, start on Baker Beach near 25th Avenue and run toward the Golden Gate Bridge until you come to the rocks. Turn around and run to the other end, next to the stairs up to Seacliff's houses. Run back to your starting point, and you'll have covered about 1½ mi.

6 *b-2*

GOLDEN GATE PARK LOOP

Paved trails in and around Golden Gate Park total more than 7 mi, but for a pleasant 5-mi run try this route: Start south of the Polo Field and run east on Middle Drive, with the Polo Field on your left. Veer left on Overlook Drive, and when it ends take two lefts to reach John F. Kennedy Drive. After you pass the golf course, turn left onto Martin Luther King Jr. Drive (you'll be heading east again). On the home stretch you'll run into another fork: the left one will put you back on Middle Drive a short distance from the Polo Fields.

2 *e-1*

MARINA GREEN

The paved path along the Marina runs a 1½-mi (round-trip) course along a flat, well-paved surface, with great views of San Francisco Bay. Extend your run by continuing along the Golden Gate Promenade (*see* The Presidio *in* Bicycling, *above*).

6 *h-1*

STOW LAKE RUN

Circle Golden Gate Park's Stow Lake, then cross the bridge and run up the path to the top of Strawberry Hill, to run a total distance of 2½ mi.

2 *a-4*

SUNSET & LAKE MERCED BIKE PATHS

The 2-mi raised bike path from Lincoln Way (the southern border of Golden Gate Park) to Sloat Boulevard (the northern border of the San Francisco Zoo) is enormously popular for running as well as biking. From Sloat Boulevard, you can pick up the Lake Merced Bike Path, which loops around the lake and the golf course, to extend your run by another 5 mi.

SAILING

On sunny days, sailing is enormously popular from the San Francisco Marina, Berkeley Marina, and Sausalito. Choose whichever starting point suits your day's plans, as all provide easy access to superb sailing on the bay's open waters. Weather permits sailing year-round, but inexperienced sailors should beware of tricky currents and strong winds. Drop by the **Eagle Café** (Pier 39, 415/433–3689) for tips on local sailing conditions. For information on guided sailing trips, *see* Boat Tours *in* Chapter 4.

3 *b-3*

CAL ADVENTURES

Cal Adventures (*see* Sports & Outdoor Activities, *above*) offers several levels of reasonably priced sailing classes and a racing program at the Berkeley Marina's South Sailing Basin. Beginners classes are available year-round. Once you're certified, you can rent the 15-ft Coronados. Call for more information during weekday business hours, as the office is closed weekends. *University Ave. and Marina Blvd., Berkeley, 510/642–4000.*

3 *b-3*

CAL SAILING CLUB

The Cal Sailing Club, not affiliated with Cal Adventures, has operated its affordable sailing school at the Berkeley Marina since the 1950s. Here, youths and adults learn how to operate 20-ft sloops or windsurf. Members, once certified, can use the club's boats. Low-cost equipment for sailing and windsurfing is also available. On the first full weekend of each month, the club hosts an open house where prospective students are invited aboard a free sailboat ride on the bay. *University Ave., across from the Marina and Shorebird Park, Berkeley, 510/287–5905.*

1 *b-2*

CASS' CHARTERS AND SAILING SCHOOL

Cass' has 22- to 75-ft sailboats and a licensed skipper to navigate them—unless you prefer to do so yourself. To rent sailboats you must have a qualified sailor in your group. Cass' also has a U.S. Sailing–certified school and a junior sailing camp. *1702 Bridgeway Ave., at Napa St., Sausalito, 415/332–6789 or 800/472–4595.*

2 *e-1*

A DAY ON THE BAY

Ideally located in the San Francisco Marina's Small Craft Harbor, A Day On the Bay provides sailing lessons, charters, and rentals. From the harbor you have easy access to the Golden Gate Bridge and open waters. *Off Marina Blvd., between Scott and Webster Sts., Marina, 415/922–0227.*

3 *b-3*

OLYMPIC CIRCLE SAILING CLUB (OCSC)

This Berkeley Marina sailing school and yacht charter service is one of the top sailing schools in the country. It offers sailing excursions lasting from one hour to several days. Forty sailboats ranging from 24 to 45 ft constitute its fleet. *1 Spinnaker Way, 510/843–4200 or 800/223–2984.*

4 *h-7*

SPINNAKER SAILING

Spinnaker Sailing has more than 40 skippered or bare-boat rentals, ranging from 22 to 90 ft. You can take lessons here, sign up for excursions such as the sunset sail tours (*see* Boat Tours *in* Chapter 4), or join the sailing club. *Pier 40, Embarcadero at Townsend St., South Beach, 415/543–7333.*

SCUBA DIVING

Scuba divers on the California coast face a unique set of rewards and challenges. The beauty of the coast's kelp beds rank them among the world's top diving experiences—and there's always the chance encounter with a migrating humpback whale. Reefs and wrecks are also plentiful. Strong currents and frigid water temperatures are the only drawbacks.

4 *g-8*

BAMBOO REEF ENTERPRISES

This dive shop offers lessons, sales, rentals, and air tank refills. An SSI basic open-water course costs $175 plus $44.95 for materials (not including any equipment). The shop has its own heated pool on the premises for diving classes. A second branch is in the divers' mecca of Monterey (614 Lighthouse Ave., 831/372–1685). The shop is closed Sunday. *584 4th St., at Brannan St., South Beach, 415/362–6694.*

SEA KAYAKING

Although you can kayak from many points on the bay, it's hard to beat Sausalito, which gives you easy access to Angel Island and lots of undeveloped coastline. Farther north of San Francisco, Point Reyes National Seashore and Tomales Bay are spectacular kayaking areas; many companies lead excursions there. Full-moon paddles are another enormously popular way to explore Bay Area waterways. In most cases, previous kayaking experience is not required.

BLUE WATERS KAYAKING

This Inverness-based company leads guided paddling trips in Marin County and the East Bay. They also provide classes and rentals. *Box 983, Inverness, 415/669–2600 or 415/669–2600.*

3 b-3
CAL ADVENTURES

Cal Adventures (*see* Sports & Outdoor Activities, *above*) offers private sea-kayaking lessons year-round at the Berkeley Marina. In addition, there are guided excursions throughout the Bay Area and weekly "group paddle" sessions for all skill levels. Rentals are available. *UC Aquatic Center at the Marina, University Ave. and Marina Blvd., Berkeley, 510/642–4000.*

1 e-3
CALIFORNIA CANOE AND KAYAK

Since 1971, this has been the East Bay's center for kayaking, providing sales, rentals, classes, and guided trips. The company is based at Jack London Square in Oakland. *Jack London Sq., Water and Franklin Sts., Oakland, 510/893–7833 or 800/366–9804 for information on classes and trips.*

7 b-3
OUTDOORS UNLIMITED COOPERATIVE ADVENTURES

This UCSF cooperative (*see* Sports & Outdoor Activities, *above*) offers low-cost classes, rentals, and guided excursions to points around San Francisco Bay. *500 Parnassus Ave., at 3rd Ave., 415/476–2078*

1 b-2
SEA TREK OCEAN KAYAKING CENTER

Based at the Schoonmaker Point Marina in Sausalito, Sea Trek leads trips to Angel Island and other San Francisco Bay destinations, as well as tours of Point Reyes National Seashore. Rentals and classes are available. *85 Liberty Ship Way, Schoonmaker Point Marina, Sausalito, 415/332–4465 (weekends), 415/488–1000 (weekdays).*

SOCCER

teams to watch

SAN JOSE CLASH

The Clash brought major-league soccer to the Bay Area in 1996. Look for the team from April through October in San Jose's Spartan Stadium (take the Story Road exit from U.S. 101). Buy tickets ($8–$35) through BASS or the San Jose State University box office. *1257 S. 10th St., at Alma Dr., San Jose, 408/985–4625 for tickets.*

where to play

Call the San Francisco Recreation and Parks Department (415/831–2700) for information about the city's soccer leagues, or to reserve one of the city's soccer fields. By permit only, groups can practice at Moscone Recreation Center or other fields.

2 e-1
MARINA GREEN

Wednesday after work, folks gather on the Marina Green for brisk pickup soccer games. *Marina Blvd., at Fillmore St., Marina.*

THE PROS

The Bay Area is proud of its top-notch professional sports teams

Golden State Warriors (Basketball)
  Look for them at the Oakland Coliseum Arena.

Oakland A's (Baseball)
  Four-time World Champions.

Oakland Raiders (Football)
  Nicknamed the "L.A. Traitors" after they spent 15 years playing in Los Angeles.

San Francisco 49ers (Football)
  A football-only stadium is being built for them.

San Francisco Giants (Baseball)
  Their brand-new stadium is under way.

San Jose Clash (Soccer)
  The Bay Area's first major-league soccer team.

San Jose Sharks (Hockey)
  Tickets to Sharks games are often sold out.

6 *d-1, e-1*

POLO FIELDS

Seven soccer pitches fields at the Polo Field in Golden Gate Park are reserved for league play only. Technically, there are no pickup games allowed. Additionally, there are three soccer fields in Golden Gate Park, behind the Beach Chalet at the far west end of the park, opposite 48th Avenue. *Middle Dr., near Martin Luther King Jr. Dr., Golden Gate Park.*

SURFING

Surfing is a quintessential California sport, and daredevil San Franciscans are quick to strap their surfboards to the roofs of their cars when a good south swell hits the coastline. Throughout the Bay Area, waves are best during fall and winter, when storms far out at sea send ripples across the Pacific. Some words to the wise: many northern California surf spots are for experts only, and along this stretch of the coastline great white sharks roam. When in doubt, check with a local surf shop about conditions. The following are great sources for information, rentals, and lessons: **Livewater** (3450 Hwy. 1, Stinson Beach, 415/868–0333); **Nor-Cal** (5460 Cabrillo Hwy., Pacifica, 650/738–9283); **O'Neil Surf Shop** (1149 41st Ave., Santa Cruz, 408/475–4151 or 408/475–2275 for surf hot line); **Wise Surfboards** (1115 41st Ave., Sunset District, 415/750–9473; surf report, 415/273–1618). In addition, champion surfer Richard Schmidt (408/423–0928) teaches beginners classes through the **Santa Cruz Parks and Recreation Department** (831/429–3663).

5 *a-1*

FORT POINT

One of two popular surf spots in San Francisco, Fort Point has cleaner waves than Ocean Beach, although the strong current and rocky shoreline may deter beginners. On the other hand, you can't beat the views of the Golden Gate Bridge. *Marine Dr., off Long Ave., Presidio.*

HALF MOON BAY

The beaches along Half Moon Bay are famous hot spots for top-notch surfers, particularly because of a monster wave that occurs every winter in a place known as Maverick's, about ½ mi off Pillar Point Beach at the north edge of Half Moon Bay (near the radar tower). Surfers trek out here from all over the globe, especially in winter. To reach Half Moon Bay from San Francisco, drive 1½ hours south of San Francisco on Highway 1.

2 *a-3*

OCEAN BEACH

Winter waves here can reach up to 25 ft ("triple overhead," to use the current surf lingo). Even when the swells are manageable, the current is extremely strong. Riptides and undertow make it suitable for experienced surfers only. *Great Hwy., between Balboa St. and Sloat Blvd., Richmond District, 415/556–8317.*

1 *a-7*

PACIFICA STATE BEACH

Pacifica breaks best at high tide, with smaller waves for beginners at the southern end of the beach, near San Pedro Point. This is sometimes also known as Linda Mar Beach. Just north of the rocky promontory, on a stretch also known as Rockaway Beach, you'll find bigger waves—but it's more crowded and competitive. To reach Pacifica, drive 45 minutes south of San Francisco along Highway 1. *Hwy. 1, Pacifica.*

SWIMMING

Although San Francisco Bay is a bracing 55°F, open-water swimming is a local institution. If you'd like to brave the chill, you can minimize the dangers of boat traffic and strong tides by hooking up with members of the two local swimming clubs: the **Dolphin Swimming & Boating Club** (415/441–9329) and the **South End Rowing Club** (415/776–7372), both at Aquatic Park (500 and 502 Jefferson St., west of Hyde St., Fisherman's Wharf). Sunday at 7 AM, look for these hardy souls, who usually wear nothing more than bathing suits, headgear, and earplugs. When there's an official swim—usually on a Sunday morning as well—participants may number in the hundreds. Both clubs have been around since the 1870s, and both sponsor biannual swims to Alcatraz Island.

For lap swimmers, the **San Francisco Recreation and Park Department** (415/831–2700) manages one outdoor swimming pool and seven indoor pools throughout the city. Admission fees at all public pools are $3 adults, 50¢ children ages 17 and under, with discount packages for 5 or 12 visits for adults; 15

visits for seniors. All public pools have swimming lessons (for children and adults) and water aerobics classes; contact the individual pools for current schedules. A few pools also host workouts for various groups of United States Masters Swimmers, a national swim league.

4 g-5

EMBARCADERO YMCA

The Y has a 25-meter pool, a gym, and spa facilities. A day pass costs $12. *169 Steuart St., between Mission and Howard Sts., South of Market, 415/957–9622.*

5 h-6

HAMILTON RECREATION CENTER

The indoor, city-run Hamilton pool is a favorite among Masters swimmers. *1900 Geary Blvd., at Steiner St., Western Addition, 415/292–2001.*

5 e-8

KORET HEALTH AND RECREATION CENTER

The well-maintained Olympic-size pool at Koret, part of the University of San Francisco, is open to the public before 2 PM daily with purchase of a $10 day pass. *Parker Ave., at Turk St., Richmond District, 415/422–6821.*

8 a-3

MISSION POOL

This is one of the three best city pools and the only outdoor public pool in the city. It has five lanes and is not usually crowded. It's open from June through September only. *19th and Linda Sts., Mission District, 415/695–5002.*

4 d-3

NORTH BEACH POOL

This indoor pool is used by all ages for lap swimming. Some mornings it opens as early as 6 AM. *Lombard and Mason Sts., North Beach, 415/274–0200.*

5 d-7

ROSSI POOL

The six lanes at this excellent indoor pool are open to lap swimmers as early as 5:30 AM on some mornings; call for the current schedule. The pool is crowded evenings 5:30 to 7. *Arguello Blvd. and Anza St., Richmond District, 415/666–7014.*

6 g-8

SAVA POOL

This is one of the more popular (and crowded) indoor city pools. It's 33⅓ yards long, with a total of six lanes. Call for the lap-swimming schedule; the most serious swimmers come to the late-night and early morning sessions. *19th Ave. and Wawona St., Sunset District, 415/753–7000.*

4 e-5

SHEEHAN HOTEL

This hotel allows nonguests to use its four-lane lap pool for a $10 entry fee, or 15 visits for $70. *620 Sutter St., at Mason St., Union Square, 415/775–6500.*

TENNIS

The Bay Area hosts the Volvo San Francisco Tennis Tournament (February) in San Francisco, the Cybase Open (February) in San Jose, and the Bank of the West women's tennis tour (October) in Oakland.

The San Francisco Recreation and Parks Department maintains more than 100 tennis courts around the city. With the exception of courts at Golden Gate Park, all are free and available on a first-come, first-served basis. For information on public tennis courts and a handy map of court locations, contact the San Francisco Recreation and Parks Department (415/831–2700). Additional tennis information is available by calling 415/753–7100.

4 c-3

ALICE MARBLE COURTS

These three free courts are unlighted, but still attract a fairly good turnout of young, tennis-playing professionals year-round. Saturday and Sunday morning there's usually a wait. *Greenwich and Hyde Sts., Russian Hill.*

7 b-1, c-1

GOLDEN GATE PARK

You may make reservations to use the 21 courts at the eastern end of Golden Gate Park on weekends or holidays (reservations are not accepted for weekday use) by calling the Tennis Reservation Line (415/753–7101). Reservations are accepted Wednesday from 4 PM to 6 PM, Thursday from 9 to 5, and Friday

from 9 to noon. Court fees range from
$2–$8 for 90 minutes of play. It's free
for those 18 years and under. Check the
bulletin board at the clubhouse for post-
ings about neighborhood clubs. *John F.
Kennedy Dr., at Middle Dr. East, Golden
Gate Park.*

5 *h-6*
**HAMILTON RECREATION
CENTER**
Tennis players from all over the city
come here to use the two free, lighted
courts—even on winter weeknights.
*1900 Geary Blvd., at Steiner St., Western
Addition, 415/292–2001.*

5 *e-5*
JULIUS KAHN PLAYGROUND
There are four free courts at the south-
east corner of the Presidio. *W. Pacific
Ave., between Spruce and Locust Sts., Pre-
sidio, 415/292–2004.*

2 *f-7*
MCLAREN PARK
These six free courts are in the southern
section of the city. *Mansell St., near University St., Visitacion Valley, 415/337–4700.*

7 *h-3*
MISSION DOLORES PARK
These six free courts make up the
largest set of lighted courts in the city.
*18th and Dolores Sts., Mission District,
415/554–9529.*

4 *a-3*
**MOSCONE RECREATION
CENTER**
There are four free, lighted courts and a
practice wall here. *1800 Chestnut St., at
Buchanan St., Marina, 415/292–2006.*

4 *d-3*
**NORTH BEACH
PLAYGROUND**
Three free, lighted courts and a practice
wall lie within this neighborhood play-
ground. *Lombard and Mason Sts., North
Beach, 415/272–0201.*

8 *e-4*
**POTRERO HILL
RECREATION CENTER**
Find two free lighted courts and a prac-
tice wall here. *22nd and Arkansas Sts.,
Potrero Hill, 415/695–5009.*

4 *f-3*
SAN FRANCISCO BAY CLUB
One of the city's premiere health clubs,
the private Bay Club has two outdoor
tennis courts. Drop-in guests must be
accompanied by a member, and pay a
$15 fee. *150 Greenwich St., between San-
some and Battery Sts., Telegraph Hill, 415/
433–2550.*

ULTIMATE FRISBEE

Call the **Ultimate Players Association**
(800/872–4384) for information about
ultimate Frisbee leagues.

5 *e-5*
JULIUS KAHN PLAYGROUND
The playground, near the southeast cor-
ner of the Presidio, hosts pickup games
Wednesday evening and Saturday morn-
ing. *W. Pacific Ave., between Spruce and
Locust Sts., Presidio.*

7 *c-1*
SHARON MEADOW
To join a free-wheeling game of Frisbee,
try Sharon Meadow, at the eastern end
of Golden Gate Park. On Tuesday and
Thursday evening and on weekend
mornings, the coed pickup games here
sometimes draw up to 40 people. *North
of Kezar Dr., Golden Gate Park.*

VOLLEYBALL

You can rent volleyball nets at **Outdoors
Unlimited Cooperative Adventures** (500
Parnassus Ave., at 3rd Ave., 415/476–
2078). The **San Francisco Recreation and
Parks Department Division of Athletics**
(415/753–7032) runs a women's adult
volleyball league; call for information.

7 *e-8*
**GLEN PARK RECREATION
CENTER**
Just south of Glen Canyon Park, you'll
find coed adult volleyball on an indoor
court twice weekly: Monday from 7 PM to
9:30 PM for advanced players and Tuesday from 10:30 AM until 1 PM for interme-
diates. The courts are free of charge and
open to all. *70 Elk St., at O'Shaughnessy
Blvd., Diamond Heights, 415/337–4705.*

2 *e-1*

MARINA GREEN

Volleyball enthusiasts bring their own nets to the Marina Green on weekends, when dozens of open games take place. *Marina Blvd., at Fillmore St., Marina.*

4 *a-3*

MOSCONE RECREATION CENTER

The Moscone Rec Center has five unlighted grass courts. High-skill two-on-two games are the norm here. They're first-come, first-served, and you must supply your own nets. *1800 Chestnut St., at Buchanan St., Marina, 415/292-2006.*

4 *e-7, e-8*

SOUTH OF MARKET RECREATION CENTER

Coed adult volleyball is played on two indoor courts Thursday from 7 PM until 9:45 PM. The level of play varies between intermediate and advanced. The courts are free of charge. *270 6th St., between Howard and Folsom Sts., South of Market, 415/554-9532.*

WHALE-WATCHING

Several fishing-charter boat services lead whale-watching trips. The **Oceanic Society** (*see* Bird-Watching, *above*) also leads excursions around the Bay Area and shorter trips to the Farallon Islands and along the Marin coast. Take motion sickness pills well in advance because the seas can be rough. Also pack a lunch, camera and film, and plastic bags to keep everything dry.

The Oceanic Society's captains know these seas well. You could easily end up seeing a humpback blow, breach, or flap its pectoral fins. You won't believe how graceful these gentle giants are when they fluke—dive down into the water and let their tail fins rise above water. Pick up a copy of the *Oceanic Society Field Guide to the Gray Whale*, or the equivalent humpback edition, which includes maps and directions to the best whale-watching sites in California. For a taste of whale-watching and other marine-life sightings, call the Oceanic Society's Whale Hotline (415/474-0488).

Dolphin Charters (Berkeley Marina, University Ave. and Marina Blvd., Berkeley, 510/527-9622), an adventure cruising company, also offers day trips to the Farallon Islands and half-day trips closer to shore.

Another option is whale-watching from shore at **Point Reyes National Seashore** (415/663-1092). From December to March, you can spot migrating whales from the self-guided Chimney Rock Trail. This 1.2-mi stretch has stunning views of Drakes Bay and the Pacific Ocean and patches of wildflowers. The trailhead is near the lighthouse, a 40-minute drive from the Bear Valley Visitor Center (off Bear Valley Rd. and Hwy. 1, in the big red barn at the entrance to Point Reyes National Seashore).

WINDSURFING

The San Francisco Bay is the third-ranked windsurfing spot in the United States, behind Hawaii's Maui island and Oregon's Hood River. The westerly winds that blow from April through August provide optimal conditions; at other times of the year, the winds are sporadic and blow either north or south. To tackle this sport in winter, you'll need a ⅜- or ⅝-mm-thick wet suit.

Many of the area's sailing schools also teach windsurfing and rent equipment (*see* Sailing, *above*). In addition, **City Front Sailboards** (2936 Lyon St., at Lombard St., Presidio, 415/929-9873), just blocks away from Crissy Field, has a beginner's instruction package as well as a full line of equipment. The **San Francisco School of Windsurfing** (Candlestick Point, 415/753-3235) has lessons for beginners and for advanced surfers at Candlestick Point.

2 *h-8*

CANDLESTICK POINT STATE RECREATION AREA

Windsurfers who crave speed launch from the beach adjacent to 3Com Stadium, where winds average 20 mph but are rumored to occasionally reach a brisk 30 mph. Beginners should be cautious. Winds can be fickle, and can leave inexperienced surfers stranded out in the bay. Parking at 3Com Stadium costs a hefty $20 on game days during football season. There are no fees on non-game days. Windsurfers also park within the state recreation area in "windsurf circle." From U.S. 101, take the 3Com exit, continue halfway around the stadium, then turn right at the first set of yellow gates.

Parking at windsurf circle is also $20 on game days, free on all other days. For more information on Candlestick Point State Recreation Area, call the ranger office (415/671–0145). The park is open daily from 8 to sunset, with shorter hours in winter. *Jamestown Ave. and Harney Way, South San Francisco.*

1 *d-8, e-8*
COYOTE POINT
South of San Francisco International Airport is another challenging windsurfing spot. The waves are choppy here, but close to shore the wind remains moderate. Follow U.S. 101 south 4½ mi past the airport exit and follow signs to the city of San Mateo's Coyote Point Park (650/573–2592). The park entry fee is $4. There are rest rooms and hot showers. *Coyote Point Dr., off Hwy. 101, San Mateo.*

5 *d-2*
CRISSY FIELD
The waters off Crissy Field, in the Presidio, are strictly for expert windsurfers. Although beach access makes launching easy, strong tides and currents can easily sweep a novice under the Golden Gate into the Pacific or across the bay to Alcatraz Island. Add heavy boat and ship traffic and you'll see why more rescues are required here than in all other Bay Area sites combined. *Hwy. 101 and Presidio Ave., Presidio.*

WRESTLING

2 *e-8, f-8*
COW PALACE
In addition to rodeos and various sporting events, the Cow Palace hosts professional wrestling matches twice each year. Call for ticket prices and show dates. *2600 Geneva Ave., at Santos St., Daly City, 415/469–6065 for box office.*

YOGA

The city's yoga institutes tailor weekend and evening classes to suit even the busiest schedule. Most welcome participants on a drop-in, pay-per-class basis, with no advance registration required. Wear loose, comfortable clothing, avoid eating one to two hours prior to class, and arrive with more than just a few minutes to spare.

7 *h-4*
INTEGRAL YOGA INSTITUTE
The Institute, founded by the Reverend Sri Swami Satchidananda, has daily classes in four levels of hatha yoga (which emphasizes breathing, posture, and meditation) and one gentle yoga class. All of the 1½-hour classes operate on a drop-in basis. Cost is $8, first-time participants and senior citizens $5. Retreats, stress management programs, and meditation workshops are held occasionally throughout the year. Six-week prenatal and mother-and-baby courses are also available. *770 Dolores St., at 21st St., Mission District, 415/821–1117 or 415/824–9600 for recorded schedule of classes.*

6 *f-7*
IYENGAR YOGA INSTITUTE OF SAN FRANCISCO
The institute offers more than 30 classes of Iyengar yoga (a type of hatha yoga) for all levels each week; call for a current schedule. Most classes run 1½ hours and cost about $12 per session (drop-ins welcome) or $40 for four. Prenatal, mother-and-baby, and seniors courses are also available. *2404 27th Ave., at Taraval St., Sunset District, 415/753–0909.*

5 *d-6*
MAGANA & WALT BAPTISTE YOGA CENTER
The oldest established yoga school in San Francisco has classes in Baptiste yoga (a type of hatha yoga) on Wednesday evening and Saturday morning. Cost is $12 for a single session, $45 for four sessions, or $110 for 12 sessions. The center also hosts several meditation programs throughout the year; these cost between $15 and $20 per session. Private instruction is also available, as are classes in Middle Eastern dance. *730 Euclid Ave., between Palm and Jordan Sts., Richmond District, 415/387–6833.*

8 *b-5*
YOGA SOCIETY OF SAN FRANCISCO
At this nonprofit community center, hatha yoga classes, with a spiritual and meditative component, cost $10 per session or $40 for five. Drop-ins are welcome. There are one or two classes most days, open to all levels. Classes are 1½ to 2 hours. Daily at 6 AM there is

a free 30-minute meditation session.
Weekdays from 7:30 PM to 9 PM the center hosts a fire ceremony (meditation and chanting) that's free and open to all. Tai chi chuan and Sanskrit classes are also available. Special events include workshops on spirituality and meditation. Call for more information. *2872 Folsom St., at 25th St., Mission District, 415/285-5537.*

fitness centers, health clubs & spa services

Many of San Francisco's dozens of fitness centers and health clubs sell day passes for $10 to $20, although some of the most luxurious remain "members only." Check the Yellow Pages under "Health Clubs" for a complete listing.

Many of the large hotels have arrangements with neighborhood health clubs, and a number of hotels have health facilities of their own. Nonguests are welcome to use the facilities at the **Fairmont Hotel** (950 Mason St., at California St., Nob Hill, 415/772–5000), where a day pass costs $10. At the **Hotel Nikko** (222 Mason St., between Ellis and O'Farrell Sts., 2 blocks from Union Square, 415/394–1153), a weekly pass costs $20 per day or $85 for seven days. Boxercise classes are also available.

CLUBS

4 *f-1*
CLUB ONE
A $20 day pass gives nonmembers access to Club One at Embarcadero Center, Club One at Citicorp Center, Club One at Yerba Buena, Club One at Nob Hill, and Club One at Fillmore Center. Like Nautilus, most of these clubs have saunas, hot tubs, and steam rooms as well as aerobics classes and a complete line of fitness equipment. The Club One at Citicorp Center has a rock-climbing wall (*see* Rock Climbing, *above*). *2 Embarcadero Center, Embarcadero, 415/788–1010.*

4 *f-5*
1 Sansome St., at Sutter St., Financial District, 415/399–1010.

1200 Clay St., at 12th St., Oakland, 510/895–1010.

2 *3-e*
1755 O'Farrell St., at Fillmore St., Western Addition, 415/749–1010.

4 *d-5*
950 California St., at Mason St., Nob Hill, 415/834–1010.

4 *f-6*
350 3rd St., at Folsom St., South of Market, 415/512–1010.

5 *g-5*
EMBARCADERO YMCA
Of the five YMCA fitness centers in San Francisco, this is the best. In fact, it ranks among San Francisco's finest health clubs, YMCA or no. There are two racquetball courts, a 25-meter swimming pool, a basketball court, a small running track, weights and cardiovascular equipment, and aerobics classes. The $12 drop-in fee includes use of the sauna, steam room, and whirlpool—plus magnificent views of the bay. *169 Steuart St., between Mission and Howard Sts., South of Market, 415/957–9622.*

5 *e-8*
KORET HEALTH AND RECREATION CENTER
On the University of San Francisco campus, Koret is open to the general public before 2 PM daily with purchase of an $10 day pass. Facilities include an Olympic-size swimming pool, basketball courts, cardiovascular and weight equipment, and aerobics classes. The pass also gives you access to showers and lockers. *Parker Ave., at Turk St., Richmond District, 415/422–6821.*

4 *c-6*
24 HOUR FITNESS CENTERS
Seven Bay Area branches of 24 Hour Fitness Centers are open to the public for a $15 day-use fee. Facilities and services vary, but most of the clubs have saunas, hot tubs, and steam rooms. Aerobics classes and use of fitness equipment are included in the price. Call for locations and hours. *1200 Van Ness Ave., at Post St., 415/776–2200 or 800/204–2400.*

4 *d-2*
350 Bay St., North Point Shopping Center, Fisherman's Wharf, 415/395-9595.

4 g-5

100 California St., Financial District, 415/ 434–5080.

4 g-6

2nd St., at Folsom St., Marathon Plaza, South of Market, 415/543–7808.

DAY SPAS

When San Franciscans need rejuvenation, there is no shortage of escapes

---

SPAS TO SLIP INTO

When the daily grind gets to be too much or your workouts are taking a toll, check into a day spa or retreat at the following resorts.

Asanté Day Spa & Holistic Health Center
Drink herbal tea and soak your feet in an aromatherapy bath while you await a raindrop massage.

Claremont Hotel & Resort
A scrub made of grape seeds from the nearby Wine Country softens your skin.

Elizabeth Arden Red Door Salon & Spa
Escape with a signature facial or body treatment with Elizabeth Arden products.

Kabuki Hot Springs
Feel like a Javanese bride with an exotic massage and rice exfoliation, and soak or wash up in beautiful Japanese communal baths.

The Lodge at Skylonda
Indulge in hot stone therapy at this exclusive weekend getaway.

Shibui Gardens
Lounge freely at privately rented hot tubs alfresco.

Sonoma Mission Inn, Spa & Country Club
Melt away tension in thermal Roman baths or with Watsu—shiatsu massage in a warm pool.

Spa Nordstrom
Escape shopping blues with a massage or beauty treatment downtown.

Tea Garden Springs
Sip hot tea in soothing garden, then cross over a symbolic stream for a holistic "ocean thermo" body wrap and facial.

---

from the daily grind. Choose from a cornucopia of massages, as well as more innovative treatments. Hot stone therapies, "ocean-thermo" wraps, goat's-cream baths, grape-seed scrubs, or ayurvedic hot oil dripping on your forehead—a "balancing" treatment based on Indian philosophies—are just a few examples.

4 b-6

ASANTÉ DAY SPA & HOLISTIC HEALTH CENTER

A one-hour massage costs $60 at this low-key, holistic day spa that operates at two locations. Ten different types of massage include a 90-minute "raindrop aromatherapy treatment," which is worth the extra cost ($95). This service relies on a unique combination of more unusual essential oils such as thyme, peppermint, oregano, marjoram, birch, basil, and cypress. You'll end up relaxed and incredibly fragrant. Herbal wraps, salt glows, and paraffin treatments are also available. With services of at least one hour, you'll enjoy a complimentary aromatherapy foot bath while you sip herbal tea. At the San Francisco location, you can also enroll in a yoga class prior to your massage. Call for schedule. *1801-B Bush St., at Octavia Sts., San Francisco, 415/775–1801; 18 Mary St., at 4th St., San Rafael, 415/460–6506.*

3 f-3

CLAREMONT HOTEL & RESORT

A traditional 50-minute Swedish massage will set you back $94 at this picturesque resort in the Oakland Hills. A wide variety of indulgences are available, including grape-seed scrubs, body wraps, and ayurvedic treatments based on Indian philosophies. The 80-minute "Rebalancer" ($129) includes a hot-oil treatment for scalp and hair, body scrub, mask, brisk massage, and hot towel wrap, as well as a short foot massage and mini-facial. Herbs and aromatic oils leave your hair and skin soft and smelling great. Beauty treatments for hair and nails are also available. Spa visitors, who shuffle around in fluffy white terry cloth robes, need not stay at the hotel to also enjoy the beautiful pool, hot tub, and saunas. Complimentary fruit and herbal drinks are available. *41 Tunnel Rd., at Claremont Ave., Oakland, 510/843–3000.*

2 g-2

ELIZABETH ARDEN RED DOOR SALON & SPA

The signature treatment at this elegant downtown day spa is a thorough, nourishing facial. You choose from 10 different kinds. Or, simply opt for a traditional 50-minute massage ($70) with your choice of essential oils. Or, for something you won't find elsewhere in town, try the $85 Ceramide Firm Lift Massage, a deep tissue rubdown using this well-known Elizabeth Arden product. Two and three-hour packages are also available, including hydrotherapies, wraps, and French body polishing. Salon services, including hair and nails, are also offered. Ask for a complimentary makeup touch-up and replenish with herbal teas and juice on the house. *126 Post St., between Grant and Kearny Sts., Union Square, 415/989-4888.*

4 a-6

KABUKI HOT SPRINGS

Traditional sit-down Japanese showers and communal baths are two unique features at this beautiful Asian-inspired day spa. Exotic services include the winning $110 Javanese Lulur Treatment: a combination massage with jasmine oil, exfoliation with tumeric and ground rice, yogurt application, and a soak with rose petals. In the candlelit bath, you sip tea- or cucumber-infused waters. Despite its fresh appearance, the Kabuki has been operating for almost 30 years, with a 55°F cold plunging pool and a 105°F *furo* soaking tub. A traditional 50-minute massage costs $70; admission to the baths is an additional $5 with a massage. Without treatment, entry is $10, from 10 AM to 5 PM. Evenings and weekends entry is $15. Sauna and steam room are included in the admission fee. Communal coed bathing, suits required, is held once a week, on Tuesday. Other days, clothing is optional but most visitors dunk in the nude. Women bathe Wednesday, Friday, and Sunday. Men are welcome Monday, Thursday, and Saturday. The schedule is subject to change. Call for updates. *1750 Geary St., at Fillmore St., Japantown, 415/922-6000.*

THE LODGE AT SKYLONDA

A traditional 60-minute massage costs $85 at this exclusive resort tucked among towering coastal redwoods. Treatments are available for overnight guests only and advance reservations are highly recommended (800/851-2222). Choose from a wide variety of massages—Thai, Trager, barefoot Japanese, or Zen shiatsu. Or opt for Jin Shin acupressure energy balancing, reflexology, or a deeply relaxing hot stone therapy. Package rates for a two-night getaway, including one massage per person, are $270 to $405 per person, per night, with double occupancy, tax, and gratuities included. Prices include gourmet spa meals, guided hikes through the Santa Cruz mountains, and yoga, stretch, or circuit training classes in a beautiful gym overlooking the forest. Afterward, relax with a swim in the majestic indoor pool, a steam or dry sauna, a dunk in the outdoor hot tub, or a private soak in your room with complimentary bath salts. Soon, you'll feel as tranquil as the floating gardenias decorating the lodge's every corner. *16530 Skyline Blvd. (Hwy. 35), Woodside, 650/851-6626.*

SHIBUI GARDENS

You can lounge freely at this earthy Marin County retreat with open-air hot tubs and dry sauna. It's been operating since the mid-1970s and still has a low-key atmosphere. Redwood decks, potted plants, and cold showers surround each hot tub. Tubs and the sauna are available for private rentals so clothing is optional. A 55-minute massage is $60, including a half-hour hot tub or sauna. Massages for 25 minutes or 85 minutes are also available. Without a massage, hot tub or sauna rentals are $7.50 per person per half hour, or $12 per person per hour. Two-for-one hot tub or sauna specials are available weekdays. *19 Tamalpais Ave., at San Anselmo Ave., San Anselmo, 415/457-0283*

SONOMA MISSION INN, SPA & COUNTRY CLUB

For $89, you get a traditional 50-minute massage in the spa at one of the oldest spas in the United States, dating from the early 1900s, with its own thermal mineral waters on the property. More than 50 treatments include soothing Watsu (a combination of water massage and shiatsu) or wraps that use evening primrose oil or goat's cream butter to moisturize your thirsty skin. For the latter, you'll lie on a soft pack table, whose tabletop descends into water, leaving you to float as if in the womb. Visitors do not need to take a room to enjoy the spa. If you do opt for an overnight stay, call for reservations (800/862–4945). *Hwy. 12 and Boyes Blvd., Sonoma, 707/ 939–2427.*

4 *e-6*

SPA NORDSTROM

This full-service day spa offers a traditional 50-minute massage for $70. A variety of services are also available, including a hot stone treatment that gently soothes sore muscles, hydrotherapy baths with your choice of aromatherapy, and massages for expectant mothers. A $366 package, up to 6½ hours long, includes a body wrap, manicure, pedicure, facial, massage, and lunch. Tea and the use of robes and slippers are complimentary, as are foot baths before most services. Ask for product samples to try at home. *San Francisco Center, 5th and Market Sts., 5th floor, 415/977–5102.*

TEA GARDEN SPRINGS

This tranquil, full-service day spa has a Zen feel and a holistic focus. You'll walk over an indoor stream as you head toward the treatment rooms, symbolically leaving your worries behind. A 55-minute massage is $70. But the spa also offers an elaborate menu of other services, such as a two-hour ocean thermo wrap, an indulgent series of treatments that begins with a detoxifying drink and steam bath. That's followed by relaxing body brushing, aromatherapy massage and wrap, seaweed and clay wrap, and a final rubdown with lavender lotion. The spa's thorough facials rely solely on natural products that smell good enough to eat. (Some of the fruit-based applications are actually edible!) There are also bath-massage packages for couples, who soak in one huge tub or side by side to simultaneously accommodate different treatments. Plan extra time for a complimentary herbal infusion served in a beautiful Chinese teapot. It's served in a peaceful indoor garden, where water runs through the tiny stream. *38 Miller Ave., near Sunnyside St., Mill Valley, 415/ 389–7123.*

chapter 4

PLACES TO
EXPLORE

galleries, gargoyles, museums & more

I t's always startling to learn that San Francisco covers only 46 square mi. But within that space exists a microcosm of the whole world: ethnic neighborhoods representing China, Japan, Spain, Italy, Russia, and beyond. The city was created by explorers and dreamers, and combing its boulevards and alleyways today reveals their legacy. From the days of the Gold Rush to the current Multimedia Gulch revolution, each group has left remnants of their time upon these hills. The 1906 earthquake and fire erased much physical history, yet the city still retains a wealthy architectural heritage ranging from Spanish Missions to gingerbread Victorians to postmodern flights of fancy. Every type of art form is available here, from Shang-dynasty bronze vessels at the Asian Art Museum to video installations at the Museum of Modern Art. Discovering San Francisco is like opening a series of Chinese boxes: each time you open one, you discover another more intimate gift waiting inside—an amazing attribute in such a tiny, but richly diverse, city.

where to go

NOTABLE NEIGHBORHOODS

CASTRO DISTRICT

The heart of the city's predominately gay neighborhood is the intersection of Castro and 18th streets, just south of Market Street. The first gay bars opened on Castro Street in the late 1960s, and in the '70s the scene exploded. Lured by national publicity, gay men and lesbian women from all over the country migrated to the Castro and Polk Street and made this their social, cultural, and political center. Today the Castro District remains one of the liveliest and most welcoming neighborhoods in the city. The streets teem with people out shopping, pushing political causes, heading to art films, and lingering in bars and cafés. Cutting-edge clothing boutiques and unique gift shops pre-

dominate, as do pairs of pretty young things holding hands.

CHINATOWN

Exotic, exuberant, and aromatic, this 14-block area is one of the largest Chinese communities outside of Asia. Housing discrimination in the past kept residents from moving outside Chinatown, and the tightly packed area has been a magnet for Chinese residents ever since. The main thoroughfare, Grant Avenue from Bush Street to Broadway, is lined with trinket shops, herbal medicine shops, produce stands, fish markets, tiny eateries turning out steaming dumplings, and about 100 restaurants. Within the narrow side streets, good-luck banners of crimson and gold hang beside dragon-entwined lampposts and street signs with Chinese calligraphy, and virtually every roof is topped with a pagoda. Listen for the sound of conversations in Cantonese or Mandarin, and the clink of mah-jongg tiles issuing from the windows of houses along quiet alleys.

FISHERMAN'S WHARF

Once shunned as the city's working-class commercial fishing center, colorful Fisherman's Wharf is now the first stopping point for tourists. Take a cable car here from downtown to see the fishing boats (the fleet arrives back in port by mid-afternoon) and to stroll through the chaotic streets, past countless seafood restaurants, sidewalk crab pots, and counters selling take-out shrimp and crab cocktails along with crusty sourdough bread. You'll also find dozens of tacky souvenir shops, talented and amusing street performers, and so-called novelty museums such as **Ripley's Believe It or Not** (175 Jefferson St., at Powell St., 415/771–6188; map 4, d-2) and the **Wax Museum** (145 Jefferson St., at Powell St., 415/885–4975; map 4, d-2). Pier 39, the Cannery, and Ghirardelli Square are historic buildings converted to shopping and entertainment complexes, and Hyde Street pier is port for a few historic ships (see Architecture & Historic Sites, below).

HAIGHT-ASHBURY

Despite its growing popularity among upscale residents and the invasion of Gap and spiffy boutiques, "the Haight," the neighborhood east of Golden Gate Park, still wears the spirit of the tie-dyed 1960s on its sleeve. Young people with flowers in their hair and peace and civil rights on their minds began moving here in the early '60s; by 1966 the Haight had become a major destination for rock bands such as the Grateful Dead, whose members moved into a big Victorian at 710 Ashbury Street, and Jefferson Airplane, whose grand mansion was at 2400 Fulton Street. These days, it's still home to a wandering tribe of Deadheads, with anarchist book collectives and shops selling incense and tie-dyes. Shops are full of folk art and funky clothes, and on sunny days the sidewalks fill with young artists displaying handmade jewelry and crafts for sale. The Haight's cafés are always filled with the young, pierced, and hip (don't these people have day jobs?), who descend on the neighborhood's many clubs and bars come nightfall.

JAPANTOWN

Around 1860 a wave of Japanese immigrants arrived in San Francisco, which they called Soko. Tragically, Japantown, which sprang up after the 1906 earthquake and fire left many of the city's Japanese immigrants homeless, was virtually disbanded when many of its residents, including second- and third-generation Americans, were forced into relocation camps during World War II. Today, Japantown doesn't feel much different from other parts of the city, and, with the exception of the Peace Pagoda and a few shops on the Japan Center Mall, the architecture in the area is fairly generic.

MISSION DISTRICT

The sunny Mission District has traditionally been a melting pot of Central Americans, Puerto Ricans, Korean, Chinese, Thai, and other various nationalities. Side-by-side on the streets are Italian restaurants and Mexican taquerías, as well as Arabic bookstores, Vietnamese markets, Filipino eateries, and trendy bars. On Mission Street, the heart of the Latino neighborhood, produce stands sell huge Mexican papayas, plantains, and garlands of chiles; this area takes center stage during important festivals such as Cinco de Mayo and Carnaval (see Events, below). The surrounding streets are filled with cafés, bookstores, secondhand clothing and furniture shops, avant-garde art galleries, live music clubs, and funky, inexpensive restaurants. In recent years a largely white, young crowd of political activists, artists, and slackers has flocked to sections of the Mission now known as New Bohemia, centered at the intersection of 16th and Valencia streets, and this group is now being supplanted by Silicon Valley imports who are rapidly gentrifying the area, creating a great deal of friction among the different factions.

NOB HILL

Once known as the Hill of Golden Promise, this neighborhood has the city's most dramatic views of downtown and the San Francisco Bay. The area was officially dubbed Nob Hill during the 1870s, after "the Big Four"—Charles Crocker, Leland Stanford, Mark Hopkins, and Collis Huntington—built their hilltop estates here. The locals below referred to the swells as "nabobs" (originally meaning a provincial governor from India), and the hill itself was called Snob Hill. The 1906 earthquake and fire destroyed most of the grand mansions, many of which were replaced by some of the city's finest hotels.

ESCAPING THE FOG

Mark Twain said the coldest winter he ever spent was a summer in San Francisco. Here's a list of places and neighborhoods where you'll find a sunny oasis.

Berkeley
The Rose Gardens in Tilden Park offer a bounty of flowers and sunshine.

China Basin
Head to the Ramp and lounge at the outdoor café.

Financial District
At the Carnelian Room, on the 52nd floor of the Bank of America Building, you can sip a cocktail and look down your nose at the fog.

Mission District
Pretend you're in Mexico and shop for papayas.

Mt. Tamalpais
At the top of the mountain you can look down at the clouds and feel like you're in heaven.

South Beach
Stroll along the marina waterfront.

Tiburon
Take the ferry over to Sam's for fish and chips.

NOE VALLEY

Noe Valley is a sedate, middle-class residential neighborhood tucked into the hills above the Mission District. Until the early 1980s, the neighborhood was predominately working class (and largely Irish), but a subsequent influx of well-shod liberals has changed the mix. Today Noe Valley feels more like a small (though prosperous) town than any other neighborhood in San Francisco. The storefronts are modest looking, everyone seems to know each other, and the pace is fairly slow; crowds gather in front of 24th Street's bagel shop and nearby coffee shops, and strollers clog the sidewalks.

NORTH BEACH

Less than a square mile in size but heavily populated, North Beach was at one time an exclusively Italian community, with as many as 125,000 Italian-American residents. Much of the area is now Chinese, but about 2,000 residents of Italian descent remain, most of them elderly. Some still regard this as the best place in the city for cappuccino, biscotti, and pasta; good-smelling authentic Italian restaurants, delicatessens, and bakeries line the streets. North Beach is also the well-known birthplace of the Beat Generation, and homages to Jack Kerouac and Allen Ginsberg appear at every turn. Along Broadway, strip joints carry on the legacy of the city's Barbary Coast days.

PACIFIC HEIGHTS

In the late 1800s, the area now know as Pacific Heights was still the domain of dairy farms—hence the name of one Pacific Heights neighborhood, Cow Hollow. Its tiny lagoon was the city's laundry basin, and until the turn of the century, tanners, slaughterhouses, and sugar factories were located here. With the invention of the cable car, however, came rapid urbanization; many of the city's most beautiful Victorians were built here at that time, and those that survived the 1906 quake and fire can still be seen on the 1700 to 2900 blocks of Broadway and the 1600 to 2900 blocks of Vallejo Street. Pacific Heights continues to this day to be one of the most exclusive districts in the city, with mansions and town houses priced at $1 million and up. From almost any point you get a magnificent view of the San Francisco Bay and the Golden Gate Bridge.

RICHMOND AND SUNSET DISTRICTS

The Richmond district's middle-class row houses are home to Eastern European, Russian, Greek, Chinese, Korean, Filipino, and Japanese residents. Interesting shops and international restaurants line Clement Street. In the Sunset, a residential area settled mainly by Chinese and Thai immigrants, ethnic shops and restaurants line Irving Street between 5th and 25th avenues.

RUSSIAN HILL

Russian Hill has long been home to wealthy San Francisco families. During the 1890s, this was the domain of a group of bohemian artists and writers, including Charles Norris, George Sterling, and Maynard Dixon; Jack London, Bret Harte, Dashiell Hammett, Jack Kerouac, and Herbert Gold have also sought and found inspiration here at one time or another. It's a beautifully scenic, highly desirable residential area with sumptuous pieds-à-terre and costly condominiums rubbing shoulders with the few remaining cottages built with $500 Red Cross loans soon after the 1906 earthquake and fire. The neighborhood is home to the renowned San Francisco Art Institute and Lombard Street, "the world's crookedest street."

SOUTH OF MARKET (SOMA)

Once an industrial area, the 2-square-mi district known as SoMa (an acronym for South of Market, as in Market Street) is a burgeoning center for the visual arts. Its heart is the San Francisco Museum of Modern Art, along with the adjoining Yerba Buena Gardens. With the arrival of *Wired* magazine to offices near South Park, SoMa has also earned the moniker "Multimedia Gulch."

TELEGRAPH HILL

Goats once grazed atop this famed 284-ft hill, and indeed they are better suited to its terrain than humans. At the east end of Lombard Street, this was the location for the first Morse code signal station in 1853, hence the name. At the crest of the hill is Coit Tower, a stone-white monument that shines as a beacon, especially at night. From Coit Tower, walk down the Filbert Street Steps, a magical winding path that leads in a nearly vertical descent, past lush gardens and vine-covered walls hiding vintage cottages, to Levi Plaza. This area is closed to cars, and, in fact, all of Telegraph Hill is better explored by foot. Your reward will be some of the finest and most unique views in San Francisco.

ARCHITECTURE & HISTORIC SITES

There are more than 200 designated historical landmarks in San Francisco, plus countless architectural gems. The following are the highlights.

1 *C-2*

ALCATRAZ

The infamous island federal prison, closed in 1963, served for 59 years as the nation's most notorious federal penitentiary for high-risk prisoners: Al Capone, Robert "The Birdman" Stroud, and Machine Gun Kelly were among its more famous inmates. In 1969, a group of Native Americans attempted to reclaim the land, saying that an 1868 federal treaty allowed Native Americans to use all federal territory that the government wasn't actively using. Named by the Spanish, Alcatraz means "pelican," but inmates called it "The Rock." Before it became a prison it was the site of the Pacific Coast's first lighthouse.

The Blue and Gold Fleet (*see* Boat Tours, *below*) provides the only public transportation to Alcatraz, with frequent departures from Pier 41 at Fisherman's Wharf beginning daily at 9:30 AM. For an additional charge, a self-guided audio-cassette walking tour of the prison is available, featuring former inmates and guards describing their experiences on Alcatraz. On the island, the National Park Service gives related talks on subjects such as escape attempts, the Island's history as a 19th-century military fort, the Native American occupation, and Alcatraz's unique properties as part of an island chain in San Francisco Bay. Advance ticket purchase is strongly advised year-round, and is essential in summer. *Blue and Gold Fleet: 415/773–1188 for information; 415/705–5555 or 800/426–8687 for advance ticket sales with $2 charge.*

4 *f-4*

ALCOA BUILDING

This 25-story "earthquake-proof" office tower designed by Skidmore, Owings & Merrill in 1964 was one of the first buildings to incorporate seismic bracing as a design element, which incorporates

---

SAN FRANCISCO'S TOP DRAWS

You can't see all of San Francisco in a single day, but if you're pressed for time, some sights shouldn't be missed.

Alcatraz (Architecture & Historic Sites)
The famous island prison, a.k.a. "The Rock."

Cable Cars (Architecture & Historic Sites)
The San Francisco treat.

Chinatown (Notable Neighborhoods)
Produce stands and pagoda-topped roofs on crowded, narrow streets.

Cliff House (Architecture & Historic Sites)
Prime spot for viewing the crashing Pacific waves.

Coit Tower (Architecture & Historic Sites)
The beacon of Telegraph Hill, with WPA murals inside.

Fisherman's Wharf (Notable Neighborhoods)
Seagulls, street performers, clam chowder, and crowds.

Golden Gate Bridge (Bridges)
The city's most majestic landmark.

Haight-Ashbury (Notable Neighborhoods)
Countercultural mecca of the '60s.

Lombard Street/"Crookedest Street" (Architecture & Historic Sites)
Eight hairpin turns in a single city block.

Mission Dolores (Architecture & Historic Sites)
Oldest building in the city, and the sixth of Father Serra's missions.

The Presidio (Architecture & Historic Sites)
Historic military base, now a splendid national park.

San Francisco Museum of Modern Art (Art Museums)
A landmark museum with a striking, Florentine-inspired design.

North Beach (Notable Neighborhoods)
The birthplace of the Beat Generation.

Twin Peaks (Viewpoints)
360° views of the San Francisco Bay Area.

"X"s along the facade. The entry lobby is two stories up, surrounded by a sculpture garden; beneath it are three levels of parking. *1 Maritime Plaza, Battery St. between Clay and Washington Sts., Financial District.*

8 *d-3*

ANCHOR BREWING COMPANY

In 1896 Ernst Baruth and Otto Schinkel founded Anchor Brewing on the basis of their one lone product, Anchor Steam, A hearty, amber-color beer. By the 1960s, tastes had changed in favor of the light lagers that made Budweiser a household name, and Anchor was ready to close its doors. Enter Fritz Maytag of washing-machine fame, who rescued the brewery in 1965 by purchasing it. The operation moved into its current facility, a 1930s building that was formerly the home of Chase and Sandborn Coffee, 20 years ago. What has never changed is the traditional methods of brewing Anchor Steam. Today Maytag is still the only owner and brewmaster for Anchor, which can be credited for beginning the 90s microbrew craze. He's added several other beers, and the old-fashioned bar in the tasting room offers samples of the full line. Brewery tours and tastings are available weekdays; reservations are required. *1705 Mariposa St., at De Haro St. , Potrero Hill, 415/ 863–8350.*

4 *f-5*

BANK OF CALIFORNIA

William Chapman Ralston, nicknamed "the man who built California," founded a commercial bank on this spot in the 1800s. By a stroke of luck, the original bank headquarters were torn down just before the 1906 earthquake and fire to make way for this Corinthian temple, completed in 1907 by Bliss & Faville. It was modeled after a bank in New York City designed by the legendary firm of McKim, Mead & White. *400 California St., at Sansome St., Financial District.*

4 *e-4, f-4*

BARBARY COAST TRAIL

In the latter half of the 19th century, San Francisco was home to one of the most infamous red-light districts ever to exist—a hotbed for the gold miners who poured into California drunk with quick fortunes (and frequently just as drunk from quick losses). Saloon keepers,

gamblers, and prostitutes all flocked to the so-called Barbary Coast, now the Jackson Square Historic District (*see* Notable Neighborhoods, *above*). This area was miraculously spared during the devastation of the 1906 earthquake and remains the oldest section of commercial buildings in San Francisco. The strip of Pacific Avenue between Sansome Street and Columbus Avenue, once called "Terrific Pacific," was the heart of the action: Every building along this street once sheltered a dance hall, saloon, gambling hall, or bordello, although by 1917 the Barbary Coast had been tamed by the Red-Light Abatement Act. In October 1996, the city designated 50 sites as stops along an official, 3.8-mi-long Barbary Coast Trail. Bronze sidewalk plaques have been installed on every street corner, starting at the Old Mint, at 5th and Mission streets, and running north through downtown, Chinatown, Portsmouth Square, Jackson Square, North Beach, and Fisherman's Wharf, ending at Aquatic Park. Pick up Daniel Bacon's *Walking San Francisco on the Barbary Coast Trail* (Quicksilver Press, $13.95) at the SFCVB Visitor Information Center (900 Market St., at Powell St., Hallidie Plaza, San Francisco 94102, 415/391–2000 or 415/391–2001 for 24-hour recorded information).

6 *b-1*

BEACH CHALET

The long-shuttered Beach Chalet, in westernmost Golden Gate Park, reopened in 1997 as part of a park renovation. The building's upper level houses the Beach Chalet brewery and restaurant (*see* American/Contemporary *in* Chapter 1) and the lower level a visitor center. The Beach Chalet was designed by noted San Francisco architect Willis Polk, and completed in 1929; sweeping murals by famed French artist Lucien Labaudt were added in the 1930s (*see* Statues, Murals & Monuments, *below*). The exquisite wooden staircase is carved with mermaids and sea creatures. *1000 Great Hwy., between Lincoln Way and Fulton St., 415/386–8439.*

CABLE CARS

San Francisco's famed cable cars have been trundling up and down its steep hills since August 1, 1873, when young engineer Andrew Hallidie demonstrated his first car on Clay Street. In 1964 the tramlike vehicles were designated National Historic Landmarks—the only ones that move. Before 1900, 500 cable cars spanned a network of 110 mi. Today there are 45 cars on three lines, and the network covers just 10 mi. Most of the cars date from the last century, although the entire network had a complete overhaul in the early 1980s. For more information on fares and routes, see Public Transportation in Chapter 7. The Cable Car Museum (see History Museums, below) examines how exactly these little red cars are able to climb "halfway to the stars."

2 a-2
CALIFORNIA PALACE OF THE LEGION OF HONOR
Spectacularly situated in Lincoln Park on cliffs overlooking the Pacific Ocean and Golden Gate Bridge, this landmark building reopened in 1995 after extensive renovations. On display is San Francisco's collection of European fine arts (see Art Museums, below). Adolph and Alma Spreckels donated the magnificent gray-stone building—designed by George Applegarth in 1924 in the style of the 18th-century Palais de Legion d'Honneur in Paris—as a memorial to the state's World War I dead. A pyramidal glass skylight in the entrance court illuminates the new lower-level galleries. *Lincoln Park, Legion of Honor Dr., 34th Ave. at Clement St., Richmond District.*

4 c-2
THE CANNERY
This three-story brick structure was built in 1894 to house what became the Del Monte Fruit and Vegetable Cannery. Today the Cannery is home to shops, art galleries, restaurants, and the Museum of the City of San Francisco (see History Museums, below). There's a glass elevator in the open-air courtyard and a constant stream of free performances by mimes, magicians, and jugglers. *2801 Leavenworth St., at Beach St., Fisherman's Wharf, 415/771–3112.*

7 f-3
CASTRO THEATRE
This 1920s Spanish Baroque movie palace, now a Castro District landmark, was the flagship of a San Francisco cinema baron who also built theaters in Noe Valley. Miller and Pflueger, one of the city's top architectural firms, designed the Castro Theatre before going on to design six others. The Castro's 1,500-seat auditorium has an elaborate plaster ceiling cast in the form of a tent, replete with sculpted swags, ropes, and tassels. This is one of the few 1920s theaters that hasn't been broken up to accommodate a multiplex (see Movie Theaters Worth Noting in Chapter 5). *429 Castro St., at Market St., Castro. 415/621–6120.*

4 e-5
CHINATOWN GATE
A pagoda-topped gate, flanked on either side of Grant Avenue by stone dragons, is the official entrance to Chinatown—a symbolic and literal transition from the rather generic downtown landscape to what could easily pass for a section of old Hong Kong. Note that the dragons are stamped MADE IN FREE CHINA—a not-so-subdued political statement. *Bush St. and Grant Ave., Chinatown.*

4 c-7
CITY HALL
San Francisco's monumental City Hall is modeled after the Capitol in Washington, D.C., although many architectural critics feel it surpasses the original as the finest French Renaissance Revival structure in the United States. The masterpiece of granite and marble, with a bronze dome taller than that of the Capitol, was built from 1913 to 1915 after the destruction of the old City Hall in the 1906 earthquake and fire. Its Paris-trained architects, Bakewell and Brown, also designed Temple Emanu-El (see Churches, Synagogues & Temples, below). The building has been witness to interesting times: Joe DiMaggio and Marilyn Monroe were married here on January 15, 1954; civil rights and freedom of speech protesters were washed down the central stairway with fire hoses in 1960; Mayor George Moscone and Supervisor Harvey Milk were murdered here on November 27, 1978; and on February 14, 1991, scores of gay couples were married on the front steps in celebration of the passage of San Francisco's Domestic Partners Act. In front of City Hall are formal gardens with fountains, walkways, and seasonal flower beds. Excellent free guided tours explain the structure's history and lead you right into the mayor's office and Board of Supervisor's chambers. *1 Dr. Carlton B. Goodlett Pl., bordered by Van Ness Ave. and Polk, Grove, and McAllister Sts., Civic Center, 415/554–6023 for tours.*

`4` c-7

CIVIC CENTER

One of the country's great governmental building complexes, the Civic Center includes City Hall, the War Memorial Opera House, the Veterans Building, the Bill Graham Civic Auditorium, and the Old San Francisco Main Library, future home of the Asian Art Museum. This Beaux Arts complex is a product of the turn-of-the-century "City Beautiful" movement—the same movement that produced the Mall in Washington, D.C. East of City Hall is United Nations Plaza, home to a colorful twice-weekly farmers' market held Wednesday and Sunday mornings. The handsome San Francisco Main Library (*see* Libraries, *below*) is just a block west of the plaza. On the west side of City Hall are the War Memorial Opera House, Davies Symphony Hall, and several other cultural institutions that are collectively referred to as the San Francisco Performing Arts Center. *Bordered by McAllister, Grove, Franklin, and Hyde Sts.*

`7` f-3

CLARKE MANSION

Built in 1891, this sprawling off-white Victorian is a beauty, with huge turrets, rounded bay windows, and lots of surrounding greenery. It was constructed on 17 acres for the flamboyant attorney Alfred "Nobby" Clarke, and earned the nickname Nobby Clarke's Folly when his wife refused to inhabit it because it was too far from fashionable Nob Hill. The Clarkes lived here a total of five years. *250 Douglass St., at Caselli Ave., Castro.*

`2` a-2

CLIFF HOUSE

At the westernmost tip of San Francisco stands one in a succession of ill-fated buildings on the same site. The original building, which dated from 1863, hosted several U.S. presidents and wealthy locals who would drive their carriages out to Ocean Beach; it was destroyed by fire on Christmas Day 1894. The second Cliff House, the most luxurious, was built in 1896; it rose eight stories and had an observation tower 200 ft above sea level. It burned down a year after surviving the 1906 quake. The present building has restaurants, a busy bar, a gift shop, and a visitor center with a display of fascinating historic photographs of the many Cliff House incarnations and the formerly glorious Sutro Baths

(*see below*). Also at the Cliff House is the Camera Obscura, an optical instrument invented by Leonardo da Vinci that was the predecessor of the camera. It casts a 360° view of Ocean Beach on a giant screen. The Musée Mécanique offers a collection of antique mechanical toys (*see* History Museums, *below*). *1090 Point Lobos Ave., at Great Hwy., Richmond District, 415/556–8642 for visitor center, 415/750–0415 for Camera Obscura.*

`4` e-3

COIT TOWER

Built in 1933 to memorialize San Francisco's volunteer firefighters, the 210-ft concrete observation tower atop Telegraph Hill is named for the heiress Lillie Hitchcock Coit (1843–1929), who bequeathed the funds to build it. During the early days of the Gold Rush, Miss Lil was said to have deserted a wedding party and chased down the street after her favorite engine, Knickerbocker Number 5, while clad in her bridesmaid finery. She was soon made an honorary member of the Knickerbocker Company, and after that always signed her name as "Lillie Coit 5" in honor of her favorite fire engine. The $3 elevator ride to the top of Coit Tower is worthwhile for its spectacular views. Inside the tower are 19 Works Progress Administration–era murals depicting laborers (*see* Statues, Murals & Monuments, *below*). Parking at the tower is limited, but Bus 39-Coit can shuttle you over from Washington Square. A strenuous hike up the charming but steep Filbert Steps or Greenwich Stairs leads to the Coit Tower. *1 Telegraph Hill Blvd., at Greenwich St., Telegraph Hill, 415/362–0808.*

`4` c-8

DAVIES SYMPHONY HALL

This well-integrated addition to the Beaux Arts Civic Center complex was designed by Skidmore, Owings & Merrill in 1980. It's a fascinating, futuristic building, with a glass-encased wraparound lobby and a curvy, pop-out balcony high on its southeast corner. Inside, 59 adjustable Plexiglas acoustical disks cascade from the ceiling. Seventyfive–minute tours of Davies Symphony Hall, the War Memorial Opera House, and Herbst Theatre are conducted on Monday, departing from the Grove Street entrance of Davies Symphony Hall. *201 Van Ness Ave., between Hayes and Grove Sts., 415/552–8338.*

7 *h-1, h-7*

DOLORES STREET

Dolores Street was once the beginning of El Camino Real, the road that the Spaniards constructed in the 18th century to connect the 21 missions founded by Father Junípero Serra. Fittingly, it's still a splendid boulevard; lining the median is a row of stately Canary Island palms where flocks of wild parrots roost. These trees were planted for the 1915 Panama-Pacific International Exposition by John McLaren, the man who for a half-century supervised the building of Golden Gate Park. The 1906 fires stopped near 20th Street, and many grandiose Victorians remain in the hills above that street. *Between Market St. and Randall St., Mission District.*

6 *b-1, b-2*

DUTCH WINDMILL AND MURPHY WINDMILL

At the very western end of Golden Gate park is the 1902 Dutch Windmill, which once pumped 20,000 gallons of water per hour to the park reservoir on Strawberry Hill. Restored in 1982, with its patina dome and wood-shingle body still intact, the mill overlooks the photogenic Queen Wilhelmina Tulip Garden (*see* Gardens *in* Chapter 3), which blooms in early spring and late summer. South of the Dutch Windmill, the unrenovated Murphy Windmill (Martin Luther King, Jr. Drive, near Great Highway) was the world's largest when it was built in 1905. It, too, pumped water to the Strawberry Hill reservoir. *John F. Kennedy Dr. between 47th Ave. and Great Hwy., Golden Gate Park.*

4 *f-4, g-4*

EMBARCADERO CENTER

Nicknamed "Rockefeller Center West" for its similarity to the famed New York City complex, the Embarcadero Center houses more than 100 shops, 40 restaurants, a five-screen cinema featuring first-run special-interest and foreign films, two hotels, the indoor-outdoor observation Skydeck (*see* Viewpoints, *below*), and office space on what was formerly the site of the city's produce market. Designed by John Portman and Associates between 1971 and 1982, it consists of a set of four neatly stacked identical concrete buildings with multilevel outdoor gardens and stages connected by walkways and bridges. A fifth tower houses the Hyatt Regency (*see*

Very Expensive Lodgings *in* Chapter 6). Its atrium lobby is 20 stories high and ringed by balconies. *Bordered by Battery, Drumm, Clay, and Washington Sts., Embarcadero, 800/733–6318.*

4 *g-4*

FERRY BUILDING

The 1898 Ferry Building was the main gateway to the city before the bridges were built; until 1958, some 170 ferries disembarked here every day. It's still a departure point for ferries to Oakland, Sausalito, Larkspur, and Vallejo. The building's 230-ft clock tower, modeled on the Giralda tower of the Seville Cathedral, was clearly visible for the first time in 30 years after the freeway blocking it was torn down following the 1989 quake. Illuminated at night, it's one of the city's loveliest sights, and a celebration marked its 100th birthday in 1998. At present the building is undergoing a major renovation. The Ferry Plaza Farmers' Market is held Saturday morning year-round across from the Ferry Building. *Foot of Market St., Embarcadero.*

4 *d-4*

FLAG HOUSE

According to local legend, this simple shingled turn-of-the-century house atop Russian Hill was saved from the 1906 earthquake and fire by alert firefighters who spotted an American flag flying from the roof and managed to quench the flames using seltzer water and wet sand. The flag had been hoisted by its owner, a flag collector, who thought his house should go down in a noble fashion, with "all flags flying." *1652 6 Taylor St., at Vallejo St., Russian Hill.*

4 *e-6*

FLOOD BUILDING

One rounded corner faces west to the Powell Street cable car turnaround, and a dramatic arched entryway faces Market Street. This 12-floor, 1904 Classic Revival building was designed by architect Albert Pissis for James Flood, Jr. (heir to the Comstock Lode fortune) to lend grandeur to the downtown area. Although the first two floors were replaced after the 1906 earthquake, the floors above remain essentially as they were constructed. It now houses a Gap on the ground floor and offices above. *870 Market St., at the Powell St. Cable Car turnaround, Union Square.*

4 a-2, b-2
FORT MASON

Spanish explorers called the site of present-day Fort Mason Punta Medanos (Black Point). It was named a U.S. military command post in 1850, but remained occupied until the Civil War. From World War I through the Korean War it was used as a depot for the overseas shipment of troops and supplies. In 1977, Fort Mason's imposing military-style warehouses were converted into a cultural center housing a collection of unique museums, galleries, performance spaces, shops, and nonprofit organizations—the Mexican Museum, Museo Italo-Americano, San Francisco African-American Historical and Cultural Society, and San Francisco Craft and Folk Art Museum—as well as the famous vegetarian restaurant Greens (*see* Vegetarian *in* Chapter 1). Most of the museums and shops at Fort Mason Center close by 7 PM, although the restaurant and theaters stay open late. Wide lawns surround the Fort Mason Center buildings, and the San Francisco Bay lies just beyond. *Marina Blvd. at Laguna St., Marina, 415/979–3010 for event information.*

5 a-1
FORT POINT NATIONAL HISTORIC SITE

Fort Point was constructed between 1853 and 1861 by the U.S. Army Corps of Engineers to protect San Francisco from sea attack during the Civil War; during World War II it was used as a coastal defense fortification post where soldiers stood watch. Ironically, the massive fort, capable of holding 500 soldiers and 126 cannons, was never called on to fire a single shot. Now a melancholy and suitably atmospheric National Historic Landmark in the shadow of the Golden Gate Bridge, the site has been converted to a museum filled with military memorabilia. You can get a superb view of the bay from the top floor. The National Park rangers lead free guided tours, show history films, and present cannon drills every day; call for times. *Marine Dr. off Long Ave., Presidio, 415/556–1693. Admission free. Closed Mon.–Tues.*

4 e-5
450 SUTTER STREET

One block north of Union Square is this Art Deco masterpiece, a 1929 terra-cotta skyscraper by Miller and Pfleuger. Although terra-cotta was chosen because it was cheaper than stone, this is now one of the city's most admired office buildings, due in part to the handsome Mayan-inspired designs that cover the building both inside and out. Inside are medical and dental offices. *Between Stockton and Powell Sts., Union Square.*

2 f-1
GHIRARDELLI SQUARE

Since 1964 Ghirardelli Square shopping center has been a favorite tourist stop for its many specialty shops, cafés, and galleries. From 1893 until the early 1960s it housed the Ghirardelli Chocolate Company, Domenico Ghirardelli's legendary candy making business. The charming complex of 19th-century red-brick factory buildings includes a fairytale 1915 clock tower, inspired by the one at the Château de Blois in France, and the 1859 Pioneer Woolen Mill building, which produced uniforms for the Union Army during the Civil War. **Ghirardelli Fountain and Candy** (415/771–4903) is an old-fashioned emporium that utilizes some of the original chocolate factory vats and ovens in making its delicious concoctions. Ghirardelli Square hosts a chocolate lover's festival every September (*see* Events, *below*). *900 North Point St., at Polk St., Fisherman's Wharf, 415/775–5500.*

7 c-1
GOLDEN GATE PARK CARROUSEL

Set in the Children's Playground, this restored historic landmark is still in operation today. In 1912 the animals and turning platform were made by the Herschell-Spillman Company in New York. The organ pipes out vintage favorites like "After the Ball Is Over" as the hand-painted menagerie of horses, dragons, giraffes, frogs, lions, and a tabby cat spin gaily. *Martin Luther King, Jr. Dr. at Kezar Dr., Golden Gate Park. Admission: $1.25 (free for children under 39 inches). Sept.–May, closed Mon.–Thurs.*

4 e-3
GRANT AVENUE

Originally called Calle de la Fundación, Grant Avenue is the oldest street in San Francisco. Here you'll find dusty bars such as **The Saloon** (1237 Grant Ave., at Columbus Ave., 415/989–7666) and the **Grant & Green Blues Club** (1371 Grant Ave., at Sutter St., 415/693–9565) that evoke the Wild West flavor of the city's Gold Rush years. Below Columbus, the wonderfully atmospheric cafés and authentic Italian delis of North Beach give way to the odd curio shops and unusual import stores of Chinatown. *Between Columbus Ave. and Filbert Sts., North Beach.*

2 *f-2*
HAAS-LILIENTHAL HOUSE

San Francisco is filled with splendid Victorian mansions, but this gabled and turreted beauty is the only one open to the public. The 1886 Queen Anne–style house, built for businessman William Haas for $18,500, was considered modest in its day. The original occupants, Alice Lilienthal, daughter of William Haas, and her husband, Samuel Lilienthal, lived here until Alice's death in 1972. One hour guided tours of the fully furnished interior shed light on turn-of-the-century tastes and lifestyles. The house is operated by the Foundation for San Francisco's Architectural Heritage, which has its headquarters here; tours are given Wednesday and Sunday. The foundation also leads Sunday walking tours of Pacific Heights (*see* Walking Tours, *below*). *2007 Franklin St., between Washington and Jackson Sts., Pacific Heights, 415/441–3004. Admission: $5 tour.*

4 *f-5*
HALLIDIE BUILDING

Regarded by many critics as the city's most important modern building, the Hallidie Building (named for cable car inventor Andrew Hallidie) was designed by Willis Polk and Co. in 1918. Its revolutionary glass-curtain wall—believed to be the world's first such structure—hangs 1 ft beyond the reinforced concrete of the frame. With its graceful all-glass facade, decorative exterior fire escapes, and Venetian Gothic detailing, this unusual building dominates the block. *130 Sutter St., between Kearny and Montgomery Sts., Financial District.*

7 *f-3*
HARVEY MILK PLAZA

This plaza, in the spiritual and physical heart of the Castro, is named in honor of California's first openly gay elected official. On November 27, 1978, City Supervisor Milk and then-mayor George Moscone were assassinated by Dan White, a disgruntled former supervisor. At his trial White launched the now-

famous "Twinkie defense," claiming that the high sugar content of his junk-food diet had altered his mental state. He was convicted of voluntary manslaughter by reason of "diminished capacity." A candlelight vigil is held at the plaza every year on the anniversary of the assassination. *Castro and Market Sts., Castro.*

5 *h-5*
HILLS PLAZA

In 1991, the 1933 Hills Brothers Coffee Building became Hills Plaza, a block-long apartment complex-cum-commercial development incorporating the original Romanesque arched-brick facade. The Hills Brothers building itself has taken on a new identity, this time as a producer not of beans, but of hops—with Gordon Biersch Brewery Restaurant (*see* American/Casual *in* Chapter 1) as its tenant. On the south end of the plaza, under the tower, is a pleasant garden with a view of the Bay Bridge. *345 Spear St., at Harrison St., South of Market.*

4 *f-5*
HOBART BUILDING

Market Street, which bisects the city at an angle, has consistently challenged San Francisco's architects. The 1914 Hobart Building successfully rises to the challenge with a tower that combines a flat facade and heavily ornamented oval sides. It is considered one of architect Willis Polk's best works in the city—and it was built under budget in a record 11 months. Although now dwarfed by surrounding high-rises, it's still a majestic sight when viewed from 2nd Street. *582 Market St., at 2nd St., Financial District.*

4 *a-6*
JAPAN CENTER

Built in 1968 with a design by noted American architect Minoru Yamasaki, this 5-acre, three-block-long complex was a multimillion-dollar endeavor—yet its static structures fail to capture the spirit and beauty of traditional Japanese architecture. The complex houses shops, teahouses, sushi bars, a public garage, a theater, and an excellent spa, all connected by partially open walkways. Its centerpiece is the five-tiered, 100-ft-tall Peace Pagoda designed by Japanese architect Yoshiro Taniguchi to convey the "friendship and goodwill" of the Japanese people to the people of the United States. (In the 1,000-year-old-tradition of Japanese architecture, miniature round pagodas symbolize eternal peace.) The pagoda overlooks the Peace Plaza, site of several annual festivals. *Post St. between Fillmore and Laguna Sts., Japantown, 415/922–6776.*

8 *a-1*

LEVI STRAUSS & CO. FACTORY

The Levi Strauss World Headquarters are downtown, in the Financial District.

LOOK-SEE, FOR FREE

Docents will lead you through San Francisco history:

**Anchor Brewing Company
(Architecture & Historic Sites)**
  Learn about a brewery that's quenched San Francisco's thirst since 1896, then quench yours.

The City Guides (Guided Tours)
  Take one of the City's 26 great bargains down the twisting path of local history—from Maiden Lane brothels to Lands End.

**City Hall
(Architecture & Historic Sites)**
  View the tallest dome in the country and the mayor's office.

**Fort Point National Historic Site
(Architecture & Historic Sites)**
  The National Park rangers lead free guided tours, show history films, and present cannon drills every day.

**Grace Cathedral
(Churches, Synagogues & Temples)**
  The interior of this grand Gothic church has a labyrinth modeled after Chartres Cathedral.

**Levi Strauss & Co. Factory
(Architecture & Historic Sites)**
  Get the skinny on the brass tacks of fashion Americana.

**Palace Hotel
(Architecture & Historic Sites)**
  The city's grand dame has hosted guests from President Warren Harding to Oscar Wilde.

**The Presidio
(Architecture & Historic Sites)**
  Experience 200 years of history, architecture, and natural beauty.

**United States Court of Appeals
(Architecture & Historic Sites)**
  View this magnificently restored Beaux Arts building.

In the Mission District, however, remains the original Levi Strauss factory built in 1906, renovated in 1970, and still turning out thousands of pairs of the world-famous blue jeans annually—making it the oldest jeans making facility in the west. Free, 1½-hour tours of the cutting and sewing areas are given Tuesday and Wednesday; reservations are required. A Levi's shop has been added on the first floor. *250 Valencia St., between 14th St. and Duboce Ave., Mission District, 415/ 565–9159.*

4 *c-3*

LOMBARD STREET ("CROOKEDEST STREET")

A must-see for visitors to San Francisco, the "crookedest street in the world" makes eight hairpin turns in a short city block as it descends the east face of Russian Hill to Leavenworth Street. The beautifully landscaped street was designed in the 1920s to mitigate the steepness of the slope. Join the line of cars waiting to drive down it, or walk down the steps on either side of the street. *Lombard St. between Hyde and Leavenworth Sts., Russian Hill.*

4 *d-3*

MACONDRAY LANE

This tiny Russian Hill street with wooden walkways is the scene for the fictional Barbary Lane of Armistead Maupin's *Tales of the City.* Edwardian cottages are tucked into vine-covered gardens, and stunning views of the bay abound—a quaint San Francisco village hidden in a big city. *Macondray La. between Leavenworth and Jones Sts. and Union and Green Sts., Russian Hill.*

4 *e-6*

MAIDEN LANE

Off the east side of Union Square is a two-block alley that was known as Morton Street in the late 19th century, when it was home to the "cribs" (brothels) that formed the center of a notoriously rowdy red-light district. After the 1906 fire destroyed the bordellos, the street was renamed Maiden Lane—it's now a quaint pedestrian mall lined with chic boutiques and sidewalk cafés, as well as the only Frank Lloyd Wright building (*see* 140 Maiden Lane, *below*) in San Francisco. *Between Stockton and Kearny Sts., Union Square.*

7 h-2

MISSION DOLORES

Mission Dolores encompasses two churches standing side by side. The humble adobe building known as Mission San Francisco de Asis was constructed between 1782 and 1791 as the sixth of the 21 California missions founded by Father Junípero Serra. The Spanish nicknamed it Dolores after a nearby stream, Arroyo de Nuestra Señora de los Dolores (Stream of Our Lady of the Sorrows), that has long since disappeared. A survivor of three major earthquakes, it is now the oldest building in San Francisco. Architecturally, it's the simplest of all the California missions—it's also one of the most intact. The ceiling depicts traditional Native American basket designs hand-painted with vegetable dyes by local Costanoan Indians. The roof consists of timbers lashed with rawhide; the walls are of 4-ft-thick sun-dried adobe mud. Next door to the original mission, the handsome multidomed Mission Dolores Basilica dates from 1913. English- and Spanish-language services are held in both the Mission San Francisco de Asis and in the basilica. There is also a small museum, and outside, a walled historic cemetery (see Cemeteries, below). The mission audio tour is extremely informative. *Dolores and 16th Sts., Mission District, 415/621–8203. Admission: $2; $5 with 45-min audio tour.*

4 f-6

MOSCONE CONVENTION CENTER

Named for slain San Francisco mayor George Moscone, the Moscone Convention Center is part of the Yerba Buena development project and has been a major revitalizing force in the SoMa district. The building, designed in 1981 by Hellmuth, Obata, and Kassabaum, contains one of the world's largest column-free exhibition halls. The Esplanade Ballroom lobby features a giant replica (25 ft by 40 ft) of the first known map of San Francisco. *747 Howard St., at 3rd St., South of Market.*

4 e-6

NEIMAN MARCUS

The department store's crowning glory is an enormous skylight stained-glass dome, a remnant of the old City of Paris dry goods store that occupied the site since the turn of the century. Many San Franciscans rallied unsuccessfully to save the old building, and continue to regard its 1982 replacement by Philip Johnson and John Burgee as inferior. *Stockton and Geary Sts., Union Square.*

4 b-4

OCTAGON HOUSE

Eight-sided houses were considered lucky in the 1850s and 1860s, and San Francisco once had around a half-dozen. Now only two remain (the other is a private residence at 1067 Green Street). This simple gray-and-white charmer was built by William McElroy in 1861 and was originally across Gough Street. In 1952 it was purchased by the National Society of Colonial Dames of America, who converted it to a museum (see History Museums, below). *2645 Gough St., at Union St., Marina, 415/441–7512. Donation requested. Closed Jan.*

4 e-4

OLD CHINESE TELEPHONE EXCHANGE

Now a branch of the Bank of Canton, this was the first building to set the style for the new Chinatown after the original buildings burned down in the 1906 earthquake and fire. The intricate three-tier pagoda, built in 1909, housed the Chinatown phone system's operators, who were famed for their great linguistic skills. (The operators were required to speak English and five Chinese dialects.) *743 Washington St., at Grant Ave., Chinatown.*

4 c-7

OLD SAN FRANCISCO MAIN LIBRARY

This beautiful Beaux Arts building is scheduled to be occupied by the Asian Art Museum in 2002. It was designed by East Coast architect George Kelham in 1915 and 1916. Just across Fulton Street is the gleaming new San Francisco Public Library. *Fulton and Larkin Sts., Civic Center.*

4 e-7

OLD U.S. MINT

The "Granite Lady" is the nickname of this fine 1869 Federal Classic Revival building, the oldest stone building in San Francisco. Although still owned by the U.S. Treasury Department, it is no longer a working mint and is closed to the public. *5th and Mission Sts., South of Market.*

4 *e-6*

140 MAIDEN LANE

San Francisco's only Frank Lloyd Wright building stands on charming Maiden Lane. With its circular interior ramp and skylights, this handsome brick structure is said to have been a model for the Guggenheim Museum in New York. It was constructed in 1948 as the Morris Store. Today it houses a gallery, Folk Art International. *140 Maiden La., between Stockton and Kearny Sts., Union Square.*

4 *f-5*

PACIFIC COAST STOCK EXCHANGE

This imposing templelike structure dates from 1915, although architects Miller and Pfleuger updated it in 1930. Around the corner, the Stock Exchange Tower (155 Sansome St., at Pine St.) is a 1930 Moderne classic by the same architects, with an Art Deco gold ceiling and a black marble wall entry. *301 Pine St., at Sansome St., Financial District.*

4 *d-5*

PACIFIC UNION CLUB

The 1906 quake and fire knocked down the palatial Nob Hill mansions of railroad barons Leland Stanford, Mark Hopkins, Collis Huntington, and Charles Crocker. The mansion belonging to silver magnate James C. Flood—the first brownstone on the West Coast, and the only one of the Nob Hill mansions that wasn't made of wood—is one of the few that survived. This attractive 45-room structure was built in 1886 by the Comstock silver baron at a reputed cost of $1.5 million. In 1909 the property was purchased by the Pacific Union Club, a prestigious private club; famous architect Willis Polk redesigned the building at that time. A small park is adjacent to the club. *1000 California St., at Mason St., Nob Hill.*

4 *c-6*

PACKARD AUTO SHOWROOM

The 1927 Maybeck structure was designed to showcase one of the 1920s' premier automobile lines. The frieze just below the roof depicts a bear, California's state animal. *901 Van Ness Ave., at O'Farrell St., Civic Center.*

5 *f-2*

PALACE OF FINE ARTS

At the far western edge of the Marina is the Palace of Fine Arts, a stunning colonnaded Roman temple designed by Berkeley architect Bernard Maybeck. The palace is the sole survivor of the 32 plaster buildings erected for the 1915 Panama-Pacific International Exposition, which celebrated the opening of the Panama Canal and the anniversary of the discovery of the Pacific. Despite the public's enthusiasm for this temporary classical city, in the ensuing 50 years it fell into disrepair. Huge private donations and legions of sentimental citizens later, the palace building was recast in concrete and reopened in 1967. The massive columns, great rotunda (dedicated to the glory of Greek culture), and swan-filled reflecting lagoon have appeared as a backdrop to countless fashion layouts and films. It now houses an unusual hands-on science center, the Exploratorium (*see* Science Museums, *below*). *Baker and Beach Sts., Marina, 415/563–7337 for palace tours.*

4 *f-6*

PALACE HOTEL

Now a Sheraton property, this is the oldest hotel in the city and also one of the grandest. The original, opened in 1875 and destroyed in the 1906 quake and fire, was replaced in 1909 with a design by architect George Kelham (who also designed the Old San Francisco Main Library). The hotel has a storied past, some of which is recounted in glass cases off the main lobby: President Warren Harding died here while still in office in 1923, and another room is thought to be haunted by the ghost of the last reigning monarch of Hawaii, who spent a night here. In the glass-dome Garden Court restaurant, a four-story skylight contains 25,000 panes, and mosaic floors replicate Oriental rug designs; here, the San Francisco Symphony occasionally performs. The Pied Piper Bar takes its name from an enormous original oil by Maxfield Parrish that hangs behind the bar. Guided tours of the hotel's grand interior take place Tuesday, Thursday, and Saturday. *2 New Montgomery St., at Market St., South of Market, 415/512–1111.*

4 *d-2*

PIER 39

Natives think the pier is tacky; tourists come in droves. A 1,043-ft former cargo pier, once abandoned and decaying, it now houses more than 100 shops and fast-food stands, 10 full-service restaurants, a 350-berth marina, a double-decked Venetian carousel, and a games arcade. Street performers vie for attention, and California sea lions gambol just offshore. Accessible validated parking and nearby public transportation ensure crowds most days. *The Embarcadero at Jefferson St., Fisherman's Wharf, 415/981–7437.*

`4` *e-4*

PORTSMOUTH SQUARE

This Chinatown square, dotted with pagoda-shaped structures, was once a lowly potato patch before becoming the plaza for Yerba Buena (the Mexican settlement that was later renamed San Francisco). On this spot, Montgomery raised the American flag in 1846, Sam Brannan started the Gold Rush by announcing gold had been discovered at Sutter's Mill, and public hangings took place in the late 1950s. These days, it's a favorite place for morning tai chi; in the afternoons elderly Chinese men gather to play chess. *Kearny St. between Washington and Clay Sts., Chinatown.*

`2` *d-2*

THE PRESIDIO

The flags of Spain, Mexico, the Bear Flag Republic, and the U.S. Army have all flown over the Presidio—one of the oldest military installations in the United States. The Presidio was established by the Spanish as a military garrison in 1776—in Spanish, *presidio* means walled fortification—and taken over by newly independent Mexico in 1822. The Americans took possession of the fort during the Mexican-American War of 1846. Since then, the Presidio has been a training ground for Civil War soldiers, a refuge for residents after the 1906 earthquake, and headquarters of the U.S. Sixth Army. In October 1994, its 1,480 acres became a national park (*see* Parks *in* Chapter 3). At the Presidio's **Visitor Information Center** (Lincoln Blvd. at Montgomery St., 415/561–4323) or the Presidio Museum (*see* History Museums, *below*), pick up the pamphlet titled "The Presidio of San Francisco Main Post Walk: 200 Years of History and Architecture" for a 1-mi self-guided walking tour of the Presidio's most important structures. One building of note is the **Officer's Club** (Moraga Ave. between Arguello Blvd. and Funston Ave.; map 5, d-4). It contains one adobe wall reputed to date from 1776, the year the base was founded. *Entrance at Lombard and Lyon Sts., Presidio.*

`4` *g-5*

RINCON CENTER

The city's old post office, built in 1939 in the Streamline Moderne style, was incorporated into a large shopping and office complex in 1989. In the Art Deco lobby where the post office's walk-up windows used to be is a controversial 27-panel WPA mural painted by artist Anton Refregier (*see* Statues, Murals & Monuments, *below*). A permanent exhibit below the murals contains interesting photographs and artifacts of life in the 1800s. The exhibit and the murals form a fascinating mini-museum and enhance what might otherwise be just another humdrum modern office space. *Spear St. at Mission St., South of Market.*

`4` *e-5*

RITZ-CARLTON HOTEL

This gleaming, 1909 Roman-Renaissance building has worn many hats, first as the Metropolitan Life Insurance Company, then as Cogswell College, then as the site of Werner Erhard's EST activities, before it became a luxury hotel (*see* Very Expensive Lodgings *in* Chapter 6). *600 Stockton St., at California St., Nob Hill.*

`4` *b-6*

ST. MARY'S CATHEDRAL

See Churches, *below.*

`4` *c-3*

SAN FRANCISCO ART INSTITUTE

The SFAI's Spanish Colonial Revival building was designed in 1926 by Bakewell and Brown, back when the school was known as the California School of Fine Arts. With its bell tower, red-tiled roofs, and courtyard graced by a Moorish-tiled fountain, it makes a pleasant addition to the neighborhood. Established in 1871, the school inhabited temporary quarters for its first two decades, then operated out of the Mark Hopkins mansion at California and Mason streets from 1893 to 1906, when it was destroyed by the earthquake and subsequent fire. The campus bustles with students during the week, and with those who come to enjoy its Walter/McBean Gallery (*see* Art Galleries, *below*), San Francisco Cinematheque, and Diego Rivera mural—one of only three in San Francisco (*see* Statues,

Murals & Monuments, *below*). The balcony offers views of San Francisco Bay. *800 Chestnut St., between Leavenworth and Jones Sts., Russian Hill.*

4 *f-6*

SAN FRANCISCO MUSEUM OF MODERN ART (SFMOMA)

Italian-Swiss architect Mario Botta, known for his skylights, has created a great slanting ellipse for the roof of the museum. The striking structure consists of a stepped-back, sienna brick facade and a central tower constructed of alternating bands of black and white stone. Inside, an imposing black-and-gray stone staircase leads up from the atrium to four floors of galleries (*see* Art Museums, *below*).

4 *e-6*

SAVINGS UNION BANK

The former Savings Union Bank of San Francisco, now occupied by Emporio Armani (*see* Clothing for Women/General *in* Chapter 2), is a classical temple inspired by the Roman Pantheon. The granite-clad steel frame has a reinforced-concrete dome, Ionic columns, and a pediment with a bas-relief sculpture by Haig Pattigan. Architects Bliss and Faville apprenticed at the legendary firm of McKim, Mead & White before designing this 1910 structure. *1 Grant Ave., at Market St., Union Square.*

4 *f-5*

SHELL BUILDING

This slender, terra-cotta tower, designed in 1929 by George Kelham, is an attractive Art Deco skyscraper in the Financial District. Look for the seashell motif, inside and out. *100 Bush St., between Battery and Sansome Sts., Financial District.*

7 *e-1*

SPRECKELS MANSION— THE HAIGHT

Not to be confused with the Spreckels Mansion of Pacific Heights, this house was built in 1898 for a member of the wealthy Spreckels family, which made its fortune in the sugar industry. The sturdy, putty-color Queen Anne Victorian stands out for its intricate "wedding-cake" detailing. Later tenants included Jack London and Ambrose Bierce. *737 Buena Vista Ave. W, between Frederick and Waller Sts., Haight.*

2 *f-2*

SPRECKELS MANSION— PACIFIC HEIGHTS

An imposing residence overlooking Lafayette Park, this Beaux Arts residence was built in 1913 for sugar heir Adolph Spreckels and his wife Alma de Bretteville Spreckels. Their former home is sometimes called the Sugar Palace, and it might as well have been constructed of sugar, as the Utah limestone is gradually dissolving into the fog. George Applegarth designed the structure, and Mrs. Spreckels also commissioned him to design the California Palace of the Legion of Honor, which was presented by the Spreckels as a gift to the city. Today the mansion is occupied by author Danielle Steele. *2080 Washington St., at Octavia St., Pacific Heights.*

2 *e-2*

STANYAN HOUSE

One of the oldest houses in the city, the Stanyan House was built in 1854 and stayed in the Stanyan family for 110 years. Only a few of the prefabricated New England houses that were sent by boat from Boston around Cape Horn have been identified with certainty; this is one of them. Compared with the city's ornate Victorians, it's a model of austerity that would look more at home on Nantucket. *2006 Bush St., at Buchanan St., Pacific Heights.*

2 *e-3*

STEINER STREET VICTORIANS

These six jewel-color, beautifully restored Queen Anne Victorians across from Alamo Square on the 700 block of Steiner Street—also known as "The Painted Ladies" and "Postcard Row"—may be the most photographed structures in San Francisco after the Golden Gate Bridge. They've been featured on hundreds of postcards and the opening credits of several TV shows set in San Francisco. Standing side by side on a steep street with the towers of the Financial District looming in the background, they make for a stunning vista combining historic and new San Francisco. Numbers 710 to 720 Steiner Street were developed in 1894 and 1895 by carpenter Matthew Kavanaugh. *Steiner St. between Hayes and Fulton Sts., Western Addition.*

2 a-3
SUTRO BATHS
Modeled after ancient Roman baths, the Sutro Baths once consisted of six enormous glass-roofed fresh- and salt-water pools, 500 dressing rooms, art galleries, several restaurants, and an amphitheater. The complex, which now resembles a set of Roman ruins, covered 3 acres just north of the Cliff House (*see above*). The baths opened in 1896, were closed in 1952 due to budget problems, and then burned down in 1966. You can explore the ruins on your own or take ranger-led walks on weekends. *Point Lobos Ave. at Great Hwy., Richmond District.*

5 f-5
SWEDENBORGIAN CHURCH
See Churches, *below.*

4 e-3
1360 MONTGOMERY STREET
Bogart fans may recognize the elegant Art Deco apartment building at 1360 Montgomery Street—indeed, it appeared in the 1947 film *Dark Passage* starring Humphrey Bogart and Lauren Bacall. It's a 1937 Moderne building with etched-glass gazelles and palms counterpointing a silvered fresco of the heroic bridge worker. The building stands at the corner where the Filbert Steps intersect with the Greenwich Steps. *1360 Montgomery St., at Alta St., Telegraph Hill.*

4 f-4
TRANSAMERICA BUILDING
When the narrow, pyramid-shape Transamerica Building was erected at the foot of Columbus Avenue in 1972, it was regarded as an architectural blunder with a $34 million price tag. Ironically, the William Pereira and Associates–designed building is now considered a landmark; indeed, it's the most-photographed modern building in San Francisco. At 853 ft tall, it's also one of the city's tallest structures. *600 Montgomery St., between Clay and Washington Sts., Financial District.*

7 d-5
TWIN PEAKS
San Francisco's second- and third-highest hills (922 ft and 904 ft, respectively) were named *Los Pechos de la Chola* (the Breasts of the Indian Maiden) by 18th-century Spanish arrivals. They now form a 65-acre park with spectacular 360° views of the San Francisco Bay. *Twin Peaks Blvd. off Portola Dr., Twin Peaks.*

4 d-7
UNITED STATES COURT OF APPEALS
In January 1997, the United States Court of Appeals for the Ninth Circuit returned to its former home in SoMa. The Beaux Arts structure, originally built in 1905 to house the federal courts and post office, had been seriously damaged during the Loma Prieta earthquake in 1989. Congress authorized $91 million for the seismic retrofitting and historical rehabilitation of the structure. Today it stands as a monument to the American Renaissance, a time in history when it was believed that the construction of opulent public buildings was a tribute to the rising wealth and importance of the nation. This sentiment is evident in the craftsmanship of the interiors: mosaic tiles covering the floors and vaulted ceilings, ornate plaster moldings, two rotundas with stained-glass medallions, white Italian marble walls, bronze window cages for the former post office. Restorationists used old photographs to recreate the original bronze light fixtures. The first floor can be viewed during business hours, 8:30 to 5 weekdays, and guided tours of the courtrooms and library are given twice a month. *7th St. at Mission St., South of Market, 415/556–9945.*

2 g-4
VERMONT STREET
Although Lombard Street has all the notoriety as "the crookedest street in the world," her sister street is equally twisted. It heads down the back side of Potrero Hill and has eight hairpin switchbacks—not a good street to attempt in the U-Haul. *Vermont St. below 20th St., Potrero Hill.*

4 c-7
WAR MEMORIAL OPERA HOUSE
Renovated in 1997, the War Memorial was built in 1932 and inaugurated on October 15 of that year with a performance of *Tosca*. The last of the city's great Beaux Arts projects, it has a marble foyer, two balconies, and a vaulted and coffered ceiling with a spectacular Art Deco chandelier that resembles a huge silver sunburst. In its long history it has heard more than just arias: this is

where the United Nations was formed in 1945, and where the treaty with Japan was signed in 1951. These days, the opera house hosts the San Francisco Opera from September through December (*see* Opera *in* Chapter 5), and the San Francisco Ballet from February through May (*see* Dance *in* Chapter 5). *301 Van Ness Ave., between Fulton and Grove Sts., Civic Center.*

2 *e-2*

WEDDING HOUSES

Dairy rancher James Cudworth had these two identical, white double-peaked homes built around the late 1870s as wedding gifts for his two daughters, who were married at the same time. These days, the twin buildings house upscale shops and a pub. *1980 Union St., at Buchanan St., Pacific Heights.*

8 *a-3*

WOMEN'S BUILDING

Since 1979, the Women's Building has acted as the hub of the female community in the Mission District. It houses offices for women's social, political, and educational organizations, and sponsors talks and readings by such noted figures as Alice Walker and Angela Davis. Before finally becoming the Women's Building, the Mission Revival–style structure had several lives. The building was erected in 1910 as Turn Hall, a German exercise club, and later became Dovre Hall, a Norwegian social club. In 1966 an Irish pub opened on the ground floor, adopting the Dovre Club as its name. After 30 years of operation and an emotional court battle, the Dovre Club was evicted and its space taken over by the landlords—the Women's Building. The building has a striking two-sided exterior mural depicting women's peacekeeping efforts (*see* Statues, Murals & Monuments, *below*). *3543 18th St., between Valencia and Guerrero Sts., Mission District, 415/431–1180. Closed weekends.*

ART GALLERIES

4 *e-6*

ARTISTS FORUM

Four shows (solo and group) per year are augmented with gallery talks, musical performances, workshops, and demonstrations at this gallery-cum-salon. All of these activities help foster the gallery's goal of giving the public greater access to artists and their ideas. *251 Post St., at Stockton St., Union Square, 415/981–6347. Closed Sat.–Mon.*

7 *g-2*

BELCHER STUDIOS GALLERY

A slickly converted early 20th-century warehouse on a residential street contains this gallery and small outdoor sculpture area. The focus is on up-and-coming local talent working in various media. The building also houses a complex of artists' studios. *69 Belcher St., between 14th St. and Duboce Ave., Castro, 415/255–8900.*

4 *e-6*

BOMANI GALLERY

Bomani showcases work with multicultural viewpoints, often by African-American artists. It's a stately place displaying folk art as well as historical and contemporary art in several rooms. You may spot Danny Glover here; he's married to gallery owner Asake Bomani. *251 Post St., at Stockton St., Union Square, 415/296–8677. Closed Sun.–Mon.*

4 *d-2*

CAMPBELL-THIEBAUD GALLERY

Paintings of the Bay Area Figurative school are displayed on two floors in a brown shingled building that previously housed a speakeasy and artists' studios. Artists include Wayne Thiebaud, Christopher Brown, and Manuel Neri. Outside is a lovely, sculpture-filled garden. *645 Chestnut St., between Columbus and Mason Sts., North Beach, 415/441–8680. Closed Sun.–Mon.*

2 *g-4*

CAPP STREET PROJECT

Although the name hails from its initial incarnation on Capp Street in the Mission District, Capp Street Project has merged with the CCAC Institute for Exhibitions and Public Programs at the California College of Arts and Crafts. Residencies and exhibitions are held four times annually on both the Oakland and San Francisco campuses of the college and encompass works by fine artists, architects, and designers. Solo shows feature internationally known contemporary artists such as Gary Hill, Mona Hatoum, and Kara Walker. *415/551–9210 for schedules and locations.*

4 *f-6*

CATHARINE CLARK GALLERY

Small but growing steadily, Catharine Clark Gallery shows contemporary painting, sculpture, and new genres with an experimental, surrealistic edge. Most of the work is by West Coast artists, but the roster has expanded to include some from Canada, New York, southern California, and beyond. *49 Geary St., at Kearny St., Union Square, 415/399–1439. Closed Sun.*

4 *f-6*

CROWN POINT PRESS

As one of the world's most respected printmaking facilities, Crown Point Press has hosted artists of international repute such as Wayne Thiebaud, Richard Diebenkorn, John Cage, Pat Steir, and Helen Frankenthaler. The sleek, ample gallery is the venue for group and solo exhibitions. *20 Hawthorne St., off Howard St. between 2nd and 3rd Sts., South of Market, 415/974–6273. Closed Sun.–Mon.*

4 *e-5*

DOROTHY WEISS GALLERY

Contemporary ceramic and glass works are on display at this well-respected, two-floor gallery. Ceramists Michael Lucero, Annabeth Rosen, and Annette Corcoran and glass artists Therman Statom, Jay Musler, and Hank Murta Adams regularly exhibit their works here, although shows usually include artists from Europe and Asia as well. *256 Sutter St., at Grant Ave., Union Square, 415/397–3611. Closed Sun.–Mon.*

4 *c-2*

DYANSEN GALLERY

Large, colorful water sculptures mark the entrance to this vast art emporium. Inside are more traditional wares, such as original paintings and prints by Peter Max, Charles Bragg, and child prodigy Alexandra Nechita. Dyansen Gallery is the original producer of Érte's sculptures, and also carries his graphic works. *799 Beach St., at Larkin St., Fisherman's Wharf, 415/928–0596.*

4 *f-6*

871 FINE ARTS

This intriguing small space specializes in printed matter—posters, Fluxus artifacts, and more. Its outstanding book-store stocks hard-to-find art publications and monographs. *49 Geary St., at Kearny St., Union Square, 415/543–5155. Closed Sun.–Mon.*

8 *a-2*

ESP

Painting, photography, collage, and even a collection of nightclub flyers by promising local talent constitute the repertoire at this small, cool gallery. Most of the artists are unknown, but invariably prove interesting. *305 Valencia St., at 14th St., Mission District, 415/252–8191. Closed Sun.–Wed.*

8 *a-2*

FOUR WALLS

Formerly a firehouse, this 1,200 square-ft, light-filled gallery with Victorian accents is a funky backdrop for group and solo shows by emerging Bay Area artists. Noted for its hip, lively openings, Four Walls sits above a bar on one of San Francisco's most bohemian blocks. *3160-A 16th St., at Albion St., Mission District, 415/626–8515. Closed Sun.–Tues.*

4 *f-6*

FRAENKEL GALLERY

San Francisco's preeminent photography gallery presents museum-quality exhibitions. Solo and group shows of modern and 19th-century masters are in three main galleries. The roster of artists include William Wegman, Nan Goldin, Hiroshi Sugimoto, Diane Arbus, and Robert Adams. *49 Geary St., at Kearny St., Union Square, 415/981–2661. Closed Sun.–Mon.*

ART AND ACTING, UNDER ONE ROOF

The following art galleries can be counted on as venues for frequent, and often intriguing, performance art events.

New Langton Arts (Art Galleries)
   The granddaddy of the city's mixed media centers.

Place Pigalle (Art Galleries)
   Combination European café–bar, art gallery, and theater.

SOMAR Gallery (Art Galleries)
   Thought-provoking theatrical pieces.

Southern Exposure (Art Galleries)
   A former cannery with plenty of space for creative performances.

8 c-5

GALERÍA DE LA RAZA

The city's premier forum for art by Chicano and Latino artists was founded in the early '70s. The gallery mounts six to eight exhibitions per year reflecting community issues: immigration, sexuality, and spirituality. Murals on the building bring the art outdoors. *2857 24th St., at Bryant St., Potrero Hill, 415/826–8009. Call for hours.*

4 f-6

GALLERY PAULE ANGLIM

In a skylighted main gallery, you can see shows by important artists such as Louise Bourgeois, Nayland Blake, Enrique Chagoya, Jess, and Melissa Porkorny. Many of the artists may have Bay Area connections, particularly the conceptual school of the 1970s, but the gallery's programming is of international caliber. *14 Geary St., at Kearny St., Union Square, 415/433–2710. Closed Sun.–Mon.*

8 d-2

GALLERY 16

Sharing facilities with a digital printing service, this innovative gallery provides artists with technological tools as well as exhibition space. The shows take place in two enormous rooms—double solo exhibitions are common—and artists are free to work in large, installation format; artist Philip Ross once created a huge sculpture that sprouted live mushrooms. The place has attracted a number of up-and-coming as well as established image-makers. *1616 16th St., 3rd floor, at Kansas St., Potrero Hill, 415/ 626–7495. Closed Sun.*

4 e-5

HACKETT FREEDMAN GALLERY

The best in contemporary realist painting is showcased in this superbly lighted, well-appointed gallery. This can mean anything from traditional floral still lifes to experimental renderings of the human figure—all by various internationally known artists. *250 Sutter St., between Grant Ave. and Kearny St., Union Square, 415/362–7152. Closed Sun.–Mon.*

4 f-6

HAINES GALLERY

Gorgeous blond-wood floors distinguish this stately gallery specializing in sleek,

high-concept painting and sculpture. Gallery artists include Andy Goldsworthy, Alan Rath, and Baochi Zhang—ask to see Goldsworthy's remarkable cracked-mud wall in the back room. *49 Geary St., at Kearny St., Union Square, 415/397–8114. Closed Sun.–Mon.*

4 f-7

HOSFELT GALLERY

The small Hosfelt Gallery showcases painting, photography, and installation. The works, by artists such as Shahizia Sikander, Richard Barnes, and Alfredo Jaar, have a conceptual and political bent and international repute. The gallery's exhibitions, receptions, and talks are crowded with the city's top curators, collectors, and art lovers. *430 Clementina St., at 5th St., South of Market, 415/495–5454. Closed Sun.–Mon.*

4 f-6

JENNJOY GALLERY

This gallery is an intellectual environment to discuss art and art making. Jennjoy promotes emerging artists from San Francisco, Boston, Los Angeles, New York, and Seattle by displaying innovative works in painting, sculpture, prints, drawing, photography, digital, and time-based media. Exhibits are combined with lectures, video screenings, and artist's talks to inspire interaction with the audience. *49 Geary, Suite 410, Union Square, 415/398–2040. Closed Sun.–Mon.*

4 e-5

JOHN BERGGRUEN GALLERY

This blue-chip showcase for modern art occupies three full floors of galleries and private viewing rooms. The emphasis is on California artists—it's a great place to investigate the Bay Area's Figurative greats—but national and European artists also appear in group and solo exhibitions. Shows range from classic modernism to contemporary mixed media, and a project room on the fourth floor is dedicated to emerging artists. *228 Grant Ave., between Post and Sutter Sts., Union Square, 415/781–4629. Closed Sun.*

8 a-2

THE LAB

Catch talented local image-makers at this spacious alternative gallery. Group art shows, performance art pieces, and a music series reflect the cultural perspectives of young, mostly Bay Area artists. In the lobby, a series of murals completed in spring 1997 commemorates San Francisco's history of progressive labor movements. *2948 16th St., at Capp St., Mission District, 415/864–8855. Closed Sun.–Tues.*

4 g-8

LIMN GALLERY

Behind the Limn Company, one of San Francisco's most respected furniture stores, is a spiffy space highlighting commercial and fine arts. Past exhibitions have included one devoted to digital art and another to the sculptural paintings of Frank Stella. Call ahead, as shows are sporadic. *290 Townsend St., at 4th St., South Beach, 415/977–1300 or 415/778–6220.*

4 e-6

THE LUGGAGE STORE

This gallery originally began in a luggage store; today it does double duty as an art venue and community center. The exhibitions explore edgy subjects—homelessness, gender issues, drugs—as perceived by emerging artists. Educational, cultural, and social events are held weekly. *1007 Market St., at 6th St., Tenderloin, 415/255–5971.*

1 b-2

MARIN HEADLANDS CENTER FOR THE ARTS

The Headlands Center for the Arts is a sprawling complex of early 20th-century military bunkers converted to studio spaces. The building itself is the biggest draw: look for David Ireland's evocative, amber-shellac wall treatment; a mess hall designed by Ann Hamilton; and a public latrine remodeled by the Interim Office of Architecture. Artists in residence, both local and international, work in more modest studios closer to the beach. You can see their artwork or witness their performance works at twice-yearly open houses. *944 Ft. Barry Rd., near Field Rd., Sausalito, 415/331–2787; or 415/331–2887 for directions from San Francisco.*

4 e-5

MARTIN LAWRENCE GALLERY

The Martin Lawrence Gallery has a slick retail edge. Even from the street, you can see, through the windows, its collection of colorful pop prints of celebrities by Andy Warhol and Steve Kaufman. Inside the clean, well-lit gallery you'll find works by other favorites such as Érte and Keith Haring. *465 Powell St., at Sutter St., Union Square, 415/956–0345.*

4 e-5

MAXWELL GALLERIES

An old-world flavor fills this established gallery of 19th- and 20th-century European and American painting. Founded in 1940, the gallery has rooms organized by theme, such as early California art; featured artists include Thomas Hill, Maynard Dixon, Edgar Payne, and Albert Bierstadt. Four times a year Maxwell mounts shows organized by theme or artist, including contemporary realist painters from the Bay Area. *559 Sutter St., at Powell St., Union Square, 415/421–5193. Closed Sun.*

4 e-5

MERIDIAN GALLERY

A nonprofit gallery founded in 1989 to promote pan-ethnic art, this intimate space is a refreshing contrast to others in this commercial neighborhood. Along with mounting nearly a dozen shows a year, Meridian hosts lecture programs, organizes international exchange shows, and operates an internship program pairing urban teens with local artists. *545 Sutter St., at Powell St., Union Square, 415/398–7229. Closed Sun.–Mon.*

0 d-5

MISSION CULTURAL CENTER FOR LATINO ARTS

The Mission Cultural Center's huge second-floor exhibition space is a venue for group installations; the smaller Salla gallery hosts solo shows, poetry readings, and video screenings. Exhibitions have included works by women, Latino gays, lesbians, and bisexuals. *2868 Mission St., between 24th and 25th Sts., Mission District, 415/821–1155. Closed Sun.*

4 f-6

MODERNISM

A broad range of trends in contemporary painting, particularly the Russian avant-garde, make up the bulk of art on display. Two concurrent solos open every six to seven weeks, with the occasional thematic group exhibition thrown in for good measure. *685 Market St., at 3rd St., Union Square, 415/541–0461. Closed Sun.–Mon.*

4 d-8
NEW LANGTON ARTS
Founded in 1975, this two-story interdisciplinary gallery is one of the city's most enduring alternative spaces. The main floor hosts five exhibitions annually, including a fall awards show and a holiday fund-raising auction. A prominent reading series, new music and jazz concerts, and performance projects take place in New Langton's theater. *1246 Folsom St., between 8th and 9th Sts., South of Market, 415/626–5416. Closed Sun.–Tues.*

4 b-8
PLACE PIGALLE
This cozy European-style café and bar also has a respectable art gallery. Funky works by subcultural artists are displayed in thematic group shows. One recent exhibition featured female tattooists; another conveyed millennium malaise through various artists' eyes. At night, the multipurpose gallery morphs

into a venue for readings, musical events, and performance art pieces. *520 Hayes St., at Octavia St., Hayes Valley, 415/552–2671.*

4 b-8
POLANCO
Mexican art fills this vibrant space, including fine art, antiques, folk crafts, jewelry, and contemporary art. Polanco mounts group and solo exhibitions of works by contemporary artists from Mexico, as well as thematic shows of folk art, vintage movie posters, Day of the Dead crafts, and other seasonal items. *393 Hayes St., at Gough St., Hayes Valley, 415/252–5753. Closed Mon.*

4 f-6
REFUSALON
The adventurous Refusalon gallery brings experimental works to downtown audiences. Its solo and group shows of Bay Area and international artists have conceptual, minimalist, or multimedia installation tendencies. A side gallery serves as a showcase for represented artists such as Pip Culbert, Gay Outlaw, and Uri Tzaig. *20 Hawthorne St., near Howard St. between 2nd and 3rd Sts., South of Market, 415/546–0158. Closed Sun.–Mon.*

4 e-6
RENA BRANSTEN GALLERY
Exhibitions range from San Francisco landscape painting and figurative works on paper to abstract painting, conceptual art, and ceramic sculpture. It's one of the few commercial galleries that also presents electronic art and video installation by internationally known artists. There's usually a solo exhibition in each of the two main exhibition spaces. *77 Geary St., at Grant Ave., Union Square, 415/982–3292. Closed Sun.–Mon.*

4 f-6
ROBERT KOCH GALLERY
Robert Koch Gallery deals in photography, with a focus on Eastern European work. There are rare prints from the 19th and early 20th centuries, as well as work by more recent artists such as Jan Saudek and Bill Owens. The mostly black-and-white images stand out against the main room's burnished blond-wood floors. *49 Geary St., at Kearny St., Union Square, 415/421–0122. Closed Sun.–Mon.*

GALLERIES AT 49 GEARY STREET

The building at 49 Geary Street is top to bottom galleries, which means you could easily spend the better part of a day browsing here.

Catharine Clark Gallery (Art Galleries)
Contemporary painting, sculpture, and mixed media.

871 Fine Arts (Art Galleries)
Posters and printed matter.

Fraenkel Gallery (Art Galleries)
The city's preeminent photography gallery.

Haines Gallery (Art Galleries)
High-concept art.

Jennjoy Gallery (Art Galleries)
Innovative works in digital and time-based media.

Robert Koch Gallery (Art Galleries)
Eastern European photos and rare prints from the 19th and early 20th centuries.

Scott Nichols Gallery (Art Galleries)
Photographic works ranging from Ansel Adams and Edward Weston.

Stephen Wirtz Gallery (Art Galleries)
Contemporary painting, sculpture, and photography.

4 c-7

SAN FRANCISCO ART COMMISSION GALLERY

The city's official art venue occupies two modest square rooms on the first floor of City Hall. Shows emphasize cultural diversity and have examined everything from surfing and skateboarding to African-American history. Writing programs and lunchtime art talks take place weekly. *401 Van Ness Ave., at McAllister St., Civic Center, 415/554–6080. Closed Sun.–Tues.*

4 a-1

SAN FRANCISCO MUSEUM OF MODERN ART RENTAL GALLERY

In addition to selling and renting an eclectic selection of works by local artists, this waterfront gallery stages group shows featuring three to a dozen artists at a time. The annual spring artists' warehouse sale is extremely popular. *Fort Mason Center, Bldg. A, Marina Blvd. at Laguna St., Marina, 415/441–4777.*

4 f-6

SCOTT NICHOLS GALLERY

This establishment grew out of Scott Nichols's personal collection of pioneering photographers, which includes works by Edward and Bret Weston, Ansel Adams, and Henri Cartier-Bresson. Today the gallery showcases a truly international repertoire of fine photographic works ranging from the 19th century to the present and maintains a large inventory. *49 Geary St., at Kearny St., Union Square, 415/788–4641. Closed Sun.–Mon.*

4 e-5

SERGE SORROKKO

In a tastefully furnished, two-story space, Serge Sorrokko shows well-known modern European and American artists. Thematic group shows often look at provocative subjects, such as the "The Last Party: Nightworld in Photographs"—a compilation of martini-swilling celebrities. *231 Grant Ave., at Sutter St., Union Square, 415/421–7770.*

4 f-6

SF CAMERAWORK

Devoted to the art of photography since 1974, SF Camerawork is a city institution, with thematic shows by emerging artists from around the world

in a 2,000-square-ft exhibition space. There's an excellent lecture program with noted photographers and critics; a small bookstore that stocks hard-to-find periodicals, monographs, and art theory books; and a 3,000-volume reference library. *115 Natoma St., between New Montgomery and 2nd Sts., South of Market, 415/764–1001. Closed Sun.–Mon.*

4 e-5

SHAPIRO GALLERY

Shapiro specializes in 20th-century black-and-white photography—particularly works by the f64 Group, which included photo luminaries Ansel Adams, Edward Weston, and Imogene Cunningham. It also represents an international roster of contemporary modernist photographers such as George Tice and Kenro Izu. At press time, Shapiro Gallery was planning to relocate to the Phelan Building at 760 Market Street. *250 Sutter St., between Grant Ave. and Kearny St., Union Square, 415/398–6655. Closed Sun.–Mon.*

8 c-1

SOMAR GALLERY

Nearly the size of an airplane hangar, this community center and arts facility gives artists room to express themselves. It has hosted a show of large paintings from the Beat era, as well as the overview show for the annual citywide Open Studios event (*see* Events, *below*). Exhibitions are sporadic, so call ahead. *934 Brannan St., between 8th and 9th Sts., South of Market, 415/863–1414. Closed Sun.–Mon.*

8 b-2

SOUTHERN EXPOSURE

A 20-year-old gallery housed in a former cannery, Southern Exposure is an important venue for emerging West Coast artists, and its annual juried show draws hundreds of submissions from all over northern California. The high ceilings and vast floor space of its main gallery allow for large group exhibitions and dinosaur-size sculptures, whereas the cozier mezzanine gallery is reserved for smaller works and shows. Provocative panel discussions, musical events, and performance pieces accompany most exhibitions. *401 Alabama St., at 17th St., Potrero Hill, 415/863–2141. Closed Sun.–Mon.*

4 f-6

STEPHEN WIRTZ GALLERY

Consistently interesting exhibitions of contemporary painting, sculpture, and photography are mostly by Bay Area artists. A spacious back room is open for viewing selections from the gallery's stable: Deborah Oropallo, Lucy Puls, Raymond Saunders, Todd Hido, Laurie Reid, and Kathryn Spence. *49 Geary St., at Kearny St., Union Square, 415/433–6879. Closed Sun.–Mon.*

1 b-1

SUSAN CUMMINS GALLERY

The best gallery north of the Golden Gate Bridge is a longtime fixture in Mill Valley's main square. Cummins has a formidable reputation for selecting choice painting, sculpture, and jewelry by predominantly Bay Area artists. *12 Miller Ave., at Throckmorton Ave., Mill Valley, 415/383–1512. Closed Sun.–Mon.*

4 f-6

TERRAIN

A quirky, compact gallery with a homey feel, Terrain shows contemporary sculpture, painting, drawing, and installations by local and international artists. The gallery directors have an interest in the-ater, so the shows often have theatrical themes. *165 Jessie St., between 3rd and New Montgomery Sts., South of Market, 415/543–0656. Closed Sun.–Tues.*

4 c-2

WALTER/MCBEAN GALLERY

Part of the San Francisco Art Institute, the Walter/McBean Gallery presents shows on two floors with raw concrete walls. In addition to hosting annual student and faculty shows, the gallery introduces young international artists—many working with alternative media—to Bay Area audiences. Past solo shows have exhibited Nicole Eisenman, Sue Williams, and David Ireland. *800 Chestnut St., between Leavenworth and Jones Sts., North Beach, 415/749–4564. Closed Mon.*

ART MUSEUMS

4 f-7

ANSEL ADAMS CENTER FOR PHOTOGRAPHY

The largest repository of art photography on the West Coast began its life in Carmel in 1967, established by Adams himself. In 1989 the center moved to SoMa, where it became the first arts organization built at the new Yerba Buena Gardens complex. Now in even larger quarters, the center showcases experimental, contemporary, and historical photography as well as changing exhibitions of Adams's work. The bookstore is outstanding. *250 4th St., between Howard and Folsom Sts., South of Market, 415/495–7000. Admission: $5, $3 students, $2 senior citizens and youth 12–17, free children under 12.*

7 a-1

ASIAN ART MUSEUM OF SAN FRANCISCO

In the same building as the M. H. de Young Museum (*see below*), this is the West Coast's largest museum of Asian art and artifacts. Collection highlights include the oldest known dated Chinese Buddha image (AD 338), the largest museum collection in the United States of Japanese *inro* (small, intricate lacquer boxes for carrying personal items), the Leventritt Collection of blue-and-white porcelain, and a superb collection of carved jade. The first floor is devoted to Chinese and Korean art; on the second floor are

---

JUST FOR SHUTTERBUGS

Fans of photography will find some excellent galleries and a museum in San Francisco:

Ansel Adams Center for Photography (Art Museums)
   The largest museum of art photography on the West Coast.

Fraenkel Gallery (Art Galleries)
   San Francisco's preeminent photography gallery.

Robert Koch Gallery (Art Galleries)
   Rare prints from the 19th and early 20th centuries.

Scott Nichols Gallery (Art Galleries)
   An international repertoire of fine photographic works.

SF Camerawork (Art Galleries)
   2,000 square ft of exhibition space, plus lectures and a library.

Shapiro Gallery (Art Galleries)
   20th-century black-and-white photography.

---

treasures from Iran, Turkey, Syria, India, Tibet, Nepal, Pakistan, Korea, Japan, Afghanistan, and Southeast Asia. The Avery Brundage Collection of nearly 12,000 sculptures, paintings, and ceramics from 40 Asian countries illustrates the major periods of Asian art. The museum is scheduled to move to the refurbished Main Library building in the Civic Center in 2002. *John F. Kennedy and Tea Garden Drs. near 10th Ave. and Fulton St., Golden Gate Park, 415/379–8801. Admission: $7, $5 senior citizens, $4 youth 12–17, children under 12 free; $1 discount with Muni transfer; free 1st Wed. of month. Closed Mon.*

3 *e-2*

BERKELEY ART MUSEUM

Although the low, concrete building may not look like much from the street, this museum houses the largest university-owned art collection in the country. It began with a bequest from the abstractionist Hans Hoffman, who donated 50 of his paintings to the University of California at Berkeley in the 1960s (these paintings now form one of the museum's most impressive permanent installations). Today the museum, which shares a building with the Pacific Film Archive, showcases Asian art and 20th-century Western painting, sculpture, photography, and conceptual art. The permanent collection is spotty and wide-ranging, but it does have some gems by Peter Paul Rubens, Albert Bierstadt, Mark Rothko, and Eva Hesse. A sculpture garden to the rear of the museum is open in summer. *2626 Bancroft Way, at College Ave., Berkeley, 510/642–0808. Admission: $6, $4 senior citizens, students, and youth 12–17; children under 12 free; free Thurs. 11–noon and 5–9. Closed Mon.–Tues.*

4 *f-6*

CALIFORNIA HISTORICAL SOCIETY

The Historical Society occasionally mounts exhibitions of paintings, drawings, and photographs pertaining to California's history. *See History Museums, below.*

2 *a-2*

CALIFORNIA PALACE OF THE LEGION OF HONOR

The artistry of this museum begins with its cliff-side location, which offers a spectacular panorama of the Golden Gate Bridge. The renovated French neoclassical building houses the city's European fine arts collection, spanning a range of 4,000 years. Included are 80 works by Rodin, as well as French, English, Flemish, and Italian painting and sculpture. Period rooms and antiquities are on view, and a new underground gallery complex houses the Achenbach collection of works on paper and the porcelain gallery. The museum restaurant offers views of the gardens and the Pacific Ocean beyond. *Lincoln Park, entrance at 34th Ave. and Clement St., Richmond District, 415/750–3600. Admission: $8, $6 senior citizens, $5 youth 12–17, children under 12 free; $2 discount with Muni transfer; free 2nd Wed. of month. Closed Mon.*

4 *e-6*

CARTOON ART MUSEUM

Colorful characters like Krazy Kat, Zippy the Pinhead, and Batman greet you as you walk in the door to the Cartoon Art Museum, the only museum on the West Coast devoted to "the funnies." The 12,000-piece permanent collection includes everything from political cartoons of the 1700s to "Far Side" and *New Yorker* cartoons of the present day. There's also a 3,000-volume library, a CD-ROM room, a children's gallery, and a gift shop overflowing with comics. Special exhibits in the past have spotlighted underground comics and Hanna Barbera studios. *814 Mission St., at 4th St., South of Market, 415/227–8666. Admission: $5, $3 senior citizens and students, $2 children 6–12, free children under 6. Closed Mon.–Tues.*

4 *f-6*

CENTER FOR THE ARTS

This remarkable arts center in the Yerba Buena Gardens complex has two main gallery spaces, a high-tech gallery, and a film and video screening room, all devoted to art with a multicultural bent. Exhibits such as the "Art of Star Wars" focus on contemporary works; many feature emerging local and regional artists. The adjacent Forum, a multipurpose room, hosts events and performances. *701 Mission St., at 3rd St., South of Market, 415/978–2787. Admission: $5, $3 senior citizens, students, and youth under 17; free 1st Thurs. of month 6 PM–8 PM. Closed Mon.*

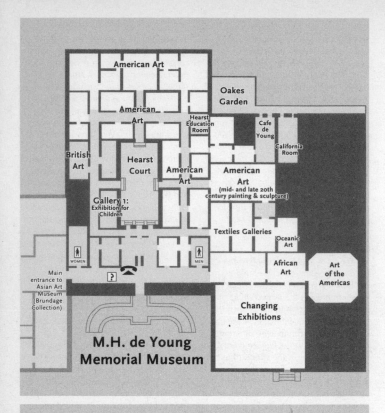

M.H. de Young Memorial Museum

American Art

Oakes Garden

Hearst Education Room

Cafe de Young

California Room

British Art

Hearst Court

American Art

American Art

American Art (mid- and late 20th century painting & sculpture)

Gallery 1: Exhibition for Children

Textiles Galleries

Oceanic Art

WOMEN

MEN

African Art

Art of the Americas

Main entrance to Asian Art Museum (Brundage Collection)

Changing Exhibitions

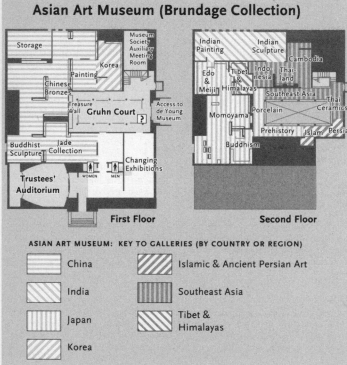

Asian Art Museum (Brundage Collection)

First Floor

Storage

Museum Society Auxiliary Meeting Room

Korea

Painting

Chinese Bronzes

Treasure Wall

Gruhn Court

Access to de Young Museum

Buddhist Sculpture

Jade Collection

Changing Exhibitions

WOMEN

MEN

Trustees' Auditorium

Second Floor

Indian Painting

Indian Sculpture

Cambodia

Edo & Meiji

Tibet & Himalayas

Indo-nesia

Thai-land

Southeast Asia

Thai Ceramics

Momoyama

Porcelain

Prehistory

Islam

Persia

Buddhism

ASIAN ART MUSEUM: KEY TO GALLERIES (BY COUNTRY OR REGION)

China

India

Japan

Korea

Islamic & Ancient Persian Art

Southeast Asia

Tibet & Himalayas

4 g-5

JEWISH MUSEUM
SAN FRANCISCO

This small museum displays the works of Jewish artists, contemporary as well as old masters, and mounts special exhibitions examining Jewish history, culture, and contemporary life. In the year 2001, the Jewish Museum plans to move into the Jessie Street Substation, an elegant industrial building in the Yerba Buena Center designed by Willis Polk. *121 Steuart St., between Mission and Howard Sts., South of Market, 415/543–8880. Admission: $3, $1.50 senior citizens and students, free children under 12; free 1st Mon. of month. Closed Fri.–Sat.*

4 a-2

MEXICAN MUSEUM

This museum has the distinction of being the first American showcase devoted exclusively to Mexican, Mexican-American, and Chicano art. Its enormous permanent collection of more than 9,000 pieces contains everything from pre-Conquest artifacts to recent works by artists such as Patssi Valdez. In 1986 the museum acquired a 500-piece folk-art collection, a gift from the Nelson A. Rockefeller estate. Temporary shows feature contemporary and historic works by Chicano, Central, and South American artists. Limited exhibition space accommodates only a fraction of the permanent collection, but the museum plans to relocate to more spacious quarters near the Yerba Buena Center in 2003. *Fort Mason Center, Bldg. D, Marina Blvd. at Laguna St., Marina, 415/441–0404 Admission: $4, $3 senior citizens and students; free 1st Wed. of month. Closed Mon.–Tues.*

7 a-1

M. H. DE YOUNG
MEMORIAL MUSEUM

The de Young has the finest collection of American art on the West Coast, including paintings, sculpture, textiles, and decorative arts from the 1670s through the 20th century. More than 200 paintings of American masters such as Copley, Eakins, Bingham, and Sargent make up the John D. Rockefeller III Collection of American paintings. Frederic Church's moody, almost psychedelic *Rainy Season in the Tropics* dominates the room of landscapes, and the marvelous gallery of American still lifes includes trompe l'oeil paintings by William Harnett. The de Young also has large collections of art, sculpture, baskets, and ceramics from Africa, Oceania, and the Americas, and textile installations on everything from tribal clothing to couture. Crafts are covered as well, thanks to a gift from Dorothy and George Saxe featuring more than 200 of the finest major works of contemporary glass, ceramics, and furniture. The de Young stands adjacent to the Asian Art Museum (*see above*) in a building constructed for the 1894 California Midwinter International Exhibition. But long-range plans are to build a new museum on the current Golden Gate Park site. Construction of the new de Young is scheduled to begin sometime in 2002 and to be completed by 2006. While the new building is under construction, the de Young will use the former space of the Asian Art Museum for temporary exhibitions once the Asian moves to its new Civic Center location in 2002. *John F. Kennedy and Tea Garden Drs. near 10th Ave. and Fulton St., Golden Gate Park, 415/863–3330. Admission: $7, $5 senior citizens, $4 youth 12–17, children under 12 free; $2 discount with Muni transfer; free 1st Wed. of month. Closed Mon.*

4 u-2

MUSEO ITALO-AMERICANO

The Museo Italo-Americano promotes Italian-American culture with a range of traveling exhibitions and events. The Museo began in North Beach, upstairs over Caffè Malvina, and what it lacks in size it makes up for in enthusiasm. Events such as Carnevale, Italian language classes, Italian regional food competitions, CIAO (Children's Italian Art Outreach), and a Frank Capra film festival demonstrate its devotion to La Dolce Vita. An important work of the rotating permanent collection is Arnaldo Pomodoro's bronze sculpture *Tavola della Memoria II* (1961). *Fort Mason Center, Bldg. C, Marina Blvd. at Laguna St., Marina, 415/673–2200. Admission: $3, $2 senior citizens and students; free 1st Wed. of month. Closed Mon.–Tues.*

3 e-7

OAKLAND MUSEUM
OF CALIFORNIA

Focusing on environment, history, and art, specifically as they relate to California, the Oakland Museum has a populist feel. It's housed in an innovative, multilevel building near Lake Merritt, and has separate sections devoted to natural history, local history, and visual arts, with excellent collections in each section. Temporary exhibits almost always have alluring themes: "History of Bicycles," "150 Years of Photography," and Woodie Guthrie. Take time to walk around the museum's terraced gardens and the nearby Sculpture Court (1111 Broadway, at Oakland City Center) for a look at some surprisingly beautiful assemblages. *1000 Oak St., at 10th St., Oakland, 510/238–2200. Admission: $6, $4 senior citizens and students, free children under 6; free 2nd Sun. of month. Closed Mon.–Tues.*

4 *e-4*

PACIFIC HERITAGE MUSEUM

The museum was established in 1984 by the Bank of Canton and is housed in the landmark U.S. Subtreasury Building, built in 1875. Selected exhibits highlight the artistic, cultural, and economic history of the Pacific Rim, rotating displays of rare art and artifacts from China, Taiwan, Japan, and Thailand. Past exhibitions have featured private collections of furniture, paintings, vases, ceramics, and calligraphy. *608 Commercial St., at Montgomery St., Chinatown, 415/399–1124. Admission free. Closed Sun.–Mon.*

4 *a-2*

SAN FRANCISCO AFRICAN-AMERICAN HISTORICAL AND CULTURAL SOCIETY

Although its collection has primarily a cultural and historical bent (*see* History Museums, *below*), the society also has an art gallery with works by African and African-American artists.

4 *a-2*

SAN FRANCISCO CRAFT AND FOLK ART MUSEUM

The changing exhibits of material culture serve as anthropology lessons, explaining the role of items ranging from ceremonial headdresses to religious shrines. Thematic shows of folk art, tribal art, and contemporary crafts from around the world span two levels at this tiny but elegant space. *Fort Mason Center, Bldg. A, Marina Blvd. and Laguna St., Marina, 415/775–0990. Admission: $3, $1 senior citizens, students, and youth 12–17; free children under 12; free Sat. 10 AM–noon and first Wed. of month 11–7. Closed Mon.*

4 *f-6*

SAN FRANCISCO MUSEUM OF MODERN ART (SFMOMA)

San Francisco Chronicle columnist Herb Caen compared the building's controversial design to "a giant toaster extruding a cheese Danish." Architect Mario Botta's creation was completed in 1995, consisting of a stepped-back, sienna brick facade and a central tower constructed of alternating bands of black and white stone. Inside, a central atrium admits natural light, and a stone staircase leads to the galleries. Traveling exhibits and films are a big part of the museum's adventurous programming agenda. The permanent collection includes works by Henri Matisse, Pablo Picasso, Georgia O'Keeffe, Frida Kahlo, Jackson Pollock, and Andy Warhol, along with respected photography, media arts, and design departments. There is also a museum store as well as a comfortable, reasonably priced café. *151 3rd St., between Mission and Howard Sts., South of Market, 415/357–4000. Admission: $9, $6 senior citizens, $5 students, free children under 13; half price Thurs. 6 PM–9 PM. Closed Wed.*

SAN JOSE MUSEUM OF ART

San Jose's museum has a vast permanent collection of 20th-century artwork, with an emphasis on post-1980 Bay Area artists. Mediums include sculpture, painting, prints, drawing, and large-scale multimedia installations, and feature artists such as Dale Chihuly, Deborah Oropallo, and Wayne Thiebaud. One portion of the museum is housed in a former post office and is connected to a new contemporary wing. On Thursday the museum stays open until 8 PM. *110 S. Market St., at San Fernando St., San Jose, 408/294–2787. Admission: $7, $4 senior citizens and students, free children under 6; free 1st Thurs. of month. Closed Mon.*

4 *f-6*

ZEUM ART & TECHNOLOGY CENTER

This museum in the Yerba Buena Gardens complex is designed for children ages 8 to 18, who can choose from a number of activities: creating computer animation, producing a multimedia show, experimenting with digital photography, and building a Web site. Changing exhibits leave much to be desired: one interactive piece promises "Tilt! is a 'multimedia fun house' in which nothing works quite the way you expect it," and displays items like a gigantic washing machine with linens spinning out of control to demonstrate "the current state of world disorder, all from the perspective of a middle-class Western household." However, this notion is made doubly ironic by the fact that the mechanical components of half the pieces don't work. *221 4th St., at Howard St., South of Market, 415/777–2800. Admission: $7, $6 seniors and students, $5 youth 5–18, free children under 5.*

BRIDGES

1 *b-3*

GOLDEN GATE BRIDGE

Since 1937, the Golden Gate Bridge has connected San Francisco with Marin County, and in the process has awed countless sightseers with its distinctive rust color and sleek Art Deco design. Created by Joseph Strauss, at 1.7 mi including its approaches, this is one of the longest suspension bridges in the world. It's also one of the strongest, made to withstand winds of more than 100 mph and the onslaught of some 40 million vehicles per year. This strength was put to the test in 1987 when the bridge was closed to cars and pedestrians were invited to walk across to celebrate the GGB's 50th anniversary. A half-million people packed the structure, dropping the level of the bridge 15 ft. Minus the crowd, walking across the bridge is the best way to experience the amazing views. (It's about a 50-minute journey one way; bundle up against wind gusts and mists.) The two raised sidewalks are open to pedestrians daily from 5 AM until 9 PM and to bicyclists 24 hours daily; follow posted instructions as to which walkway, east or west, to use. You can park near the toll stations on the San Francisco side, or at Vista Point on the Marin side. If you cross by car, note that the $3 toll is paid only on the southbound approach into the city. *U.S. 101 Hwy.*

4 *h-8*

"LEFTY" O'DOUL BRIDGE

Formerly known as the 3rd Street Bridge, this structure was designed by Joseph Strauss, the designer of the Golden Gate Bridge. It's the city's only drawbridge, and a beauty, too. The bridge is still raised and lowered so crafts may pass from the Mission Creek Marina into China Basin and the San Francisco Bay. In 1999, the bridge underwent major seismic retrofitting and an updating of controls and mechanisms, and got upgraded pedestrian walkways leading to the new ballpark. *3rd St. near Berry St., South of Market.*

1 *c-3, d-3*

SAN FRANCISCO–OAKLAND BAY BRIDGE

Charles H. Purcell's design is considered less glamorous than the Golden Gate Bridge; however, it opened six months earlier and is nearly five times as long. Connecting San Francisco and Oakland, the Bay Bridge stretches 8¼ mi, making it one of the longest steel bridges in the world. The twin suspension bridge runs from the city to Yerba Buena Island in the middle of the bay, and cantilever and truss spans complete the bridge to Oakland. A major retrofitting is underway for the western portion leading from San Francisco, scheduled to be completed in 2007. An entirely new eastern span will be built, and then the old span will be torn down. A $2 toll is collected from westbound traffic only. *I–80.*

CEMETERIES

7 *h-2*

MISSION DOLORES CEMETERY

This picturesque walled cemetery is one of the oldest sites in San Francisco. Ornate tombstones—bordered by wrought-iron fences and colorful nasturtiums—tell the story of the city's early history: the names of Spanish and Mexican pioneers and Irish immigrants who died young as a result of the harsh life in the territory. Among the San Francisco notables buried here are Don Francisco de Haro, San Francisco's first mayor, and Don Luis Antonio Arguello, the first governor of Alta California. Kim Novak paid a memorable visit in the 1958 Alfred Hitchcock thriller *Vertigo*. The $2 admission fee is good for entrance to both the cemetery and the adjacent Mission Dolores (*see* Architecture & Historic Sites, *above*). *Dolores and 16th Sts., Mission District, 415/621–8203.*

5 *c-2*

PRESIDIO PET CEMETERY

The Presidio is home to one of the most unique sites in San Francisco. Since the 1940s, military personnel stationed at the base have buried their beloved departed pets in this small plot shaded by a grove of pine trees. Tombstones run the gamut from hand-carved wooden dog biscuits to engraved granite, and messages like this one say it all: "Skipper/ The best damned dog we ever had/ 1967." *Chrissy Field Ave. at McDowell Ave., Presidio.*

5 *e-7*

SAN FRANCISCO COLUMBARIUM

Laid to rest on the four ornately decorated stories of this fine 1898 burial vault are some of San Francisco's most illustrious families: the Magnins, Folgers, Turks, and Eddys. *1 Loraine Ct., off Anza St. between Arguello Blvd. and Stanyan St., Richmond District, 415/752–7891.*

5 *c-3, d-3*

SAN FRANCISCO NATIONAL CEMETERY

Just west of the Main Post in the Presidio is a cypress-shaded 19th-century cemetery that is the final resting place for some 30,000 American servicemen and women. Headstones here predate the Civil War. Contact the Presidio Visitors Center (415/561–4323) for information about occasional docent-led walking tours of the cemetery. *Lincoln Blvd. at Sheridan Ave., Presidio, 415/561–2008.*

CHURCHES, SYNAGOGUES & TEMPLES

4 *e-4*

BUDDHA'S UNIVERSAL CHURCH

This five-story temple, completed in 1961, was hand built using exotic woods. It's decorated with tile mosaics and murals and topped with a roof garden. The church is open to visitors on the second and fourth Sunday of the month, except in February and March, when it presents a bilingual costume play on Saturday and Sunday to celebrate the Chinese New Year. *720 Washington St., at Kearny St., Chinatown, 415/982–6116.*

4 *d-6*

GLIDE MEMORIAL UNITED METHODIST CHURCH

The dynamic Reverend Cecil Williams has made this the city's most famous church, known for its gospel and rock-and-roll services with a funky band and choir. It's also respected widely for its social programs; among them are a daily free meal program, an HIV/AIDS project, a families in crisis center, recovery programs for men and women, and women's health services. Sunday services at 9 and 11 AM are a joyous experience. *330 Ellis St., at Taylor St., Tenderloin, 415/771–6300.*

4 *d-5*

GRACE CATHEDRAL

It took 53 years to build this grand Gothic cathedral, the seat of the Episcopal Church in San Francisco, on the site of Charles Crocker's mansion. The east entrance doors were taken from casts of Ghiberti's *Gates of Paradise*, which are on doors to the famed Baptistery in Florence, Italy. The twin towers are 170 ft high, and the north tower contains 44 working bells. The AIDS Memorial Chapel, dedicated in 1995, contains a sculpture by the late artist Keith Haring and rotating panels from the AIDS Memorial Quilt. The church's ⅓-mi-long Labyrinth is a replica of the 13th-century stone labyrinth on the floor of the Chartres Cathedral. Visitors are welcome for the singing of vespers every Sunday at 3:30 PM or Thursday at 5:15 PM. Guided tours of the cathedral are free (donations accepted). *1100 California St., at Taylor St., Nob Hill, 415/749–6310.*

4 *b-4*

HOLY TRINITY ORTHODOX CATHEDRAL

The oldest Eastern Orthodox church in the country was founded in 1857. Tours are available by appointment. *1520 Green St., at Van Ness Ave., Pacific Heights, 415/673–8565.*

4 *e-4*

KONG CHOW TEMPLE

America's oldest Chinese Buddhist temple was established in 1851 and moved to its present location in 1977. Amid the statuary, flowers, richly colored altars (red signifies "virility," green "longevity," and gold "majesty"), and plumes of incense are a pair of plaques announcing that MRS. HARRY S. TRUMAN CAME TO THIS TEMPLE IN JUNE 1948 FOR A PREDICTION ON THE OUTCOME OF THE ELECTION. . . THIS FORTUNE CAME TRUE. A $1 donation is requested. *855 Stockton St., 4th floor, at Clay St., Chinatown, 415/434–2513.*

7 *h-2*

MISSION DOLORES

See Architecture & Historic Sites, *above.*

4 *e-5*

OLD ST. MARY'S CATHEDRAL

Built of granite quarried in China, this structure was dedicated in 1854 and served as the city's first and only Catholic cathedral until 1891. It survived both the 1906 quake and a 1966 fire. Look for classical chamber music concerts on Tuesday and Thursday afternoon, following noontime mass (*see* Concert Halls *in* Chapter 5). *660 California St., at Grant Ave., Chinatown, 415/777–3211 for concert information.*

4 *b-6*

ST. MARY'S CATHEDRAL

In 1962 a devastating fire destroyed the 72-year-old mother church of the city's Catholic archdiocese. To replace it an ultramodern Catholic house of worship was designed in the Italian travertine style by a team of local architects and Pierre Nervi of Rome. It was dedicated in 1971 and affectionately dubbed by locals "Our Lady of the Maytag" for its resemblance to an old-fashioned washing-machine agitator. The four magnificent 139-ft-long stained-glass windows that cross in the massive dome represent the elements: the blue north windows, water, the light-color south windows, sun, the red west windows, fire; and the green east windows, earth. Above the altar is a spectacular freestanding sculpture by Robert Lippold made of 7,000 aluminum rods that symbolize ascendant prayer. *1111 Gough St., at Geary St., Japantown, 415/567–2020.*

4 *e-3*

STS. PETER AND PAUL CHURCH

The splendid Romanesque church on Washington Square is also known as the Italian National Cathedral. Completed in 1924, it has a pair of fanciful turreted stone towers that are local landmarks. Sunday masses are said here in English, Italian, and Chinese. On the first Sunday of October a mass followed by a parade to Fisherman's Wharf celebrates the annual Blessing of the Fleet. *666 Filbert St., at Powell St. facing Washington Square Park, North Beach, 415/421–0809.*

5 *f-5*

SWEDENBORGIAN CHURCH

This beautifully detailed 1894 church is the stunning product of the California Arts and Crafts movement. Bruce Porter provided the original design and the stained-glass windows, and Bernard Maybeck was responsible for the pegged wooden chairs with seats of woven rushes—said by Gustav Stickley to be the inspiration for his Mission-style furniture. The roof is supported by rough-hewn trunks of madrone trees and shelters a giant brick fireplace. Adjacent to the church is a raised, walled garden full of flowers, shrubs, and trees from every continent. *2107 Lyon St., at Washington St., Pacific Heights, 415/346–6466.*

5 *d-6*

TEMPLE EMANU-EL

Temple Emanu-El's congregation dates from 1850. The current building, a striking Levantine design combining Byzantine, Roman, and Mediterranean influences, was dedicated in 1926. Within the impressive 150-ft domed interior are several stained-glass windows depicting Fire and Water; these were created in 1972 to 1973 by San Francisco artist Mark Adams. Tours are given weekdays. *2 Lake St., at Arguello Blvd., Laurel Heights, 415/751-2535.*

4 *a-3*

VEDANTA SOCIETY OLD TEMPLE

This 1905 structure, the first Hindu temple in the West, is a pastiche of colonial, Queen Anne, Moorish, and Hindu opulence; its turrets are oddly juxtaposed with onion domes and Victorian detailing. The design is appropriate: Vedanta, the highest of the six Hindu systems of religious philosophy, maintains that all religions are paths to one goal. The interior is closed to visitors. *2963 Webster St., at Filbert St., Cow Hollow.*

HISTORY MUSEUMS

4 *d-4*

CABLE CAR MUSEUM

Not only is this a museum, but it's also the control center for the city's famous cable car system. From the mezzanine gallery you'll see (and hear) the four sets of huge power wheels that drive the entire system. You can also go downstairs for a glimpse of the cables running under the city streets. A 15-minute video describes how the system works (cables must be replaced every 75 to 250 days!); the design is so simple it seems almost unreal. The museum is chockfull of photographs, scale models, signposts, ticketing machines, diagrams, drawings, and vintage cars—including cable car inventor Andrew Hallidie's prototype car dating from 1873. It's all housed in a tri-level redbrick cable car barn, circa 1907—the last of some 14 cable car barns that once operated around the city. *1201 Mason St., at Washington St., Nob Hill, 415/474–1887. Admission free.*

FREEBIES

There's no admission charge at the following history museums:

Cable Car Museum
  Control center for the city's famous cable car system.

Chinese Historical Society of America
  The history of Chinese immigrants and their descendants.

Musée Mécanique
  Antique toys and carnival gadgets (bring quarters to operate them).

**Museum of Money
of the American West**
  A mini-museum at the Union Bank of California.

National Maritime Museum
  Ship models, carved figureheads, maps, and more.

Pacific Heritage Museum
  Rare art and artifacts from Asian nations.

Presidio Museum
  History of the city's military base in the midst of a national park.

Randall Museum
  Children's museum with hands-on nature and science exhibits.

San Francisco History Center
  Small history museum at the San Francisco Main Library.

Wells Fargo Museum
  Gold mining tools and treasures, and an old Concord stagecoach.

---

4 *f-6*
CALIFORNIA HISTORICAL SOCIETY

The state's official historical society, founded in 1871, has amassed an awesome collection of Californiana: some 500,000 photographs; 150,000 manuscripts; thousands of books, periodicals, prints, and paintings; and Gold Rush paraphernalia. The building itself is a former hardware store converted to an airy, skylighted space with a central gallery, two adjacent galleries, the North Baker Research Library, and a storefront bookstore. Exhibitions, all exploring California's history, change every two to three months. Call before visiting, as the galleries close between exhibitions. *678 Mission St., at 3rd St., South of Market, 415/357–1848. Admission: $2, $1 senior citizens and students. Closed Sun.–Mon.*

4 *f-4*
CHINESE HISTORICAL SOCIETY OF AMERICA

The fascinating Chinese Historical Society moved to the historic Chinatown YWCA building (*see* Architecture & Historic Sites, *above*) in 1999. Photos and graphics, accompanied by moving explanations, document the little-publicized history of Chinese immigrants and their descendants from the early 1800s to the present. Among other artifacts, you'll view an altar built in the 1880s and a parade dragon head from 1909. *644 Broadway St., between Grant and Stockton Sts., 415/391–1188. Admission free (donations requested). Closed Sun.–Mon.*

5 *a-1*
FORT POINT NATIONAL HISTORIC SITE

This historic site has been converted to a museum of military memorabilia (*see* Architecture & Historic Sites, *above*).

4 *c-2*
HYDE STREET PIER

Between the Cannery and Ghirardelli Square is this bustling pier, one of the best bargains at Fisherman's Wharf. The highlight of the pier is its collection of fully restored historic ships, all of which can be boarded. The ***Balclutha*** is an 1886 full-rigged, three-mast sailing vessel that was built in Scotland and sailed around Cape Horn 17 times; comedian Jonathan Winters was once briefly institutionalized

In case you want to see the world.

At American Express, we're here to make your journey a smooth one. So we have over 1,700 travel service locations in over 130 countries ready to help. What else would you expect from the world's largest travel agency?

do more   AMERICAN EXPRESS

In case you want to be welcomed there.

We're here to see that you're always welcomed at establishments everywhere. That's why millions of people carry the American Express® Card – for peace of mind, confidence, and security, around the world or just around the corner.

do more

Cards

To apply, call 1 800 THE-CARD
or visit www.americanexpress.com

In case you're running low.

We're here to help with more than 190,000 Express Cash locations around the world. In order to enroll, just call American Express at 1 800 CASH-NOW before you start your vacation.

do more

Express Cash

And in case you'd rather be safe than sorry.

We're here with American Express® Travelers Cheques.

They're the safe way to carry money on your vacation,

because if they're ever lost or stolen you can get a refund,

practically anywhere or anytime. To find the nearest

place to buy Travelers Cheques, call 1 800 495-1153.

Another way we help you do more.

do more **AMERICAN EXPRESS**

Travelers Cheques

after he climbed its mast and hung from it, shouting "I am the man in the moon!" The newly restored 1890 paddle-wheel ferry **Eureka** once carried passengers around the waters of San Francisco Bay. The 1895 three-master schooner **C. A. Thayer** was used to transport lumber, whereas the 1891 schooner **Alma** hauled hay. Hyde Street Pier is part of the San Francisco Maritime National Historical Park, which also includes the National Maritime Museum (see below). At the foot of Hyde St. off Jefferson St., Fisherman's Wharf, 415/556–3002. Admission: $4, $2 youth 12–17, free senior citizens and children under 11, $7 Family Ticket (2 adults and up to 4 youth or children), $19 Combo Family Ticket (2 adults and up to 4 youth or children for both Hyde St. Pier and USS Pampanito).

2 a-3

MUSÉE MÉCANIQUE

This quirky penny arcade museum brims with antique mechanical games and carnival contrivances: player pianos, peep shows, pinball machines, marionettes, nickelodeons, and a mechanical laughing lady. Bring a roll of quarters to play with all the old gadgets, and don't miss the miniature amusement park built out of toothpicks by San Quentin inmates. Step outside to take a peek at the Farallon Islands, 30 mi offshore, through the magical lens of the museum's camera obscura. 1090 Point Lobos Ave., at Great Hwy., Richmond District, 415/386–1170. Admission free.

11 e-2

MUSEUM OF THE CITY OF SAN FRANCISCO

The first independent museum on the history of the city displays historic items, maps, and photographs, including the 700-pound head of the Goddess of Progress statue, which was removed from City Hall in 1909 due to damage from the 1906 earthquake. Other exhibits trace the history of Chinatown, Golden Gate Park, and the Sutro Baths, as well as the earthquakes of 1906 and 1989. The Cannery, 3rd floor, 2801 Leavenworth St., at Beach St., Fisherman's Wharf, 415/928–0289. Suggested donation: $2. Closed Mon.–Tues.

4 f-5

MUSEUM OF MONEY OF THE AMERICAN WEST

The Union Bank of California operates this mini-museum in their Financial District branch. Exhibits tell the story of banking in the Old West, and include samples of privately minted money used before the U.S. Mint was established. There's also a display of counterfeit coins and detection devices. 400 California St., at Sansome St., Financial District, 415/765–0400. Admission free.

4 b-2

NATIONAL MARITIME MUSEUM

Housed in a sturdy, round Art Deco structure, this museum exhibits painstakingly crafted ship models, photographs, carved figureheads, scrimshaw, diaries, maps, ship's logs, and other artifacts chronicling the development of San Francisco and the West Coast through maritime history. The museum is part of the San Francisco Maritime National Historical Park, which also includes Hyde Street Pier (see above). 900 Beach St., at Polk St., Fisherman's Wharf, 415/556–3002. Admission free (donation requested).

2 f-2

OCTAGON HOUSE

The National Society of Colonial Dames operates a charming little museum inside this unusual eight-sided house (see Architecture & Historic Sites, above), with antique American furniture, decorative arts (paintings, silver, and rugs), and documents from the Colonial and Federal periods. It's open only on the second Sunday and the second and fourth Thursday of the month. 2645 Gough St., at Union St., Pacific Heights, 415/441–7512. Donation requested. Closed Jan.

5 e-3

PRESIDIO MUSEUM

The Presidio Museum is housed in a circa-1860 former hospital, the oldest building on the base put up by the U.S. Army. Its collection illustrates the role of the military in the development of San Francisco from 1776 to the present. Behind the museum are two "earthquake cottages" that were used to house refugees from the 1906 earthquake and fire—5,000 such structures filled the Presidio and Golden Gate Park following the disaster. Lincoln Blvd. at Funston Ave., Presidio, 415/561–4331. Admission free. Closed Mon.–Tues.

`4` *a-2*

SAN FRANCISCO AFRICAN-AMERICAN HISTORICAL AND CULTURAL SOCIETY

The only museum of black culture on the West Coast has a research library (*see* Libraries, *below*), an art gallery, and permanent exhibits on the history of blacks in California and in the Civil War. An intriguing gift shop sells jewelry and artifacts. *Fort Mason Center, Bldg. C, Marina Blvd. at Laguna St., Marina, 415/441–0640. Admission: $2, $1 senior citizens and students. Closed Mon.–Tues.*

`4` *c-7*

SAN FRANCISCO HISTORY CENTER AT THE SAN FRANCISCO MAIN LIBRARY

The main branch of the San Francisco Public Library maintains a small history museum with frequently changing exhibits on its sixth floor. The focus is usually on book arts, such as calligraphy and illustration, as well as rare books and special editions. *Larkin St. at Grove St., Civic Center, 415/557–4400 for Main Library, or 415/557–4567 for San Francisco History Center. Admission free. Closed Mon.*

`4` *h-6*

SS JEREMIAH O'BRIEN (NATIONAL LIBERTY SHIP MEMORIAL)

Of a great fleet used to carry troops and supplies to Normandy, this is the last unaltered World War II Liberty Ship freighter that is still seaworthy. On board, volunteers answer questions and lead tours. To keep the ship in sailing shape, its steam engine is fired up dockside on special "steaming weekends" (the third weekend of the month). Full-day bay tours depart during Fleet Week and Memorial Day Weekend (*see* Boat Tours, *below*). *Pier 32 at the foot of Brannan St., South of Market, 415/441–3101. Admission: $5, $3 senior citizens, $2 youth 10–18, $1 children under 10.*

`1` *d-2, d-3*

TREASURE ISLAND MUSEUM

The museum on Treasure Island presents highlights of the three sea services—the Navy, the Marines, and the Coast Guard—from 1813 to the present. Other exhibits take a look at the Golden Gate International Exposition of 1939–40, the China Clipper flying boats of the '30s, and the history of Treasure Island, the only manmade island in San Francisco Bay. The superb views of San Francisco and the bridges are reason enough to make the trip. *410 Ave. of Palms, Treasure Island, 415/395–5067. Suggested donation: $3.*

`4` *c-1*

USS PAMPANITO WORLD WAR II SUBMARINE

Built in 1943, this 312-ft-long submarine saw plenty of action in the Pacific during World War II. These days it's a floating museum where you can go below deck to explore the crew quarters, galley, and control room. The admission fee includes an excellent self-guided audio tour. *Pier 45 at the foot of Taylor St., Fisherman's Wharf, 415/929–0202. Admission: $5, $3 senior citizens and children 6–12, $15 Family Ticket (2 adults and up to 4 youth under 18), $19 Combo Family Ticket (2 adults and up to 4 youth under 18 for both USS Pampanito and Hyde St. Pier).*

`4` *f-4*

WELLS FARGO MUSEUM

For a short course in the history of Wells Fargo, California's oldest bank (it opened its first San Francisco branch in 1852), as well as a look at the picturesque Pony Express and Gold Rush–era banking practices, visit this small museum on the street level of Wells Fargo Bank's headquarters. The showpiece is a century-old Concord stagecoach that in the mid-1850s carried 18 passengers from St. Joseph, Missouri, to San Francisco in three weeks. The museum also displays samples of nuggets and gold dust from mines, a mural-size map of the Mother Lode, mementos of the poet bandit Black Bart ("Po8," as he signed his poems), an old telegraph machine on which you can practice sending codes, and many other artifacts. *420 Montgomery St., between California and Sacramento Sts., Financial District, 415/396–2619. Admission free. Closed weekends.*

LIBRARIES

`4` *c-5*

ALLIANCE FRANCAISE

The alliance contains 25,000 volumes in French—mostly literature. *1345 Bush St., at Polk St., Nob Hill, 415/775–7755. Admission free. Closed Sun.*

`4` *c-7*

BLIND AND PRINT HANDICAPPED LIBRARY

More than 6,000 four-track cassette tapes are available at the Blind and Print Handicapped Library, part of the Library of Congress. It is housed in the San Francisco Main Library (*see below*). *100 Larkin St., between Fulton and Grove Sts., Civic Center, 415/557–4253. Admission free. Closed weekends.*

`4` *g-7*

CALIFORNIA GENEALOGICAL SOCIETY

Here is an extensive collection for those interested in tracing their ancestors. *300 Brannan St., Suite 409, at 2nd St., South Beach, 415/777–9936. Admission: $5 nonmembers, $35 annual membership. Closed Mon., Tues., Fri., and Sun.*

`4` *e-5*

GOETHE INSTITUT

The Goethe Institut's library contains some 12,000 items—books, magazines, newspapers, CDs, videos—of or about Germany. Most of the collection is in German. *530 Bush St., at Grant Ave., Union Square, 415/391–0428. Admission free. Closed Sat.–Mon.*

`7` *a-2*

HELEN CROCKER RUSSELL LIBRARY OF HORTICULTURE

The Strybing Arboretum and Botanical Gardens (*see Gardens, in Chapter 3*) operates this horticultural library, whose 18,000-plus volumes make it the largest such collection in northern California. *9th Ave. and Lincoln Way, Golden Gate Park, 415/661–1316. Admission free.*

`7` *a-1*

MAILLARD REFERENCE LIBRARY

Within the California Academy of Sciences (*see Science Museums, below*) is the Mailliard Reference Library, with 180,000 natural sciences volumes, plus CD-ROM databases and, in its Special Collections department, more than 1 million visual and audio items such as slides, photos, magazine articles, and videotapes. There is a small lending library here as well. *Music Concourse, near John F. Kennedy and Tea Garden Drs., Golden Gate Park, 415/750–7102 for Mailliard Library, 415/750–7122 for Special Collections. Admission free. Closed weekends.*

`4` *a-2*

NATIONAL MARITIME MUSEUM LIBRARY

Operated by the National Maritime Museum, this library at Fort Mason Center is a reference center and public reading room, with more than 25,000 books, newspapers clippings, and pamphlets relating to naval history. There's also a large collection of ship plans, and some 250,000 photographs. *Fort Mason Center, Bldg. E, 3rd floor, Marina Blvd. at Laguna St., Marina, 415/556–9870. Admission free. Closed Sun.–Mon.*

`4` *f-6*

NORTH BAKER RESEARCH LIBRARY

The California Historical Society's research library, open by appointment only on Wednesday, has 35,000 books and pamphlets dating from 1535 to the present; 150,000 manuscript items; a 500,000-piece photographic collection; a collection of *The San Francisco Chronicle* dating from 1906; and maps, posters, periodicals, newspapers, microfilm, and ephemera. *678 Mission St., at 3rd St., South of Market, 415/357–1848. Admission: $5 nonmembers, $3 students.*

`4` *a-2*

SAN FRANCISCO AFRICAN-AMERICAN HISTORICAL AND CULTURAL SOCIETY

The society maintains a research library and historical archive with books, magazines, computer databases, and rare print material. *Fort Mason Center, Bldg. C, Marina Blvd. at Laguna St., Marina, 415/441–0640. Admission: $2, $1 senior citizens and students. Closed Mon.–Tues.*

`4` *c-7*

SAN FRANCISCO MAIN LIBRARY

The new main library, which opened in April 1996, is one of the most technologically advanced in the country: It has 300 computer terminals, many with free access to the Web and the library's CD-ROM databases. The building is a striking, modernized version of the old Beaux Arts library that sits just across Fulton Street (which is scheduled to become the new site of the Asian Art Museum in 2002). In addition to its collection of books, records, and CDs, the new space also contains several specialty rooms, including the Wallace Stegner Environmental Center, an art gallery, a café, a center for people with hearing and visual impairments, a children's library, a gay and lesbian history center, African-American and Asian centers,

WHEN IT'S FREE

What better incentive to brush up on your facts about Degas and Descartes than a free day at one of the Bay Area's better art and science museums?

Asian Art Museum of San Francisco (Art Museums)
Free first Wednesday of the month.

Berkeley Art Museum (Art Museums)
Free every Thursday 11–noon and 5–9.

California Academy of Sciences (Science Museums)
Free first Wednesday of the month, except for Morrison Planetarium and Laserium.

California Palace of the Legion of Honor (Art Museums)
Free second Wednesday of the month.

Center for the Arts (Art Museums)
Free first Thursday of the month 6 PM–8 PM.

Exploratorium (Science Museums)
Free first Wednesday of the month.

Jewish Museum San Francisco (Art Museums)
Free first Monday of the month.

Lawrence Hall of Science (Science Museums)
Free every Thursday, excluding Planetarium shows.

Mexican Museum (Art Museums)
Free first Wednesday of the month.

M. H. de Young Memorial Museum (Art Museums)
Free first Wednesday of the month.

Museo Italo-Americano (Art Museums)
Free first Wednesday of the month.

Oakland Museum of California (Art Museums)
Free second Sunday of the month.

San Francisco Craft and Folk Art Museum (Art Museums)
Free Saturday 10 AM–noon and all day on the first Wednesday of the month.

San Francisco Museum of Modern Art (Art Museums)
Half-price Thursday 6 PM–9 PM.

and a rooftop garden and terrace. The new San Francisco History Room and Archives is full of historic photographs, maps, and other memorabilia. At the library's center is a five-story atrium with a skylight, a grand staircase, and murals painted by local artists. *Larkin St. between Grove and Fulton Sts., Civic Center, 415/557–4400. Admission free.*

7 *b-8*
SAN FRANCISCO PERFORMING ARTS LIBRARY AND MUSEUM (PALM)

This library and research center is a virtual clearinghouse for information on the performing arts world, particularly the performing arts of the Bay Area. It's the largest collection of its kind on the West Coast, with more than 8,000 books and periodicals and nearly 2,000 radio interviews with performers. A small gallery has fascinating quarterly exhibitions of programs, photographs, manuscripts, costumes, and other memorabilia from the collection. PALM also hosts an excellent lecture series. *399 Grove St., at Gough St., Civic Center, 415/255–4800. Admission free. Closed Sun.–Tues.*

SCHOOLS

STANFORD UNIVERSITY

The "Ivy League university of the West Coast," also nicknamed "The Farm," occupies the former 8,180-acre South Bay horse farm of Big Four railroad baron Leland Stanford. Together with his wife, Jane, Mr. Stanford founded the school in 1891 in honor of their beloved only son Leland Stanford, Jr., who died at age 15. Frederick Law Olmsted designed the campus, whose yellow Spanish Mission–style sandstone buildings and red-tile roofs give it a distinctly western feel. Stanford currently enrolls 13,144 students at seven nationally top-ranked schools, and proudly claims a $3.6 billion endowment. Daily campus walking tours take in campus attractions such as the stately Romanesque Memorial Church, known for its Venetian mosaic; 285-ft Hoover Tower, with its observation deck; the Rodin Sculpture Garden, known for its awe-inspiring bronze reproduction of the *Gates of Hell*; the Stanford Museum of Art; and the Stanford Medical Center, one of the country's finest. Science buffs will want to visit the Stanford Linear Accelerator

(SLAC), a research facility with a 2-mi-long electron accelerator used for elementary-particle research. The outdoor Stanford Shopping Center is one of the Bay Area's finest. *University Ave. off Hwy. 101, or Sand Hill Rd. off Hwy. 280, Palo Alto, 650/725-3335.*

3 d-2, e-2

UNIVERSITY OF CALIFORNIA AT BERKELEY

Established in 1868 as the first branch of the statewide University of California system, UC Berkeley is one of the top public academic institutions in the United States, with 300 degree programs and 31,000 students representing every state and some 100 foreign countries. Its wooded, 1,232-acre campus overlooking San Francisco Bay has seen its share of history: At Sproul Plaza, on the west side of campus, the Free Speech Movement began in 1964. Another campus highlight is Sather Tower (more commonly known as the Campanile), a 307-ft clock tower modeled after the one in Venice's Piazza San Marco. On permanent display in the administrative office of Bancroft Library is a gold nugget purported to have started the California Gold Rush when it was discovered on January 24, 1848, at Sutter's Mill. Free campus tours depart daily from the Visitor Center, on the west side of campus (University Hall, Room 101, 2200 University Ave., at Oxford St., 510/642-5215; map 3, d-2); self-guiding tour maps are also available here. *Bancroft Ave. at Telegraph Ave., Berkeley, 510/642-6000.*

SCIENCE MUSEUMS

7 a-1

CALIFORNIA ACADEMY OF SCIENCES

One of the country's top-five natural-history museums, this huge complex is subdivided into several blockbuster sights, including the Morrison Planetarium (*see below*), the excellent Steinhart Aquarium (*see Zoos & Aquariums in* Chapter 3), and the Natural History Museum. The latter has separate halls devoted to plants, animals, gems, and minerals; the most popular among the natural science exhibits is the Hall of Fossils, with dinosaur bones and a brontosaurus skull. One of the best exhibits is the African Hall, depicting animals (real but stuffed) specific to Africa in

their native vegetation; don't miss the sights and sounds of the African watering hole at the end of the room. You can also experience the vibrations of an 8.0-magnitude quake in the "earthquake room" of the Space and Earth Hall; learn the story of evolution from the beginnings of life on earth to the age of mammals in the innovative Life Through Time Hall; or explore the languages, physical features, and learning habits of birds with the Birds of a Feather exhibit. In the Wild California Hall, a 14,000-gallon aquarium tank shows underwater life at the Farallones (islands off the coast of northern California), life-size elephant-seal models, and video information on the wildlife of the state. A cafeteria is open daily until one hour before closing time. *Music Concourse and John F. Kennedy Dr. near 8th Ave. and Fulton St., Golden Gate Park, 415/750-7145. Admission to Natural History Museum and Steinhart Aquarium: $8.50, $5.50 senior citizens and youth 12–17, $2 children 4–11, children under 4 free; $1 discount with Muni transfer; free 1st Wed. of month. Separate admission fee required for Morrison Planetarium and Laserium (see below).*

5 f-2

EXPLORATORIUM

A world-famous interactive museum housed in the Palace of Fine Arts (*see* Architecture & Historic Sites, *above*), the Exploratorium contains more than 650 hands-on exhibits, many computer-assisted, about science and technology. Laser beams, miniature tornadoes, soap bubbles, holograms, microbes, and other interactive exhibits make it a fun place for both children and adults to explore the world of science. Reservations are required for the museum's enormously popular Tactile Dome (415/560-0362), a series of dark, small rooms in which you walk, crawl, and slither through materials of different textures. *3601 Lyon St., between Marina Blvd. and Lombard St., Marina, 415/561-0360 for recorded information. Admission: $9, $7 senior citizens, $5 youth 6–17, $2.50 children 3–5, free children under 3; $12 Tactile Dome; free 1st Wed. of the month. Labor Day–Memorial Day, closed Mon. (except holidays).*

3 f-1

LAWRENCE HALL OF SCIENCE

The University of California at Berkeley's Lawrence Hall of Science is a memorial to Ernest O. Lawrence, the university's first Nobel laureate and an inventor of the atomic bomb. Its exhibits are mostly

---

MUSEUMS FOR KIDS OF ALL AGES

San Francisco offers a bevy of collections and activities that will appeal to youngsters:

Cartoon Art Museum (Art Museums)
A special children's gallery features cartoon characters from "Peanuts," activities, and classes.

Exploratorium (Science Museums)
Hands-on opportunities to learn about everything from soap bubbles to tornadoes.

Laserium (Science Museums)
Young and old rockers enjoy laser light shows choreographed to classics like Dark Side of the Moon.

M. H. de Young Memorial Museum (Art Museums)
Gallery One is just for kids, with free Saturday art classes for ages 3 through 12.

Morrison Planetarium (Science Museums)
For children ages 6 to 8, the Neighbors in Space exhibit offers the Sky Show starring real stars, the moon, and planets.

Musée Mécanique (History Museums)
Children play with the types of toys that amused their grandparents.

Museo Italo-Americano (Art Museums)
CIAO (Children's Italian Art Outreach) provides free instruction in Italian art and culture.

Natural History Museum/ California Academy of Sciences (Science Museums)
Climb a platform to view T. Rex, see a taxidermic gorilla, and build a structure and test it for earthquake stamina.

Randall Museum (Science Museums)
On Saturday children can see the model railroad exhibit, participate in drop-in classes, or see live native California animals up close.

Zeum Art & Technology Center (Art Museums)
Children ages 8 to 18 experiment with technology.

---

hands-on and geared toward children, with an emphasis on biology, chemistry, and astronomy. On weekends, and daily during summer, you can catch films, lectures, laboratory demonstrations, and planetarium shows. A wind organ, a set of 36 long, slender pipes, sticks out of the ground in the hillside beyond the rear patio: you'll hear their music if you walk among them when the wind is blowing. You can also play with their tones by turning one of six moveable pipes. On clear Saturday nights from 8 PM to 11 PM, employees and amateur local astronomers bring their telescopes here to give you a free peek at the moon, planets, star clusters, and galaxies; call the Hall's Astronomy and Night Sky Information Line (510/642–5132) for details. *Centennial Dr. near Grizzly Peak Blvd., Berkeley, 510/642–5132. Admission: $6, $4 senior citizens and students, $2 children 3–6; free Thurs.*

7 *a-1*

MORRISON PLANETARIUM/ LASERIUM

For astronomy buffs, the Morrison Planetarium presents one-hour sky shows daily on the 65-ft dome of the Sky Theater. Discussions range from scientific explanations of the night sky to the mythology behind it. Laser light shows, accompanied by tunes from such bands as the Doors, the Rolling Stones, and Pink Floyd, are held most evenings at the Laserium and some days at the Morrison Planetarium. The Laserium is also the venue for special 3-D shows. *Music Concourse and John F. Kennedy Dr. near 8th Ave. and Fulton St., Golden Gate Park, 415/750–7141 for Planetarium, 415/750–7138 for Laserium. Admission: Planetarium $2.50, $1.25 senior citizens and youth, free children under 5. Laserium $7, $6 senior citizens and students, $4 youth, free children under 5.*

7 *f-2*

RANDALL MUSEUM

This small children's museum in Corona Heights Park near Buena Vista Park features changing hands-on nature and science exhibits, including minerals to touch, dinosaur bones to view, working seismograph, chemistry, and biology labs, exhibits on California Indians, and more. The museum's Animal Room has live owls, snakes, and raccoons that kids can view up close. Saturday classes offer kids and parents fun opportunities like playing Casey Jones while running one of California's largest model trains, art workshops, hikes, and nature classes. *199 Museum Way, at Roosevelt Way, Castro, 415/554–9600. Admission free. Closed Sun.–Mon.*

THE TECH MUSEUM OF INNOVATION

This mango-colored building sitting off Highway 280 is sure to become a Silicon Valley Mecca to technocrats the world over. Nearly all the exhibits at the Tech are original or custom designed, letting you experiment with millions of dollars worth of computer technology by using interactive, cutting-edge tools such as the Space Station Simulator software. The museum's 132,000 square ft of space is shared by four major theme galleries, an educational center for workshops, and the Hackworth IMAX Dome Theater. *201 South Market St., at Park Ave., near I–280 and Hwy. 87, San Jose, 408/795–6100. Admission: $8, $7 senior citizens, $6 children 3–12, free children under 3.*

STATUES, MURALS & MONUMENTS

8 *b-5*

BALMY ALLEY

In the tradition of the great Mexican muralist Diego Rivera, Mission District artists have transformed their neighborhood with message-minded paintings on walls, buildings, fences, and alleys. The best example is the one-block Balmy Alley, filled with a series of murals. A group of local children working with adults started the project in 1971; since then, dozens of artists have steadily added to it, with the predominant themes being peace in Central America, community pride, and AIDS awareness. (Be extremely alert here: the north end of Balmy Alley adjoins the back of a severely crime-ridden and dangerous housing project.) *Bordered by 24th, 25th, and Harrison Sts. and Treat Ave., Mission District.*

6 *b-1*

BEACH CHALET

The Beach Chalet's sweeping murals depicting San Francisco city life were added in the 1930s by famed French artist Lucien Labaudt, with funding from the WPA Federal Art Project. Labaudt covered almost the entire interior of the chalet—a roughly 1,500-square-ft surface—with frescoes done in 9-ft-high panels. There are scenes of picnickers and swimmers at Ocean Beach, fishermen at the Wharf, and the construction of the Bay Bridge; many of the subjects are famous people of the day, or friends and relations of Labaudt. Sculptor Michael Von Meyer created the whimsical sea-creature motifs on the carved wood staircase. (*See* also Architecture & Historic Sites, *above*.) *1000 Great Hwy., at John F. Kennedy Dr., Golden Gate Park.*

7 *h-1*

CALIFORNIA VOLUNTEERS' MEMORIAL

The 1903 California Volunteers' Memorial is a classic equestrian statue of a heroic rider—complete with raised sword—mounted on a charging steed. Douglas Tilden, perhaps the city's most talented outdoor sculptor, was the designer; heavyweight architect Willis Polk is responsible for the base. Behind the statue commences the grand stretch of Dolores Street, with a stately row of palm trees along its median strip. *Dolores St. at Market St., Mission District.*

4 *g-7*

CAPP STREET PROJECT

The highly regarded Capp Street Project sponsors three controversial murals South of Market. *Inner City Home* (6th and Brannan Sts., South of Market; map 4, f-8) comments on homelessness; *One Tree* (10th and Brannan Sts., South of Market; map 8, c-1) provokes thought about deforestation; and *Extinct* (5th and Folsom Sts., South of Market; map 4, f-7) takes on the issue of endangered animal species. *525 2nd St., between Bryant and Brannan Sts., South of Market, 415/495–7101.*

4 *e-3*

COIT TOWER

Standing in front of Coit Tower is *Discoverer of America,* an impressive bronze statue of Christopher Columbus, donated by the local Italian community in 1957. Inside the tower are 19 WPA-era murals painted by 25 artists depicting California's laborers in a Socialist-Realist style pioneered by Diego Rivera. The U.S. government commissioned the murals as a Public Works of Art project, and the artists were each paid $38 a week. On Saturday morning you can view the second-floor murals that are normally closed to the public by signing up for a tour of

Coit Tower with City Guides (*see* Guided Tours, *below*). An illustrated brochure for sale in the Coit Tower gift shop explains the various murals for those who prefer the self-guided route. *Telegraph Hill Blvd. at Greenwich St., Telegraph Hill, 415/362–0808.*

4 *f-5*

DONAHUE MONUMENT

Holding its own against the skyscrapers that tower over this intersection is the Donahue Monument—an homage to waterfront mechanics created by a noted California sculptor, Douglas Tilden. The plaque below the monument marks the spot as the location of the San Francisco Bay shoreline in 1848. *Market and Battery Sts., Financial District.*

4 *c-7*

DOUBLE L EXCENTRIC GYRATORY

Outside the main entrance to the San Francisco Main Library, spinning slowly in the breezes, is *Double L Excentric Gyratory,* an 18-ft stainless-steel kinetic sculpture by American artist George Rickey. The 1982 artwork consists of two delicately balanced "L"-shape pieces perched atop a "Y"-shape base. The sculpture was a gift of Carl Djerassi, the Stanford University professor who pioneered the birth control pill. He allegedly placed the sculpture in the Civic Center to symbolize "literature, literacy, law, and liberty." *Larkin and Fulton Sts., Civic Center.*

7 *a-1*

FRANCIS SCOTT KEY MONUMENT

Opposite the band shell on Golden Gate Park's Music Concourse stands the impressive Francis Scott Key monument, the first monument in the United States to the author of the *Star Spangled Banner.* Sculpted by William Story, the work was commissioned by the city's philanthropist James Lick in 1888, and was moved several times before coming to rest here. The monument's sides are inscribed with phrases from the song such as "long may it wave." *Music Concourse near John F. Kennedy and Tea Garden Drs., Golden Gate Park.*

2 *b-3*

THE HOLOCAUST

Just north of the California Palace of the Legion of Honor is George Segal's **The Holocaust,** a sobering monument whose white-plaster figures lie sprawled and twisted on the ground, while one lone figure peers out from behind barbed wire. *Lincoln Park, entrance at 34th Ave. and Clement St., 415/750–3600, Richmond District.*

4 *a-6*

JAPAN CENTER FOUNTAINS

At the center of the open-air Japan Center Mall are twin origami-like fountains by local artist Ruth Asawa. Squat, circular structures are made of fieldstone, with three levels for sitting and a brick floor that also serves as a drain. *Buchanan St. between Post and Sutter Sts., Japantown.*

4 *g-4*

JUSTIN HERMAN PLAZA

A favorite with office workers on their lunch breaks, this little plaza is also the delight of admirers of art. In Armand Vaillancourt's huge building-block fountain you can walk under, around, and over streams of falling water. Nearby is Jean Dubuffet's mammoth stainless-steel sculpture, *La Chiffonière. Market and Steuart Sts., South of Market.*

4 *c-8*

LARGE FOUR PIECE RECLINING FIGURE

In front of Davies Symphony Hall is this valuable Henry Moore bronze sculpture, in Moore's trademark abstract style. It is one of only seven editions of this piece completed by the great British artist before his death in 1986. *Van Ness Ave. at Grove St., Civic Center.*

1 *f-6*

LOTTA'S FOUNTAIN

The nondescript Lotta's Fountain has lion's head spigots that no longer function, and the monument receives little attention from passersby as they rush to and fro on Market Street—although it is on the National Register of Historic Places. It was presented to the city in 1875, on the 25th anniversary of California's statehood, by Lotta Crabtree, a Mae West prototype and the most highly paid American singer of her time. Her "brash music-hall exploits" so enthralled San Francisco's early population of miners that they were known to shower her with gold nuggets and silver dollars after her performances.

The buxom Ms. Crabtree is depicted in one of the Anton Refregier murals in Rincon Center (*see below*). *Bordered by 3rd, Market, Kearny, and Geary Sts., Financial District.*

4 *f-6*

MARTIN LUTHER KING, JR. MEMORIAL

The focal point of the Yerba Buena Gardens complex is a Martin Luther King, Jr. Memorial. At the north end of a grassy, spacious esplanade, the memorial consists of 12 glass panels, all behind a shimmering waterfall, engraved with quotes from Dr. King in English and in the languages of each of San Francisco's sister cities. The powerful waterfall is meant to mirror the enduring force of King's words that are carved on the stone walls and on glass blocks behind the waterfall. *Bordered by 3rd, 4th, Mission, and Howard Sts., South of Market.*

7 *f-3*

NAMES PROJECT VISITOR CENTER AND PANELING WORKSHOP

Panels from the *NAMES Quilt*—made as a memorial to those who have died of AIDS—are displayed at the NAMES Project Foundation's Visitor Center and Paneling Workshop.The project started in 1987 when gay rights activist Cleve Jones organized a meeting with several others who had lost friends or lovers to AIDS; they decided on a quilt with each panel made by the loved ones of an individual who has died of AIDS. The gigantic quilt now contains more than 44,000 hand sewn and decorated panels, portions of which are displayed in San Francisco and several other cities around the world. Those who are interested may create a panel during one of the center's weekly "quilting bees," or send one by mail. *2362A Market St., at Castro St., Castro, 415/863–1966.*

4 *f-5*

PACIFIC COAST STOCK EXCHANGE

Flanking the entrance to the Pacific Coast Stock Exchange (*see* Architecture & Historic Sites, *above*) are a pair of 21-ft-tall Art Deco statues, *Earth's Fruitfulness* and *Man's Inventive Genius*, created in 1930. The monumental granite pair are both by Ralph Stackpole. *301 Pine St., at Sansome St., Financial District.*

4 *c-7*

PIONEERS MONUMENT

The city's largest historical monument stands just north of the San Francisco Main Library. The monument was completed in 1894 and stood firm in the 1906 earthquake and fire, even when City Hall was leveled. Historians believe that a time capsule is buried at the base—but nobody knows for sure. The monument's 30-ft-high granite shaft is topped by a bronze figure whose spear, shield, and bear symbolize California. Figures and bas-reliefs at the base depict scenes from early California and important personalities from that time, such as James Fremont, James Lick, Sir Francis Drake, John Sutter, and Father Junípero Serra. *Fulton St. between Larkin and Hyde Sts., Civic Center.*

4 *e-4*

PORTSMOUTH SQUARE

The focal point of this historic square (*see* Architecture & Historic Sites, *above*) is this bronze galleon atop a 9-ft granite shaft. Designed by Bruce Porter, the sculpture was erected in 1919 in memory of Robert Louis Stevenson, who often visited the site during his residence from 1879 to 1880. On the lower level of Portsmouth Square, in the children's play area, is an installation by Mary Fuller of six animal sculptures significant to Chinese astrology: the tiger, ram, serpent, monkey, rabbit, and dragon. *Kearny St. between Washington and Clay Sts., Chinatown.*

8 *h-6*

PRECITA EYES MURAL ARTS CENTER

A nonprofit arts organization begun in 1977, the mural center is the best resource if you are interested in exploring and understanding the approximately 80 murals that can be found within an eight-block area in the south east Mission District, including Balmy Alley (*see above*). Muralists-in-residence lead bus, bike, and walking tours, along with an introductory slide show (*see* Walking Tours, *below*). The center also sells a handy "Mission Mural Walk" map ($1.50 donation). *348 Precita Ave., between Folsom and Harrison Sts., Mission District, 415/285–2287.*

4 g-4
PROMENADE RIBBON
North of the Ferry Building at Pier 5 is the initial section of the 5-ft-wide, 2½-mi-long glass-and-concrete Promenade Ribbon, billed by the city as the "longest art form in the nation." The ribbon spans the waterfront from the base of Telegraph Hill to South Beach. At various points along the way it curls up to form tabletops and park benches; at night it lights up to ensure a safe pathway for pedestrians. *Along the Embarcadero.*

4 g-5
RINCON CENTER
Anton Refregier spent eight years creating the 27-panel mural in the lobby of Rincon Center (*see* Architecture & Historic Sites, *above*). Because it depicts the history of California, including the oppression of Native Americans and the exploitation of workers by capitalist overlords, the mural was criticized by conservative groups, who claimed that Refregier's "radical" approach to the subject matter seemed to espouse Communist principles; to win federal approval, the artist was required to make more than 85 changes to the work. *Spear St. at Mission St., South of Market.*

4 e-5
RUTH ASAWA'S FANTASY FOUNTAIN
On the plaza in front of the Grand Hyatt Hotel, look for this 14-ft circular fountain. Children and friends helped sculptor Ruth Asawa shape these hundreds of tiny figures from baker's clay; they were then assembled on 41 large panels that were used as molds for the casting of the bronze. See if you can spot all of the city's famous hills, bridges, and unusual buildings within its wonderland of real and mythical creatures. Sculptor Ruth Asawa's work can also be found at the Japan Center Mall (*see above*), and there's a delightful mermaid fountain of hers in Ghirardelli Square. *345 Stockton St., between Sutter and Post Sts., Union Square.*

8 c-5
ST. PETER'S CATHOLIC CHURCH
A stunning mural adorns the rectory building of St. Peter's Catholic Church, made all the more stunning by the irony of its message. The mural, titled "500 Years of Resistance," portrays the strug-gle of the indigenous people of Central and South America to retain their unique cultures after the arrival of the Spaniards—and, of course, the Spaniards' Catholic church. It was painted in 1993 by master muralist Isaias Mata of El Salvador. *24th and Florida Sts., Mission District.*

4 e-6
SAMUELS CLOCK
The charming 12-ft-tall Samuels Clock appeared on Market Street in front of the Albert S. Samuels Jewelry Company just in time for the opening of the Panama-Pacific International Exposition (which also saw the building of the Palace of Fine Arts). It was built in 1915, and Albert Samuels was one of its principal designers. *865 Market St., between 4th and 5th Sts., Financial District.*

4 c-3
SAN FRANCISCO ART INSTITUTE
Of the three murals painted by Mexican master Diego Rivera in San Francisco, the one at the San Francisco Art Institute is the most accessible and impressive. The seven-section fresco, painted in 1931, is titled *The Making of a Fresco Showing the Building of a City* and features Rivera himself in the foreground, with his back to the viewer and surrounded by his assistants. They are surrounded by construction scenes and laborers, as well as city notables such as sculptor Robert Stackpole and architect Timothy Pfleuger. The gallery is to your left as you enter the institute. *800 Chestnut St., between Leavenworth and Jones Sts., Russian Hill.*

4 h-7
SEA CHANGE
The 10-ton, 70-ft-tall *Sea Change* sculpture, a bright-red and steel work with a crown that moves gracefully in the wind, soars above South Beach Park. The artist, Mark di Suvero, came to San Francisco as an eight-year-old immigrant from Shanghai, and later worked as a welder on the San Francisco waterfront. *The Embarcadero between Townsend, 2nd, and King Sts., Embarcadero.*

4 f-4, g-4
SKY TREE
Embarcadero Center (*see* Architecture & Historic Sites) has a collection of some two dozen works of art by nationally

renowned artists, and guided art tours are available. Most notable is Louise Nevelson's dramatic 54-ft-high black-steel sculpture, *Sky Tree*, which stands guard over Building 3. *Embarcadero Center, Bldg. 3, bordered by Battery, Drumm, Clay, and Washington Sts., Embarcadero.*

4 e-5
SUN YAT-SEN STATUE
In tranquil St. Mary's Square, across the street from Old St. Mary's Cathedral, is a 12-ft statue of the founder of the Republic of China, done in stainless steel and rose-color granite by local sculptor Beniamino (Benny) Bufano. The heroic statue of Sun Yat-sen was installed in 1937 on the site of the Chinese leader's favorite reading spot during his years of exile in San Francisco. *Pine, Quincy, and California Sts., Chinatown.*

4 f-4
TRANSAMERICA REDWOOD GROVE
In the Transamerica Redwood Grove is a statue of children playing leapfrog. Named *The Puddlejumpers,* this is the work of sculptor Glenna Goodacre, who was also responsible for the new Women's Vietnam war memorial in Washington, D.C. *Columbus Ave. at Montgomery St., Financial District.*

4 e-6
VICTORY MONUMENT
Center stage at Union Square is Robert Ingersoll Aitken's soaring *Victory Monument,* which commemorates Commodore George Dewey's victory over the Spanish fleet at Manila in 1898. The 97-ft Corinthian column, topped by a bronze figure symbolizing naval conquest, was dedicated by Theodore Roosevelt in 1903 and withstood the 1906 earthquake. The city's famous philanthropist and iconoclast, Alma Spreckels, was the model for the Victory figure at its top. *Bordered by Stockton, Powell, Geary, and Post Sts., Union Square.*

5 g-1
WAVE ORGAN
It's an artwork, but it's also a functioning musical instrument. The sea-powered organ was built by artists with help from the Exploratorium (*see* Science Museums, *above*) and consists of a set of pipes that run along the waterfront and extend into the bay. Take a seat at one of the stone benches, place your ear on a pipe, and listen to the soothing tones created by lapping waves. Acoustics are best at high tide. *At the end of the jetty on Yacht Rd., north of Marina Blvd., Marina.*

8 a-3
WOMEN'S BUILDING
A striking two-sided mural on the exterior of this community center (*see* Architecture & Historic Sites, *above*) depicts women's peacekeeping efforts over the centuries. *Maestrapeace* was painted by seven principal artists, all Bay Area women, and assisted by 10 guest artists and some 80 volunteers, also all women. All of the images are of women, as well: look for Audre Lorde, Georgia O'Keeffe, and Rigoberta Menchú among many others. This is the largest of the Mission District mural projects, completed in 1994. *3543 18th St., between Valencia and Guerrero Sts., 415/431–1180, Mission District.*

VIEWPOINTS

There are so many to chose from, but these are some of the best.

2 b-2
BAKER BEACH
The Golden Gate Bridge looms to your right, the ocean extends endlessly to your left, and the mountainous Marin Headlands rise before you. It's one of the city's most beautiful views, and also a popular beach (*see* Beaches *in* Chapter 3).

4 e-5
CALIFORNIA AND POWELL STREETS
The view down the California Street hill from this Nob Hill intersection is simply breathtaking, particularly if you're aboard a cable car.

2 a-3
CLIFF HOUSE
Although natural disasters have wreaked havoc on the buildings on this site (*see* Architecture & Historic Sites, *above*), the splendid views of Ocean Beach, the Pacific Ocean, Seal Rock, and the Marin Headlands remain.

4 e-3
COIT TOWER
For wonderful 360° views of the city, make a pilgrimage to the landmark Coit

Tower (*see also* Architecture & Historic Sites, *above*), at the summit of Telegraph Hill. For $3, an elevator inside the 210-ft concrete observation tower will take you to the top for a drop-dead view of the Golden Gate Bridge, the Bay Bridge, and Alcatraz.

49-MILE DRIVE

Follow the blue-and-white signs (marked with a seagull) along this scenic drive developed for San Francisco's 1939–40 Golden Gate International Exposition and inaugurated by President Franklin D. Roosevelt. The drive starts at Civic Center and wends its way through Japantown, Union Square, Chinatown, Nob Hill, North Beach, and Telegraph Hill; then, skirting Fisherman's Wharf, it goes past the Marina and the Palace of Fine Arts. The southern approach to the Golden Gate Bridge is one of the best viewpoints; the Presidio and Golden Gate Park also provide sweeping vistas of the Pacific. In the final stretch, the drive climbs Twin Peaks, descends to Mission Dolores, and returns past the Bay Bridge, the Ferry Building, and the Financial District. A free map is available at the San Francisco Visitor Information Center.

2 *b-2*
LINCOLN PARK

Here you can view the Golden Gate Bridge from atop a 200-ft cliff (*see* Parks *in* Chapter 3).

7 *c-7, c-8*
MT. DAVIDSON

This sylvan summit is 16 ft higher than the much more famous Twin Peaks (*see below*). It's also the site of an ongoing court battle: the largest steel-and-concrete cross in the country, placed on its top in 1934, was lighted every evening until 1989, when a multifaith group challenged its constitutionality. Easter Services are still held here, but the cross is now dark. You can hike to the summit by taking the steps between 919 and 925 Rockdale Drive and keeping to the left at every fork, or drive up to the intersection of Myra and Dalewood Ways to get fairly close to the top.

2 *b-2*
SEACLIFF

On sunny days you can catch some of the city's finest views of the San Francisco Bay in between the houses in the exclusive Seacliff neighborhood. Take the stairway off El Camino del Mar, just west of the end of 32nd Avenue, to a circular viewing deck with wonderful vistas of the whole Seacliff neighborhood, plus the Golden Gate Bridge and the Marin Headlands. *Bounded by Lake St. and 25th and 33rd Aves., Richmond District.*

4 *f-4*
SKYDECK

This indoor-outdoor observation deck on the 41st floor of Embarcadero Center opened in 1996. Come here for 360° views of the city, plus interactive multimedia presentations of San Francisco history and culture. Buy tickets on the ground floor; the elevator departs from the Mezzanine Level. Call for current hours. *1 Embarcadero Center, Battery and Sacramento Sts., Embarcadero, 800/733–6318 for Embarcadero Center information, 888/737–5933 for SkyDeck hot line, 415/772–0591 for SkyDeck ticket booth. Admission: $5, $3.50 senior citizens and students, $3 youth 5–12, free children under 5.*

2 *a-3*
SUTRO HEIGHTS PARK

This magnificent park—once the grounds of May Adolph Sutro's mansion—overlooks the Cliff House, the Great Highway, and endless Pacific Ocean. Pick up the trail at Balboa Street across from the end of La Playa and head north up the path. *Off Balboa St. near La Playa, Richmond District.*

7 *d-3*
TANK HILL

A footpath leads to a high, craggy overlook where you can gaze at the city to your heart's content. *End of Belgrave Ave. off Stanyan St., Twin Peaks.*

1 *d-2, d-3*
TREASURE ISLAND

See the familiar San Francisco skyline from a slightly different angle by taking the Treasure Island exit from the Bay Bridge, then parking at the water's edge. *Ave. of Palms, Treasure Island.*

7 *d-5*
TWIN PEAKS

The peaks' crest, at the top of winding Twin Peaks Boulevard, is often windy and notoriously chilly, and it can get crowded with tour buses. But the prime panoramic views of the city and Bay are nothing less than breathtaking. *Twin Peaks Blvd. off Portola Dr., Twin Peaks.*

7 *e-6*

UPPER MARKET STREET
A close second to nearby Twin Peaks, this viewing point at the base of Market Street takes in the city and the East Bay. *Portola Dr. at base of Market St., Diamond Heights.*

guided tours

Reservations are recommended, and often required, for the following tours.

AIR TOURS

SAN FRANCISCO HELICOPTER TOURS
Downtown San Francisco and Alcatraz, the Golden Gate Bridge, the Pacific Coast, Tiburon, and Angel Island are a few of the destinations covered on these scenic helicopter flights. Special wine country flights include lunch, and evening flights around San Francisco include dinner or a dinner-and-dancing boat cruise. All flights depart from San Francisco International Airport. *415/635–4500 or 800/400–2404.*

SAN FRANCISCO SEAPLANE TOURS, INC.
Seaplane flights take off from the water, departing from either Pier 39 or Sausalito. The Golden Gate Tour from Pier 39 takes in Alcatraz, Angel Island, the Marin Headlands, the Golden Gate Bridge, and the city of San Francisco. The Coast Tour from Sausalito includes all points of interest along the San Francisco Bay as well as Mt. Tamalpais, Stinson Beach, and the Marin County coastline. There's also a sunset champagne flight. *415/332–4843 or 888/732–7526.*

SCENIC AIR TOURS
Scenic Air specializes in full-day airplane tours to Yosemite National Park, including private tour bus and guide within the park in addition to the scenic flight (45 minutes each way). The company also offers the only full-day air tour to Grand Canyon National Park, a 2½-hour one-way flight from the Bay Area. *415/922–2386, 800/957–2364.*

BICYCLE TOURS

BAY BICYCLE TOURS
Sign up for the 3½-hour tours across the Golden Gate Bridge to Sausalito. Tours depart from the Cannery shopping center at Fisherman's Wharf. *415/436–0633 for recorded schedule information or 415/923–6434.*

BREAKAWAY
Guided mountain biking tours explore Bay Area state parks, with destinations varying by season. *415/203–9910.*

BOAT TOURS

ADVENTURE CAT SAILING CHARTERS
San Francisco's only catamaran sailing vessel used for public excursions departs from Pier 39 for 1½-hour tours of the San Francisco Bay. *415/777–1630.*

BLUE AND GOLD FLEET
The Blue and Gold Fleet's 45-minute "Bay Cruise" takes you past the Golden Gate Bridge, Angel Island, Alcatraz, and the San Francisco waterfront. Blue and Gold also provides ferry service to Oakland, Alameda, Sausalito, Tiburon, Vallejo, and Angel Island; the only service to Alcatraz Island (*see* Architecture & Historic Sites, *above*); and package tours, including ferry and bus transportation, to the wine country and Muir Woods. Between mid-April and mid-December there are three-hour "Dinner-Dance Cruises" on Friday and Saturday nights. Tours depart from Pier 41 at Fisherman's Wharf. *415/773–1188 for information; 415/705–5555 or 800/426–8687 for advance ticket sales with $2 service charge.*

HORNBLOWER DINING YACHTS
Enjoy a weekend brunch cruise or an afternoon or dinner-dance cruise aboard the 183-ft *California Hornblower*, patterned after the classic steamers of the early 1900s. In summer and occasionally at other times, the same company operates Monte Carlo Cruises, which give you a taste of riverboat gambling (with play money), along with dancing and karaoke singing. Tours depart from Pier 33 at Fisherman's Wharf. *415/394–8900.*

MISS FARALLONES

One-hour scenic bay tours aboard the 38-passenger *Miss Farallones* take in the San Francisco waterfront, Golden Gate Bridge, and Alcatraz Island and are narrated in person. The boat is docked at Space 6 (Jefferson St. between Taylor and Jones Sts.) at Fisherman's Wharf. *415/346–2399 or 510/352–5708.*

OCEANIC SOCIETY EXPEDITIONS

The nonprofit Oceanic Society sponsors excursions to the Farallon Islands National Wildlife Refuge on an 85-ft boat, *New Superfish,* that leaves the Yacht Harbor at the Marina Green from June through November. You may see dolphins, sea lions, blue and humpback whales, birds, and other marine life. From December through April, the society also organizes whale-watching trips. *415/474–3385 or 800/326–7491.*

RED AND WHITE FLEET

Red and White Fleet's "Round the Rock" tour is a 45-minute narrated ferry cruise around Alcatraz Island. As you slowly circle the island you'll hear stories about famous prisoners, daring escapes, and other penitentiary lore. Also popular is the one-hour "Golden Gate Bridge Cruise," which passes Hyde Street Pier, Fort Mason, Fort Point, the Presidio, Alcatraz, Angel Island, and Sausalito and then crosses under the Golden Gate Bridge to view the Marin Headlands. The company also offers discount land and water tour packages in conjunction with Gray Line (*see* Bus Tours, *below*). Tours depart from Pier 43½ at Fisherman's Wharf. *415/673–2900.*

RENDEZVOUS CHARTERS/ SPINNAKER SAILING

Romantic sails around the San Francisco Bay are given aboard the 78-ft, square-rigged brigantine *Rendezvous,* built in 1933 in the classic style of the tall ships of the 19th century. There are three-hour Sunday brunch cruises aboard the *Rendezvous,* as well as two-hour Sunday afternoon cruises aboard either the *Rendezvous* or the smaller *Yukon Jack;* all depart from South Beach Harbor's Pier 40. *415/543–7333.*

SS JEREMIAH O'BRIEN (NATIONAL LIBERTY SHIP MEMORIAL)

Five days a year, during Fleet Week and Memorial Day Weekend, this historic ship (*see* History Museums, *above*) goes out for full-day bay tours, complete with gourmet lunch and dance band. Buy tickets far in advance.

BUS TOURS

CABLE CAR CHARTERS

Here's your chance to ride a motorized cable car. The one-hour "Heart of San Francisco" tour takes you to Fisherman's Wharf, Union Square, Chinatown, and North Beach; the two-hour "Golden Gate Bridge" tour takes in the bridge, Fisherman's Wharf, the Presidio, and Union Street boutiques. Tours depart from in front of Sabella's Restaurant (Taylor and Jefferson Sts., Fisherman's Wharf; map 4, d-2). *415/922–2425, 800/ 562–7383.*

GRAY LINE OF SAN FRANCISCO

Deluxe motor coaches and London double-deckers make excursions within San Francisco and the Bay Area, and also to Yosemite, Monterey, Carmel, Santa Cruz, Hearst Castle, and the wine country. The San Francisco Trolley Hop tour, aboard a motorized cable car, covers Fisherman's Wharf, Union Street, the Presidio, Fort Point, and North Beach. *415/558–9400, 800/826–0202.*

GREAT PACIFIC TOUR COMPANY

Twelve-passenger minivans provide an intimate touring experience, with daily departures year-round for Muir Woods and Sausalito in Marin County, as well as extensive city tours of 13 neighborhoods. Farther-flung tours take you to the wine country, as well as Monterey and Carmel. *415/626–4499.*

SUPER SIGHTSEEING TOURS

Tours of the city, Alcatraz and the San Francisco Bay, Muir Woods and Sausalito, Monterey and Carmel, the wine country, and Yosemite Valley are on board deluxe motor coaches. *415/777– 2288 or 888/868–7788.*

TOWER TOURS

Tower makes the same excursions as Super Sightseeing (*see above*), also aboard deluxe motor coaches. *415/434– 8687.*

SPECIALIZED TOURS

Most specialized tours require advance reservations.

A DAY IN NATURE

Experienced naturalists lead this company's intimate, customized, half-day tours of Marin County's scenic areas. Group size is limited to four people at most. 415/673–0548.

ARTICULATE ART: 1930s SAN FRANCISCO

Masha Zakheim, a City College humanities professor for 30 years, leads short, informative tours focusing on artists of the 1930s; destinations include Coit Tower, the Beach Chalet, the murals of Diego Rivera, and other locales. Tours range in length from one hour to a half day. 415/285–0495.

ESCAPE ARTIST TOURS

Unusual customized adventures cover the Bay Area and beyond. Favorites are the ranch tour of the gold country and the haunted bed-and-breakfast tour. 415/726–7626 or 800/728–1384.

EXPLORERS' CLUB

The Explorer's Club tours are designed especially for children between the ages of 6 and 12, with or without their parents. The "Mission Salsa" tour takes the children to the Mission Cliffs climbing gym for play time, *panaderías* (bakeries) for snacks, Mission Dolores for a short history lesson and tour, and the Precita Eyes Mural Art Center to create art with help from a professional artist. Other tours go to the Exploratorium, Golden Gate Park, Chinatown, or on a bay cruise. Tours range in length from four to seven hours. 415/566–7014 or 800/360–7727.

SHOPPER STOPPER

This 6½-hour tour takes shoppers to warehouses and other outlets normally closed to the public. Prices are lowest in January and February, when all merchandise is marked for clearance. Refreshments are served, and drawings for cash and prizes are held throughout the day, giving these tours a party atmosphere. The expert guides willingly give wardrobe-planning advice. 707/829–1597.

3 BABES AND A BUS NIGHTCLUB TOURS

A wonderful way to sample the city's vibrant nightlife is with 3 Babes and a Bus, run by a stockbroker who started the company in 1990 with two of her friends. The 50-person luxury bus rolls out every Saturday and some Friday nights, and stops at clubs to hear various types of music: '70s disco, Top 40, '80s dance music, urban dance music, blues, R&B, Motown, Brazilian music, and salsa. San Francisco residents celebrating birthdays and bachelorette parties often jump on the bandwagon. Pickup is at New Joe's Restaurant (347 Geary St., between Powell and Mason Sts., Union Square; map 4, e-6). 415/552–2582.

WALKING TOURS

For self-guided walking tours, consult *Bay Area at Your Feet* (Lexikos, $8.95) or *The New San Francisco at Your Feet: Best Walks in a Walkers City* (Grove/Atlantic, $12.95): the finest of *San Francisco Chronicle* writer Margot Patterson Doss's "Sunday Punch" columns appear in these two collections. Also recommended is Adah Bakalinsky's *Stairway Walks in San Francisco* (Wilderness Press, $9.95). All three are available in most local bookstores. *Walking San Francisco on the Barbary Coast Trail*, by Daniel Bacon (Quicksilver Press, $13.95), is a guide to the city's official historical walking trail.

Almost all of the following guided tours require advance reservations.

ALL ABOUT CHINATOWN!

Longtime Chinatown resident Linda Lee emphasizes history, culture, and traditions on her daily 2½-hour tours. Stops take in Chinese temples, a fortune cookie factory, and a tea shop; a sumptuous dim sum luncheon is the grand finale. 415/982–8839.

BAY VENTURES

You can't go wrong with Bay Ventures' various specialist-led tours. Standouts: "Movie Hike of San Francisco," which covers famous movie sites; "Herb Caen Way," which explores the haunts of the city's beloved late columnist; and "Stairways to the Gods," which solves the mystery of why streets in Buena Vista are named after deities. Other tours explore downtown landmarks, Victorian houses, and former grave sites. 510/234–4834.

THE CITY GUIDES

Friends of the San Francisco Public Library sponsor 26 intriguing tours each week, covering the history, architecture, and culture of almost every corner of town. "Roof Gardens and Open Spaces," the "Telegraph Hill Hike," "Gold Rush City," "Art Deco Marina," "History of Haight-Ashbury," and "Mission Murals" are just a few tour topics. For a list, stop by any San Francisco public library, or send a self-addressed, stamped envelope to City Guides, Main Library, Civic Center, San Francisco 94102. Tours are free, although donations are requested. *415/557–4266 for recorded information.*

CRUISIN' THE CASTRO FROM A HISTORICAL PERSPECTIVE

Trevor Hailey's highly recommended tour clues you in on how and why San Francisco became a gay mecca, with stops at various Castro District landmarks, followed by brunch. *415/550–8110.*

FLOWER POWER HAIGHT-ASHBURY WALKING TOUR

It's always the Summer of Love on these 2½-hour tours of the famous hippie district, Haight-Ashbury. Tours take place Tuesday and Saturday morning

and cover more than just the landmarks and history of the heady '60s: under the guidance of longtime Haight residents Pam and Bruce Brennan, a brother-and-sister team, you'll also look at Victorian architecture and get the scoop on the neighborhood's best bars, restaurants, cafés, and shops. *415/863–1621.*

FRIENDS OF RECREATION AND PARKS

On weekends from May through October, free one- to two-hour guided walking tours explore the history, flora, and fauna of glorious Golden Gate Park. Choose from the "Japanese Tea Garden Tour," "Strawberry Hill Walk," "Windmill to the Beach Chalet Walk," "McLaren's Walk," "Grand Concourse Walk," and "Lloyd Lake Tour." Less-frequent tours explore Stern Grove and McLaren Park. *415/263–0991 for recorded information.*

GLORIOUS FOOD CULINARY WALKTOURS

Retired caterer-chef Ruby Tom, one of the original graduates of the California Culinary Academy, and her husband Ben Tom lead tours of Chinatown (including a dim sum lunch), the Italian neighborhood of North Beach (including cappuccino and biscotti), and, when the Ferry Building farmers' market is in full swing, the south Embarcadero waterfront. The emphasis is on culture, history, and, of course, food. *415/441–5637.*

HERITAGE WALKS

This tour will teach you the difference between Italianate, Eastlake, and Queen Anne Victorians, as well as provide fascinating insight into the city's history. On Sunday the expert guides of the Foundation for San Francisco's Architectural Heritage lead two-hour walking tours of Pacific Heights' vintage homes. Also recommended are the one-hour tour of Yerba Buena Gardens, and the hour-long, docent-led tour of the interior of the Haas-Lilienthal House (see Architecture & Historic Sites, *above*), the foundation's headquarters. *415/441–3000.*

JAVAWALK

These two-hour tours depart twice weekly from the Mark Rubin Gallery and take in the best of the North Beach coffeehouses, with plenty of time for sipping cappuccinos and discussing history. *415/673–9255.*

A TASTE OF SAN FRANCISCO—LITERALLY

There's no better way to explore San Francisco than by a walking tour—unless it's a walking tour accompanied by a delicious meal:

All About Chinatown!
Tours end with a dim sum luncheon.

Cruisin' the Castro from a Historical Perspective
Fascinating Castro District tour followed by brunch.

Glorious Food Culinary Walktours
Cruise North Beach, Chinatown, and the Ferry Building farmers' market with one of the original graduates of the California Culinary Academy.

Javawalk
A walk through historic San Francisco neighborhoods, latte by latte.

Wok Wiz Chinatown Tours and Cooking Company
The "I Can't Believe I Ate My Way Through Chinatown" tour is a perennial favorite.

ONE DOLLAH STATUEWALKS

Local history buff Peter Garland leads these entertaining weekend tours (the suggested price is more than a dollar these days, but still a bargain) from June through September. The five-hour Saturday tour starts at Civic Center, and the 1½-hour Sunday tour starts at the Ferry Building (at the foot of Market Street on the Embarcadero). Tours cover important statues, monuments, murals, and city history. *510/834–3617.*

PRECITA EYES MURAL ARTS CENTER

Two-hour walking tours every Saturday explore many of the Mission District's 80 or so colorful murals. Less-frequent tours range farther afield, by bicycle, BART, or on board the center's "Mexican Bus." All tours are led by one of the center's expert muralists in residence. The center also publishes a "Mission Mural Walk" map for self-guided tours. No reservations are necessary; call for a current schedule. *415/285–2287.*

SAN FRANCISCO AFRICAN-AMERICAN HISTORICAL AND CULTURAL SOCIETY

African-American history is the focus of these 45 minute to two hour walking tours through downtown San Francisco, with stops at companies owned and run by black businesspeople. *415/441–0640.*

A SAN FRANCISCO WALKABOUT WITH GARY HOLLOWAY

These twice-monthly California Historical Society tours are led by guide extraordinaire Gary Holloway, a native Californian who's led more than 1,000 historic and architectural walking tours of San Francisco. His two-hour rambles take in Chinatown, North Beach, and downtown. Tour price includes admission to the California Historical Society museum. *415/357–1848.*

SUNSET HIKES

Jeff Morris, a naturalist and Marin County native, leads these small-group nature hikes of Muir Woods, Mt. Tamalpais, and the Marin Headlands. Tours last about 3½ hours and are customized to participants' interests and fitness levels. *415/258–9434 or 800/848–8607.*

VICTORIAN HOME WALK

Jay Gifford, a 19-year resident of San Francisco and member of the city's Victorian Alliance, leads daily 2½-hour tours covering Fisherman's Wharf, Union Street, Telegraph Hill, North Beach, and Chinatown, with an emphasis on Victorian-era history and architecture. The leisurely small-group tours include a café break and trolley ride. Tours depart from the lobby of the Westin St. Francis Hotel (Powell St. between Post and Geary Sts., Union Square; map 4, e-6). *415/252–9485.*

WOK WIZ CHINATOWN TOURS AND COOKING COMPANY

The enormously popular "I Can't Believe I Ate My Way Through Chinatown" tour, led by chef and cookbook author Shirley Fong-Torres, visits restaurants and markets, ending "when the first person explodes." Wok Wiz also leads several other tours focusing on folklore, history, and food. *415/981–8989.*

events

JANUARY

CHINESE NEW YEAR CELEBRATION AND GOLDEN DRAGON PARADE

The city's biggest festival lasts two weeks, usually from late January through early February, with pageantry, outdoor and cultural programs, and fireworks in Chinatown, and the spectacular Golden Dragon parade from Market and Second streets to Columbus Avenue. *415/982–3000.*

MARTIN LUTHER KING JR. BIRTHDAY CELEBRATION

Speeches by civic leaders and other events take place at the Yerba Buena Center on January 15, Dr. King's birth date. *415/771–6300.*

NAPA VALLEY MUSTARD FESTIVAL

In late January when the wild mustard blooms in the vineyards, the Mustard Festival begins in Napa and is held in different locales throughout the valley. The festival lasts two months, with events ranging from a black-tie opening-night gala to family events showcasing wine and gourmet foods to a photography competition and exhibit. *707/259–9020.*

SAN FRANCISCO BALLET GALA OPENING

America's oldest ballet company begins its season of performances of eclectic, full-length neoclassical and contemporary ballets. The season runs through May at the War Memorial Opera House. 415/865–2000.

SAN FRANCISCO SPORTS AND BOAT SHOW

This nine-day show in mid-January at the Cow Palace is one of the West Coast's biggest expos for boats, fishing tackle, and camping and hunting gear. 415/469–6065.

SAN FRANCISCO TRIBAL, FOLK, AND TEXTILE ART SHOW

More than 100 dealers of folk and ethnic art set up shop at Fort Mason to sell North American pottery, basketry, textiles, and jewelry. 310/455–2886.

TET FESTIVAL

On the Saturday closest to the Vietnamese New Year, the Tet Festival features traditional food and performances by Vietnamese, Cambodian, and Laotian singers and dancers in the Tenderloin and Civic Center. 415/351–1038.

WHALE-WATCHING

Between January and April, hundreds of gray whales migrate along the Pacific Coast. The best place to watch is on the Marin Headlands. Contact the California Office of Tourism for details. 800/862–2543.

FEBRUARY

CALIFORNIA INTERNATIONAL ANTIQUARIAN BOOK FAIR

For rare and antiquarian books, visit the Concourse Exhibition Center in mid-February, when more than 215 booksellers converge. 888/208–8889.

CHINESE NEW YEAR

See above.

GOLDEN GATE KENNEL CLUB DOG SHOW

The Cow Palace is a dog lover's heaven during the first weekend in February. 415/469–6065.

PACIFIC ORCHID EXPOSITION

San Francisco Orchid Society's dazzling orchid displays fill Fort Mason for this annual event usually held in late February. 415/546–9608.

RUSSIAN FESTIVAL

For two days in mid-February, the Russian Center is the site of folk singing, dancing, opera, painting, and other crafts, as well as traditional food and flavored vodkas. 415/921–7631.

TULIPMANIA

More than 40,000 tulips from all over the world bloom at Pier 39 in late February and early March. You can walk around on your own, or join a free guided tour. 415/705–5500.

MARCH

EASTER PARADE AND CELEBRATION

The city's annual Easter Parade, held in March or April depending on when Easter falls, brings the Easter bunny and children's activities to Union and Fillmore streets. 415/775–5703.

EASTER SUNRISE SERVICE

Since 1923, Mt. Davidson, west of Twin Peaks, has been the setting for this interdenominational sunrise Easter Sunday service, held in March or April, depending on when Easter falls. The service takes place at the base of a controversial 103-ft cross at Dalewood Avenue and Myra Way. 415/564–7535.

ST. PATRICK'S DAY CELEBRATION

The Irish celebrate their day with religious services at St. Patrick's Church and a gala parade from Civic Center to Spear Street on the Sunday before March 17. The parade begins at 12:30 PM. 415/661–2700.

SAN FRANCISCO FLOWER AND GARDEN SHOW

Hosted at the Cow Palace each year, this show showcases cutting-edge landscape design and high-quality exhibits of plants and superior gardening products. 800/829–9751.

SAN FRANCISCO INTERNATIONAL ASIAN AMERICAN FILM FESTIVAL

This film festival at the AMC Kabuki 8 theater in Japantown shows Asian films and videos, including world premieres, documentaries, and experimental films. 415/863–0814.

APRIL

AMERICAN CONSERVATORY THEATER

One of the country's premier repertory theater companies performs from April through June at the Geary Theater. *415 Geary St., at Mason St., Union Square, 415/749–2228.*

CHERRY BLOSSOM FESTIVAL

Tea ceremonies, martial arts, calligraphy, floral arranging demonstrations, nearly 400 Japanese performers, and numerous exhibits of Japanese art bring the Japantown Center to life over two consecutive weekends in mid April. Most popular are the taiko drum performance and the parade from Civic Center to Japantown. *415/563–2313.*

GOLDEN GATE PARK BAND

Since 1882, the Golden Gate Park Band has performed regularly in the park in spring. Pack a picnic and head to the Music Concourse to enjoy this perennial pleasure free of charge. *415/666–7107.*

OPENING DAY ON THE BAY

On the first day of Daylight Savings Time the Bay Area celebrates the start of the sailing season with a parade of decorated yachts and local fireboats. *415/381–1128.*

SAN FRANCISCO GIANTS BASEBALL SEASON

In early April the Giants step up to the plate at the new PacBell Park for another season of Major League Baseball. The season runs through September. *800/ 734–4268.*

SAN FRANCISCO INTERNATIONAL FILM FESTIVAL

Spanning two weeks in April and early May, the nation's oldest film festival features seminars and screenings of 100 films and videos from some 30 countries. Screenings take place at the Kabuki 8 and the Castro Theatre in San Francisco, the Pacific Film Archive in Berkeley, and other locations in the South Bay and Marin. *415/931–3456.*

SAN FRANCISCO SYMPHONY

The Symphony's season begins in April and runs through June, with performances at Davies Symphony Hall. The Symphony celebrates its 87th season in 2000. *415/864–6000.*

MAY

ARTS AND CRAFTS BY THE BAY

Pier 29 is the setting for this late May festival, with live entertainment, food and drink, and about 200 artists and craftspeople selling their wares. *415/ 956–5316.*

CARNAVAL

This raucous Río-style shindig is held in the Mission District on Memorial Day weekend, with food, craft booths, a costume contest, and performances by dozens of Latin American musical groups. The parade starts at 10 AM on Sunday at Bryant and 24th streets, travels along Mission Street, and ends at Harrison Street between 16th and 22nd streets, where the party begins. *415/ 826–1401.*

CINCO DE MAYO CELEBRATION

Vibrant mariachi bands and colorful Mexican *folklórico* dancers congregate in the Mission District on the weekend nearest May 5 to celebrate the anniversary of Mexico's defeat of the French at the Battle of Puebla. On Sunday at 11 AM there's a parade through the neighborhood, starting at 24th and Bryant streets and ending on Harrison Street. *415/826–1401.*

NEIGHBORHOOD FESTIVALS

The best way to get a sense of what San Francisco's all about is to drop by one of the many neighborhood festivals:

Blues and Art on Polk (September)
   Groove your way down Polk Street.

Castro Street Fair (October)
   Kick up your heels in the gay Castro district.

Haight Street Fair (June)
   Music and art in the Haight.

Jazz and All That Art on Fillmore (July)
   Jazz and blues in the Fillmore.

North Beach Festival (June)
   Come see the "World's Biggest Salami."

Union Street Spring Festival Arts and Crafts Fair (June)
   Swing dancing and fine wine in Cow Hollow.

POLISH SPRING FESTIVAL

Look for polka dancing and Polish food and crafts at the San Francisco County Fair Building in mid-May. *415/285–4336.*

SAN FRANCISCO EXAMINER BAY TO BREAKERS FOOTRACE

The world's largest foot race attracts about 70,000 participants, many of whom don zany costumes to run the 7½-mi course from the Financial District to Ocean Beach. The year 2000 will mark the 89th race, which takes place on the third Sunday every May. *415/777–7770.*

ETHNIC FESTIVALS

You could easily plan your calendar around San Francisco's many ethnic heritage celebrations.

Cherry Blossom Festival (April)
   Celebrates Japanese culture and customs.

Chinese New Year Celebration (January)
   The sensational Golden Dragon Parade is a highlight of the city's largest festival.

Cinco de Mayo (May)
   In remembrance of Mexico's defeat of the French on May 5, 1862.

Día de los Muertos (November)
   The Mexican tradition of Day of the Dead.

Festival de las Americas (September)
   Celebrating eight Latin American nations.

Filipino American Fair (July)
   The crescendo is the Pearl Parade.

Italian Heritage Parade and Festival (October)
   Columbus Day festivities in North Beach.

Juneteenth (June)
   June 19, the day Lincoln's Emancipation Proclamation was read in Galveston, Texas.

Polish Spring Festival (May)
   Polka dancing and Polish food.

St. Patrick's Day Celebration (March)
   A gala parade and religious services at St. Patrick's Church.

Tet Festival (January)
   Vietnamese New Year celebrations.

SAN FRANCISCO SYMPHONY BLACK & WHITE BALL

Proceeds from the city's most elegant affair benefit the San Francisco Symphony. It's a semiannual black-tie block party on the Embarcadero waterfront with gourmet food, dancing to live music on 15 stages, and 12,000 guests. *415/864–6000 or 510/762–2277 for tickets.*

SAN FRANCISCO YOUTH ARTS FESTIVAL

This annual festival held in Golden Gate Park celebrates the creativity of San Francisco students with city school, museum, and library artwork and competitions. *415/759–2916.*

STRYBING ARBORETUM ANNUAL PLANT SALE

Held at the San Francisco County Fair Building, this event in early May is always well attended by the city's green thumbs. Up for sale are plants rare and common, for indoors and out. *415/661–3090.*

JUNE

ANIMAL WINGDING

The San Francisco SPCA (Society For the Prevention of Cruelty to Animals) sponsors this one-day festival in early June for furred and feathered folk and their owners. After the games and live music, a parade winds down the Mission District. *415/554–3050.*

ETHNIC DANCE FESTIVAL

With 900 talented dancers and musicians performing, there's something new every weekend in June at the Palace of Fine Arts Theater. Previews are held on Saturday in late May and early June at Ghirardelli Square in Fisherman's Wharf. *415/474–3914.*

FREE FOLK FESTIVAL

This feel-good festival takes place on a June weekend at the John Adams Campus of City College. Bring your guitar, harmonica, or fiddle to the workshops and impromptu jam sessions that spring up between concerts of folk, blues, and international music. It's a very loosely organized event; check newspaper entertainment listings for details.

HAIGHT STREET FAIR

On a Saturday in mid-June, the fair on Haight Street between Masonic and

Stanyan streets features local bands playing rap, jazz, and rock, along with booths by neighborhood merchants, artists, and craftspeople. 415/661–8025.

JUNETEENTH CELEBRATION

Celebrating the day when Lincoln's Emancipation Proclamation was read in Galveston, Texas (June 19, 1865), Oakland's big festival features big-name blues and R&B acts and children's activities at Lake Merritt's Lakeside Park (510/238–3866). A smaller festival on Fillmore Street in San Francisco is sponsored by the Supporters of the Western Addition Cultural Center (415/386–1186).

LESBIAN, GAY, BISEXUAL, TRANSGENDER PRIDE CELEBRATION

Known as San Francisco Pride for short (and formerly known as the Gay and Lesbian Freedom Day Parade), this celebration on the third or fourth weekend in June features dancing, music, food, speeches, arts and crafts held citywide, and the famed Sunday 11 AM parade from Market and 8th streets to Justin Herman Plaza on the Embarcadero. The Annual Dyke March down Castro and Market streets takes place on the preceding Saturday, and draws more than 40,000 women. 415/864–3733.

MIDSUMMER MOZART FESTIVAL

The music of one of the world's best-known and best-loved composers is performed at venues throughout the city from late June through late July. 415/391–4400.

NORTH BEACH FESTIVAL

Come see the "World's Biggest Salami" at the country's oldest urban street fair, held on a weekend in mid-June on Washington Square. Added attractions: arts and crafts, chalk street painting, small-press booksellers, all kinds of live music, and of course plenty of delicious Italian food. 415/989–6426.

SAN FRANCISCO INTERNATIONAL LESBIAN AND GAY FILM FESTIVAL

The second-largest film festival in California showcases more than 350 films and videos from all over the world during the week preceding the Lesbian, Gay, Bisexual, Transgender Pride Celebration (see above). Screenings take place at the Castro Theatre and various other venues. 415/703–8650.

STERN GROVE MIDSUMMER MUSIC FESTIVAL

A San Francisco tradition since 1937, the Stern Grove Midsummer Music Festival features free live performances of classical, jazz, pop, world music, and more in beautiful Stern Grove. Performances take place from mid-June through August, Sunday at 2 PM. 415/252–6252.

STREET PERFORMERS FESTIVAL

Look for comedians, jugglers, and unicyclists strolling the streets at this weekend-long event at Pier 39 in Fisherman's Wharf. 415/705–5500.

SUMMER FESTIVAL

This annual festival celebrates a changing roster of musical greats. Put on by the San Francisco Symphony at Davies Symphony Hall, it takes place in the latter half of June. 415/864–6000.

UNION STREET SPRING FESTIVAL ARTS AND CRAFTS FAIR

In the Marina district's chic Cow Hollow neighborhood on Union Street between Gough and Steiner streets, the spring festival features big bands, a swing dance contest, wine and gourmet food, a garden party, and the San Francisco Waiter's Race. It takes place on the weekend after Memorial Day (usually the first weekend in June). 415/346–9162.

JULY

BOOKS BY THE BAY

At the Ferry Building on a Saturday in mid-July, this is a reader's delight, with booths representing 40 bookstores, plus readings, book signings, and fun activities for children. 415/927–3937.

COMEDY CELEBRATION DAY

During this annual rib-tickling event on a Sunday in mid-July, more than a dozen of the nation's top comedians entertain for free at Sharon Meadow in Golden Gate Park. 415/249–4625.

FILIPINO AMERICAN FAIR

The city's Filipino community throws a joyous outdoor festival at the Center for the Arts at Yerba Buena Gardens on a weekend in mid-July. It concludes with Perlas ng Silangan (Pearl Parade) down Market Street on Sunday at noon, starting at the Embarcadero and ending at Yerba Buena Gardens. 415/436–9711.

FOURTH OF JULY WATERFRONT FESTIVAL

The biggest Independence Day celebration in the Bay Area takes place along the San Francisco waterfront, from Aquatic Park to Pier 39. Live entertainment and a children's program start at 1 PM, and fireworks light the skies at 9:30 PM. *415/777–8498.*

JAZZ AND ALL THAT ART ON FILLMORE

In the 1940s, '50s, and '60s, Fillmore clubs were famous for sizzling jazz and blues. National jazz talents—old-time musicians and young ones, too—revive those heady days on the first weekend in July, with outdoor jazz, wine, food, and art on Fillmore Street between Post and Jackson streets. *415/346–9162.*

JEWISH FILM FESTIVAL

The world's largest Jewish film festival runs for two weeks at the Castro Theatre and at Berkeley's UC Theater. *415/621–0556.*

SAN FRANCISCO CABLE CAR BELL RINGING COMPETITION

On the third Thursday every July, the city's cable car operators square off at Union Square to compete for highly coveted prizes. Out-of-towners love this event. *415/923–6217.*

SAN FRANCISCO MARATHON

On a Sunday in mid-July some 3,000 hardy spirits race a scenic 26.2-mi course that starts at the Marin side of the Golden Gate Bridge and ends at Kezar Stadium in Golden Gate Park. *415/296–7111*

SAN FRANCISCO SYMPHONY POPS

Some of the world's greats perform at Davies Symphony Hall from July through early August. *415/864–6000.*

SUMMER EVENING ARTWALK

Thirty member galleries showcase emerging artists with an evening of exhibitions and receptions. *415/626–7498.*

AUGUST

NIHONMACHI STREET FAIR

The fall celebration of Japanese culture, at Japantown on a weekend in early August, features lion dancers and taiko drummers in addition to live entertainment, food, and crafts. *415/771–9861.*

RENAISSANCE PLEASURE FAIRE

On weekends from mid-August through September at Blackpoint Forest in the city of Novato, the Renaissance fair is a pleasure fest for anyone fascinated by 16th-century Elizabethan England. It's a jousting, dancing, outdoor theater with nearly 1,500 costumed performers. Jousting, dancing, and performances in the outdoor theater with nearly 1,500 costumed performers are among the festivities. *800/523–2473.*

SAN FRANCISCO 49ERS FOOTBALL SEASON

The 49ers strap on their helmets and prepare for another winning season of pro football at 3Com Stadium. The season runs through December. *415/468–2249 or 415/656–4900 for tickets and game schedule.*

SEPTEMBER

BLUES AND ART ON POLK

In mid-July, ease on down Polk Street between Jackson and Bush streets during this weekend festival with plenty of blues music, arts, crafts, and food. *415/249–4625.*

FESTIVAL DE LAS AMERICAS

This mid-month Mission District festival, celebrating the independence of Mexico and seven other Latin American countries, attracts more than 80,000 people to 24th Street between Mission and Hampshire streets. The alcohol-free, family-oriented, one-day event promotes pride in the Latino community, with Latino musicians, ethnic food, and booths selling original crafts. The El Grito Celebration (*415/585–2043*) is usually the following day, and marks Mexican Independence Day with mariachi music and folklórico dancers. *415/826–1401.*

FESTIVAL OF THE SEA

Sail- and rope-making demonstrations, seafaring music, and a parade of tall ships and yachts along the San Francisco waterfront celebrate San Francisco's maritime tradition. The free festival takes place at San Francisco's

Hyde Street Pier on a weekend in mid- or late September. 415/561–6662.

FOLSOM STREET FAIR

One of the city's most popular—and controversial—street fairs put on by the gay leather crowd features music, comics, dancing, a beer garden, and lots of leather and flesh. People crowd the blocks of Folsom Street between 7th and 12th streets strutting their latest leather-wear, usually on a Sunday in late September. 415/861–3247.

GARDENS GALLERY WALK

On a day in early September the Center for the Arts at Yerba Buena Gardens sponsors an arts mega-tour, with museums, sculptures, and two dozen galleries on the agenda. 415/541–0312.

MILL VALLEY FALL ARTS FESTIVAL

For more than 40 years, this community event has been held in Mill Valley to showcase the work of local artists. It's held under the redwoods in Old Mill Park. 415/381–0525.

OPERA IN THE PARK

The San Francisco Opera kicks off the opera season with a free concert in Golden Gate Park's Sharon Meadow on the Sunday after the first performance of the season, usually the week after Labor Day. 415/864–3330.

RINGLING BROTHERS BARNUM & BAILEY CIRCUS

The famed three-ringed circus visits San Francisco's Cow Palace for five days in early September. 415/469–6065.

SAN FRANCISCO BLUES FESTIVAL

Local talent as well as big-name musicians like B. B. King and Robert Cray perform at America's oldest blues festival, held on the third weekend in September at Justin Herman Plaza and at Fort Mason's Great Meadow. Advance ticket purchase is advised. 415/979–5588.

SAN FRANCISCO FRINGE FESTIVAL

The city's 10-day festival of offbeat and avant-garde performing arts is held at various downtown venues. 415/931–1094.

SAN FRANCISCO OPERA SEASON

The Opera, celebrating its 78th season, runs from September through January.

Performances are in the newly renovated War Memorial Opera House. 415/864–3330.

SAUSALITO ART FESTIVAL

This excellent, expansive exhibition of original artworks from all over the world is worth a trip across the Golden Gate Bridge to Sausalito on Labor Day weekend. More than 10,000 works are displayed. 415/332–3555.

STOLI À LA CARTE, À LA PARK

The annual mouthwatering, stomach-filling food festival hosted by Stolichnaya Vodka with dishes from 50 of the city's top restaurants, plus drinks by California wineries and microbreweries, takes place in Golden Gate Park over Labor Day weekend. 510/762–2277.

A TASTE OF CHOCOLATE

Enter the chocolate-tasting or chocolate-sculpting contests, or just come to eat the chocolate concoctions at this sweet-as-can-be festival at Ghirardelli Square in early September. 415/775–5500.

OCTOBER

CASTRO STREET FAIR

On the first Sunday of the month, the Castro Street Fair brings crafts vendors; booths run by community, health, and social organizations; and musical entertainment to the city's gay community. 415/841–1824.

FLEET WEEK

During a mid-October week, San Francisco salutes its sailors with activities and booths on Fisherman's Wharf, a parade of ships under the Golden Gate Bridge, and a Blue Angels air show. 415/705–5500.

GRAND NATIONAL RODEO, HORSE, AND STOCK SHOW

San Francisco revisits its western heritage every October at the Cow Palace, in a cowboy and bronco bonanza that runs 10 days. 415/469–6065.

GREAT HALLOWEEN AND PUMPKIN FESTIVAL

This is a fun weekend festival on Polk Street in mid-October, with a pumpkin-carving and pie-eating contest, pony rides, arts and crafts sale, and a costume parade. 415/249–4625.

HALLOWEEN NIGHT

After nearly two decades in the Castro district, San Francisco's flamboyant Halloween parade and party recently relocated to Civic Center. About 300,000 revelers attend each year, in an event sponsored by the city's lesbian, bisexual, transgender, and gay community. 415/826–1401.

INTERNATIONAL VINTAGE POSTER FAIR

Held at Fort Mason Center, this is the oldest and largest vintage poster fair in the world. It features American and European posters from the 1890s to the 1980s. 415/546–9608.

ITALIAN HERITAGE PARADE AND FESTIVAL

The Columbus Day festivities in North Beach, the city's Italian community, include a landing pageant, coronation of Queen Isabella, a 1 PM parade up Columbus Avenue, and the traditional blessing of the fishing fleet at Aquatic Park. 415/989–2220.

SAN FRANCISCO FALL ANTIQUES SHOW

About 60 antiques dealers from all over the world exhibit and sell upscale fine and decorative arts at Fort Mason for five days in late October. The opening party is held at the Fort Mason Festival Pavilion the Wednesday before the fair and benefits the Enterprise for High School Students. 415/546–6661.

SAN FRANCISCO JAZZ FESTIVAL

Local and national jazz performers perform at venues all over the city in this 12-day jazz festival, one of the country's finest. 415/398–5655 or 800/627–5277.

SAN FRANCISCO OPEN STUDIOS

Here's a monthlong opportunity for the art-loving public to visit and shop the ateliers of more than 500 artists citywide. Most studios are open weekends only. 415/861–9838.

WORLD PUMPKIN WEIGH-OFF

Pumpkins from all over the world vie for the heavyweight title at this one-day festival sponsored by the International Pumpkin Association. The weigh-off takes place on a Saturday at the Ferry Building farmers' market. 415/346–4561.

NOVEMBER

A CHRISTMAS CAROL

A theatrical version of Dickens's holiday classic is performed by the American Conservatory Theatre every November and December. 415/749–2228.

CHRISTMAS TREE– LIGHTING CEREMONIES

In November and December, tree-lighting ceremonies take place at Ghirardelli Square (415/775–5500), at Pier 39 (415/981–8030), and in Golden Gate Park at Fell and Stanyan streets (415/831–2700). Contact each directly for more information.

DÍA DE LOS MUERTOS

The Mexican tradition of Day of the Dead, derived from Aztec rituals and the Catholic All Souls' Day, is celebrated in early November in San Francisco's Mission District with art exhibitions and a parade. 415/826–1401.

FILM ARTS FESTIVAL OF INDEPENDENT CINEMA

Between 60 and 80 films by independent local artists are screened. 415/552–8760.

HARVEST FESTIVAL & CHRISTMAS CRAFTS MARKET

On two weekends in mid-November at the Concourse Exhibition Center, this arts and crafts fair lets you get an early start on holiday shopping. 707/778–6300.

THE NUTCRACKER

A holiday favorite, Tchaikovsky's *Nutcracker* is performed every November and December by the San Francisco Ballet at the War Memorial Opera House. 415/865–2000.

RUN TO THE FAR SIDE

On the Sunday after Thanksgiving, more than 13,000 people dressed as their favorite Gary Larson characters compete in this 10K run/5K walk through Golden Gate Park. The event benefits the California Academy of Sciences' environmental education programs. 415/759–2690.

SAN FRANCISCO BAY AREA BOOK FESTIVAL

Bibliophiles rejoice at this gargantuan festival held at the Concourse Exhibition Center on the first weekend in November. More than 300 booths represent small, alternative presses as well as big publishing houses; many sell books at a discount. Nearly 250 authors also show up to sign books, hold readings, or participate in discussions. *415/908–2833.*

SAN FRANCISCO INTERNATIONAL AUTO SHOW

For one week in late November, **the Moscone Convention** Center is the showroom for next year's models and space-age, futuristic cars. *415/332–2016.*

DECEMBER

CELEBRATION OF CRAFTSWOMEN

Glasswork, leather work, and wearable art are displayed at Fort Mason on the first two weekends of December. In addition to crafts demonstrations and sales, child care, entertainment, and refreshments are provided. *415/431–1180.*

A CHRISTMAS CAROL

See November, *above.*

CHRISTMAS AT SEA

On a weekend in mid-December, head to Hyde Street Pier for holiday cheer: there's caroling, hot cider, a Santa Claus, and plenty of other surprises for children. *415/561–6662.*

CHRISTMAS TREE– LIGHTING CEREMONIES

See November, *above.*

THE NUTCRACKER

See November, *above.*

SING-IT-YOURSELF MESSIAH

Raise your voice in a chorus of hallelujahs at the Louise M. Davies Hall, in a rousing performance of Handel's *Messiah.* No previous singing experience is required. *415/864–6000.*

day trips out of town

ANGEL ISLAND STATE PARK

One of San Francisco Bay's famous islands is a former prison; the other is an exquisite state park. With 750 acres, Angel Island is an oasis of sandy beaches, old military installations, and spectacular views—all just a ferry ride away from San Francisco. Start your tour at the ferry landing in Ayala Cove, where the visitor center (415/435–1915) distributes a brochure on the history and geography of the island. Then set out for any of the scenic and historic sites that lie along the 5-mi perimeter road that rings the island; or, better yet, ride your bike along the entire route (*see* Bicycling *in* Chapter 3). A mile north of Ayala Cove is Camp Reynolds, which functioned as an army camp from the Civil War to World War II. On the other side of the island is an immigration station, once known as "The Ellis Island of the West," where immigrants (mostly Asian) were detained when trying to enter the United States between 1910 and 1940. There are plenty of picnic tables and barbecue grills around the island (bring your own charcoal, as wood-gathering is not allowed). For information on ferry transportation to and from the island, *see* Chapter 7.

BERKELEY

This vibrant, liberal-minded East Bay town is the storied home of the original University of California, a hotbed of student activism in the tumultuous 1960s. In addition to visiting the beautiful—and now tranquil—campus, make it a point to dine at one of its famous but expensive restaurants, such as Chez Panisse (*see* American/Contemporary *in* Chapter 1), ground-zero of California cuisine. The university's Berkeley Art Museum (*see* Art Museums, *above*), Botanical Garden (*see* Gardens *in* Chapter 3), and Lawrence Hall of Science (*see* Science Museums, *above*) are all worthy attractions in town. Berkeley lies 10 mi east of San Francisco and is accessible via the Bay Bridge, BART, or Transbay bus service. *Berkeley Convention and Visitors Bureau, 2015 Center St., Berkeley 94704, 510/549–7040 or 510/549–8710.*

CARMEL

Carmel, once a Spanish mission town, was founded for a second time in 1904 by a group of artists and writers. Its reputation as an arts colony has grown in the decades since, bringing many charming shops and galleries, although strict zoning laws have been enacted to preserve its old-time charm. Drive the cypress-lined "17 Mile Drive" to Monterey for a peek at the lifestyles of the area's rich and famous, as well as views of the famed Pebble Beach and Cypress Point golf courses. The town lies on the Monterey Peninsula just south of Monterey. *Carmel Business Association, Box 4444, Carmel 93921, 408/624–2522.*

MARINE WORLD AFRICA USA

Opened in 1986, this 160-acre oceanarium and wildlife park features performing dolphins and killer whales, sea lions, tigers, elephants, and exotic birds, as well as shows by world-class water skiers. There are camel and elephant rides, an exhibit filled with free-flying tropical butterflies, and a petting zoo where children can talk to the animals. Discount ticket packages are available with purchase of roundtrip fare aboard the Vallejo Baylink Ferry (*see* Ferry *in* Chapter 7) from San Francisco. *Marine World Pkwy. (Rte. 37) off Hwy. 80, Vallejo, 707/643–6722. Closed Mon.–Tues. in winter.*

MONTEREY

The Monterey Peninsula juts out into the Pacific south of Monterey Bay, and the spectacular shoreline with its white sand beaches, craggy rocks, and twisted cypress trees is unsurpassed for scenic beauty. The town of Monterey was the capital of California in 1777 when the area was under Spanish and Mexican rule; today, Monterey State Historic Park preserves several centuries of buildings and habitations. Also in Monterey are a colorful Fisherman's Wharf, historic Cannery Row, and the spectacular Monterey Bay Aquarium, one of the world's largest, with more than 500 species of sea creatures. The breathtaking "17 Mile Drive" links Monterey with neighboring Carmel (*see above*). Monterey is approximately 140 mi south of San Francisco on Highway 101. *Monterey Peninsula Chamber of Commerce and Visitors and Convention Bureau, 380 Alvarado St., Monterey 93940, 408/649–1770.*

MUIR WOODS NATIONAL MONUMENT

This stunning 550-acre redwood grove is just 17 mi northwest of the city—a 45-minute drive when traffic isn't heavy. With redwoods nearly 250 ft tall and 1,000 years old, this grove was saved from destruction in 1908 and named for naturalist John Muir. It's a pedestrians-only park with 6 mi of easy trails; no cars are allowed in the redwood grove itself. Crowds (and attendant parking problems) make an early morning or late-afternoon visit advisable. Muir Woods is off Highway 1. *Muir Woods National Monument, Mill Valley 94941, 415/388–2595.*

NAPA VALLEY

A trip to the sunny vineyards of Napa Valley is the perfect escape from the fog. Just 30 years ago, Napa's land was predominately used for cattle ranches and plum orchards. Only a handful of wineries had survived Prohibition by making sacramental altar wine. Today Napa has become the premier wine destination in the world, with more than 250 wineries creating everything from gold-medal winning champagnes to robust Italian-style reds. And although wine is the main attraction, the region offers more than the joys of the grape. Picnicking at the wineries or Bothe State Park is a popular pastime, or dine at one of Napa's famed gourmet restaurants. Hike Mt. St. Helena, float over the vineyards in a hot air balloon, ride through the valley aboard the Wine Train, wallow in a mud bath in Calistoga, or shop for antiques in the town of Napa. The American Center for Wine, Food and The Arts, a cultural institution celebrating the area's heritage, is scheduled to open in 2001. Weekend travelers take note: most lodging requires a two-night minimum stay, and in summer Highway 29 is clogged to a standstill. Some wineries still offer free tastings, but many charge a fee, which varies from $2 for several wines, to $25 for a single glass. *Napa Valley Conference and Visitors Bureau, 1310 Napa Town Center, Napa 94559, 707/226–7459.*

OAKLAND

The largest city in the East Bay is Oakland, a major West Coast port whose rich heritage is celebrated in festivals throughout the year, including the Bay Area's largest Juneteenth celebration (*see* Events, *above*). Visit the Oakland Museum (*see* Art Museums, *above*); beautiful Lakeside Park and Lake Merritt; the waterfront Jack London Square for dining, shopping, and nightlife; and the newly refurbished downtown with Art Deco and Victorian buildings. Oakland is 10 mi east of San Francisco, accessible via the Bay Bridge, BART, or Transbay bus service. *Oakland Convention and Visitors Authority, 550 10th St., Suite 214, Oakland 94607, 510/839–9000.*

POINT REYES NATIONAL SEASHORE

The 63,500-acre Point Reyes, the West Coast's only National Seashore, is a favorite for hiking, whale-watching, and solitude-seeking, and also for sea kayaking (*see* Chapter 3) on adjacent Tomales Bay. High rolling grasslands above spectacular cliffs and miles of sandy beaches and tidal pools make this an area of outstanding beauty. The main attraction is the 1870 Point Reyes Lighthouse, a scenic 30- to 40-minute drive from the visitor center. Point Reyes is north of San Francisco in Marin County, accessible via winding Highway 1. *Superintendent, Point Reyes National Seashore, Point Reyes 94956, 415/663–1092.*

SANTA CRUZ

This mellow seaside town has 26 mi of sunny beaches surrounded by ancient redwood forests. At its center is the never-ending carnival of the Santa Cruz Beach Boardwalk, the West Coast's largest seaside amusement park, with its 1924 Giant Dipper wooden roller coaster. Santa Cruz lies 75 mi south of San Francisco (about a two-hour drive), accessible by Highway 1 or 17. *Santa Cruz Area Chamber of Commerce, Box 921, Santa Cruz 95060, 408/423–1111.*

SAUSALITO

Charming Sausalito (Spanish for "little willow"), with its winding streets, rustic houses, waterfront shops, and outdoor dining, is the perfect day trip from San Francisco. It's 8 mi north of San Francisco in Marin County, accessible by Blue and Gold Fleet ferries (*see* Ferry *in* Chapter 7), or by Highway 101 across the Golden Gate Bridge. Just offshore in Richardson Bay are some 400 houseboats; these quirky abodes comprise one of the Bay Area's most famous views. An excellent time to visit is Labor Day weekend, during the renowned Sausalito Art Festival (*see* Events, *above*). *Sausalito Visitors Center, 777 Bridgeway, Sausalito 94965, 415/332–0505.*

SILICON VALLEY: SAN JOSE AND SANTA CLARA

Sprawling San Jose, the largest city in the suburban South Bay and fourth-largest city in California, blends in with its neighbor Santa Clara. Together these two cities have earned the nickname Silicon Valley for their plethora of aerospace, technology, and electronics firms. San Jose has become an increasingly recognized cultural center, with excellent performing arts organizations, gardens, the fine San Jose Museum of Art (*see* Art Museums, *above*), the Tech Museum of Innovation, and the Winchester Mystery House—a bizarre, 160-room Victorian mansion built over a period of 38 years by Sarah Winchester, the rifle heiress, in an attempt to calm the spirits of those killed with Winchester firearms. Smaller Santa Clara is home to the popular Paramount's Great America theme park, with five giant roller coasters. The two cities lie approximately 50 mi south of San Francisco and can be reached by Highways 101 and 280. The San Jose Convention and Visitors Bureau provides information about both cities as well as the rest of Silicon Valley. *San Jose Convention and Visitors Bureau, McEnery Convention Center, 150 W. San Carlos St., San Jose 95113, 408/977–0900.*

SONOMA VALLEY

Sonoma is Napa's more rural country cousin. Sonoma County borders the Pacific Ocean, a fact that lends the topography a cooler climate, plus generous doses of mountains, redwoods, and scenic drives. Its vineyards were initially planted by Catholic missionaries, and share with Napa the distinction of producing some of America's finest wines. The atmosphere of the tasting rooms is more relaxed and rustic than the bustle of Napa's Highway 29. The town of

Sonoma offers a glimpse of the area's history when it was still a colony of Mexico. Built around a central plaza in 1834, it still contains many vintage adobe structures, including General Vallejo's Sonoma Fortress. Healdsburg, also designed around a town square, offers a bit of picturesque Americana. Glen Ellen lies in a forested canyon, where Jack London's ranch remains today, featuring a collection of London's artifacts. Armstrong Redwoods State Reserve offers a primeval 700-acre redwood forest, a wide variety of wildlife, and 20 mi of equestrian trails (horse rentals available). At the north end of the county in the coastal foothills lies tranquil Lake Sonoma. Here you can rent a canoe, camp by the water, hike 40 mi of trails, or fish for bass. *Sonoma Valley Visitors Bureau, 453 1st St. E, Sonoma 95476, 707/ 996–1090.*

TIBURON

On a peninsula called Punta de Tiburon (Shark Point) by Spanish explorers, Tiburon is a beautiful Marin County community with a villagelike atmosphere. San Francisco is directly south, 6 mi across the bay—which makes the views from waterfront restaurants sublime. Like its neighbor, Sausalito, Tiburon is connected to San Francisco by Blue and Gold Fleet ferries (*see* Ferry *in* Chapter 7) and by Highway 101 across the Golden Gate Bridge. Sunday brunch is an institution here, and there are plenty of attractive, upscale shops and galleries to make for an afternoon's browsing. *Tiburon Chamber of Commerce, 96B Main St., Tiburon 94920, 415/ 435–5633.*

YOSEMITE NATIONAL PARK

This 1,169-square-mi natural wonder is in the Sierra Nevada, 210 mi southeast of San Francisco—making it a better destination for a weekend trip. Elevation within the park ranges from 2,000 ft near the park's west entrance to 13,014 ft at the summit of Mt. Lyell. The main attraction, spectacular Yosemite Valley, was carved by glaciers during the Ice Age and is now filled with cascading waterfalls and the famous El Capitan, Cathedral Spires, and Half Dome mountains. Activities include fishing, hiking, bicycling, horseback riding, and, in winter, ice skating and cross-country skiing. Accommodations range from tent camping to a luxury hotel. A free bus shuttle service takes you where passenger cars may not. *Superintendent, Box 577, Yosemite National Park 95389, 209/ 372–0200.*

chapter 5

ARTS, ENTERTAINMENT & NIGHTLIFE

S an Francisco has a first-class cultural calendar. The San Francisco Opera, Symphony, and Ballet are among the best in the nation, and many smaller performing arts organizations put on innovative performances throughout the year. Whether you want to dress up for an evening on the town or bundle up against the fog to see Shakespeare performed in Golden Gate Park, your options are wide open.

Theater and music groups are centered around (but by no means limited to) the Civic Center and Union Square areas, but you'll find that bars and dance clubs abound all around town. South of Market has long been a nightlife hot spot, and you'll still find dozens of dance clubs and live music venues here, despite the area's increasing number of high-priced residential lofts. The Mission District is another hugely popular area for bar-hopping, despite its past reputation as a downmarket spot for dive bars and grungy live-music joints; its gentrification in the past several years has also brought a cascade of swanky retro and theme bars. In the Castro, virtually every other storefront is a gay bar. The Marina, Pacific Heights, and Russian Hill, although less densely packed with bars, cater to a well-dressed professional crowd. North Beach is a mix of tourist haunts, local neighborhood bars, and atmospheric old spots that have served San Francisco drinkers for decades. The Tenderloin is possibly San Francisco's seediest neighborhood, but has a number of good live music venues and bars for those with an adventurous streak or those who want to see what parts of the city looked like before rents went sky high.

The best guide to arts and entertainment events in San Francisco is the "Datebook" section, printed on pink paper, in the combined Sunday Examiner and Chronicle. The free alternative weeklies, the Bay Guardian and SF Weekly, available at cafés and in boxes all over the city, are stronger for information on bars, dance clubs, and the alternative scene. The free weeklies Bay Times and Bay Area Reporter have extensive listings for gay and lesbian entertainment.

performing arts

For information on the fine arts, see Art Galleries, Art Museums, Guided Tours, and Events in Chapter 4.

CONCERT HALLS

4 f-6

CENTER FOR THE ARTS THEATER

The 750-seat state-of-the-art facility at Yerba Buena Center for the Arts has superb acoustics and lots of souped-up technological gadgets. The programming is an adventurous mix of dance, theater, performance art, and music. *Yerba Buena Center for the Arts, corner of Howard and 3rd Sts., South of Market, 415/978–2787.*

4 a-1

COWELL THEATER

With good sight lines and acoustics, the 400-seat Cowell Theater has become increasingly popular with small classical and other ensembles, as well as local dance groups. You can also see spoken word performances and live radio shows here. *Fort Mason Center, Pier 2, Laguna St. at Marina Blvd., Marina, 415/441–5706.*

4 c-8

DAVIES SYMPHONY HALL

The home of the San Francisco Symphony also hosts programs by San Francisco Performances (500 Sutter St., Suite 710, 415/398–6449), a company that presents the world's best musicians and dancers, with high-powered events held at various locations from October through May. *201 Van Ness Ave., at Grove St., Civic Center, 415/864–6000.*

4 c-7

GREEN ROOM

In the same building as the larger Herbst Theater, this small room provides an intimate setting for chamber and vocal ensembles. *Veterans Bldg., 401 Van Ness Ave., at McAllister St., Civic Center, 415/621–6600.*

4 | c-7

HERBST THEATER

World-class soloists, chamber and choral groups, and San Francisco Performances (*see* Davies Symphony Hall, *above*) present their works at the elegant Herbst, in the Veterans Building downtown. Although the theater is plush, the acoustics are mediocre. *Veterans Bldg., 401 Van Ness Ave., at McAllister St., Civic Center, 415/621–6600.*

4 | d-5

MASONIC AUDITORIUM

This large hall is used by San Francisco Performances and others for symphonic and other musical events. *1111 California St., at Taylor St., Nob Hill, 415/776–4917.*

8 | c-3

THEATER ARTAUD

A cavernous converted cannery that still has an industrial air, Artaud is one of the most interesting performance halls in town. The excellent local and traveling shows—often dance, drama, and music all at once—usually have an experimental flavor. *450 Florida St., at 17th St., Mission, 415/621–7797.*

CONCERTS IN CHURCHES

4 | d-5

GRACE CATHEDRAL

Free, late-afternoon organ recitals, choral concerts, and other events take place often, usually on Sunday. Sight lines are poor and the acoustics a bit rumbly, but it's one of the most beautiful places in the city to see a concert. *1100 California St., at Taylor St., Nob Hill, 415/749–6300.*

7 | h-2

MISSION DOLORES

The church next to this historic mission has become a popular site for a cappella and other choral recitals, including performances by top groups such as Chanticleer. *16th St. at Dolores St., Mission, 415/621–8203.*

4 | b-5

OLD FIRST CHURCH CONCERTS

This well-respected Friday evening and Sunday afternoon series at Old First Presbyterian Church includes chamber and orchestral music, vocal soloists, and world music and dance. Call for tickets or visit the TIX booth in Union Square (*see* Tickets, *below*). *1751 Sacramento St., at Van Ness Ave., Pacific Heights, 415/474–1608.*

4 | b-6

ST. MARY'S CATHEDRAL

San Franciscans have a love-hate relationship with this unusual modern building, popularly known as "Our Lady of Maytag" (it looks like a washing machine agitator). Organ recitals and choral concerts are often held on Sunday afternoon. *1111 Gough St., at Geary St., Western Addition, 415/567–2020.*

4 | f-6

ST. PATRICK'S CHURCH

Take a break from the workaday grind by attending Noontime Concerts, a year-round series of solo and chamber music concerts on Wednesday afternoon at 12:30. Solo pianists and vocalists form the bulk of the programs. A $5 donation is suggested for each concert. *756 Mission St., between 3th and 4th Sts., South of Market, 415/777–3211 for concert information.*

DANCE

4 | n-4

DANCERS' GROUP STUDIO THEATER

This small space is packed most Friday and Saturday nights with audiences enjoying the creativity of local choreographers. Many performances incorporate text with music and movement to explore personal and political themes. *3221 22nd St., at Mission St., Mission, 415/824–5044.*

4 | f-6

LAWRENCE PECH DANCE COMPANY

Formed in 1996, this company has gained the reputation of being a rising star in the Bay Area dance scene. Founder and artistic director Pech danced with the American Ballet Theatre and San Francisco Ballet and before turning to choreography. *Yerba Buena Center for the Arts Theater, corner of Howard and 3rd Sts., South of Market, 415/978–2787.*

4 f-6

LINES CONTEMPORARY BALLET

Founded in 1982 by choreographer Alonzo King, LINES creates and presents original, contemporary ballets to ardent crowds at Yerba Buena Center for the Arts Theater, as well as in New York City and Los Angeles. Recent collaborations with musicians like Zakir Hussain have enhanced its reputation. *Yerba Buena Center for the Arts Theater, corner of Howard and 3rd Sts., South of Market, 415/863–3040.*

4 f-6

MARGARET JENKINS DANCE COMPANY

This experimental troupe has a loyal following. Its namesake has collaborated with a number of internationally recognized talents, including Yoko Ono. It often performs at the Center for the Arts Theater (*see above*). *Yerba Buena Center for the Arts Theater, corner of Howard and 3rd Sts., South of Market, 415/826–8399.*

3 d-7

OAKLAND BALLET

Perhaps even more respected than the San Francisco Ballet, this company founded in 1965 often performs revivals of early 20th-century classics, as well as new works set to contemporary music.

EAST BAY ARTS

San Franciscans tend to be little snobbish about arts organization in the East Bay; with so many events in the city itself, they rarely make it across the bay for an evening out. That's a shame, because several of Berkeley's and Oakland's arts organizations are first-rate.

Berkeley Opera (Opera)
    Many of its lead singers come from the San Francisco Opera Chorus.

Berkeley Repertory Theatre (Theaters & Theater Companies)
    It won the 1997 Tony Award for Best Regional Theater.

Berkeley Symphony Orchestra (Orchestras & Ensembles)
    Music Director Kent Nagano is world-renowned.

Oakland Ballet (Dance)
    Some people prefer this group to the San Francisco Ballet.

Performances are held in the grand old Paramount Theater (510/465–6400) in downtown Oakland. *2025 Broadway, at 19th St., Oakland, 510/452–9288.*

8 b-3

ODC/SAN FRANCISCO

ODC, which stands for Oberlin Dance Collective, presents the works of the collective's choreographers, including Brenda Way. It dances *The Velveteen Rabbit* to sold-out crowds each Christmas. *3153 17th St., at Shotwell St., Mission, 415/863–6606, 415/863–9834 for box office.*

2 f-8

ROBERT MOSES' KIN

Founder Robert Moses collaborates with other choreographers, musicians, and even authors to explore social issues such as race, class, and gender through dance. Ballet, jazz, hip-hop, and traditional African dance are all reflected in its programs, usually lauded by the press. In San Francisco, it most frequently performs at Theater Artaud. *171 Hahn St., at Sunnydale Ave., Visitacion Valley, 415/586–1466.*

4 b-7

SAN FRANCISCO BALLET

Although the nation's oldest ballet company has never been known for cutting-edge performances, it has started attracting more notice for its staging of modern works under the artistic direction of Helgi Tomasson. The season runs from February through May. *Box office: 455 Franklin St., at Grove St., Civic Center, 415/865–2000.*

5 f-3

SAN FRANCISCO ETHNIC DANCE FESTIVAL

The city's biggest dance festival, featuring dozens of ethnic dance companies yearly, is held for several days in late June at the Palace of Fine Arts Theater. Check the *Bay Guardian* for schedules and dependable recommendations. *Palace of Fine Arts Theater, 3301 Lyon St., at Bay St., Marina, 415/474–3914.*

SMUIN BALLETS/SF

Led by former San Francisco Ballet Director Michael Smuin, the group is renowned for its fluidity. The company regularly integrates nonclassical music into its performances—it even once danced the first ballet set to mambo music. The group has no regular venue, but it sometimes performs at the Center for the Arts Theater (*see above*). 415/665–2222.

4 *a-6*
UNBOUND SPIRIT DANCE COMPANY

The resident modern dance company of Asian American Dance Performances stages 10 performances every year throughout the Bay Area and Hawaii. Most of its repertoire consists of original works by ethnically diverse Asian-American choreographers. *1840 Sutter St., Suite 207, between Buchanan and Webster Sts., Japantown, 415/441–8831.*

FREE ENTERTAINMENT

7 *a-1*
GOLDEN GATE PARK BAND

The band has put on free concerts every Sunday, weather permitting, since 1882. Concerts start promptly at 1 PM. *Golden Gate Park Band Shell, at west end of Music Concourse, Golden Gate Park, 415/831-2700.*

MAKE-A-CIRCUS

This new vaudeville-style group tours area parks and recreation centers every summer. All the kids in attendance are invited to learn circus skills at Intermission, then join in during the second act. 415/242–1414.

6 *g-5*
SAN FRANCISCO CONSERVATORY OF MUSIC

Many of the conservatory's recitals, student-performed and otherwise, are free of charge. Most are held at either of the conservatory's two smallish concert halls. Call for a schedule of upcoming events. *1201 Ortega St., at 19th Ave., Sunset District, 415/759–3475.*

SAN FRANCISCO MIME TROUPE

Scathing musical satires are performed for free in area parks from the weekend of July 4 through September; the first one usually takes place in Dolores Park. When the mimes pass the hat at the end of the performance, remember that audience donations keep this 40-year-old group afloat. Call for its current whereabouts. 415/285–1717.

7 *b-1*
SAN FRANCISCO SHAKESPEARE FESTIVAL

This popular festival plays at Liberty Tree Meadow in Golden Gate Park, and a few other East Bay and South Bay locations. It usually hits Golden Gate Park around Labor Day, but watch the papers or call for exact dates. Arrive early for the San Francisco shows and bring warm clothing, as the weather in this part of the park is almost invariably cool. *Across Conservatory Dr. from Flower Conservatory, Golden Gate Park, 415/422–2221.*

6 *g-8*
STERN GROVE FESTIVAL

From mid-June to mid-August, the nation's oldest continual free summer

---

CULTURE FOR KIDS

Who says kids don't like opera? Well, maybe that's pushing it, but San Francisco does have plenty of cultural options tailored to the little dears with a short attention span.

Golden Gate Park Band (Free Entertainment)
 Combine this free concert with an afternoon in the park.

Make-A-Circus (Free Entertainment)
 Kids are invited to learn circus skills and then show them off.

The Marsh (Theater & Theater Companies)
 Call for information about special kids' programs.

Oakland Ballet (Dance)
 The December Nutcracker performances tend to sell out.

San Francisco Mime Troupe (Free Entertainment)
 Kids may miss some of the political satire, but they'll still love the show.

San Francisco Symphony (Orchestras & Ensembles)
 Look for the "Music for Families Series."

Sony Theatres Metreon (Movie Theaters Worth Noting)
 A huge IMAX screen makes everyone feel like a little kid.

Stern Grove Festival (Free Entertainment)
 Family-friendly performances in an outdoor setting.

music festival hosts Sunday afternoon performances of music and dance in a fabulously atmospheric amphitheater in a eucalyptus grove. Come early to stake out your patch of grass, and bring warm clothing, as the fog is apt to roll in at any moment. *Sloat Blvd., at 19th Ave., Sunset District, 415/252–6252.*

WOMAN'S WILL

You've never seen Shakespeare like this before; all-women casts perform a single work by the Bard in Bay Area parks each summer. The emphasis is on acting and on the text rather than fancy sets and costumes (this *is* free theater after all). *415/567–1758 during business hrs only.*

4 *f-6*

YERBA BUENA CENTER FOR THE ARTS GARDEN

Any type of performance may make an appearance in the lush, green garden of the Center for the Arts: dance, music, theater, or spoken word. Many of these performances take place on weekday afternoons around 12:30, attracting Financial District workers, but there are occasional evening performances as well. *Corner of Howard and 3rd Sts., South of Market, 415/978–2787.*

MOVIE THEATERS WORTH NOTING

4 *c-6*

AMC 1000 VAN NESS

Even if you usually skip the fancy, new movie theaters for the older, historic treasures, you might like to come here for the guilty pleasure of sitting in big, comfy seats on such a steep slope you'll be able to see the screen no matter what the hairdo of the person in front of you. It was voted "Best First-Run Movie House" in the *Bay Guardian*'s 1999 poll. *1000 Van Ness Ave., at O'Farrell St., Tenderloin, 415/931–9800.*

8 *a-4*

ARTISTS' TELEVISION ACCESS

Not exactly a movie theater, the ATA is more like a fringe media center dedicated to showing low-budget and experimental films, mostly by local artists. The facilities here are strictly garage sale—folding metal chairs and a small screen—but the films shown here are

almost impossible to see elsewhere. *992 Valencia St., at 21st St., Mission, 415/824–3890.*

4 *f-3*

THE CASTING COUCH MICRO CINEMA

True to its name, this 46-person screening room, used exclusively for independent films, has sofas instead of regular seats—and the staff serves chocolate-chip cookies to boot. Arrive 15 minutes before show time to secure a seat. *950 Battery St., between Green and Vallejo Sts., Embarcadero, 415/986–7001.*

7 *g-3*

CASTRO THEATRE

Built in 1922 and still the most beautiful place to see a film in San Francisco, the Castro shows a wide selection of rare, foreign, and unusual films. The man who plays the Wurlitzer organ before performances consistently gets a rousing cheer from the patrons who clap along with his rendition of "San Francisco." The theater's specialties are camp and classics of all genres. *429 Castro St., between Market and 18th Sts., Castro, 415/621–6120.*

4 *f-6*

CENTER FOR THE ARTS THEATER

Open since 1993, the Center for the Arts shows local and international works, often highly experimental, in its 100-seat film and video screening room. *Yerba Buena Center for the Arts, corner of Howard and 3rd Sts., South of Market, 415/978–2787.*

7 *d-7*

THE RED VIC

Film buffs either love this cozy co-op theater, where you can enjoy herbal tea while watching the movie on one of the couches, or hate it, complaining about the small screen and strange repertoire. Films here are usually artsy, ultrafunky, or rare. *1727 Haight St., between Cole and Shrader Sts., Haight, 415/668–3994.*

8 *a-2*

THE ROXIE

This slightly run-down Mission theater shows political, cult, and otherwise bent films of widely varying quality. Although some fabulous films pass through here, there's also a fair share of silly old flicks that might just as well be forgotten. *3117 16th St., at Valencia St., Mission, 415/ 863–1087.*

8 *c-3*

SAN FRANCISCO CINEMATHEQUE

Founded in 1961, the Cinematheque showcases experimental films at about 75 screenings each year from fall to spring. Expect to see historical international films, independent documentaries, conversations with filmmakers, and a little bit of the unexpected. *480 Potrero Ave., between 17th and Mariposa Sts., Potrero Hill, 415/558–8129.*

4 *e-6*

SONY IMAX THEATER

San Francisco's first IMAX theater has the largest screen on the West Coast— 80 ft tall by 100 ft wide. Some films are show in 3-D. *Metreon, 4th and Mission Sts., South of Market, 415/369–6200.*

4 *e-6*

SONY THEATRES METREON

Many locals avoid the glitzy new Metreon, where tourists congregate to spend the day at the high-tech shops, multimedia exhibits, and the movie theater. But with 15 movie screens and 3,900 rocking stadium-style seats, it has no problem attracting crowds. *Metreon, 4th and Mission Sts., South of Market, 415/369–6200.*

5 *d-7*

UNITED ARTISTS CORONET

If you've just got to see a loud action flick, the UA Coronet impresses with its huge capacity, large screen, and Sony Dynamic Digital Sound. *3575 Geary Blvd., at Arguello Blvd., Richmond District, 415/752–4400.*

OPERA

3 *e-3*

BERKELEY OPERA

The opera performs several fully staged shows each season in the intimate Julia Morgan Theater, a treat for operagoers used to nosebleed seats at larger opera houses. Many of its lead singers come from the San Francisco Opera Chorus; a few of them have gone on to the Met. *2640 College Ave., at Derby St., Berkeley, 510/841–1903.*

POCKET OPERA

Since 1977, this company has carved a niche for itself by presenting chamber operas in original English translations from February through June. Although performances may lack the polish of those at the San Francisco Opera, they are unfailingly lively and entertaining. Concerts are held at various locations in San Francisco, Marin, the South Bay, and the East Bay. *415/575–1102.*

4 *c-7*

SAN FRANCISCO OPERA

One of the most important companies in the United States outside New York, the Opera presents a full season of grand-scale originals and revivals from the first Friday after Labor Day through mid-December. Watch for frequent coproductions with European opera companies. *War Memorial Opera House,*

HISTORIC SAN FRANCISCO

With bars, movie theaters, and supper clubs opening every other day, it's easy to forget some of San Francisco's beloved older venues that seem to exude a sense of the city's history.

Beach Blanket Babylon (Cabaret)
Playing since 1974, with topical references to the city.

Castro Theatre (Movie Theaters Worth Noting)
Built in 1922, it's many San Franciscans' favorite theater.

Eli's Mile High Club (Blues)
The birthplace of West Coast blues, and still going strong.

The Fillmore (Pop/Rock)
San Francisco's most famous rock music venue.

Finocchio's (Cabaret)
Featuring female impersonators since 1936.

Mission Dolores (Concerts in Churches)
Concerts in a church next to the city's most famous historic mission.

Tosca (Bars & Lounges)
Worthwhile for its elegant and historic ambience.

Vesuvio (Bars & Lounges)
Popular Beat era hangout.

301 Van Ness Ave., at Grove St., Civic Center, 415/864–3330.

ORCHESTRAS & ENSEMBLES

3 *e-2*

BERKELEY SYMPHONY ORCHESTRA

The Berkeley Symphony Orchestra has managed to hang onto Music Director Kent Nagano, a world-famous conductor who spends part of the year with the renowned Lyon Opera in France. The emphasis is on 20th-century composers, such as Witold Lutoslawski and Luciano Berio. Performances take place in Berkeley's Zellerbach Hall and various other East Bay locations from August to June. *Corner Bancroft and Telegraph Aves., Berkeley, 510/841–2800.*

PHILHARMONIA BAROQUE ORCHESTRA

The orchestra performs works by composers of the 17th and 18th centuries at venues throughout the area. Its season lasts from fall through spring. *415/495–7445.*

SAN FRANCISCO CONCERT CHORALE

Since 1973, the chorale has been singing both the standard choral repertoire and Bay Area premieres of contemporary works. Recently it collaborated with the Margaret Jenkins Dance Company, Kronos Quartet, and Bay Area Women's Philharmonic. Performances are held in churches and concert halls throughout San Francisco and the South Bay. *650/589–3276.*

6 *g-5*

SAN FRANCISCO CONSERVATORY OF MUSIC

The city's major music school has something going on almost nightly, whether it's a performance by students, faculty, or the Conservatory Orchestra. The performances by the Conservatory Opera Theatre are a relatively low-cost introduction to this often pricey art. Most student recitals are free. *1201 Ortega St., at 19th Ave., Sunset District, 415/564–8086.*

4 *f-6*

SAN FRANCISCO CONTEMPORARY MUSIC PLAYERS

The best contemporary company in the area and one of the oldest in the United States stages only about six performances a year at the Yerba Buena Center for the Arts. Concerts generally feature cutting-edge new works by contemporary composers. Ticket prices include a preconcert discussion with composers and other guests. *701 Mission St., at 3rd St., South of Market, 415/252–6235.*

4 *c-8*

SAN FRANCISCO SYMPHONY

California-born conductor Michael Tilson Thomas has attracted near-superstar fame since he became music director in September 1995. Innovative programs of 20th-century American works are the symphony's strong suit. Additional programming includes performances by the youth orchestra, a concert series for families, and chamber music. *Davies Symphony Hall, 201 Van Ness Ave., at Grove St., Civic Center, 415/864–6000.*

4 *c-7*

SAN FRANCISCO WOMEN'S PHILHARMONIC

After a nearly two-year hiatus, this talented group of performers resumed advancing the work of women composers, conductors, and performers in 1997. Performances, held at Herbst Theater, are often preceded by a discussion with the artists. *Herbst Theater, 401 Van Ness Ave., at McAllister St., Civic Center, 415/437–0123, or 415/392–4400 for reservations.*

THEATERS & THEATER COMPANIES

4 *e-5*

ACTOR'S THEATRE

Both classic American plays and contemporary works by emerging playwrights make an appearance in this 99-seat theater. *533 Sutter St., between Powell and Mason Sts., Union Square, 415/296–9179.*

4 *d-6*

AMERICAN CONSERVATORY THEATER (ACT)

One of the nation's leading regional theaters, ACT presents about eight plays annually, from October through late spring, in the newly renovated Geary Theater. In December, it stages a much-loved version of Charles Dickens's *A*

Christmas Carol. 415 Geary St., at Mason St., Union Square, 415/749–2228.

4 *a-6*

ASIAN AMERICAN THEATER COMPANY

This company presents the works of Asian and Asian-American playwrights. *1840 Sutter St., Suite 207, between Buchanan and Webster Sts., Japantown, 415/440–5545.*

4 *b-5*

AUDIUM

Not a theater in the traditional sense of the word, this place was specially designed by composer Stan Shaff as a "theatre of sound-sculptured space"; theatergoers sit in concentric circles in the dark while experimental music coming from 169 speakers encircles them. At each performance, Stan himself mans the control board, and he's happy to tell you about his art before or after the performance. *1616 Bush St., at Franklin St., Pacific Heights, 415/771–1616. Closed weekdays.*

3 *d-2*

BERKELEY REPERTORY THEATRE

Across the San Francisco Bay, the Berkeley Rep was awarded the 1997 Tony Award for Best Regional Theater. It performs an adventurous mix of classics and new plays from fall through spring in a modern, intimate theater near BART's downtown Berkeley station. *2025 Addison St., at Milvia St., Berkeley 510/845–4700.*

8 *c-5*

BRAVA!

Brava! For Women in the Arts is the full name of this theater company that develops and produces works by women playwrights. It frequently showcases the work of Latina authors. *2789 24th St., at York St., Potrero Hill, 415/641–7657.*

4 *d-6*

CURRAN THEATRE

Big Broadway-style shows come to this large theater. *445 Geary St., at Mason St., Union Square, 415/551–2000.*

8 *a-5*

EL TEATRO DE LA ESPERANZA

The resident company of the Mission Cultural Center produces bilingual work based on the Chicano experience. *2868 Mission St., between 24th and 25th Sts., Mission, 415/821–1155.*

4 *e-6*

EXIT THEATRE

Absurdist theater and multimedia productions are the draw at this two-stage café-theater. *156 Eddy St., at Mason St., Union Square, 415/673–3847.*

4 *d-e*

FOOTLOOSE

Footloose produces a wide variety of original works—theater, dance, cabaret, comedy, poetry, and music collaborations—with an emphasis on emerging artists. Performances are at Venue 9, where the lobby art gallery contains the work of local artists. *252 9th St., between Howard and Folsom Sts., South of Market, 415/298–2000.*

4 *c-8*

42ND STREET MOON

This company produces delightful staged concerts of rare chestnuts from the golden age of Broadway musicals. It's especially known for doing little-performed works by composers like Jerome Kern, Cole Porter, and Rodgers and

---

WOMEN IN THE ARTS

San Francisco is a welcoming spot for women who want to expand their role in the traditionally male-dominated worlds of theater and music. The following are some groups whose mission includes furthering women in the arts.

**Brava!
(Theaters & Theater Companies)**
　　Develops and produces works by women playwrights.

**Luna Sea
(Theaters & Theater Companies)**
　　Producing a variety of women-oriented events, including art, performance art, and plays.

San Francisco Women's Philharmonic (Orchestras & Ensembles)
　　One of its goals is to advance the work of women composers, conductors, and performers.

Woman's Will (Free Entertainment)
　　Performing works by the Bard with all-women casts.

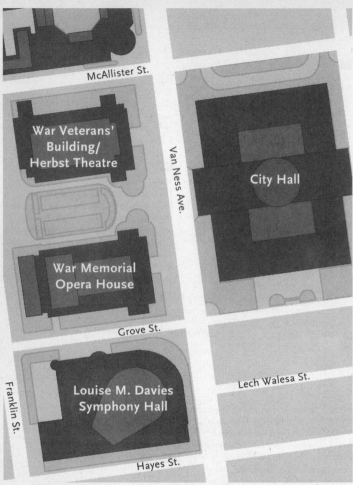

McAllister St.

War Veterans'
Building/
Herbst Theatre

Van Ness Ave.

City Hall

War Memorial
Opera House

Grove St.

Lech Walesa St.

Franklin St.

Louise M. Davies
Symphony Hall

Hayes St.

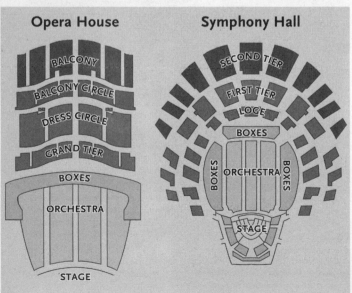

Opera House

BALCONY

BALCONY CIRCLE

DRESS CIRCLE

GRAND TIER

BOXES

ORCHESTRA

STAGE

Symphony Hall

SECOND TIER

FIRST TIER

LOGE

BOXES

BOXES

ORCHESTRA

BOXES

STAGE

Hart. Performances are usually at the New Conservatory Theatre, but it also performs elsewhere in the city. *25 Van Ness Ave., between Fell and Oak Sts., Civic Center, 415/861–8972.*

4 *d-7*
GOLDEN GATE THEATRE
The program consists primarily of musicals, including "Best of Broadway" shows, at this stylishly refurbished theater. *Golden Gate Ave., at Taylor St., Tenderloin, 415/551–2000.*

8 *a-2*
INTERSECTION FOR THE ARTS
Plays, mostly contemporary, poetry readings, and performance art are presented by Intersection in its stark 65-seat space. Unusual sound and visual installations take place in the gallery upstairs. The 32-year-old Intersection is San Francisco's oldest alternative art space, and its shows are consistently good. *446 Valencia St., between 15th and 16th Sts., Mission, 415/626–2787.*

LAMPLIGHTERS MUSIC THEATRE
This group presents lavish productions of Gilbert and Sullivan and other operettas at theaters throughout the Bay Area. Its venues are usually small, the better to appreciate the often whimsical costumes and sets. *415/227–1797 or 415/227–0331 (City Box Office) for tickets.*

4 *d-5*
THE LORRAINE HANSBERRY THEATRE
Experimental, musical, and classical works by African-Americans and other writers of color are performed at this consistently high-quality theater. *620 Sutter St., at Mason St., Union Square, 415/474–8800.*

8 *h-2*
LUNA SEA
There's an ever-changing lineup of women's projects, including visual arts displays, performance art, and readings, at this smoke- and alcohol-free gallery and theater space. Its newest project is presenting full-length plays by lesbian playwrights. Some events are for women only. *2940 16th St., between Capp St. and S. Van Ness Ave., Mission, 415/863–2989.*

4 *a-2*
MAGIC THEATRE
Once Sam Shepard's favorite showcase, the Magic is now San Francisco's leading showcase for new plays, presenting works by the latest rising American playwrights. *Fort Mason Center, Bldg. D, Laguna St. at Marina Blvd., Marina, 415/441–8822.*

8 *a-4*
THE MARSH
Alternative theater, performance, comedy, puppetry, and musical acts come to this "breeding ground for new performance." The 99 house seats include a cozy corner of sofas, and you can purchase freshly baked treats and coffee at intermission. *1062 Valencia St., at 22nd St., Mission, 415/826–5750.*

4 *c-8*
NEW CONSERVATORY THEATRE CENTER
Three theaters seating from 50 to 132 form the heart of this complex where you can see plays produced by the center itself, as well as works by visiting companies like 42nd Street Moon (*see above*). The center's "Pride Season" features contemporary gay- and lesbian-themed works. *25 Van Ness Ave., between Oak and Fell Sts., Civic Center, 415/861–8972.*

4 *d-8*
NEW LANGTON ARTS
In operation since 1975, an eternity for a nonprofit experimental arts organization, New Langton hosts art exhibits upstairs and theater productions downstairs in its 80-seat space. Look for a frequently changing lineup or minimally staged pieces, plus slightly more elaborate productions by visiting companies. *1246 Folsom St., between 8th and 9th Sts., South of Market, 415/626–5416.*

4 *d-7*
ORPHEUM
This 2,500-seat theater, a former vaudeville house, is used for the biggest touring shows. *1192 Market St., at Hyde St., Civic Center, 415/551–2000.*

8 *b-3*
THEATRE OF YUGEN
Synthesizing traditional Japanese and Western forms of theater, Theatre of

Yugen stages theater and multimedia projects in its home, the Noh Space in the Project Artaud complex. *2840 Mariposa St., between Florida and Alabama Sts., Mission, 415/621–7978.*

`.4.` d-6

THEATRE ON THE SQUARE
Smaller touring dramas and musicals are staged here. *450 Post St., at Mason St., Union Square, 415/433–9500.*

`8` a-2

THEATRE RHINOCEROS
The oldest active lesbian and gay theater company in the country, Theatre Rhinoceros stages reliably good plays in its tiny performance space. Some events benefit nonprofit organizations supporting the gay and lesbian communities. *2926 16th St., at Capp St., Mission, 415/861–5079.*

`8` c-3

A TRAVELING JEWISH THEATRE
Look to this company for productions with Jewish themes. *470 Florida St., between 17th and Mariposa Sts., Mission, 415/399–1809.*

`4` f-7

ZEUM THEATER
The performance space in the new interactive art and technology center in South of Market stages high-tech spectacles that appeal to families. *4th and Howard Sts., South of Market, 415/820–3353.*

TICKETS

The city's charge-by-phone ticket service is **BASS** (510/762 2277), which also operates the separate **BASS Charge Performing Arts Line** (415/776–1999). The latter sells tickets to all but the smallest cultural venues in the Bay Area; its operators are more knowledgeable about arts events than those at the main number. You can purchase tickets in person at the BASS outlets in **Tower Records** and **Wherehouse** stores throughout the Bay Area, as well as at the TIX Bay Area booth (*see below*).

Since BASS adds a per-ticket charge to all purchases, you might want to visit venue box offices in person. By calling the numbers given above for each venue and organization, you can get information about box-office hours or mail-order purchase of tickets, if available. Many venues give discounts for students and senior citizens; perhaps the best deal is with the San Francisco Opera, where $20 and a student ID or senior status can get you excellent seats to some shows on the day of performance only. Call ahead for availability.

For same-day, half-price discounts, try the **TIX Bay Area** (251 Stockton St., between Post and Geary Sts., 415/433–7827) booth on Union Square. Open from 11 to 6 Tuesday through Thursday and from 11 to 7 on Friday and Saturday, the booth requires in-person sales; you cannot get information about half-price ticket sales over the phone. Only cash and traveler's checks are accepted for half-price tickets. Half-price tickets for Sunday and Monday shows are sold on Saturday. TIX is also a full-service ticket agency and BASS outlet selling full-price, advance-purchase tickets for arts, culture, and sports events around the Bay Area.

nightlife

BARS & LOUNGES

`4` f-8

ANNIE'S COCKTAIL LOUNGE
Perhaps it's just because it's on a particularly desolate alley South of Market, but when you enter Annie's you feel like settling in for a while. It's as comfortable as could be, lit by the glow of red lightbulbs and plenty of candles. Most nights the jukebox continually plays eclectic tunes, but Tuesday night brings a smattering of folks for karaoke. *15 Boardman Pl., between 6th and 7th and Bryant and Brannan Sts., South of Market, 415/703–0865. Closed Sun.*

`8` a-5

THE ATTIC
The Mission has plenty of hip bars, but this one is possibly the hippest, with jet-black walls and a mellow noir atmosphere. Fairly crowded even on weeknights, this tiny spot hosts occasional alternative arts events, like found footage film nights and live jazz combos. *3336 24th St., between Mission and Valencia Sts., Mission, 415/643–3376.*

4 c-7

BACKFLIP

From the transvestite doorperson in 5-inch platform shoes to the vinyl dresses on the wait staff, everything at Backflip seems designed for maximum visual impact. The place is outrageously decorated with shag carpet, a preponderance of shiny blue vinyl, and fuzzy tufted stools in the rest rooms. You can make reservations for dinner, or just order from the menu of elaborate cocktail food. 601 Eddy St., at Larkin St., Tenderloin, 415/771–3547. Closed Mon.

5 h-3

BALBOA CAFÉ

A young and upwardly mobile crowd mingles over burgers at this lively hangout. But its atmosphere makes it a cut above your average yuppie singles bar, wood paneling, brass railings, and a comfy sofa fill this bar that has been here since 1914. 3199 Fillmore St., at Greenwich St., Cow Hollow, 415/921–3944.

4 f-4

BAMBOO HUT

Next to the swinging Hi-Ball Lounge, the new Bamboo Hut has all the usual elements of a tiki bar: bamboo furniture, Polynesian decor, and fruity drinks served in coconut shells. The crowd is mostly young, well-dressed folks taking refuge from the packed swing and jazz clubs in the neighborhood. 479 Broadway, between Kearny and Montgomery Sts., North Beach, 415/397–9464.

8 a-3

THE BEAUTY BAR

Retro hair products like Toni home permanent kits are lined up against the pink, sparkly walls at this kitschy postmodern cocktail lounge where your seating options include old-fashioned hair dryers. Most evenings a manicurist is on duty to paint the nails of men and women alike. 2299 Mission St., at 19th St., Mission, 415/285–0323.

8 a-2

BLONDIE'S BAR AND NO GRILL

A jukebox with a great selection of jazz and French doors looking out over Valencia Street make Blondie's a sleek spot for a cocktail. A mixed bar most of the week, Blondies' plays host to "Red," an all-women's night, every Sunday. 540

Valencia St., between 16th and 17th Sts., Mission, 415/864–2419.

4 c-2

BUENA VISTA

Unlike most establishments in the area, this bar near Fisherman's Wharf has a loyal local following. The Buena Vista strenuously claims to have introduced Irish coffee to the New World; whether or not that's true, the bartenders do make a mean version, sure to warm you up after your waterfront wanderings. 2765 Hyde St., at Beach St., Fisherman's Wharf, 415/474–5044.

4 d-6

C. BOBBY'S OWL TREE

One of the oddest theme bars in the city is covered floor to ceiling with owl items: '70s macramé owls, painted owls, ceramic owls, stuffed owls, stained-glass owls. The eponymous Bobby, recognizable by his pompadour, mixes drinks while patrons pick Sinatra tunes from the jukebox. 601 Post St., at Taylor St., Union Square, 415/776–9344.

8 d-1

CAFÉ MARS

An increasingly upscale crowd of Russian Hill and Marina residents comes to this somewhat remote corner of SoMa to have a really good time. Sip Martian Martinis, made with Finlandia Cranberry Vodka and a dried cranberry twist, or order a plate of surprisingly good food. The back patio is often booked for private parties. 798 Brannan St., at 7th St., South of Market, 415/621–6277.

4 f-5

CARNELIAN ROOM

On the 52nd floor of the Bank of America Building, the Carnelian Room has what is perhaps the loftiest view of San Francisco's skyline. Dress up if you don't want the staff to look down their noses at you; dinner patrons are required to wear a jacket. 555 California St., at Kearny St., Financial District, 415/433–7500.

7 d-1

CLUB DELUXE

One of the many new, slick retro bars in the city, the Deluxe is unusually free of pretension. Still, patrons enjoy donning their finest '40s duds, sipping martinis, and acting very cool. The place is usually booked by swing bands, but sometimes you'll find owner Jay Johnson himself crooning a few tunes. *1511 Haight St., between Ashbury and Clayton Sts., Haight, 415/552–6949.*

4 *c-4*

THE COUP CLUB

Having taken over the location where *über*–singles spot Johnny Love's used to be, the Coup Club attracts a similar yuppie clientele. Deejays spin a variety of tunes, but you can usually count on the music being mellow enough to allow a civilized conversation. End of the week happy hours start early: Friday at 2 PM. *1500 Broadway, at Polk St., Russian Hill, 415/922–2582. Closed Sun.–Tues.*

8 *a-2*

DALVA

At first glance, it's hard to see why Dalva was voted "Best Bar" by *Bay Guardian* readers in 1999. It's basically just a dark bar lighted by candles on each table and with hip but not-too-

---

SKYLINE BARS

For sightseeing in comfort, nothing beats a skyline bar. You'll find them on the top floor of many of San Francisco's major hotels, as well as in private establishments such as the Carnelian Room.

Carnelian Room, Bank of America Building (Bars & Lounges)
The best of the best, from the 52nd floor; jackets required.

Crown Room, Fairmont Hotel (Hotel Bars)
The crown of the Fairmont, reached by a glass-enclosed elevator.

Equinox, Hyatt Regency (Hotel Bars)
A revolving room provides 360-degree views.

Harry Denton's Starlight Room, Sir Francis Drake Hotel (Hotel Bars)
Live jazz and swing—or taped Frank Sinatra—in swanky, '50s-style digs.

Top of the Mark, Mark Hopkins Inter-Continental (Hotel Bars)
A classic.

View Lounge, San Francisco Marriott (Hotel Bars)
Live piano or R&B and blues.

---

trendy patrons in their twenties and thirties packing both the front room and the quieter back lounge. Then you realize it has achieved the perfect balance of comfort and chic. *3121 16th St., between Valencia and Guerrero Sts., Mission, 415/262–7740.*

8 *a-4*

DOC'S CLOCK

The huge neon sign reading "Doc's Clock Cocktail Time" beckons local barflies to this long and narrow bar. What's possibly the only shuffleboard table in any bar in San Francisco sets this place apart. *2575 Mission St., at 21st St., Mission, 415/824–3627.*

4 *g-6*

EL ROYS

This cavernous two-story, indoor-outdoor restaurant and bar is the site of San Francisco's cruisingest yuppie scene. Packed on weekends and for postwork fêtes on Thursday and Friday, El Roys attracts Financial District workers looking for a date: men are largely in suits, women in clingy little dresses. *300 Beale St., at Folsom St., South of Market, 415/882–7989.*

4 *e-4*

15 ROMOLO

When it first opened in 1998, this gem on an obscure alleyway was the favorite hideaway of scenesters in the know. A slick interior, comfy booths, diverse patrons, and the sense you had escaped all the tourists strolling around just outside made it a cult favorite. Alas, the crowds around the bar are now three deep on weekends, although you can still get a sense of its original, uncrowded charm on weekdays. *15 Romolo St., off Broadway, between Columbus Ave. and Kearny St., North Beach, 415/398–1359.*

7 *h-3*

THE 500 CLUB

A huge neon martini sign outside attracts neighborhood bar flies to this tiny bar on weekdays; weekends, the crowd is younger, trendier, and more social. Two cramped pool tables and three comfy vinyl booths are just about all there is to this bar, so show up early on weekends, when it's difficult to find a place to stand. *500 Guerrero St., at 17th St., Mission, 415/861–2500.*

4 *f-4*

HARRINGTON'S

This family-owned Irish drinking saloon is the place to be on St. Patrick's Day. The rest of the year, the occasional Celtic rock group provides live music. The bar attracts a Financial District crowd unwinding after work on weekdays. *245 Front St., near Sacramento St., Financial District, 415/392–7595. Closed Sun.*

4 *g-5*

HARRY DENTON'S

Packed with well-dressed young professionals after work, Harry Denton's was once voted "Best Place to Pick Up a High-Powered Executive, or a PR Weasel Who Looks Like a High-Powered Executive" by the *Bay Guardian*. Live bands and dancing begin after 10 every night except Sunday. It's also a great place to enjoy stunning views of the bay—especially from the back bar. *161 Steuart St., between Howard and Mission Sts., Embarcadero, 415/882–1333.*

4 *e-4*

HI-BALL LOUNGE

In the midst of some of North Beach's sleazier sex clubs, this swank bar attracts a retro-dressed crowd with its leopard-skin drapery and red velvet booths. Live swing bands (and accompanying swing dance lessons) are a big draw; unfortunately, the tiny dance floor is so packed it's tough to dance most weekend nights. *473 Broadway, between Kearny and Montgomery Sts., North Beach, 415/397–9464.*

4 *g-4*

HOLDING COMPANY

Suited-up workers from the Financial District gather here after work. The kitchen and bar are open weekdays. *2 Embarcadero Center, Embarcadero, 415/986–0797.*

4 *f-6*

HOUSE OF SHIELDS

This old-fashioned saloon, with big wooden booths downstairs and less-atmospheric tables upstairs, fills up after work with an older, buttoned-up crowd. Frequent live jazz music enlivens the place. A cozy wine cellar downstairs is available for private parties. *39 New Montgomery St., between Market and Mission Sts., Financial District, 415/392–7732. Closed weekends.*

8 *a-4*

LATIN AMERICAN CLUB

Graduate students, local intellectuals, and just plain folks come to this Mission District standby that's not too trendy, not too divey, not too loud, and not too sleepy. Quirky Christmas lights over the bar and Formica-topped tables set a no-fuss mood. Mellow Latin American music and patrons who mind their own business make it a good spot for a solo drink. *3286 22nd St., between Valencia and Mission Sts., Mission, 415/647–2732.*

8 *e-3*

LI-LO LOUNGE

This newcomer in Potrero Hill plays up the Polynesian theme to the hilt, with wicker chairs, palm trees, and slowly rotating ceiling fans. Weekdays, multimedia freelancers who live in the neighborhood's new lofts share scorpion bowls and other tropical drinks sprouting long straws. Weekends, the crowd gets younger and trendier. *1469 18th St., between Missouri and Connecticut Sts., Potrero Hill, 415/643–5678.*

4 *e-4*

LI PO'S

The dark, cavernous setting and incense-burning Buddhist shrine lend an oddly mystical feel to this bar on the edge of Chinatown. By 1 AM the coveted back booths are filled with boisterous escapees from the crowded bars of North Beach. Extroverts can take part in

---

LEI À LA DON HO

If swing dancing was the hottest trend a few years ago, Polynesian-themed tiki bars seem to be the thing of the moment. San Francisco offers both old standbys and new additions.

Bamboo Hut (Bars & Lounges)
You probably won't spy any Hawaiian shirts at the trendiest tiki joint.

Li-Lo Lounge (Bars & Lounges)
Hang ten at this newcomer in Potrero Hill.

The Tonga Room (Hotel Bars)
A simulated rainstorm blows through the room every half hour.

Trad'r Sam (Bars & Lounges)
The booths are named after tropical destinations.

occasional karaoke. *916 Grant Ave., between Washington and Jackson Sts., Chinatown, 415/982–0072.*

7 *h-4*

THE LONE PALM

Put on some classy duds if you want to feel at home here, where a '40s retro atmosphere, tables with white table-cloths, and skilled cocktail shakers behind the bar set the scene. This is the perfect setting for sipping martinis with that certain someone. *3394 22nd St., at Guerrero St., Mission, 415/648–0109.*

7 *g-2*

LUCKY 13

If the young, black-clad crowd at Café du Nord (*see Jazz, below*) is a bit too hip for you, head a few doors down to Lucky 13, where a laid-back, tattooed, and pierced set drinks one of the many beers avail-able on tap. Its location at the cross-roads of the Castro, the Mission, and the Lower Haight ensures a diverse but slightly scruffy crowd. *2140 Market St., between Church and Sanchez Sts., Castro, 415/487–1313.*

8 *a-4*

THE MAKE OUT ROOM

The dark, quiet street and beckoning marquee may have you convinced that

this is a shady strip joint. In fact, it's a perfectly reputable bar, whose fairly cav-ernous space is enigmatically decorated with antlers on the wall. The spacious floor means you won't get jostled too unmercifully on crowded weekend nights. Expect to pay a cover for most DJ and live band performances. *3225 22nd St., at Mission St., Mission, 415/ 647–2888.*

7 *h-1*

THE MINT

Here you'll find a mixed gay and straight crowd that really loves their karaoke: earnest and often surprisingly good singers get up on stage to sing every-thing from Broadway favorites to Rolling Stones songs to Celine Dion tunes. There's a two-drink minimum at the tables during karaoke, but it's rarely enforced when the bar isn't crowded. Karaoke starts at 9 PM Monday through Thursday, 8 PM on Friday, and 4 PM on weekends. *1942 Market St., between Duboce and Laguna Sts., Hayes Valley, 415/626–4726.*

7 *g-1*

MOLOTOV

A grungy group of Lower Haight regu-lars comes here to release its angst with a beer and game of pool. It's more a place to drink than to see and be seen—perhaps because it's so dark inside you can barely see who's standing next to you. *582 Haight St., between Fillmore and Steiner Sts., Lower Haight, 415/558–8019.*

7 *d-1*

MURIO'S TROPHY ROOM

Upper Haight slackers and bikers usu-ally crowd this low-key bar. When the conversation lags, you can always resort to the pool table, jukebox, or TV. *1811 Haight St., between Shrader and Stanyan Sts., Haight, 415/752–2971.*

7 *g-1*

NOC NOC

Step inside this Lower Haight institution and you'll find yourself in a postmodern cave complete with chunky Flintstones-style furniture and a very eclectic music repertoire—lots of acid jazz and house. Despite its wild decor and raucous Lower Haight location, it's usually just a mellow place to enjoy a beer or wine (there's no full bar). *557 Haight St., between Fillmore and Steiner Sts., Lower Haight, 415/861–5811.*

KARAOKE BARS

Whether you're a musically inclined extrovert or a timid shower warbler you can find your 15 minutes of fame at any of the following spots.

**Annie's Cocktail Lounge
(Bars & Lounges)**
   It's worth a trip to this out-of-the-way spot for Tuesday karaoke.

Bahia Cabana (Dance Clubs)
   Singing replaces dancing every Tues-day night.

Li Po's (Bars & Lounges)
   Tunes are occasionally belted out in this faintly mystical Chinatown bar.

**The Metro
(Gay & Lesbian Bars & Clubs)**
   It's mostly gay men at their Tuesday night session.

The Mint (Bars & Lounges)
   Karaoke seven nights a week for those who just can't get enough.

---

7 h-1
ORBIT ROOM
In this smart-looking café-bar with a high ceiling, you can enjoy a leisurely cocktail at the bar, a better choice than the leg-crunching, conical-shape tables. The subdued lighting and high-tech design make you feel as if you're on display at an art gallery. *1900 Market St., at Laguna St., Hayes Valley, 415/252–9525.*

5 d-7
PAT O'SHEA'S MAD HATTER
One of the better sports bars in a city where sports bars get no respect, Pat O'Shea's is a good choice if you just gotta see the game on a big-screen TV. The crowd, enthusiastic about Bay Area teams to say the least, still seems to tolerate the occasional dissenter. *3848 Geary Blvd., at 3rd Ave., Richmond District, 415/752–3148.*

4 u-4
PERRY'S
This upscale singles bar-restaurant is usually jam-packed with a well-dressed Cow Hollow and Marina crowd. It serves great hamburgers as well as more substantial fare. *1944 Union St., between Laguna and Buchanan Sts., Cow Hollow, 415/922–9022.*

7 d-1
PERSIAN AUB ZAM ZAM
Quirky barely begins to describe this old-time bar, where the cantankerous bartender opens and closes the bar seemingly at whim, occasionally dismisses people from his bar, telling them that they'd "be more comfortable" at the bar down the street, and seems put out if you order anything other than a martini. Though some can't understand why anyone would put themselves through this ordeal just for a cocktail, others wouldn't have a martini any place else. *1633 Haight St., between Clayton and Belvedere Sts., Haight, 415/861–2545.*

4 b-8
PLACE PIGALLE
The vibes are hip and European at this sleek, French-owned wine bar and gallery space where you can lounge in anonymity in the dark front room or get a good look at your date in the brightly lit back. DJs spin Wednesday, Thursday, and Saturday, and occasional spoken-word performances are held during the week. *520 Hayes St., between Octavia and Laguna Sts., Hayes Valley, 415/552–2671.*

7 g-5
THE RAT AND RAVEN
Probably the most popular bar in the relatively bar-free Noe Valley, the Rat and Raven attracts a loyal bunch of neighborhood regulars most nights of the week. Although occasionally it can resemble a frat party, the crowd is friendly and laid back. A patio out back is a plus. *4054 24th St., between Noe and Castro Sts., Noe Valley, 415/285–0674.*

4 d-6
RED ROOM
A hyper-hip, well-dressed crowd frequents this cocktail bar attached to the Commodore Hotel. Its impressive entrance opens to a curved wall of red bottles stacked to the ceiling, and a shockingly red interior. Dress in black, the better to be seen. *827 Sutter St., at Jones St., Tenderloin, 415/346–7666.*

8 b-3
THE RITE SPOT
The piano in the corner, candlelit tables, and understated decor all lend a sense of class to this outer Mission bar that's a favorite among locals. The light meals served here are a cut above most bar fare. *2099 Folsom St., at 17th St., Mission, 415/552–6066.*

4 c-4
ROYAL OAK
Comfy leather-clad bar stools and large tables encourage you to lounge at this capacious bar attracting well-to-do professionals. Tiffany-style lamps, red velvet couches, and dozens and dozens of plants have set the mood here since the 1970s. *2201 Polk St., at Vallejo St., Russian Hill, 415/928–2303.*

4 e-2
ROYALE
This new North Beach hangout is owner John Loufas's attempt to create a comfortable spot for locals to enjoy a drink away from the crush of tourists usually found in this neighborhood. Blue lights dimly illuminate the velvety gray banquette that runs the length of the bar and the dark hardwood floor. The manager is proud of his jukebox, stocked with eclectic tunes from Sinatra to the

Clash. *1326 Grant St., between Green and Vallejo Sts., North Beach, 415/433–4247.*

8 b-3
SACRIFICE

Unlike most of the trendy new spots in the Mission District, Sacrifice is a no-attitude place where more people swig Budweiser than anything sipped from a sugared-rimmed cocktail glass. Couples huddle at the dimly lighted tables over kitschy Latin American prayer candles, while a small crowd congregates around the pool table in the back. Attached is a

---

DRINKING AL FRESCO

With fog rolling in almost every summer evening, it's often too cold to drink outside in San Francisco. This makes it all the more enjoyable to spend that rare balmy evening enjoying a drink outside.

Backflip (Bars & Lounges)
Sip drinks next to a swimming pool outside the funky Phoenix Hotel.

**Blondie's Bar and No Grill
(Bars & Lounges)**
The seats by the open French doors are highly prized.

Bottom of the Hill (Pop/Rock)
Escape to the patio when you tire of the alternative rock.

**The Café
(Gay & Lesbian Bars & Clubs)**
Beyond the mirrors and neon is a balcony facing Market Street.

El Río (Dance Clubs)
Salsa dancing and margaritas are the preferred activities on the patio.

Mad Dog in the Fog (Pubs)
Indulge in a tasty Irish breakfast—in the fog?

**The Metro
(Gay & Lesbian Bars & Clubs)**
The balcony overlooks a busy corner in the Castro.

**Potrero Brewing Company
(Brewpubs & Microbreweries)**
The heated decks are a great place for lunch on sunny days.

The Rat and Raven (Bars & Lounges)
The back patio is packed on sunny summer evenings.

Zeitgeist (Bars & Lounges)
A crowd spills outside in the afternoons.

---

casual restaurant selling Cajun and Caribbean food. *800 S. Van Ness Ave., at 19th St., Mission, 415/641–0990.*

4 e-3
SAVOY-TIVOLI

A youngish upscale crowd fills this cavernous North Beach institution. The large, covered front patio opens when the weather's nice, making the Savoy prime territory to drink wine and watch the world go by. If it's raining, you can shoot pool in the back. *1434 Grant Ave., between Union and Green Sts., North Beach, 415/362–7023. Closed Sun.*

8 a-2
SKYLARK

In the midst of a densely packed cluster of nightspots, Skylark is the classiest of the bunch: this is the place to drink martinis and romance that special someone, especially if you can grab one of the two huge booths next to the front windows. Be sure to look up at the whimsical ceiling mural. *3089 16th St., at Valencia St., Mission, 415/621–9294.*

4 e-4
SPECS'

To call this North Beach bar low key would be an understatement; patrons sometimes seem almost comatose as they quietly nurse their beverages. Still, it's a friendly, no-attitude sort of place where you can gaze for hours at the quirky memorabilia papering the walls. *12 Adler Pl., off Columbus Ave., next to Tosca (see below), North Beach, 415/421–4112.*

7 g-1
THE TORONADO

As divey as you would expect from a Lower Haight bar, the Toronado attracts a leather-clad and slacker set with one of the widest selections of microbrews in the city. The jukebox blares a refreshing mix of kitschy country and western in addition to the standard grunge anthems. *547 Haight St., between Fillmore and Steiner Sts., Lower Haight, 415/ 863–2276.*

4 e-4
TOSCA

Like Spec's and Vesuvio nearby, Tosca holds a special place in San Francisco history. A mostly opera jukebox and a beautiful old espresso machine create an elegant environment—no wonder celebrity patrons (including Francis Ford Coppola, Sam Shepard, and Mikhail Baryshnikov) are occasionally spotted in the enormous red booths. Try one of the excellent liqueur-laced coffee drinks. *242 Columbus Ave., at Broadway, North Beach, 415/391–1244.*

2 *b-3*

TRAD'R SAM

Locals in the know who don't mind driving to the outer Richmond have a kitschy good time at this over-the-top tiki bar. Each of the booths here is labeled with a tropical destination like Samoa or Hawaii. That along with the wicker furniture will get you into the mood to order a rum punch, Singapore Sling, or one of those silly drinks served frothing with dry ice. *6150 Geary Ave., at 26th Ave., Richmond, 415/221–0773.*

4 *e-4*

VESUVIO

A bohemian hangout during the Beat era (along with City Lights Bookstore next door), Vesuvio is the ideal place to discuss the city's history with the regulars at the bar. The best seats, though, are upstairs all the way in the back, where large windows look out on Columbus Avenue. *255 Columbus Ave., at Broadway, North Beach, 415/362–3370.*

8 *a-1*

ZEITGEIST

Don't be intimidated by the number of motorbikes outside this bar, the crowd is friendly, even if you got here on four wheels. In the afternoon it's popular with bike messengers and neighborhood slacker types; by night the BMW motorbike crowd clogs the outdoor deck, waiting its turn at the pool table. Occasional bands make up for their lack of talent by turning up the volume. *199 Valencia St., at Duboce St., Mission, 415/255–7505.*

BLUES

4 *d-6*

BISCUITS AND BLUES

Southern cuisine and southern blues make a great combination at Biscuits and Blues. Unlike at many clubs, all seats have an unobstructed view of the stage, and all ages are welcome. *401 Mason St., at Geary St., Union Square, 415/292–2583.*

4 *d-6*

THE BLUE LAMP

A friendly downtown hole in the wall, the Blue Lamp books blues, jazz, folk, and rock bands nightly. The crowd is a mix of laid-back regulars and music hounds following their favorite bands. *561 Geary St., at Taylor St., Union Square, 415/885–1464.*

3 *d-5*

ELI'S MILE HIGH CLUB

The reputed birthplace of West Coast blues remains a consistently good bet, continuing to highlight promising local acts, and some more-renowned performers. It's a small club with a pool table, soul food, and music, usually Thursday through Sunday. *3629 Martin Luther King Jr. Way, between 36th and 37th Sts., Oakland, 510/655–6661.*

4 *e-6*

GOLD DUST LOUNGE

Although its Union Square location means it's often packed with tourists, the Gold Dust Lounge is a good choice—if you like Dixieland jazz. Settle back into one of the large, comfy booths, order a stiff cocktail, and listen to the live music performed every night of the week. This historic bar has been open since 1933. *247 Powell St., at O'Farrell St., Union Square, 415/397–1695.*

4 *e-3*

GRANT AND GREEN BLUES CLUB

A welcome contrast to the very civilized cafés and coffeehouses that dominate North Beach, the dark, smoky Grant and Green Blues Club hosts raucous blues shows seven nights a week. *1731 Grant Ave., at Green St., North Beach, 415/693–9565.*

4 *a-6*

JOHN LEE HOOKER'S BOOM BOOM ROOM

Blues musicians take the stage here seven days a week. The club's namesake makes occasional appearances. *1601 Fillmore St., at Geary St., Western Addition, 415/673–8000.*

5 *c-6*

LAST DAY SALOON

Blues, Cajun, rock, funk, country, and jazz artists frequent this always-packed club. *406 Clement St., between 5th and*

6th Aves., Richmond District, 415/ 387–6343.

4 *f-3*

PIER 23

A restaurant by day, Pier 23 turns into a club by night, with live music that tends toward Motown, blues, and reggae. *Pier 23 at the Embarcadero, Embarcadero, 415/362–5125.*

4 *e-4*

THE SALOON

The patrons are sometimes as entertaining as the tip-top performers at this blues and R&B hangout in North Beach. Local R&B favorites Johnny Nitro and the Doorslammers play here frequently. *1232 Grant Ave., at Columbus Ave., North Beach, 415/989–7666.*

8 *b-1*

SLIM'S

One of the most popular live music venues in town, Slim's specializes in what it labels "American roots music"— blues, jazz, classic rock—with a sprinkling of alternative rock and roll. Although tickets and drinks are not cheap, co-owner Boz Scaggs helps bring in the crowds and top-notch talent. *333 11th St., between Folsom and Harrison Sts., South of Market, 415/255–0333.*

BREWPUBS & MICROBREWERIES

2 *a-3*

BEACH CHALET

Murals depicting San Francisco in the 1930s produced by the Works Project Administration decorate the walls of this hot new restaurant and microbrewery in a beautiful Willis Polk–designed Art Deco building overlooking the Pacific Ocean. The beers run the gamut from a light pilsner to Playland pale ale, named after a former amusement park that was nearby. *1000 Great Hwy., near Martin Luther King Jr. Dr., Golden Gate Park, 415/386–8439.*

4 *h-5*

GORDON BIERSCH BREWERY AND RESTAURANT

Inside the old Hill Brothers Coffee factory, this brewery, with soaring ceilings and sleek industrial decor, is a favorite of the twenty- and thirtysomething set. Better-than-average bar food and excellent microbrew beers, such as the malty Blonde Bocke and Golden Export, a refreshing dry lager, make all the other well-dressed patrons look even better. *2 Harrison St., at Embarcadero, Embarcadero, 415/243–8246.*

8 *c-3*

POTRERO BREWING COMPANY

The payoff for coming to this formerly industrial spot at the edge of the Mission District is space: the brewery is spread out over a spacious bi-level loft with not one but two heated outdoor decks. The house-made brews—from refreshing wheat beers to hearty oatmeal stouts—come with food you wouldn't expect to find at a brewpub, such as polenta, oysters, and gourmet Italian sandwiches. *535 Florida St., at Mariposa St., Mission, 415/552–1967.*

4 *e-4*

SAN FRANCISCO BREWING COMPANY

A thirtysomething crowd, equal parts jazz lovers and beer connoisseurs, frequents this popular brewery. The frequent mellow jazz ensures that the excellent beers—taste the Alcatraz Stout or the Gripman's Porter—go down smoothly. *155 Columbus Ave., at Pacific St., North Beach, 415/434–3344.*

8 *b-1*

20 TANK BREWERY

Serving up a large selection of microbrews and some hearty bar food such as pizzas and nachos, this former warehouse is a good place to fuel up before heading across the street to Slim's (*see* Blues, *above*). A mix of frat boys and Gap-clad twentysomethings don't seem to mind the cheesy '80s tunes. *316 11th St., at Folsom St., South of Market, 415/ 255–9455.*

CABARET

4 *d-8*

ASIASF

This sophisticated SoMa bar and restaurant is the hottest place in town for saucy, sexy fun. The entertainment, as well as gracious food service, is provided by "gender illusionists." These gorgeous men don daring dresses and strut in impossibly high heels on top of the bar, which serves as a catwalk, vamping to show tunes and disco favorites. The creative Asian-influenced cuisine is excellent. *201 9th St., at Howard St., South of Market, 415/ 255–2742.*

4 *e-3*

BEACH BLANKET BABYLON

This zany San Francisco revue has been selling out most nights since 1974, with talented musicians and a wacky script that changes to incorporate topical references and characters. Although the choreography is colorful and the songs witty, the real stars are the comically exotic costumes and famous ceiling-high headgear. Those under 21 may attend Sunday matinee performances only. *Club Fugazi, 678 Green St., at Powell St., North Beach, 415/421–4222.*

4 *e-4*

FINOCCHIO'S

This world-famous club has been generating confusion with its female impersonators since 1936. The decor hasn't changed much since then. To add to the retro mood, show tunes comprise the bulk of the repertoire. Shows are Thursday through Saturday only. *506 Broadway, at Kearny St., North Beach, 415/ 982 9388.*

7 *g 2*

JOSIE'S CABARET AND JUICE JOINT

In the predominantly gay Castro, Josie's stages everything from serious theatrical pieces to stand-up comedy, drag acts, and cabaret. Drag chanteuse Musty Chiffon and cabaret singer Samantha Samuels have both made appearances here. *3583 16th St., at Market St., Castro, 415/861 7933.*

4 *d-6*

PLUSH ROOM

This cabaret space at the York Hotel (a.k.a. the "Empire," one of Kim Novak's hideaways in Alfred Hitchcock's *Vertigo*) has long been a place for torch singers and jazz divas. In recent years, small comedies and monologues have been performed here, too. *940 Sutter St., between Leavenworth and Hyde Sts., Tenderloin, 415/885–2800.*

CIGAR BARS

4 *f-4*

850 MONTGOMERY STREET

Since all the staff has an ownership stake in the bar, this is one of the few spots in town where you can smoke both indoors and out. Pick out a premium cigar from the humidor, some cognac, or one of several wines available by the glass and settle down at one of the tables with the other well-dressed cigar fans. *850 Montgomery St., between Jackson and Pacific Sts., Jackson Square, 415/291–0850. Closed Sun. and Mon.*

4 *e-6*

THE IRON HORSE

This old-fashioned restaurant-bar morphs at night into a live music venue with a smoking lounge upstairs. While DJs play '70s, funk, and R&B tunes in the main room, smokers of both cigarettes and cigars enjoy the enclosed smoking room with a small humidor. *19 Maiden La., between Kearny St. and Grant Ave., Union Square, 415/982–2582.*

SINGLES BARS

If you want to see San Franciscans wearing their best clothes and flirting like mad, check out the scene at the following places.

The Coup Club (Bars & Lounges)
The new spot that replaced the old standby, Johnny Love's.

El Roys (Bars & Lounges)
A cavernous spot that's hyper-trendy.

Gordon Biersch (Brewpubs & Microbreweries)
A tried-and-true brewpub-restaurant with tasty homemade brews.

Harry Denton's (Bars & Lounges)
Live bands and dancing spice up the scene.

Holding Company (Bars & Lounges)
The Embarcadero location means it's packed with suits come happy hour.

Perry's (Bars & Lounges)
Pacific Heights and Marina residents mingle here.

4 *d-5*

MURRAY'S CIGAR AND COGNAC LOUNGE

Comfortable chairs and good ventilation in the glassed-in cigar room make this cigar lounge inside the Canterbury Hotel a favorite meeting place of the San Francisco Cigar Society. Food and drinks from the adjacent restaurant and bar can be brought into the lounge, where a relaxed atmosphere prevails. *740 Sutter St., between Jones and Taylor Sts., Nob Hill, 415/474–6478.*

COMEDY

4 *a-2*

BAY AREA THEATRESPORTS

This group stages shows of improvised skits that range from the side-splitting to the frankly silly. The annual improv festival each August features innovative formats like competitive grudge matches against improv teams from L.A. Also call to ask about improv workshops. *Fort Mason Center, Bldg. B, Laguna St. at Marina Blvd., Marina, 415/474–8935.*

4 *c-2*

COBB'S COMEDY CLUB

This well-established club books national performers, such as Jake Johannsen, Rick Overton, and Janeane Garofalo. *The Cannery lower courtyard, 2801 Leavenworth St., at Beach St., Fisherman's Wharf, 415/928–4320.*

KILLING MY LOBSTER

This new comedy collective, performing in San Francisco only since 1997, has been making a name for itself with riotously funny sketch comedy mixing slapstick, satire, and sometimes music. Its members are also responsible for wacky short films like *Space Chocolate* and *Bonjour Sandwich*. *415/267–0642.*

4 *f-4*

THE PUNCH LINE

Big-name comics sometimes perform at this club, once a launching pad for the likes of Jay Leno and Whoopi Goldberg. The Sunday Showcase, a bargain at $5, features up-and-coming Bay Area comics. *444-A Battery St., 2nd floor, between Clay and Washington Sts., Financial District, 415/397–7573.*

4 *a-2*

TRUE FICTION MAGAZINE

Audience members suggest titles and themes, and the True Fiction crew improvises a story on the spot: no two shows are ever alike. If you want to get a taste of what it does, listen for one of the frequent appearances on the public radio program West Coast Live. Performances are usually at Fort Mason's Bayfront Theater. *Fort Mason Center, Laguna St. at Marina Blvd., Marina, 415/441–8822.*

DANCE CLUBS

4 *c-8*

BAHIA CABANA

A multigenerational, international crowd dances at this tropical downtown supper club with mural-covered walls. Thursday and Friday are salsa nights; other evenings expect Brazilian, Caribbean, Jamaican, and Latin bands. Tuesday night the karaoke machine gets fired up. *1600 Market St., at Franklin St., Hayes Valley, 415/861–4202.*

4 *d-8*

THE CAT CLUB

Formerly Cat's Alley Bar & Grill, this newly remodeled dance space with two dance floors, a huge DJ booth, and plenty of nooks for sitting attracts an eclectic group for different dance parties every night of the week. Particularly popular is Wednesday night's "Bondage A Go-Go," the oldest fetish dance club in California—it's a light introduction to the real S&M subculture. Thursday night's "1984" blares '80 pop tunes all night. *1190 Folsom St., at 8th St., South of Market, 415/431–3332.*

4 *h-7*

CLUB TOWNSEND

Local DJs churn out sounds for a mostly gay male crowd at this vast SoMa disco. The popular Club Universe on Saturday nights is a crush of buff and shirtless men. The first Friday night of the month is Club Q, a dance club for lesbians featuring "mixtress" Page Hodel. *177 Townsend St., between 2nd and 3rd Sts., South of Market, 415/974–6020.*

4 *f-7*

COVERED WAGON

Mixed crowds gather here early in the evening before continuing on to other

SoMa haunts, but as the night wears on the crowd becomes increasingly lesbian. Live funk, soul, and ska some nights attracts a crowd that's happy to get sweaty; other nights it's DJs dancing under the glow of black lights, against a backdrop of cheesy Western decor. *917 Folsom St., at 5th St., South of Market, 415/974–1585.*

8 *a-6*
EL RÍO
A healthy mix of men and women, straight and gay, turns up at this casual neighborhood hangout for different dance parties every night of the week, when DJs spin a variety of tunes and alternative rock bands play. On Sunday you can work off the beer with some salsa dancing on the back patio. Particularly popular are same-sex salsa and swing dancing nights, preceded by dance lessons. *3158 Mission St., at Cesar Chavez St., Mission, 415/282–3325.*

4 *e-8*
THE ENDUP
This primarily gay club has a pool table, a gazebo, and a waterfall, all surrealistically situated almost underneath U.S. 101. Sunday starting at 5:30 AM, look for the hugely popular "Sunday T-Dance," a gay dance party that lasts until 2 AM Monday morning—a tradition for nearly a quarter of a century. Monday and Wednesday night is "Club Dread," a reggae DJ dance party. *995 Harrison St., at 6th St., South of Market, 415/357–0827 Closed Tues.*

8 *a-2*
ESTA NOCHE
Esta Noche plays a good mix of hard-pumping Latin, house music, and '70s disco to a crowd of mostly Latin gay men plus a handful of drag queens. Women, however scarce, are welcome. *3079 16th St., at Valencia St., Mission, 415/861–5757.*

4 *h-7*
KING STREET GARAGE
Every night brings a different music and a different crowd to this dark and cavernous dance club. The biggest crowds show up for Asia, when DJs spin tunes for gay Asian men the second and fourth Friday of the month, and for Futura, when gay Latinos dance to Latin and house music on the second and

fourth Saturday. *174 King St., between 2nd and 3rd Sts., South Park, 415/974–6020.*

8 *d-2*
METRONOME BALLROOM
Turn up any night of the week for lessons in swing, Latin, and almost every other type of ballroom dance. The place is at its most lively on weekend nights, when dancers come to this alcohol-free, smoke-free environment to practice their dance steps. *1830 17th St., at DeHaro St., Potrero Hill, 415/252–9000.*

7 *g-1*
NICKIE'S BBQ
Red-vinyl booths and Christmas lights decorate this unpretentious Lower Haight hole-in-the-wall. DJs spin something different every night—usually hip-hop on Thursday, '70s funk on Friday, funk and soul on Saturday, and reggae on Sunday. Patrons have a good time dancing, despite the elbow-to-elbow crush most nights. *460 Haight St., between Webster and Fillmore Sts., Lower Haight, 415/621–6508.*

FREE DANCE LESSONS

If you're looking to pick up a few dance pointers, the following clubs and bars give free lessons (although there's sometimes a cover to get in), usually before the band starts playing. Always call to confirm times and types of lessons; they change frequently.

Bahia Cabana (Dance Clubs)
Join in salsa classes on Thursday.

Café du Nord (Jazz)
Lessons in swing are the most popular.

Hi-Ball Lounge (Bars & Lounges)
Some people here are so good you wonder why they're taking lessons.

**Rawhide II
(Gay & Lesbian Bars & Clubs)**
The only club in the city with two-step and line dancing lessons.

Roccapulco (Dance Clubs)
Wednesday night salsa lessons prepare you to hit the dance floor weekends.

330 Ritch Street (Dining & Dancing)
Swing lessons take place Wednesday.

8 *a-6*

ROCCAPULCO

Formerly Cesar's Latin Palace, Roccapulco got a face-lift and a spit shine and is once again bringing in crowds. Wednesday night you can take some serious salsa lessons (call ahead for exact times). Then, put your skills to use Friday through Sunday nights, when the city's most dedicated dancers come to dance all night long. The crowd is mostly young, well-dressed Latinos. *3140 Mission St., at César Chavez (Army) St., Mission, 415/648–6611.*

4 *e-8*

1015 FOLSOM

This mixed gay and straight SoMa spot, one of the largest in the city, was under threat of closing at press time, inspiring a heated debate about the rash of club closings in the rapidly gentrifying South of Market area. If it survives, it's the best place to dance to drum and bass and other electronica. *1015 Folsom St., at 6th St., South of Market, 415/431–1200.*

DINING & DANCING

4 *f-4*

BROADWAY STUDIOS

If you're tired of getting stepped on in tiny dance clubs like the Hi-Ball Lounge, the large wooden dance floor here will come as a welcome surprise. The food is fairly basic—mostly burgers and pastas—but will keep you fueled up for the hours of dancing ahead. Swing classes most nights of the week come in two flavors: beginning and intermediate. Saturdays the club is closed for private events. *435 Broadway, between Montgomery and Kearny Sts., 415/291–0777. Closed Sat. and Mon.*

4 *c-4*

RED DEVIL LOUNGE

This plush, trendy supper club features local and up-and-coming live funk, rock, and jazz acts, along with the occasional DJ dance night. Intimate tables line the narrow balcony overlooking the dance floor. *1695 Polk St., at Clay St., Polk Gulch, 415/921–1695.*

4 *g-7*

330 RITCH STREET

Open Wednesday through Sunday, this popular SoMa dinner club attracts a classy crowd with its stylish decor, extensive tapas menu, wooden dance floor, and occasional live music and diverse lineup of DJ dance parties. There's a sizable following for Thursday's Popscene, with BritPop, mod, and indie rock. A little-known fact: in the 1970s, this space was a hard-core sex club. *330 Ritch St., between Townsend and Bryant Sts., South of Market, 415/541–9574. Closed Mon. and Tues.*

4 *e-8*

UP AND DOWN CLUB

Sleek deco digs give this multilevel SoMa supper club the feel of a New York lounge. Upstairs you'll find a DJ laying down tracks, but little room to dance. Downstairs, Latin jazz and acid jazz heat up the room. *1151 Folsom St., between 7th and 8th Sts., South of Market, 415/626–2388. Closed Sun.*

FOLK & ACOUSTIC

3 *c-2*

FREIGHT AND SALVAGE COFFEE HOUSE

One of the best folk clubs in the country and certainly the best in the Bay Area merits a trip across the bridge to Berkeley. In this alcohol-free, smoke-free spot you can see some of the country's most talented performers of folk, blues, bluegrass, and world music. *1111 Addison St., near San Pablo Ave., Berkeley, 510/548–1761.*

7 *g-5*

NOE VALLEY MINISTRY

One of the city's more eclectic venues hosts everything from chamber music to world music to folk tunes. Although it's an atmospheric spot for unamplified concerts, sight lines are poor. Call ahead for tickets. *1021 Sanchez St., at Elizabeth St., Noe Valley, 415/282–2317.*

GAY & LESBIAN BARS & CLUBS

7 *g-3*

THE CAFÉ

This large, lively bar with mirrored walls and neon lights used to cater mainly to lesbians, but these days you'll find plenty of gay men as well. Dancing and a quiet chat are equally popular diversions here. The rare outdoor balcony makes it a favorite for smokers. *2367 Market St., at Castro St., Castro, 415/861–3846.*

4 *c-4*
THE CINCH

Except for the music, which is culled from a hip collection of CDs behind the bar, this is a Wild West–themed gay men's bar with amazingly cheap drinks. Memorable touches include a cigar store Indian, swinging doors, fake cacti, Navajo rugs, and wagon wheels. *1723 Polk St., between Clay and Washington St., Polk Gulch, 415/776–4162.*

4 *d-8*
COCO CLUB

A variety of acts comes through this narrow, cozy, woman-owned restaurant and performance space south of Market—everything from acoustic rock to avant-garde jazz and blues. The club is largely lesbian, but all are welcome. The entrance is tucked away on Minna Street. *139 8th St., at Minna St., South of Market, 415/626–2337. Closed Mon.*

7 *g-3*
THE DETOUR

Minimally decorated with a chain-link fence and pool table, this bar attracts a young, good-looking gay clientele. Urgent techno house music and Saturday-night go-go dancers set the racy mood, as do the dim blue lights. If you forget the address, listen for the music, since the black-on-black sign is impossible to see at night. *2148 Market St., between Castro and Noe Sts., Castro, 415/861–6053.*

4 *c-5*
KIMO'S

This laid-back gay men's club has floor-to-ceiling windows that provide a great view of busy Polk Street. On Friday and Saturday nights, drag, cabaret, and comedy shows take place upstairs. *1351 Polk St., at Pine St., Polk Gulch, 415/885–4535.*

8 *a-3*
LEXINGTON CLUB

This is the Mission District's neighborhood lesbian bar, where a low-key crowd hangs out drinking beer, shooting pool, playing pinball, and poring over the jukebox selections. Although the crowd is mostly gay women, men and straight women will also feel comfortable. *3464 19th St., at Lexington St., Mission, 415/863–2052.*

7 *g-2*
THE METRO

More upscale than the nearby Detour and filled with guppies (gay yuppies), the Metro has a balcony that overlooks the intersection of Noe, 16th, and Market streets. The Tuesday night karaoke is wildly popular. A line usually forms on weekends. *3600 16th St., at Market St., Castro, 415/703–9750.*

7 *f-3*
MIDNIGHT SUN

Two large video screens help alleviate the need for conversation in this crowded gay men's bar, one of the oldest in the Castro. A mix of campy TV shows and music videos play on the giant video screens. The thirtysomething crowd tends toward the clean-cut and upscale. *4067 18th St., at Castro St., Castro, 415/861–4186.*

4 *c-6*
MOTHERLODE

The city's most popular transvestite haven, Motherlode is *the* place for transvestites, transsexuals, and their admirers. It's sometimes seedy, and always entertaining. Free drag shows draw a crowd on Friday and Saturday nights. *1002 Post St., at Larkin St., Tenderloin, 415/928–6006.*

4 *e-8*
RAWHIDE II

If the Texas two-step is your thing, there's no place like the Rawhide, where gay men and women, mostly in their thirties and forties, come to dance to country and western music. The dance floor is packed with couples in cowboy boots twirling each other around. Most of the dancers here look like they've been practicing their moves for a long time, but if you're not so experienced you might want to show up for the two-step or line dancing lessons that take place many evenings. *280 7th St., between Howard and Folsom Sts., South of Market, 415/621–1197.*

8 *b-1*
SF-EAGLE

One of the few SoMa gay bars remaining from before the area's gentrification, this bar hosts innumerable campy contests, like Mr. SF Leather, most of which are AIDS benefits. The Sunday afternoon "Beer Busts" (3 PM–6 PM) have been hugely popular for years. *398 12th St., at Harrison St., South of Market, 415/ 626–0880.*

8 *c-1*

THE STUD

One of the city's oldest gay bars, with a gender-bending mix of straight, gay, and bisexual patrons, The Stud is a reliable choice any night of the week. The club's DJs mix up-to-the-minute music with carefully chosen hits from the glory days of gay disco. The Tuesday-night club Trannyshack is especially popular, when cross-dressers enjoy "make-up tips and cheap cocktails." Friday nights the crowd is mostly women. *399 9th St., at Harrison St., South of Market, 415/252–7883.*

7 *f-3*

TWIN PEAKS

This casual, loungelike gay bar beckons with comfy-looking pillows stacked in the window seats. The Peaks has been around for more than 15 years and proudly claims to have been the first gay bar in the city with clear—as in, not tinted—floor-to-ceiling windows. On weekends expect big crowds of mostly older men. *401 Castro St., at Market St., Castro, 415/864–9470.*

2 *f-6*

WILD SIDE WEST

Wild it may not be, but Wild Side West is an excellent place to while away an evening. Although this mellow neighborhood bar out in residential Bernal Heights has a large lesbian contingent, all are welcome; it was voted the "Best Lesbian Bar for Everybody" by the *San Francisco Bay Guardian.* *424 Cortland Ave., between Mission and Bayshore Sts., Bernal Heights, 415/647–3099.*

HOTEL BARS

4 *e-5*

CLUB 36

On the top floor of the Grand Hyatt, Club 36 has piano music and a view of North Beach and the bay—both draws for out-of-towners. The decor is corporate blah, but if you park yourself in front of one of the windows, you probably won't notice. *345 Stockton St., between Post and Sutter Sts., Union Square, 415/398–1234.*

4 *d-5*

CROWN ROOM

This aptly named lounge on the 23rd floor of the Fairmont Hotel is one of the city's more luxurious skyline bars. Those prone to vertigo may want to close their eyes while riding up the glass-enclosed elevator. *Fairmont Hotel, California and Mason Sts., Nob Hill, 415/772–5131.*

4 *g-4*

EQUINOX

On the 22nd floor of the Hyatt Regency, this is the city's only revolving skyline bar. You can sightsee, eat, and drink, all without even swiveling your chair. *5 Embarcadero Center, at Market St., Embarcadero, 415/788–1234.*

4 *e-5*

HARRY DENTON'S STARLIGHT ROOM

On the 21st floor of the Sir Francis Drake Hotel, this most romantic of rooftop lounges re-creates the 1950s high life with velvet booths and dim lighting. A live swing combo plays weekends. Come well dressed (jackets are preferred for men) and with plenty of money for cover charges and high-priced cocktails. *450 Powell St., between Post and Sutter Sts., Union Square, 415/ 395–8595.*

4 *e-5*

THE LOBBY LOUNGE

The lobby lounge in the Ritz-Carlton, the city's most elegant hotel, features a harpist during high tea (weekdays 2:30–4:30, weekends 1–4:30). Piano music, with occasional vocal accompaniment, takes over during cocktails—until 11:30 weeknights and 1:30 AM weekends. *600 Stockton St., at California St., Nob Hill, 415/296–7465.*

4 *d-5*

NEW ORLEANS ROOM

Although this bar in the Fairmont Hotel has a somewhat tacky 1960s hotel-bar ambience, it's still a low-key place to enjoy a pricey cocktail along with show tunes by the pianist. *950 Mason St., at California St., Nob Hill, 415/772–5259.*

4 b-7
OVATION

In the Inn at the Opera Hotel, Ovation is perhaps the most romantic lounge in the city, with dim lighting, sumptuous Victorian decor, and a crackling fireplace. The most popular time to come (and most difficult time to get in) is after symphony and opera performances. *333 Fulton St., between Franklin and Gough Sts., Hayes Valley, 415/553–8100.*

4 d-6
REDWOOD ROOM

The Clift Hotel's Art Deco lounge is a classic favorite, especially among martini drinkers. The low-key but sensuous ambience is enhanced by Klimt reproductions and the warm redwood walls that give the bar its name. Mellow music from the grand piano fills the room. *Clift Hotel, 495 Geary St., at Taylor St., Union Square, 415/775–4700.*

4 d-5
THE TONGA ROOM

Tropical drinks are served with little paper umbrellas at this absurdly kitschy bar, where quasi-Polynesian decor and an artificial lagoon draw locals and out-of-towners. Every 30 minutes or so, a simulated rainstorm blows through the bamboo-and-palm-filled room, and at 8 PM most nights, an almost comically bad soft-rock band performs from a thatched hut in the middle of the lagoon. *Fairmont Hotel, 950 Mason St., at California St., Nob Hill, 415/772–5278.*

4 d-5
TOP OF THE MARK

The bar at the top of the Mark Hopkins Inter-Continental hotel was immortalized by a famous magazine photograph as a hot spot for World War II servicemen on leave or about to ship out. Now you can dance to the sounds of that era on weekends, in a room with a view. Crowds are a bit sedate, and drink prices high, but the views and quality of the swing, jazz, and standards are superb. *Mark Hopkins Inter-Continental, 999 California St., at Mason St., Nob Hill, 415/392–3434.*

4 e-6
VIEW LOUNGE

Enjoy live R&B or blues, or simply some jazz tunes played on piano, on the 39th floor of the San Francisco Marriott. The views through the fan-shape windows more than compensate for the uninspired corporate hotel–style decor. *San Francisco Marriott, 55 4th St., at Mission St., South of Market, 415/896–1600.*

JAZZ

4 d-3
BIMBO'S 365 CLUB

A large, plush room swathed in red draperies, Bimbo's retains a retro ambience apt for the "Cocktail Nation" programming that keeps the dance floor hopping. Tickets to big-name progressive jazz and alternative rock bands often sell out in advance, but you can usually get tickets to shows by local acts at the door. *1025 Columbus Ave., at Chestnut St., Russian Hill, 415/474–0365.*

4 e-4
BLUE BAR

A well-heeled crowd in their thirties and forties lounges in funky aqua armchairs at this tiny spot tucked beneath the retro Beat-generation restaurant Black Cat. A blue light infuses the space with a dreamy feel. Live jazz bands perform nightly, and a scaled-down version of Black Cat's cuisine is served until 1 AM. *501 Broadway, at Columbus Ave., North Beach, 415/981–2233.*

11 a-3
BRUNO'S

Restored in 1995 after years of neglect, Bruno's is a slice of retro heaven in a happening neighborhood. In one room, diners eat elaborately presented meals at enormous red booths; next door, well-dressed hipsters order swanky cocktails at the long bar and listen to the local jazz and swing bands. *2389 Mission St., between 19th and 20th Sts., Mission, 415/550–7455. Closed Sun.*

7 g-2
CAFÉ DU NORD

The atmosphere in this basement bar is decidedly casual, but the music, provided mostly by local talent, is strictly top-notch. The newest trend here is DJ nights featuring drum and bass. Those more interested in playing pool or socializing can do so in the front of the bar, while music lovers groove uninterrupted in the back. Dinner is served

Wednesday through Saturday night. *2170 Market St., between Church and Sanchez Sts., Castro, 415/861–5016.*

8 *a-3*

THE ELBO ROOM

This popular Mission watering hole becomes unmanageably crowded as the night progresses. Head upstairs for some of the best local live jazz, hip-hop, or occasional DJs and world music acts, or join the locals packed around the pool table. Happy hour stretches from 3 PM until 9 PM. *647 Valencia St., between 17th and 18th Sts., Mission, 415/552–7788.*

4 *e-4*

ENRICO'S

The city's hippest North Beach hangout for a long spell after its 1958 opening, Enrico's is once again all the rage. The indoor–outdoor café has a mellow ambience, a fine menu (tapas and Italian), and mellow nightly jazz combos. *504 Broadway, at Kearny St., North Beach, 415/982–6223.*

4 *e-4*

JAZZ AT PEARL'S

This sedately romantic North Beach joint is one of the few reminders of North Beach's days as a hot spot for cool tunes. The talent level is remarkably high, featuring mostly traditional jazz in a dimly lit setting. There's no cover, but during shows there's a two-drink minimum. *256 Columbus Ave., near Broadway, North Beach, 415/291–8255. Closed Sun.*

5 *h-8*

JUSTICE LEAGUE

Live acid jazz and hip-hop groups alternate with DJ dance nights at this club that's high on energy and low on pretension. But you'd best show up early on weekend nights, unless you want to be one of the people standing in the long line out front. The funky interior of the club was hand-painted by local graffiti artist Twist. *628 Divisadero St., near Hayes St., Western Addition, 415/440–0409.*

4 *c-2*

LOU'S PIER 47

Although it's near one of the city's most touristed locations, Lou's waterfront bar attracts a laid-back local crowd with cool jazz and hot Cajun food. It's a fine place for a break in the middle of the day, as

it's open daily from 6 AM until 9 PM. Most days see two bands perform: one in the late afternoon and one in the evening. *300 Jefferson St., at Jones St., Fisherman's Wharf, 415/771–0377.*

4 *f-3*

PIER 23

A waterfront restaurant by day, Pier 23 turns into a packed, unpretentious club at night. Musical arts range from jazz to salsa, Motown to reggae. *Embarcadero and Pier 23, Embarcadero, 415/362–5125.*

5 *f-8*

STORYVILLE

Storyville switched gears and names in early 1996, going from the rock palace Brave New World to a dressy, classic jazz club. Both front and back rooms have live music from Tuesday through Saturday. The kitchen serves Cajun cuisine. *1751 Fulton St., between Central St. and Masonic Ave., Western Addition, 415/441–1751.*

3 *d-8*

YOSHI'S

Serious jazz aficionados make the trip to Oakland to see big names and local favorites perform at Yoshi's. Blues and Latin stars put on shows frequently. *510 Embarcadero St., between Washington and Clay Sts., Oakland, 510/238–9200.*

PIANO BARS

7 *h-1*

MARTUNI'S

Groups of gay men and straight couples enjoy the low light, copious floral arrangements, velvet curtains, and overall swank atmosphere of this attractive bar with attractive bartenders in white shirts and black vests. Have a seat at the semicircular bar and order one of the creative variations on the martini; particularly odd versions include the chocolate martini and sour apple martini. Piano players tickle the ivories in the back room on weekends. *4 Valencia St., at Market St., Mission, 415/241–0205.*

4 *c-5*

THE SWALLOW

For those who have had it with the young and buffed, this quiet, posh bar at the foot of Nob Hill caters to an older gay male clientele. Pianists play standards nightly from 9 PM, and patrons are often invited to croon along. *1750 Polk St., between Washington and Clay Sts., Nob Hill, 415/775–4152.*

POP/ROCK

8 *e-2*

BOTTOM OF THE HILL

Squeeze into this bar at the bottom of Potrero Hill to hear promising local talent and touring bands. The atmosphere is ultra low-key, although the occasional nationally known act turns up here from time to time. It's one of the city's best bets for quality alternative rock bands. *1233 17th St., at Texas St., Potrero Hill, 415/621–4455.*

2 *e-3*

THE FILLMORE

One of San Francisco's most famous rock music halls serves up a varied menu of national and local acts: rock, reggae, grunge, jazz, comedy, folk, acid house—you name it. To avoid paying steep service charges for events here, stop by the box office Sundays between 10 and 4. *1805 Geary Blvd., at Fillmore St., Western Addition, 415/346–6000.*

4 *c-6*

GREAT AMERICAN MUSIC HALL

A gorgeous old theater that serves as a midsize concert venue, the Music Hall books an innovative blend of rock, blues, folk, jazz, and world music. The beautiful marble-pillared building (constructed in 1907 as a bordello), the balcony on which to avoid the madding crowd, and top-notch acts make it many San Franciscan's favorite live-music venue. A bar menu is available most nights. *859 O'Farrell St., between Polk and Larkin Sts., Tenderloin, 415/885–0750.*

4 *f-7*

HOTEL UTAH

All manner of local rock, jazz, and acoustic bands perform at this casual SoMa bar. The room in the back where bands play is so small that many patrons end up at the long wooden bar, supposedly shipped from Belgium during the Civil War. The crowd is eclectic and friendly—you'll find lawyers, bikers, and slackers—and the pub grub is almost reason enough to come. Many shows, including Monday open mike nights, are free. *500 4th St., at Bryant St., South of Market, 415/421–8308.*

8 *a-2*

KILOWATT

Saturday and Sunday, Kilowatt hosts indie rock bands reaching maximum noise levels. Other nights, it's just a good place for a cheap drink and game of pool. The dark, smoky bar is usually filled with a mix of neighborhood locals. *3160 16th St., between Valencia and Guerrero Sts., Mission, 415/861–2595.*

8 *b-1*

PARADISE LOUNGE

There are three different stages to choose from here; Monday-night poetry slams and beyond-the-fringe theatrical performances at the connecting Transmission Theatre are just a small sampling. Although the quality of music varies widely, the broad selection ensures that there's always something worth hearing. *1501 Folsom St., at 11th St., South of Market, 415/861–6906.*

4 *e-7*

WARFIELD

This former movie palace was transformed into one of the city's largest

ROMANTIC RENDEZVOUS

San Francisco is arguably the most romantic city in the United States. If you're not a true believer, try one of the following places.

Harry Denton's Starlight Room (Hotel Bars)
The most romantic of the city's rooftop bars.

The Lone Palm (Bars & Lounges)
A retro atmosphere and excellent cocktails.

Martuni's (Piano Bars)
Floral arrangements and velvet curtains make you glad you dressed up.

Ovation (Hotel Bars)
A fireplace illuminates the sumptuous Victorian decor.

Redwood Room (Hotel Bars)
A classy Art Deco lounge with mellow jazz music to set the mood.

Tosca (Bars & Lounges)
A historic charmer with huge red booths.

venues for mainstream rock and roll. If you sit downstairs at the tables and chairs there's usually a two-drink minimum. Upstairs is a balcony with theater seating. Performers range from Porno for Pyros to Suzanne Vega to Harry Connick, Jr. *982 Market St., between 5th and 6th Sts., Tenderloin, 415/775–7722.*

PUBS

7 *g-1*

AN BODHRÁN

One of the city's newer Irish bars, this is a good place for a pint and some mellow conversation. Sunday afternoon, the bar is packed with Guinness drinkers enjoying cheap pints and an Irish music session. *668 Haight St., between Pierce and Steiner Sts., Lower Haight, 415/431–4724.*

4 *b-3*

BLACK HORSE PUB

Owner Joe Gilmartin likes to call his pub "the smallest bar on the West Coast," and he just may be right; his tiny spot accommodates only 15 people. The beers, all British or Irish imports, change monthly; traditional English bitters are a big draw. *1514 Union St., between Van Ness Ave. and Franklin St., Cow Hollow, 415/928–2414. Closed Tues.*

8 *b-3*

DYLAN'S

Named after Wales's most famous poet, this Potrero Hill pub is plastered with Welsh memorabilia. You may not understand the bartender's thick accent, but he'll understand you when you order a pint. Jazz music on Wednesday night draws a big crowd. *2301 Folsom St., at 19th St., Mission, 415/641–1416.*

4 *c-6*

EDINBURGH CASTLE

If you're willing to brave the dicey neighborhood, this British pub with a beautiful bar is an excellent choice. Thick-accented U.K. and Irish types congregate to play darts, eat fish-and-chips, and drink pints of Guinness and Boddingtons. Local bands make occasional appearances, as do Irish and British writers for occasional spoken word performances. *950 Geary St., between Polk and Larkin Sts., Tenderloin, 415/885–4074.*

4 *c-4*

FIDDLER'S GREEN

Tourists and local Irish expats alike find their way to this bi-level bar near Ghirardelli Square. Downstairs is the place for a mellow pint of Guinness or Strongbow. Upstairs is a dance floor, which gets packed during DJ events when British house music is the choice. *1333 Columbus Ave., at Beach St., Fisherman's Wharf, 415/441–9758.*

7 *d-2*

FINNEGANS WAKE

One of the only bars in sedate and residential Cole Valley, Finnegans Wake attracts all the neighborhood barflies with the usual pub accoutrements: a pool table, darts, and perfectly pulled pints. A Ping-Pong table in back is usually in use all night long. *937 Cole St., at Parnassus St., Cole Valley, 415/731–6119.*

4 *e-5*

THE IRISH BANK

Known as the Bank of Ireland before it was forced to change its name by the Bank of Ireland, this Financial District institution is a chummy, attitude-free spot for an after-work drink. Irish memorabilia lines the walls, Irish beers are on tap, and Irish bartenders are usually serving up the pints. The back room is a restaurant serving full Irish meals. *10 Mark La., off Grant Ave. between Sutter and Bush St., Financial District, 415/788–7152.*

4 *g-6*

KATE O'BRIEN'S

Although the patrons are mostly Multimedia Gulch types stopping in for a hearty lunch or a postwork pint, a few authentic Irish regulars are usually seated at the bar chatting with the Irish bartenders and waitress. The pub food (Irish stew, fish-and-chips, and the like) is a cut above the usual, and weekends DJ dance parties take place upstairs. *579 Howard St., between 1st and 2nd Sts., South of Market, 415/882–7240.*

7 *g-1*

MAD DOG IN THE FOG

A crowd of Guinness-drinking Brits frequents this pub in the Lower Haight. On warm summer mornings or afternoons, the beer garden outside is the perfect place for a greasy breakfast like the

Greedy Bastard (bacon, sausage, baked beans, scrambled eggs, and tomato). Best of all, dishes of at least $6 include a free pint until 2:30 PM. Team trivia contests on Monday and Thursday are all the rage. *530 Haight St., between Fillmore and Steiner Sts., Lower Haight, 415/ 626–7279.*

4 e-3
O'REILLY'S IRISH BAR AND RESTAURANT
Gleaming brass railings and wooden snugs (booths) set this Irish bar apart from others in the city. Everything about O'Reilly's is classy, from the unusually good Irish breakfasts (no soggy tomatoes here) to the well-dressed crowd and irresistible Irish coffee. *622 Green St., at Columbus Ave., North Beach, 415/ 989–6222.*

5 f-7
THE PIG AND WHISTLE
Although this is a fine place to just relax with a pint of Harp amid English memorabilia, many come to take advantage of the pool table in the back room or the professional dartboard in the front. Frequent pool and darts tournaments attract big crowds. The bar-sponsored cricket team uses the game as an "excuse to go out on sunny weekends, hit a few stumps, and down copious amounts of beer in the process." *2801 Geary Blvd., at Wood St., Richmond, 415/ 885–4779.*

5 d-6
PLOUGH AND THE STARS
The city's Guinness-loving Irish drink at this very plain but authentic pub. It's also the center of traditional Irish music in the city, with live music most nights and Irish music sessions on Sunday and Tuesday night. *116 Clement St., between 2nd and 3rd Aves., Richmond, 415/751–1122.*

WINE BARS

4 f-4
BUBBLE LOUNGE
A postwork Financial District crowd fills this upscale yet comfortable champagne bar on weeknights. Upstairs, young executives nestle into wingback chairs and overstuffed couches, while downstairs a lively atmosphere surrounds the pool table and another bar. Champagne is this bar's raison d'être and the selection is excellent, with more than 300 types to choose from. A full bar is also available, as are sushi and other light fare. *714 Montgomery St., at Washington St., Financial District, 415/434–4204.*

4 e-4
CAFÉ NIEBAUM-COPPOLA
Sitting at one of the tables outside Francis Ford Coppola's new café–wine bar you could almost imagine you're in Italy—if it weren't for the cold wind howling down Columbus Avenue. Appetizers like pizza and caponata go well with the Italian and California wines. Of course you can get Coppola's own vintages as well, sold by the bottle, the glass, or a four-wine "flight." *916 Kearny St., at Columbus Ave., North Beach, 415/ 291–1700.*

7 d-2
EOS WINE BAR
Attached to the restaurant of the same name, this snug (and usually packed) little wine bar sells hundreds of wines by the bottle and many by the glass. Frequent tastings group wines thematically, or order some of Eos's knockout food to go with your wine selections. *901 Cole St., at Carl St., Cole Valley, 415/566–3064.*

4 h-8
HAYES AND VINE
Hayes and Vine has a broad selection of wines by the glass, many of them moderately priced. After-opera visitors mingle with younger wine aficionados looking for a classy night away from the Lower Haight or the Mission. Although there is no kitchen, you can order plates of cheese, pâté, and caviar. *377 Hayes St., between Franklin and Gough Sts., Hayes Valley, 415/626–5301.*

4 f-4
LONDON WINE BAR
This cozy Financial District spot, open on weekdays only, pours 40 wines by the glass from a cellar of 8,000 bottles. The clubby interior, with large, private booths, attracts serious dealmakers who come to seal the deal after hours. *415 Sansome St., between Sacramento and Clay Sts., Financial District, 415/788–4811.*

chapter 6

HOTELS

Not surprisingly, San Francisco, the tourist capital of the United States, has hotel rooms of every size, style, and swankiness: small bed-and-breakfasts with the bath down the hall, opulent luxury hotels on Nob Hill, and everything in between. The bad news is that rooms don't come cheap. First-time visitors are often surprised to find that except for a few rare bargains, even relatively bland hotel rooms in central neighborhoods can go for $150 a night or more.

The largest concentration of accommodations is around Union Square, where mostly ritzy hotels are convenient to the city's best shopping, theaters, and public transportation. A few blocks uphill from Union Square, Nob Hill is the city's preferred address, its prestigious hotels looking down upon the city. Another cluster of hotels, all held down to four stories or fewer due to city ordinances, is found around Fisherman's Wharf. Rooms here are on the bland side but command high prices because of the location. The other main hotel area is along Lombard Street, the main corridor leading to the Golden Gate bridge. Although Lombard Street is close to the waterfront and gives you easy access to Marin County, it's not one of the city's more attractive areas for its plethora of tacky hotel neon and fast-food joint signs, and traffic noise can be a problem.

Don't overlook San Francisco's more residential neighborhoods. Atmospheric North Beach is packed with Italian restaurants and cafés but has surprisingly few hotels. Still, a few small B&Bs hide on the neighborhood's side streets. The Castro, the most prominent gay neighborhood in the United States, offers gay- and lesbian-friendly accommodations ranging from motels to B&Bs to small hotels. Haight-Ashbury, with its flower power history, attracts those hoping to recapture the '60s. The upscale residential Marina District and neighboring Pacific Heights draw visitors looking for a quiet neighborhood and views of the bay and the Golden Gate Bridge.

Whenever you come, make reservations as far in advance as possible for the best possible selection. This is especially important in late summer and early fall. And when calculating your expenses, don't forget to figure in the 14% hotel tax that will take an extra bite out of your wallet. Most San Francisco hotels, especially those around Union Square, the Financial District, and Nob Hill charge hefty rates for parking—often around $25 a night. The price categories used below refer to a standard room for two people during peak season (summer and fall). At most of these places you can find suites or deluxe rooms for considerably more, and occasionally you can score a smaller room for somewhat less.

Except for some tiny B&Bs, most hotels in San Francisco have at least a few rooms, and often several entire floors, where smoking is prohibited.

price categories

CATEGORY	COST*
Very Expensive ($$$$)	over $200
Expensive ($$$)	$150–$200
Moderately Priced ($$)	$100–$150
Budget ($)	under $100

*All prices are for a standard double room, excluding 14% tax.

VERY EXPENSIVE LODGINGS

4 e-5
CAMPTON PLACE
Highly attentive service is the hallmark of this small, top-tier hotel behind a simple brownstone facade. Although many rooms are small, all are supremely elegant, with light earth tones and pearwood accents, and all have stylishly modern baths featuring open-design limestone shower/baths. Multipane windows do a good job of keeping city noises out (a plus in this active neighborhood). The Campton Place Restaurant is famed for its lavish breakfasts

and country French dinners, and the hotel's lounge is popular at cocktail time with the downtown crowd. *340 Stockton St., between Post and Sutter Sts., Union Square, 94108, 415/781–5555 or 800/235–4300, fax 415/955–5536. 101 rooms, 9 suites. Restaurant, bar, in-room safes, minibars, room service, laundry service and dry cleaning, concierge, business services, meeting rooms, parking (fee). AE, DC, MC, V.*

3 f-3,   h-4
THE CLAREMONT

Nestled in the Berkeley Hills about 20 minutes from downtown San Francisco, this luxurious European-style resort has provided refuge from the urban fray since 1915. Treat yourself to an herbal bath or therapeutic massage in the spa. Dine poolside at the Bayview Café or at upscale Jordan's with a great view of San Francisco and the Bay. Rooms vary from quite small to spacious, but all have a refined look that reflects the hotel's respectable age. *41 Tunnel Rd., near Ashby and Claremont Aves., Berkeley, 94705, 510/843–3000 or 800/551–7266, fax 510/848–6208. 247 rooms, 32 suites. 2 restaurants, bar, café, in-room data ports, minibars, room service, 2 pools, wading pool, beauty salon, massage, sauna, steam room, 10 tennis courts, health club, jogging, shops, nightclub, laundry service and dry cleaning, concierge, business services, meeting rooms, parking (fee). AE, D, DC, MC, V.*

4 d-6
THE CLIFT

The lobby's dark paneling and enormous chandeliers lend a note of grandeur to this quiet, handsome hotel with a well-deserved reputation for superior service. Rooms, some rich with dark woods and burgundies, others refreshingly pastel, have large writing desks, plants, and flowers. The art deco Redwood Room, paneled with wood from a single 2,000-year-old tree, is the place for power breakfasts and draws an upscale crowd at the end of the working day for cocktails and dinner. *495 Geary St., at Taylor St., Union Square, 94102, 415/775–4700 or 800/652–5438, fax 415/441–4621. 218 rooms, 108 suites. Restaurant, bar, in-room data ports, minibars, room service, exercise room, laundry service and dry cleaning, concierge, business services, meeting rooms, parking (fee). AE, DC, MC, V.*

5 g-5
EL DRISCO

This historic little Pacific Heights hotel (Eisenhower once stayed here), unheard of by most San Franciscans, is known for unfailingly attentive service and a genteel ambience. Wonderful views of the bay from the upper floors are another perk, as are a complimentary Continental breakfast and visitor's pass to the Presidio YMCA. Eleven of the rooms are rented on a monthly basis. *2901 Pacific Ave., at Broderick St., Pacific Heights, 94115, 415/346–2880 or 800/634–7277, fax 415/567–5537. 24 rooms, 19 suites. Breakfast room, laundry service. AE, D, DC, MC, V.*

4 d-5
THE FAIRMONT

Commanding the top of Nob Hill like a European palace, the Fairmont, which served as the model for the St. Gregory in the TV series *Hotel*, has experienced plenty of real drama including its triumph over the 1906 earthquake and the creation of the United Nations Charter here in 1945. Rooms in the Tower are generally larger, and all rooms have

---

ROMANTIC GETAWAYS

San Francisco oozes romance even with one hand tied behind its back, but for those extra-special occasions when you want to play it to the hilt, try one of the following extravagant hotels to get you in the mood.

The Archbishop's Mansion (Expensive)
  Hold your honey under the chandelier used in Gone With the Wind.

Hotel Bohème (Expensive)
  Near many romantic Italian restaurants.

Hotel Majestic (Expensive)
  Straight out of a storybook, with gas fireplaces and claw-foot tubs.

Inn at the Opera (Expensive)
  Curl up by the fireplace for afternoon tea or evening wine.

Sherman House (Very Expensive)
  The city's most romantic hotel, bar none.

Union Street Inn (Expensive)
  Soak in your own private whirlpool tub.

handsome marble baths. An impressive array of amenities and services (including free chicken soup if you're under the weather), plus legendary performance venues like the Tonga Room and Venetian Room, keep loyal (and royal) guests coming back. *950 Mason St., at California St., Nob Hill, 94108, 415/772–5000 or 800/527–4727, fax 415/837–0587. 531 rooms, 65 suites. 4 restaurants, 5 bars, room service, barbershop, beauty salon, spa, health club, laundry service and dry cleaning, concierge, business services, car rental. AE, D, DC, MC, V.*

4 *d-6*
HOTEL MONACO
Unquestionably the hippest hotel north of Market Street, Hotel Monaco surprises you with a dramatic lobby, where a French inglenook fireplace climbs almost two stories toward the three huge domes of a whimsically painted vaulted ceiling. Although small, the rooms are comfortable and inviting, with a riot of stripes and vivid colors. A complimentary wine and appetizer hour each evening in the lobby features a tarot reader and massage therapist. The ornate Grand Cafe and bar, featuring a French-California menu, gives hotel guests preferred seating. *501 Geary St., at Taylor St., Union Square, 94102, 415/292–0100 or 800/214–4220, fax 415/292–0111. 177 rooms, 24 suites. Restaurant, bar, in-room data ports, in-room safes, minibars, room service, massage, sauna, exercise room, laundry service and dry cleaning, business services, parking (fee). AE, D, DC, MC, V.*

4 *e-6*
HOTEL NIKKO SAN FRANCISCO
A piano player provides live nightly entertainment at Z Bar in the Nikko Hotel—a nod to the civilized atmosphere of Union Square. Rooms have diamond-patterned wallpaper, teak desks, and terra-cotta colored furniture. The excellent fitness facility has dry saunas, traditional *ofuros* (Japanese soaking tubs), a *kamaburo* (Japanese sauna), a glass-enclosed swimming pool, and a whirlpool. Restaurant Anzu pairs beef dishes with sushi. *222 Mason St., between Ellis and O'Farrell Sts., Union Square, 94102, 415/394–1111 or 800/645–5687, fax 415/394–1106. 492 rooms, 32 suites. Restaurant, in-room data ports, minibars, beauty salon, massage, sauna, exercise room, laundry service and dry cleaning, concierge, business services, meeting rooms, parking (fee). No pets. AE, D, DC, MC, V.*

4 *d-5*
THE HUNTINGTON
Across from Grace Cathedral and the small but captivating Huntington Park, the redbrick Huntington provides a quiet alternative to the larger, flashier Nob Hill hotels. The highly attentive staff is known for personal service and protecting the privacy of its celebrity guests. Individually decorated rooms are spacious and traditional, with opulent materials such as raw silks and velvets in deep shades of cocoa, gold, and burgundy. T-1 phone lines yield fast Internet connections. *1075 California St., between Taylor and Mason Sts., Nob Hill, 94108, 415/474–5400 or 800/227–4683; 800/652–1539 in CA; fax 415/474–6227. 100 rooms, 40 suites. Restaurant, bar, in-room data ports, in-room safes, room service, laundry service and dry cleaning, concierge, meeting rooms, parking (fee). No pets. AE, D, DC, MC, V.*

4 *g-4*
HYATT REGENCY
The 20-story Hyatt at the foot of Market Street is the focal point of the Embarcadero Center, where more than 100 shops and restaurants cater to the Financial District. The spectacular 17-story atrium lobby is a wonder of sprawling trees, a running stream, and a huge fountain. Rooms, some with bay-view balconies, mix deep gold, blue, and russet colors with blond-wood furniture. The Equinox restaurant is the city's only revolving rooftop restaurant. *5 Embarcadero Center, at Market St., Embarcadero, 94111, 415/788–1234 or 800/233–1234, fax 415/398–2567. 745 rooms, 60 suites. 2 restaurants, bar, lobby lounge, room service, exercise room, concierge, concierge floor, parking (fee). No pets. AE, D, DC, MC, V.*

4 *f-5*
MANDARIN ORIENTAL
In the heart of the city's Financial District, the Mandarin Oriental occupies the top 11 floors of a 48-story building, with two towers connected by a dramatic glass sky bridge. Sedate, off-white textured wallpaper, walnut armoires, and large writing desks don't detract from the rooms' stupendous views. The real showstoppers are the 22 Mandarin

rooms, where enormous marble bathrooms have floor-to-ceiling windows next to extra-deep soaking tubs. A pianist performs in the first-floor lounge every evening from 4:30 to 8:30. *222 Sansome St., between California and Pine Sts., Financial District, 94104, 415/276–9888 or 800/622–0404, fax 415/433–0289. 154 rooms, 4 suites. Restaurant, lobby lounge, in-room data ports, minibars, room service, exercise room, laundry service and dry cleaning, concierge, business services, meeting rooms, parking (fee). No pets. AE, DC, MC, V.*

4 *d-5*
MARK HOPKINS INTER-CONTINENTAL

The circular drive of this towering Nob Hill architectural landmark leads to a graceful mirrored and marble-floored lobby. The dramatic, neoclassical rooms glow with warm earth tones, and bathrooms are lined with Italian marble. Rooms on the upper floors have views of either the Golden Gate Bridge or the downtown cityscape, and the venerable yet vibrant rooftop lounge, the Top of the Mark, features cocktails, live music, and dancing, with an almost 360° view of the city. *999 California St., at Mason St., Nob Hill, 94108, 415/392–3434 or 800/662–4455, fax 415/421–3302. 362 rooms, 30 suites. 2 restaurants, 2 bars, room service, exercise room, laundry service and dry cleaning, concierge, business services, car rental. No pets. AE, D, DC, MC, V.*

4 *e-5*
NOB HILL LAMBOURNE

Although this urban retreat is designed with the traveling executive in mind—rooms have computers, fax machines, and spacious desks—it's also a great choice if you're eager to unwind. The on-site spa lends out "wellness" videos on topics such as yoga and tai chi, and exercise equipment may be brought to your room on request. Rooms have queen-size beds with hand-sewn mattresses, luxurious silk damask bedding, and contemporary furnishings in muted colors. Turn-down service features vitamins and chamomile tea on your pillow. A deluxe Continental breakfast and evening wine service are complimentary. *725 Pine St., at Stockton St., Nob Hill, 94108, 415/433–2287 or 800/274–8466, fax 415/433–0975. 15 rooms, 5 suites. Breakfast room, in-room data ports, kitchenettes, in-room VCRs, spa, laundry service and dry cleaning, business services, parking (fee). No pets. AE, D, DC, MC, V.*

4 *f-6*
THE PALACE HOTEL

This landmark 1875 hotel—once patronized by the likes of Enrico Caruso, Woodrow Wilson, and Amelia Earhart—wows first-time visitors with its stunning entryway. The belle epoque–style Garden Court restaurant has graceful chandeliers and a lead-glass ceiling, and the Pied Piper Bar is named for its 1909 Maxfield Parrish mural. Rooms, with twice-daily maid service and nightly turn-down service, feature high ceilings, antique furnishings, and marble bathrooms with luxury bath products. The hotel's 20-yard lap pool is the longest hotel pool in the city. The Kyo-ya restaurant is widely considered the city's best Japanese restaurant. *2 New Montgomery St., at Market St., South of Market, 94105, 415/392–8600 or 800/325–3535, fax 415/543–0671. 517 rooms, 33 suites. 3 restaurants, bar, lobby lounge, in-room data ports, in-room safes, minibars, room service, indoor lap pool, sauna, exercise room, laundry service and dry cleaning, concierge, business services, meeting rooms, parking (fee). No pets. AE, D, DC, MC, V.*

4 *e-6*
PALOMAR

Slipped into the top five floors of SoMa's 1908 Pacific Place Building is this urbane and luxurious oasis, where a cool, clean '30s look prevails. After checking in at the spare ground-floor lobby, you are whisked up to the 5th floor, where a clubby lounge gives way to the aptly named Fifth Floor, serving modern French cuisine. Soundproofed rooms have muted leopard-print carpets, raffia-weave walls, bold navy and cream–striped drapes, armoires of dark polished wood, and fluffy beds with quilted comforters and down pillows. Baths sparkle with polished granite countertops and ivory and silver wallpaper and feature Aveda products. Cordless phone, CD player, fax/copy machine, shoe shine, and morning paper are only the beginning of the high level of amenities and personal service on offer, guaranteed by butlers on every floor and the exclusive preference-tracking system. Adventurous bathers can even partake of the "Tub Menu," with everything from aromatherapy infusions to cigars and brandy. *12 4th St., South of Market, 94103, 415/348–1111, fax 415/348–0302. 182 rooms, 16 suites. Restaurant, piano bar, in-room data ports, minibars, refrigerators, room service, exercise room, dry cleaning, laundry service, concierge, business services, meeting rooms, parking (fee). AE, D, DC, MC, V.*

4 *d-6*

PAN PACIFIC HOTEL

Exotic flower arrangements fill the hushed common areas of this supremely tranquil and refined business-oriented hotel—including the atrium, which rises 21 stories above a sculpted bronze fountain. Bathrooms lined with Portuguese marble are the highlight of the guest rooms, which have soft green and beige color schemes and black and gold quilted bed covers featuring Asian block print designs. The hotel's restaurant, Pacific, is well regarded for its contemporary regional cuisine. *500 Post St., at Mason St., Union Square, 94102, 415/771–8600 or 800/327–8585, fax 415/398–0267. 311 rooms, 19 suites. Restaurant, bar, lobby lounge, in-room data ports, minibars, room service, exercise room, piano, laundry service and dry cleaning, concierge, business services, meeting rooms, parking (fee). No pets. AE, D, DC, MC, V.*

4 *d-6*

PRESCOTT HOTEL

Although not as famous as many hotels in the area, the Prescott has several advantages: the relatively small size means personalized service, and its relationship with Postrio, the Wolfgang Puck restaurant attached to its lobby, means you get preferred reservations. Rooms are traditional, with a rich hunter-green theme. The fireplace in the hunting lodge–style living room is a perfect setting for the complimentary coffee service and evening wine receptions. The more expensive Club Level rooms include complimentary expanded Continental breakfast and afternoon cocktails with Puck's pizza. *545 Post St., between Taylor and Mason Sts., Union Square, 94102, 415/563–0303 or 800/283–7322, fax 415/563–6831. 134 rooms, 30 suites. Restaurant, bar, in-room data ports, minibars, room service, exercise room, concierge, business services, meeting rooms, parking (fee). No pets. AE, D, DC, MC, V.*

4 *a-6*

RADISSON MIYAKO HOTEL

East meets West at this pagoda-style hotel near the Japantown complex, where you can choose either a Western-style room or a Japanese-style room, which have tatami mats, futon beds, and deep tubs. Some guest rooms are in the tower building; others are in the garden wing, which has a traditional Japanese garden with a small waterfall. The hotel's award-winning Yoyo Bistro specializes in Asian fusion cuisine. *1625 Post St., at Laguna St., Japantown, 94115, 415/922–3200 or 800/533–4567, fax 415/921–0417. 209 rooms, 9 suites. Restaurant, bar, in-room data ports, room service, exercise room, laundry service and dry cleaning, business services, meeting rooms, parking (fee). No pets. AE, D, DC, MC, V.*

4 *e-5*

RENAISSANCE STANFORD COURT

Built in 1912, this Nob Hill landmark has a reputation as one of the city's toniest hotels. The lobby is dominated by a stained-glass dome, a dramatic mural depicting scenes of early San Francisco, and high-quality arts and antiques—it's the perfect setting for afternoon tea. Rooms invariably achieve understated elegance with a mix of English country manor–style furnishings accented with Asian artwork and accessories. Fournou's Ovens is consistently rated as one of the nation's top restaurants. *905 California St., at Powell St., Nob Hill, 94108, 415/989–3500 or 800/227–4736; 800/622–0957 in CA; fax 415/391–0513. 384 rooms, 9 suites. Restaurant, piano bar, in-room data ports, room service, exercise room, piano, laundry service and dry cleaning, concierge, business services, meeting rooms, car rental, parking (fee). No pets. AE, D, DC, MC, V.*

4 *e-5*

RITZ-CARLTON, SAN FRANCISCO

Rated the top hotel in San Francisco for the fifth year in a row by *Condé Nast Traveler* magazine, the Ritz-Carlton defines opulence and attentive service: as you enter the grand lobby, white-gloved staff members present themselves, at the ready. Rich cream colors and top-quality contemporary and antique reproduction furnishings give the spacious guest rooms a luxurious feel, and baths are of Italian marble. The hotel's deluxe fitness center, complete with swimming pool and saunas, is a destination in its own right, as is the renowned Dining Room (see French in Chapter 1). 600 Stockton St., at California St., Nob Hill, 94108, 415/296–7465 or 800/241–3333, fax 415/291–0288. 276 rooms, 60 suites. 2 restaurants, 2 bars, lobby lounge, in-room data ports, in-room safes, minibars, room service, indoor pool, sauna, health club, laundry service and dry cleaning, concierge, business services, meeting rooms, car rental, parking (fee). AE, D, DC, MC, V.

4 e-6

SAN FRANCISCO MARRIOTT

When this 40-story hotel opened in 1989, critics alternately raved about and condemned its distinctive design—modern art deco, with large fanlike windows across the top (it's been compared to a parking meter and a jukebox). The flashy lobby features a mirrored ceiling and a huge beaded crystal chandelier. An adjacent five-story, glass-topped atrium encloses a dining court lush with palm trees, tropical plants and a cascading fountain. If you are an art buff, you're in good company: a heavy-hitter art collection is installed throughout, and the hotel is very close to the San Francisco Museum of Modern Art and the Yerba Buena Gardens complex. The pastel rooms are small but functional. Conventioneers often stay here. 55 4th St., at Mission St., South of Market, 94103, 415/896–1600 or 800/228–9290, fax 415/896–6177. 1,366 rooms, 134 suites. 3 restaurants, bar, 2 piano bars, in-room data ports, minibars, room service, indoor pool, sauna, exercise room, laundry service and dry cleaning, concierge, business services, convention center, car rental, parking (fee). AE, D, DC, MC, V.

5 h-4

SHERMAN HOUSE

This magnificent 1876 Italianate mansion at the foot of residential Pacific Heights is San Francisco's most luxurious small hotel. Decadence reigns, from the canopied four-poster feather beds to the wood-burning fireplaces and sumptuous bathrooms, some with whirlpool baths. Every room is different, but all are a tasteful mix of Biedermeier, English Jacobean, or French Second Empire antiques. Though one of the priciest properties in San Francisco, it's also the single most romantic place to stay in the city. 2160 Green St., between Fillmore and Webster Sts., Pacific Heights, 94123, 415/563–3600 or 800/424–5777, fax 415/563–1882. 8 rooms, 6 suites. Dining room, room service, in-room VCRs, piano, concierge. No pets. AE, DC, MC, V.

4 f-6

W SAN FRANCISCO

Epitomizing cool modernity and urban chic, the W's prime spot next door to the SFMOMA and its bi-level XYZ restaurant—one of the hottest in town—make it the place to drink, dine, and stay. Stone, frosted glass, corrugated metal, and other industrial elements are offset by polished mahogany, floor-to-ceiling yellow-green mohair drapes, and broad-stripe carpeting. A pool and hot tub gurgle away in a glass-covered atrium and a tree-filled outdoor terrace is attached. Guest rooms redefine urban chic, with pale colors and simple, spare furnishings such as a dark-wood desks, dark-wood slab headboards, and pillow-top beds with goose down comforters and more pillows. Each room has a cozy sitting area or a padded window seat perch overlooking the city. Minibar selections are imaginative, from trail mix to Gummi bears to local microbrewed beers. Amenities include cordless phones, Ethernet modem connections, stereos with in-room CD library, Aveda bath products, and plush robes. 181 3rd St., at Howard St., South of Market, 94103, 415/626–0777 or 877/946–8357, fax 415/817–7848. 418 rooms, 5 suites. Restaurant, bar, café, in-room data ports, in-room safes, minibars, room service, in-room VCRs, indoor pool, hot tub, massage, exercise room, laundry service and dry cleaning, concierge, business services, meeting rooms, parking (fee). AE, D, DC, MC, V.

4 e-6

WESTIN ST. FRANCIS

The grande dame of San Francisco hotels is the preferred destination of visiting royalty and world leaders (all the U.S. presidents since Taft have stayed here), as well as convention and tour groups. The original 1904 building, with its beautiful black marble-columned lobby, has been augmented with a 32-story tower. Many rooms in the original building are small by modern standards, but all retain their original Victorian style moldings. Rooms in the modern tower are larger, with an Asian motif. *335 Powell St., between Post and Geary Sts., Union Square, 94102, 415/397–7000 or 800/228–3000, fax 415/774–0124. 1,108 rooms, 84 suites. 3 restaurants, 2 bars, in-room data ports, in-room safes, minibars, room service, exercise room, nightclub, concierge, business services, meeting rooms, travel services, car rental, parking (fee). AE, D, DC, MC, V.*

8670 95 331

EXPENSIVE LODGINGS

4   *a-8*

THE ARCHBISHOP'S MANSION

Everything at the Archbishop's Mansion is extravagantly romantic. This Second Empire–style mansion, built in 1904 for Archbishop Patrick Riordan, faces Alamo Square and its brightly painted Victorian homes. In the cavernous sitting room, a chandelier used in the

---

HOTEL ORIGINALS

A new breed of boutique theme hotels is burgeoning in San Francisco. Much more than mere places to sleep, these hotels distinguish themselves with unique styles and attitudes that often conjure up escapist fantasy lands, from the tropics to the Far East.

Hotel Monaco (Very Expensive)
   A chic, 1940s theme.

Hotel Triton (Expensive)
   A mecca for the avant-garde.

Mandarin Oriental (Very Expensive)
   Bathing has never been so luxurious!

The Mansions (Expensive)
   A pig collection and a campy magic show.

Nob Hill Lambourne (Very Expensive)
   An urban retreat geared toward health and wellness.

Phoenix Hotel (Moderately Priced)
   Kitschy tropical decor and a celebrity clientele.

Radisson Miyako Hotel (Very Expensive)
   Some rooms have tatami mats and futon beds.

The Red Victorian (Budget)
   Request the Summer of Love room.

---

movie *Gone With the Wind* hangs over Noël Coward's Bechstein piano. Individually decorated guest rooms are full of ornate antiques; some have whirlpool tubs or fireplaces. The complimentary Continental breakfast can be taken in your room; there's also an afternoon wine service. *1000 Fulton St., at Steiner St., Western Addition, 94117, 415/563–7872 or 800/543–5820, fax 415/885–3193. 10 rooms, 5 suites. Breakfast room, in-room VCRs, piano, free parking. No pets. AE, MC, V.*

5   *h-7*

CHÂTEAU TIVOLI

Although there are a lot of bright "painted ladies" on Alamo Square, perhaps none is as conspicuous as this late 19th-century château, painted in no fewer than 22 colors. The dramatic rooms vary in style but are large, comfortable, and loaded with antiques and knickknacks; a few have fireplaces, and one of the suites has a kitchenette. You are treated to an expanded Continental breakfast on weekdays and a champagne brunch on weekends. *1057 Steiner St., at Golden Gate Ave., Western Addition, 94115, 415/776–5462 or 800/228–1647, fax 415/776–0505. 5 rooms, 3 with bath, 4 suites. Dining room. No pets. AE, MC, V.*

4   *f-5*

GALLERIA PARK

The black marble facade of Galleria Park is a few blocks east of Union Square, convenient to the Financial District, the Chinatown Gate, and the Crocker Galleria—one of San Francisco's most upscale shopping complexes. The comfortable rooms all have floral bedspreads and stylish striped wallpaper. The third floor rooftop Cityscape Park features an outdoor running track. *191 Sutter St., at Kearny St., Financial District, 94104, 415/781–3060 or 800/792–9639, fax 415/433–4409. 162 rooms, 15 suites. 2 restaurants, in-room data ports, minibars, room service, exercise room, jogging, concierge, business services, meeting rooms. No pets. AE, D, DC, MC, V.*

4   *g-5*

HARBOR COURT

Within shouting distance of the Bay Bridge and the many nightclubs and restaurants of SoMa, this cozy hotel is noted for exemplary service. Guest rooms are small but fanciful, with faux-

textured walls, partially canopied upholstered beds layered with throw pillows,
reproductions of turn-of-the-century
nautical and nature prints, and armoires
with TVs. Some guest rooms overlook
the bay; others face a garden courtyard.
In the evening complimentary wine is
served in the snug, earth-tone lounge,
sometimes accompanied by live guitar.
You have free access to the excellent
YMCA facilities flanking the hotel on
one side, and cover charges are waived
at Harry Denton's nightclub and restaurant, on the other side of the hotel. *165
Steuart St., between Howard and Mission
Sts., Embarcadero, 94105, 415/882–1300
or 800/346–0555, fax 415/882–1313. 130
rooms, 1 suite. Restaurant, in-room data
ports, minibars, room service, business services, parking (fee). No pets. AE, D, DC,
MC, V.*

4 e-3

HOTEL BOHÈME

In the middle of historic North Beach,
the Bohème gives you a taste of the past
with coral-color walls, bistro tables, and
Beat generation memorabilia. Allen
Ginsberg, who stayed here many times,
could in his later years be seen sitting in
a window tapping away at his laptop.
Screenwriters from Francis Ford Coppola's nearby American Zoetrope stay
here often, as do poets and other
artists. Beds feature unnecessary but
fun mosquito netting. Enjoy complimentary sherry in the lobby while you delib-
erate over the many nearby Italian
restaurants and cafés. Rooms in the rear
are quieter. *444 Columbus Ave., at Vallejo
St., North Beach, 94133, 415/433–9111, fax
415/362–6292. 15 rooms. Parking (fee). No
pets. AE, D, DC, MC, V.*

4 e-6

HOTEL DIVA

A striking black granite and crackled
green glass facade beckons you into the
Diva's small lobby, where a 1920s ocean
liner motif takes over. Nautical touches
in the rooms include cobalt blue carpets
and brushed steel headboards echoing
the shape of waves. The Diva's proximity to the city's theaters attracts those
with an artistic bent, and the hotel is
also popular with families, who entertain themselves with the in-room Nintendo and VCRs. *440 Geary St., at
Mason St., Union Square, 94102, 415/
885–0200 or 800/553–1900, fax 415/346–
6613. 79 rooms, 32 suites. Restaurant, in-*

room data ports, in-room safes, exercise
room, business services, meeting room.
AE, D, DC, MC, V.

4 g-5

HOTEL GRIFFON

Occupying a stately 1906 building, the
Hotel Griffon attracts business travelers
with its proximity to the Financial District and pleasure travelers with its views
of the Bay Bridge from eight of the
rooms. Rooms are quietly elegant, with
beige tones and cherry or mahogany
pieces. In-room CD players are a nice
touch. *155 Steuart St., between Mission
and Howard Sts., Embarcadero, 94105,
415/495–2100 or 800/321–2201, fax 415/
495–3522. 56 rooms, 6 suites. Restaurant,
in-room data ports, minibars, room service, laundry service and dry cleaning, business services, meeting room, parking (fee).
No pets. AE, D, DC, MC, V.*

4 b-6

HOTEL MAJESTIC

One of San Francisco's original grand
hotels and the decade-long residence of
screen stars Joan Fontaine and Olivia de
Havilland, this five-story, white 1902
Edwardian is extremely romantic. Most
of the guest rooms have gas fireplaces,
a mix of French and English antiques,
and canopied beds; some have original
claw-foot bathtubs. In the afternoon,
guests enjoy complimentary sherry and
homemade biscotti in the lobby, where
black marble stairs, antique chandeliers,
and a white marble fireplace make a
statement. Café Majestic offers California cuisine with an Asian touch, and the
bar features a large collection of rare
butterflies from Africa and New Guinea.
*1500 Sutter St., at Gough St., Western
Addition, 94109, 415/441–1100 or 800/
869–8966, 415/673–7331. 48 rooms, 9
suites. Restaurant, bar, in-room data
ports, minibars, room service, laundry and
dry cleaning, concierge, business services,
meeting rooms, parking (fee). AE, DC,
MC, V.*

4 e-5

HOTEL REX

The spirit of salon society and literary
and artistic creativity are the causes
célèbres at the stylish Hotel Rex, where
thousands of books line the clubby,
1920s-style lobby—the site of frequent
book readings and round-table discussions. Upstairs, quotations from works
by California writers are painted on the

terra-cotta-color walls of the generously sized rooms, which are outfitted with checkered bedspreads and playful hand-painted lamp shades. *562 Sutter St., between Powell and Mason Sts., Union Square, 94102, 415/433–4434, fax 415/433–3695. 92 rooms, 2 suites. Bar, lobby lounge, in-room data ports, minibars, laundry service and dry cleaning, concierge, parking (fee). AE, D, DC, MC, V.*

4 *e-5*
HOTEL TRITON
A playfully conceived lobby of three-legged furniture, star-patterned carpeting, and inverted gilt pillars give you a hint of the zaniness to come: the rooms are decked out with pink and gold paint, S-curved chairs, and oddball light fixtures. The yellow rubber ducky is yours to take home. The fashion, entertainment, music, and film-industry types who frequent this place don't seem to mind the uncommonly small rooms or the uneven service. *342 Grant Ave., at Bush St., Financial District, 94108, 415/394–0500 or 800/433–6611, fax 415/394–0555. 133 rooms, 7 suites. In-room data ports, exercise room, laundry service, business services, meeting room, parking (fee). AE, D, DC, MC, V.*

4 *e-5*
HOTEL VINTAGE COURT
This bit of the Napa Valley two blocks from Union Square has quiet, cheery rooms—some with sunny window seats—decorated with jade and rose floral fabrics. Complimentary wine served every evening in front of the lobby fireplace and a deluxe Continental breakfast have created a congenial atmosphere without driving up prices. Guests get preferred reservations at adjoining Masa's, the city's most celebrated French restaurant. *650 Bush St., between Powell and Stockton Sts., Union Square, 94108, 415/392–4666 or 800/654–1100, fax 415/433–4065. 107 rooms, 2 suites. Restaurant, bar, minibars, refrigerators, laundry service, meeting rooms, parking (fee). No pets. AE, D, DC, MC, V.*

4 *b-7*
INN AT THE OPERA
Highly recommended for its tranquil, intimate setting, this European-style hotel a block or so from Davies Hall and the War Memorial Opera House hosts the music and dance greats that perform at these venues. Creamy pastels and dark-wood furnishings give the rooms an air of warmth, and terry-cloth robes, fresh flowers, and a basket of apples are homey touches. A major attraction is the sumptuously romantic, dimly lighted Ovation Restaurant and Lounge, where a free buffet breakfast is served. *333 Fulton St., between Franklin and Gough Sts., Hayes Valley, 94102, 415/863–8400 or 800/325–2708; 800/423–9610 in CA; fax 415/861–0821. 30 rooms. Restaurant, piano bar, kitchenettes, room service, laundry service and dry cleaning, concierge, valet parking. No pets. AE, DC, MC, V.*

4 *e-6*
INN AT UNION SQUARE
With its tiny but captivating lobby, where trompe l'oeil bookshelves are painted on the walls, this inn is a more personal alternative to the neighborhood's larger hotels. Half of the rooms are decorated in a Georgian style, half are more contemporary. All have sumptuous touches like goose down pillows and fine toiletries, plus such practical features as electronic door keys, work desks, and two phones per room. Guests like to lounge in front of the fireplaces found in each floor's tiny sitting area, and they enjoy the Continental breakfasts and evening wine and hors d'oeuvres included in the room rate. Tips are not accepted, and this is an entirely no-smoking hotel. *440 Post St., between Powell and Mason Sts., Union Square, 94102, 415/397–3510 or 800/288–4346, fax 415/989–0529. 23 rooms, 7 suites. Laundry service and dry cleaning, parking (fee). No pets. AE, D, DC, MC, V.*

7 *f-3*
INN ON CASTRO
A mixture of antiques and pop art is cheerily set around this beautiful B&B in an 1896 Edwardian. Complimentary brandy in each room can be sipped by the fireplace when weather warrants, and an excellent full breakfast gives you the chance to socialize. Its location in the busiest part of the Castro ensures a largely gay and lesbian clientele. *321 Castro St., at Market St., Castro, 94114, phone/fax 415/861–0321. 8 rooms, 7 with bath. Breakfast room. No pets. MC, V.*

4 *a-5*
JACKSON COURT
On a stately and quiet residential block in tony Pacific Heights, Jackson Court is a B&B and time share in a converted

brownstone mansion built in 1900, as well as a truly serene oasis within this busy city. The light, spacious decor features a mixture of antique and contemporary furnishings with plenty of fresh flowers. A standout is the Garden Court room, with handcrafted wood paneling and a picture window overlooking the garden patio. Continental breakfast is served in the sunny little kitchen. *2198 Jackson St., at Buchanan St., Pacific Heights, 94115, 415/929–7670, fax 415/ 929–1405. 8 rooms, 2 suites. No pets. AE, MC, V.*

4 *e-6*

KING GEORGE HOTEL

Built in 1914 for the Panama-Pacific Exposition, the King George has a reputation among its loyal European guests for warm hospitality; the staff is adept at catering to your every whim. The compact, classic English–style rooms have walnut furniture and royal red and green color schemes. A proper English high tea is served in the hotel's Windsor Tea Room. *334 Mason St., between Geary and O'Farrell Sts., Union Square, 94102, 415/ 781–5050 or 800/288–6005, fax 415/391– 6976. 141 rooms, 2 suites. Room service, laundry service, meeting rooms, parking (fee). No pets. AE, D, DC, MC, V.*

4 *a-5*

THE MANSIONS

An arresting combination of funky elegance and eccentricity, the Mansions is a lavish, slightly faded, but very fun hotel housed in a twin-turreted 1887 Queen Anne. Fresh flowers and antique furnishings decorate the rooms, one of which Barbra Streisand stayed in. The hotel's own museum has quirky holdings ranging from historic documents to various "porkabilia" (pigs, pigs, and more pigs). Rates include a full breakfast and a campy magic show in the evening. Dinner in the colorful stained-glass dining room features desserts dusted with 24-karat gold flakes. This is a pet-friendly hotel. *2220 Sacramento St., at Laguna St., Pacific Heights, 94115, 415/ 929–9444 or 800/826–9398, fax 415/567– 9391. 15 rooms, 6 suites. Breakfast room, dining room, billiards, laundry service, parking (fee). AE, D, DC, MC, V.*

4 *d-5*

THE MAXWELL

Formerly the Raphael, the Maxwell was completely refurbished in 1997 and is

now a stylish hotel just a few blocks from Union Square. Behind the dramatic black and red curtains, the Victorian-style lobby welcomes you with a green velvet sofa and boldly patterned chairs. Rooms have a clubby, art-deco feel. Max's On The Square serves American breakfast, lunch, and dinner, as well as after-theater drinks and supper. *386 Geary St., at Mason St., Union Square, 94102, 415/986–2000 or 888/734–6299, fax 415/397–2447. 122 rooms, 31 suites. Restaurant, bar, in-room data ports, in-room safes, room service, laundry service, concierge, parking (fee). No pets. AE, D, DC, MC, V.*

4 *b-6*

THE QUEEN ANNE

This four-story Victorian is one of the city's beautiful Painted Ladies. In the spacious lobby, guests gather in front of the fire to drink sherry or eat home-baked goods for breakfast. Rooms come in all shapes and sizes: there's a tiny top-floor room with slanted ceilings, a two-bedroom town house with private deck, and everything in between. Most have English antiques, and some have fireplaces. *1590 Sutter St., at Octavia St., Japantown, 94109, 415/441–2828 or 800/ 227–3970, fax 415/775–5212. 44 rooms, 4 suites. Laundry service, meeting room, parking (fee). No pets. AE, D, DC, MC, V.*

1 *d-2*

RADISSON HOTEL AT FISHERMAN'S WHARF

A striking bayfront location at Fisherman's Wharf is the major drawing card here. The higher-priced rooms on the upper floors overlook a courtyard and pool or have balconies with unobstructed views of the bay and Alcatraz. Rooms are simple and bright, with tan carpeting, black and tan striped drapes, and cherry wood furniture. The complex the hotel is housed in includes several restaurants and shops. *250 Beach St., at Powell St., Fisherman's Wharf, 94133, 415/ 392–6700 or 800/578–7878, fax 415/986– 7853. 355 rooms. Restaurant, in-room data ports, minibars, pool, laundry service, concierge, meeting rooms, parking (fee). No pets. AE, D, DC, MC, V.*

4 *d-6*

SAVOY HOTEL

If you want to be near Union Square— it's about three blocks away—but don't want to spend $250 a night, you will appreciate this good-value European-style hotel. The French country–style rooms are simple but very comfortable, with featherbeds and down pillows. The attached restaurant, Brasserie Savoy, is well regarded for its seafood and basic brasserie fare. *580 Geary St., at Jones St., Union Square, 94102, 415/441–2700 or 800/227–4223, fax 415/441–0124. 70 rooms, 13 suites. Restaurant, minibars, laundry service, concierge, meeting room, parking (fee). No pets. AE, D, DC, MC, V.*

4 *e-5*
SIR FRANCIS DRAKE
Beefeater-costumed doormen welcome you into the regal lobby of this 1928 landmark, with wrought-iron balustrades, chandeliers, and Italian marble. Rooms, some awkward in design, have a neoclassical look featuring boldly striped fabrics and mahogany and cherry wood furnishings. On the top floor, Harry Denton's Starlight Room is one of the city's plushest skyline bars, and the hotel's affordable restaurant, Scala's Bistro, serves excellent Italian food in its dramatic, bi-level dining room. *450 Powell St., between Post and Sutter Sts., Union Square, 94102, 415/392–7755 or 800/227–5480, fax 415/391–8719. 394 rooms, 23 suites. Restaurant, café, in-room data ports, minibars, exercise room, nightclub, laundry service and dry cleaning, concierge, business services, meeting rooms, parking (fee). No pets. AE, D, DC, MC, V.*

4 *d-2*
TUSCAN INN
The faux stone exterior of the inn, with a mural of the Tuscan hills, gives some indication of the charm of the small guest rooms. Whitewashed Italian-style pine armoires, writing tables, and chairs; wooden plantation-style shutters; large mirrors; pale-green–striped wallpaper; and richly colored floral carpeting and bedspreads evoke the Tuscan countryside. The staff is friendly and attentive, and complimentary perks include morning coffee, tea, and biscotti in the lobby, wine service in the early evening, and a limousine to the Financial District. Café Pescatore, the Italian seafood restaurant off the lobby, provides room service on summer evenings. *425 N orth Point St., at Mason St., Fisherman's Wharf, 94133, 415/561–1100 or 800/648–4626, fax 415/561–1199. 209 rooms, 12 suites. Restaurant, room service, meeting rooms. AE, D, DC, MC, V.*

5 *h-4*
UNION STREET INN
With the help of many precious family antiques and unique artwork, the innkeepers— Jane Bertorelli and David Coyle, who was once a chef for the Duke and Duchess of Bedford—made this ivy-draped 1902 Edwardian a delightful B&B inn. Equipped with candles, fresh flowers, and wineglasses, rooms are popular with honeymooners and romantics. The Carriage House, with its own hot tub, is set off from the main house by an old-fashioned English garden with lemon trees. An elaborate breakfast is included, as are afternoon tea and evening hors d' oeuvres. Late sleepers should avoid the English Garden room, a bit noisy mornings. *2229 Union St., between Fillmore and Steiner Sts., Cow Hollow, 94123, 415/346–0424, fax 415/922–8046. 6 rooms. Breakfast room, parking (fee). No pets. AE, MC, V.*

4 *e-3*
WASHINGTON SQUARE INN
This little charmer in the heart of North Beach in perfect for those who want to try out the many Italian restaurants and cafés in this convivial neighborhood. Rooms, although small, are tastefully decorated with antiques. Continental breakfast and afternoon tea are complimentary. *1660 Stockton St., at Filbert St., North Beach, 94133, 415/981–4220 or 800/388–0220, fax 415/397–7242. 13 rooms, 2 suites. Breakfast room, parking (fee). No pets. AE, D, DC, MC, V.*

4 *d-5*
WHITE SWAN INN
A library with book-lined walls and a crackling fire is the heartbeat of the wonderfully inviting White Swan. Home-baked snacks and afternoon tea are served in the lounge, where comfortable chairs and sofas also invite lingering. Each of the good-size rooms, filled with reproduction Edwardian furniture, has a fireplace and refrigerator. The gourmet breakfasts here are famous, and the entire inn is no-smoking. *845 Bush St., at Taylor St., Union Square, 94108, 415/775–1755 or 800/999–9570, fax 415/775–5717. 23 rooms, 3 suites. Breakfast room, refrigerators, library, laundry service, parking (fee). No pets. AE, DC, MC, V.*

4 d-6

YORK HOTEL

Hitchcock fans may recognize the exterior of this reasonably priced hotel—it's the building where Kim Novak, as Judy Barton, stayed in *Vertigo*. Its other claim to fame is the popular cabaret on the premises, the Plush Room—a favorite among the gay travelers and Europeans who frequent the hotel. Inside, moderate-size rooms are a tasteful mix of Mediterranean styles. Although this is not the worst part of the Tenderloin, walking around the surrounding blocks at night is discouraged. *940 Sutter St., at Leavenworth St., Tenderloin, 94109, 415/885‑6800 or 800/808‑9675, fax 415/885‑2115. 91 rooms, 5 suites. Bar, in-room data ports, in-room safes, minibars, exercise room, nightclub, laundry service, concierge, parking (fee). AE, D, DC, MC, V.*

MODERATELY PRICED LODGINGS

4 c-7

THE ABIGAIL HOTEL

Built in 1926, this relatively unknown charmer has a lobby with a tiled Art Deco floor, faux-marble front desk, an old-fashioned telephone booth, and a vintage gated elevator. It's handy to major Civic Center music and performance venues. Rooms feature English lithographs and antiques. The always crowded Millennium Restaurant, right off the lobby, serves food so delicious it's hard to believe it's vegan (made without meat or dairy). Room rates include Continental breakfast. *246 McAllister St., between Hyde and Larkin Sts., Civic Center, 94102, 415/861‑9728 or 800/738‑7477, fax 415/861‑5848. 60 rooms, 1 suite. Restaurant, laundry service, parking (fee). AE, D, DC, MC, V.*

6 h 8

ALAMO SQUARE INN

Three buildings encircle a flower-filled patio at this B&B on picturesque Alamo Square. Two of the buildings date from the late 19th century, and rooms are decorated in Victorian style with antiques and Oriental rugs. Excellent full breakfasts and afternoon wine or tea promote relaxation. *719 Scott St., at Fulton St., Western Addition, 94117, 415/922‑2055 or 800/345‑9888, fax 415/931‑1304. 9 rooms, 4 suites. Breakfast room, free parking. No pets. AE, MC, V.*

4 d-6

THE ANDREWS HOTEL

Two blocks west of Union Square, this Queen Anne–style abode began its life as the Sultan Turkish Baths in 1905. Down comforters, lace curtains, and fresh flowers make up for the small size of the forest green and beige rooms,

---

HIPSTER HANGOUTS

Hip is cool, and cool is hot, and these hotels don't need the famous fog to make them cool when the cool crowd makes them oh so hot. They're hip, man.

Commodore International (Moderate)
The all-crimson Red Room hosts well-dressed slicksters late into the night.

Hotel Bohème (Expensive)
A place where artists and writers (including Beats like Allen Ginsberg) are repeatedly struck by the Muse.

Hotel Monaco (Very Expensive)
Whimsical high style from lobby to penthouse, as well as the outlandishly appointed and popular Grand Cafe.

Hotel Rex (Expensive)
Stylish and clubby, the Rex revives the spirit of 1920s salon society, when it was hip to be literate.

Hotel Triton (Expensive)
Zany avant-garde decor and trendy people buzzing through in a busy downtown location at the gates of Chinatown.

The Maxwell (Expensive)
Stylish Art Deco surroundings lend theatrical flair, and Max's On The Square hosts the play-going crowd for cocktails and pre- or post-theater suppers.

Phoenix Hotel (Moderate)
An arty, kitschy, tropical urban oasis and rock star haunt the aquatic-themed Backflip restaurant and lounge.

The Red Victorian (Budget)
If you mean "hip" as in hippy dippy, relive the Summer of Love in this Haight Street hotel and peace center.

W San Francisco (Very Expensive)
Sophisticated international urban chic in a high-art neighborhood.

which have equally tiny bathrooms (many have showers but no tub). A buffet-style Continental breakfast is served on each floor, and there's complimentary wine in the hotel restaurant, Fino, in the evening. *624 Post St., at Jones St., Union Square, 94109, 415/563–6877 or 800/926–3739, fax 415/928–6919. 43 rooms, 5 suites. Restaurant, concierge, parking (fee). AE, DC, MC, V.*

4 *a-4*

BED AND BREAKFAST INN

Hidden in an alleyway off the trendiest part of Union Street is this ivy-covered Victorian, which opened in 1976 as San Francisco's first B&B. Rooms carry out the Victorian theme with antiques, plants, and floral paintings. Those with shared bath are quite small. The large Garden Suite, with a delightful, full country kitchen, solarium, and whirlpool bath, easily accommodates four. *4 Charlton Ct., off Union St. between Buchanan and Laguna Sts., Cow Hollow, 94123, 415/921–9784, fax 415/921–0544. 9 rooms, 5 with bath, 2 suites. Breakfast room, parking (fee). MC, V.*

4 *d-6*

CLARION BEDFORD HOTEL

The tallest on the block at 17 stories, and a bright-golden counterpoint to its gray neighbors, this handsome 1929 building provides spectacular city and bay views. Avant-garde film posters from 1920s Russia, crystal chandeliers, and a ceramic-tile floor adorn the sun-yellow lobby with an adjoining restaurant-café. The light and airy rooms are decorated in yellow and peach with white furniture and vibrant floral bedspreads. Baths are rather small. There is an evening wine reception in the lobby. *761 Post St., between Leavenworth and Jones Sts., Union Square, 04109, 415/673–6040 or 800/227–5642, fax 415-563–6739. 137 rooms, 7 suites. Restaurant, bar, lobby lounge, in-room data ports, minibars, room service, laundry service and dry cleaning, parking (fee). AE, D, DC, MC, V.*

4 *d-5*

COMMODORE INTERNATIONAL

Billing itself as an "urban adventure," the Commodore provides a giddy alternative to its more stately neighbors: neo-deco chairs in the lobby suggest an ocean liner; the Titanic Cafe is studded with goldfish bowls and bathysphere

light fixtures; and the hotel's Red Room is a startlingly scarlet nightclub filled with well-dressed hipsters. In the fairly large rooms, all painted in soft yellows and golds, framed photographs of San Francisco landmarks add character. *825 Sutter St., at Jones St., Union Square, 94109, 415/923–6800 or 800/338–6848, fax 415/923–6804. 112 rooms, 1 suite. Restaurant, in-room data ports, nightclub, laundry service and dry cleaning, parking (fee). AE, D, DC, MC, V.*

4 *e-5*

CORNELL

This small, French country–style hotel is a bargain, especially considering its convenient location a few blocks north of Union Square and the Theater District. Reproduction French paintings hang in the plain but comfortable rooms. The owners also operate a small restaurant, Jeanne d'Arc, in the atmospheric cellar, with medieval trappings on the walls. *715 Bush St., between Powell and Mason Sts., Union Square, 94108, 415/421–3154 or 800/232–9698, fax 415/399–1442. 58 rooms, 48 with bath. Restaurant, in-room safes, parking (fee). No pets. AE, D, DC, MC, V.*

7 *h-3*

DOLORES PARK INN

On a sedate street not far from Dolores Park, near the border of the Mission and the Castro, this 1874 Italianate Victorian is consistently rated one of the city's best B&Bs. Rooms vary from quite small to practically palatial (the suite). All are comfortable and attractive, with a smattering of antiques. Service is cordial and excellent, and full breakfast, afternoon tea, and evening wine are complimentary. The management requires a two-night minimum. *3641 17th St., at Dolores St., Mission, 94114, phone/fax 415/621–0482 or 415/553–6060. 3 rooms, 1 suite. Breakfast room. No pets. MC, V.*

4 *d-6*

HALCYON HOTEL

Three blocks from Union Square, in an unassuming 1912 white-brick building, this small hotel is known for its compact but amazingly well-equipped rooms. They are simply furnished, each in a different style, and contain a refrigerator, coffeemaker, toaster, microwave, dishes and utensils, a small sink, TV, cassette player, and phones with private voice mail and unlimited free local calls. The beds are covered in quilted spreads, and an occasional antique has been added to the mostly modern furnishings. Some of the rooms have bay windows overlooking this steepish block of Jones Street, which can get noisy. A washer and dryer are in the basement for guests' use, and the staff are friendly and helpful, though there is no central desk. Guests are issued a lock code to enter the front door. The manager lives on-site; you can page him or knock on his door for assistance. *649 Jones St., between Post and Geary Sts., Union Square, 94102, 415/929–8033 or 800/627–2396, fax 415/441–8033. 25 rooms. In-room safes, coin laundry, parking (fee). No pets. MC, V.*

4 *a-3*

HOTEL DEL SOL

Once a typical '50s-style motor court, the Del Sol is now an anything-but-typical artistic statement playfully celebrating California's vibrant (some might say wacky) culture. The sunny yellow and blue, three-story building and courtyard, a riot of stripes and bold colors, are literal eye candy. Rooms open onto the courtyard's heated pool and hammock, lazing under palm trees, and evoke a beach-house mood with plantation shutters, tropical-striped bedspreads, and rattan chairs; some have brick fireplaces. The baths are small with bright-yellow tiling. *3100 Webster St., at Greenwich St., Marina, 94123, 415/921–5520 or 877/433–5765, fax 415/931–4137. 47 rooms, 10 suites. In-room data ports, in-room safes, pool, sauna, laundry service, concierge, free parking. AE, D, DC, MC, V.*

8 *b-4*

INN SAN FRANCISCO

On the eastern outskirts of the city's lively Mission, this B&B is housed in a strikingly pink 1872 Italianate Victorian. Antiques, featherbeds, and a hot tub out back make it a particularly inviting spot for romantics. Fresh flowers and gourmet chocolates in each room are a welcoming touch, as are the complimentary breakfast buffet and afternoon tea and sherry service. Some rooms have deep soaking tubs. *943 S. Van Ness Ave., between 20th and 21st Sts., Mission, 94110, 415/641–0188 or 800/359–0913, fax 415/641–1701. 22 rooms, 1 suite. Breakfast room, outdoor hot tub, parking (fee). AE, D, DC, MC, V.*

4 *d-5*

NOB HILL INN

Guests regularly return to the Nob Hill Inn for its simple, stately style and surprisingly reasonable prices. The 1907 Edwardian has smallish rooms, but each has attractive, mostly 19th-century furnishings. You can mingle in the living room during afternoon tea and Continental breakfast in the inn's own wine cellar. *1000 Pine St., at Taylor St., Nob Hill, 94109, 415/673–6080, fax 415/673–6098. 21 rooms. No pets. AE, MC, V.*

4 *d-5*

PETITE AUBERGE

The dozens of teddy bears in the reception area may seem a bit precious, but

---

LOUNGING IN STYLE

In this city of high real-estate properties and tiny hotel rooms, an inviting hotel lobby can be a real boon for visitors who want to meet friends before dinner. The following hotels have some of the city's most elaborate lobbies.

The Archbishop's Mansion (Expensive)
> *Wildly ornate antiques and chandeliers.*

The Fairmont (Very Expensive)
> *A soaring vaulted ceiling and a grand staircase.*

Hotel Monaco (Very Expensive)
> *A fireplace climbs almost two stories toward the domed ceiling.*

Hotel Rex (Expensive)
> *Antiquarian books and a clubby, 1920s mood.*

Hotel Triton (Expensive)
> *Brightly colored velvet couches and three-legged furniture.*

Hyatt Regency (Very Expensive)
> *A 17-story garden atrium, with full-size trees and a running stream.*

The Palace Hotel (Very Expensive)
> *A stained-glass ceiling, towering Ionic columns, and crystal chandeliers.*

Pan Pacific Hotel (Very Expensive)
> *A 21-story atrium with an elegant bronze fountain.*

Renaissance Stanford Court (Very Expensive)
> *A stained-glass dome and dramatic paintings.*

the rooms in this re-creation of a French country inn never stray past the mark. Rooms are small, with bright flowered wallpaper, an old-fashioned writing desk, an armoire, and only one teddy bear. Larger rooms have wingback chairs in front of a gas fireplace. A copious homemade breakfast buffet invites you to linger in the lounge—or in bed. *863 Bush St., at Taylor St., Union Square, 94108, 415/928–6000 or 800/365–3004, fax 415/673–7214. 25 rooms, 1 suite. Breakfast room, parking (fee). No pets. AE, DC, MC, V.*

4 c-7
PHOENIX HOTEL

This lively hotel is a kitschy tropical paradise on the edge of the Tenderloin. Rooms, which open onto a courtyard pool with a mural by Francis Forlenza on its bottom, are simple, with bamboo furniture, tropical-print bedspreads, and original local artwork. Although its location in the seedy Tenderloin District tends to scare off visitors, adventurous travelers come here hoping to spot one of the hotel's famed rock-star celebrity guests. *601 Eddy St., at Larkin St., Tenderloin, 94109, 415/776–1380 or 800/248–9466, fax 415/885–3109. 41 rooms, 3 suites. Restaurant, bar, pool, massage, nightclub, laundry service, free parking. AE, D, DC, MC, V.*

7 d-2
STANYAN PARK HOTEL

This three-story 1905 Victorian hotel with bay windows and a cupola across from Golden Gate Park is a welcome respite from the Haight's usual intense energy. Americana touches such as quilts give the Victorian-style rooms a homey mood; many also have fireplaces, which look nice but are nonfunctional. The large suites, with two bedrooms and full kitchens, are perfect for families. *750 Stanyan St., between Waller and Beulah Sts., Haight, 94117, 415/751–1000, fax 415/668–5454. 30 rooms, 6 suites. Dining room, parking (fee). No pets. AE, D, DC, MC, V.*

4 d-6
TOUCHSTONE TULIP INN

Although the rooms are somewhat plain, this hotel is ideally located in the middle of the Theater District, a few blocks from Union Square. It's attached to David's Delicatessen, San Francisco's most famous New York–style noshery, where patrons have been coming for knishes for more than 40 years. Hotel guests receive a 50% discount at David's, and the hotel provides free pickup from San Francisco International Airport if you stay two nights or more. *480 Geary St., at Taylor St., Union Square, 94102, 415/771–1600 or 800/524–1888, fax 415/931–5442. 42 rooms. Restaurant, parking (fee). No pets. AE, D, MC, V.*

5 g-8
VICTORIAN INN ON THE PARK

This fancifully ornamented 1897 Queen Anne Victorian is one of the finer B&Bs in the city. Pass through the grand entrance with oak parquet floors, into the formal parlor (where wine is served each evening), and you'll think you've gone back in time. Guest rooms have Eastlake antiques and distinctive wall treatments. Complimentary sherry is available anytime, and Continental breakfast (also included) always features home-baked items. *301 Lyon St., at Fell St., Western Addition, 94117, 415/931–1830 or 800/435–1967, fax 415/931–1830. 12 rooms. Breakfast room, meeting room, parking (fee). No pets. AE, D, DC, MC, V.*

7 h-2
WILLOWS

Bent willow furnishings give the name to this quiet B&B, where antiques and floral fabrics add to the charm. Rooms have washbasins and kimonos for your use (showers and toilets are down the hall), and there is nightly turn-down service. In the sitting room, evening beverage service and an expanded Continental breakfast buffet are good opportunities to mingle. Unlike some other B&B's, the front desk here is staffed from 8 AM to 10 PM for your needs. The location in the Castro means it's very popular with gay men and lesbians. *710 14th St., at Market St., Castro, 94114, 415/431–4770, fax 415/431–5295. 11 rooms with shared bath, 1 suite. Parking (fee). No pets. AE, D, MC, V.*

BUDGET LODGINGS

4 d-6
ADELAIDE INN

The bedspreads at this quiet retreat may not match the drapes or carpets, but the rooms are sunny, clean, and remarkably cheap. Tucked away in an alley just minutes from Union Square, the funky European-style pension hosts many guests from Germany, France, and Italy, some of whom congregate in the common area over coffee and snacks. *5 Isadora Duncan Ct., at Taylor St. between Geary and Post Sts., Union Square, 94102, 415/441–2474 or 415/441–2261, fax 415/441–0161. 18 rooms with shared bath. Breakfast room, parking (fee). No pets. AE, MC, V.*

4 d-7
AIDA HOTEL
The low-grade motel decor is by no means impressive, but the rooms are clean, large, and, on the top floor, quite sunny. Guests are attracted by the low prices and the central (if not terribly scenic) location near the Civic Center BART station, not too far from downtown or the clubs in SoMa. This is a good choice for serious budget travelers who forgot to reserve in advance, as rooms are often available at the last minute. *1087 Market St., at 7th St., Civic Center, 94102, 415/863–4141 or 800/863–2432, fax 415/863–5151. 174 rooms, 100 with bath. No pets. AE, D, MC, V.*

5 h-3
BEL-AIRE TRAVELODGE
This neat, white-with-blue-trim motel is a block away from busy Lombard Street and much quieter than many on the "main drag." It's made up of twin L shape buildings facing each other across Steiner Street, with exterior corridors and outside parking. Rooms are furnished in typical contemporary motel-style blond furniture. Bathrooms have showers only. Amenities include coffeemakers, cable TV, and free local calls. *3201 Steiner St., at Greenwich St., Marina, 94123, 415/921–5162 or 800/280-3242, fax 415/921–3602. 32 rooms. Free parking. AE, D, DC, MC, V.*

7 c-2
BOCK'S BED AND BREAKFAST
If peace and quiet are more important to you than a central location, consider this B&B in Parnassus Heights, two blocks from Golden Gate Park and just a few blocks south of Haight Street. The 1906 Edwardian is simple but comfortable, with redwood paneling and hardwood floors. Some rooms have decks and city views. There is a two -night minimum, and the entire property is no-smoking. *1448 Willard St., at Parnassus Ave., Haight, 94117, 415/664–6842, fax 415/664–1109. 3 rooms, 1 with bath. No pets. No credit cards.*

4 e-5
GOLDEN GATE HOTEL
Captain Nemo, a big black and white cat, serves as unofficial doorman to this homey, family-run B&B three blocks northwest of Union Square. Built in 1913 as a hotel, the four-story Edwardian has an original "birdcage" elevator that lifts you to hallways lined with historical photographs and guest rooms with antiques and wicker pieces. Complimentary Continental breakfast and afternoon English tea and cookies are served fireside in the cozy parlor. *775 Bush St., between Mason and Powell Sts., Union Square, 94108, 415/392–3702 or 800/835–1118, fax 415/392–6202. 25 rooms, 14 with bath. Parking (fee). No pets. AE, DC, MC, V.*

4 e-5
GRANT PLAZA
An exceptional value and popular with visiting families, Grant Plaza is on one of Chinatown's liveliest streets near the Financial District. The small rooms each have private bath, electronic lock, phone with voice mail, and satellite TV. Bathrooms are tiny, basic, and immaculate. Rooms on the top floor are newer, slightly brighter, and a bit more expensive; for a quieter stay, ask for one in the back. *465 Grant Ave., at Pine St., Chinatown, 94108, 415/434–3883 or 800/472–6899, fax 415/434–3886. 72 rooms, 1 suite. Laundry service, concierge, parking (fee). No pets. AE, MC, V.*

4 a-3
MARINA INN
Five blocks from the Marina, this place feels a little like a B&B but is priced like a motel. (It's especially reasonable between November and March.) English country–style rooms are simply appointed but have queen-size two-poster beds. Some rooms facing the street have nice bay windows with window seats, but the rooms in back are quieter. A simple but complimentary Continental breakfast and afternoon sherry are served in the sitting room. *3110 Octavia St., at Lombard St., Marina, 94123, 415/928–1000 or 800/274–1420, fax 415/928–5909. 40 rooms. Barbershop, beauty salon. No pets. AE, MC, V.*

5 g-3

MARINA MOTEL

This quiet motel, owned and run by the same family for more than 60 years, is one of the best of the many motels along congested Lombard Street. Half the 1930s-style rooms have fully equipped kitchens, and free garage parking makes it an even better deal. The courtyard garden is bright with pink bougainvillea and colorful murals by local artists, and a fountain gurgles pleasantly. *2576 Lombard St., at Divisadero St., Marina, 94123, 415/921–9406 or 800/346–6118, fax 415/921–0364. 38 rooms. Kitchenettes, free parking. MC, V.*

7 f-1

METRO HOTEL

Although the large, clean, high-ceilinged rooms are some of the nicest for the money in the city, many visitors never make their way to the Metro Hotel, due to its location in the somewhat depressed Western Addition. It does have a sizable following among the European crowd, however, and a French café downstairs serves breakfast and lunch on a sunny outdoor patio. *319 Divisadero St., between Oak and Page Sts., Western Addition, 94117, 415/861–5364, fax 415/863–1970. 24 rooms. Café. No pets. AE, D, DC, MC, V.*

5 f-3

PRESIDIO TRAVELODGE

After 90% of the west-bound traffic on Lombard Street veers off onto the Golden Gate Bridge approach, Lombard continues for two much quieter blocks, leading up to one of the entrance gates to San Francisco's 1,500-acre Presidio, a former army base, now woodsy national parkland. It's a terrific location for this humble gray and blue three-story motel, which features clean comfortable rooms furnished with blond furniture and standard motel amenities such as coffeemakers and cable TV. *2755 Lombard St., between Lyon and Baker Sts., Marina, 94123, 415/931–8581, fax 415/776–0904. 27 rooms. Refrigerators, free parking. AE, D, DC, MC, V.*

7 d-1

THE RED VICTORIAN

An immensely popular Haight Street landmark originally built as a resort hotel in 1904, the budget-priced Red Vic evokes San Francisco of the '60s: request the Summer of Love Room,

decked out with a tie-dyed canopy and '60s concert posters. Rooms are more quirky than fancy, but all are clean, and the staff takes good care of the guests. *1665 Haight St., between Belvedere and Cole Sts., Haight, 94117, 415/864–1978, fax 415/863–3293. 18 rooms, 6 with bath. No pets. AE, D, DC, MC, V.*

4 e-5

SAN FRANCISCO RESIDENCE CLUB

In contrast to its palatial and grand neighbors, the S. F. Residence Club, once an apartment building, is a humble guest house with million-dollar views, a money-saving meal plan, and a pleasant garden patio. The building has seen better days, and most of the modest rooms share baths, but many have sweeping bay views and some have TVs and refrigerators. The international clientele ranges from leisure travelers and business professionals to longer-term residents who enjoy the full American breakfast *and* dinner included in the daily, weekly, or monthly room rate. *851 California St., between Powell and Stockton Sts., Nob Hill, 94108, 415/421–2220, fax 415/421–2335. 84 rooms, 6 with bath. Dining room, coin laundry. No pets. No credit cards.*

4 d-2

SAN REMO

A three-story, blue and white 1906 Italianate Victorian between Fisherman's Wharf and North Beach, the San Remo has smallish, reasonably priced rooms and a slightly tatty elegance reminiscent of a quaint European hotel. Guests share the scrupulously clean bathrooms, and there are no phones or TVs in rooms. Honeymooners often request the Penthouse, which has a 360° view of the city and a private bath, and it must be booked well in advance. *2237 Mason St., between Francisco and Chestnut Sts., North Beach, 94133, 415/776–8688 or 800/352–7366, fax 415/776–2811. 61 rooms, 1 suite. Parking (fee). No pets. AE, DC, MC, V.*

4 e-6

STRATFORD HOTEL

Location is what it's all about at this budget find half a block from Union Square. The fresh rooms are white and yellow with pine furniture and gold drapes and bedspreads. There's a second-floor tearoom where both complimentary afternoon tea and Continental breakfast are served, and you have free access to an indoor pool and exercise room at the nearby Sheehan Hotel. *242 Powell St., between O'Farrell and Geary Sts., Union Square, 94102, 415/397–7080 or 888/504–6835, fax 415/397–7087. 95 rooms, 3 with bath. Laundry service and dry cleaning, concierge. No pets. AE, D, DC, MC, V.*

4 *a-3*

TOWN HOUSE MOTEL

What this family-oriented motel lacks in luxury and ambience, it makes up for in value: the simple rooms have dark-blue carpeting, earth-tone walls, and modern oak furniture. Continental breakfast is complimentary. *1650 Lombard St., between Gough and Octavia Sts., Marina, 94123, 415/885–5163 or 800/255–1516, fax 415/771–9889. 24 rooms. Free parking. AE, D, DC, MC, V.*

7 *g-2*

24 HENRY

Rooms are colorful and cozy at this friendly, gay- and lesbian-oriented guest house comprising three different turn-of-the-century properties in the Castro. The apartment suite with a full kitchen is an especially good deal if you want to do your own cooking. Complimentary breakfast is served in Victorian-style double parlors. Because of parking concerns and great public transportation here, guests are discouraged from bringing a car. *24 Henry St., between Noe and Sanchez Sts., Castro, 94114, 415/864–5686 or 800/900–5686, fax 415/864–0406. 10 rooms, 3 with bath, 1 suite. No pets. AE, MC, V.*

HOSTELS

4 *e-6*

AYH HOSTEL AT UNION SQUARE

A crowd of international students fills this huge hostel, perhaps San Francisco's best equipped—and certainly its best located if you want to be near Union Square. Most rooms have two or three bunk beds; a few suites are reserved for families. Facilities include a TV room, smoking room, library, kitchen, and computer room with Internet access. *312 Mason St., between O'Farrell and Geary Sts., Union Square, 94102, 415/788–5604 or 800/909–4776,*

ext. 02. 260 beds, including 12 family suites. MC, V. $

4 *d-8*

EUROPEAN GUEST HOUSE

Its South of Market location, near many of the city's best nightspots, is a draw for many wide-eyed club kids amazed at nightlife in the big city. The common rooms, including a kitchen and sundeck, are comfortable if not always immaculately maintained, and there is a computer for Internet access. Rooms have two or four beds. *761 Minna St., near Mission St. between 8th and 9th Sts., South of Market, 94103, 415/861–6634, fax 415/621–4428. 76 beds. Laundry. AE, MC, V. $*

4 *b-2*

FORT MASON INTERNATIONAL HOSTEL

If it weren't for its spectacular views of the Golden Gate Bridge, you might forget you're in San Francisco when you stay at this Fort Mason hostel, smack in the middle of an expanse of bay-front warehouses and lawns that feels removed from the rest of the city. Make reservations in advance or show up early on the day you want to stay. Travelers of all ages are welcome here, and facilities include a pool table, kitchen, clothes washers, and that rare commodity—free parking. Complimentary continental breakfast is served in the café. *Fort Mason, Bldg. 240, near Franklin and Bay Sts., Marina, 94123, 415/771–7277 or 800/909–4776, ext. 03, fax 415/771–1468. 160 beds. Kitchen, laundry. MC, V. $*

4 *d-6*

GLOBETROTTER'S INN

This hostel's small size makes it more personable than many of the others, and a mostly under-40, international clientele can be found here, although all are welcome. The building is a bit old and creaky but generally well maintained. Common areas include a fully equipped kitchen, TV room, and smoking rooms. Guest rooms have one to four beds. *225 Ellis St., between Mason and Taylor Sts., Union Square, 94102, 415/346–5786. 48 beds. Kitchen, laundry. No credit cards. $*

4 *e-4*

GREEN TORTOISE GUEST HOUSE

The only hostel at the edge of North Beach, Green Tortoise is American-friendly but so popular with European backpackers it's often tough to get a bed, so call ahead. Perks include unusually clean rooms, a nice kitchen, friendly staff, free Internet access, and, best of all, no curfew or lockout. Double rooms are also available, and rates include breakfast. *494 Broadway, between Montgomery and Kearny Sts., North Beach, 94133, 415/834–1000, fax 415/956–4900. 110 beds. Kitchen, laundry. No credit cards. $*

4 *e-8*

INTERCLUB GLOBE HOSTEL

Although this hostel is intended for international travelers, U.S. residents can get in by flashing a passport and a smile. A relaxed atmosphere for all ages, a South of Market location, and the international clientele make it a lively place to socialize, especially on the pleasant sundeck. Rooms have four or five beds and an adjoining bath. *10 Hallam St., near Folsom St. between 7th and 8th Sts., South of Market, 94103, 415/431–0540, fax 415/431–3286. 144 beds. Laundry. No credit cards. $*

1 *a-2*

MARIN HEADLANDS HOSTEL

If you have a car and don't mind a bit of a drive, this hostel in the Marin Headlands is ideal for a mellow, relaxing stay. In addition to endless hiking trails and breathtaking scenery just steps outside the door, guests enjoy a communal kitchen, laundry room, tennis court, Ping-Pong table, pool table, and a common room with a fireplace. Private rooms are often available. *Ft. Barry, Bldg. 941, just up hill from visitor center, Sausalito, 94965, 415/331–2777 or 800/909–4776, fax 415/331–6943. 103 beds. Kitchen, laundry. D, MC, V. $*

4 *c-8*

NEW CENTRAL HOTEL AND HOSTEL

This former flophouse in a central if a little seedy location has been transformed into a decent hostel. A pool table, TV room, kitchen, and free coffee keep the stay-at-homes occupied, but the location is great for forays into other parts of the city. All visitors, even Americans, must show a passport to stay here. *1412 Market St., at 10th and Fell Sts., Civic Center, 94102, 415/703–9988, fax 415/703–9986. 250 beds. Kitchen, laundry. AE, D, MC, V. $*

4 *e-5*

PACIFIC TRADEWINDS

The smallest of San Francisco's hostels, this homey spot in Chinatown is near some of the city's best restaurants, budget and otherwise. Guests, who are almost exclusively young international backpackers, have access to a kitchen

---

HOTELS WITH GREAT GRUB

These hotel restaurants really cut the mustard by garnering praise for the hotel they're partnered with, as well as being top-notch dining destinations in their own right.

The Abigail Hotel (Moderately Priced)
Innovative vegan concoctions at the Millennium.

Campton Place (Very Expensive)
The preeminent power breakfast spot.

The Clift (Very Expensive)
Close the deal in the sedate Redwood Room.

Hotel Vintage Court (Expensive)
Affiliated with Masa's, the city's most acclaimed French restaurant.

Inn at the Opera (Expensive)
Ovation Restaurant is sumptuously romantic.

Mandarin Oriental (Very Expensive)
Silks restaurant has innovative California-Asian cuisine.

The Palace Hotel (Very Expensive)
Kyo-ya, for top-notch Japanese.

Pan Pacific Hotel (Very Expensive)
California cuisine at its best.

Prescott Hotel (Very Expensive)
Attached to Postrio, the famed Wolfgang Puck restaurant.

Ritz-Carlton, San Francisco (Very Expensive)
Consistent thumbs up for the Dining Room.

Touchstone Tulip Inn (Moderately Priced)
You get a discount at the 40-year-old David's Deli downstairs.

W San Francisco (Very Expensive)
Be seen among the hip, artsy crowd at XYZ.

and common room. Ask for a key (deposit required) if you want to stay out past midnight. *680 Sacramento St., at Kearny St., Chinatown, 415/433–7970, fax 415/291–8801, 94111. 35 beds. Kitchen, laundry. MC, V. $*

HOTELS NEAR THE AIRPORT

very expensive lodgings

1 *d-8*

EMBASSY SUITES SAN FRANCISCO AIRPORT– BURLINGAME

One of the most lavish hotels in the airport area, this one set on the bay has up-close views of planes taking off and landing (although rooms are remarkably quiet). All guest rooms are suites that open onto an atrium and tropical garden; each has a desk area, sleeper sofa, wet bar, television, microwave, and refrigerator. Full American breakfast and evening cocktails and snacks are included in the room rate. *150 Anza Blvd., at Airport Blvd., Burlingame 94010, 650/342–4600 or 800/362–2779, fax 650/343–8137. 339 suites. Restaurant, bar, refrigerators, room service, indoor pool, hot tubs, sauna, exercise room, laundry service and dry cleaning, business services, airport shuttle, free parking. AE, D, DC, MC, V.*

HOTEL SOFITEL– SAN FRANCISCO BAY

Parisian lampposts and a kiosk covered with French posters bring a bit of Paris to this hotel 10 mi south of the airport. Nightly turn-down service yields a fresh rose and Evian water, and at checkout you receive a French baguette. The French-theme public spaces—the Gigi Brasserie, Baccarat restaurant, and La Terrasse bar—have an open, airy feeling that extends to the rooms. A small sitting area in each room is a welcome perk in this city of tiny hotel rooms. *223 Twin Dolphin Dr., at Ralston Ave., Redwood City 94065, 650/598–9000 or 800/221–4542, fax 650/598–0459. 379 rooms, 42 suites. 2 restaurants, bar, lobby lounge, pool, spa, health club, laundry service, concierge, meeting rooms, airport shuttle, free parking. AE, DC, MC, V.*

1 *d-8*

SAN FRANCISCO AIRPORT MARRIOTT

Five minutes south of the airport, the Marriott has a recreation area with an indoor pool, sauna, and whirlpool. Good-size guest rooms are decorated in autumn colors, with Scandinavian furniture. *1800 Old Bayshore Hwy., Burlingame 94010, 650/692–9100 or 800/228–9290, fax 650/692–8016. 663 rooms, 21 suites. 2 restaurants, bar, in-room data ports, room service, indoor pool, sauna, exercise room, piano, laundry and dry cleaning, business services, meeting rooms, car rental, airport shuttle. AE, D, DC, MC, V.*

1 *d-7*

THE WESTIN HOTEL– SAN FRANCISCO AIRPORT

Although geared toward business travelers, the Westin has an atrium-enclosed swimming pool and bay-front location that make it a fine choice for anyone who wants to be near the airport. The medium-size guest rooms have Asian accents in gold, green, and rose. *1 Old Bayshore Hwy., at Millbrae Ave., Millbrae 94030, 650/692–3500 or 800/937–8461, fax 650/872–8111. 390 rooms, 3 suites. Restaurant, coffee shop, lobby lounge, in-room data ports, minibars, room service, sauna, exercise room, business services, airport shuttle, free parking. No pets. AE, DC, MC, V.*

expensive lodgings

1 *i-8*

THE CLARION HOTEL SAN FRANCISCO AIRPORT

This busy hotel, a mile south of San Francisco International Airport, is a favorite of business travelers who pop into town for quick meetings. In the lovely garden area, wrought-iron benches, a heated pool, and a whirlpool tub are set among pine trees. Rooms in the Garden Building are slightly larger although older, whereas the newer Tower rooms have better views and comfortable pillow-top mattresses. A popular running trail winds alongside the bay. *401 E. Millbrae Ave., off U.S. 101, Millbrae 94030, 650/692–6363 or 800/223–7111, fax 650/697–8735. 430 rooms, 10 suites. Restaurant, room service, pool, outdoor hot tub, exercise room, coin laun-*

dry, laundry service and dry cleaning, business services, meeting rooms, airport shuttle, parking (fee). No pets. AE, D, DC, MC, V.

moderately priced lodgings

1 d-8

HYATT REGENCY
SAN FRANCISCO AIRPORT

The spectacular 29,000-square-ft, eight - story lobby atrium of this dramatic Hyatt Regency 2 mi south of the airport encloses a world of water, light, and air that makes you feel like you're outdoors and the weather is always perfect.

Almost every service and amenity you could think of is available, and rooms are modern and well equipped. The featured restaurant, Scalini, serves upscale northern Italian fare. 1333 Old Bayshore Hwy., at Burlingame Ave. (Millbrae exit off Hwy. 101), Burlingame 94010, 650/347–1234, fax 650/696–2669. 793 rooms, 42 suites. Restaurant, café, deli, lobby lounge, piano bar, sports bar, in-room data ports, room service, pool, outdoor hot tub, exercise room, jogging, laundry service and dry cleaning, concierge, business services, convention center, meeting rooms, airport shuttle, car rental, free parking. AE, D, DC, MC, V.

1 c-6

LA QUINTA MOTOR INN

Right off Highway 101, this is a good moderately priced choice for travelers who just staggered off a late flight. Typical chain motel rooms with floral touches are well insulated from the freeway noise. Continental breakfast is complimentary. 20 Airport Blvd., off U.S. 101, South San Francisco 94080, 650/583–2223 or 800/531–5900, fax 650/589–6770. 169 rooms, 3 suites. Pool, hot tub, exercise room, coin laundry, free parking. AE, D, DC, MC, V.

budget accommodations

1 d-8

RED ROOF INN

Rooms at this popular budget hotel are plain but very clean, with light-wood furnishings. The pool makes it popular with families. Upper floors facing the airport and San Francisco have better views, but are noisier when planes start flying early in the morning. 777 Airport Blvd., at Anza Blvd., Burlingame 94010, 650/342–7772 or 800/843–7663, fax 650/342–2635. 212 rooms. Restaurant, pool, free parking. No pets. AE, DC, MC, V.

HOTELS IN THE WINE COUNTRY

expensive lodgings

GAIGE HOUSE

The charming "something old, something new" quality of the hamlet of Glen Ellen is mirrored in one of its finest and most stylish small inns. Gaige House is a handsome 19th-century creekside home that has been totally modernized

---

GAY-POPULAR HOTELS

Gay couples can count on a warm welcome from almost any San Francisco hotel, but the following are particularly popular with gay and lesbian visitors.

The Archbishop's Mansion (Expensive)
Popular for weddings, both gay and straight.

Bock's Bed and Breakfast (Budget)
A quiet inn in a quiet neighborhood, frequented by lesbians.

Hotel Diva (Expensive)
Big among those in the arts.

Hotel Monaco (Very Expensive)
A slick hotel with outré decor.

Hotel Rex (Expensive)
Clubby decor and warm service.

Hotel Triton (Expensive)
Avant-garde decor and a trendy crowd.

Inn on Castro (Expensive)
Relax in this 1896 Edwardian B&B on bustling Castro Street.

Phoenix Hotel (Moderately Priced)
Home away from home for celebs and pop icons.

24 Henry (Budget)
Cozy rooms in the Castro.

W San Francisco (Very Expensive)
Next door to SFMOMA and ultra chic.

Willows (Moderately Priced)
A serene hotel with willow furnishings.

York Hotel (Expensive)
There's a cabaret on the premises.

and decorated with West African and Indonesian touches from its owners' extensive travels. Some rooms have whirlpools, fireplaces, or decks, and all guests enjoy the pool, gourmet breakfasts, evening wine tastings, and full concierge service. *13540 Arnold Dr., Glen Ellen 95442, 707/935–0237 or 800/935–0237, fax 707/935–6411. 11 rooms, 2 suites. Breakfast room, pool, outdoor hot tub, concierge. No pets. MC, V.*

INDIAN SPRINGS RESORT & SPA

At California's oldest continually operating pool and spa facility, Indian Springs' three hot geysers have been pumping their famous 212°F waters into its mineral pools, steam rooms, and mud (actually volcanic ash) baths since 1871. Overnight guests stay in charming bungalows built in the 1940s with gas fireplaces, quaint full kitchens, and hammocks and barbecues outside. A full array of spa services including massage and facials is available, and guests have free use of the naturally heated Olympic-size pool year-round. *1/12 Lincoln Ave., Calistoga 94515, 707/942–4913, fax 707/942–4919. 18 suites. Picnic area, kitchenettes, refrigerators, pool, hot springs, massage, mineral baths, spa, steam room, tennis court, croquet, Ping-Pong, bicycles, recreation room. No pets. D, MC, V*

MADRONA MANOR

Madrona Manor's ornate 1881 Victorian mansion sits atop a wooded knoll in pastoral Healdsburg, providing a storybook setting, gracious rooms, and fine dining. Eighteen of the 21 rooms, some in the main house and some in outbuildings, have fireplaces, and a few have balconies or decks. Furnishings range from antiques and Persian carpets to Nepalese rosewood and rattan. The lovely buildings, grounds, and gourmet breakfasts exemplify California elegance. *1001 Westside Rd., Healdsburg 95448, 707/433–4231 or 800/258–4003, fax 707/433–0703. 18 rooms, 3 suites. Restaurant, pool. AE, D, DC, MC, V.*

VILLAGIO INN AND SPA

One of the newest inn and spa complexes in the Napa Valley, Villagio has Tuscan-style gardens, frescoes, fountains, and waterways, even a Roman-style "ruin." It's next to vineyards and a short walk from downtown Yountville's many lauded eateries. Rooms, decorated in subtle earth tones, all have fireplaces and a patio or balcony. A champagne Continental breakfast buffet is included. The spa facility offers a huge range of pricey services including skin care, massage, body treatments, and fitness and meditation classes. *6481 Washington St., Yountville 94599, 707/944–8877 or 800/351–1133, fax 707/944–8855. 90 rooms, 22 suites. Restaurant, lobby lounge, refrigerators, room service, pool, outdoor hot tub, massage, sauna, spa, tennis court, aerobics, exercise room, health club, bicycles. AE, DC, MC, V.*

moderately priced lodgings

BELTANE RANCH

Outside of Glen Ellen, on a pastoral slope of the Mayacamas Mountains, the Beltane Ranch is a working vineyard, olive orchard, cattle ranch, and grand 1892 yellow and white ranch house with wraparound verandas. The lovely rooms all have outside entrances, antique furniture, and private baths, but the real attraction is miles and miles of hiking trails with stunning scenery and bird- and wildlife-viewing opportunities. Full breakfast is included. *11775 Sonoma Hwy. (Hwy. 12), Glen Ellen 95442, 707/996–6501. 6 rooms. Tennis court, hiking, horseshoes. No credit cards.*

SONOMA MISSION INN AND SPA

Two miles north of Sonoma, this beautifully landscaped resort built in the 1920s has a Mediterranean-cum-California Mission style, European spa, par-72 golf course, and two good restaurants. The spa features an elaborate Roman coed bathing area, herbal steam rooms, and a full array of personal beauty, fitness, and relaxation options, from grape-seed body polishing and seaweed wraps to yoga, meditation, and nutrition classes. Service, including twice-daily maid service in guest rooms, is excellent. *Hwy. 12, at Boyes Blvd., Box 1447, Sonoma 95476, 707/938–9000 or 800/862–4945, fax 707/938–4250. 168 rooms, 60 suites. Restaurant, café, bar, lobby lounge, refrigerators, room service, pool, outdoor hot tub, massage, mineral baths, sauna, steam room, 18-hole golf course, aerobics, exercise room, health club, jogging. AE, DC, MC, V.*

THE WINE COUNTRY INN

Off a rural lane and overlooking rolling hills, stone bridges, and miles of vineyards north of St. Helena, the Wine Country Inn is a tranquil and comfortable getaway. Rural antiques fill the rooms, most of which have a fireplace and a patio, balcony, or deck, but no television. Some rooms have private hot tubs. Wine tastings take place in the afternoon, and a hearty country breakfast buffet is also included in the room rate. *1152 Lodi La., off Hwy. 29, St. Helena, 94574, 707/963–7077 or 800/ 473–3463, fax 707/963–9018. 21 rooms, 3 suites. Pool, outdoor hot tub. MC, V.*

B&B RESERVATION SERVICES

In addition to the regular hotels, motels, hostels, and B&B inns, there are lots of lodgings in San Francisco available in private homes, apartments, and even houseboats. They may not be advertised or listed, except through booking agencies that function as travel agencies but deal with accommodations only. If you're looking for a more personal (and sometimes significantly cheaper) overnight experience in a residential neighborhood, investigate this alternative. Accommodations, amenities, service, and privacy may not be the same as you get in more mainstream lodgings, so do check out all the details. Many B&Bs of this sort also enforce a two-night minimum stay, especially on weekends and holidays. Be sure to ask your booking agency about breakfast and other food service; some B&Bs provide sumptuous spreads, while others don't serve breakfast, despite the name.

B&Bs booked through either of the following services may be hosted (you are the guest in someone's occupied residence) or unhosted (you have full use of the residence, including kitchen privileges). The latter option is sometimes more expensive. Make reservations as far in advance as possible; the best rooms book up quickly, especially in summer and fall.

Bed and Breakfast California (Box 2247, Saratoga 95070, 408/867–9662 or 800/ 872–4500, fax 408/867–0907).

Bed and Breakfast San Francisco (Box 420009, 94142, 415/899–0060 or 800/ 452–8249, fax 415/899–9923).

chapter 7

CITY SOURCES

getting a handle on the city

basics of city life

BANKS

The following are all full-service banks, members of the FDIC. For the address of the nearest ATM accepting Cirrus cards, call the **Cirrus Cash-Machine Locator** (800/424–7787). For help finding an ATM that accepts Plus cards, call the **Plus ATM Locator** (800/843–7587).

Bank of America. More than 60 branches in San Francisco, all with ATMs accepting Plus, Star, and Interlink cards. Most are open Saturday 9–2. Additional freestanding B of A ATMs are located at 3Com Park, the San Francisco International Airport, San Francisco Shopping Centre, and in many Lucky supermarkets. *415/615–4700 for 24-hr service.*

Bank of the West. Six citywide branches with ATMs accepting Cirrus, Star, and Explore cards. Branch hours are weekdays 9–5; some branches are open Saturday 9–1. *800/488–2265.*

Bayview. Twelve branches in San Francisco, with ATMs accepting Plus, Star, and Interlink cards. Branches are open Monday to Thursday 9–5 and Friday 9–6; some open Saturday 9–1. *800/229–8439 for 24-hr service.*

California Federal Bank. More than 15 branches, most with ATMs accepting Plus, Star, and Explore cards. Several CalFed branches are open Saturday, although hours vary. Branches are open Monday to Thursday 9–5, Friday 9–6, and Saturday 9–2. *800/843–2265.*

Citibank. Ten branches in San Francisco, all with ATMs accepting Cirrus cards. Branches are open Monday to Thursday 9–6 and Friday 9–6; one branch is open Saturday 9–1. *800/756–7047.*

Washington Mutual Bank. Twenty-six branches citywide, with ATMs accepting Plus and Star cards. Branch hours are weekdays 9 to 5; some branches are open Saturday 9–1. *800/788–7000.*

Wells Fargo. "Anytime, anywhere banking" at more than 20 branches citywide, all with ATMs accepting Star, Cirrus, Explore, Maestro, and Global Access cards. Additional ATMs are located at many Safeway supermarkets. Hours are weekdays 9–6, and Saturday 9–2 at select branches. *800/869–3557.*

DRIVING

San Francisco's relatively small size and extensive and smooth-running public transportation system translate into one important rule: you don't need a car to get around. The one exception is if you live in the Avenues (the outer Richmond or Sunset districts), where public transportation and cabs can be scarce. If you head out of town often, having a car is handy, but renting is always an option.

The speed limits in San Francisco are 25 mph on city streets and 55 mph on highways inside the city limits. Unless otherwise noted, it is permissible to turn right at a red light.

licenses

To get a license plate, you must fill out an application form called the "Application for Plates, Stickers, Documents" at the DMV and make an appointment to have the application processed. The cost is $8. Call 415/557–1179 to make an appointment. It is notoriously difficult to get through on the phone, so the other (better) option is to make an appointment in person when you pick up your application form.

DEPARTMENT OF MOTOR VEHICLES
California Department of Motor Vehicles (DMV). *1377 Fell St., at Baker St., 415/557–1179.*

traffic

San Francisco's two top traffic magnets are, without a doubt, the Golden Gate Bridge and the Bay Bridge, particularly during rush hour (6 AM to 9 AM and 3:30 PM to 6:30 PM) if you are traveling in the direction of traffic (heading across the bridges into San Francisco in the morning, and then back in the afternoon).

Van Ness Avenue is one of the main thoroughfares in San Francisco, so expect to find traffic jams during rush hour. Two worthwhile alternatives that run parallel to Van Ness Avenue are Gough Street (if you are traveling south), and Franklin Street (if you are heading north). Battery Street in the Financial District is another major thoroughfare, so try to avoid it during the afternoon rush hour. Your best bet when heading into the Financial District is to take public transportation, because it is a BART and Muni hub and parking is particularly difficult downtown.

Another traffic hot spot in the city is the area of Broadway and Columbus Street in North Beach, particularly on Friday and Saturday night.

A note of caution: if you are traveling in the direction of the bay and the SF Ferry Building (northeast), beware of Market Street (the city's best-known thorough-fare) at any time of the day because it is virtually impossible to make a left (northwest) off it. It's better to drive on a street that runs parallel to Market Street, such as Folsom Street.

In anticipation of the April 2000 open-ing of the new Pacific Bell Park, the pub-lic transportation options in the China Basin area have more than doubled. If you are driving on game day, your best bet is to park in a cheap lot elsewhere in the city (or in a Bart station that has a parking lot) and then take public trans-portation the rest of the way. Stay away from the main streets leading to the ball park—Townsend, King, 3rd, and 4th streets—and take side streets instead.

GAS STATIONS

Castro Street Chevron. Open 24 hours. *2399 Market St., at Castro St., 415/621-2570.*

Downtown Union 76. Open 24 hours. *390 1st St., near Harrison St. at the Bay Bridge on-ramp, 415/957-1754.*

Fisherman's Wharf Union 76. Open 24 hours. *490 Bay St., at Taylor St., 415/771-7730.*

Lombard Union 76. Open 24 hours. *2498 Lombard St., at Divisadero St., 415/931-4040.*

Valencia Chevron. Open 24 hours. *1198 Valencia St., at 23rd St., 415/695-8743.*

GEOGRAPHY

San Francisco sits at the tip of a 32-mi-long peninsula surrounded on three sides by the San Francisco Bay and the Pacific Ocean. The city is 46 square mi, surprisingly small considering its mighty international reputation. Steep hills are San Francisco's most notable geograph-ical feature. There are approximately 40 of them; some—Nob Hill, Russian Hill,

Telegraph Hill—are quite famous. The hills cleave the city into distinct areas that are the foundation of its distinctive neighborhoods. They also make for some hair-raising descents. You'll come face-to-face (literally) with several of the city's steepest hills when exploring downtown San Francisco.

Union Square, the downtown shopping district, is at the heart of San Francisco. From here, prime destinations such as Chinatown, North Beach, Fisherman's Wharf, Civic Center, and the Financial District are easy to reach by cable car, by bus, or (for those who don't mind a lit-tle climbing) on foot. The city's two beloved parks, Golden Gate Park and the Presidio, lie several miles west of the downtown area, along the Pacific Ocean. The neighborhoods surrounding the parks are primarily residential. San Francisco's famous Golden Gate Bridge extends from the tip of the Presidio north to wealthy Marin County.

Most of San Francisco's neighborhoods are laid out along a neat grid, so it helps to know the nearest cross street when searching for an address. An exception to the city's tidy pattern is Market Street, the main downtown thoroughfare, which runs diagonally through the heart of the city. Downtown, on the south side of Market Street (SoMa), a series of numbered streets begins with 1st and continues south to 30th. The first 12 streets run southeast–northwest, and the remaining ones run east–west. Far west of downtown are the Richmond and Sunset districts; the numbered avenues in these districts run north-south, starting with 2nd and ending near the ocean with 48th. The avenues intersect with a series of alphabetically named east–west streets, which begin with Anza and Balboa and continue south to Wawona and Yorba (there's no X or Z Street) just north of Sloat Boule-vard. Be careful not to confuse streets and avenues when reading addresses.

The major east–west streets north of Market Street are Geary Boulevard (it's called Geary Street until Van Ness Avenue), which runs to the Pacific Ocean; Fulton Street, which begins at the back of the Opera House and con-tinues along the north side of Golden Gate Park to Ocean Beach; and Fell Street, whose left two lanes cut through Golden Gate Park and empty into Lincoln Boulevard. The latter continues on the park's south side to the ocean.

The longest street in San Francisco, Mission Street, heads southwest from the Embarcadero to Van Ness Avenue, then turns due south to Army Street, after which it resumes a southwest course into Daly City.

Among the major north–south streets are Divisadero Street, which becomes Castro Street at Duboce Avenue and continues past Army Street; Van Ness Avenue (it becomes South Van Ness Avenue a few blocks south of City Hall); and Park Presidio Boulevard, which empties into 19th Avenue.

HOLIDAYS

During the following holidays, all offices of the city and county of San Francisco are closed, as are many other places of business. *See* the "Events" section of Chapter 4 for information on holiday events and celebrations.

New Year's Day (January 1).

Martin Luther King, Jr. Day (third Monday in January).

President's Day (third Monday in February).

Memorial Day (last Monday in May).

Independence Day (July 4).

Labor Day (first Monday in September).

Columbus Day (the Monday closest to October 12).

Veteran's Day (November 11).

Thanksgiving Day (fourth Thursday in November).

Christmas Day (December 25).

LIQUOR LAWS

Packaged alcoholic beverages may be purchased daily from 6 AM to 2 AM at liquor stores, grocery stores, and some drug stores. During the same hours, most San Francisco restaurants, bars, and nightclubs are licensed to serve a full line of alcoholic beverages by the glass or bottle. However, some hold permits to sell beer and wine only. The legal age for purchase and/or consumption is 21; proof of age is required.

NO SMOKING

Almost all hotels and motels have no-smoking rooms; in larger establishments entire floors are reserved for nonsmokers. Most bed-and-breakfasts do not allow smoking on the premises.

In accordance with California law, San Francisco restaurants and bars do not permit smoking. Smoking is not allowed in office buildings, stores, malls, and theaters. Smoking is permitted in the streets.

PARKING

rules and enforcement

The best advice if driving into the city: park it, and rely on your feet and the city's excellent public transportation system. Downtown, limited metered parking is available, but most meters limit parking to 30 minutes or one hour. Additionally, certain streets have designated tow-away zones during rush hours (7 AM–9 AM and 3 PM–6 PM). If your car is towed, take the registration or rental agreement papers to the nearest police station. You'll be required to pay the parking fine plus a $100 towing fee to free your vehicle. In outlying neighborhoods, watch for street-cleaning signs indicating when parking is prohibited. Some areas require resident parking permits, and nonresident parking is severely restricted.

Throughout the city, pay attention to curb colors. The colors painted on the curbs indicate rules: red means no stopping or parking at any time; yellow is for loading and unloading vehicles with commercial plates only; green has a 10-minute parking limit for all vehicles; white, for passenger loading and unloading, has a five-minute limit that is in effect during the adjacent business's hours of operation; blue is for vehicles displaying a California disabled-person plate or placard. In all parts of the city except Fisherman's Wharf, parking regulations are not enforced on New Year's Day, Memorial Day, Independence Day, Labor Day, Thanksgiving, and Christmas Day. New Year's Day, Thanksgiving, and Christmas are the only meter-free days at Fisherman's Wharf.

If you insist on parking on one of San Francisco's famous hills, the law requires that you curb your wheels—

that is, turn them toward the street if the car is facing uphill, toward the curb if facing downhill. Remember to set the car's emergency brake, and if it's a stick shift, leave the car in gear. Failure to curb a vehicle's wheels on a hill earns a $23 parking ticket. For more information on parking in San Francisco, call the city's **Department of Parking and Traffic** (415/554–7275).

parking lots

Parking garages are plentiful but expensive. The three best downtown garages—a bargain for shoppers, since they average only $1.50 per hour—are the Fifth and Mission Garage, the Ellis-O'Farrell Garage (across from Macy's), and the Sutter-Stockton Garage. The garages listed below are all near shopping and tourist attractions.

CHINATOWN
Holiday Inn Parking. 750 Kearny St., at Washington St., 415/781–3942.

Portsmouth Square Garage. 733 Kearny St., between Clay and Washington Sts., 415/982–6353

Sutter-Stockton Garage. 444 Stockton St., at Sutter St., 415/982–7275.

CIVIC CENTER/OPERA PLAZA
Civic Center Plaza Garage. Civic Center, McAllister St., between Polk and Larkin Sts., 415/863–1537.

Opera Plaza Garage. 601 Van Ness Ave., between Golden Gate Ave. and Turk St., 415/771–4776.

DOWNTOWN
Ellis-O'Farrell Garage. 123 O'Farrell St., at Stockton St., Union Square, 415/986–4800.

Embarcadero Center Garage. 1–4 Embarcadero Center, at Battery St., Embarcadero, 800/733–6318.

5th & Mission Garage. 833 Mission St., South of Market, 415/982–8522.

FISHERMAN'S WHARF
Pier 39 Garage. 2550 Powell St., across from Pier 39, Embarcadero, 415/705–5418.

The Wharf Garage. 350 Beach St., between Taylor and Mason Sts., 415/921–0226.

GHIRARDELLI SQUARE
Ghirardelli Square Parking Garage. 900 North Point St., between Larkin and Polk Sts., 415/929–1665.

PARKS INFORMATION

For information on city parks, call the **San Francisco Recreation and Parks Department** (415/831–2700) or send a self-addressed, stamped envelope to: Recreation and Parks, McLaren Lodge, Golden Gate Park, 501 Stanyan St., San Francisco 94117. The McLaren Lodge visitor center is open weekdays 8–5.

California State Parks in the San Francisco area include Angel Island, Mt. Tamalpais, and Samuel P. Taylor. *California State Parks and Recreation Dept., Bay Area District Office, 250 Executive Park Blvd., Suite 4900, San Francisco 94134, 415/330 6300.*

The vast **Golden Gate National Recreation Area,** administered by the U.S. Department of the Interior's National Park Service, encompasses much of the San Francisco and Marin coastline: beaches, redwood groves, historic forts, the Presidio, and more. For information, contact the National Park Service (Western Regional Information Center, Bldg. 201, Fort Mason, San Francisco 94123, 415/556–0561). This office handles all national parks in California, Oregon, and Washington. The Fort Mason Visitors Center is open weekdays 9.30–4.30. A smaller office on the lower level of the Cliff House (1090 Point Lobos Ave., at Great Hwy., Richmond District, 415/556–8642.) is open daily 10–5.

PERSONAL SECURITY

As in any city these days, it's important to use common sense on the street. Be wary in the Tenderloin, parts of the Mission (around 14th Street, for example), the lower Haight, and SoMa (South of Market) if you aren't on the main thoroughfare, where clubs and nightlife are centered. When going out at night, know your destination, how you are getting there, and most importantly, how you are getting back: cabs are scarce and therefore difficult to hail on the street, but hotels, restaurants, clubs, and bars will call one for you on request.

PUBLIC TRANSPORTATION

The TravInfo Hotline offers up-to-the-minute information on public transit lines, highway traffic conditions, carpooling, parking, and airport transit for all nine Bay Area counties. The *Regional Transit Guide* ($3.95) is an excellent resource listing Bay Area transportation agencies, lines, and frequency. It's available in bookstores as well as the San Francisco Visitor Information Center at Hallidie Plaza. *415/817–1717, 510/817–1717, 650/817–1717, and 408/817–1717.*

muni system

Muni (Municipal Railway) is a network of diesel buses, electric trolley buses, Muni Metro streetcars, historic streetcars, and the world-famous cable cars. The 80 Muni routes include 16 express lines, plus special service to 3Com Park and Pacific Bell Park on game days. Service operates 24 hours daily, but is limited after midnight; during weekdays buses run approximately 10–15 minutes apart. For a comprehensive map of all Muni routes send $2.50 (check or money order payable to San Francisco City and County) to Muni Map (949 Presidio Ave., Room 238, San Francisco 94115). The map is sold at many stores in San Francisco and throughout the Bay Area. *415/673–6864, 415/923–6336 for 24-hr route assistance, 415/923–6168 for lost and found.*

The adult fare for Muni-system buses and streetcars is $1. For senior citizens and youth 5–17, the fare is 35¢. Exact change is required. **Transfers** are issued free on request at the time the fare is paid for bus or streetcar service, and are valid for 90 minutes for two boardings in any direction. There are a number of discount travel plans: the **Fast Pass** ($35) is an adult monthly pass good for all Muni transport, including cable cars, as well as BART and CalTrain within San Francisco. The Fast Pass for youth and senior citizens costs $8 (proper identification required). The **Weekly Pass** ($9) is valid from Monday through Sunday on all Muni buses and streetcars, and each cable car ride is an additional $1. **Passport** passes allow unlimited access to Muni buses, streetcars, and cable cars for one day ($6), three days ($10), or seven days ($15). Passport passes are also good for discounts at tourist attractions around San Francisco, including the museums in Golden Gate Park. Purchase passes at the Visitor Information Center at Hallidie Plaza, or at the Muni booth next to the cable-car turnarounds at Powell and Market streets and at Fisherman's Wharf.

CABLE CARS

San Francisco's charming cable cars have delighted residents and visitors since 1873. Cable car fare for all riders is $2. Senior citizens (65 and older) pay $1 daily between 9 PM and 7 AM (at other times they pay the full fare). Tickets are purchased aboard the car. Exact change is not required, and transfers are neither issued nor accepted. (With a valid Muni Fast Pass or Passport there is no additional charge to ride the cable cars.) Each car has seats for up to 100 passengers; standing and straphanging are also allowed. To board a cable car midway along its route, move toward it quickly as it pauses, wedge yourself into any available space and hold on tightly. Cable cars operate daily from 6 AM until 1 AM.

The **Powell–Mason line** (No. 59) runs from downtown (Market and Powell streets) through Union Square, Nob Hill, Chinatown, and North Beach, ending at the east end of Fisherman's Wharf. The **Powell–Hyde line** (No. 60, the most scenic route), which also begins at Powell and Market streets near Union Square, runs through Nob Hill, Chinatown, and Russian Hill, and ends at the west end of Fisherman's Wharf. The wait to board at either Fisherman's Wharf or the cable-car turnaround at Powell and Market streets can often exceed an hour. The **California Street line** (No. 61) runs from Van Ness Avenue and California Street through Nob Hill, Chinatown, and the Financial District; it ends at the Embarcadero Muni station, at Market and California streets. Although the views on this line are not as spectacular, there are fewer crowds.

bus

AC Transit (Alameda–Contra Costa Transit) provides bus service in Alameda and Contra Costa counties, and transbay service between these counties and San Francisco via the Bay Bridge. Use AC Transit buses to reach Berkeley, Oakland, and Treasure Island. Buses depart from San Francisco's Transbay Terminal (Mission St., between 1st and Fremont

Sts.). Call for schedules and information. 415/817–1717.

Golden Gate Transit Bus service in San Francisco, Marin, and Sonoma counties, and connecting service between the counties. Buses depart from the Transbay Terminal (Mission St., between 1st and Fremont Sts.) and several other points in San Francisco. Fares are calculated on a zone system; call for schedules and information. 415/923–2000.

SamTrans Buses serve all of San Mateo County, with local and commuter express routes traveling as far south as Palo Alto. Additional buses run to SFO and the Transbay Terminal (Mission St., between 1st and Fremont Sts.) in downtown San Francisco. 800/660–4287.

subway

BART (Bay Area Rapid Transit) is a smooth, air-conditioned subway and commuter rail system that operates between San Francisco and the East Bay. It's best for moving from city to city around the San Francisco Bay rather than traveling between points in San Francisco itself. The five color-coded lines are Richmond to Fremont; Richmond to Daly City/Colma via San Francisco; Pittsburg/Bay Point to Colma via San Francisco; Fremont to Daly City via San Francisco; and Dublin/Pleasanton to Daly City via San Francisco. BART will take you from San Francisco to Oakland, Berkeley, and Concord, as well as the Oakland Coliseum and Oakland International Airport. Each line operates under a different schedule, but trains generally run every 10 to 20 minutes until midnight, with service starting up again at 4 AM weekdays, 6 AM Saturday, and 8 AM Sunday. Evenings, Sunday, and holidays only the Richmond–Fremont, Pittsburg/Bay Point–Colma, and Dublin/Pleasanton–Daly City lines operate. 650/992–2278 in San Francisco, 510/465–2278 in the East Bay, and 510/464–7090 for lost and found.

Fares run from $1.10 to $4.70, depending on length of journey, although transfers between the lines (at designated transfer stations) are free. Ticket vending machines at each station allow you to buy tickets worth $1.10 to $60, the newest machines accept ATM cards as well as cash. Insert your ticket into the fare gate, then keep it in a safe place after it pops out the top—you'll need your ticket to exit. The fare is automatically deducted from your ticket at the exit gate; any amount left unused can be used on your next ride, as you can add fare to old tickets. If you're planning to take a Muni or AC Transit bus after your BART ride, pick up a bus transfer slip at one of the specially marked white vending machines as you exit the BART station.

Several discount BART fare packages are available. Adults can purchase the **High-Value Ticket**—$48 worth of rides for $45 (a $3 savings); or the **Blue Ticket,** $32 worth of rides for $30. The **Red Ticket,** for children between the ages of 5 and 12, is $16 worth of rides for $4 (a $12 discount). The **Green Ticket,** for senior citizens 65 years and older, is also $16 worth of rides for $4. Appropriate identification is required for purchase of Red or Green tickets. You can buy High-Value Tickets at all Safeway and Lucky grocery stores, and at the Montgomery Street BART station office weekdays 7 AM–7 PM and at the Lake Merritt BART station office Monday–Thursday 7:30 AM–5 PM, and Friday 8:30 AM–5 PM. **BART Plus** tickets can be purchased from machines in most BART stations and provide substantial discounts on local bus systems: a $28–$61 ticket (eight different values) entitles you to $15–$50 worth of BART rides plus unlimited rides on any Bay Area bus system for either the first or last two weeks of the month.

bicycle

In 1996, the **S.F. Bicycle Program** (415/585–2453) began marking the most bicycle-friendly of San Francisco's streets with numbered route signs. North–south routes have odd numbers, whereas east–west routes are even-numbered; the numbers go up as you move west and south. The route map is printed in the San Francisco Yellow Pages. Purchase the "San Francisco Biking/Walking Guide" ($2), an excellent biking map that shows street grades and routes, at select city stores or the **Berkeley TRiP Commute Store** (2033 Center St., 1 block west of Berkeley BART, Berkeley, 510/644–7665). For personalized route maps, safety information, a list of Bay Area bicycle advocacy groups, commuter information, and updates about the San Francisco Bicycle Program, call the San Francisco Department of Parking and Traffic's **Bicycle Information Hotline** (415/585–2453). The grassroots **San Francisco Bicycle Coalition** (1095 Market St., Suite 215, San Francisco 94103, 415/431–2453) provides information on activities, advocacy, cycling groups, routes, and public transportation options.

You can take your bicycle on Bay Area transit systems with varying degrees of hassle. Muni currently allows bikes on more than 10 buses (17, 35, 36, 37, 39, 53, 56, 66, 76, and 91 OWL); note that Line 76 travels to the Marin Headlands. BART allows bikes in all but the first car of each train, except during commuter rush hours (6:30 AM–9 AM and 3:30 PM–6:30 PM). During these hours, a bike shuttle ($1) operates every 30–45 minutes between MacArthur BART and the Transbay Terminal (Mission St., between 1st and Fremont Sts.); call CalTrans (510/286–0669) for more information. For details on bikes on BART call the BART Office of Passenger Service (510/464–7127). All ferries, except the Blue and Gold Fleet's bay cruises, accept bicycles on a first-come, first-served basis. For a summer weekend jaunt to Angel Island State Park, you'll want to line up well before departure time to secure a spot for your bike.

ferry

In San Francisco, the main point of departure is the landmark **San Francisco Ferry Building** (on the Embarcadero, at the foot of Market Street). In most cases, you purchase your ticket after you board. All ferries are equipped with snack bars and toilets. Your ferry ticket acts as a free transfer to buses on both sides of the bay.

Alameda–Oakland Ferry Service (510/522–3300 for 24-hour FerryFone, or 415/705–5555 for group reservations) runs ferries from the SF Ferry Building to Alameda (2990 Main St.) and Oakland's Jack London Square (Clay St., at the Embarcadero). One-way fare is $4.50, senior citizens $2.75, children 5–12 $1.75, under 5 free. There is no service on Thanksgiving, Christmas, or New Year's Day. Call for a current schedule.

Weekends from May through early September the Alameda–Oakland Ferry Service operates ferries from Alameda and Oakland to Angel Island State Park. Round-trip fare (park admission included) is $14; senior citizens and youth 13–18 pay $10, and children 5–12 pay $6.50. A limited number of bikes is allowed on board at no additional charge, on a first-come, first-served basis. Call for a schedule.

Blue and Gold Fleet (415/773–1188 for 24-hour recorded information or 415/705–5555 for ticket purchase) sends ferries to Tiburon, Sausalito, Angel Island State Park, and Alcatraz. The weekday commuter ferry to Tiburon (20 minutes) departs from the SF Ferry Building. All other departures are from Pier 41 at Fisherman's Wharf, including weekend service to Tiburon (30 minutes) and daily service to Sausalito (30 minutes), Angel Island (20 minutes), and Alcatraz (15 minutes). One-way fare to Sausalito or Tiburon is $6, and $3 for children 5–11. To Angel Island, round-trip fare (including park admission) is $11, $10 for youth 12–18, $6 for children 5–11, free for children under 5. Bikes are allowed on board at no additional charge, although space is limited. To Alcatraz, fare includes a worthwhile audio tour: $14.50, $12.75 for senior citizens, $9.25 for children 5–11**, free kids under 5**. Without the audio tour the cost is $11, $9.25 for senior citizens, $7.75 for children 5–11, free for children under 5. There is no service on Thanksgiving or Christmas. Call for a current schedule.

Golden Gate Ferry Service (415/923–2000, or 415/455–2000 in Marin County) ferries passengers from the SF Ferry Building to Sausalito and Larkspur in Marin County. To Larkspur, one-way fare is $2.85 weekdays, $4.80 weekends and holidays. To Sausalito, one-way fare is $4.80. Senior citizens ride at a 50% discount at all times; children 6–12 receive a 25% discount. There is no service on Thanksgiving, Christmas, or New Year's Day. Call for a current schedule.

Harbor Bay Ferry (510/769–5500) shuttles between Harbor Bay Isle in the East Bay, near the Oakland International Airport, and both the San Francisco Ferry Building and Pier 41. Fare is $4.50, $3.50 senior citizens, $1.25 children 5–12. The Harbor Bay Isle ferry to San Francisco operates weekdays year-round and weekends from May to October. Ferry service to Giants games has been canceled and postponed indefinitely to 49ers games.

Vallejo Baylink Ferry (707/643–3779 for recorded information, or 707/648–4349 for group reservations) provides service between San Francisco, Angel Island,

and Vallejo with connecting shuttles to Marine World Africa USA. In San Francisco, ferries leave from the SF Ferry Building and Pier 39. One-way fare from San Francisco to Vallejo is $7.50, or $3.75 for senior citizens, persons with disabilities, and children 6–12. The Marine World Africa USA Package, which includes round-trip ferry transportation between San Francisco and Vallejo, a shuttle bus between the Vallejo Ferry Terminal and Marine World, and park admission, costs $42 (no discounts for senior citizens), $28.50 for children 5–12. Round-trip fare from Vallejo to Angel Island State Park (park admission included; ferries make this trip only on the weekends) is $14, $9.50 for senior citizens and children 6–12. The Vallejo Baylink Ferries can carry between 25 and 30 bikes each, on a first-come, first-served basis. Call for a current schedule.

taxi

Taxis charge $2.50 for the first ⅙ of a mile, $1.80 for each additional mile, and 40¢ for every minute in stalled traffic. The appropriate tip for good service is 15%. A ride from downtown to San Francisco International Airport averages $30 plus tip. Taxis are scarce on San Francisco streets, and particularly difficult to hail during rush hours. Look for the lighted sign on the cab roof, wait for one at the taxi stand of a major hotel, or call for a reservation. It is safest to stick with a city-licensed taxi denoted by the city insignia on the front door. Check the Yellow Pages under taxis for a number of choices. Two reliable companies are **Veteran's Cab** (415/552–1300) and **Yellow Cab** (415/626–2345).

In the East Bay you'll pay a $2 base fee, plus $2 per mile; a ride from Oakland to San Francisco can cost $30 or more. Call **Friendly Cab** (510/536–3000) or **Yellow Cab** (510/841–8294).

commuter rail

CalTrain (800/660–4287) commuter train service operates between San Francisco and Gilroy, with many stops in San Mateo and Santa Clara counties. On weekdays, Muni express shuttle buses connect the CalTrain station (4th and Townsend Sts.) with San Francisco's Financial District, South of Market, and Levi's Plaza. Call for schedules and information. A free CalTrain–SFO shut-

tle operates daily between the Millbrae Station and the airport; call **SFO Rides** (800/736–2008) for information about this service.

PUBLICATIONS

daily

San Francisco Chronicle. The city's main newspaper is published each morning. The Sunday paper, published jointly with the *Examiner*, contains the must-read "Datebook" (the Pink Section). It's chock-full of reviews and listings for museums, galleries, performing arts, movies, nightlife, restaurants, and festivals.

San Francisco Examiner. The *Examiner* hits newsstands every afternoon except Sunday, when a morning paper is published jointly with the *San Francisco Chronicle*. For extensive listings of city events, pick up Friday's "Weekend" section.

The Hearst Corporation bought the *Examiner* in late 1999, and at press time reports were that the *Examiner* would merge with the *Chronicle*.

on-line

www.bayarea.citysearch.com. This handy Web site has listings galore for San Francisco, including restaurants, shops, bars, clubs, and more.

www.sanfran.com. Here you can take advantage of some of *San Francisco Magazine*'s past special theme issues ("Cheap Eats in San Francisco") by searching through its archives.

www.sfbg.com. Log onto the Bay Guardian's Web site, and you can search through its extensive restaurant, bar, and club listings.

www.sfweekly.com. *SF Weekly*'s website offers a quick way to browse through its always thorough, in-the-know events calendar.

weekly and monthly

Bay Area Reporter. The city's free gay weekly is published each Thursday. It features local and national news, as well as listings of local events.

Bay Guardian. This free, alternative weekly (published Wednesday) has in-depth cultural listings, and occasional daring investigative pieces. Look for its "Best of the Bay Area" special every August and the "Insider's Guide" issue in February.

San Francisco Magazine. This glossy monthly magazine covers arts, style, dining, and shopping.

SF Weekly. This free, alternative weekly, published on Wednesday, has extensive, beyond-the-mainstream cultural events listings.

RADIO STATIONS

Due to the Bay Area's many hills, not all of the stations listed here will be in range all of the time.

fm

KZSC (88.1) Eclectic

KQED (88.5) NPR news, public affairs

KUSP (88.9) NPR news, variety

KCEA (89.1) Big Band

KLEL (89.3) Rock

KOHL (89.3) Top 40

KPOO (89.5) Third World

KFJC (89.7) College radio, eclectic

KZSU (90.1) Eclectic

KUSF (90.3) College radio, eclectic

KSJS (90.5) College radio, variety, jazz

KALX (90.7) College radio, variety

KCSM (91.1) NPR news, jazz

KKUP (91.5) Eclectic

KALW (91.7) International news, variety

KLOV (91.9) Christian music

KZWC (92.1) Spanish music

KSJO (92.3) Album-oriented rock

KZSF (92.7) Spanish music

KRQC (92.7) '70s hits

KYCY (93.3) Country

KAXT (93.5) Country

KPFA (94.1) Eclectic

KUFX (94.5) Classic rock

KYLD (94.9) Hits, dance

KRTY (95.3) Country

KOYT (95.7) Adult contemporary

KSQQ (96.1) Portuguese

KOIT (96.5) Light rock

KWAV (96.9) Adult contemporary

KLLC (97.3) Adult contemporary

KBGG (98.1) '60s to '80s classic rock

KOME (98.5) Modern rock

KSOL (98.9/99.1) Spanish pop

KFRC (99.7) '60s and '70s rock

KBAY (100.3) Adult contemporary, light rock

KTOM (100.7) Country

KKHI (100.9) Classical

K101 (101.3) Adult contemporary

KXDC (101.7) Light jazz

KDFC (102.1) Classical

KBLX (102.9) Jazz

KSCU (103.3) College radio, alternative rock

KKSF (103.7) Adult contemporary

KISE (103.9) Oldies

KRAY (103.9) Spanish music

KMBY (104.3) Alternative rock

KFOG (104.5) Album-oriented rock

KBRG (104.9) Spanish music

KOCN (105.1) Oldies

KITS (105.3) Modern rock

KARA (105.7) Oldies

KMEL (106.1) Hits, dance

KLUE (106.3) Adult contemporary

KEZR (106.5) Adult contemporary

KEAR (106.9) Christian talk, music

KVRG (107.1) Spanish talk, music

KPIG (107.5) Country, rock

KSAN (107.7) Classic rock

am

KSFO (560) *Sports, talk*

KFRC (610) '60s and '70s rock

KSTE (650) Talk

KNBR (680) Talk, sports

KVRG (700) Spanish music

KCBS (740) News

KGO (810) News, talk

KNEW (910) Country

KABL (960) Big Band

KCTY (980) Spanish music

KATD (990) Christian contemporary

KIQI (1010) Spanish music

KOFY (1050) Spanish music

KSCO (1080) News, talk

KFAX (1100) Christian music, talk

KZSJ (1120) Spanish dance music

KLOK (1170) Spanish music

KDFC (1220) Classical

KNRY (1240) News, talk, oldies

KOIT (1260) Adult contemporary, light rock

KAZA (1290) Spanish rock

KDIA (1310) Soul

KLBS (1330) Portuguese, Spanish

KOMY (1340) News, talk

KKSJ (1370) Nostalgic

KTOM (1380) Country

KVTO (1400) Asian programming

KRML (1410) Jazz

KNTA (1430) Spanish

KEST (1450) Chinese

KSJX (1500) Vietnamese

KNOB (1510) Jazz

KMPG (1520) Spanish music

KPIX (1550) Country

KTGE (1570) Spanish music

KLIV (1590) News

RECYCLING

Once a week, San Francisco's "Curbside Recycling Program" picks up all recyclables that have been placed in their signature blue bins (issued by the program) and left on the curb. If an apartment building contains more than six units, the program issues large recycling bins that can be found in the garage, garbage, or laundry area of the building. The cans/bottle container can include aluminum foil and cans, glass jars and bottles, plastic bottles, and paint and aerosol cans. The paper container can include newspapers, junk mail, magazines, paper bags and paper packaging, and telephone books. For more information, call the **San Francisco Recycling Program** 24-hour hot line (415/554–7329).

TAX & TIP

sales tax and beyond

The California State Tax on all purchased items (except food for preparation and items purchased for out-of-state delivery) is 8.5%. Although there is no sales tax on hotel rooms, there is a 14% "transient occupancy tax" added to your bill. The rate quoted will not normally include this tax.

tipping

The average tip for good service in a restaurant is 15%–20% of the bill. The average tip in a taxi is 15%. For those who carry your bags at the airport or hotel, the going rate is $1–$2 a bag.

TELEVISION

networks

KTVU (Fox/Oakland) 2

KRON (NBC/SF) 4

KPIX (CBS/SF) 5

KGO (ABC/SF) 7

KQED (PBS/SF) 9

KNTV (ABC/San Jose) 11

KBHK (Independent/SF) 12

KDTV (Spanish/SF) 14

KOFY (WBN/SF) 20

KCNS (Independent/SF) 23

KTSF (Independent/SF) 26

KMTP (Independent/SF) 32

KICU (Independent/SF) 36

KPST (Independent/SF) 66

cable

A&E (Arts & Entertainment) 44

AMC (American Movie Classics) 34

BAYTV (Bay TV) 35

BET (Black Entertainment Television) 42

BRAVO (Bravo) 46

CNBC (Consumer News & Business Channel) 39

CNN (Cable News Network) 17

COM (Comedy Central) 39

COURT (Court TV) 75

CSPAN (House of Representatives) 25

DISC (Discovery Channel) 36

DISN (The Disney Channel) 31

E! (The Entertainment Channel) 38

ENC (Encore) 92

ESPN (Entertainment Sports Network) 14

ESPN2 (Entertainment Sports Network 2) 88

FAM (The Family Channel) 47

FX (FX Channel) 37

HBO (Home Box Office) 8

HIST (History Channel) 77

KNO (Knowledge TV) 82

LIFE (Lifetime) 22

LRN (The Learning Channel) 51

MAX (Cinemax) 0/98

MSNBC (Microsoft NBC) 19

MTV (Music Television) 21

NASH (The Nashville Network) 49

NICK (Nickelodeon) 15

NOST (Nostalgia) 64

PLAY (The Playboy Channel) 25

SFC (Sci-Fi Channel) 54

SHOW (Showtime) 10

SPT (Sports Channel) 59

STARZ (Starz) 73

TBS (Turner Broadcasting System) 28

TMC (The Movie Channel) 1/99

TNT (Turner Network Television) 18

TRAV (The Travel Channel) 81

USA (USA Network) 20

VH-1 (Video Hits One) 41

WC (Weather Channel) 28

VOTER REGISTRATION

Call the **California Voter Registration Hotline** (800/345–8683) to receive a voter registration form. You need to reregister every time you move, change your address, or wish to change your political party.

WEATHER

San Francisco is blessed with a temperate marine climate and mild weather year-round. It's rarely warmer than 70°F, or colder than 40°F. The warmest months are May, September, and October. In summer, morning and evening fog rolls in over the bay; they bring a chill but dissipate quickly. December through March is the rainy season (annual rainfall averages 19.24"), making an umbrella essential. Note that the weather in San Francisco is known for its changeability and actually varies within the city; the bay side of Twin Peaks and Mt. Davidson are warmer and drier areas than those along the Pacific. It's best to dress in layers.

The rest of the Bay Area is divided into myriad microclimates, with temperatures in northern Marin, Napa, the Contra Coast, and the South Bay running between 15°F and 20°F warmer than the city. In the East Bay highs average 72°F, lows 43°F. Marin County's weather varies from town to town: The coast is usually fogged in, the bay-side towns of Tiburon and Sausalito get a cool breeze, and San Rafael checks in at a solid few degrees warmer than most of the Bay Area, with an average summer high of 82°F. In the South Bay, average summer highs, both on the coast and inland, hover in the 80s. In the winter, things cool down to a medium rare, with lows dipping to 40°F.

For updated local weather reports, call the **National Weather Service's Bay Area Forecast office** (650/364–7974). **Doc!** (415/512–5000 or 415/808–5000, ext. 3000) has local and national weather reports. The **SFCVB Information Hotline** (415/391–2000 or 415/391–2001) provides local weather updates. For ski conditions in northern California, Tahoe, or the Sierras, call the **California State Automobile Association's Ski Report Hotline** (415/864–6440).

January

Daily mean maximum: 56.1°F

Daily mean minimum: 46.2°F

Rainfall total inches: 4.48″

February

Daily mean maximum: 59.4°F

Daily mean minimum: 48.4°F

Rainfall total inches: 2.83″

March

Daily mean maximum: 60.0°F

Daily mean minimum: 48.6°F

Rainfall total inches: 2.58″

April

Daily mean maximum: 61.1°F

Daily mean minimum: 49.2°F

Rainfall total inches: 1.48″

May

Daily mean maximum: 62.5°F

Daily mean minimum: 50.7°F

Rainfall total inches: 0.35″

June

Daily mean maximum: 64.3°F

Daily mean minimum: 52.5°F

Rainfall total inches: 0.15″

July

Daily mean maximum: 64.0°F

Daily mean minimum: 53.1°F

Rainfall total inches: 0.04″

August

Daily mean maximum: 65.0°F

Daily mean minimum: 54.2°F

Rainfall total inches: 0.08″

September

Daily mean maximum: 68.9°F

Daily mean minimum: 55.8°F

Rainfall total inches: 0.24″

October

Daily mean maximum: 68.3°F

Daily mean minimum: 54.8°F

Rainfall total inches: 1.09″

November

Daily mean maximum: 62.9°F

Daily mean minimum: 51.5°F

Rainfall total inches: 2.40″

December

Daily mean maximum: 56.9°F

Daily mean minimum: 47.2°F

Rainfall total inches: 3.52″

resources for challenges & crises

BABY-SITTING SERVICES

Aunt Ann's Agency. *731 Market St., 415/ 974–3530.*

Bay Area Child Care. *758 San Diego Avenue, Daly City, 650/991–7474.*

Bay Area Second Mom Nanny Agency. *555 Geary St., 415/346–2620.*

CATERING

grown-up parties
Beyond Expectations. *3613 Sacramento St., 415/567–8696.*

Creighton's Catering. *673 Portola, 415/753–0750.*

Knight's Catering. *550 Alabama St., 415/861–3312.*

MacArthur Park Catering. *607 Front St., 415/398–5703.*

Work of Art. *1226 Folsom St., 415/552–1000.*

CHARITIES

You can donate old clothing, old furniture, and old computers to the **Salvation Army** (800/958–7825) either by arranging for a pickup or by dropping it off at the nearest center. Call for the address of the Salvation Army nearest to you. It also accepts used cars.

Goodwill (1500 Mission St., 415/575–2133) accepts old clothing and furniture. Call and arrange for a pickup, or drop it off at its headquarters on Mission Street. To donate your used car, you must have all the ownership papers; if the car needs any mechanical or body repairs, the cost cannot exceed $250.

Catholic Charities of the Archdiocese of San Francisco (814 Mission St., 415/844–4800) is one of San Francisco's largest charitable organizations, with a wide range of services including counseling and help for the sick and the elderly. They accept donations of old clothing, furniture, and computers and other appliances. Call 800/733–8000 to donate a used car.

CHILD CRISIS

Family Service Agency of San Francisco. Twenty-four-hour child-abuse prevention hot line. *415/441–5437.*

San Francisco Child Abuse Council. Education services and referrals to counselors. *415/668– 0494.*

San Francisco Department of Human Services, Child Protective Services Emergency Hotline. *415/558–2650.*

CITY GOVERNMENT

complaints
San Francisco Board of Supervisors. *1 Dr. Carlton B. Goodlett Pl., Room 244, 415/554–5184.*

Muni Complaint Hot Line. *415/923–6164.*

state assembly representatives
Carole Migdin, 13th District, Democrat. *455 Golden Gate Ave., Ste. 14300, 415/557–3000.*

Louis J. Papan, 19th District, Democrat. *660 El Camino Real, Ste. 214, Millbrae, 650/866–3940.*

Kevin Shelley, 12th District, Democrat. *455 Golden Gate Ave., Ste. 14600, 415/557–2312.*

COAST GUARD

United States Coast Guard. *510/437–3700 (general information) or 415/556–2103 (emergencies only).*

CONSUMER PROTECTION

Better Business Bureau. Provides information about business reliability and other consumer issues; files consumer complaints. *510 16th St., Ste. 550, Oakland, 94612-1584, 415/243–9999.*

Consumer Credit Counseling. Money-management counseling for people with credit problems. *77 Maiden La., 415/788–0288.*

Consumer Information Center, Department of Consumer Affairs. Receives and investigates complaints against businesses. *400 R St., Sacramento, 800/952–5210.*

San Francisco District Attorney, Consumer Protection Unit. Receives, investigates, and mediates consumer complaints. *732 Brannan St., 415/553–1814.*

COUNSELING & REFERRALS

aids advice
AIDS/HIV Nightlife. Answered from 5 PM until 5 AM. *415/434–2437.*

AIDS Legal Referral Panel. 415/291–5454.

Project Open Hand. Two meals a day are delivered to those who are ill with AIDS. 415/447–2300.

San Francisco AIDS Foundation. An umbrella organization that can direct people to the appropriate AIDS-related group. 10 United Nations Plaza, 415/487–8000, or 415/863–2437 for hot line.

San Francisco Department of Public Health, AIDS Health Project. Free, anonymous HIV testing. 415/502–8378.

alcoholism treatment

Alcoholics Anonymous. 1540 Market St., 415/621–1326.

Haight Ashbury Free Clinic Alcohol Treatment Services. 425 Divisadero St., 415/487–5634.

National Council on Alcoholism and Other Drug Addictions (NCADA). Their 24-hour hot line provides information, assessment, and referral. 944 Market St., 3rd floor, 415/296–9900.

crime victims

Critical Incident Response Team. Emotional support for families of young people who have been killed or injured in violent acts. 415/671–1010.

Domestic Violence Hot Line. 415/864–4722.

Riley Center Crisis Center. Offers all levels of help to women who are victims of domestic violence, including shelter, referrals, and individual and group counseling. 3543 18th St., 415/831–3535.

Victims of Crime Resource Center. Legal information and referrals to local organizations. 800/842–8467.

drug abuse treatment

Cocaine Anonymous. 415/821–6155.

Haight Ashbury Free Clinic Drug Detox Program. 588 Clayton St., 415/487–5632.

National Council on Alcoholism and Other Drug Addictions (NCADA). 24-hour hot line for information, assessment, and referral. 944 Market St., 3rd floor, 415/296–9900.

San Francisco Health Department 24-hour Drug Line and Information. 415/362–3400.

mental health information & referral

Patient Rights Advocacy Program. Advocacy services for people receiving mental health care. 415/552–8100.

San Francisco General Hospital, Psychiatric Emergency Services. 415/206–8125.

San Francisco Health Department Mental Health Programs Information and Referral Access Line. Answered 24 hours. 415/255–3737.

Therapist Network. Gives referrals to mental health-care providers. 800/843–7274.

rape victims

San Francisco General Hospital 24-Hour Rape Treatment Center. 415/206–3222.

SF Women Against Rape. 415/647–7273.

DOCTOR & DENTIST REFERRALS

California State Medical Board Complaints. 800/633–2322.

California State Medical Board, Verification of Licenses. 916/263–2635.

Davies Medical Center Physician Referral Service. 415/565–6333.

1-800 DENTIST. 800/336–8478.

Physician Referral Service, CHW Bay Area, Saint Francis, St. Mary's, and Seton Medical Centers. 800/333–1355.

St. Luke's Hospital Physician Referral Service. 415/821–3627.

San Francisco Dental Society Referral Service. 415/421–1435.

San Francisco Dentist. 415/433–0265.

UCSF Stanford and UCSF/Mount Zion Physician Referral Service. 415/885–7777.

EMERGENCIES

ambulance

American Medical Response Ambulance Service. 415/931–3900.

King-American Ambulance Company. 415/931–1400.

St. Joseph's Ambulance Service. 415/921–0707.

hospital emergency rooms

California Pacific Medical Center. *2333 Buchanan St., at Sacramento St., 415/923–3333.*

St. Luke's Hospital. *3555 Cesar Chavez St., at Valencia St., 415/641–6625.*

St. Mary's Medical Center. *450 Stanyan St., 415/750–5700.*

UCSF Stanford Health Care Medical Center. *505 Parnassus Ave., at Stanyan St., 415/476–1037.*

UCSF Stanford/Mount Zion Medical Center. *1600 Divisadero St., 415/885–7520.*

poison control center

California Poison Control Center. *800/876–4766.*

suicide prevention

San Francisco Suicide Prevention Hot Line. *415/781–0500.*

FAMILY PLANNING

Crisis Pregnancy Center of San Francisco. *415/753–8000.*

Planned Parenthood of San Francisco. *415/441–5454.*

San Francisco General Hospital Family Planning Clinic. *415/206–3410.*

San Francisco Health Department Family Planning Information. *415/554–9611.*

GAY & LESBIAN CONCERNS

Bay Area Lawyers for Individual Freedom (Gay and Lesbian Bar Association). *415/956–5764.*

Communities United Against Violence. *973 Market St., Suite 500, 415/777–5500, hot line 415/333–4357.*

Gay & Lesbian Alliance Against Defamation (GLAAD). Media Resource Center *1360 Mission St., 415/861–2244, hot line 800/429–6334.*

Lavender Youth Recreation and Information Center. Peer support group for people 23 and under. *127 Collingwood St., 415/703–6150, hot line 415/863–3636 or 800/246–7743.*

HOUSE CLEANING HELP AGENCIES

Cinderella's Housekeeping. *45 Franklin St., Suite 301, 415/864–8900.*

New Dimensions Housekeeping Agency. *415/731–4900.*

Rainbow Home Cleaning. *415/565–0383.*

INTERIOR DESIGNER AND ARCHITECT REFERRALS

Bradford Interiors. *780 Joost Ave., 415/584–7215.*

Holly Hulburd Interior Design and Architecture. *1763 Green St., 415/440–0801.*

Thompson Studio Architects. *435 Brannan St., 415/495–6492.*

The Wiseman Group Interior Design, Inc. *636 San Bruno Ave., 415/282–2880.*

LANDLORD/ TENANT ASSISTANCE

California Department of Fair Employment and Housing. Handles housing discrimination complaints. *800/884–1684.*

Housing Rights Committee of San Francisco. A tenant rights counseling and advocacy organization. *115 Jones St., 415/398–6200.*

San Francisco Tenant's Union. Tenants' rights counseling services. Members receive phone counseling; nonmembers attend a drop-in clinic. *558 Capp St., 415/282–6622.*

U.S. Department of Housing and Urban Development Housing Discrimination Hot Line. Provides information on housing rights and accepts discrimination complaints. *800/669–9777.*

LEGAL SERVICES

American Civil Liberties Union. *415/621–2493.*

La Raza Centro Legal. Legal information and referrals in both English and Spanish. *474 Valencia St., 415/575–3500.*

Lawyer Referral Service of the Bar Association of San Francisco. Provides refer-

rals to attorneys and attorney media-
tors. 415/989–1616.

Legal Aid Society of San Francisco.
Gives legal referrals and information,
especially for low-income families. 1663
Mission St., Ste. 400, 415/986–7511.

**State Bar of California, Attorney Com-
plaint Hot Line.** Provides information
about common attorney–client problems and accepts complaints against
attorneys. 800/843–9053.

LOST & FOUND

at airlines & airports
Oakland International Airport. 510/577–
4095.

San Francisco International Airport.
650/876–2261.

San Jose International Airport. 408/277–
4759.

on other public transportation
BART. 510/464–7090.

Muni. 415/923–6168.

lost animals
Look in the local papers, including the
San Francisco Chronicle, SF Weekly, and
Bay Guardian, for notices regarding lost
and found animals.

**San Francisco Animal Care and Control
Center.** Call to locate your lost pet. 415/
554–6364.

**San Francisco Society for the Prevention
of Cruelty to Animals.** Call if you've
found a cat with an SPCA tag on it. For
all other animals and cats without SPCA
tags, call the San Francisco Animal
Care and Control Center (see above).
415/554–3084.

lost credit cards
American Express. 800/528–4800.

Diner's Club. 800/234–6377

Discover. 800/347–2683

MasterCard. 800/307–7309

Visa. 800/847–2911

lost traveler's checks
American Express Travelers Cheques.
800/221–7282.

Citicorp Travel Payment Services. 800/
645–6556.

Mastercard Global Service Center. 800/
223–9920.

Visa Global Refund. 800/227–6811.

ON-LINE SERVICES

Activa.Net. 415/863–6965.

Slip.Net. 415/784–0150.

Wired Digital Incorporated. 415/276–
8400.

PETS

adoptions
**Pets Unlimited Hospital and Adoption
Center.** 2343 Fillmore St., 415/563–6700.

San Francisco SPCA. 2500 16th St., 415/
554–3000 (general information).

grooming
The Barking Lot. 209A Sanchez St., 415/
431 0969.

Bill's Doggie Bath-O-Mat. 3928 Irving
St., 415/661–6950.

Pet Wash. 1840 Polk St., 415/928–8788.

Pets Unlimited. 2343 Fillmore St., 415/
563–6700.

training
Dog Gone Good. 415/437–0848.

Top Quality Obedience School. 1427
Clement St., 415/566–4141.

veterinary hospitals
Irving Street Veterinary Hospital. 1434
Irving St., 415/664–0191.

Pets Unlimited. 2343 Fillmore St., 415/
563–6700.

Vet on Wheels. 415/333–4673.

veterinarian referrals
Marina Pet Hospital. 2024 Lombard St.,
415/921–0410.

Mission Pet Hospital. *720 Valencia St., 415/552–1969.*

Pets Unlimited. *2343 Fillmore St., 415/563–6700.*

PHARMACIES OPEN 24 HOURS

Walgreens Drugstore. *3201 Divisadero St., 415/931–6415; 498 Castro St., 415/861–6276; 42 Geary St., 415/386–0706.*

POLICE

For emergencies, dial 911. For nonemergencies, call the police departments at the following numbers.

Brisbane Police Department. *415/467–1123 for police and fire calls.*

Broadmoor Police Department. *650/755–3838 or 650/755–5666 for fire calls.*

Colma Police Department. *650/997–8320 or 650/755–5666 for fire calls.*

Daly City Police Department. *650/991–8119 or 650/991–8092.*

San Francisco Police Department. *415/553–0123 or 415/558–3268.*

POSTAL SERVICES

Civic Center Post Office. Hours are weekdays 9–5:30. *101 Hyde St., 94142, 800/275–8777.*

U.S. Postal Service Answer Line. Twenty-four-hour automated information line for post office hours, postal rates, zip codes, and more. *800/725–2161.*

fed ex

Call 800/463–3399 for pickups. There are 12 Fed Ex offices in San Francisco, including these three main facilities:

127 Kearny St. Open weekdays 9–8.

555 California St. Open weekdays 9–8.

120 Bush St. Open weekdays 9–8.

ups

The office is open weekdays 9:30–7. *320 San Bruno Ave., at 16th St., 800/742–5877.*

SENIOR CITIZEN SERVICES

Department of Human Services, Elder Abuse Reporting. *415/557–5230.*

Friendship Line for the Elderly. Answered 24 hours a day. *415/752–3778.*

Gray Panthers of San Francisco. Senior citizen advocacy group. *415/552–8800.*

Senior Citizen Information Line. Provides referrals to organizations for senior citizens throughout the Bay Area. *415/626–1033.*

TELEVISION— CABLE COMPANIES

AT&T Cable Services. *800/436–1999 to order, 415/863–9600 for repairs.*

satellite-installation companies

Birdview Satellite Antennas. *800/854–6166.*

Dish Network. *800/333–3474.*

Signal International. *800/367–7722.*

UTILITIES

Public Utilities Commission, Inquiries and Complaints. *415/703–1170.*

gas

Pacific Gas and Electric Company. *800/743–5000 (24-hr emergency and customer service) or 800/743–5002 (24-hr information on electric outages).*

electric

Pacific Gas & Electric. *863 Clay St., 2435 Mission St., 415/973–7000.*

telephone

Pacific Bell. *800/310–2355 for residence customer service; 800/214–8433 for 24-hr recorded information; 611 for repair calls.*

water

City and County Water Department of San Francisco. *425 Mason St., 415/923–2420.*

VOLUNTEERING

how to

Most of San Francisco's community service agencies and churches gladly accept the help of volunteers. Depending on the agency and on the time of year, there are a wide range of volunteer opportunities, from serving food to the homeless to tutoring and counseling.

Volunteer Center of San Francisco. A clearinghouse for nonprofit agencies throughout the Bay Area that matches up volunteers with agencies. *425 Jackson St., 415/982–8999.*

organizations

Dolores Street Community Services. Provides food and shelter for the homeless and those with HIV/AIDS. *938 Valencia St., 415/282–6209.*

Episcopal Community Services. Provides food and shelter for the homeless and assistance to low-income families. *201 8th St., 415/863–3893.*

Glide Memorial United Methodist Church. One of San Francisco's oldest and best-known churches, with more than 40 programs and services, including assistance for the homeless and those with HIV/AIDS, recovery programs, job training and placement, and scholarships. *330 Ellis St., 415/771–6300.*

La Casa de las Madres. San Francisco's oldest and largest shelter for battered women and their children. *1850 Mission St., Suite B, 415/503–0500.*

St. Anthony's Foundation. Provides food and shelter for the homeless. *121 Golden Gate Ave., 415/241–2621.*

Shanti Project. Provides a wide range of services to people with HIV/AIDS. *730 Polk, 3rd floor, 415/674–4700.*

ZONING & PLANNING

San Francisco Planning and Zoning Information. Planning and zoning information, planning application status. *415/558–6377.*

learning

ACTING SCHOOLS

American Conservatory Theater. *30 Grant Ave., 415/834–3200.*

Bay Area Theatresports School of Improvisation. *Fort Mason Center, Bldg. B, 415/474–8935.*

Full Circle Productions. *1045 Sansome St., 415/982–2024.*

Rob Reece Actors Workshop. *466 Geary St., 415/928–8929.*

ADULT EDUCATION IN PUBLIC SCHOOLS

City College of San Francisco Public Information Office. *50 Phelan Ave. E200, 415/241– 2300.*

Extension Center, University of California. *1995 University Ave., Berkeley, 510/642–4111. Also: 55 Laguna St., San Francisco.*

San Francisco State University, College of Extended Learning. *425 Market St., 415/405–7700.*

ART & PHOTOGRAPHY SCHOOLS

Academy of Art College. *79 New Montgomery St., 415/274–2222.*

San Francisco Art Institute. *800 Chestnut St., 415/771–7020.*

San Francisco School of Art. *667 Mission St., 415/543–9300.*

UC Berkeley Extension Art and Design Programs. *55 Laguna St., 510/642–4111.*

papermaking

California College of Arts and Crafts Fine Arts. *5212 Broadway Ave., Oakland, 415/703–9500.*

printmaking

See Papermaking, *above.*

Zip Codes

N

PACIFIC OCEAN

94129

West Pacific Ave.

94121

17th Ave.

94118

Fulton St.

Fulton St.

GOLDEN GATE PARK

Lincoln Way

Lincoln Way

94122

94143

7th Ave.

94131

Ortega St.

94116

Dewey Blvd.

94127

Sloat Blvd.

Monterey Blvd.

Junipero Serra Blvd.

Lake Merced

94132

0   1 mile
0   1 km

94112

Orizaba Ave.

SAN FRANCISCO
CITY/COUNTY LINE

SAN MATEO COUNTY

94015

94014

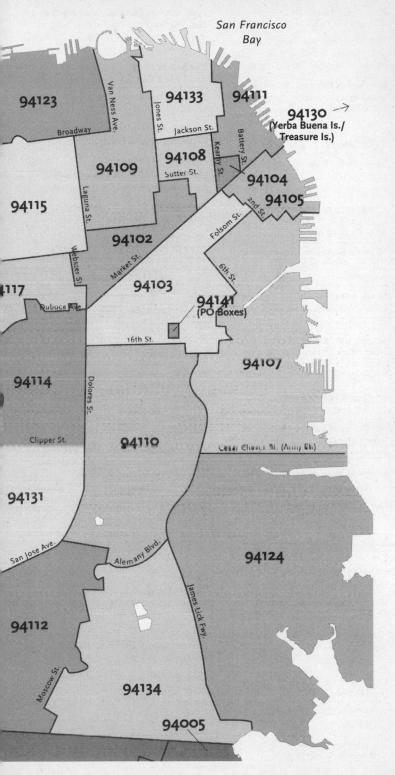

San Francisco
Bay

94123

Van Ness Ave.

Broadway

94133

Jones St.

Jackson St.

94111

Battery St.

94130
(Yerba Buena Is./
Treasure Is.)

94109

94108

Sutter St.

Kearny St.

94104

Laguna St.

94115

2nd St.

94105

94102

Webster St.

Market St.

Folsom St.

6th St.

4117

Duboce Ave.

94103

94141
(PO Boxes)

16th St.

94114

Dolores St.

Clipper St.

94110

Cesar Chavez St. (Army St.)

94107

94131

San Jose Ave.

Alemany Blvd.

94124

James Lick Fwy.

94112

Moscow St.

94134

94005

BALLROOM DANCING

Metronome Ballroom. Individual and group classes, including ballroom, swing, and salsa. *1830 17th St., 415/252–9000.*

Renaissance Ballroom. Individual and group lessons, including ballroom and Latin. *285 Elise St., 415/474–0920.*

BOOKBINDING

Center for the Book. *300 De Haro St., 415/565–0545.*

CHILDREN'S EDUCATION PROGRAMS

St. John's Educational Center Tutoring. (children grades four through nine) *415/864–5205.*

San Francisco Public Library's Fisher Children's Center. *Larkin and Grove Sts., 415/557–4554.*

San Francisco Public Schools General Information. *415/241–6000 (general school district information).*

COMMUNITY COLLEGES

City College of San Francisco Public Information Office. *50 Phelan Ave. E200, 415/239–3000.*

College of Alameda. *555 Atlantic Ave., Alameda 94501, 510/522–7221.*

College of Marin. *1800 Ignacio Blvd., Novato 94949, 415/883–2211.*

College of San Mateo. *1700 W. Hillsdale Blvd., San Mateo 94402, 650/574–6161.*

Laney College. *900 Fallon St., Oakland 94607, 510/834–5740.*

Merritt College. *12500 Campus Dr., Oakland 94619, 510/531–4911.*

Vista College. *2020 Milvia St., Berkeley 94704, 510/841–8860.*

COMPUTER TRAINING

CompuTrain. *870 Market St., Suite 1005, 415/433–7370.*

The Digital University. *220 Bush St., Suite 1400, 415/616–9559.*

New Horizons Computer Learning Centers. *1 Embarcadero Center, Suite 200, 415/421–5151.*

COOKING SCHOOLS

California Culinary Academy. *625 Polk St., 800/229–2433.*

City College of San Francisco Hotel and Restaurant Department. *50 Phelan Ave., 415/239–3152.*

HomeChef Cooking School. *3525 California St., 415/668–3191.*

Tante Marie's Cooking School. *271 Francisco St., 415/788–6699.*

CPR & FIRST AID CERTIFICATION

American Red Cross Bay Area Chapter. *800/520–5433.*

City Aid First Aid and Safety. *415/474–2551.*

DANCE

San Francisco Ballet School. *455 Franklin St., 415/861–5600.*

San Francisco Dance Center. All-level adult classes in ballet, modern, jazz, and flamenco. *50 Oak St., 415/863–3360.*

Sunset Academy of Dance. All levels, all ages; classes include tap, jazz, and ballet. *1337 Riving St., 415/731–9921.*

LANGUAGE SCHOOLS

Berlitz Language Centers. *180 Montgomery St., 415/986–6464.*

chinese
Chinese Language Instruction. *117 Stanyan St., 415/387–0851.*

esl
Brandon College English Instruction. *830 Market, 7th floor, 415/391–5711.*

Golden Gate University English Language Institute. *536 Mission St., 415/442–6598.*

french
Alliance Française. *1345 Bush St., 415/775–7755.*

german

Goethe Institut. *530 Bush St., 415/391–5194.*

italian

Italingua Institute. *447 Sutter St., 415/362–6025.*

japanese

Aisea Japanese Language Services. *110 Sutter St., 415/296–9295.*

russian

Russian Language Lessons. *1371 31st Ave., 415/564–7155.*

spanish

Casa Hispana. *110 Gough St., 415/861–1223.*

MUSIC SCHOOLS

Blue Bear School of American Music. *Fort Mason, Bldg. D, 415/673–3600.*

San Francisco Conservatory. *1201 Ortega St., 415/564–8086.*

WINE PROGRAMS

Pacific Rim Wine Education Center. Offers a regular series of wine appreciation classes in various locations throughout San Francisco. *801 4th St. 415/512–9318.*

San Francisco State University Wine Tasting Series. Offers wine tasting and appreciation classes every semester. *1600 Holloway Ave., 415/405–7700.*

University of California at Berkeley Extension Center, Wine Appreciation Course. *1995 University Ave., Berkeley, 510/642–4111. Also: 55 Laguna St., San Francisco, 415/252–5221.*

vacation & travel information

AIRLINES

See Lost & Found, *above,* for airport lost-and-found departments.

Air Canada. *800/776–3000.*

Air France. *800/237–2747.*

Alaska Airlines. *800/426–0333.*

American. *800/433–7300.*

America West. *800/235–9292.*

British Airways. *800/247–9297.*

China Airlines. *800/227–5118.*

Continental. *800/525–0280.*

Delta. *800/221–1212.*

Frontier Airlines. *800/432–1359.*

Japan Airlines. *800/525–3663.*

Mexicana Airlines. *800/531–7921.*

Northwest. *800/225–2525.*

Southwest. *800/435–9792.*

TWA. *800/221–2000.*

United. *800/241–6522.*

USAirways. *800/428–4322.*

AIRPORTS

San Francisco International Airport (SFO). Major gateway to San Francisco, about a half hour south of the city off U.S. 101. *650/876–2377.*

Oakland International Airport. Serviced by several domestic airlines. It's the same distance from San Francisco as SFO (across the bay via I–880 and I–80), although traffic on the Bay Bridge may add to travel time. *510/577–4000.*

San Jose International Airport. About an hour north of San Jose, near Santa Clara, sandwiched between I–880 and U.S. 101; allow much more time during commuter hours. The bulk of its flights are to domestic destinations, although it does have some international flights. *408/277–4759.*

getting there by public transportation

SAN FRANCISCO INTERNATIONAL AIRPORT (SFO)

By Bus and Train. From the Transbay Terminal (Mission St. between 1st and Fremont Sts.), SamTrans Buses 292 (1 hour, $2.20 to the airport; $1.10 from the airport) and KX (45 minutes, $2.30)

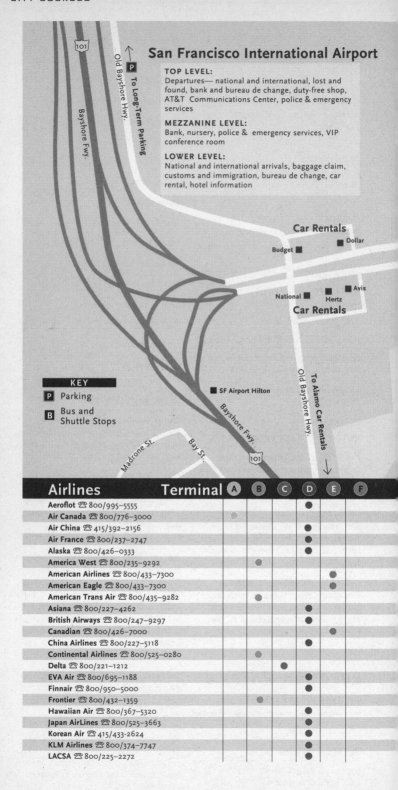

San Francisco International Airport

TOP LEVEL:
Departures— national and international, lost and found, bank and bureau de change, duty-free shop, AT&T Communications Center, police & emergency services

MEZZANINE LEVEL:
Bank, nursery, police & emergency services, VIP conference room

LOWER LEVEL:
National and international arrivals, baggage claim, customs and immigration, bureau de change, car rental, hotel information

Car Rentals

Dollar

Budget

Avis

National Hertz

Car Rentals

KEY
P Parking
B Bus and Shuttle Stops

SF Airport Hilton

Airlines Terminal	A	B	C	D	E	F
Aeroflot ☎ 800/995–5555				●		
Air Canada ☎ 800/776–3000	●					
Air China ☎ 415/392–2156				●		
Air France ☎ 800/237–2747				●		
Alaska ☎ 800/426–0333				●		
America West ☎ 800/235–9292		●				
American Airlines ☎ 800/433–7300					●	
American Eagle ☎ 800/433–7300					●	
American Trans Air ☎ 800/435–9282		●				
Asiana ☎ 800/227–4262				●		
British Airways ☎ 800/247–9297				●		
Canadian ☎ 800/426–7000					●	
China Airlines ☎ 800/227–5118				●		
Continental Airlines ☎ 800/525–0280		●				
Delta ☎ 800/221–1212			●			
EVA Air ☎ 800/695–1188				●		
Finnair ☎ 800/950–5000				●		
Frontier ☎ 800/432–1359		●				
Hawaiian Air ☎ 800/367–5320				●		
Japan AirLines ☎ 800/525–3663				●		
Korean Air ☎ 415/433-2624				●		
KLM Airlines ☎ 800/374–7747				●		
LACSA ☎ 800/225–2272				●		

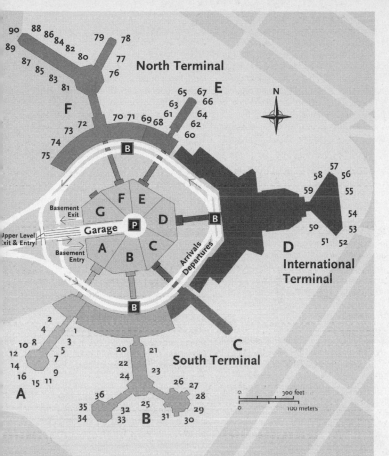

Airlines (cont.) Terminal	A	B	C	D	E	F
Lufthansa ☎ 800/645–3880				●		
Mexicana ☎ 800/531–7921				●●		
Midwest Express ☎ 800/452–2022	●					
Northwest (Domestic) ☎ 800/225–2525			●			
(International) ☎ 800/447–4747				●		
Philippine Air Lines ☎ 800/435–9725				●		
Reno Air ☎ 800/736–6247			●			
Rich International	●					
Shuttle by United ☎ 800/748–8853						●
Singapore Airlines ☎ 800/742–3333				●		
Skywest/Delta Connection ☎ 800/221–1212			●			
Southwest Airlines ☎ 800/435–9792	●					
TACA ☎ 800/535–8780				●		
Tower Air ☎ 800/221–2500				●		
TWA ☎ (Domestic) ☎ 800/221–2000	●					
(International) ☎ 800/892–4141	●					
United (Domestic) ☎ 800/241–6522						●
(International) ☎ 800/538–2929				●		
United Express ☎ 800/241–6522						●
US Airways ☎ 800/428–4322	●					
US Airways Express ☎ 800/428–4322	●					
Virgin Atlantic ☎ 800/862–8621				●		
Western Pacific ☎ 800/930–3030					●	

provide direct service to the airport. Bus KX is an express bus that allows one carry-on piece of luggage. From the Colma BART Station, SamTrans Bus BX (15 minutes, $1.10) also has direct service to SFO. At the CalTrain station in Millbrae, a free airport shuttle service (10 minutes) connects with all arriving and departing trains. For more information on SamTrans and CalTrain services, call 800/660–4287.

By Shuttle Van. For most San Franciscans, the preferred method of travel to SFO is by shuttle van; 12 such companies provide 24-hour, door-to-door service between the airport and addresses in San Francisco. Most shuttle services require reservations only three hours in advance. Average cost ranges from $10 to $15 per person one-way. A few companies also offer services between the airport and the East Bay, Marin County, and along the Peninsula, but prices are then hiked substantially and can range anywhere from $20 to $60 per person. Reliable companies include **SuperShuttle** (415/558–8500), **Bay Shuttle** (415/564–3400), and **Quake City** (415/255–4899). **Airport Commuter** (510/841–0150) requires reservations 24 hours in advance. For others, check the San Francisco Yellow Pages under "Airport Transportation Service."

By Express Bus. One private company runs express bus service between SFO and major San Francisco hotels. The **SFO Airporter** (415/495–8404) stops at points around Union Square and downtown. The average cost is $10 per person one-way.

By Taxi and Limousine. Taxi service to SFO costs approximately $35 from downtown San Francisco or $34 from Fisherman's Wharf, plus tip. Taxis may carry a maximum of five people. The city has nine registered limousine services that provide transport to SFO. The minimum charge is $40 for one hour; average cost from downtown is $60. Limousines may carry up to 12 people. For a list of companies, check the San Francisco Yellow Pages under "Airport Transportation Service."

OAKLAND INTERNATIONAL AIRPORT

The **Air-BART Shuttle** (510/569–8310) runs every 15–20 minutes between the airport and the Coliseum BART Station.

Buy tickets ($2) at the BART station or airport terminal before you board. AC Transit Bus 58 ($1.25) follows the same route, continuing into downtown Oakland. Most of the city's private shuttle services operate between San Francisco and the Oakland International Airport; expect to pay between $20 and $35 per person one-way. A taxi to downtown San Francisco from Oakland International Airport generally ranges from $30 to $35.

SAN JOSE INTERNATIONAL AIRPORT

From San Francisco, take the CalTrain to the Santa Clara Station, and from there **Bus 10** (free) runs every 10 minutes to the airport.

getting there by car

SAN FRANCISCO INTERNATIONAL AIRPORT (SFO)

San Francisco International Airport (650/876–2377) lies 15 mi south of downtown San Francisco off I–101. For information on transportation options to and from the airport, call **SFO Rides** (800/736–2008).

Airport Parking. Long- and short-term parking are available at SFO. Long-term parking is located near the San Bruno Avenue East exit off I–101; the cost is $12 per day for a maximum of seven days, plus $15 for each additional day. Free shuttles transport passengers between the long-term lot and the airport terminals. This lot tends to fill up during peak travel times, especially on three-day holiday weekends. Call the airport's **Parking Hot Line** (650/877–0227) to check on parking availability, rates, directions, and valet parking.

OAKLAND INTERNATIONAL AIRPORT

Oakland International Airport (1 Airport Dr., off Hegenberger Rd., 510/577–4000) is 6 mi south of downtown Oakland, off I–880. From San Francisco, take I–80 east across the Bay Bridge to I–980 south, then continue following signs south on I–880.

Long-term airport parking (510/633–2571) is $10 for 24 hours or $8 in the economy lot next to Terminal 1. A free shuttle carries passengers between the parking lot and the airport terminal.

CAR RENTAL

A standard, mid-size car rents for $27–$51 per day from a major agency; rentals from a local agency can be cheaper, about $25–$35 per day. SUVs rent for about $60 a day from national chains, generally cheaper than at a local agency (from $70). Most rental car agencies offer unlimited daily mileage, though you might find special deals that give a cheaper day rate if you stay under a certain mile limit. If you plan to drive your rental car outside of San Francisco (or the state), it's obviously best to go with a national company because you can drop off the car at any of its offices nationwide. Also, major agencies have offices at the San Francisco and Oakland airports, and local rental agencies do not.

major agencies

Alamo. 800/327–9633.

Avis. 800/331–1212.

Budget. 800/527–0700.

Dollar. 800/800–4000.

Enterprise. 800/325–8007.

Hertz. 800/654–3131.

National. 800/227–7368.

Thrifty. 800/367–2277.

local agencies

A-One Rent-A-Car. 434 O'Farrell St., 415/771–3911.

City Rent-A-Car. 1748 Folsom St., 415/861–1312.

Reliable Rent-A-Car. 349 Mason St., 415/928–4414.

CURRENCY EXCHANGE

All of the currency exchange offices listed below buy and sell traveler's checks and foreign currency, although it's best to call ahead to check on availability, particularly if you require special denominations or large amounts of currency.

American Express. Currency exchange at all three locations. 800/461–8484 for general information; 560 California St., at Kearny St., Financial District, 800/825–8578; 455 Market St., at 1st St., Financial District, 800/551–0210; 333 Jefferson St., at Jones St., Fisherman's Wharf, 415/775–0240.

Bank of America. Foreign currency services offices are on the main level of the Bank of America building. 345 Montgomery St., at California St., Financial District, 415/622–2451.

Bank of America at SFO. On the departure level of the international terminal at San Francisco International Airport. 650/742–8081.

Foreign Exchange, Ltd. Convenient downtown location between Chinatown and the shopping district of Union Square. 415 Stockton St., at Sutter St., Union Square, 415/677–5100.

Mutual of Omaha/Travelex at SFO. On the departure level of the International Terminal at San Francisco International Airport. 415/266–9420.

Thomas Cook. 75 Geary St., 1 block north of Market St., Union Square; 800/287–7362 for general information.

EMBASSIES & CONSULATES

Australia. 1 Bush St., Suite 700, 415/362–6160.

Austria. 41 Sutter St., 415/951–8911.

Bolivia. 870 Market St., 415/495–5173.

Brazil. 300 Montgomery St., Suite 1160, 415/981–8170.

Chile. 870 Market St., Suite 1058, 415/982–7662.

Colombia. 595 Market St., Suite 588, 415/495–7195.

Costa Rica. Box 7643, Fremont 94537, 510/790–0785.

Dominican Republic. 870 Market St., Suite 982, 415/982–5144.

Ecuador. 455 Market St., 415/957–5921.

Egypt. 3001 Pacific Ave., 415/346–9700.

El Salvador. 870 Market St., Suite 721, 415/781–7924.

Finland. 333 Bush St., 415/772–6649.

France. 540 Bush St., 415/397–4330.

Germany. 1960 Jackson St., 415/775–1061.

Great Britain. *1 Sansome St., 415/981–3030.*

Greece. *2441 Gough St., 415/775–2102.*

Guatemala. *870 Market St., Suite 1057, 415/788–5651.*

Honduras. *870 Market St, Suite 451, 415/392–0076.*

Indonesia. *1111 Columbus Ave., 415/474–9571.*

Ireland. *44 Montgomery St., Suite 3830, 415/392–4214.*

Israel. *456 Montgomery St., 21st floor, 415/398–8885.*

Italy. *2590 Webster St., 415/931–4924.*

Japan. *50 Fremont St., 23rd floor, 415/777–3533.*

Luxembourg. *1 Sansome St., Suite 830, 415/788–0816.*

Malta. *2562 San Bruno Ave., 415/468–4321.*

Mexico. *870 Market St., Suite 528, 415/392–5554.*

Monaco. *100 Pine St., Suite 2540, 415/749–1663.*

Netherlands. *1 Maritime Plaza, Suite 1106, 415/981–6454.*

Norway. *20 California St., 415/986–0766.*

Panama. *870 Market St., Suite 551, 415/391–4268.*

Peru. *870 Market St., Suite 579, 415/362–5185.*

Philippines. *447 Sutter St., 6th floor, 415/433–6666.*

Portugal. *3298 Washington St., 415/346–3400.*

Republic of Korea. *3500 Clay St., 415/921–2251.*

Russia. *2790 Green St., 415/202–9800.*

Singapore. *1670 Pine St., 2nd floor, 415/928–8508.*

Spain. *1405 Sutter St., 415/922–2995.*

Sweden. *120 Montgomery St., Suite 2175, 415/788–2631.*

Switzerland. *456 Montgomery St., Suite 1500, 415/788–2272.*

Venezuela. *455 Market St., Suite 220, 415/512–8340.*

INOCULATIONS, VACCINATIONS & TRAVEL HEALTH

Centers for Disease Control's International Travelers' Hotline. Provides health warnings and inoculation information for locations around the world. *404/332–4559.*

San Francisco International Airport Medical Clinic. *International Terminal, ground floor, 650/794–5600.*

UC San Francisco Traveler's Clinic UCSF Medical Center. *400 Parnassus Ave., 415/476–5787.*

PASSPORTS

San Francisco Passport Agency. First-time applicants must have proof of U.S. citizenship, a valid driver's license (or employee or military ID), and two identical passport photos taken within the last six months. Payment ($60 for new passport, $40 for renewals and for children) may be made with cash (exact change required), personal check, or money order. Passports routinely take three to four weeks to process. *95 Hawthorne St., 5th floor, 415/538–2700.*

passport photos agencies

Fotek. *3499 Sacramento St., 415/563–3896.*

Leetone. *615 Sansome St., 415/391–9890.*

ROUTING SERVICE FOR U.S. TRIPS

AAA. This Automobile Association of America branch offers all the usual services, including emergency road service, author insurance, and maps. Membership is $63 for the first year and $46 for renewal every year. *150 Van Ness Ave., 415/565–2012.*

SIGHTSEEING INFORMATION FOR SAN FRANCISCO

Redwood Empire Association. The association has a visitor center in the Cannery shopping center, closed Sunday. Its staff provides free information on San Francisco and surrounding areas. Their 48-page *Redwood Empire Visitor's Guide* has useful maps, events listings, and recreation highlights for San Francisco, the wine country, redwood groves, and the north coast. To receive a copy by mail, send $3 (cash, check, or money order). The guide is free and can be picked up at the association's visitor center, at the airport, and at the San Francisco Visitor Information Center (*see below*). Also worth obtaining is the association's handy free booklet "How to Get There from Union Square," which explains how to reach approximately 50 points of interest in downtown San Francisco by public transportation. *2801 Leavenworth St., 2nd floor, San Francisco 94133, 415/394–5991 or 888/678–8507.*

TOURIST INFORMATION

for local information

California Office of Tourism. Answers questions about travel in the Golden State. Call or write for a free copy of the "California Visitors Guide," which includes a calendar of statewide events. *801 K St., Suite 1600, Sacramento 95814, 916/322–2881 or 800/862–2543.*

San Francisco Convention and Visitors Bureau. *201 3rd St., Suite 900, 415/974–6900.*

SFCVB Visitor Information Center. In the lower level of Hallidie Plaza, next to the Cable Car Turnaround and Powell Street BART Station. Write or call for a free copy of its complete "Visitor Information Package," which includes tips on city lodging, sightseeing, shopping, dining, entertainment, sports, and arts. Or stop by the center for free maps, brochures, and sightseeing guides, as well as discount public transportation passes, all dispensed by a helpful, multilingual staff. The office closes at 2:45 weekends. *900 Market St., at Powell St., Hallidie Plaza, San Francisco 94102, 415/391–2000 or 415/391–2001 for 24-hr recorded information.*

The San Francisco Bay Area encompasses dozens of towns, and many of them have chambers of commerce that are happy to provide you with information. A few of the largest are the following:

Berkeley Convention and Visitors Bureau. *2015 Center St., Berkeley 94704, 510/549–7040 or 510/549–8710 for recorded information.*

Marin County Convention and Visitors Bureau. *1013 Larkspur Landing Circle, Larkspur 94939, 415/499–5000.*

Oakland Convention and Visitors Authority. *475 14th St., Ste. 120, Oakland 94612, 510/839–9000, 800/262–5526.*

San Jose Convention and Visitors Bureau. *McEnery Convention Center, 150 W. San Carlos St., San Jose 95113, 408/977–0900, 888/847–4875, or 408/295–2265 for 24-hr recorded entertainment and events listings.*

for planning your travels

Hawaii Visitors and Convention Bureau. *180 Montgomery St., Ste. 2360, 415/248–3800 or 800/464 2924.*

Irish Tourism Information. *3195 California St., 415/621–2201.*

Japan National Tourist Organization. *360 Post St., 415/989–7140.*

Philippine Department of Tourism. *447 Sutter St., 415/956 4060.*

U.S. CUSTOMS

U.S. Customs Service. *San Francisco Port Office, 33 New Montgomery St. 415/782–9210.*

VISA INFORMATION & TRAVEL ADVISORIES

American Express Global Assist. Provides travel advisory information and emergency doctor and lawyer referrals to American Express cardholders traveling abroad. *800/554–2639, or 301/214–8228 collect outside U.S.*

Department of State's Office of American Citizens Services. Provides travel warnings for dangerous destinations, and alerts on current conditions and visa requirements. Helps citizens in distress abroad. *202/647–5225.*

DIRECTORIES

restaurants by neighborhood

THE HAIGHT

Axum (Ethiopian), 23
Crescent City Café
(Cajun/Creole), 16
Eds Restaurant & Wine
Bar (Fusion), 30
The Ganges (Indian), 32
Massawa (Ethiopian), 23
North Beach Pizza
(Pizza), 49
Rosamunde Sausage Grill
(American/Casual), 6

HAYES VALLEY

Caffé delle Stelle (Italian),
34
Hayes Street Grill (Sea-
food), 51
Jardinière (American/
Contemporary), 11
Suppenkuche (German;
breakfast & brunch),
3, 31
Vicolo (Pizza), 50
Zuni Café & Grill
(Mediterranean;
Burgers; Espresso; fire-
place), 8, 10, 31, 44

JAPANTOWN

Juban (Japanese), 39
Kushi Tsuru (Japanese),
39–40
Maki (Japanese), 40
Mifune (Japanese; child-
friendly), 16, 40
New Korea House
(Korean), 42
Sanppo (Japanese), 40
Seoul Garden (Korean),
42
Sushi-A (Japanese), 41

LOWER HAIGHT

Indian Oven (Indian), 32
Kate's Kitchen
(American/Casual;
breakfast & brunch),
3, 5
Mad Dog in the Fog
(English; views), 23, 34
Pasta Pomodoro (Italian),
36
Spaghetti Western
(American/Casual), 6
Squat and Gobble
(American/Casual), 6
Thep Phanom (Thai), 55

LOWER PACIFIC HEIGHTS

Café Kati (Fusion), 29–30
Florio (French), 27
Pasta Pomodoro (Italian),
36–37

LOWER POTRERO

Slow Club (American/
Contemporary), 13

THE MARINA

Bistro Aix (French), 24
Café Marimba (Mexican),
45
Fuzio (Eclectic), 22
Greens (Vegetarian;
views), 34, 56
Home Plate (American/
Casual; breakfast &
brunch), 3, 5
Izzy's Steak & Chop
House (Steak), 54–55
Lhasa Moon (Tibetan),
55–56
Pasta Pomodoro (Italian),
36
World Wrapps (Eclectic),
23
Zinzino (Italian), 38

MISSION DISTRICT

Angkor Borei
(Cambodian), 17
Amira (Middle Eastern),
46–47
Bombay Ice Cream and
Chaat (Indian), 31–32
Brisas de Acapulco
(Mexican), 44
Bruno's (Mediterranean),
42
Burger Joint (American/
Casual; Burgers), 4, 10
Cha Cha Cha at
McCarthy's (Caribbean;
Tapas), 17, 42
Charanga (Caribbean;
Tapas), 17, 42
Chava's (Mexican; break-
fast & brunch), 3, 45
Delfina (Italian), 34
El Nuevo Frutilandia
(Caribbean), 17
El Zocalo (Salvadoran;
late-night), 25, 50
Elephant Bleu (Vietnam-
ese), 57
Esperpento (Spanish;
Tapas), 42, 53
Fina Estampa (Peruvian),
49
Foreign Cinema (Amer-
ican/Contemporary), 9
La Paz Restaurant
(Salvadoran), 50
La Santaneca
(Salvadoran), 51
La Taqueria (Mexican;
child-friendly), 16, 45
Los Jarritos (Mexican), 45

North Beach Pizza
(Pizza), 49
Pancho Villa (Mexican),
45–46
Papalote Mexican Grill
(Mexican), 46
Pauline's Pizza (Pizza),
49
Pinxtos (Spanish; Tapas),
42, 53
St. Francis Fountain
(American/Casual;
child-friendly), 6, 16, 46
Slanted Door
(Vietnamese), 58
Taqueria Cancun
(Mexican), 46
Taqueria San José
(Mexican), 46
Ti Couz (French), 29, 46
Timo's (Spanish; Tapas),
42, 53–54
Tokyo Go Go (Japanese),
41
Truly Mediterranean
(Middle Eastern), 47
Watergate (French), 29
Vineria (Italian;
Espresso), 31, 37–38

NAPA

Bistro Don Giovanni
(Italian), 20, 33
Mustard Grill (American
Casual), 5

NOB HILL

Acquerello (Italian), 33
Charles Nob Hill
(French), 26
Ritz-Carlton Dining Room
and Terrace (French;
breakfast & brunch), 3,
29, 56
Swan Oyster Depot
(Seafood), 46, 52, 54

NOE VALLEY

Hamano Sushi
(Japanese), 39
Speckmann's (German),
30–31

NORTH BEACH

Albona Restaurant
(Eastern European), 22
Bix (American/
Contemporary), 7–8
Black Cat (American/
Contemporary), 8
Café Jacqueline (French;
romantic), 25, 38
Café Niebaum-Coppola
(Italian), 33–34

shops by neighborhood

index